92 D7372

Diedrich, Maria.

Love across color lines
: Ottilie Assing and
1999.

DATE			

LOVE ACROSS COLOR LINES

LOVE ACROSS COLOR LINES

Ottilie Assing and Frederick Douglass

MARIA DIEDRICH

HILL and WANG

A division of Farrar, Straus and Giroux

New York

Hill and Wang
A division of Farrar, Straus and Giroux
19 Union Square West, New York 10003
Copyright © 1999 by Maria Diedrich
All rights reserved
Distributed in Canada by Douglas & McIntyre Ltd.
Printed in the United States of America
Designed by Jonathan D. Lippincott
First edition, 1999

Library of Congress Cataloging-in-Publication Data
Diedrich, Maria.
    Love across color lines : Ottilie Assing and Frederick Douglass /
by Maria Diedrich.
        p.   cm.
    Includes bibliographical references and index.
    ISBN 0-8090-1613-3 (alk. paper)
        1. Douglass, Frederick, 1817?–1895—Friends and associates.
2. Assing, Ottilie, 1819–1884.   3. Abolitionists—United States—
Biography.   4. Afro-American abolitionists—Biography.
5. Journalists—United States—Biography.   6. Women journalists—
United States—Biography.   7. United States—Race relations.
8. Afro-Americans—Relations with Germans—History—19th century.
I. Title.
E449.D57   1999
973.8′092—dc21   98–25224
[b]

Acknowledgments

Research and the writing of books can—perhaps must—be a lonely business. Yet it is also the kind of work that cannot be done without exploring new roads. Most important, however, we cannot reach our goal without the support of others, without moving within an extended network of experts, colleagues, and friends; and, if we are fortunate, these encounters lead to new friendships. I consider myself fortunate indeed for all the support I have received—stimulating, encouraging, and empowering in the best sense of the word.

Ottilie Assing was a citizen of the world, and as I traced her itinerary she challenged me to turn in new directions and communicate in new ways. This was perhaps the most enlightening part of writing this book. It all started with Maria Zwiercan and her staff at the Biblioteka Jagiellonska in Krakow. I consider our Polish-German cooperation a fine example of the kind of intellectual companionship that transcends national borders and the borderlines established by our national memories.

The staff of the Schiller-Nationalmuseum/Deutsches Literaturarchiv in Marbach am Neckar guided me through their voluminous collections; Günter Kroll from the Stadt- und Universitätsbibliothek Frankfurt combed through the Gutzkow Papers for me. Other German archives scrupulously answered letters and requests for material: the Archiv Bibliographia Judaica in Frankfurt, the Bayrische Staatsbibliothek in Munich, the Bibliothek der Jüdischen Gemeinde Hamburg, the Herzog August Bibliothek and the Niedersächsische Staatsarchiv Wolfenbüttel, the Institut für die Geschichte der deutschen Juden in Hamburg, the Museum für Hamburgische Geschichte, the Salomon Ludwig Steinheim-Institut für deutsch-jüdische Geschichte in Duisburg, the Schleswig-Holsteinische Landesbibliothek in Kiel, the Staatsarchiv Hamburg, the Staatsbibliothek zu Berlin—Stiftung Preussischer Kulturbesitz, the Stadtarchiv Braunschweig, the Sudentendeutsche Archiv in Munich, the Stadt- und Landesbibliothek Dortmund.

Marion Brandt from the Steinheim-Institut, and Jutta Dick from the Moses Mendelssohn Akademie Halberstatt, both experts on the Varnhagen and Assing circles, offered generously from the treasures they had collected. Jörg Kudlich shared his family memories with me and sent me photographic material for my book. My colleague and friend Geneviève Fabre from the University of Paris VII appointed a young scholar, Tessa C. Spargo, who combed the archives of Paris for clues on Assing's suicide and translated the documents for me.

In the United States, I had marvelous support. James H. Cook from the Frederick Douglass Papers at West Virginia University and I exchanged dozens of messages on the Douglass family. Karl Kabelac, Manuscript Librarian at the Rush Rhees Library at the University of Rochester, gave me a crash course in local history and advised me on my research at the Rochester Historical Society and the Public Library. Judy Throm at the Archives of American Art in Washington guided me through the Sylvester Rosa Koehler Papers, thus enabling me to reconstruct Ottilie Assing's post-Douglass years. The owners of Between the Covers—Rare Books, Inc. graciously allowed me to illustrate my book with material from their wonderful collection of African Americana.

Whenever I went to an archive in the United States, I met knowledgeable individuals eager to assist me—at the Library of Congress, the Schomburg Center for Research in Black Culture, the Leo Baeck Institute, the public libraries in Boston, New York, Hoboken, and Rochester, the (state) historical societies in New York, Rochester, Hartford, St. Louis, Newark, and Madison, the Western Reserve Historical Society in Cleveland, the Amistad Research Center, the Boston Athenaeum, the Ferguson Library at Stamford, Connecticut, the Hoboken Museum, Harvard's Widener and Houghton Libraries, the Schlesinger Library at Radcliffe College, the Sterlin Memorial Library at Yale University, the Moorland-Springarn Research Center, the Philadelphia Jewish Archives Center, the Presbyterian Historical Society, the Schaffer Library of Union College in Schenectady, the Syracuse University Library, the Special Collections Library of the University of Michigan, the Rutherford B. Hayes Library in Fremont, Ohio, the German Society of the City of New York, the Hoboken Board of Education.

During my years of research I was offered an intellectual home and the company of critical minds at Harvard's W. E. B. Du Bois Institute for Afro-American Research. Its director, Henry Louis Gates, Jr., proved an enthusiastic and impatient observer and a pertinent critic, with a wonderful sense of humor. My colleagues at the Institute—especially Allan Austin, Mary Hamer, Michael Hanchard, Sieglinde Lemke, Elizabeth McHenry, Richard Newman, Susan Reverby, Barbara Solow, Patricia Sullivan, Hal Weaver, Jean Fagan Yellin—never tired of giving me constructive criticism.

William McFeely's brilliant biography of Frederick Douglass inspired me to take a close look at Assing's life. As my book took shape, his pertinent questions were cautioning and encouraging. Nell Irvin Painter shared her experience of writing Sojourner Truth's biography and pointed out strategies of reading the minds of those who have left no written documentation. The information on the burning of Douglass' mansion provided by Richard H. White, Director of the African American History Project at Port Crane, New York, helped me gain an understanding of the atmosphere in which Assing and Douglass moved during their Rochester years. Of utmost importance were my friends from the Collegium for African American Research (CAAR)—especially Geneviève Fabre, Fritz Gysin, Christopher Mulvey, Carl Pedersen, Alessandro Portelli, Werner Sollors, and Justine Tally. Then there were young colleagues who shared their research with me: Britta Behmer, Volker Depkat, Stephen Engle.

I am especially grateful to those colleagues and friends who took it upon themselves to read the text of my book in its various manuscript stages. They accompanied me through that treacherous labyrinth of interpretation, warned me against the pitfalls of wishful thinking, shared their expertise with me—even polished my English. They encouraged me in ways that cannot be translated into words: Karen and David Blight, Joanne Braxton, Randall Burkett, Jutta Dick, Lois and James Horton, Christoph Lohmann, Sylvia Mayer, Deborah McDowell, Patrick Miller, Waldo Martin, Jr., Marian Cannon Schlesinger.

In 1996 Christoph Lohmann came to Münster to discuss his plans of translating Assing's *Morgenblatt* reports into English. Our interest in Assing became the foundation of a warm working relationship. I will forever be grateful to Chris not only for relieving me of the work of translating Assing's articles, but especially for those wonderful days of intense intellectual exchange on Nantucket which he and his wife Pamela offered to me.

The illustrations for this book would have been all too conventional had it not been for Cathy Ingram, curator at the Frederick Douglass National Historical Site, who showed me unidentified photos that turned out to be items from the albums Assing had willed to Douglass. Frank Faragasso, supported by Douglas Stover, from the National Park Service, contributed uncountable hours in helping me to gain access to this material. He introduced me to Jeanne Levelle from the Museum and Archeological Research and Supplies at Glen Dale, whom I thank for her skill in reproducing superb photographic material. Faragasso gave abundantly of his inside knowledge of Douglass. To paraphrase Toni Morrison: it is a blessing when you meet a person who is a friend of your mind.

I would not have been able to complete this book in a relatively short time had it not been for the diligence of my "crew" at the University of Hannover—Anette Bickmeyer, Karsten Fitz, Antje Ruppelt—and for the devotion of Kirsten Raupach, my research assistant from the University of Münster. Kirsten's enthusiasm inspired the team in Münster—Gesine Farnsworth, Claudia Hölscher, Oliver Heinichen, Sylvia Mayer. I could not have escaped to the Du Bois Institute were it not for my colleagues at the English departments in Hannover and Münster who supported me by taking upon themselves the work I left behind when I withdrew to Massachusetts.

I want to express my gratitude to Jill Kneerim and her staff at Palmer & Dodge in Boston, who guided me conscientiously through the dark alleys of American publishing toward the safe haven of Hill and Wang and Elisabeth Sifton. When I signed my contract many people told me that among American editors Elisabeth Sifton is the most challenging and the best. She is—no need for a fact-fiction debate in that. Through her proposals for revision I discovered the book I had intended to write all along. It was a privilege and an inspiration to work with her.

Last but not least there is my family, who were served Assing-Douglass fare for breakfast, lunch, and dinner, and for years. Perhaps this is why there was no word of protest when I was in Massachusetts.

I will forever be grateful to all the people and institutions who encouraged and assisted me in writing this book. Needless to say, the responsibility for whatever errors occur on the following pages is exclusively mine.

In grateful memory of

Nathan I. Huggins

Contents

Introductory Remarks: Snooping in Other People's Lives   xv

I   A Mount Calvary of Joy: Ottilie Assing's Childhood and Youth   3

II   If Only I Were a Bird: Vagrant Years   43

III   Pilgrim-Fool: American Beginnings   89

IV   Irresistible Attractiveness and Distinction: Appropriating Frederick Douglass   131

V   The I and the Other: Ottilie Assing and the Douglasses   169

VI   Of Emerald Islands and Magic Gardens: The Antebellum Years   199

VII   The Iron Arm of the Black Man: The Civil War Years   231

VIII   A Delightful Time, Admirably Spent: The Reconstruction Years   259

IX   *La Donna è mobile?* Years of Suspense   301

X   Hagar's Shadow: Separation and Suicide   331

Concluding Remarks: Aequanimitas   377

Notes   383

Bibliography   423

Illustration Credits   465

Index   467

i found god in myself

& i loved her

I loved her fiercely

　　—Ntozake Shange

INTRODUCTORY REMARKS

Snooping in Other People's Lives

This is exactly how I imagined the man I would love some day! Oh how long, how painfully and how longingly have I searched for him—at home, in my fatherland, I could not find him; these civilized Europeans have wiped off that divine enamel from their soul; they have become so much part of humanity that they have lost their touch of the divine. And my soul longed to meet a whole human being, to love a man who has not yet been marked and branded by the world, in whose soul the divine fire of truth is still glowing, who can still feel with the whole freshness of the natural.
—CLARA MUNDT, *Aphra Behn*

> For heart of man though mainly right,
> Hides many things from mortal sight
> Which seldom ever come to light
>   Except upon compulsion.
> —FREDERICK DOUGLASS, "What am I to you?"

Ottilie Assing (1819–84), German-American, "half-Jew," journalist, teacher; Frederick Douglass (1818–95), African-American, abolitionist, editor, civil rights advocate. For twenty-eight years, between 1856 and 1884, a companionship existed between these two that violated the nineteenth-century boundaries separating black and white and challenged Victorian sentiments about morality, gender, and class. The participants in this unusual *pas de deux* moved in a semi-public realm, yet Americans chose to ignore their performance. Not so the German public. In 1884, only months after Ottilie Assing's death, Carlos von Gagern, a German aristocrat and professional revolutionary, informed his readers that Assing, "to prove her lack of prejudice," had "entered into an intimate friendship with a full-blooded Negro."[1] Only four years later Heinrich Zeise, a poet from Hamburg, treated his audience to a sketch of Assing's unconventional relationship to an African-American man when writing about "the hard struggles of life and the peculiar circumstances"[2] of her death. However, the most fanciful rendering of this interracial relationship appeared in Germany in the mid-1890s, in the memoirs of the famous actress and courtesan Helene von Racowitza, *Von Anderen und Mir* (Of Others and Me). "Two names are ringing in my ears—Ottilie Assing and Fred Douglas,"* Racowitza, who associated with the couple in New York in the late 1870s, remembered. Never known for too close an adherence to fact, she offered a most imaginative, sensational rendering of a love across the color line she claimed she had been privileged to observe. She portrayed Assing as a white Harriet Tubman, as heroic liberator of slaves, and as Douglass' intellectual mentor. As for Douglass, he was

> a strikingly attractive, tall, glorious type of man, built like a lion, in whom race mixing . . . has created the most fortunate potion. Of an enticing charm, he had— despite his extraordinary, universal learning . . . —lost nothing of the gentleness of character that characterizes the Negro in his folk songs and that makes men and women of this race such popular domestics. Our old friend Ottilie Assing had taught him perfectly polished manners. In short, we found in him one of the most interesting and agreeable people among our acquaintances. Wit and a humorous approach to life were as much in his command as deep seriousness and erudition.

For Racowitza it would have been almost unnatural had her friend Ottilie not fallen in love with this "glorious type of man." "The aging heart of our good Ottilie was, as was only human and natural, entwined in passionate love with the beautiful dark Fred—this creature of her mind. But she honored his marriage bond and—probably hoped that, once his black wife's death had liberated him, he would lay this freedom at her feet." Yet the romance ended in tragedy: "The poor woman was bitterly disappointed."[3]

Life transformed into fiction and Germany's notorious "Red Countess" as its author—how Ottilie Assing and Frederick Douglass would have chuckled at the idea, how they would have raged at the racist implications of Racowitza's invention! Yet theirs was a story that begs to be told. In 1855 the British abolitionist Julia Griffiths, who had helped Douglass edit his journal, *The North Star*, returned to England, painfully aware that their friendship was being used

---

*Racowitza persistently misspelled Frederick Douglass' name, as did several of the journals to which Ottilie Assing submitted her articles.

to disparage the abolitionist cause. Only a few months after her departure the German journalist Ottilie Assing traveled to Rochester. She had read Douglass' autobiography *My Bondage and My Freedom* (1855) and wanted to interview the author. The encounter changed the lives of both. During the next twenty-six years Douglass was a frequent guest in Assing's home in Hoboken, and Assing, in turn, spent all her summers in the Douglass residences in Rochester and Washington; she translated his autobiography into German; and she began to inform the German reading public about the plight of African-Americans.

It was an intimate, mutually enriching, but also tragic relationship. Douglass was enchanted with his German companion, but he never again forgot that any liaison with a white woman could prove fatal to his political mission. As America's representative and most visible black man, he had to be a paragon of bourgeois respectability, offering to the world "a priesthood, occupying the highest moral eminence,"[4] as he attested in 1855. Neither an extramarital affair nor a divorce was compatible with this role. Assing respected the burden he had taken upon himself. She defied conventional notions of morality and became both intellectually and physically intimate with this extraordinary man, certain that eventually he would marry her. She would be grievously disappointed: after his wife, Anna Murray, died in 1882 Douglass remarried in January 1884— not Ottilie Assing but his secretary, Helen Pitts. In August 1884 Assing committed suicide in Paris, leaving her estate to Douglass.

If theirs was a story begging to be written, the protagonists' attitude toward this possibility was highly ambivalent and subject to change. Assing herself wrote one version in the portraits of Douglass she contributed to the German journal *Morgenblatt für gebildete Leser*[5] and in her preface to the German edition of *My Bondage and My Freedom*, in hundreds of letters she sent to Douglass, in her correspondence with her sister Ludmilla, in letters to friends in Europe and in the United States. Douglass wrote another version in his letters to Assing, her "weekly allowance,"[6] as she called them, to his children, and to a small group of friends, and in references to her in his third autobiography, *The Life and Times of Frederick Douglass*. Yet in her will the woman who had been so determined to document this relationship decreed: "All the letters which will be found in my possession, are to be destroyed immediately,"[7] a wish that was honored when Dr. Hermann C. Kudlich, one of her former pupils and now executor of her will, burned her papers.[8] Only one of Douglass' letters to Assing, a fragment of 1874, survived. Douglass, too, saw to it that almost no trace of Ottilie Assing would remain in his papers. The Frederick Douglass Papers contain only twenty-eight Assing letters, dated between 1870 and 1879. It is possible that Douglass never archived her letters as conscientiously as she did his; it is possible that he destroyed them after Assing's suicide; it is also possible that they were discarded by heirs anxious that posterity apotheosize the icon rather than understand the man. Also, with the exception of two, all of Assing's letters to him after their first encounter in 1856 were lost when the Douglass residence in Rochester went up in flames in June 1872. There can be no doubt that Douglass wanted biographers to write his life, that his wife and children were eager for historians to do justice to the great man, but there was also a strong intention to control the shape this portrait would take. After all, he left three autobiographies, a signal of the irony implicit in what Henry Louis Gates, Jr., calls "the re-creation of successive fictive selves."[9] "No man," Peter Walker asserts, "more assiduously guided future biographers along the paths that he wanted them to follow."[10] Expurgating his papers was another safe means of presiding over the shape his public representation would assume. Like the families of James Fenimore Cooper, Nathaniel Hawthorne, Charles Dickens, and others, convinced they were "shaping materials for a public shrine, not displaying, let alone dissecting, illustrious cadavers,"[11] Frederick Douglass and his heirs seem to have intervened to conceal and correct history; it was a well-established custom of the day.

So Assing's papers were destroyed, Douglass' probably expurgated. What escaped, however, were the many articles which Assing published in German magazines and her preface to his autobiography. These were public texts, but they contain a private subtext that invites us to decode it and that offers us glimpses into the writer's private realm. What also survived were letters from Douglass to his children; letters from his daughters and sons to him; some of the correspondence between Douglass and German-Americans he had befriended during his many visits to Hoboken, letters which Ottilie Assing sent to these acquaintances; letters she wrote to German relatives and friends; and the correspondence between these addressees and their comments on the liaison. Much of this material was, of course, written in German.

The most continuous and revealing representation of the Assing-Douglass relationship is to be found in Ottilie's letters to her sister Ludmilla. The relationship between the sisters was warped by intense personal rivalry expressed in years of silence. But when Ottilie Assing emigrated to the United States in 1852, the sisters corresponded sporadically; Ludmilla discarded Ottilie's early American letters. Then, after the Civil War, Ottilie resumed and intensified this correspondence, and Ludmilla, then living in Florence, archived many of them. Thus ninety-one letters from Ottilie to Ludmilla, written between 1865 and 1877, usually between four and twelve pages in length, and all of them in an exquisite old German handwriting, were preserved as part of the extensive Varnhagen von Ense Collection at the Jagiellonian Library in Krakow, Poland.

The narrative that emerges from the sources available is almost exclusively Ottilie Assing's—that is, her construction and interpretation of her relationship with Douglass. Documentation of Douglass' perspective, of his feelings and his attitude toward Assing, of his motives, went up in smoke with Assing's papers. There is his autobiography, a few letters to his children and to his German-American friends; we can make connections from his travel itinerary; and we can draw conclusions from the number of visits he paid to Hoboken, the frequency with which he invited Assing to join him in Rochester and Washington, and the length of her stays. Still, what remains is an imbalance between her representation and his.

Any attempt to reconstruct their liaison is further complicated by the fact that although Ottilie Assing provided something like a continuous narrative, for long periods we have to rely almost exclusively on her public texts, especially on the American columns she wrote for the *Morgenblatt*, plus third-person perspectives, while at other times the material revolves around only private statements. And in reading Ottilie Assing's letters to her sister Ludmilla we have to keep in mind that the sisters were estranged, which obviously affected the information they exchanged. Aware that her German family perceived her emigration to the United States as a defeat, as the self-imposed exile of a fallen woman, it was essential for Ottilie's sense of self that she portray her venture as a success story, both on the professional and on the private level. As Mary A. Favret's *Romantic Correspondence*[12] reminds us, epistolary discourse transgresses the boundaries between public and private spheres in its effort to construct and represent an authentic self via dialogue, in the carefully chosen postures the participants adopt. The self-creating and self-authenticating voice we hear in letters is always also half somebody else's.[13] Ottilie Assing's invention in her letters to Ludmilla of a perfect interracial romance, of love across the color line and in defiance of institutionalized morality, thus was not just another expression of what Peter Gay describes as a nineteenth-century bourgeois penchant for baring the heart;[14] it was central to her self-construction and self-justification, and it was essential to the rebel persona she cultivated for herself and others. In this correspondence between warring sisters, fighting for self against the other was just as important as the dynamics of agreement and the common code they shared.

The narrative Ottilie Assing constructed was more than a chronology of events; she was restructuring, rearranging, rereading experience; she was molding, selecting, and deleting memory, until the story of her life became compatible with the persona she invented. Like Douglass, she masked interpretation as representation. The letters she wrote, the constructions of "self"[15] she portrayed, thus need to be read as a balancing act between fiction and fact—*Dichtung und Wahrheit*, to use the title of Johann Wolfgang Goethe's memoirs she so adored. In approaching her texts we must try to wrestle with both, her representations of herself and Douglass as historical presence and as individual human being.

Are we talking about a love story, or are we imposing twentieth-century, post-Freudian expectations on a friendship between a German-American woman and an African-American man that was just that, a friendship? Ottilie Assing died childless; there were no reporters peeping through Douglass' or Assing's bedroom windows, nor witnesses sitting on their bedside to provide graphic evidence. All we have are words and texts—words and texts, moreover, written in a nineteenth-century context that avoided explicit reference to the body, to intimacy, to sexuality. As we attempt to decode the meaning of Victorian public and private discourse, we must remember that the spoken and the written word for people in the nineteenth century had meanings that differed substantially from today's usage. In addition, we are dealing with many different codes which the main narrator of our tale, Ottilie Assing, used: a public code she shared with her German middle-class and liberal readers, playing with conventions of representation, with established metaphors, images, tropes, symbols, in written work that, moreover, was submitted to the dictates of a publisher trying to stay clear of government censorship and that was exposed to drastic editorial changes;* the private code she and Douglass created for themselves; the encrypted code Ottilie and Ludmilla shared as sisters; and the semi-public, semi-private code that characterized the correspondence among Assing, Douglass, and their German-American friends. We are forced to read silences, discontinuities, contradictions, ambiguities in a discourse that sought to transform and transcend the boundaries between a familiar "self"—Ottilie Assing: woman, "half-Jew," German-American, and thus white—and an "other"[16]—Frederick Douglass: man, African-American, and thus black. Ottilie Assing contended that she and Douglass lived "unmarried . . . and yet united in a deeper love than

---

*The manuscripts held by the Cotta Archives reveal that Assing's *Morgenblatt* editor frequently replaced *Frau*, meaning "woman," with the derogatory *Weib*, meaning "female" (or even "old hag"), thus drastically changing the tone and message of her text.

many who are married"; she portrayed herself as "intimately connected with *one* man";[17] she used the term "friend" in the contemporary German sense that encompassed friend, lover, and husband; she mobilized a powerfully eroticizing language whenever she referred to Douglass, especially in her letters to him, thus bolstering her claim that she and Douglass were living as husband and wife. Yet how much authority and authenticity may we attribute to the voice of a woman who tried to reinvent herself and the man she loved as a modern American Aphra Behn and Oronooko, who continually crossed back and forth between fact and fiction?

Like the archaeologist's, it is the biographer's task to retrieve what we have lost from memory, to reclaim the past, and to build a bridge between this past and our present. We unearth bits and pieces of information—"evidence," we call it—and we rearrange and piece together these fragments, hoping that what we reassemble will bear a semblance to the actual events and help us understand what actually happened—in spite of the inevitable gaps and fissures. In fact, these gaps and fissures are as important as the pieces we were able to recover. Any biographer struggles to narrow the range of that which can never be recovered with certainty, and in doing so we must draw a dividing line between what is possible and probable, between what is improbable and impossible,[18] even as we realize that fact and fiction, memory and interpretation, are intimately intertwined. In the end we have to acknowledge that much of the person into whose life we delve must necessarily elude us, and, perhaps even more significant, that much of the life we reimagine and reconstruct is about our own life, our own prejudices, dreams, agonies, and joys. We are made aware of our own potentials and limitations as we try to come to terms with another human being's potentials and limitations. This is the humbling aspect of writing biography. It is also what makes biography "the most seductive and the most untrustworthy of literary genres."[19]

The reconstruction of the Assing-Douglass relationship cannot take the form of a traditional history. It is of necessity a difficult balancing act between narrative and interpretation, between fact and fiction. This intricate choreography is reflected in the formal structure of this book. Each chapter opens with a text printed in italics; many of these italicized passages—about the death of Ottilie's mother, Ottilie's departure to America, her visit to an African-American camp meeting, her first arrival at the Douglass residence, a morning in Douglass' orchard, the New York draft riots—dramatize a key scene, and though they are inventions, they are always based on Assing's own accounts or those of her acquaintances. Some of them are translations from narratives—Racowitza's memoirs, Clara Mundt's novel; others—newspaper reports, Assing's letter to Ludwig Feuerbach—are documentary. Most chapters are also prefaced by an epigraph from Clara Mundt's *Aphra Behn*, the novel which was so essential to the ways in which Ottilie Assing perceived and represented her friendship with Frederick Douglass.

This book is filled with questions I cannot possibly answer. It tells a story full of contradictions, for it revolves around individuals who were full of contradictions: courage and loyalty, love and brutality, ruthlessness and hatred, ambition and devotion, the public and the private, duty and inclination, humanitarian commitment and blatant racism, black and white cohabiting and in constant warfare. Both Assing and Douglass were children of relationships that transgressed established notions of race, class, or religious alliance, and they spent a lifetime negotiating identity: Ottilie Assing was taught by her Christian mother and her Jewish father, a convert, that the difference between Christians and Jews was exclusively cultural. Consequently these parents insisted that for her, a child of this relationship, identity was a matter of choice, and she became an enthusiastic advocate of intermarriage.* Yet German society ostracized the "half-Jew." And even Ottilie Assing and her parents, despite their rhetoric of culture and their egalitarian and universalist creed, were not immune to essentialist and racialized assessments of "the Jew," "the German," "the Negro." We simply have to acknowledge that Germans of the day, and that includes the Assing family as victims of German anti-Semitism, saw and treated Jews as a people apart, which made Ottilie's subjective experience of being a "half-Jew" very like a "racial" experience.† Only emigration to the United States transformed Ottilie Assing into a German, and it was America that eventually redefined her as white.

It was as a white woman with all the privileges of whiteness, yet seasoned

---

*In one of her first articles for the *Morgenblatt* she commented on the legalization of Jewish-Gentile intermarriage as follows: "The law, which from now on will allow marriage between Christians and Jews in Hamburg, has been passed by the city council by the ridiculous plurality of only two votes, to our great surprise and despite the resistance of the orthodox Christian and Jewish parties, which campaigned against it almost daily in the news with quotations from the Old and New Testaments, Moses and the prophets, all of which shows how little people supported the initiative. It is said that several fundamentalist Jews attended a city council meeting for the first time in their lives in order to vote against the bill, which, however, found an advocate in Dr. Hertz, one of the best and most brilliant local lawyers, against whom all that small-mindedness came to naught."[20]

†To characterize the dichotomy between the Assings' cultural definitions and the racialized assessment of the dominant German discourse of the day, the words "race," "racial," and "interracial" will be in quotation marks whenever the Jewish-Gentile connection is evoked.

with the wisdom of the "half-breed," that she reached out to Frederick Douglass, who, like her, was suspended between both and neither. "Within him there were two people and two imperatives," Peter Walker argues: "Harriet Bailey, carrying that which was brought out of Africa through a slave culture to her son, and Aaron Anthony the master, heir to the 'Anglo-Saxonism' which Douglass scathingly arraigns in *Bondage and Freedom* and the *Life and Times*, but does not mention in the *Narrative*."[21] There is no consistent Ottilie Assing, nor will there be a consistent Frederick Douglass on these pages. How could we impose unity, continuity, or closure on this narrative without doing violence to its unnervingly complex, its proudly defiant, its stunningly unconventional protagonists?

Both Ottilie Assing and Frederick Douglass obviously launched their expurgation campaigns only after their relationship deteriorated in the late 1870s and early 1880s. Before that, as long as Assing hoped that someday she would be Douglass' wife, she was careful to preserve their correspondence. It is significant that the first will she wrote in 1871 contained no instructions for the destruction of her papers.[22] At this point she was still intent on documenting their romance and martyrdom for posterity—that is, for those who would someday reconstruct the life of the heroic black liberator and his equally heroic white companion. It is even possible that Douglass did the same. After all, their relationship was never one of those secretive affairs, carefully concealed from the public gaze. Though they were always discreet, theirs was a liaison that embraced bright daylight. Ottilie Assing and Frederick Douglass knew each other for twenty-eight years: for twenty-six years they corresponded on a weekly basis; every summer Assing lived in the Douglass residence for several months; they promenaded arm in arm through the streets of Rochester, New York, Hoboken, Philadelphia, and Washington; they entertained friends together; they attended meetings, lectures, parties, dances, and dinners together; they visited the theater, the opera together; they worked together. Their families, their friends and acquaintances, their colleagues, their communities—all were aware of this relationship. Why, then, did it escape the eyes of Douglass' biographers for so long? What accounts for their silence? Equally important: how do we explain the curious abstinence of the sensation-hungry contemporary American press?

When Julia Griffiths came to live with the Douglasses, American newspapers reveled in rumors of a scandalous interracial and extramarital affair; when Frederick Douglass married Helen Pitts the newlyweds were caught in what Douglass described as a "freeze of popular disfavor."[23] But Douglass' long-term and semi-public liaison with Ottilie Assing either escaped or was ignored by the American press. There is no conclusive explanation for this silence. It seems relevant, though, that the vicious campaign against Douglass' friendship with Griffiths was launched not by nosy reporters or a proslavery press but by his former allies—namely, by William Lloyd Garrison and other abolitionists—in an attempt to discredit and punish him. Only after these ex-friends had broken the "news" did other newspapers jump on the wagon. Equally it was Douglass' former political allies, and thus individuals familiar with his private world—namely, Rochester's radical Republicans—who, disappointed when he did not join them in their rebellion against President Grant in 1872, took revenge by "parading his board and bedding matters before the public."[24] Douglass was a prominent public figure, a government official, a man in the spotlight when he married Helen Pitts, and Pitts was not only white but also twenty years younger than he.[25] But in the decades between? The press reported on Douglass' public appearances—his lectures and speeches, his involvement in the John Brown raid on Harpers Ferry—that is, on the public figure Frederick Douglass, on activities that affected their white readers. Is it possible that America's conservative press simply was not interested in a black man's private life, that their antagonists' racialized vision protected Ottilie Assing and Frederick Douglass against their intrusive gaze, while the liberal and abolitionist press carefully abstained from spreading information that might be counterproductive to its mission? Is it possible that his opponents deigned not to look while his allies averted their eyes? By the time Douglass took office in Washington and entered a more precarious public space, he was fifty-nine and Assing fifty-eight—hardly material for public scandal in a society that associated a woman's sexuality with youth.

If Frederick Douglass and Ottilie Assing lived their relationship in a semi-public realm, if it was virtually public property, why did it not surface in the Douglass biographies that were written right after Douglass' death by biographers who had personal memories of him and who still could interview family, friends, colleagues—James M. Gregory (1893), Frederick May Holland (1895), Charles W. Chesnutt (1899), and Booker T. Washington (1906)? Like nineteenth-century autobiography, biographies of famous individuals focused almost exclusively on the protagonist's public persona. They were written to document and celebrate an individual's achievement and contribution to the world. There was no room for family life—with the exception of a standardized and token bow to the faithful helpmate and to domestic bliss; and even though bourgeois reticence was increasingly replaced by a desire to reveal all, as Peter Gay documents in *The Private Heart,* there was little tolerance for anything that would taint the image of the celebrity, and no taste for the more controversial, even seedy aspects of life.[26] The first generation of Douglass biographers were raised in this laudatory tradition, and they wrote his life to celebrate a great African-American, a heroic black liberator and freedom fighter. What Peter Walker attributes to the Douglass constructs of Quarles and Foner thus also holds true for their predecessors, that they wrote "in the classical biographical tradition that resolves the problems of human unruliness not by grappling with them but by avoiding them. Rather than attempting to pierce the mysteries of the hidden springs of human action and reconcile the cross-purposes and para-doxes that exist in every life, biographers sought a complemental cluster of traits which provided the key to personality."[27] Also, these first-generation writers were reconstructing Douglass' life in a period in which the African-American community was tottering under its worst setback since the end of Reconstruction: the Supreme Court's *Plessy* v. *Ferguson* decision of 1896 holding that segregation was constitutional; blacks suffered disfranchisement, lynching, exploitation; they were battling scientific racism and Ku Klux Klan violence. The need for a black icon was real and urgent, and Douglass' biographers pro-vided it. If they knew of Ottilie Assing, they chose to exorcise her. Still, in 1899 Charles W. Chesnutt wrote "The Wife of His Youth," the tale in which the light-skinned Mr. Ryder, a prominent businessman and politician, has to choose between a young light-skinned Molly Dixon and the much older black woman Liza Jane, whom he had married before the Civil War; he acknowledges Liza Jane. Was Chesnutt signifying Douglass in this story published the same year as his Douglass biography?

Later Douglass biographers—Quarles (1948), Foner (1964), Bontemps (1971), Blassingame (1976), Huggins (1980), Martin (1984), Blight (1989), to name only a few—no longer had access to the private memory and spoken words of Douglass' contemporaries. They had to work with expurgated papers which contained almost no clues that might have induced them to look into the Assing connection. Their silence on Assing can no longer be construed as a pro-tective gesture; it was not respect for an icon, fear that discussing a relationship would taint the image of an immaculate black hero. After all, these biographies deal with the Griffiths affair and with other rumors of Douglass' extramarital interests. There were simply too few clues left. Even if they had tried to follow the Assing lead in *Life and Times of Frederick Douglass,* the Assing papers had disappeared and, with them, the memory of Ottilie.

The history of these papers is almost as fascinating as the story they tell.[28] Ot-tilie and Ludmilla Assing were nieces of Rahel Levin Varnhagen, the famous

Jewish salonnière of turn-of-the-century Berlin who converted to Christianity in 1814, and of Karl August Varnhagen von Ense, an influential diplomat and writer and enthusiastic collector of autographs. At his death in 1858 he gave his collection to Ludmilla, who had lived with him since 1842, and she willed the collection, plus the papers she had added to it, to the Royal Library in Berlin upon her death in 1880; this is the voluminous and famous Varnhagen Collection.* While many German libraries, archives, and collections were destroyed in World War II during the Allied bombardment of German cities, the Varnhagen Collection was preserved because it was of special value for the Nazis: since Varnhagen von Ense was married to a formerly Jewish woman and through her had excellent connections to Jewish intellectuals and converts all over Germany, the Nazis misused his extensive biographical notes to "prove" the Jewish lineage of German intellectuals. Varnhagen's commitment to reconciliation between Jews and Gentiles was a lifelong passion, and his memories were thus perverted into a murderous instrument during the Nazi period.

In 1941, after a bomb attack damaged the State Opera next to the State Library in Berlin, the Nazis decided to deposit the most valuable parts of the library's holdings in twenty-nine depository sites, most of which were located east of the river Elbe, as the Eastern Front was still considered safe. Together with what was later called "the world's most important collection of missing music,"[30] the Varnhagen Collection was deposited in a Benedictine monastery in the village of Grüssau, in a section of Silesia that was ceded to Poland in 1945. This monastery was destroyed by fire, but monks later testified that the 505 crates containing Varnhagen's papers had been evacuated in Polish army trucks in 1946, before the blaze; nobody knew where they had been taken. For decades they were given up as lost. Most of the collection survived, however, and was eventually rediscovered in the Jagiellonian Library in Krakow, Poland, in the 1970s. In the 1980s the library began to make some of this material available to scholars from the West. Boxes of Assing family papers were included, material Ludmilla had assembled, among them the ninety-one letters that Ottilie wrote to her from the United States between 1865 and 1877.

I cannot claim the honor of having discovered these papers, and I have profited from the skill, perseverance, and diligence of scholars and colleagues who paved the way for me. In 1989 Terry H. Pickett's "The Friendship of Frederick Douglass with the German, Ottilie Assing" was published in *The Georgia Historical*

---

*The 1911 guide to the collection has 963 pages.[29]

Quarterly. A Varnhagen von Ense biographer,[31] he had unearthed the Assing-Douglass connection while assessing the Varnhagen Collection at the Jagiellonian Library. His article was the first tentative documentation of this friendship, and it was based on Ottilie's letters to Ludmilla. William McFeely followed Pickett's lead in his extensive references to Assing in his exquisite Douglass biography (1991). Since then Jutta Dick and Tamara Felden have written articles on Assing's American adventures and her contribution as a journalist, and Maria Wagner included some of Assing's *Morgenblatt* columns in her anthology of German-American journalism.[32] Slowly Ottilie Assing is reemerging from the darkness and silence that buried her.

I did not discover the Assing papers or the Assing-Douglass relationship, nor am I the one to snatch Ottilie Assing from total oblivion. Yet in years of the most joyful detective work, which took me to libraries and archives all over Europe and the United States and made me aware of how truly Ottilie Assing was a citizen of the world, I have unearthed new, relevant, and extensive documentation for the story, and I hope to suggest new assessments. Dick, Felden, McFeely, and Pickett base their representation of Ottilie Assing and her friendship with Frederick Douglass almost exclusively on her letters to Ludmilla and her *Morgenblatt* columns. I took this correspondence as a starting point that helped me trace and reestablish the complex international network of relationships within which this remarkable woman moved. Literally hundreds of Assing letters, lectures, and columns emerged. To top it all, Ottilie Assing's personal photo albums, which she willed to Frederick Douglass, were discovered and identified as hers in Douglass' final home, Cedar Hill; most of the illustrations in this book are from her own collection.

This is not yet another Douglass biography, but an attempt to assess the Assing-Douglass relation by moving Ottilie Assing to center stage, by reconsidering this interracial relationship from her perspective. Here, Ottilie Assing is at the center of a drama which revolves around the relationship between her and Douglass, two fascinating and complex individuals.

On the one hand, I trace the chronology of this liaison, the extravagant choreography Assing and Douglass designed for their twenty-eight-year *pas de deux,* the word-castle they built for it, the interplay they enjoyed between romance and intellectual partnership, between the eroticism of secrecy and the joy of open defiance. On the other hand, I delineate the effect of this union and, especially, Douglass' perspective on the American images that Assing invented for her German readers in her articles, as well as the influence which Assing, in turn, had on Douglass' intellectual development and his political career. To un-

derstand Assing's approach to race relations in the United States in general as
well as her personal relationship to Douglass, one must scrutinize carefully her
Old World background and its influence on the American images she created
for herself before her emigration. We need this information to investigate and
assess accurately the effects her intimate exposure to the African-American experience and perspective, which she obtained through Douglass and his family,
had on her perceptions and representations of the New World. Frederick Douglass taught Ottilie Assing about what today's parlance calls polyphony; he made
her aware of the connection between power and discourse. He invited her to
join him in challenging the white "master narrative" and to defy contemporary
beliefs in history's monologic closure. Ottilie Assing became his guide on his
encounter with non-English European literature, philosophy, and social theory;
she challenged him to transcend his intellectual American focus. She became
the medium through which his powerful voice could be heard, his interpretations discussed, in the German-speaking world. I hope, then, that this book establishes an international context for Frederick Douglass and Ottilie Assing.
What may at first appear as simply an enchanting interracial romance invites us
to reconsider major social and intellectual issues of the New World and the Old
in the past century. And the dynamics of the Assing-Douglass relationship challenge us to acknowledge that many of the idiosyncrasies in racial mixing that
we may tend to see as an American phenomenon transcend this national frame.

They also invite us to rethink gender and race in the nineteenth century.
Assing and Douglass performed their interracial romance in a quasi-public
realm, and they lived their liaison in the Douglasses' domestic setting, in the
very space that was occupied by Douglass' wife Anna Murray and their children. The story that unfolds thus is not so much a *pas de deux* as perhaps a ring
shout, polyphonic, but also vibrating with choral silences, and with an elaborate choreography of many.

Ottilie Assing and Frederick Douglass spent a lifetime pretending that race
was not an issue in their relationship. And yet race was central to the way they
perceived and approached each other; it was a powerful, eroticizing magnet in
their liaison; it influenced the decisions they made about their life together; it
shaped their contemporaries' attitude toward them. Loving Douglass made Assing guilty by association to many of her contemporaries; she violated dominant
notions of racial purity. Loving Assing made Douglass a traitor to his race, especially to black women. "We have no further use for him," wrote one African-
American correspondent after Douglass' marriage to a white woman.[33] Race is a
definer in the assessment of their story we attempt today. As Douglas Lorimer

has shown, we like to presume that "a fundamental discontinuity exists between our present and the Victorian past,"[34] yet Ann duCille's eye-opening *Coupling Convention* and Werner Sollors' pathbreaking *Neither Black Nor White* force
us to admit that "amalgophobia" or "mixophobia" is not a nineteenth-century
phenomenon, nor have we answered the question which version of identity is to
be preferred or if either should be privileged in the first place. Where do we
place this story in our contemporary battle about "authenticity," about versions
of self and identity, with its conventional assertions of stifling and limiting para-
digms?

This narrative of a nineteenth-century interracial relationship has to be
placed and understood in a racialized setting. I try to do justice to the ambitious professional woman and the vivacious, aggressively rebellious private individual who was Ottilie Assing, and I hope to redefine the relationship between
the public persona and the private man who was Frederick Douglass. This does
not undermine his place in American history, his importance to race relations in
the United States, to the liberation of "his race," and to the moral regeneration
of an erring American nation. In fact, it shows that his analytical power and hu-
manizing wisdom transcended American boundaries. So I hope I have continued what the biographical studies of Blight, Davis, Gates, Leverenz, Martin,
McFeely, Preston, and Yarborough and the defamiliarizing analyses of McDowell, Franchot, and Washington encouraged us to do: to move beyond the "self-
given consistent personality"[35] Douglass created for us, beyond the remote icon,
and to rediscover and embrace a complex human being. The Frederick Douglass
who shaped American history was not a loner, frozen on a pedestal. He was a
man among women and men, black and white, shaped by them and shaping
them. I hope this book will familiarize us with two exceptional individuals,
who were heroic in stature just as they were human in scale.

Interracial plot lines like the one in this narrative still challenge the boundaries within which we prefer to think and move, our definitions of "self" and
"other," of "authenticity" and "hegemony." They clash with our power structures. "Race is the tar baby in our midst," Marita Golden reminds us in her introduction to *Skin Deep;* "touch it and you get stuck, hold it and you get dirty,
so they say."[36] However, theirs is a story that color blindness cannot tell. Race
does matter.

LOVE ACROSS COLOR LINES

A MOUNT CALVARY OF JOY

Ottilie Assing's Childhood and Youth

And you, who pretends to be a stranger!
You renegade—denying
The pious race of your ancestors
Ashamed of your Father and your Mother.
You deny the customs of your stricken people
And join, you traitor,
The enemy with words of ridicule:
So that your ruthless children,
An alienated race, throw stones
At your Father's head
And tousle his gray beard.
—SALOMON LUDWIG STEINHEIM, "Gesänge aus der Verbannung,
welche sang Obadiah ben Amos im Lande Ham"
(Songs from Exile, sung by Obadiah ben Amos in the Land of Ham)

Slowly, hesitantly the young woman came into the room.[1] The blue curtains of the only window in this small, sparsely furnished chamber were drawn, as if to banish the warm glow of the setting sun outside, but on this unusually bright afternoon of 22 January 1840, the sun was still powerful enough to penetrate the dark cloth, and consequently the room was tinged a surreal, watery blue. Did the woman realize that she was crossing the room on tiptoe? As if in slow motion, she pulled back the curtains, and a warm light fell on the face of the elderly woman who could now be seen lying on the bed. She had the look of one who is just awaking from a restful afternoon nap. For a long time the young woman stood motionless; she seemed unwilling to disturb the other's rest and fascinated with the healthy rosiness which the sun painted on that still face. Finally she walked toward the bed, again on tiptoe, and gently brushed a lock of gray hair from the sleeper's face.

Rosa Maria Assing had died the night before, just before sunrise, surrounded by her husband David, her daughters Ottilie and Ludmilla, and their maid, Cappel. Seven months before, a sharp pain had forced her to her sickbed, but although David, a physician, had warned her to stay in bed and rest, she had ignored his worried face and had soon insisted on taking up her usual routine of supervising her household and on welcoming the many friends who came to express their relief at her recovery. Then the pain had returned, sharper than before, and, with it, a paralyzing exhaustion. Dr. Salomon Steinheim was consulted, the Jewish physician from Altona who was one of the family's most intimate friends, and he confirmed what David refused to accept: Rosa Maria obviously suffered from cancer; there was no hope. Every day she found it harder to fight the longing for rest that had begun to penetrate her body. Every day it became more difficult to ridicule her daughters for their concern, to force an encouraging smile on David's face. Why was she so relieved when friends whose companionship she had enjoyed for years left her bedside after the briefest visit, when, finally, David denied them access to the sickroom? Knowing her love of nature, these friends hoped that death would wait to claim her till spring, so that the fertile, reawakening soil, which she had celebrated in a song— "adorned like a bride, bathed in full blessing / I see the soil resplendent with the luster of spring"[2]—would embrace and cover her. She died on 22 January 1840, in "a savagely stormy night, with the thunder of the cannon warning of the dangers of the rising flood tide of the Elbe River."[3]

Ottilie had secluded herself in her room all day, as had her younger sister Ludmilla, while their father had sat by his wife, unable to part from the woman who had just left him. Ottilie had heard the footsteps and the soft voices of friends and relatives who came to pay their last respects. Finally, Dr. Steinheim had arrived, Uncle Steinheim, as the Assing girls called him, and with his quiet, firm authority he had taken David to his room.

Now, as she looked down on her mother's face, Ottilie experienced relief bordering on joy. None of the contortions of pain which had marred Rosa Maria's mature beauty in the last weeks of incessant torture, none of the artificial smiles for her daughters, none of the dead vacancy produced by morphine remained. Only peace, and the warm glow of the evening sun. Brushing back her mother's hair behind her ears Ottilie bent over the still face and calmly removed the aquamarine earrings Rosa Maria had worn ever since her mother had passed them on to her on her wedding day. Ottilie had always associated her mother with those earrings. In fact, it would be hard to say what had first found entrance into the baby girl's nascent memory as her eyes began to focus and differentiate—that smiling face with its abundant blond hair and bright blue eyes, or those light blue flowers, like forget-me-nots from which a petal seemed to drop. How cool these stones had always seemed to her prying little fingers! Yes, they were hers, hers from a memory that knew no beginning, and hers as the elder daughter. Rosa Maria would have given them to her on her wedding day, just as she, in turn, had received them from her mother. Rosa Maria was dead, and Ottilie her legitimate heiress. From now on she was an adult—no longer just Rosa Maria's child but a woman in her own right and responsibility.

Ottilie removed the shawl which covered the mirror in the dead woman's chamber and attached the blue flowers to her earlobes. How familiar they looked on her! Her mother's face had once been bright and healthy, surrounded by blond tresses too abundant to be tamed, and on her the aquamarines had competed with the deep blue of her vivacious, sparkling eyes. Ottilie resembled her mother: her face was as full as Rosa Maria's, and she prided herself on her skin of the same warm texture. Her hair was darker blond, but just as rich and untamable. On her the aquamarines seemed darker, almost the color of the cornflowers she so loved. Ottilie smiled at what she saw in the mirror, for this transformation made them all hers. She could hardly remove her eyes from the empowering image the mirror reflected.

So absorbed was she in herself that not a sound escaped her even when she turned around to leave the room and walked right into Ludmilla, standing motionless in the doorway. Like white marble. Cold. Silent. Breathless. Ottilie quickly recovered her composure and, throwing back her head in a movement of proud defiance, walked past her sister, invested with all the dignity of her new role. Suddenly Ludmilla's hand shot up, slapping Ottilie across the face. All the tension that had grown in two decades between sisters competing for their parents' love now exploded over the possession of a pair of blue flowers.

Cappel, who had separated the fighting sisters since their first toddler wars, stormed upstairs, breathless with horror at the two young ladies screaming, biting, scratching in the presence of their mother's corpse. But her authority failed her in the face of this unstoppable torrent. Ottilie and Ludmilla did not notice that David's door had opened. "Stop. Please." It was an utterance soft as a breath, and it did not penetrate their enraged minds. Then the command was repeated, in a voice which, always gentle and somber, was now so lifeless that it pierced through their screams. They stopped abruptly and turned toward this pale stillness, two as one. For an eternity they faced each other, David's eyes seemed unable to focus, yet when they finally caught the familiar coolness of the aquamarines, a smile played around his lips. Without saying a word he approached Ottilie and took her in his arms. Then, stepping back, grasping both her hands, his eyes fastened on hers, he took leave of his child to acknowledge the presence of a woman. There was no doubt that he approved the metamorphosis caused by loss, and without speaking a single word he passed the authority that had been Rosa Maria's and his to the daughter who had already claimed it. He knew it was in good hands, and he was relieved, for this would make it easier for him to follow the one who just departed.

Ludmilla stood motionless as David resumed his watch at Rosa Maria's bed and Ottilie returned to her room. The girls' childhood was over. The sisters' rivalry had turned to hatred.

In February 1818[4] Harriet Bailey, a slave woman in Talbot County, Maryland, gave birth to a baby boy. She named him Frederick August Washington Bailey. Not long after, mother and son were separated, Harriet Bailey toiling away for a Mr. Stewart, to whom she had been hired out, and Frederick being handed over to his grandparents Betsy and Isaac Bailey, in whose cottage he spent his early childhood days. Frederick was six years old when his grandmother took him by the hand to walk with him to the Great House, delivering the property to its owner. Unable to bear the pain of separation that would be certain to overwhelm the little boy, she stole away as Frederick was playing with his half sisters and brothers. "Almost heart-broken at this discovery, I fell upon the ground and wept a boy's bitter tears," he would remember many years later. "I had never been deceived before and something of resentment mingled with my grief at parting with my grandmother."[5] At only six, Frederick discovered his existential loneliness. He was a slave, the property of a white man, yet whose child was he? His mother sometimes walked miles to see him, arriving after dark, after a full day's work, sitting with him as he drifted off to sleep, but she was gone in the morning. A cherished moment with her came one night when she protected him against the wrath of the plantation cook. For the first time in his life Frederick knew "that I was not only a child, but *somebody's* child."[6] But then she stayed away, and somebody told him she had died. There was no father to embrace the boy as his. There were rumors about Aaron Anthony, the general plantation superintendent of the Lloyd property,[7] the man who had savagely beaten Frederick's aunt Hester for choosing a black lover over him, who had punished Frederick when he did not perform properly, and who sometimes patted him on the head, calling him his "little Indian boy."[8] Anthony died in 1827, only a year after Harriet Bailey. His daughter, Miss Lucretia—Frederick's half sister?—took pleasure in treating the bright little slave to an extra ration of food, and at times she even had a caress for him. He was somebody's property; he was somebody's plaything. He was nobody's child.

At age eight he was sent to Baltimore, to serve the Hugh Auld family as a companion to their little boy, Thomas. Sophia Auld gave in to Frederick's urgent pleas to teach him his ABCs, but her husband interfered, believing that an educated black boy made a bad slave. Frederick did what his proud mother had done before him: he stole what his white masters withheld from him—the written word. He used those words to learn about human rights, to teach other slaves the skills whites claimed as their prerogative, to write freedom passes. He was a man unfit for slavery, a man whom the slave-breaker Covey might terrorize but whose thirst for freedom and knowledge no white master, no whip could stifle.

He was twenty when, disguised as a sailor and equipped with money from the free black woman Anna Murray, he escaped to the free North on 3 September 1838. He renamed himself Frederick Douglass. He was twenty-three, married to Anna Murray, and the father of two children when he launched his career as an abolitionist orator in the Garrisonian camp and devoted his life and skills to the liberation of his enslaved race. The slave child Frederick Bailey had not only reimagined himself as a human being and liberated himself; he had not only educated himself. At an age when contemporary white American men were usually just beginning to understand their adult responsibilities, he had already transformed himself into the liberator of America's bondspeople and race leader.

Nothing could be more different from Frederick Douglass' first two decades than Ottilie Assing's childhood and youth. She was born in Hamburg, Germany, on 11 February 1819, as the oldest child of a highly respected middle-class family. The Assings were almost prototypes of what we today call the educated German bourgeoisie. Ottilie and her sister Ludmilla, born on 22 February 1821, grew up in an intellectual environment in which education was regarded as a secular form of individual salvation, and their parents, Rosa Maria Antoinette Pauline Assing (1783–1840) and Assur David Assing (1787–1842) provided them with a training highly conducive to the children's natural intellectual curiosity and their longing for autonomy.

Rosa Maria Assing came of a well-known family of German physicians with strong liberal, if not openly radical, leanings.[9] She was born to parents who spent a lifetime defying convention: her mother, Anna Maria Varnhagen, née Kunz (1755–1826), was the well-educated daughter of a magistrate from Strasbourg, baptized in the Lutheran faith; her father, Johann Andreas Jakob Varnhagen (1756–99), was a physician from Düsseldorf and a Catholic. Contemporaries denounced intermarriage between Catholics and Protestants as misalliances that challenged established religious boundaries, yet these controversies failed to deter the young couple. And their defiance did not stop there:

violating the regulations of the Roman Catholic Church that children of mixed marriages be raised in the Catholic faith, the couple respected each other's convictions enough and cared too little about religion to bring up their firstborn, Rosa Maria, as a Lutheran, her brother, Karl August Varnhagen von Ense (1785–1858), as a Catholic! Defiance became a family tradition.

Though born in Düsseldorf on 28 May 1783, Rosa Maria grew up in Strasbourg, her father having accepted a teaching position at the university there. Her parents became enthusiastic disciples of the French Revolution. "To belong to the new empire of Liberty and Law, of the bourgeoisie and of brotherly love seemed the most happy fate intelligent, noble people could partake of,"[10] their son remembered. When the Revolution actually reached Strasbourg in 1792, however, the university was shut down and Varnhagen had to leave the city. He was appalled by the violence that he believed was perverting the original idea of the Revolution, and when he said so publicly, he was told in no uncertain terms that he had better make a home elsewhere. After an odyssey through several German states he and his son finally settled in Hamburg, where he struggled to make a living as a physician. He was a man who had lost his place: on the one hand, his critical attitude toward the perversions of the Revolution forced him to leave France; on the other hand, his German contemporaries suspected him of being a French spy. Rosa Maria and her more militant mother,[11] who was appalled at her husband's skepticism, remained in Strasbourg, residing at Monsieur Kunz's house on the Place du Corbeau. Here the girl was educated by her mother and by excellent private tutors. At a very early age, she was bilingual in French and German; she soon gained an easy command of English and Italian; and she could read Latin as well as Greek and Old French. Her mother not only encouraged her to read without restriction but also emboldened her to write.

In 1796 the women joined Johann and Karl August in Hamburg, reluctantly, for they hated to give up their freedom and mobility, and also because their political differences had caused a rift between husband and wife. It was only a brief reunion: Johann died in June 1799, receiving a Protestant burial in Hamburg's pauper cemetery. The small amount of money the family had went to Karl August, who went off to Berlin to enter a Prussian cadet school, while Anna Maria Varnhagen supported herself by needlework.[12] Rosa Maria seemed to have no future, but she was well prepared to fend for herself: despite her youth—she was sixteen—her superior education enabled her to get a position as a live-in governess for the two daughters of a wealthy Jewish family in Hamburg. Upper-class Jews of the day often preferred to have German tutors for their children, hoping this would increase their chances for integration. A German teacher represented command of literate German, and she or he could be expected to provide the social skills that were essential in polite German society.[13] Through her employers, Rosa Maria soon began to associate with the city's Jewish intelligentsia and was a frequent guest in the Hertz mansion, where Fanny Hertz ruled as the city's most distinguished salonnière. The relationship to the Hertzes became even more intimate when Rosa Maria's brother was hired as the children's tutor and a love interest developed between him and the capricious Fanny.[14]

Rosa Maria's life was anything but lonely; her education and her lively interest in intellectual pursuits, in politics and literature, in art and social matters as well as her own writing made her an attractive companion to the young intellectuals to whom her brother introduced her—the poet, dramatist, and society lion Adalbert von Chamisso; aspiring poets of the young Romantic school, Justinus Kerner, Ludwig Uhland, Gustav Schwab, and Karl Mayer. Her excellent French made her a well-liked guest in the homes of many refugees who had come to Hamburg in the wake of the Revolution.[15] Contemporaries described her as an engaging woman, her attraction coming less from physical beauty than from her generous and vivacious nature. She was of medium height, well proportioned, with fair, curly hair and blue eyes, and her friends frequently praised the fresh and healthy texture of her skin.

While living in a luxurious Jewish mansion next to the famous Hamburg puppet theater, Rosa Maria made friends who were to accompany her for the rest of her life: Amalie Weise (Schoppe) and Justinus Kerner. Amalie, six years younger and also a governess, adored the more mature Rosa Maria, who not only embraced her as a sister but also introduced her to her lively circle of friends. No doubt it was this group that awakened in Amalie a desire to compete with what they all did profusely—writing. After a brief disastrous marriage to her former tutor, Dr. Schoppe, Amalie Schoppe, now the mother of three boys, eventually became one of Germany's most prolific writers.[16] Schoppe was later to call her friend, who had pointed out this road to her, "the gem of my life, the rose without thorns, who beautifies and elevates the wreath of my happiness through fragrance, form, and color to the utmost."[17] Her love of Rosa Maria was passionate enough for contemporaries to suspect lesbian motivations.[18]

Even more important for Rosa Maria's future was her relationship to Justinus Kerner, a young physician and aspiring poet of the Romantic School from Tübingen. After graduating from university, he was touring Germany and Austria, and in 1809 he spent a few months with his brother Georg in Hamburg.

Rosa Maria fell passionately in love with this tall, gaunt, pale young man, and for a time at least Kerner seemed to share her feelings. She was a woman unconventional enough to encourage his wildest dreams, so how could he not be attracted to her? In a letter to his poet friend Uhland he raved: "By God, to have a puppet theater would be my truest joy, and you could live well on it. Rosa would immediately tour with me. . . . What a divine life that would be, and we[19] would ridicule every husband in his marital bed!" The enamored young woman was too happy to heed her friends' warning against this liaison: "rather would I suffer a bitter death / than languish from this kind of longing!"[20] she wrote in her poem "Romance." A true daughter of Romanticism, she accepted love as the great definer, and she was determined to live her conviction by giving herself unconditionally. In a short, untitled poem of this period she confessed:

> In a fragrant forest
> Through which a pure spring rippled,
> Songs and flowers sprouted,
> And where the sun shone brightly through the green,
> There we became one . . .[21]

Love, she claimed in lines that eroticized nature, was not just a dreamlike state of emotional ecstasy but tangible, physical. She celebrated sexual consummation in "Song of Spring"—"With a thousand pleasures / My love life had begun"—and she embraced the desire and passion she experienced, affirming that "we drifted in an ocean of lust."[22]

Her happiness did not last, for very soon she had to realize that Kerner regarded their relationship only as an affair; he offered friendship where she was "consumed by hot amber inside."[23] He tried to soften the blow by treating her with unwavering kindness, but his friendliness only increased her pain. Referring to a popular literary theme of the time, the death of a lover on the battlefield, she insisted that the loss of the lover to friendship is as terrifying to the one left behind as a loss through death:

> I, too, have lost my lover,
> But not on a bloody field;
> Healthy and full of joy he walks
> About our town.[24]

The poetry she composed during the years following this encounter was permeated with images of suffering, wasting, and death.

Kerner left Hamburg in September 1809 for Berlin, Nuremberg, and Vienna, then returned to Swabia, where he practiced medicine in Weinsberg and, together with Uhland, Schwab, and Mayer, became a prominent member of the Swabian Romantic School. Rosa Maria and he corresponded regularly, and her poetry, simply signed "Rosa Maria," was published in the annual poetry anthologies which he and his friends edited. Kerner later named his eldest daughter Rosa Maria.

Justinus Kerner introduced Rosa Maria to the man with whom she chose to spend the rest of her life: David Assur,* a Jewish physician from Königsberg, in East Prussia.[25] His parents, wealthy merchants, were orthodox Ashkenazim, his mother, Caja, née Mendel, coming from Courland, his father, Ascher (or Assur) Levy, from Posnania. In her autobiography of 1860–61 David Assur's niece, the novelist Fanny Lewald,† mentioned miniature portraits of David's parents:

> Grandmother's was of a pale woman with a quiet clever gaze, dressed all in white, a lace kerchief covering her throat and breast, and wearing a white lace headdress that fit closely to her forehead and temples and let not a single strand of hair show. She wore beautiful large pearl earrings and a matching necklace. Grandfather had a refined face with light blue eyes, a small powdered wig, a blue coat with large buttons; they were both the very picture of cozy cleanliness and peace. There was something solemn about their physiognomies . . . [26]

His enormous wealth enabled Ascher Levy, Sr., to retire early and live off his investments; at a time when it was hardly common practice for Christians to associate with Jews, prominent citizens of Königsberg, among them the philosopher Immanuel Kant, treated him with the greatest respect. Though frugal in their private life, the Assurs were eager to display a splendid outer appearance, and David later described to Ottilie and Ludmilla their spacious mansion, situated across from the royal bank, near the Green City Gate, on the corner of Kneiphof Langgasse and Magisterstrasse, which boasted a salon with furniture covered in yellow damask and huge mirrors. Here his parents lavishly entertained their masked and unmasked guests at Purim, the Jewish carnival.

Jewish customs were carefully respected; Passover, the Festival of Booths,

---

*Sources use two different spellings, Assur and Azur. Rosa Maria used Assur.

†Fanny Lewald (1811–89) was the eldest daughter of David Assur's youngest sister, Zippora Assur Markus, and the merchant David Markus. Markus later adopted the name Lewald for his family so that his sons would not be identified as Jews when attending university.

and the Day of Atonement were solemnly observed. David's youngest sister
Zippora later told her children

> how our grandparents had summoned all their children on the eve of Yom Kippur
> and blessed them, how Grandmother, in a white dress edged with exquisite lace,
> would accompany Grandfather to the synagogue, how they would not return until
> late in the evening, how a servant would quietly divest Grandmother of her stylish
> yellow-lined black taffeta, how they would fast on the following day, and not break
> the fast until the stars appeared that night. Then life had resumed its normal
> course.[27]

David Assur was born on 12 December 1787, the youngest of five sons in a
family that eventually boasted twelve children. Following the tradition of well-
to-do upper-class Jews, the girls were taught what Lewald ridiculed as "French,
music, dancing, and other superficial skills,"[28] and they even hired a tutor for
"charm," but as their father considered women's education a luxury, their tutoring was stopped immediately after their mother's death. The boys, however, received superior training, for wealthy Jewish fathers, successful but uneducated
merchants, prided themselves on their ability to educate their male offspring
for the professions—as professors, physicians, writers, intellectuals. David, a
small, frail boy, spent more time than any of his siblings with his tutor, reading
voraciously and writing his own poetry; and his father eventually sent him to
Halle, Tübingen, Göttingen, and Vienna to study medicine. On 26 August
1807, David Assur received his medical doctorate from the university of
Königsberg.[29]

Though raised in an orthodox Jewish environment, David, growing up in
Kant's Königsberg, could not avoid being exposed to Enlightenment philosophy, and to his father's chagrin he became a disciple of the Enlightenment
and its Jewish counterpart, represented by leading intellectuals like Moses
Mendelssohn and Gotthold Ephraim Lessing. The creed David Assur eventually
adopted combined a firm Enlightenment belief in human equality with popular
contemporary notions of cultural hierarchy and progress. He was not alone
among the Jewish intelligentsia in seeing the Jewish subculture as inferior to
German bourgeois culture. Like many prominent Jewish intellectuals of his day
who adopted the Enlightenment concept of moral individualism,[30] he assumed
that large parts of the German Jewry had degenerated, and, convinced that degeneration was largely a cultural phenomenon, the result of poverty and discrimination, he hoped that new social and educational ideals could be devised
by an enlightened generation to initiate and support a process of regeneration.

Jews, he argued in unison with other prominent Jewish intellectuals, must emulate the superior German culture in order to achieve political and moral equality. He was convinced that members of a subculture could educate themselves into the mainstream, into the system.

These notions of cultural hierarchy were strengthened by the Enlightenment assumption that each generation "possessed a higher religious truth than that which preceded it."[31] It was a belief that acknowledged the historical superiority of Christianity over Judaism, which was regarded as "a dying remnant of the past," an "outmoded form which produced an unpleasant and unnecessary separation between himself and his gentile environment."[32] Many years later David's wife, in her novella "The Chimney Sweeper" (1834), represented his view of the relationship between Jewish and Christian cultures as embodied in two statues that the medieval sculptor Sabina von Steinbach had created for the cathedral at Strasbourg:

> This crowned virgin, who holds the cross in the right hand, the chalice and the host in the left, personifies Christian religion; on the left we have the symbol of Jewish religion, also personified by a virgin, who in her entire attitude seems dazzled by the superior radiance and conquered by a power much stronger than hers. She stands with her head bowed and blindfolded, a broken arrow in her right hand and Moses' commandment tablets in her left; her crown has dropped to her feet.[33]

There are many signs that David Assur's attitude toward his Jewish background, like that of his famous sister-in-law Rahel Levin Varnhagen,[34] was characterized by ambivalence both before and after his conversion in 1815. A disciple of Enlightenment humanism on the one hand, and in the face of an all-pervasive German anti-Semitism and the degrading misery in which most Jews in Germany lived on the other, he could not help experiencing his Jewishness as a stigma and a burden, yet even after his conversion he continued to affirm his Jewish background. Instead of "passing"—that is, camouflaging his Jewish birth, he openly converted, thus maintaining a link between past and present. Together with his wife and daughters he sought the company of other Jews, and they lived in a Jewish neighborhood. It seems he never found a true home in the Christian doctrine; his melancholy, his tendency to withdraw, his dark prophetic nature may have been expressions of his spiritual dislocation. His intimate friendship with the Jewish physician and philosopher Salomon Steinheim, who was outspoken in his disapproval of conversion, gave him a partner with whom he could discuss the anguish caused by his proselytism, but it almost seems he sought this relationship out of a kind of intellectual masochism,

determined that the wound should never heal, the pain never cease. To the end
he struggled to create a place for himself in realms where both his Jewish heritage and his enlightened humanism could transcend established religious and
"racial" boundaries; he accepted his responsibility as a successful physician for
suffering, uneducated Jews who had not escaped the ghetto as he had. Together
with Jewish notables of the city,[35] he supported Jewish welfare societies, offered
medical aid to the Jewish poor, and advocated Jewish emancipation. It was always important to him to instill in his daughters pride in their Jewish background, awareness of anti-Semitism or any expression of racism, as well as a
sense of responsibility, and to familiarize them with Jewish beliefs and rituals.

David Assur seemed a man in the grip of depression and incessant doubt
even during his years as a student of medicine. His friend Ludwig Uhland, who
was a great admirer of Assing's dark poetry, called him "a spirit of misery," "this
depressive, narcotic Assur," and later "this melancholy, black-spotted sacrificial
lamb," associating his melancholy with his Jewishness.[36] The brooding manner
he adopted during his mature years, his self-isolation in his laboratory, his intellectual conservatism, his avoidance of intellectual combat, and finally his sui-
cidal behavior after his wife's death together suggest a torn and haunted man.

Assur, then, had many reasons for leaving Königsberg: he must have realized that he could not live out his Enlightenment creed and his anxieties in his
hometown, where they were bound to cause pain and embarrassment to the
members of his family who remained true to their orthodox faith. Another reason for his departure may have been the strict *numerus clausus* regulations which
Prussia enforced against Jews: each Jewish household which had been granted a
permanent-residence permit on Prussian territory could pass on this privilege to
one child only. The Assur family had given theirs to their eldest daughter, hoping this would attract a husband to this rather plain woman.[37] Thus David had
no choice but to seek a new start on new territory. For a few months he toured
Austria, and hiked through the Steiermark in true Romantic fashion. In September 1810 he showed up in Tübingen. The young Swabian intellectuals
among whom he moved, especially Kerner, challenged the Jewish disciple of
the Enlightenment with their Romantic creed, enticing him to travel in yet another direction. One year later, in September 1811, he was on his way to Hamburg, equipped with letters of introduction for Rosa Maria from Kerner,
Uhland, and Varnhagen von Ense, whom he had met in Vienna.

By the time David Assur arrived in Hamburg, Rosa Maria had left her Jewish
employers to open an academy in the neighboring community of Altona. She

offered a warm welcome to the young physician about whose eccentric but kindly nature she had heard from her brother and Kerner. Rosa Maria and David both loved literature, both wrote poetry, both became disciples of Romanticism, both favored long excursions into the countryside—the older and more experienced Rosa Maria drafting the itinerary. They thoroughly enjoyed each other's company. Assur was enchanted by the Hamburg to which Rosa Maria introduced him so generously. Probably the most prosperous community in Germany, it was a city of merchants and patricians, of a proud and free bourgeoisie. One of its historians, Feodor Wehl, claims that it had about 180,000 citizens in 1760. He mentions the city's cleanliness, its broad avenues, its wealth and the absence of beggars; in celebration of its many parks it was called the garden city. The musical historian Charles Burney, who spent some time in Hamburg, used the terms "contentment," "prosperity," and "freedom" when characterizing the "Hansestadt." In the anonymously published *Briefe über Hamburg* another admirer wrote in 1794: "You will encounter a luxury which not only is appropriate to the wealth and the respectable professions of these first houses of the city but often reaches beyond that; you will find elegant carriages, numerous servants, splendidly furnished rooms, palace-like garden houses and friendly meals, which would honor every noble or royal table."[38]

Another important point of attraction in the Free and Hanseatic City of Hamburg was its large Jewish community. Since the early seventeenth century, the city had tolerated the Sephardim, prosperous Jews of Spanish and Portuguese origin, hoping to profit from their international trade connections, and these were joined by large groups of Ashkenazim. In the early nineteenth century they constituted the largest Jewish community on German territory, boasting more than 9,000 members.[39] Despite the discrimination they suffered—they were compelled to live in restricted areas; they could not buy land or houses; they had to pay extra taxes; the guilds excluded them; they were exposed to pogroms—Jews in Hamburg were privileged in comparison to Jews in other German towns. In Altona they fared even better, for Altona was under Danish rule: the town had no *numerus clausus*; Jews could purchase landed property, the Crown guaranteed religious toleration and gave them autonomy in many realms of public life, thus enabling them to live according to their norms.

Only two months after they met, Rosa Maria's and David's friendship had to face its first major challenge: experimenting in his laboratory, Assur was hurt by a chemical explosion. For weeks he believed he had lost an eye; fortunately the fire had only burned the lid. Still, Assur was desperate. According to contemporary definitions of beauty he had never been an attractive man. He was small and lean, with a dark complexion, and deep furrows marred his face even as a young man. The solemnity of his appearance was intensified by his black hair worn shoulder length. After the accident his lidless eye gave his face an uneven, haunted expression, and people likened his features to those of an eagle. Rosa Maria stood unflinchingly by him in those difficult months, and on 12 January 1812, she wrote to Kerner: Assur "has become rather dear to me, and I thank you once again for sending him to me; he is a very excellent human being with a superior mind, and consequently it hurts all the more to see him so melancholy and unhappy."[40] Assur's suffering and Rosa Maria's caring loyalty established a new bond between them. They began to write poetry together, most of which was eventually published in anthologies edited by the Swabian Romantics.*

We do not know when Rosa Maria and David became lovers; in letters to Kerner and Schoppe she called him her "friend" and physician as late as 1815. Yet there is a poem called "Farewell and Covenant," probably written in 1813, which suggests that the outbreak of the German War of Independence against Napoleon (1813–15), bringing separation and the fear of irreparable loss, caused them to articulate their feelings. Rosa Maria's first poem describing their love was free from the romantic ravings that had characterized her love poems to Kerner. They concerned a relationship that germinated in soil polluted by war, lovers prematurely matured by a world of violence and death, a love that carried in it the potential of extinction:

> Neither through joking nor flirting
> Did love reveal itself as love;
> Full of dark foreboding in a somber hour
> The covenant of our love was sealed.[41]

Assur, like most young Romantics deeply committed to the idea of German independence and unity, decided to return to Prussia, offering his service as a physician first to the Russian hospitals in Berlin and then with the Prussian army.[42] At the end of the summer of 1814 he returned for a brief visit and talked Rosa Maria into spending a few weeks in Berlin with him. They had begun to discuss a future they hoped to mold together, knowing that their relationship might scandalize many of their acquaintances.[43]

---

*At first, Kerner was reluctant, calling Assur's poems "strange," though Rosa Maria praised them as "original, deep." Yet the more of Assur's poetry the editors read, the more they appreciated them, and he was represented in each anthology.

Perhaps their decision to marry was also influenced by the wedding of the famous Jewish salonnière Rahel Levin and Rosa Maria's brother Varnhagen on 27 September 1814. Four days before their wedding Rahel, fourteen years older than Varnhagen and his lover for many years, had been baptized as Friederike Antonie Robert. For herself, her husband, and her friends Rahel remained Rahel after her conversion; for outsiders she became Mrs. Varnhagen: the notorious Jewish mistress had been transformed into the respectable Christian wife of a German diplomat. But the German elite never forgave Varnhagen for this breach of etiquette; his career as a diplomat soon came to an end.[44] Rosa Maria and David, however, saw only that this kind of union was possible and desirable.

In 1814 Rosa Maria moved her academy to Hamburg; in 1815 Assur returned to Hamburg to establish himself officially as a physician; he was baptized David Assing; and he and Rosa Maria announced their engagement. They knew they were inviting social ostracism, the moral censure of both conservative Germans and Jews; they were aware that they would have to give up many connections and habits, that they would lose family and friends, yet what they found in each other weighed more than what they risked. From its very beginning tolerance and mutuality were the definers of their union: David converted so that he could marry Rosa Maria; Rosa Maria agreed to move into a Jewish neighborhood. For once in his life the deeply troubled Assing seemed happy. Though she was four years his senior, his bride's joyous nature and her indomitable high spirits, her love of laughter and her optimism rejuvenated a man who appeared so prematurely aged. In a letter to Kerner, the poet Gustav Schwab, who spent some time with the couple in November 1815, described David as a man succumbing to joie de vivre: "without saying a word about it, he loves—and I can see this from his songs and conversation—Rosa Maria beyond description."[45] They were married on 1 May 1816.

It was a happy marriage, celebrated by both partners as well as those who observed them as an ideal relationship as it was defined in the Romantic Age: a union of a woman and a man whose bodies, minds, and souls seemed made for each other. Both had sensuous natures, and their physical enjoyment of each other was increased by the intellectual, emotional, and moral harmony between them. Their sensuality was unapologetic, inventive, and uninhibited, yet also, as their self-stylization as lover-wife and lover-husband denotes, domesticated. In that, their marriage defied the separation between eroticism and respectability upon which much of the contemporary discourse of love versus sexuality rested. Nowhere in Rosa Maria's writing can we find traces of the popular dichotomy of woman as angel-to-be-married and whore-to-be-enjoyed. In 1817, at the age of thirty-four, Rosa Maria gave birth to their first child, a son, whom she glorified as a child of love and passion in a poem of 1818:

> From the fire of our love we jubilantly saw
> a little flame rising purely
> In the beloved, sweet child's life.[46]

The conventional piety this poem expressed was firmly intertwined with her jubilant celebration of sexuality. But the joy of parenthood was of only short duration: the boy died in the spring of 1818. Rosa Maria and David were numb with pain, yet they found solace in each other. Not their religion but their romantic notion of sacrifice and mystic challenge sustained them. As their friend Amalie Schoppe commented: "The happiness which these two beloved people give each other often elicits tears of emotion from me; and that they made a costly, unforgettable tribute to the deepest sorrow through the loss of their first child, calms me regarding the permanence of such happiness."[47]

Soon Rosa Maria was pregnant again, and on 11 February 1819 she gave birth to Ottilie. Two years later the couple's second daughter, Ludmilla, was born. They rented an unassuming house with a tiny garden in 15 Poolstrasse, a street in a Jewish neighborhood in the center of Hamburg's Neustadt (New Town), which would eventually boast a Jewish synagogue, hospital, and businesses.[48] The dramatist Karl Gutzkow, who befriended the family in the 1830s, compared the Assings' small garden of less than twenty square meters to a hatbox crammed with flowers, with a pear tree and apple tree, raspberry shrubs—a little Garden of Eden complementing the house. The Assings' was a small place, but there was always room for guests, and the girls, who loved animals, had their private mini-zoo of cats, dogs, birds, hamsters. In a love poem brimming with references to sensual delight, which Rosa Maria wrote as a birthday tribute to David in 1824, she painted a haven of domestic bliss:

> Early in the morning and with golden rays
> The sun greets a house,
> From which two lovely faces
> Of sweet children look out.
> Their mother, she stands behind them
> With blessed delight on her face . . .[49]

In numerous poems dedicated to her husband she expressed her gratitude for and happiness about a marriage that not only gave her the fulfillment of motherhood but in which husband and wife continued to be lovers. In April 1825, after nine years of marriage and the birth of three children, she wrote:

> Spring is approaching! And there is always
> Spring in our happiness and our minds![50]

In their own sensuous world, their various individualities—Rosa Maria's gentle cheerfulness and optimism, David's melancholy and mature sense of humor, Ottilie's irreverent laughter and boisterous rebelliousness, Ludmilla's angry brooding and sarcasm—found expression in a domestic oneness they enjoyed in all its diversity. The family came to personify the Romantic concept of harmony, without, however, stifling individuality or denying difference. The stabilizers in this family were the passionate love and deep emotional and intellectual commitment between husband and wife, and the intimate bond between Rosa Maria and the girls—more like that between sisters than that between mother and daughters. As Ottilie remembered in a letter to her uncle Varnhagen: "I don't think it is possible to find . . . another relationship like the one that existed between Mother and us; not a single night were we apart, no thought we did not communicate. And she was just as open toward us, had given us all her love, so that it sometimes seemed to me that I myself had the memory" of events from "thirty years ago."[51]

Yet despite the joy they found in each other, this perfect family was a construct of their minds. Ottilie's obituary letter shows that the circle of love Rosa Maria evoked in her poems in reality consisted of two entities—husband and wife on the one hand and mother and daughters on the other, with no comparable link between the father and his children. Even more important: Ottilie's and Ludmilla's biographies reveal that "the two lovely faces" of which Rosa Maria sang were those of children who had begun to hate each other despite their parents' religion of love. The Assings never doubted that both their daughters were gifted, and they carefully encouraged and guided their intellectual endeavors. There is evidence, however, that they paid more attention to Ottilie and always regarded her as the more gifted of the two. They were thrilled when, at the age of five, Ottilie demanded adamantly that she be taught to read and write, and Rosa Maria enthusiastically recorded her progress in her diaries.[52]

Studies of parent-child relationships show that most parents spend considerably more time with their firstborn than with subsequent children, and the Assings were no exception. Yet their preference of Ottilie was probably also a recognition of her intellectual and emotional vivacity, and a response to her close resemblance with her mother. Like her mother, she was small and delicately built; she had the same abundant blond hair; she had inherited her mother's rosy skin, and her blue eyes sparkled with laughter and mischief. Extroverted, cheerful, merry, and full of energy, adventure, and deviltries, she charmed everybody so much that they even accepted her belligerence and tantrums as expressions of a strong personality. The authority her mother assumed over her was one that encouraged her individuality without permitting what was considered eccentric, that set limits without stifling growth and mobility. A diary entry of 1827 is typical of her approach. Describing a pleasant visit at the Steinheims' she wrote: "All of a sudden Ottilie had the idea to undo her braids; she looked stunningly beautiful with her abundant fair hair, but I did not want to tolerate this little expression of vanity, forbade her and Ludmilla, who was about to follow her sister's example, to do this, and immediately braided her hair again."[53] Ottilie received constant attention and praise, from which she developed a sense of self, an inner strength that enabled her to defy convention, to map out and profit from the unusual paths she chose for herself. As a lover she could afford to be generous, giving, nurturing.

Ludmilla appeared to be the very opposite of her elder sister. Like David, she was small and skinny, with rather sharp features. She had brunet hair, dark eyes, and a very pale complexion. Although she loved company, she was more introverted than Ottilie and certainly more docile—possibly hoping to cater to her parents' love by her submissiveness. Her diary entries show that she worked hard to compete intellectually with Ottilie; she was convinced that she was superior to her in every way. Ludmilla suffered from what she perceived as her parents' misjudgment, and she struggled fiercely to attract their attention and appreciation.[54] Yet she needed their love too much to blame them, venting her frustration on Ottilie instead. Her need for love was insatiable, and the love she offered as a mature woman was possessive and dominating, stifling rather than nurturing.

Friends and relatives frequently commented upon the antagonism between the sisters. In his obituary for David Assing, Karl Gutzkow played with conventional day and night metaphors to illustrate the fundamentally different natures of the Gentile Rosa Maria and the Jew David Assing. "If sunshine always sparkled on Rosa Maria's sympathetic face, you always felt like looking into the night when looking at her husband's,"[55] he claimed. The same dichotomy of light and darkness seems to have characterized their children. The parents spontaneously worshipped the sun. More than that: their preference for the fair Ot-

Karl August Varnhagen von Ense
Ottilie Assing's maternal uncle, Karl August Varnhagen von Ense, was the shining white knight of her childhood years. However, after living in his household in Berlin for one year she ridiculed him as "the personification of egotism and vanity," calling him a man "whose entire life is devoted exclusively to self-love and self-glorification, without regard, without respect for others, who regards the slightest doubt in his greatness as a crime."

Rahel Varnhagen von Ense, née Levin
In Rahel Levin's famous salon in turn-of-the-century Berlin, intellectuals, aristocrats, artists, and actors—Jews, Christians, freethinkers—met to discuss literature, art, and politics. This salon provided a model for the gatherings which the Assings arranged in their home in Hamburg.

Salomon Ludwig Steinheim
Steinheim openly despised Jews who converted to Christianity, denouncing them as "traitors" and their children as "an alienated race." Still, he and his wife Johanna were among the Assings' most intimate friends. The Assing girls called them "uncle" and "aunt."

Amalie Schoppe
Amalie Schoppe was one of Rosa Maria Assing's most intimate friends. After Rosa Maria's death, Amalie's meddling nature caused tensions between her and the surviving Assing sisters. She emigrated to the United States in 1850 and invited Ottilie Assing to live with her in Schenectady. When Ottilie rejected all her offers, Amalie ridiculed the young woman as "pilgrim-fool."

tilie betrays the degree to which they obviously had internalized the contemporary racialized discourse and its related concept of beauty. Ottilie's rosy skin, fair tresses, and blue eyes were living proof of their cherished conviction (based on the late-eighteenth-century theory of "hybrid vigor"[56] later popularized in Victor Hugo's novel *Bug-Jargal* [1826]) that "interracial" procreation would improve humanity. Theirs was an unshakable belief in a universal and egalitarian humanism, and they defied a contemporary discourse that explained the differences between the Jewish and the German cultures as a hierarchy based on racial qualities, yet beneath this enlightened rhetoric their biases lurked. Their pride in Ottilie illustrates that the progress of humankind they envisioned was racial rather than cultural, and it was not about two "races" intermingling to create a higher "race." It was all about redeeming inferior Jews by elevating them to the level of the superior German "race." Rosa Maria and David saw their daughters not as children of two cultures or as individuals uniting in themselves features of both their mother's and their father's ancestries; they reimagined them as individuals whom "racial" mixing freed from the stigmata of inferiority. Ottilie seemed a paragon of that glorious transformation—a child who showed no traces whatsoever of being half-Jewish. Unaware of the racial bias that influenced their feelings and conduct, Rosa Maria and David adored Ottilie's "Germanness" while unconsciously recoiling in disappointment from the "Jewishness" in Ludmilla's features.

The alienation of Ottilie's and Ludmilla's later years no doubt had its roots in these childhood experiences. There is no sign, however, that Rosa Maria and David were aware how serious their daughters' rivalry was. They encouraged them to express themselves openly, and consequently they also accepted conflict, but their love blinded them to the dangerous undercurrent of what they explained away as natural childish squabble. It is also possible that their need for harmony and their doctrine of love made them deny and close their eyes to expressions of a destructive, violent passion in two girls they loved above all else. Like many middle-class families of the day, they no doubt felt but could not acknowledge what Peter Gay calls "the tug between love and hate deeply felt," subjecting themselves to that kind of unconscious censorship and repression "that makes for neurosis. The ideology of unreserved love within the family was attractive but exhausting."[57]

In accordance with his Jewish upbringing, David wanted his wife to be absolute mistress of the house, while he devoted his energies to his professional life. In many ways this was a conservative arrangement: the husband's was the public, the wife's was the private realm. Yet Rosa Maria was a mature woman who had made an independent living ever since she was a teenager, a woman who had successfully managed her own business. Her expertise, her strength, and her creativity enabled her to reconceptualize her conventional wifely role according to her needs, to submit it to her definitions. She became David's lodestar, in Gutzkow's words his "partner of many years, the organizer of his own impractical confusion and unsuitability for the demands of daily life, the guiding hand, who built a playground for his eccentric nature,"[58] but she also remained a woman in her own right. She could give so generously, love so abundantly because she did not give up her own precious self, because she loved herself. Rosa Maria defined and managed the children's education, the family's social activities, and the household affairs (with the help of one maid). Later, when the girls were older, Ottilie and Ludmilla were well trained in all domestic chores; they were prepared to supervise servants but also learned to cope on their own, to cook, bake, clean, and sew. Rosa Maria raised daughters willing and able to think, feel, and fend for themselves in both the domestic and public realms, women who claimed the world as their property and their autonomy as their birthright.

Rosa Maria had been a governess all her adult years; now she made her daughters' education her life's mission. She started reading fairy tales and poetry to them as soon as they displayed their first signs of understanding, and she taught them to read and write long before they could have entered elementary school at the age of six. She encouraged them to read as widely and freely as she had in her youth. Her diaries mention Goethe as well as George Sand, Kleist as well as Shakespeare, the classics and contemporary texts. The family library was open; the Assings guided their children's reading without suffocating their curiosity. Also, Rosa Maria, with her easy command of French, regularly communicated with them in that language, so that Ottilie and Ludmilla learned to speak, read, and write French fluently. Later, tutors were hired to teach them English, Italian, and Latin, and as a rule either their mother or their father attended these lessons. A Romantic, Rosa Maria did not restrict her teaching to the nursery turned classroom but saw nature as the ideal academy. She was a disciple of the Swiss educator Pestalozzi, practicing his method of object instruction, based on the insight that a child's training cannot rely on language and text alone but must include observation and sense impression. On daily outings, which Rosa Maria recorded in her diaries, the girls were familiarized with plants and animals, with planting, ripening, and harvesting, with birth and death; they were given factual information, and they learned to feel and respect nature.

Rosa Maria continued to teach Ottilie and Ludmilla beyond the age when other children of their class went to school. Precocious children, they were well ahead of their age group, and so their parents decided to educate them at home. They knew the girls would be bored with the meager intellectual diet that schools offered in those days—especially to girls, if they taught them at all. And they would be outsiders in more than one way: since they had been encouraged by their parents not only to think independently but to speak their mind, their conduct was likely to clash with the ideal of absolute obedience and docility that was basic to the German educational system. Used to their maternal teacher, whose approach was one of challenge and admiration, provocation and praise, they might well have balked at the corporal punishment, incarceration, and verbal insults to which many German teachers regularly resorted.

More important still: in school the girls would have had to learn in the most brutal way that they were different, that they did not belong. Their father may have been baptized; he may have believed that the individual could educate her- or himself into the mainstream. Yet his German fellow citizens refused to invite his children to birthday parties, for to them mere baptism had not transformed their father into a German. He highlighted ethics, universalism, culture; their parochialism saw only difference and inferiority. In their eyes he would forever be a Jew, the eternal "other," which rendered Ottilie and Ludmilla "half-breeds," *Halbjüdinnen*, and his wife a voluntary Jew, a Jew by association, which was even worse. At a crucial point in his life David Assur, configuring the differences between Jews and Christians exclusively in cultural terms, made the decision that from now on he would be David Assing, adopting a Christian and German identity, and it is likely that this decision posed a dilemma for him, as it did for his sister-in-law Rahel Levin Varnhagen and later for the Viennese Jewish philosopher Ludwig Wittgenstein. No such dilemma emerged for those contemporaries, however, who simply closed their doors to his daughters, the "half-Jews." Enlightenment and Romantic philosophies might insist that identity was a matter of free choice; the reality of German anti-Semitism taught a different lesson. The term "half-Jew," coined for children of mixed marriages, should have warned Assing that the people around him conceived Jewishness not as a cultural but as a racial category, and that baptism would only make him a Lutheran Jew, that his children would continue to be half-Jews. "Half-Jews," not "half-Germans"—the construction "half-German" never made it into the vocabulary. The German sense of racial superiority rendered biological integration impossible.

"Hybrid vigor" was not a theory to which most of his reluctant fellow citizens subscribed; they preferred to denounce these mixed marriages as a violation against nature, as a threat to humanity. As H. L. Malchow contends, the "terms 'half-breed' and 'half-caste' are double, hyphenated constructions resonating with other linguistic inadequacies and incompletes—with 'half-wit' or 'half-dead,' with 'half-naked' or 'half-truth,' and of course with 'half-civilized.' The half-breed is, by the word that defines him or her, not a true or authentic being, not a member of a 'race' for which there is a word."[59] Assing's descendants would remain Jews or "half-Jews" as long as a neighbor remembered their Jewish genealogy. Rosa Maria and David Assing daily lived out their belief in an egalitarian humanism, but only six months after Ottilie's birth, in August 1819, a mob roamed the streets of Hamburg, harassing and maltreating Jews, attacking Jewish businesses, causing havoc in Jewish neighborhoods, until the city council sent the militia to suppress the riots. Eleven years later a mob celebrated the July Revolution in France by raiding Hamburg's Jewish quarters. Time and again the Assings were forced to listen to the notorious "Hep-Hep" cries of the mob.[60] Disdain and fear of the underclass, which Ottilie Assing harbored throughout her life, had its roots in these confrontations with the anti-Semitic mobs of her childhood. Small wonder also that she would have no problems understanding when America confronted her with the "one drop" doctrine!

One way of dealing with the violence and hostility that surrounded the Assings was to turn a blind eye and deaf ear to them, to seek solace in the domestic realm, and to focus exclusively on that reliable circle of friends who shared their lifestyle and their beliefs. Rosa Maria and David Assing confronted German racism as part of their daily routine, but they continued to teach their daughters that the authority to define identity lay in them as individuals, that for them identity was a matter of choice. Rosa Maria, as Gutzkow wrote in his obituary, was a woman with a "talent to select 'the most pleasant' from all that life has to offer"; her memories were always "decorated with wreaths," and her tales were "a Mount Calvary of joy": "Everything genuinely human, everything individual for her was a revelation of the divine. She saw in the human being a piece of art so exquisite that she needed no hereafter to fill a gap in her life." She defended this creed against all odds and recoiled from anything perceived as "roughness, worldliness, raw passion."[61] And David was too grateful for her gift of compromise, reconciliation, and humor to disrupt the peace she created by imposing his darker moods, his anger and frustration, on her optimistic images. He, too, after all, was characterized by "tolerance of dissenting minds, his tendency to believe in virtue when confronted with ambiguous rumors about fellow human beings, his shrinking at each mortifying word that would wound an opponent's personality."[62] On the issue that was outside their control, the Assings asked silence to rule supreme.

What was within their control, however, was the way in which their daughters perceived their Jewish heritage. Unlike his sister Zippora, David Assing did not despise his Jewishness; if there was self-hatred in him, it was directed against the self as convert rather than his Jewish self. As a young woman Zippora had been a victim of the Prussian *numerus clausus* against Jews, and her frustration was vented in fierce hatred of her Jewishness. Her children did not know they were Jews until others told them, and their parents eventually made them convert. Their daughter Fanny Lewald was later to blame this Jewish self-hatred for much of the anti-Semitism that permeated nineteenth-century Europe:

> The prejudiced individual and the prejudiced mass of people in Germany and England do not forget and forgive the Jew for being a Jew, even today, and they have a right to scorn him as long as he does not have the self-confidence to assert his human dignity to them as equal to theirs, as long as he is ashamed of his origin. . . . We cannot expect another to respect in us what we do not value in ourselves.[63]

The Assings, however, saw no reason why their daughters should deny their paternal heritage. David familiarized them with the orthodox creed, and as the family joined Jewish friends—the de Castros, who were of Portuguese background, the Steinheims,[64] the Friedländers, the dramatist and critic Feodor Wehl, the family of David's brother—on religious holidays, Ottilie and Ludmilla knew Jewish rituals and traditions by heart. The girls spent every Monday with Johanna and Salomon Steinheim, both strict opponents of the Jewish Enlightenment, yet intimate enough with the Assings to identify themselves as their aunt and uncle. David had moved away from orthodox Judaism, but he wanted his children to accept it as an important segment of their past, an essential part of their composite present identity.

Neither David's incontestable reputation as one of Hamburg's best physicians nor the family's secure income nor David's conversion to Lutheranism protected the family against anti-Semitic prejudices and social isolation. The Assing girls, ostracized by conservative Germans on the one hand, and orthodox Jews on the other, may have suffered severe "category" crises. They learned the painful lesson that identity was not a matter of choice but defined by those who held the power to define, yet they clung to the creed they had inherited from their parents. The ostracism to which they were exposed sharpened their eyes for all expressions of discrimination, but it also burdened them with a need to belong, at times overwhelming. The almost excessive pride they took in the elitist circles they moved in, the arrogance they displayed against petty bourgeois and "philistine" people may have been a self-protective mask: in a society that avoided them, they reconstituted themselves as architects of their social realm, claiming they wielded the instrument of choice, had decided whom to exclude and whom to embrace. Thinking of themselves as exceptionally sophisticated, they proclaimed it as only natural that their circle of friends would be small—exclusive.

Ottilie and Ludmilla received a superior education because their parents believed in the intellectual equality of women and men, because they knew that as "half-Jews" of superior education but middling wealth it would be hard for their daughters to find suitable husbands, because their father's experience had taught him that flexibility and the ability to improvise were essential survival techniques for men or women with a Jewish background.[65] Sharing the conviction of their feminist sister-in-law Rahel Varnhagen that women have the same right to professional training as men, the Assings prepared their daughters for active professional lives, and this meant that they were not only encouraged to write but taught to write well. They not only learned to make good conversation but memorized and practiced the rules of classic rhetoric. They not only went to the theater, opera, and art exhibitions but were expected to offer assessments of what they had seen. They acquired foreign languages so they could make a living anywhere in the world. Their mother instructed them in the art of teaching so they could enter the most popular and respectable profession for women. While most contemporary women of their class were taught merely enough to enhance their value on the marriage market, Ottilie and Ludmilla were given the skills to make them independent. The model woman which Rosa Maria evoked for her daughters combined features of their aunt Rahel, whose intelligence and vivacity had enabled her to assemble Berlin's social and intellectual elite in her salon and who, with her demands for a woman's right to education and professional training, became a pioneer for women's liberation in Germany; of George Sand, with her courage to live what she preached, a woman in whom writing skill and imagination formed a harmonious one; and of the fourteenth-century sculptor Sabina von Steinbach, daughter of the architect Erwin von Steinbach, who designed and chiseled many of the statues decorating the facade of the cathedral at Strasbourg. This unconventional training provided by their parents, but especially by their mother, eventually enabled both sisters to work abroad as journalists and, in Ottilie's case, as a teacher. Their physical and intellectual mobility was at odds with contemporary designations of womanhood.

Parallel to the rational acquisition of factual data and professional skills, which the Assings regarded as essential to their children's upbringing, ran an education defined in terms of the Romantic concept of inner life (the German term is *Gemütsbildung*), directed toward perfection of the girls' emotional and moral perceptions; both parents considered traveling and literature as ideal training grounds to achieve this end. On the one hand, traveling was the best way to familiarize the children with their "fatherland" and its various regional cultures—after all, their parents, like most Romantics, dreamed of a united German nation and enthusiastically supported the nationalism that found expression, for example, in the Hambach Festival;* on the other hand, it helped them transcend a narrow nationalism and mature into proud citizens of the world. The Assings wanted their daughters to understand that history is composed of and nourished by many cultures which are not confined to one specific place or time. In the 1830s Rosa Maria and her daughters took extended excursions to Berlin, where they were guests of the Varnhagens and of David's brother; to Swabia, where they stayed with the Kerner family; to Heidelberg and Mannheim; and finally to Strasbourg, where they met Rosa Maria's relatives, successful merchants, magistrates, and professors. As faithful disciples of the Romantic School, regarding Uhland, Chamisso, Schwab, Achim von Arnim, Clemens Brentano, and Ludwig Tieck as both their models and mentors, Rosa Maria introduced her adolescent daughters to the circle she admired so much during several trips to Swabia. Their friend Feodor Wehl later confirmed the importance of these connections when he said, "Ludmilla and Ottilie were as if begotten and raised under the spell of the muses. They had a fine sense and a tender understanding for everything that had poetic talents." He remembers their "bated breath and red cheeks" when they listened to readings of poetry.[66] Paris was their goal in 1835, and Ottilie immediately embraced the "City of Light" as hers: "From the very first moment it seemed more familiar to me than any other foreign city, for I had read so much about it."[67] How much she felt at home in Paris became clear twenty-five years later, when she tried to make it the haven to which she and Douglass would escape from the American gaze in early 1860. In 1835 the Assing women spent days in a row at the Louvre and the Palais Luxembourg; they saw Heinrich Heine; and they made a special pilgrimage to worship the goddess of their literary and feminist dreams, George Sand. These trips were the highlight of Ottilie's young life. No matter how great the hardships they encountered on the road, in letters to Varnhagen she complained about only one thing: that the trips had to end.[68] The excursions with her mother generated a passion for traveling that never died.

---

*The Hambach Festival, which took place at Hambach Castle in the Palatinate on 27–30 May 1832, was the first mass rally for a free and united Germany. More than 30,000 people attended.

For Rosa Maria, preparing her children for life also meant teaching them about what for her was its defining center—love between woman and man. As Ottilie and Ludmilla grew, their mother not only familiarized them with German folk tales, folk songs, and ballads, with classic and contemporary literature but—being too much a writer merely to read and retell tales created or collected by others—wrote her own ballads and tales for them, fairy tales for bright children, she called them. And the center of all her texts was love—"love and pride and controlled passion."[69] The pattern of all these texts is identical: beautiful young lovers of a sensuous innocence encounter violent opposition to their relationship from their elders, who plan to marry them off to socially suitable partners, and they either overcome this opposition by faithful perseverance, defy convention by consummating their love against official morality, or escape into death. In his obituary of Rosa Maria, Karl Gutzkow defined her concept of love as "a return to the liberal ways of the Age of Troubadours," a time "when love was regarded as superior to the law."[70] In that, Rosa Maria reconceptualized and rewrote the novels of her favorite, Goethe, who, in novels like *The Sorrows of Young Werther* (1774–87) and *Elective Affinities* (1809), insisted on the priority of marriage as a legal institution over the individual's inner inclinations and preached self-abnegation. For Rosa Maria, love demanded and deserved consummation, fulfillment, happiness, and if that was not possible, death was preferable to a marriage of convention, which for her was identical with a loveless relationship. In one of her songs to the river Rhine, a noble virgin escapes an arranged marriage by committing suicide as the wedding party crosses the Rhine. Rather than sacrificing her purity to her despised groom she offers herself to the river god:

> The maiden felt embraced by an invisible power,
> Which pulled her down with strong hands.
> Trembling she sinks down, hardly conscious,
> Into the waves and to the god's bosom.[71]

Ottilie and Ludmilla were taught by their mother, who knew of the suicide epidemic sparked by Goethe's *Werther*,[72] that in such a situation, suicide, far from being a sin, a crime, an act of escapism, or a sign of weakness, can express individual autonomy, personal integrity, and strength—an act of self-liberation, a sensuous embrace.

Though she depicted suicide as a viable alternative to a loveless life, Rosa Maria's tales and ballads for her children celebrated life. In "The Young Lady and the Fisherman" a count's daughter, bored by the luxury with which her parents surround her, and appalled by her effeminate aristocratic suitors, develops a passionate longing for a young fisherman whom she observes from her window. He, first seeing her when delivering fish to the castle kitchen, falls desperately in love. On her appointed wedding day a storm sinks the ship on which the ceremony takes place; while the noble groom and aristocratic guests are saved, the bride vanishes in the waves. The fisherman, who continues the search, finds her dead body and carries her back to his cabin, covering the beloved maid with hot tears and kisses. His passion revives her; the lovers, the noble white maiden and the dark-skinned fisherman, finally united, decide that her "death" shall be her liberation and their salvation. Dead and lost for her parents and husband, she will live her true love in the fisherman's cabin in happy defiance of convention:

> Here with you I will seek a new, more beautiful life,
> Sweet happiness in a quiet valley![73]

As a rule, the decision to place love above public morality was made by the women in these narratives, and it is obvious that Rosa Maria glorified this determination to choose as an act of woman's self-liberation and self-elevation. The male lover is usually lower-class, but always nature's gentleman: his noble features, natural intelligence and charm, moral integrity, industry, and courage are designed to compensate for his social shortcomings, rendering the very notion of social hierarchy as absurd. As long as the man of lower social status was able and willing to accept the notions of culture which the Assings and their friends represented as their norm, as long as he was able and willing to become "like us," he was embraced as an equal.

Rosa Maria's "The Chimney Sweeper" is a perfect illustration of this approach. In this novella, published in Strasbourg in 1834, a chimney sweeper overcomes social prejudice in conservative Strasbourg in marrying a magistrate's daughter. Society regarded marriage outside an individual's class as a violation of social decorum, outside of religious denomination, "race," or ethnicity as unnatural, but this daughter of a Catholic-Lutheran misalliance, this woman of a German-Jewish intermarriage, Rosa Maria Assing, taught her daughters that class and race were irrelevant when love was based on physical, intellectual, and moral compatibility—provided always that the lower-order lover be willing and able to educate her- or himself into the higher rank. Rosa Maria's dark chimney sweeper, a man of physical beauty and strength, personal courage and integrity, intellectual curiosity and mobility, saves the city from a fire by his heroic and skillful intervention; he educates himself and establishes a successful business before he claims his prize: the magistrate's fair daughter. For

Rosa Maria, as for David, the Enlightenment concept of human equality and nineteenth-century notions of cultural hierarchy existed side by side, and there is no sign that they were aware of potential tensions or contradictions between the two.

In the last decades of the eighteenth and the first decade of the nineteenth century, the Jewish upper and middle classes in Germany increasingly adopted the lifestyle of the bourgeoisie. They entertained lavishly and graciously, opened their doors to Christians who deigned to communicate with them, and often encouraged their children to convert. For a brief interval Jewish and German intellectuals, representatives of the German nobility and bourgeoisie, actors and artists came together for sophisticated conversation and unconventional liaisons in the salons of Jewish women like Rahel Levin and Henriette Herz in turn-of-the-century Berlin. In *Zeit und Menschen*, Feodor Wehl, the Jewish literary critic and friend of the Assings and Varnhagens, assessed these salons:

> At the beginning of this century, the lifestyles and moral attitudes of the French Louises still influenced the great and high society in Germany. The mistress business was well tolerated and hardly ever in harsh moral disrepute. Rahel Levin had no problem in being in intimate contact with such people. Their underrating of marriage, female virtue, and civil honor was very relaxed and open, and this made a very heterogeneous social life possible. In this mixed society modern Jewry was first accepted, thanks to its biting humor, its inspiring spirit, and the enormous quickness of repartee of its conversations. Especially beautiful women like Henrietta Herz, Friederike Robert and, above everybody else, Rahel Levin, distinguished themselves by that.[74]

This openness prospered under the impact of the Enlightenment and Hardenberg's reform policy toward Jews,* though it remained always a minority position and did not survive the conservative resurgence initiated by the Napoleonic Wars and Restoration policy. German polite society, the majority of which had defied Hardenberg's reforms anyway, happily resumed an attitude they had never willingly questioned: treating aspiring Jews with contempt and keeping their doors firmly closed to them. Gutzkow, who lived in Hamburg in the 1830s, reported that Germans might accept an invitation to Jewish mansions like Salomon Heine's or Fanny Hertz's, but there were no return invita-

---

*Count Karl von Hardenberg, as the King of Prussia's principal minister, issued new regulations intended to speed up the transition of Prussia from absolutism to liberalism. In 1812 a *Judenedikt* (Jews' edict) decreed that, as a rule, Jews were citizens with equal rights.

tions; literary and social circles and clubs remained segregated.[75] In 1837 the *Allgemeine Zeitung des Judenthums* reported: "The hatred of Jews, or rather the scorn of Jews, here really reaches unbelievable dimensions, and although Christian families cannot totally dissociate themselves from contact with rich Jews, it always appears as if they condescended to do so."[76]

Keeping this background in mind, the Assing house in the Poolstrasse was indeed a haven of multicultural encounters. Imitating the example of Rahel and her salon culture, Ottilie's parents continued to live the concept of Romantic social life in Restoration Germany almost two decades after it had been stifled in Berlin, and while most of Germany succumbed to the conservative pressure of the Restoration, the Assing home in Hamburg became a regular meeting place for members of the Jewish and German intelligentsia like the dramatist Friedrich Hebbel, the novelist Amalie Schoppe, the poet Heinrich Zeise, the Friedländers, de Castros, and Steinheims. Here Gabriel Riesser, a pioneer of Jewish emancipation, found an eager audience, preaching to the converted, and representatives of the radical Young Germany movement like the poet Heinrich Heine, the dramatist and novelist Karl Gutzkow, and members of the Hamburg theater sought out each other. Actors, ostracized by Hamburg's polite circles, who still associated theater with immorality, found a warm welcome. At the Assing salon one debated political and social issues, read and discussed contemporary literature, staged plays, and had concerts. Many years later Feodor Wehl remembered the Assing home as a meeting place for those who loved to move beyond the conventional, and Rosa Maria as the one who challenged them all to soar. From their childhood onward, Ottilie and Ludmilla were encouraged, especially by their mother, to join these groups of some of Germany's most unconventional minds. In this highly intellectual and politicized atmosphere, the girls became familiar with the politics of the day. Born in Restoration Germany, they were, in intellectual terms, children of the most progressive elements of the German Enlightenment and German Romanticism, and they reached maturity as participants in the tragic events of 1848.

The Assing home gave the girls a sense of place and security without entombing them in the kind of stasis that characterized the domestic life of so many German middle-class women of the time. Its doors were thrown wide open, inviting the world outside to join its vivacious circle, and to encourage those within to explore the enticements beyond its walls.[77] Theirs was a domestic environment of openness, generosity, and creative vitality, of intellectual curiosity and adventurousness, of heated debates and boisterous laughter, and it was all their mother's making. Rosa Maria chose, invited, and entertained, and people came to visit Rosa Maria. As Ottilie and Ludmilla grew up, she invited them to share the role of hostess with her. To visitors David always seemed like an outsider in his own house during these events, as Feodor Wehl recalled: "The study was his world, and when he appeared at parties in his own house, it seemed as if he had dropped in by chance."[78] Gutzkow agreed: "Assing isolated himself, he made no use of his domestic privileges, but let his family rule while he sat in his narrow study. He tested each new acquaintance his family made with an almost distrustful coldness, and it often took a while before he could make friends with a guest whom the others had long accepted and welcomed daily."[79] While his friends discussed poetry and George Sand's latest novel or played silly games, he would interrupt them with quotations from Goethe; while his guests and daughters devoured Strauss and Ruge, he held on to Homer and Plato and sought solace in a Kernerian mysticism; while Heine and Gutzkow fought over the future of Germany, he indulged in memories of his personal past and in a romantic reinvention of the Middle Ages à la Uhland. His motto, "The physician, however, perceives the horrible," corresponded perfectly with his dark style. His wife and children moved happily among an intellectual elite, indulging in their egalitarian and radical rhetoric; he administered to the needs of poor Jews. Rosa Maria and her daughters looked out on life from the "Mount Calvary of Joy" they invented; David Assing perceived the world through Gothic lenses.

Friends unanimously agreed that, while Rosa Maria loved to surround herself with the most rebellious minds of the day, David Assing seemed more conservative in his taste. The radicalism and aggressiveness of the Young Germans frightened him. He seemed appalled by their love affairs, their irreverence about religion, their challenge to marriage as an institution, and he worried about the effect these associates might have on his already unruly daughters. He was especially apprehensive when religious controversy moved center stage. In 1835 the Assing salon was boiling with debates over David Friedrich Strauss's *The Life of Jesus*. Strauss, then a left-wing Hegelian, not only deconstructed most of the Gospel as myth but reconceptualized the historical Jesus as a reality, as the personification of the idea of humanity. This pantheistic approach saw God as "the eternal," and immortality was a mere construct of the mind. Religion, Strauss taught, is inseparable from history, and he defended pantheism as an appropriate expression for the modern human mind.[80] As Gutzkow later reported, the Assing circle's response was ambivalent. On the one hand, "the myth of Christ, devised from oriental parallels and the messianic prophecies of the Jews, unmasked a lot of other matters in state and church, science and life, as myths," yet Strauss's focus on myths could not satisfy the rationalists among them. "The mythic Christ dissolved into nothing, in a fog . . . Even in the most enlightened circles we had the need for a historical Christ, for a noble, virtuous, enthusiastic human being, for a martyr who remained interesting and respectable even for neologues."[81]

A few years later their debates received new impetus when Arnold Ruge[82] and Theodor Echtermeyer published their manifesto *Der Protestantismus und die Romantik* (1839–40), a vigorous attack on the religious notions of Romanticism. The Romantics' glorification of "genius," their celebration of a fake medievalism, their vacant negativity, and their intellectual arbitrariness turned them into defenders of the most reactionary forces in Germany, the authors charged. All these debates were important steps which Ottilie, unable to find a home either in mysticism or in skepticism, welcomed as stepping-stones on her road to what she eventually accepted as her true creed: *Unglauben*, unbelief, atheism.

Assing's friend Dr. Salomon Steinheim was the only one in this circle who shared his skeptical uneasiness, and he later explicitly warned Ottilie and Ludmilla against a radicalism that would not only threaten their reputation but also subvert and pervert their most intimate relationships. In a letter which he wrote to the sisters on the anniversary of their father's death, Steinheim claimed that "one of the rare complaints he articulated in conversations with me was the absence of respect in the young generation. This caused his insurmountable aversion against so many of the excellent individuals, so many of the celebrities, who received a welcome in your home."[83] Yet it seems that either David never interfered with his wife's and daughters' social activities or they dismissed his arguments. There are no reports of controversies between husband and wife over these issues, and the only sign we have of David's silent disapproval was his refusal to join company he did not appreciate. Gutzkow, one of the most aggressive Young Germans, remembered: "His eyes were always turned toward the past. New developments, fermenting elements of the future he calmly ignored. He even closed his mind methodically against the just germinating, and so it happened that those around him embraced the newest developments while he himself lived only for the old."[84] And yet his closest friends and especially his family knew that this first impression told only half the truth, for he could also enjoy thoroughly the rich social life to which "his womenfolk" exposed him every day. Though stern and sober, he was a loving husband and father and a generous host. Wine never failed to soften his nature, and then his love of laughter, his playfulness, his sense of humor shone. He was a lively actor and a sensitive reader, a hilariously funny satirist. He might look like an outsider most of the time, but he knew, as did his family, that he belonged.

Ottilie never forgot how privileged she was to grow up in this environment. Her parents' was a dynamic partnership, a never-ending struggle to make the marriage work despite substantial differences in personality and attitude. It became the model according to which Ottilie and Ludmilla later strove to define their relationships to men. They spent a lifetime seeking for partnerships based on openness and honesty, passion and intellectual challenge.

The house in the Poolstrasse was a haven for those who lived in it and for those who visited, but it was also an island, surrounded, it often seemed, by a stormy sea. Rosa Maria's diaries, which she kept during all those years, as well as the letters which Ottilie and Ludmilla wrote to their uncle Varnhagen von Ense in Berlin[85] document that the family could never overcome the segregation that reigned in Hamburg. Germans were a minority in their inner circle—Amalie Schoppe, Karl Gutzkow and his wife, Heinrich Zeise (all of them writers united by love of literature)—and they hardly ever mention social gatherings in Christian homes. They regularly visited the family of their Lutheran minister, but other social contacts with Germans took place outside of Hamburg: in Amalie Schoppe's house on the island of Fehmarn, in Varnhagen's Berlin, in Swabia, Strasbourg, and Paris. The Assings' most intimate friends were Jews, the Steinheims and de Castros; they were entertained by and, in turn, invited Fanny Hertz, Dr. Salomon Heine, the Friedländers. Obviously these Jewish acquaintances understood that David Assing's conversion was neither an act of opportunism nor a defection; it was the result of sincere intellectual struggle that deserved respect.

It is impossible to determine from the sources available to us whether this dominance of Jewish acquaintances resulted from personal preferences or was a response to German prejudices. They never discussed the issue in either their private writings or their public utterances. Anti-Semitism as a force that shaped their lives in such an ugly way—after all, they lived through pogroms in 1830 and 1835[86]—was absent from their texts. If mentioned at all, it came up as a discrimination from which other Jews, usually the poor, suffered. This is all the more revealing inasmuch as three of the family's closest friends, Salomon Steinheim, Gabriel Riesser, and Karl Gutzkow, were leading figures in the controversy over Jewish emancipation which raged in Hamburg in the 1830s and culminated in the 1840s. Steinheim, a Jewish physician, philosopher, and musician, was a fierce critic of the Jewish Enlightenment, challenging his contem-

poraries to seek personal salvation within Jewish doctrine, in revelation rather
than analysis. At the same time he demanded immediate Jewish emancipation.
Conversion for him was an act of betrayal: "It is always a wretched thing to
deny one's nationality," his wife reported him as saying; "it is all the more criminal when this is an oppressed and terrorized people."[87] His most powerful Jewish opponent and ally, all in one, was Gabriel Riesser (of whom Gutzkow wrote
that he had "the hair of a Negro. Fair, but so tightly curled that you would
think it was wool"[88]). Riesser had broken with orthodox Judaism and called
himself an enlightened Deist. He was a militant spokesman for immediate and
full emancipation of Jews, demanding a separation of church and state, and
thought Jewishness should be expressed exclusively in terms of religious community. Gutzkow, meanwhile, who later in life became notorious for anti-
Semitic statements, took a gradualist stand, arguing that German biases against
Jews were a natural response to expressions of Jewish cultural inferiority; consequently equal rights for Jews, though desirable, should not be imposed on Germans until the Jews had improved themselves.[89]

Ottilie observed these debates between three of her closest friends and intellectual mentors attentively, and there can be no doubt that this intellectually
curious woman did not relegate herself to the position of neutral and silent observer, but we have no documentation of what position she adopted. Her later
life shows that her alternative to these disputed doctrines, in relation to religious issues, was freedom of the mind, as Gutzkow's eponymous Uriel Acosta
claimed it for himself in his play. After his rejection of both Judaism and Christianity as untruth, he charges:

> To words you shackle the intellect, to words
> You shackle the eternal God, to this worldly creation,
> Which your eye can barely understand.
> We want to shake off this old yoke!
> Only reason be the symbol of faith,
> And when we doubt to find the truth,
> It is better to seek for new gods,
> Instead of cursing with the old, instead of praying.[90]

Raised in the midst of religious controversy, Ottilie Assing became a belligerent freethinker.

We can trace as a leitmotif in all of Ottilie's public and private writings
the stubborn insistence that in a free and enlightened society, identity is—or,
better, must be—a matter of free choice. The definer of her discourse was un-

wavering belief in the Enlightenment concept of human equality and, as its companion, fierce opposition to any social or racial ascription that stigmatized difference. This creed determined her attitude toward members of other races, nations, ethnicities, and classes, her relationship to the American women's movement, to trade unions, and to the socialist struggle in Europe. This made her ridicule women's claims to innate purity, to moral superiority, and for special protection. This caused her to demand equal rights rather than special training for the underprivileged. This enabled her to love Frederick Douglass—to embrace the African-American as the white woman's equal, and, equally important, to perceive herself as a woman equal to the man she loved. The society she was raised in defined difference hierarchically; her response was a militant denial of innate difference. And yet her representation of African-Americans, Irish-Americans, Germans, Chinese-Americans and Native Americans, of the women's movement, and of class issues in later years shows that her adherence to egalitarian principles never really protected her against essentialist assessments of race. The competition in her between her two readings of human diversity did not cease, yet there is no sign that she was aware of the contradictions.

In the winter of 1839–40 the delicate but strong web of human relationships which the house in the Poolstrasse represented for all who associated with it was destroyed with one violent blow: Rosa Maria's illness and death. To the last, Rosa Maria, now fifty-seven and thus, by contemporary standards, an old woman, a matron, saw her life as defined by love, and this love made it almost impossible for her to believe the end could be approaching. Here she was—still loving and longing, full of desire. How could death possibly call upon one who felt so deeply, so passionately? Was it not unnatural to claim a life that experienced a bride's joy in walking on virginal blossoms (and ignored the reality that painted the falling leaves of winter approaching)? "Have we already reached autumn?" she asked in a tone that bespoke bewilderment rather than fear:

> This is what I ask myself, for truly, I do not know,
> Are the leaves already falling? Is the air already rough?
> Why do you look at me amazed? For me love sprinkles blossoms,
> Therefore I believe that around me the most glorious Spring blooms![91]

Death may have claimed her prematurely, but it could not deprive her of the richness she experienced. At the very end she triumphed:

Hail to me, the happy one! I call out in joy at the end of my life,
For I have not lived in vain, for I have known love!

In a résumé written on her deathbed, she insisted:

You, Amor, I served always.
Of all the gods you reigned supreme.[92]

For months Ottilie and Ludmilla, aged twenty-one and nineteen, nursed their mother on her sickbed, surrounded her with their love; their letters and diaries show no sign of awareness that her illness was fatal. When the end came, they were devastated by the loss. "Our sun, which animated and warmed everything, has set, and with that everything is annihilated," Ottilie wrote to Varnhagen in a letter of 10 February 1840. "How we shall continue to live I really don't know." True, they were surrounded by friends who did their utmost to sustain them, but Ottilie was ambivalent about the help and advice they offered. She was enraged at a colleague of David's who counseled him at the funeral to take "an experienced petticoat into the house immediately." Does he really think "we would allow a strange element to force her way between us and Father?" she fumed. But even more gentle and thoughtful advice—to stop dwelling on the past, to go on with their lives—roused her ire: how could one discard memories "of an almost perfect happiness of twenty years" for what could only be "an empty, cold future"?[93] Her annoyance was more than an expression of the mourner's right to weep and remember; it was also that of a woman determined to shape her future without interference from any outsider, perhaps more experienced but certainly meddling.

The letter shows, too, that only two weeks after her mother's death Ottilie had taken control of her life and of the realm of which she was now in charge. And there is ample evidence that her new sense of self and place was defined not just in terms of mourning and duty. She had inherited her mother's love of life, her sense of humor, her ability to make the best out of whatever life offered. She could not do what society expected of her—that is, bury herself in her room and weep; she had to take on life on her own terms. Only a month after Rosa Maria's funeral the sisters hired a teacher to improve their English, and they resumed their music lessons; they asked their father to read to them regularly;[94] they begged his friends in Swabia to distract their father with a visit—everything to keep him and themselves busy and from feeling too deeply.

As soon as the prescribed year of mourning was over, Ottilie and her sister again participated in the social life they so loved. The autobiography of Heinrich Zeise contains several playbills of February 1841 which show Ottilie and Ludmilla starring as actresses in comedies, sketches, and tragedies performed—or, rather, read, for the participants sat in a circle—at the Steinheim and Gutzkow homes. Zeise remembers the Ottilie of these days as "a beautiful girl with an opulent body, next to Gutzkow . . . the best reader of the circle,"[95] and he even suggests that she later performed onstage. Still, everything was different: the house in the Poolstrasse had ceased to be a magnet and a meeting place. The Assing sisters, trained as hostesses, found themselves in the role of guest. After a few futile attempts to force some rays of sunshine back into the dark Assing home by gathering in this familiar setting, most of their acquaintances had given up. Whenever Ottilie, Ludmilla, and their friends became too boisterous or enthusiastic, "a deep sigh, an almost painful groan from that part of the large salon which could not be reached by the lamp dampened our spirits," Zeise reported. The center of intellectual and social activities was now the Steinheim mansion in Altona, a vast Renaissance building surrounded by a beautiful park and overlooking the river Elbe.

The mourning David Assing whom Zeise evoked was the prototypical "melancholy Jew":

> Here a bent, gaunt man paced up and down, nervously restless; his long black hair hung over his face and fell over the large hollow eyes; he wrung his hands, pressed them to his face, heavy drops penetrated between his thin fingers. And so I always saw him, many hours in a row, dissolving in his pain, inaccessible to solace, a lost man. . . . Never again have I seen a man in such devouring, deathly pain—it was a ghostly sight.[96]

David Assing reimagined himself as the Romantic mourner, and the role became his only reality. "Do you know what did me some good for a little while? To see my name joined with Rosa Maria's on the black cross on her grave," he wrote in a letter to his brother-in-law; soon he would follow his wife, he said, joining her in death as she had once joined him in life. He envisioned this final reunion erotically: "She came to live with me, my Rosa, I remembered . . . , and I will soon move in with her—and I know the comfort that lies in this desire, in this hot longing."[97] Rosa Maria's lifelong romantic flirtation with death, which had permeated her poems and tales, had been just that—flirtation. With her every movement, her every thought, she had celebrated life, and when death approached, she had fought to her last moment. But her husband's attitude was fundamentally different. He had been beset by depression, guilt feelings, and self-doubt since his youth, and the romantic glorification of dying as *ars moriendi* seemed to atone for the death wish he carried with him always. Rosa Maria, with her love and joie de vivre, had stood between him and these dark longings, keeping him away from the abyss, but with her no longer there, his death wish took possession of him. His melancholy, conflated with the roles of tragic lover and Romantic mourner, created a deadly potion.

The last two years of David's life were devoted entirely to Rosa Maria. To outsiders it seemed that David wasted these months in aimless wanderings, caught in a bottomless pit of extreme pain. In reality he spent hours in the isolation of his study assembling his wife's poetry and tales, just as Varnhagen von Ense had edited Rahel's letters immediately after her death. Comparing Rosa Maria's poems to flowers that death had prevented her from winding into a beautiful wreath, he offered to finish this task for her as a token of his love—only to realize, as he admitted in his introductory poem, that pain deprived him of the strength and creativity to give to his wife what his love challenged him to offer. The dedication poem culminated in a cry of despair:

> Oh, without you no effort can succeed:
> How, then, could a wreath be closed!—
> Only tears flow without you,
> Just like my fading life![98]

The magic circle she had conjured was broken, and he had no place left but the grave. *Rosa Maria's poetischer Nachlass* was published in 1841. A tribute of David's love to his deceased wife, not only does it contain her private and public poetry as well as the romantic tales and ballads she composed for her daughters but, being arranged in chronological order, the collection also invites us to retrace the most important steps of Rosa Maria's life.

With his uncompromising openness David Assing then declared that he had decided to die. "When a nature who did not progress with time and only enjoyed memories of the past is attached to life with loosely tied strings anyway, Rosa Maria's death had severed them totally," Gutzkow observed. Assing even lost interest in his daughters. Perhaps, without Rosa Maria's softening interpretations, he saw how far they had drifted from him. "Oh, if only you knew how I love him, this father," Ludmilla wrote to Varnhagen; "since Mother's death he has withdrawn so much from us and, despite his affection, showed so little interest in our lives, in our thoughts and our feelings that we usually had to fend for ourselves."[99] In the fall of 1841 Assing came down with an inflammation of the respiratory tract and took to his bed. In January 1842 Ottilie reported to Varnhagen—she sent him long reports throughout these months—that his health had improved enough for him to move about the house, yet a few weeks later he suffered a relapse. Ottilie and Ludmilla nursed him day and night, but David refused nourishment and soon could no longer recognize his daughters. It was clear to everybody that he had willed himself to die. His friend Dr. Steinheim called in a colleague, Dr. Stietzing, for support, hoping that a stranger's authority might help. To no avail. David Assing died on 25 April, 1842, at 4 p.m.[100] He was fifty-five years old. On 30 April he was buried at 5 a.m., one day before Rosa Maria's and his twenty-sixth wedding anniversary. As was the custom of the day, his daughters did not accompany the casket but remained at home. "I followed him with my eyes," Ottilie wrote to her uncle. "On many of his ways I have followed him thus from the doorsteps."[101]

II

IF ONLY I WERE A BIRD

Vagrant Years

⊙══╋══⊙

I want to live, live at any cost, even if living may mean suffering.
—CLARA MUNDT, *Aphra Behn*

I cannot give up my Germany, but I have little hope for its unity, for it is so divided. That is true. Liberty cannot be devoured, and someday it will surface brightly and be a light for those who follow after us. . . . Like a letter cast in ore Germany is locked into my heart; it will always be that heart because the ore cuts so hard and deeply into it. —RAHEL DE CASTRO, Letter to Ludmilla Assing

⊙══╋══⊙

*D*arkness *had already begun to settle on 16 August 1852, when Ottilie Assing stood at the rail of the* Indian Queen, *her face turned toward the city of Hamburg. As the huge vessel was pulled out of the harbor, moving away from the waving, cheering, weeping crowd on shore, beginning its long journey down the river Elbe to the open space of the North Sea, she turned her eyes away from the docks, as if nobody was there for her, away from the city, as if it contained nothing dear to her.*

Her friends Mrs. Baison and her daughters, as well as Ludmilla, had accompanied her on board, they had watched the sunset together, and over a glass of wine they had spent hours reveling in the past and conjuring up the future. Ottilie had not been able to cry, even as she saw tears running down the girls' faces. Situations like this made her tense, angry, irritable. Ludmilla had looked at her with a mixture of pity and contempt. "Unhappy as a result of her circumstances, unhappy as a result of her own character traits, which will always accompany her!" Ludmilla wrote to Varnhagen the following day. It was with a peculiar emptiness in her stomach that Ottilie watched the darkness swallow up her sister and friends when they left the vessel, yet the flowers and the candy, the shawl and the pillow they had left in her cabin made her breathe freely again. These gifts were more than reminiscences of ties severed; they were promises of new connections she would make in her American life ahead. She would sleep soundly on board.

There was no sadness in Ottilie's face as she turned to observe her fellow passengers, rather compassion and curiosity. What kind of people were taking this transatlantic passage? She saw before her a curious quilt of humanity, a good sample, it seemed, from the divided, heterogeneous Germany they were leaving behind: Bavarians, Hessians, Rhinelanders, Jews from Slesingia, Prussians, Saxonian Slavs; representatives of all classes, with those from lower strata dominating: farmers, teachers, physicians, artisans, field hands, peddlers, artists, ministers, factory workers, maids. Men in their prime were in the majority, and women in their late teens and early twenties. All were wearing their best outfits, well groomed to make a good last impression on the people who stayed behind. Ottilie saw a few smiling faces: a couple of honeymooners on the upper deck, a few slightly tipsy young men from the second level, clearly tourists. Most of the travelers seemed somber, and tears were blinding many eyes; people showed a strange melancholy, an almost desperate anxiety. Even the children on board had this mood, clinging to their mothers' frocks, distressed by the pain in their parents' eyes; some were wailing, but most were silent, like their elders. Last messages were called across the water as the vessel picked up speed, addressed to loved ones whose faces could no longer be identified in the crowd. Familiar features of Hamburg began to lose their contours, as in a fog, and sobs of desperation escaped those who had no new pictures to replace the old ones drifting out of sight. Ottilie Assing was among the few who could smile. She had convinced herself that the New World was her destiny, and after a painfully futile quest for a place in Germany she was determined to make it bright.

Her eyes fell on a huge black cat sleeping on a bright white deck chair, still warm from the sun. Ottilie was overjoyed. Slowly she approached, anxious not to frighten the beast into flight. But she need not have worried: he was on his territory, and no passenger could dislodge him. Especially not this one. He seemed to know she was a friend from the way she moved, and didn't even bother to open an eye for her; he simply started purring. Ottilie held her hand in front of his nose so that he could smell her. Smiling at his apparent approval, she sat down on the deck next to him, lay her face by the cat's warm fur, and gently stroked his back. She decided to call him "Cat with a Social Rank."[1] Their friendship lasted until the Indian Queen *arrived in the New World. Both Cat and Ottilie were pleased, dozing as the movement of the vessel gently rocked them, enjoying the sea breeze. It would be a good trip.*

Ottilie Assing's Hamburg lost its luster at her mother's death; it disappeared with her father. On Wednesday, 4 May 1842, only days after David Assing's funeral, Ottilie and Ludmilla were awakened by fire bells: Hamburg was in flames. For four days the fire raged, destroying one block after another.

By the time the fire came to a halt at the western bank of the river Alster, 4,219 houses had been burned, 20,000 people were homeless, and 51 people had lost their lives.[2] The Assing sisters anxiously watched the wall of flames as it moved toward their home, coloring the sky bright red; explosions shook the city as desperate firefighters tried to stop the blaze by destroying dozens of houses; looters roamed the streets. Ludmilla was almost paralyzed with fear, but Ottilie went out into the streets to find a cart; they loaded their most valuable possessions on it and then joined the procession of fugitives. They found shelter at the Steinheims' house in Altona, but on Friday, Ottilie, unable to bear the suspense, returned to the Poolstrasse. To her great relief, she found the house blackened but unharmed, and she immediately took possession of it. Still, she could barely recognize the city, now a wasteland. The city hall, sixty schools, the famous church of St. Nikolai, Salomon Heine's mansion on the Jungfernstieg, the Portuguese-Jewish synagogue which the de Castros attended, the Old Exchange—everything was destroyed.

Among the people who lost their homes were the family of Dr. Wilhelm Birkenstock, a colleague of Ottilie's father, and when they heard of their friends' plight the Assing sisters offered to share their house with them. The way Ottilie managed the details of this arrangement shows her inner strength and sense of self. Instead of allowing the grief over her father's death and the pain of Hamburg's destruction to paralyze her, she reached out compassionately to others. But more: aware that she could not endure continuous contacts with relative strangers, and sensing that the Birkenstocks might feel they should take on the role of mature advisers to the "poor fatherless girls," she divided up the house so as to provide each family with space of its own; in addition, she decided, "in order to be freer and to avoid too close proximity, we would always have our lunch in a restaurant, which also means we avoid all cumbersome accountancy."[3] Ottilie was establishing control over her life.

The destruction of Hamburg reinforced a decision that Ottilie and Ludmilla must already have begun to discuss in the months of their father's final illness: to leave Hamburg. In her letter to her uncle Varnhagen describing her father's last days, Ottilie mentioned that she had given notice to her landlord for the coming November, and on 12 May she told him that the sisters were determined to move to Berlin: "It is our provisional plan to sell most of our things . . . and to rent two or three rooms near you and, so we can live independent of the landlady and landlord, to hire a maid." Ottilie had drawn up a solid financial plan that showed exactly what they could afford to do: "We are used to a simple lifestyle, not the least spoiled, and know how to adapt and to moderate ourselves, so that we may hope to make our capital do, which now consists of 22,000 marks . . . then some Prussian and Hamburgian state bonds . . . so that our total income amounts to approximately 1,100 marks, which is, on an average, half of our former budget. I do not believe life in Berlin will be more expensive than here."[4] Ottilie Assing knew what she was doing and would not be stopped.

Possibly it was this strongly expressed need for mobility and autonomy that made her leave Hamburg. There were many intimate older friends around who were eager to protect and help the Assing sisters. Frederick Douglass, orphaned at seven and denied parental love ever since, ran from slavery at the age of twenty, struggling to escape from a system that stifled his growth and manhood; Ottilie Assing was twenty-three when she escaped from Hamburg and all its volunteer mothers and fathers whose love threatened to keep her in perpetual childhood, especially the paternalistic Steinheim, who would not see that she was now a fully grown woman, eager to fend for herself, and kept on calling her and Ludmilla his "birds of paradise," his "dear evil girls," his "beloved children."[5] For many years Ottilie had been her mother's most reliable partner in running the household; she had been totally in charge since Rosa Maria's death. Now she was ready and determined to have her way. True, she began her letter to Varnhagen with a gesture of submission, affirming that "only your approval, your satisfaction can give me inner autonomy and some self-reliance; only you do I want to ask about everything; usually few can influence me."[6] Yet the text of what followed spoke another language: she did not ask for anything; she politely explained her plans, paid verbal tribute to his male vanity, and then told him what was up.

Varnhagen's biographers claim that he was the one who talked his nieces into moving to Berlin, but Ottilie's letters show that nothing could be further from the truth. It was only after she acquainted him with her decision that Varnhagen offered his hospitality and protection. Ottilie's response was an enthusiastic assent. "How glad Father and Mother would be had they been able to read your letter, had they seen such a future opening up for us," she exclaimed, and she quickly accepted his offer to stay with him: "How can you even imagine the possibility that we would not like it at your place? Everything shall be as you say, and we only ask that you not put yourself out and that as few changes as possible be made in your realm."[7] How do we explain this abrupt reversal of her plans? She seems to have taken her uncle's proposal pragmatically as a change that would favor their budget. As to Varnhagen, she never considered him a man who would bother to interfere with her personal freedom. On the contrary: rather than entangle her in a new dependence, this relocation would strengthen her. Varnhagen was a widower (his wife, Rahel, had died in 1833) who lived alone with his elderly maid, Rahel's faithful Dore. Ottilie imagined herself in the glorious role of a new Rahel, new mistress of the famous Varnhagen household, glamorous hostess of a revived salon. The changes in Varnhagen's daily routine would be dramatic; she would see to that!

Her letters of the following months show that the ever energetic Ottilie was invigorated by these anticipations. She arranged the sale of the furniture and had their library shipped to Berlin; for weeks she worked in the garden to make up for the neglect it had suffered during her father's sickness; she invested her and Ludmilla's money. Varnhagen may have had second thoughts about her promise of no changes when she told him she would bring her dog, Frisch, a big black mixed breed, "for he has been used to us for eleven years and can hardly adapt to strangers."[8] To reward themselves for all this hard work, the sisters went on a long vacation to the island of Helgoland in June, to stay with their old friend Rahel de Castro. In early September they accepted Karl Gutzkow's invitation to spend a few days with him and his wife in Frankfurt.[9]

Surely Ottilie's enthusiasm would have been dampened considerably had she realized that her uncle was less devoted to his relatives than she assumed. While Varnhagen scrupulously recorded in his diaries every sneeze that emanated from the Prussian court, he did not waste a single word on his brother-in-law's sickness and death that spring, and made no references to his nieces and their fate, though he had a long response to the great fire of Hamburg and comments on the helping hand extended by the King of Prussia. Even if we concede that Varnhagen was a public figure using his diary as a record of public events, this silence signaled an indifference that did not bode well.* Still, the prospect of having his two lively nieces help him cope with the loneliness that characterized the private life of the publicly lionized intellectual was not without attraction for Varnhagen. "For the winter, which I always dreaded so much, a new life is being readied for me there [in Berlin], for Ottilie and Ludmilla will be with me, one hopes forever,

---

*Several of Varnhagen's contemporaries commented on his lack of personal warmth. Alexander von Sternberg, for example, wrote in his autobiography: "Despite his attractive conduct it appears as if Mr. von Varnhagen was unable to make lasting friends. His character emanated a certain coldness which hurt and roughly brought you back to your senses, if initially you had been overly impressed by the brilliance of his external appearance. There was a biting harshness in his judgments and expectations, and often a cold ignoring of the reasons and words his opponents expressed. His sarcasm was never benevolent and always enriched with an acid brine . . . You see, Satan does not lose his face in good society."[10]

if they do not dislike it there," he wrote to Justinus Kerner. The sentence that followed can almost be read as a foreshadowing of the conflict to ensue in that it suggests paternalism, describing as children two women who were moving to Berlin in pursuit of personal autonomy: "These children lost their parents so prematurely, when this rare happiness of four people was so rapidly dissolved."[11]

There was only one minor setback during these parting months, and it reveals much about Ottilie's personality and her relationships to other people. While arranging their possessions the sisters noticed that many little items were missing—pieces of jewelry, china, silver, a shawl, and, what really upset them, "especially Father's golden chain, which had been taken from a locked drawer." To their consternation they discovered that the young maid, Lisette, whom they had hired during Assing's illness, who had nursed their father devotedly, and whom they intended to take to Berlin, was stealing from them regularly and shamelessly. They warned her, but she simply continued. Finally they had her arrested, though Ottilie was desperately torn by the guilt of having ruined another woman's life. She tried to explain it away: ". . . everybody says we had no choice," she told Varnhagen, "but I cannot bear the thought that somebody has been thrown into prison through us. A liberal conscience balks at this! This may be more a mishap than a misfortune, but it has upset me deeply and follows me day and night; and I am only glad that Father did not live to experience this."[12]

There is no hint in the sisters' letters of how the relationship between them was evolving during these months of leave-taking. Almost all the letters to Varnhagen then came from Ottilie, who used the plural "we" whenever she discussed decision making yet left no doubt that she was in charge. During that same year, Ludmilla's diary discloses that she had fallen in love with Theodor Mundt, one of the most distinguished professors of literature in Germany, but Mundt had just married Clara, a successful young novelist, and Ludmilla was almost in a state of emotional paralysis at his marriage. Apparently she was unaware of Mundt's anti-Semitism, which would never have allowed him to marry a woman of Jewish descent.[13] She was doubtless still hurt by Ottilie's conduct at her mother's deathbed, and chafing under the matter-of-course way the elder one took control. Whatever may have happened between the sisters during these months, they kept their feelings to themselves.

Varnhagen was fifty-seven years old when, in October 1842, his nieces invaded his huge apartment in the palace-like building that was 36 Mauerstrasse.[14] Fanny Lewald described his home as follows:

It was a large house with an attractive portal, perfect for the reception of guests. The wide entrance, the broad, slowly ascending stairway, the entrance door masked with mirrors, on the second floor, the benches for servants-in-waiting, all of this had the aura of hospitality. But when you stepped from this entrance hall into Varnhagen's room you were . . . in a huge library, and the cosmopolitanism and learning which united in [him] were thus represented as in a picture immediately upon your entry.

Although he had lost his position in the diplomatic service many years before, Varnhagen was a public figure in Restoration Berlin, someone whose name everybody knew, whom everybody bragged about having met at least once, who was spoken of sometimes with admiration, more often with envy. He was still an attractive man: "it was a pleasure to observe the delicate, active play of his features," Fanny Lewald wrote of her first encounter with him, which occurred soon after the Assings arrived in Berlin. "His face was round and in forms and colors had preserved its youthful quality, and his full gray hair still was slightly curled, so that you could easily imagine how attractive a young man, how charming an officer he had been, and how pleasant his presence must have appeared in the diplomatic salons if it continued to possess such charm in late years."[15]

Ludmilla described their welcome by Varnhagen in glowing terms in a letter of 15 October to Johanna Steinheim: "Our uncle was so impatient that he had risen at 3 a.m., and he approached us full of love and cordiality."[16] And perhaps Varnhagen was thrilled to have the company of two attractive nieces, vivacious, bright as silver dollars, well educated, and, moreover, eager to make a good impression on him and the society to which he introduced them, women also who respected his need for privacy because they cherished theirs. Perhaps he appreciated the chance to give proof of his enlightened generosity to his friends and enemies. Remarkably, however, he did not record their arrival in his diary or ever mention their presence during the first year. Also, the joy, if it ever existed, was of short duration, for the sisters' battle for domination which had raged through their childhood flared up now that they entered new territory and were staking new claims. Fierce arguments were exchanged almost daily, and sometimes it came to blows. It was an ugly situation, and there was no solution in sight. For a while Varnhagen tried to remain neutral, yet when he felt he had to intervene, he took sides with Ludmilla. Ottilie, who had adored her uncle with an almost childish hero worship, and who had been his faithful correspondent for more than a decade, was furious, though not surprised. His attitude only confirmed for her what she had realized almost immediately upon her arrival: that he was not the semi-god she had invented.

Ottilie soon understood that there were two Varnhagens—a private and a public one, personae that seemed incompatible to her. The public man was still an impressive figure: sophisticated, witty, well informed, tolerant, the graceful and physically attractive center of every party, a magnet for upcoming young intellectuals, a generous, ageless patriarch. Yet the private man was a sickly creature, full of real and imagined ailments, who spent hours lying in a kind of stupor on the hard, uncomfortable sofa in his library, covered with a silk blanket, allowing his maid, Dore, to pamper him like a sick child. Ottilie was disgusted, and she did not hide her feelings. In a letter to Gutzkow she later called her uncle's conduct "incrementally ridiculous."[17] But Ludmilla loved to sit by him during those hours of repose, read to him, humor him, competing with Dore in endeavors to make him comfortable. She was a bright woman, yet tense and insecure, easily hurt. Feodor Wehl, who was so close to her in those early Berlin years that many suspected him of being her lover, described her as a woman who had "little of that which makes a woman attractive; she was of small build and skinny, had a large mouth and small yet lively eyes, a common forehead and a pointed chin. The goddesses of charm certainly had not been her godmothers. Without being ugly in any way, she was without physical beauty, but intellectually very superior: always inspiring and vivacious, full of bright thoughts and challenging ideas."[18] Perhaps Varnhagen sensed her loneliness and desperation; he certainly appreciated her intellectual qualities. He reached out to her and embraced her as his daughter. Ludmilla was enchanted. She became his daughter, his secretary, his public relations officer, his editor. In his memoirs one of their friends, Julius Rodenberg, spoke of a symbiosis between uncle and niece in which the "I" lost herself in the other: "She was totally engrossed in him. She thought like, spoke like him, and even in her most delicate handwriting she imitated his to such perfection you could hardly distinguish between them."[19] Yet Ludmilla's need for love was as demanding as it was insatiable, and no matter how much she received, it did not restore her inner balance. Her deep-rooted insecurity made her envious even of the attention Varnhagen paid to Dore,[20] which helps us understand her aggressive conduct toward her sister.

Together with George Sand, Rahel Levin Varnhagen had been Rosa Maria Assing's idol, and she had passed this attitude on to her daughters. After Rahel's death Varnhagen compiled excerpts from her letters and diaries, and the little volume, *Rahel. Ein Buch des Andenkens für ihre Freunde* (1833), became the Assing girls' feminist bible. Rahel's room in Varnhagen's apartment was like a sanctuary: nothing had been changed or moved in it. In the decade since her death Varnhagen had transformed his wife into a cult figure and himself into the faithful Cerberus at her shrine. Ottilie and Ludmilla learned that he had even respected her most eccentric last wish—namely, not to be buried for thirty years (she had had a great fear of being buried alive). For a while the Assing sisters became willing disciples in this cult, but Ottilie soon defected. Not that she discarded her model, but she balked at Varnhagen's using his dead wife to glorify himself as her high priest and legitimate heir. Her uncle had too many enemies, and Ottilie had too many talkative friends for her not to know that he had had other women during his married years; shortly after Rahel's death he became engaged to Marianne Saaling but broke it off when Saaling insisted on a marriage without sex; rumors associated him with Jenny von Pappenheim, Jérôme Bonaparte's illegitimate daughter, and Jette Mendelssohn, principal of a girls' school in Paris; Ottilie knew of his intimate friendship with Henriette Solmar, a relative of Rahel's. With the moral rigidity of inexperienced youth she despised her uncle's prolonged self-portrayal as bereaved husband as a self-serving pose. How shallow this seemed after David Assing's pain! Also, Ottilie was devoted to life, to the here and now, as her response to her parents' deaths shows, and she disliked a devotion that came alive only when it turned to the past. She was too young to live retrospectively. Ludmilla, however, enthusiastically joined Varnhagen's Rahel worship. She eventually helped him edit and publish Rahel's papers, and her familiarity with Rahel's thoughts increased her admiration of this unconventional woman as it endeared her to her uncle. Eventually, Rahel's room became Ludmilla's. She had arrived.

Ottilie's aversion to Varnhagen increased when she became aware of how he positioned himself politically. Rosa Maria had represented her brother as a champion of human equality, a fearless revolutionary, a pioneer of social justice and liberalism, a radical willing to make sacrifices for his convictions. For many years he was all that; as his biographer Terry Pickett suggests, he was "a man psychologically suited for the opposition . . . a man who continued to function in the face of a political and social order with which he was out of tune."[21] By the time Ottilie came to live with him, however, he had made his peace with the world around him, living comfortably on a pension he was drawing from the much-despised Restoration government. He had successfully reimagined himself as sophisticated elder statesman, mediator between hostile parties, interpreter of events. He still claimed the right to have it all—to admire Bakunin and to welcome Prussian court representatives in his house; he was on intimate terms with King Frederick Willliam's advisers, and he encouraged the radical Young Germans' hero worship of him. As Fanny Lewald remembered:

... he was more courageous and optimistic than the youngest, and more radical in his attitudes than most; but his radicalism was of a more theoretical nature. In practical matters he was paralyzed by the inner character of his being. Varnhagen's was so receptive and soft a nature that all the people with whom he had lived and all the eras when he had been active had left traces of their defining characteristics. This made him versatile, understanding, and tolerant. Yet tolerance is a virtue as well as a weakness.[22]

Even people who frequently sought his company, like Clara and Theodor Mundt, became disgusted at

the conflicting nature of this old diplomatic hypocrite, coquettish toward all parties, flattering and unprincipled, who secretly writes for the *Nationalzeitung* and the *Urwähler* in the morning and who can spend his evenings in sweetest company with Sternberg and all kinds of revolutionaries, yet who, at a time when it became dangerous to associate with aristocrats, canceled even the evenings he usually spent at his lady friend Solmar's because he met so many detestable reactionaries there.[23]

Varnhagen's ambivalence, flexibility, and mature openness were qualities that Ottilie, who was attracted to the militancy of the Young Germans and associated closely with them in Berlin, interpreted as senility, opportunism, or, worse, duplicity. As a thirteen-year-old she had observed her parents' enthusiasm over the Hambach Festival; as a teenager she had spent whole evenings listening to and participating in debates among Gutzkow, Riesser, and Heine, Steinheim and Zeise on the political fate of the German Confederation, still divided into dozens of little monarchies and miniature states; she had internalized the radical slogans of Young Germany. It was her first major political involvement, and her youthful enthusiasm, as that of most new converts, left no room for ambivalence. The cause demanded commitment and sacrifice, not diplomacy. Ottilie might well have agreed with Friedrich Engels' verdict on Varnhagen: "That fellow is nevertheless an utter and cowardly rascal . . ."[24]

Ottilie Assing had hoped she would inherit Rahel's role as hostess of one of Berlin's finest salons—a sign of both her self-confidence and her naiveté. After all, Rahel's salon had seen its zenith decades before, during the 1790s and the first years of the nineteenth century. The few participants who were still alive now gathered at Henriette Solmar's home above the Royal Bank, and to Ottilie's consternation these people had aged and softened along with her uncle. The women and men who had once been pioneers of progress, irreverent intellectuals, restless noblemen and noblewomen, romantic lovers defying convention, were now shadows, puppets reenacting a stale choreography, elderly salon lions with no teeth living in nostalgic reveries, nourishing their egos on what they had once been, surrounding themselves with brainless disciples, unable to perceive the vacuum of their lives. Ottilie's mind was too independent, her nature too vivaciously irreverent to join this circle. With Fanny Lewald she disliked them as historical anachronisms, and she hated their pretense and arrogance:

> I cannot imagine anything more boring than the society we live in. A cold morality, a virtuous indolence or indolent virtue, plenty of hypocrisy in that silence—in truth, a display of dull tolerance—which they maintain while scandalized about the minor weaknesses of others, every once in a while a relaxed indignation at this or that, which, however, will never be inflamed by real anger or hatred, whether against people or situations; no passionate affection, no passionate dislike, no real pressure, no real liberty. All of that combined with a miserable prosperity, no beautiful luxury, no élan, no real joie de vivre, and all of that doused with the cheapest kind of dry interest in literature and art.[25]

Ottilie's frustration transformed Berlin, a city of "Markian sand, dull walks in the Thiergarten, . . . the goldfish pond and the noble boredom of this provincial town . . ."[26] Ludmilla, again, took a different stand. She appreciated the generosity with which Varnhagen's friends embraced her; despite her radical Young German rhetoric she shared his partiality for members of the nobility; she was willing to venerate them for what they had been for Rahel and Varnhagen. In letters to the Steinheims, Gutzkow, and Gottfried Keller, she bragged about being on intimate terms with Countess Elise von Ahlefeld, Bettina Brentano von Arnim, the von Pücklers—all of them of her parents' generation, all of them of noble birth. She achieved what Ottilie obviously was no longer interested in doing: a revival of the social gatherings in the Varnhagen home, which made it all the easier for Varnhagen to love her as the daughter he never had.

Ottilie quickly realized how prophetic had been her skepticism about her new life, expressed in a letter to Karl Gutzkow before her departure from Hamburg. "Sometimes I grow rather uneasy when I think of the new life toward which we are moving, and of the things that we will encounter and that lie ahead," she had mused on 21 September 1842. "There is no way I could make friends dearer than the ones I already have, and that's the best thing one can find anywhere."[27] The home she had left behind had offered security and affirmed mobility. The house in which she now awakened so roughly from her dreams was a borrowed place in which she could not take root. The pool of her disenchantment with the new life in Berlin was filled with many ripples: Berlin was buzzing with life, just as she expected, with elegant, sophisticated people, with theaters, the opera, libraries, discussion circles, literary clubs. It was, after all, not only the political but the cultural center of Germany. But it was also a city under the spell of Restoration conservatism, of Biedermeier, the German version of oppressive Victorianism, which made it difficult for unmarried young women as independent-minded and unconventional as Ottilie Assing to make friends, or even to move about the city unescorted. The society, of mostly his own generation, to which Varnhagen introduced her bored her, yet both sisters were choosy when it came to younger people. They saw themselves as superior to most of their age group. A letter from Ludmilla to her confidant Feodor Wehl in 1853 is revealing: "It is terrible that with most people you encounter you must be happy to know that you are not one of them,"[28] she sighed in the make-believe despair of the discouraged radical. Equally, Ottilie's feminism made her ridicule conventional women of her own age, and they, in turn, rejected her as eccentric, arrogant, unwomanly. Like one of those "unnatural women" with "German names and French habits"[29] so abhorred by the German sociologist W. H. Riehl, she smoked cigars and drank champagne in public, courted scandal, and then marveled why women of her age and class were reluctant to associate with her. Most young men were nervous about a woman who set such high intellectual standards, who refused to parrot their opinions, whose sense of humor and irreverent laughter undermined their self-confidence. And then everybody knew—or was promptly informed—that Ottilie's heroines were Rahel Levin and George Sand: love, champagne, cigars, and revolution! Her loneliness and disorientation surfaced in a letter to her old *intimus* Gutzkow: "I believe when somebody has been as happy as we once were in our family life and so close to many friends, you cannot help experiencing life as cold, when all of that is over, the one destroyed, the other scattered all over the globe."[30]

Though she continued to associate with some of Varnhagen's friends, Ottilie generated her own circle, women and men of her generation and intellectual background who shared her political creed, but it was not easy. Her impatience with Biedermeier Berlin, shared by her cousin Fanny Lewald, helped to establish a feeble bond between the young women, and this was a beginning. Fanny, eight years older than Ottilie, had come to Berlin in 1839 and had already launched a career as one of Germany's most prolific woman novelists. Her tales, insisting on the priority of love over the institution of marriage, protesting violently against marriages of convenience, and advocating the right to divorce, earned her the name of "the German George Sand."[31] A converted Jew from Königsberg, she openly discussed the moral dilemma for women who converted, giving voice to a problem that the Assing family had always wrapped in silence. And she was so fascinated with the Assings' family story as Ottilie and Ludmilla told it to her that she used elements of it in her novel *Jenny* (1842). Ottilie and Fanny never became close friends, but they enjoyed each other's company.

Of greater importance to Ottilie was the vivacious Clara Mundt,[32] who, under the pen name of Luise Mühlbach, wrote novels and tales about the self-liberation of women. Her candid cordiality soon made her the unhappy young woman's confidante and adviser. She seemed to be the only one who understood how much Ottilie chafed under the restrictions imposed on her as a woman. Clara recognized the enormous potential and energy which turned to poison when there was no creative outlet for it. "To me, Ottilie always appears like some happily frizzled parsley, which got mixed up with some hemlock leaves that imperceptibly poison her," Mundt tried to explain to Ludmilla, after one of the sisters' clashes. "Oh God, if only we knew a Socrates who would drain this cup of hemlock." Mundt could only describe Ottilie in terms of maleness, and it was as a man manqué that she accepted her. "Ottilie's is a very significant stature which, for her own bad luck and mishap, was put into a girl's body, though she was given everything that would make a very merry lad. And when I imagine her as a boy manqué, then I find much in her that I respect and much I excuse."[33]

Both Fanny Lewald and Clara Mundt understood Ottilie's restlessness, and they became role models for her: their careers proved that a woman with skills and willpower could be independent even in an inhospitable, narrow-minded society. Ottilie had no lack of skills, and she certainly had a powerful will, as her mother's diaries testify and Varnhagen, to his chagrin, confirmed. She was determined to move on. Perhaps it was her restlessness, her strong competitiveness, even envy that made it impossible for her to establish lasting relationships beyond polite interest in Clara Mundt or Fanny Lewald, but during Ottilie's Berlin years they were important.

Ottilie was anything but lonely. Gutzkow came to Berlin while she was there, and he introduced her to Heinrich Laube, an aspiring dramatist who was to become a member of the Frankfurt Parliament in 1848 and director of the Burgtheater in Vienna. When they met, he, like Gutzkow, was deeply involved with Young Germany. And there were other young intellectuals as fascinated with politics as she was. All these acquaintances made life in Berlin bearable, if not attractive, but they could not help Ottilie cope with her domestic problems. The sisters fought almost daily, and ugly scenes ensued between Ottilie and Varnhagen.[34] In the early spring of 1843, on a cold, wintry day, the powder keg exploded.[35] In the course of an argument, Varnhagen slapped Ottilie, and she ran from the house in a rage. When night came, Ottilie had not returned. Varnhagen, now deeply worried, sent out messengers to inquire about her whereabouts—to no avail. In the midst of the search only Ludmilla remained remarkably calm, suggesting to Theodor Mundt, who had joined the posse, that her sister was only trying to frighten them; she would be back when she felt she had made her point; it was all comedy, and a cheap one at that. But Ottilie did not return that night, and finally Varnhagen's friends gave up.

The next day at noon, when Clara Mundt returned to her home in the Marienstrasse from a visit, she was met at the door by a deeply upset maid telling her that Ottilie was waiting in the living room. Mundt was shocked when she saw her young friend: deathly pale, she lay more than sat in an armchair, too weak to rise. The tension which Clara had accumulated during a night of futile search and endless waiting erupted in anger rather than relief, and she greeted her guest with a haughty, "Well, Ottilie, Ludmilla was right after all: you put on an act?" Ottilie responded with embarrassment and exhausted wrath: "So you know everything?" Clara Mundt nodded. "But this you do not know!" With a dramatic gesture Ottilie removed the shawl she had wrapped herself in, displaying a dress soaked with blood from three deep wounds in her chest. Quickly she was taken to bed and a physician was called; he later told Mundt that it was a miracle she was still alive.

Only after the doctor left did they get the full story: from her uncle's place Ottilie had run to the Tiergarten, Berlin's most popular public park, and there, concealed in the shrubs and brushwood, she had stabbed herself three times with a knife. She had lain unconscious all night, until ants, crawling across her face, had awakened her. She had then dragged herself to the Mundt home, not only because it was closest to the park but also because she believed Clara would understand. Did she also hope that Clara would find the tragedy fascinating enough to use in a novel? Would this not be a most sophisticated form of revenge on Varnhagen and Ludmilla?

There are a number of remarkable parallels between Ottilie Assing's first suicide attempt in 1843 and her successful suicide more than forty years later. For the outside world she was a strong, independent woman, able to handle the problems that confronted her, a woman with a good sense of humor and, more important, the ability to laugh at herself. She *was* all of that, but there was also that other, equally demanding and legitimate self who needed to be loved, who tired of always being in charge, yet incapable, unwilling, or afraid of admitting weakness. She could not build a bridge between the powerful public persona she had created and those other needs, which she tried to suppress because she mistook them for weakness. When frustrations mounted between these two natures—which she perceived as warring, rather than as being two sides of a complex, healthy personality—until she could no longer handle them, she sought escape in death. Her suicide attempt had a performance quality—performance as a way of constructing an identity that is threatening to dissolve, a violent means of reenacting her own materiality. Had not her mother taught her that in certain situations suicide was an act of courage and self-determination? Had not the Romantics glorified suicide as self-elevation and self-purification? Had not some of the greatest writers, some of her favorite heroes from literature—Karoline von Güderode, Goethe's Werther—chosen this path? And more: was not suicide the most powerful way of punishing those who were responsible for her pain? A childish notion, perhaps, but a response most human beings never outgrow.

In both her first and second suicide attempts Assing tried to put an end to herself in public. Instead of crawling away to a quiet place or locking herself in her room, she betook herself to one of the city's most popular places. She wanted to make sure she was found. More than forty years later, in Paris, again she chose a park; her death would make for news that Douglass could not ignore. One might think that this public mode suggests a last desperate appeal to the world for help, a sign that she desired to live, but her mode of destroying herself seems to undermine this interpretation. In Berlin her stab wounds were so deep that her physician called her survival a miracle. In Paris she saw to it that the miracle would not be repeated: she took a large dose of cyanide.

What occurred in the hours following her arrival at the Mundts' reveals how deeply alienated Ottilie was from Ludmilla and Varnhagen, and they from her. They rushed over to be with her, yet Ludmilla remained unmoved. "She only wants to give herself airs," she shrugged. Clara Mundt was appalled, and, neglecting all rules of decorum, told her so in the clearest words possible. Belatedly realizing that she might be alienating a woman with considerable influence in Berlin's polite society, Ludmilla quickly changed her tactics, wailing, "My sister, oh, my sister!"

Varnhagen's response was shaped by one concern only—to avoid a public scandal by all means. If he feared anything, it was the loss of his reputation. His suggestion was to have Ottilie declared insane! For this, Ottilie never forgave him. Fourteen years later, in an article in the *Morgenblatt*, she called him "the personification of egotism and vanity," a man "whose entire life is devoted exclusively to self-love and self-glorification, without regard, without respect for others, who regards the slightest doubt in his greatness as a crime."[36] The dramatist Friedrich Hebbel, who had been a member of the Assings' inner circle in the 1830s, but who disliked Ottilie and Ludmilla as pretentious feminists, pseudo-critics, and would-be intellectuals after they had compared him with Goethe and found him wanting, saw his aversion justified by these events, commenting: "Is that not like a view into a veritable nest of vipers? Two sisters who, under the mask of love, hate each other with a deadly hatred, and an uncle who nurses [Ottilie] tenderly out of regard for the world while he would love to poison her!"[37] Try as he might, however, Varnhagen could not keep the story quiet. The people he associated with were of the leisured classes and demanded to entertain and be entertained; what better way was there than with gossip? Ottilie's behavior did not help, either. Her conduct seemed to confirm the rumors that she had staged her suicide to embarrass her uncle and sister: instead of hiding her shame, she talked about it openly—bragged of her courage, so less well-disposed contemporaries charged. But this was a role she could not sustain. She had only two choices: to accept her place in the second tier as a tolerated guest in the Varnhagen home or to sever the bonds with those to whom she could no longer relate. In the fall of 1843 Ottilie Assing was back in Hamburg, desperately longing for a second chance.

Even after her sister's departure Ludmilla tried to maintain a facade of domestic harmony by adopting the persona of the loving sister. "My dear Uncle Steinheim, if you want to do me a great favor, drop me a line on how Ottilie is faring," she wrote to Salomon Steinheim on 20 October 1843; "you know that she always suffered from pallor, and that seems to have increased here to a point that she was unwell lately; now in her letters she assures me of her full recovery, but as she does not like to admit when being not well, I rely exclusively on you . . ."[38] The art of hyperbole, cultivated in the polite circles in which Ludmilla now habitually moved, could hardly find a better example. A suicide attempt was natural pallor, and the sister who had ceased to communicate with her relatives was a caring sibling, lying to protect her kin from worrying too much!

In the years that followed the sisters made several attempts at reconciliation—traveling together, spending vacation time with relatives in Hamburg, corresponding. But they always ended up hurting each other. With each confrontation the willingness to reach out and make compromises decreased, while their hurt, emotional frustration, and exhaustion grew. Friends tried to calm the waves by offering to be intermediaries: Georg Schirges begged them to write letters to him as one, "for I can and do not want to imagine you as separate."[39] He reminded Ludmilla that ever since Rosa Maria's death "there was something like maternal tenderness in her [Ottilie's] love for you."[40] On the first anniversary of David Assing's death, while Ottilie and Ludmilla were still both living in the Varnhagen home, their paternal friend Salomon Steinheim tried to breach the gap between the alienated sisters in the *Jahrzeit* ritual, the Jewish tradition of honoring a parent's demise in a memorial service on the death day. As of a Jewish surrogate father, he warned them that the unlimited freedom which they were claiming for themselves in imitation of George Sand's libertinism and under the influence of their unruly Young German friends would cause warfare between those whom their Creator saw as one. He admonished them in a letter:

> This is the sickness of our times, that . . . we have ceased to submit even to legitimate authority, and that is why they are so rough and cold, and that is why all relationships are so evil, so antagonistic, so repulsive, because we lack inner humility, voluntary submission, and instead enforced submission in its evil form has taken over. This gnaws away at our happiness; this generates enmity and hatred; this pits brother against brother, and sister against sister. We all want to be republicans, want to be free! We have no right to be so before we have overcome our egotism and our pride.

The letter was an implicit critique of the free spirit which Rosa Maria had encouraged in her daughters, a dark warning about the challenge of tradition and authority that the Young Germans personified. His letter culminated in a passionate entreaty to reform, to listen to the voice of their blood rather than to that of artificial associations: "Love each other, dear children, and may each of you remember to seek to find fault in herself whenever you believe to be in the right, so that your father and I may see you in peace and joy. . . . I cannot bear to see you separate, for in your father as well as in my soul, you two are one and united!"[41] This letter from their venerated adoptive uncle reminded Ottilie and Ludmilla in no uncertain terms that their warfare violated their parents' memory, but it could not wipe out their envy and bitterness.

The sisters could not live together, yet they could not let go, either. After all, they were not totally immune to conventional notions of family and kin. Also, there were not many sophisticated women like them, so they held on to the few intellectually compatible relationships they had, however tense. Sometimes they did not correspond for months, but they asked friends for reports; they fought when sharing a home, but when living apart they keenly experienced the loss of an intimacy for which there was no substitute. Each blaming the other's evil temper for the alienation, they shared a sense of guilt in remembering their parents' harmonious lifestyle and their dreams for their daughters. Both made efforts to reach out, and sometimes it seemed that the elaborate choreography they designed would enable them not to clash, yet clash they inevitably did. In 1845, two years after Ottilie's return to Hamburg, the loving intercession of Rahel de Castro, an old family friend, promised success when the three women went off on an extensive summer tour to Leipzig, Dresden, Carlsbad, and Prague. "I am very pleased with my travel companions," an unusually cordial and relaxed Ludmilla reported to Feodor Wehl. "Ottilie is so enterprising and indefatigable that even I, whom Clara [Mundt], as you well know, so often upbraids for my vigor and health, can hardly compete with her, and Miss de Castro is good-natured and accommodating . . ."[42] It was such a pleasant summer that friends hoped it would be the beginning of a more stable relationship. But, in fact, the sisters got along only because they both escaped into an activism that left them neither time nor energy for personal confrontation. Excursions to the countryside, parties, visits with friends, evenings at the theater and the opera, days in museums and galleries—every minute was filled with activity, every step was with or among friends, personal encounters were staged as public performances, personal feelings were stifled by a determined embrace of convention.

How thin the ice they danced on! Less than a year later, during a quiet summer with paternal relatives in rural Eimsbüttel, near Hamburg, the bubble burst. It seems that Ottilie's refusal to shape her life according to her relatives' notions of propriety was at the center of the new controversy. Ludmilla, writing to Wehl, put all the blame on Ottilie: ". . . hers is a character, of which I have come to realize that I would not want anything in common with, false, perfidious, icy cold, of a gruesome passionateness; she seeks to harm me as if I were her greatest enemy, she tries to deprive me of my dearest friends, wherever she can."[43] To her uncle she wrote the same day: "I realize that she is my worst enemy who tries to harm me wherever she can."[44] For Ludmilla, this encounter was the culmination point of her sibling martyrdom, and she told the world she was through with her "evil" sister. "If only you knew how many years it took me until I was strong enough to turn away from her, to realize that I could indeed be burdened by such a sister," she complained to Wehl. "I made so many attempts to approach her, to believe in something good in her. She is my only sister. I assure you that from no one in the world have I suffered so much, that nobody has deprived me of so much happiness, that I had so much patience with nobody but Ottilie, but to no avail—she exhausts all patience."[45]

Ottilie Assing mentioned this clash in a letter to Karl Gutzkow: "Ludmilla in her most tender sisterly love has stopped writing to me completely. How they will probably blacken my name for you! Unfortunately the one absent is always at a disadvantage, and I can only say, do not believe without further ado what you hear! Oh, I have to see you and tell you everything, for I am unhappy when you believe false things about me."[46] We do not have Ottilie's side of the story; it is revealing, however, that Clara Mundt, who witnessed the fight, wrote a letter to Ludmilla urging her to reach out to her sister, to which Ludmilla replied by complaining of her "taking so erroneous and false an interpretation of things."[47] It is also significant that their paternal friend Steinheim frequently ridiculed Ludmilla for her "poisonous tongue."[48] Emilie Nickert, a cousin of the sisters, insisted that "Ottilie does not give the tiniest bit of information"[49] whenever Ludmilla asked her how she felt toward her. As late as the mid-1870s, when Ludmilla was again to accuse Ottilie of smearing her reputation, Johanna Steinheim gently reminded her that Ottilie had never made a negative remark about her in her presence. But no matter what caused the original enmity between the sisters or widened the gap between them, it seems clear that these two were unable to walk through life hand in hand. The painful internal struggle between their need to love and be loved, on the one hand, and their siblings' rivalry, hatred, and struggle for dominance, on the other, marred their relationship even beyond their graves.

It is extremely difficult to document Ottilie's life after she returned to Hamburg. Evidently she did not communicate with her relatives in Berlin for several years; if she did, the letters either were lost or Ludmilla did not preserve them. Ludmilla usually spent each summer with relatives, the Wolffs, in Hamburg, and her letters to Varnhagen always contained information on Ottilie, but she can hardly be seen as a reliable narrator when it comes to Ottilie. There are a few scattered letters from Ottilie to friends, between 1850 and 1852, some letters to Varnhagen, but there is no continuous report.

We do know that upon her return to Hamburg, Ottilie found a provisional home with Maria and Dr. Wilhelm Christian Birkenstock, whose daughter Marie was one of her most intimate friends, and they helped her to find a position as a tutor in a well-to-do family. This was not difficult, for despite their Jewish background the Assings had been respectable and well liked. Rosa Maria had run a successful school, and Ottilie was known to be a bright, vivacious woman with a superior education and distinguished manners who moved in the best social circles. To hire a governess with such gifts was an asset for any family.

Karl Gutzkow

The German writer Karl Gutzkow was a frequent guest at the Assing home. His religious skepticism, expressed in his play *Uriel Acosta*, had a great influence on the young Ottilie Assing.

Fanny Lewald

Ottilie Assing's paternal cousin, the novelist Fanny Lewald, provided a motto for her: "Our self-abnegation almost always makes us unhappy, and it does not make happy the one for whom we make the sacrifice."

Clara Mundt, alias Luise Mühlbach

Clara Mundt, a close friend of Ottilie Assing's during the 1840s, spoke of Assing as "some happily frizzled parsley, which got mixed up with some hemlock leaves." In 1849 Mundt published her novel *Aphra Behn*, at the center of which was the romantic involvement of the eponymous heroine with the rebellious African slave Oronooko—a novel that influenced Assing's perception of Douglass.

Ottilie was not under pressure to find work immediately, for she lived modestly and could easily survive on the money her parents left her. Yet she wanted to work and was eager to prove herself to the world. Tutoring children was not glamorous enough: she craved a more public setting, wanted response from a wider audience. Soon she began to write reviews on literature, art in general, and cultural events in Hamburg. Her friends Therese von Bacheracht, Amalie Schoppe, and Karl Gutzkow as editor of the *Telegraph*, as well as his successor Georg Schirges, saw to it that her columns appeared in local newspapers and journals like the *Hamburger Correspondent*, the *Telegraph*, the *Privilegierte wöchentlich gemeinnützige Nachrichten von und für Hamburg*, and the *Jahreszeiten*. From her letters to Gutzkow we can deduce that she wrote regularly and drew a small income from this work. All of these texts appeared anonymously, and only isolated pieces have been identified.

The few articles we know about explain why Ottilie Assing would never become popular in her native town: hers was a campaign against Hamburg's lack of culture, against the materialism of the city's rich "Pepperbags" (*Pfeffersäcke*)—that is, people with plenty of money but deficient, according to her, in education, taste, and intellectual aspirations. She considered herself an intellectual, and she prided herself in despising both the Biedermeier petty bourgeoisie and the moneyed bourgeoisie with their exclusively commercial associations. Like her hero Heinrich Heine, like Gustave Flaubert, she used "bourgeois" as an insult; she fought against what Heine called "*Spiessbürgerlichkeit*," a philistinism that nauseated her. Hypocrisy hunting was a favorite sport among young intellectuals like her who, as a matter of course, were proud to display their own freedom from hypocrisy in every way imaginable.[50] But these writings are more than philistine-bashing; they prove that Assing had a deep understanding of literature and art, she had obvious critical and journalistic skills, the courage to speak up, and the knowledge and the wit to do so in an engaging way. Yet she also revealed arrogance and lack of patience toward people who had had the opportunity to educate themselves and live a culturally rich life but neglected or refused to do so.

Her attacks on Hamburg's bourgeoisie became more acute after 1845, when the city was shaken by what literary historians called the Theater War. During the early nineteenth century the city's Municipal Theater was regarded as one of the best playhouses anywhere on German-speaking territory. Wehl later praised the Hamburg audience as "one of the most enlightened, refined and decent audiences in Germany," quiet and attentive, visiting the theater regularly, embracing "beauty without hot enthusiasm." And they were definitely ahead of their times, for they "enjoyed Shakspeare [sic] when almost all of Germany could not yet understand him."[51] The theater hired the most distinguished actors and directors, and dramatists vied with each other to have their plays produced on this stage. In 1843, as the city was being rebuilt after the great fire, the city council was given plans for a second theater for more popular productions; convinced that this wealthy metropolis could easily support two major stages, the council agreed. The Thalia Theater opened on 9 November 1843—with catastrophic effects. As a result of the competition between the two theaters production costs skyrocketed. Assing claimed that 30,000 marks or 12,000 thalers monthly would have been needed to cover production costs alone. Even the most supportive audiences could not sustain that. Directors resigned, actors blackmailed their respective institutions, the press fumed. In 1847 the city council made a desperate attempt to calm the waters: two directors were appointed in a joint venture—the Alsatian entrepreneur Maurice, who had run a popular tavern stage before the fire and was one of the initiators of the Thalia plans, and Jean Baptiste Baison, star of the Municipal Theater, who was nationally renowned for his Hamlet performances; cooperation was the motto of the day. Again Hamburg was disappointed. The businessman and the highly sensitive actor soon clashed violently, and for years Hamburg's theaters were paralyzed by ugly warfare.

Ottilie Assing, whose most precious childhood memories were those of evenings at the theater and opera, and who was a passionate lover of contemporary and classical drama, took up the cudgel. For her, a worshipper at the shrine of high culture, the choice was easy: her hero was Baison. In numerous columns she extolled Baison as a pure representative of art, and denounced the cheap materialism, nasty scheming, cultural blindness, and ruthlessness of his opponents.

It did not take long for those critics who sided with Maurice to identify the author of these fiery reviews, for not only were Ottilie Assing's skills and sarcasm as a critic known and feared by then; she was also living in the Baison household. Officially she was tutor of Baison's daughters, Josefine and Caroline, but especially after his wife, the former actress Caroline Sutorius Baison, left her family to live in Düsternbrook, near Kiel, rumors spread about this unusual domestic arrangement. In 1847–48 a series of columns appeared in *Der Lumpensammler* (The Ragpicker), a journal explicitly created in response to the Theater War, in which journalists hostile to Baison tried to destroy his character, personality, and merits as an actor with devastating reviews and gossip "that extended even to the internals of Baison's domestic situation."[52]

Assing and Baison had probably met as early as 1835, during the actor's first engagement in Hamburg. Together with her parents Ottilie saw several of his performances, especially his debut as Hamlet on 2 April, and she had been in the enthusiastic crowd that celebrated the attractive young actor. "It was especially the ladies who raved about him and declared him irresistible," she later remembered. "A beautiful young woman from one of the most respectable families went so far in her passion that she did not rest till a novel with all his triumphs and tribulations, excitements and entanglements had been written."[53] Is it possible that this young beauty was Ottilie herself? In February 1848 Amalie Schoppe wrote to Ludmilla: "She [Ottilie] is writing a novel, the papers say, which unfortunately, to my dismay, but as had to be expected, pay far too much attention to her in response to her relationship to these plebeian comedians."[54] If this novel was written, whether in the mid-1830s or later 1840s, it was never published, and no trace of the manuscript has been found. As Assing frequently masked her own adventures, especially if they were of a shady quality, as those of "a young lady," there is reason to assume that she was indeed the author; it is also possible that she used parts of the manuscript for the biography of Baison she wrote several years later.

During Baison's visits at the Assing and Gutzkow homes between 1835 and 1837 Ottilie had been able to observe this shy and hypersensitive man in a more intimate, relaxed setting and to hear him talk about the theater and his glamorous work from an insider's perspective. It is possible that the sixteen-year-old fell in love with him then; at twenty-three, Baison was not only an exceptionally talented actor but a man whose features, lifestyle, and conduct must have been magnetically attractive. In a letter to Feodor Wehl of 11 July 1844 Gutzkow lauded Baison as "a capable, stylish, educated actor" distinguished by his "knowledge, his love of art, his respect for literature."[55] Even Ludmilla, who hardly ever found a kind word for Ottilie's friends, praised him as "a remarkable artist, who combines in the best way thorough knowledge with natural talent, and who performs most exceptionally in Shakespeare's and Goethe's plays."[56] In her book about Baison, which was published in 1851, Ottilie characterized him as a man whom Nature herself—following German tradition she personified Nature as a woman—must have designed especially for his profession, "for she had equipped him lavishly with all those advantages which she usually bestows upon her favorites only when she is in an exceptionally good mood. His tall, slim figure had an innate grace which was ennobled by a perfect physique, and his exquisitely and regularly formed features mirrored each emotion with lightning speed."[57]

In the book, she reimagined Baison's life as the romantic quest of an actor by nature's choice. Born on 24 October 1812 in Hattersheim near Mainz, he was the son of an abusive, alcoholic father and a mother broken by her spouse's irascibility; the family was of Huguenot descent. Jean Baptiste grew up in abject poverty, in an environment defined by violence and neglect. "Fate, who had equipped him with every potential to reach the highest goal, at the same time did not provide him with external happiness, and step by step, by incessant struggle, he had to wrest each success from her,"[58] she wrote. The rags-to-riches narrative matched the romantic plots in her mother's tales.

Her precocious, gifted hero could acquire an education only because his parents donated him to the church to train him as a priest. The boy endured this physical and intellectual bondage, realizing that he had no alternative if he wanted to satisfy his craving for knowledge. Assing portrayed the youth as routinely spending his nights in an unheated chamber, absorbed in books—the conventional image of the devoted scholar. This romantic topos shapes the chapters on the protagonist's childhood and youth, all the more effectively as Assing combined it with an equally popular literary motif—that of warring natures: though his performances as a pupil amazed his superiors, though he excelled at the tasks set him, Baison was a torn creature—brilliantly gifted, on the one hand, extremely passionate, on the other. It must be a heroic man of superior nobility, Assing insisted, who could reach artistic perfection under these conditions, "for the same energy which enabled him to elevate himself to that height, which is so admirable under these circumstances, could easily have dragged him into the abyss of vice, even crime, had he turned it toward evil."[59] He personified Assing's belief in the superiority of the free will, in the inevitability of human progress. Nothing can stop the human being determined to make her or his way, neither hereditary burdens, the father's alcoholism, the mother's weakness, nor external boundaries established by contemporary social views.

Baison entered a theological seminary only to realize that he could no longer wear the shackles his elders had imposed on him, and he decided to free himself from his religious chains. In February 1831 he escaped from the institution. Years of wandering followed, a man's quest for his place, his vocation, his self. Determined to become an actor, he apprenticed himself to traveling stock companies, taking on any role they allowed him to play, and adapting himself to their roving lifestyle: to the ridicule and abuse "respectable" citizens heaped on them, their poverty, their homelessness, their pariah status. Once he felt that he had the necessary skills, and once the audience's responses began to confirm his belief that he had promise, he went to established directors, who quickly recognized his talent. Only four years after he had run from the seminary the audiences in Hamburg were lionizing him for his Hamlet. Ottilie Assing had found her hero: he was "one of the few artists who owed his success only to his own talent and to the recognition of the audience."[60] Could there possibly be a more perfect representation of the egalitarian creed? Rosa Maria's brown fisherman, her noble chimney sweeper reincarnated in flesh and blood! Small wonder that Ottilie Assing fell in love; small wonder also that she felt delicious pangs of recognition and knew she was entering familiar territory when she read Frederick Douglass' *My Bondage and My Freedom* twenty years later.

Ottilie Assing may have been in love with Baison as early as 1835, but the teenager was no competition for a more mature woman who entered his life during his Hamburg sojourn: Caroline Sutorius, the star at the Municipal Theater, became his mentor, directing his wild enthusiasm into constructive and creative channels. In the fall of 1836 they married; in 1837 they left Hamburg for a triumphant odyssey which took Baison to Leipzig, Dresden, Vienna, Frankfurt, and Berlin; in 1844, shortly after Ottilie had returned to the city, he signed a contract with Hamburg.

When Baison and Ottilie Assing saw each other again after seven years, it was an encounter between a self-confident, independent teacher and critic and a mature artist, between adults who shared the same passion for literature, who were devoted to the world of the theater and who loved to perform. We do not know how the relationship developed, nor do we have reliable information when or if they became lovers. What we do know is that in the summer of 1846 Assing made plans for "leaving the Birkenstocks, as she will move in as a governess with her latest friends, the Baisons,"[61] as a scandalized Ludmilla wrote to Wehl, and by late 1846 Assing was living in the Baison home. To Gutzkow she wrote on 28 January 1847: "I have to inform you that I moved in with Baison after all. . . . now I feel as comfortable (touch wood, a thousand times!) as I have not in many years."[62] Caroline started to spend long periods of time in Düsternbrook, leaving Ottilie in charge of her household, her children, and her husband—and, what was most shocking to the people watching in wonder, remaining on the friendliest terms with the new mistress of the place!

Ottilie's paternal relatives, Otto and Adolf Wolff from Eimsbüttel, were shocked when Ottilie told them she was going to live with the Baisons. Not only did her conduct challenge their morality, family pride, and social respectability; they were businessmen skeptical of theater people and artists in general, of people who didn't live what they considered a useful life, and they distrusted Baison. In the past, the Baisons had borrowed money from them, and the Wolffs had been disturbed by the lax way the actor had paid his debt. To lose their niece to an illegitimate relationship was bad enough; to lose her to this kind of charlatan was unbearable. Ludmilla, though she virtually apotheosized her romantic rebel-lovers Rahel Levin and Elise von Ahlefeld, was disgusted. It was all right to invite actors to a salon, but one did not fraternize with them. As always, Ottilie had gone too far—the whole hog.

Hamburg was scandalized at conduct that disregarded conventional public notions of propriety. But Ottilie seemed to Rahel de Castro, who visited her regularly, as relaxed, happy, active, full of good spirits, and conquering all with her fine sense of humor. We cannot do justice to Ottilie and her sense of right and wrong unless we bear in mind that she was a child of the Victorian Age only in regard to chronology; intellectually and morally she was a daughter of the most radical segment of the German Enlightenment and of German Romanticism, and the models she chose were proud members of a small elite of exceptionally, aggressively unconventional individuals of turn-of-the-century salon culture in Berlin. Living with a lover was regarded as perfectly legitimate, even fashionable in the circles the Assing girls had been taught to idealize by their mother, provided that the lover was of an "exotic" background and had the right attitude.

Rahel's famous salon had been a meeting place not only for intellectuals and artists, radicals and noblemen, but for Jews, Christians, and freethinkers; parallel to sophisticated discussions of literature and politics, a young poet could make advances to a Jewish femme fatale, a nobleman flirt with an actress, a married woman signal her interest in a would-be revolutionary. What Feodor Wehl (who never really made it into the inner circle) later denounced as that "business of mistresses," those violations of "race" boundaries, was central to the self-definition of these salons. Rahel Levin herself had had several passionate affairs with Karl Graf Finck von Finckenstein and with the Spanish diplomat Raphael d'Urquijo before her involvement with Varnhagen, which went on for several years before they married. To be a man's mistress had not been her choice; from her diaries and letters we know that she desperately wanted to be married to the one she loved, railing against arranged marriages rather than marriage as an institution when she exclaimed: "Negro [not slave] trade, war, marriage!—and they wonder and make patch repairs!"[63] We also know that being a woman and a Jew imposed this situation upon her. Yet the public persona that she successfully created for herself and that Rosa Maria Assing later praised to her daughters had no room for defeat and humiliation; for the world that watched in wonder, disgust, and admiration she reinvented her personal trials in terms of challenge and triumph: she was not a kept woman; her affairs were her creations, her choice.

For years Louis Ferdinand, Prince of Prussia, attended Rahel's gatherings with his lover Pauline Wiesel. Here Dorothea Mendelssohn-Veith's divorce and her love of Friedrich Schlegel, as well as Schlegel's frank delineation of their sex life in *Lucinde* (1799), were discussed, as were Wilhelm von Humboldt's friendship with Charlotte Diede. There was no need for secrecy, for they all had a model that was beyond criticism: Johann Wolfgang von Goethe. Their lives roused the ire and envy of more conventional contemporaries, but they were celebrated as pioneers of human freedom, as liberated spirits anticipating and shaping a gloriously sensuous future. Their pride and confidence is well expressed in the many published accounts of their relationships—their letters, diaries, and autobiographies.*

True to their Cartesian feminism and Romantic notions of womanhood, these radically elitist circles claimed that women were the ones who made the decisions, women who challenged convention, women who were the active ones. The concept of human nature which the German Enlightenment and early Romantics developed would not have been possible without the intense debates on the nature of woman as found in Friedrich Schlegel, Friedrich E. D. Schleiermacher, Friedrich von Schiller, Goethe, and Johann Gottlieb Fichte. They pictured woman as an independent being equal in value to man, yet also innately different. The male still represented the norm, while the female in her uniqueness was extolled as the high priestess and bearer of humanity.[64] It was an ideal that women like Rahel and Rosa Maria could embrace, for it seemed to affirm a woman's right to an autonomous personality in any social, and especially any love relationship, yet it was in reality an elegant, gallant, and rather eccentric concept of womanhood defined according to male norms and needs. The tragic fate of the women in Rahel's salon—the men usually discarded their mistresses in favor of marriages with "decent" women of their own class and "race"—is ample testimony to the disastrous consequences of women's emancipation, the conceptualization of which had been left to men.

Ottilie saw neither the humiliations to which her heroines had been exposed nor the exigency that defined their conduct, nor their ultimate victimization. She admired them for their determination to live their creed and their love against all odds, and she interpreted their failure as delicious romantic suffer-

---

*Varnhagen published Rahel's correspondence with her lovers, and Humboldt's letters to Diede came out in 1847.

ing. For her the relations between men and women in Rahel's salon, as she learned of them from Rosa Maria's accounts, expressed woman's self-liberation and free choice, showed woman as sculptor and definer. But she did not and perhaps could not see that Rahel's true rebellion lay not so much in her defiance of convention as in her ability to redefine liabilities as assets.

Ottilie's espousal of this lifestyle was further confirmed by choices that her friends made, many of them young radicals demanding political and sexual liberation. Karl Gutzkow, married father of several children, entered into a passionate relationship with Therese von Bacheracht, seven years his senior and wife of the Russian General Consul in Hamburg; the Assings continued their close friendship with Gutzkow, his wife Amalie, *and* Therese von Bacheracht[65] during this stormy period, and Rosa Maria especially saw no reason why their daughters should not observe and judge for themselves. Equally, the aspiring poet Friedrich Hebbel, introduced to this vivacious circle by Amalie Schoppe, lived openly with his mistress, an older woman named Elise Lensing, and in November 1840 Lensing gave birth to their son.[66] Again, the Assings kept their door open to these violators of convention, although they had difficulty perceiving Lensing, whom Hebbel ultimately left, as a romantic heroine. The Assings were not advocates of free love, but they believed in the individual's right to search for that perfect love until she/he found it, even if this meant several changes of partners and divorce. A woman loves only once, Rosa Maria taught her daughters, but not necessarily the man she fell for first time around or, for that matter, second or third! They would know that one love when it came, and the urge to rove would cease.

Ottilie Assing's "training" continued in Berlin. There she was on intimate terms with the countess Elise von Ahlefeld, then in her fifties, who notoriously had divorced her husband to live with the dramatist Karl Immermann, then director of the theater in Düsseldorf. After years he suddenly left her to marry a very young woman. Immermann died only a year later, and Ahlefeld paid a pension to his widow. The Assing sisters were so fascinated with this story that Ludmilla eventually wrote a laudatory biography of Ahlefeld.

Even closer to Ottilie's heart was the fate of her cousin Fanny Lewald, whose first novel, *Clementine* (1843), a *roman à thèse* against marriages of convenience, deeply impressed her. Lewald, who had refused to enter into an arranged marriage at the age of twenty-six, had her protagonist complain of the institution of marriage: "And what has now happened to marriage? A thing, the mention of which makes well-bred girls lower their eyes, poke fun at men, and smile to themselves secretly when they look at women. The marriages I see being entered into daily before my eyes are worse than prostitution."[67] In 1845, during a trip to Italy, Lewald met the love of her life, a professor named Adolf Stahr, the married father of five. Still, they became lovers, spending delightful months in Rome. When Stahr had to return to his family they continued to meet in Berlin, Paris, and Hamburg; for ten years they lived in this makeshift relationship until Stahr finally divorced. In her reminiscences of this period Lewald claimed that she suffered frightfully from self-doubt and moral scruples during the initial phase but finally decided that it would be unnatural and thus also immoral to sacrifice a relationship between partners who harmonized so well, in body and soul, for a stale marriage in which husband and wife had drifted apart. On 27 June 1849 she confided to her diary: "Our self-abnegation almost always makes us unhappy, and it does not make the one happy to whom we make the sacrifice. If we do not renounce, we would, instead of two sufferings, have one happiness and one unhappiness, and that would be much better."[68] Ottilie Assing knew of all these changes in Lewald's life and her attitude toward them. Again, a woman she admired was refusing to deny her self and her needs for society's sake "A woman's reputation is very important and well worth considering, but it is not the final criterion of her worth."[69]

These various examples come from a small segment of eighteenth- and nineteenth-century German society, but they suggest the need to revise our images of the age. No doubt the individuals Ottilie tried to imitate were exceptional—in class, education, religious inclinations, political attitudes; they lived in a social and political environment that historians legitimately describe as reactionary and repressive. Yet despite censorship and violently negative reviews, they published their radical messages and their plays were performed; their contemporaries were scandalized at their conduct and gossip flourished, but they continued to socialize with them; society condemned extramarital relationships, yet Lewald and Stahr, George Eliot and George Henry Lewes, George Sand and Franz Liszt, Dorothea Veit and Friedrich Schlegel, prospered; sentimental novelists might decry the fate of the fallen woman and kill her in childbirth, yet the rate of illegitimate births increased steadily; scientists denied the sexual needs of women or denounced them as perverse, yet the private and public writings of Rosa Maria Assing, the Brontë sisters, Emily Dickinson, Margaret Fuller, Elizabeth Gaskell, Fanny Lewald, and George Sand tell a different story. Assing's and her friends' conduct affirms what Peter Gay suggests about the Victorian Age, that the "boundaries between the permissible and the impermissible . . . were uncertain and remained little explored."[70] When Ottilie moved into the Baison house, friends like Johanna Steinheim, Amalie Schoppe, and

Rahel de Castro worried that she might suffer, yet they continued to cherish her as a friend. "There is nothing we can do, and faithful opinion and advice must watch passively as she ruins herself," Schoppe complained. "This is a great pain."[71] "Ottilie really is in good hands at the Baisons," Clara de Castro insisted. "I like Madame Baison very much, and the children are very nice."[72] The extrovert Ottilie enjoyed the role of rebel, but above all she did what she truly believed to be her birthright.

The new role was demanding and time-consuming. She took on all the responsibilities of the housewife except one—public representation; on social occasions she was introduced as the journalist and governess of Baison's children, Ottilie Assing. She supervised the household; she became mother and teacher to the daughters and trained his dog, Sultan; she was Baison's partner, nurse, and probably his lover, and she continued her work as a journalist. The relationship was special from the start as it developed during the most painful years of Baison's career. He was hurt by the slanderous press reports, frustrated at having to waste his energy on management and public relations; he became morose and ill. Ottilie shared all that, trying to help him by wielding her pen in his favor, relieving him of domestic responsibilities, encouraging him to recover his strength during vacations on Helgoland. Her well-informed and knowledgeable articles document that Baison respected her professionalism, for he obviously shared details of his work with her, asked her advice and discussed strategies. Ottilie's biography of Baison shows, too, that he also entrusted her with the most intimate details of his life, talking about his childhood, giving her the diaries he had written during his apprenticeship, letting her read his letters. There are many passages in this book which only a person intimately involved in his daily life, in his dreams and nightmares, could have written. Theirs was an intense and dynamic working relationship, just as Ottilie would later work side by side with Frederick Douglass. Yet no matter how anxious Assing was to describe it in terms of mutuality and equality, no matter how important freedom of choice was in her self-representation, the relationship was asymmetric, for it was always Ottilie Assing adapting to Baison's needs and moves. "She talks almost exclusively of the theater and certainly ranks herself with the board of directors," Ludmilla suggested sardonically. Yet even she had to admit that obviously Ottilie was in her element: "Never before have I seen her so happy and satisfied as now."[73]

It is legitimate to assume that Assing was key in Baison's last triumph as an actor and director. In response to his close encounters with representatives of the

Jewish community in Hamburg, his friendship with David Assing, and his exposure to the debates on Jewish emancipation raging all over Germany, Karl Gutzkow wrote a play about a young Jewish intellectual caught between the temptations of his personal religious creed, the demands of his orthodox community, and his love of a Christian woman: *Uriel Acosta*. Ottilie was deeply moved by this, for it articulated many of the issues that powerfully shaped her own and her family's lives. Her review of the play, which appeared in the *Privilegierte wöchentlich gemeinnützige Nachrichten von und für Hamburg* on 9 January 1847, is one of the few statements revealing her thorough familiarity with Jewish traditions, institutions, and rituals, her fascination with the problems of conversion, her interest in relations between Jews and Germans. She praised Gutzkow's faithful delineation of Jewish family life but criticized his use of the generalized term "the Jew,"[74] his ignorance of Jewish rituals, and his inability to translate religious issues into dramatic events; still, she was grateful that finally a competent dramatist had had the courage to pose the question of Jewish identity in post-Enlightenment Germany. It is possible that it was she who talked Baison, an old yet now alienated friend of Gutzkow's, into producing it in Hamburg; Baison himself played the role of Uriel Acosta, and he sent the laurel wreath, presented to him by the audience after the fifth performance, to Gutzkow as a token of respect.[75]

In her review Assing mentioned that "during the last two acts" of the opening performance on 2 February 1847, "a physical indisposition seemed to weaken his [Baison's] strength." It was the first sign of a tragedy ahead of them. Assing later called Baison's decision to accept the directorship of the Hamburg theater his tragic fallacy:

> Inspired with honest artistic desire, he forgot that you must never open your camp to the archenemy, that each contact with baseness—even for the best of ends—carries its own curse. . . . Naively, glowing with enthusiasm for art, to which he devoted his life, he still betrayed it; it was a betrayal for which, as soon as he saw what he had done, he atoned for by heroic battles at the price of his peace and health, his property, even his life.[76]

Although she saw that he had chosen the wrong path for himself, Assing did everything in her power to ease his lot and to support him. In early 1848 Ludmilla, reporting the latest Hamburg gossip to Wehl, suggested not only that Baison was facing bankruptcy, having lost more than 100,000 marks in a year, but that Ottilie had sought an interview with the board of directors to plead for its financial and political support—an unprecedented move.[77] People went on whispering that she gave him a good part of her inheritance to help him save his theater, to protect him against financial ruin, and to restore his peace of mind, a rumor which Rahel de Castro contested. In conversations with German friends Ottilie always denied that she lost her money in the Theater War, but the fact that she later quarreled with Mrs. Baison over unpaid interests and arrived in New York almost penniless confirms the gossip. Only later, in the United States, when struggling to make a living as a seamstress, did Ottilie finally confide her secret to a friend, who immediately spread the news. Pretending he was acting out of concern over her financial plight, he told everyone that she "had given her estate to a theater director, who died and the theater went bankrupt; now she cannot even get her interest, and she might as well forget the money; it is totally lost."[78] But however much money she may have given him, it was too late for Baison.[79] Soon he was suffering from violent headaches, continuous indisposition, and shortness of breath. They even sent the children off to a boarding school so that Ottilie could devote herself totally to Baison's needs, but it was to no avail.

Ottilie was worried, yet too many things happened in the weeks and months that followed for them to focus exclusively on their personal problems. Their tribulations faded into the background as they watched their dreams for a united, free Germany and for a liberated Europe collapse. The beginning was hope: the revolution that flared up in Paris in February 1848 spread all over Europe. In many small German states of the German Confederation, a broad revolutionary movement forced the rulers to set up liberal ministries, and when the King of Prussia tried to save his skin by granting the "patent"—that is, freedom of the press and other reforms—an enraged mass told him it was too late for him to grant anything. For the first time in German history a German parliament met in the Paul's Church in Frankfurt. Still, failure seemed programmed: the members of this parliament were almost all university professors; there were no representatives of the working classes. It was a bourgeois, not a proletarian revolution. And the parliament lacked a standing army, an administration, and revenue. They had no political parties, no committees, and no experience—only devotion, enthusiasm, brilliant minds, as well as many warring opinions and personalities. While they endlessly debated over a large or small united Germany, monarchy or republic, federalist or centralized structure, for or against Jewish emancipation, for or against the franchise for women, King Frederick William of Prussia had his troops occupy Berlin. Rebellions in Saxony, the Palatinate, and Baden met gory ends; the parliament dissolved.[80] Though Baison was more ambivalent than Ottilie about the revolution, they both were enthusiastic when their friends Gabriel Riesser and Heinrich Laube were elected to the Frankfurt Parliament, and they despaired when it failed. Ottilie, who had been aware of the anti-Semitism and machismo of many of her revolutionary friends, turned away in disgust when they betrayed potential yet unloved allies.[81] Assing and Baison realized it would take a long time for Germany to rise from the abyss into which the country had been thrown.

Personal tragedy followed the nation's: in October 1848, after months of vicious struggle over the theater and an abortive vacation in Helgoland, Baison collapsed; within weeks typhoid brought him to the brink of the grave. In December there was new hope, for it seemed as if his youth might conquer the disease, and on 22 December they celebrated with a short outing: it took them past the cemeteries near the Dammtor, and Baison exclaimed good-humoredly: "Well, I luckily escaped from you!" His triumph was premature. In the night of 11 January he was awakened by a fierce pain in his abdomen that no medicine could relieve, and died in the early morning hours of 13 January. In death, Ottilie Assing insisted, he reclaimed the beauty of which he had been deprived as "a victim of materialism." She wrote of the joy that she and his friends experienced—she actually used the word *geniessen*, or "relish"—at the sight: "The noble, regular features were unchanged, the painful expression of the past days had disappeared, to be replaced by a serene peace and transfiguration; everyone there admired these features, of an antique beauty which the black beard . . . framed picturesquely and which repeatedly evoked the remark that you could not find a more perfect model for a Christ figure."[82]

Ottilie's liaison with Baison was a curious episode that in many ways anticipated her relationship with Frederick Douglass. She fell in love with a man whose social background made him exotic in the eyes of his middle-class mistress; a man already married to another woman and a father; a man who was a public figure and celebrity. The only socially and morally acceptable, and respectable, response for Ottilie Assing would have been self-abnegation, a response also glorified in the literature Rosa Maria had taught her to cherish. Goethe's Werther suffered in a way that captivated generations of readers; had not the lovers in the romantic ballad "Es waren zwei Königskinder" (There were two royal youths) been ennobled by a love of eternal longing and by beautiful death? But Ottilie rejected this denial for respectability's sake. She accepted, indeed enjoyed, the spotlight of scandal. Yet once the radical step was taken, her conduct was conservative, for she accepted the responsibilities of a legitimate wife, though she lacked her rights. She was faithful, for her liberation was not for free love but to give herself freely to the man she loved. Her survival strategy was adopted from Rahel Varnhagen: to redefine liability as asset; to embrace as choice what others would decry or belittle as victimization; to wear what might be a stigma as a badge of honor. She defined, and so identified with, her role that she seemed unaware of its ambivalence, its duality, its precariousness. But she was also the prisoner, the victim, of the persona she created.

How did Ottilie Assing cope after Baison's death? Though she wrote to her sister to tell her of the tragedy,[83] her pride kept her from approaching Ludmilla and Varnhagen for moral support; the Steinheims had left Hamburg in 1844 and were now living in Italy; Rahel de Castro extended sisterly solace, yet how open could Ottilie be with a friend who corresponded regularly with Ludmilla? Amalie Schoppe was in a state of emotional paralysis after the death of two sons and the imprisonment for fraud of her youngest; still, she reached out to Ottilie. "The long-expected blow has finally been dealt to our Ottilie: Baison is dead! I wrote her immediately and asked her warmly to come to me; she promised but never showed up." Ottilie never liked Schoppe's efforts to interfere with her life. Schoppe continued: "You know how fearful I am that she might have thrown her estate into this chasm, and her staying away seems to confirm this fear. And that when she needs the advice and help of an experienced friend more than ever. With Madame Baison she is . . . worse off than she probably was with the diseased husband. I have no idea what I should do with her, and yet I so want to help her." She even asked that Varnhagen "write a few lines to me in which he urges me to look after Ottilie's money. With that I could confront Madame Baison, what I would not dare now, for fear of her impertinence."[84] Small wonder that Ottilie stayed away!

What sustained Ottilie Assing was, first, that she did not lose a home, and second, that she was not alone. Madame Baison had moved out when Ottilie moved in, but she evidently did not regard the young woman as her enemy or rival. During her husband's final illness Caroline Baison returned to Hamburg, and wife and mistress shared the responsibility of nursing the invalid; after his death they shared the state of widowhood. Caroline Baison became a virtual sister, and with the sister came a family, came obligations. Like Jean Baptiste, Caroline Baison was an artist who lived in a world of her own creation that had little in common with the real world. Ottilie Assing had proved her skills as a domestic manager after Rosa Maria's death and during her years with Baison; now she took on the management of the Baison family. It was her experience and advice that ultimately enabled Madame Baison to reach a reasonable settlement with the Hamburg city council. For eight years Caroline Baison received an annual pension of 800 thalers, and she was offered a contract as an actress for an additional 500 thalers per year.[85] But a fierce and bitter struggle continued against the management on Madame Baison's behalf, and it finally rendered Ottilie persona non grata in her beloved theater. "She and Madame Baison both live in a never-ending and totally useless world of theater intrigues and gossip, seeking with antlike diligence to render themselves obnoxious and hated in these circles. Their sense for everything beyond that setting is lost in these activities,"[86] Ludmilla wrote. But frantic activism can be a way of escaping pain that threatens to overwhelm.

In August 1849, when the Prussian army marched into Hamburg, it was welcomed by conservative citizens as guarantor of law and order, and bombarded with stones by those still willing to defend the remnants of a dead revolution. Early in 1851 it was succeeded by more than 4,000 Austrian troops, and the city groaned under the financial burden of this military billeting. Ottilie was indifferent to the world around her and to these political events. "Nations may fall, and you hardly notice," she wrote, "but two eyes, closed forever, make the whole world appear in a new light and cause an external and internal transformation in the lives of those close to and distant from him." The suffering was all the more acute inasmuch as she refused to seek solace in religion. In fact, it appears that Baison's death consolidated her atheist commitment. "You know that I was never of that so-called positive religion which teaches us to submit patiently to any disaster, humbly stooping in the dust," she wrote to Gutzkow, "and so I cannot shake the feeling that Baison's death is an injustice, an expression of fate's brutality, which, before destroying him, chose to play its deliberate game with him and us." "How indifferent, how trivial do events of global import appear—revolution or counterrevolution, first republic or monarchy—when such a life is at stake!"[87]

Memories of her father's response to Rosa Maria's death finally helped Ottilie through this painful period: she withdrew to write Baison's biography, translating her sorrow into words, turning her pain outward so that it would not consume her. Instead of focusing on death she devoted herself to reconstructing and celebrating the life of a man she had loved and to sharing the inspiration and beauty she believed he had given her. She used the anonymous "An Actor" instead of her name, but when the book was published in Hamburg in 1851 she was immediately identified as the author.[88] David Assing had thought of his edition of Rosa Maria's writings as a last gesture of love to his wife, his final offering to the world he was determined to leave. His daughter shouldered her biographical task as a test of her willpower and her literary skills. The book enabled her to embrace her loss creatively, and empowered her to go on with her life. Also, she was working in a time-honored family tradition: not only had her father preserved Rosa Maria's memory in a book, but Varnhagen had immortalized Rahel's with an edition of her letters; many years later, when Ludmilla Assing's lover, Piero Cironi, died, she, too, wrote a biography, *Vita di Piero Cironi* (1865).[89]

Ottilie reached out in many ways: Baison's death softened her, it seems. Suddenly it seemed important to achieve some sort of reconciliation with Ludmilla and Varnhagen. They had hardly written to each other since Ottilie's departure from Berlin, but they had stayed in touch through Rahel de Castro. In the summer of 1849 Ludmilla and Varnhagen spent a vacation in the Hamburg area, and Varnhagen's diaries record several outings with Ottilie. Then, on an early morning in February 1850, Ludmilla's bedroom door flew open and Ottilie stormed in. She was spending a week in Berlin with a friend of hers, a Miss Grahe, and had decided that one day should be devoted to her sister. To avoid any occasion for quarrel, Ottilie planned it as a day of incessant activity: shopping, visits with friends, theater, galleries. Somehow in between she also had a conversation with Varnhagen, who was so pleased with the sober way she conducted herself that he gave her a silk dress and a velvet mantilla. It almost seemed as if "she had given up her strange aversion to our uncle and is again on good terms with him," a stunned Ludmilla reported to Johanna Steinheim.[90] Yet Ottilie gave no sign that she would like to spend more than one day with the family, and after eight days she returned to Hamburg, "very pleased with her excursion." She resumed her correspondence with her relatives in Berlin, but her letters, though friendly, remained noncommittal. We can deduce from the content of the four letters written between 1850 and 1852 in the Varnhagen Collection that there must have been more; Ludmilla must have discarded them—another sign of how far the sisters had drifted apart.

Although she was still living at the Baisons', Ottilie Assing's activities in the early 1850s document that she was struggling to regain her independence. As an adolescent she had taken painting lessons; now she hired a tutor to help her polish her skills. When Ludmilla came to Hamburg in June 1852, she found her sister painting away happily, convinced she would be able to make a decent living at it. For Ludmilla it was difficult to take Ottilie's efforts seriously: "I found her in very good spirits . . . totally absorbed in her paintings, which she showed me in great numbers; naturally we need not even mention their aesthetic merits, but they seem to impress the amateur and are produced with excessive speed."[91] In a letter a month later she added that Ottilie had been furious at her criticism and fiercely rejected her claim "that she seems to have no knowledge whatsoever about the composition of colors."[92] For peace's sake the sisters continued to meet politely, but their good manners could not hide the violent emotions that boiled beneath the surface.

In 1851 Ottilie Assing departed on yet another new venture: she began writing for the *Morgenblatt für gebildete Leser*, one of Germany's most distinguished journals, published by the house of Cotta,[93] which had become famous as the publishing house of Goethe, Schiller, and other classic German writers as well as of contemporary literature. In their republican enthusiasm they had printed the novels of the German-American writer Charles Sealsfield as well as the narratives of Herzog Paul Wilhelm von Württemberg and many other travelers in America. In addition, the Cottas were newspaper pioneers, publishing the *Augsburger Allgemeine Zeitung*, the first German daily that reported internationally like the *Times* and *New York Tribune*, and they enraged the authorities by the liberal views they advocated. The paper first called *Morgenblatt für gebildete Stände* (Morning Paper for the Educated Classes), then renamed *Morgenblatt für gebildete Leser* (Morning Paper for Educated Readers) in 1837, was addressed to well-educated readers of the middle and upper classes, and especially people in positions where they could spread what they learned from the paper. This gave it an enormous influence in Germany, although sales hardly went beyond 1,500. Ottilie Assing's parents had subscribed to it, and for many years their poems appeared regularly in it as well. On 12 July 1851 Carl Cotta received a letter from Ottilie Assing in which she announced: "On friendly recommendation from Mrs. Dr. Schoppe I hereby send you a correspondent's report from Hamburg."[94] It is not clear whether Cotta remembered her parents as faithful contributors, whether he wanted to do a favor to his long-standing writer Amalie Schoppe, or whether he was impressed by Assing's lively, moving, witty—just as the occasion demanded—report or by its cynicism and proud subjectivity.[95] But her column was printed that same month. In the next fourteen years, at least 125 articles of hers, usually three or four two-column pages, appeared in the *Morgenblatt*. The unwritten agreement between Cotta and Assing ended only when financial problems forced the publisher to discontinue the *Morgenblatt* in 1865. All her commentaries were published anonymously, but Cotta, a conscientious bookkeeper, kept a list in which he recorded author, title of contribution, and remuneration, so authorship is traceable. From this list we can see that she was indeed privileged to work for the house of Cotta, for not only did the *Morgenblatt* have an excellent reputation but Cotta paid his authors generously, about

35 or 36 gulden per published sheet,[96] or the equivalent of $14 at a time when a ship's carpenter in New York made $2 or $3 a day and a second-class transatlantic passage cost $80. From now on Ottilie could count on a reliable income from this source. It was a big step toward true independence. Slowly she achieved what many other women writers and emerging journalists of her day and class were struggling for: to transform themselves from someone being written about to someone writing.[97]

It was an irony that Ottilie Assing began her career as a *Morgenblatt* correspondent with an article on German emigration to the United States. On 11 July 1851 the sixty-year-old Amalie Schoppe boarded the *Franklin* for the New World, following her only remaining son, who had emigrated the year before after his release from prison.[98] Ottilie Assing accompanied her on board, and she could therefore describe the conditions under which thousands of her countrywomen and -men crossed the Atlantic each year. She wrote about the confined luxury of the first-class salon and the tomblike quality of their cabins, and then about the potential hell of the lower deck into which human beings were crowded like sardines. What has our country come to, she asked, to make people embrace this danger, this discomfort, this loss of place and space? What has happened when brave and active women like Amalie Schoppe and her friend Madame Paulsen, the founder of Hamburg's Women's Club, turn their back on it? What have we come to when our healthy, industrious farmhands, our workers, our teachers, our ministers and artists cross the ocean to offer their service to a nation whose language they do not even speak? Each question was an accusation to which her audience, she affirmed, knew the answer. Of equal importance was the other question that followed the travelers on their long journey—the question of what it was the New World had to offer, so that thousands followed its clarion call, like the children the Pied Piper of Hamelin in the famous German folk tale. People sailed to America because their homeland chained them to the here and now, to drudgery without perspective, she claimed; they left in quest of a future—a future like a blank piece of paper for the desperate ones, and hope for those who had not yet lost the ability to dream. Yet wasn't that what all people wanted: the right to dream, to hope? she asked. Was that really asking too much? What paralyzed our country so that the word "hope" has been eliminated from our discourse?[99]

Did Ottilie Assing divine, when she asked these questions, that only thirteen months later she would join this human odyssey and follow her friend? It is likely, for Germany held no future for her, either: its narrowness stifled her. "Submission to morality and manners is boosted to a point at which it severely impedes social encounters, narrows down your range of vision and tolerates no free attitude toward the world and toward life,"[100] she complained in the *Morgenblatt* in January 1852. Her parents were gone, and she could no longer relate to her closest kin; her great hope for national regeneration and rejuvenation had collapsed with the revolution; the counterrevolution had driven friends into exile, others into the inner immigration of silence. The Hamburg Senate, like other administrations all over Germany, passed laws that restricted the freedom of the press which the revolution of 1848 had given to some regions, and Ottilie Assing refused to become an accommodationist journalist. Anti-Semitism gained new virulence among conservatives, who railed against Jewish revolutionaries like Heine, Riesser, and Marx, and it was virulent even among Young Germans like Gutzkow, who blamed their Jewish fellow revolutionaries for their political debacle.[101] "There is a gulf between the Jewish and the Christian which cannot be filled with words," Gutzkow had claimed as early as 1842; "education and humanity can jump across it, friendship and an individual's enlightened, true value can build a free-floating, secure bridge across it that makes the most intimate encounter possible; but from the point of view of the naturally rooted population all these motives are like water off a duck's back."[102] This upsurge of anti-Semitism among the Young Germans taught Assing that Gutzkow had been wrong: intellectuals were not immune to the epidemic; the hope for reconciliation in a purified Germany died. She had lost her companion, and, through him, her reputation; as a consequence, she was deprived of her ability to make a living as a teacher outside the Baison home, for who would hire a fallen woman to tutor their children? It is likely that she had given a large percentage of her inheritance to Baison and lost it when he died. Yet Johanna Steinheim was probably wrong when she blamed the Baison affair for Ottilie's political ideas: "Without this unfortunate relationship to the Baison family she would never have developed such quixotic ideas."[103] Despite all she had suffered, Ottilie Assing was determined never to give up her personal creed that the power to define the self lay in the individual. Her American sojourn was an attempt to recover this precious power of self-definition.

Ottilie's sister and uncle may have been relieved when she told them of her decision to leave the Old World, but there is evidence that they also dreaded the gossip this departure was bound to cause. So embarrassed was Varnhagen by his niece's moves that as late as one month before her departure he had not even told his most intimate friend, Henriette Solmar, of this most recent act of defiance. And, as always, Ottilie's behavior did not contribute to his peace of mind either, for she talked about her travel plans to everybody willing to listen, staging her American adventure, just as she had staged her suicide attempt. "Should Miss Solmar inquire about Ottilie's voyage, she will most certainly get all the details, if not from us, then from others, for Ottilie talks about it wherever she goes," Ludmilla wrote. "Wouldn't it be more diplomatic to tell the truth, especially since Miss Solmar inquires more from sympathy than curiosity?"[104] Ludmilla, who was in Hamburg for the summer, went with Ottilie when she inspected American boats, Varnhagen sent money to help with clothing for the trip and to ensure that Ottilie had enough funds for travel. Ottilie finally decided to book passage on the *Indian Queen*, due to leave Hamburg on 15 August.[105]

In the last weeks before her departure Ottilie Assing had to sustain another major disappointment—this time from someone whom she had spent years defending against slander. After Ottilie had seen to it that Caroline Baison got her pension, her friend agreed that Ottilie should at least receive interest on the money she had invested in Baison's tragic venture. Now, shortly before her departure, Ottilie had to acknowledge that Madame Baison could not be relied on to keep this promise. Not only had she gone off for the summer, leaving Ottilie to manage the household and "forgetting" to leave sufficient money, but she had also made up all kinds of excuses for not paying Ottilie's interest. The young woman knew she would lose control over the situation once in America unless she commissioned Varnhagen to see after her claims. But that was impossible, for she had always denied giving her money to Baison in the first place. She was caught in a trap of her own making, and in desperation vented her rage against anybody who dared touch on the issue—first and foremost Ludmilla, who obviously enjoyed rubbing it in.[106]

Many losses and frustrations accumulated before Ottilie Assing decided to leave Germany for good, and yet we would do her an injustice if we interpreted her emigration exclusively in terms of flight. Far more important was that America spelled promise, a new beginning—life in the best sense of the word. If we follow Janis Stout's argument that journeys to foreign lands are either exploration, flight, or search for a new home,[107] Ottilie's must be said to have contained elements of all three motives, with the last dominating. In that, she joined a pilgrimage of hope that had given hundreds of thousands of Europeans the courage to face the transatlantic passage. Ever since Christopher Columbus articulated his famous boast "I have discovered Paradise," Europeans had claimed their human right to dream in this way. Millennia before, the Greeks had redefined their utopia after their first encounter with India; after the "discovery" of America, Europeans realized that their speculations about a Golden

World could have a definite geographical locale. Happiness, they exclaimed, could be achieved in the here and now. Whether we read Thomas More's *Utopia*, Shakespeare's *Tempest*, or the poetry of Marvell, Drayton, Herbert, Swift or Blake, Heine or Goethe—they all subscribed to this dream. In the late eighteenth century Europe was again shaken out of its political lethargy by the American Revolution. Sensing what Alexis de Tocqueville predicted in his *Democracy in America* (1835), that the doctrines and practices represented by these young United States were bound to transform the entire Western world,[108] apologists of the old order and the radicals and restless alike decided to go and see for themselves. The questions they asked of the object of their curiosity document their objectives: in the words of the historian Henry Steele Commager, "Can men govern themselves? Is it possible to reconcile liberty and order, the individual and the state? Can men of different races, tongues, and faiths live amicably side by side? . . . Can art, literature, and philosophy flourish in a society which substitutes the verdict of the majority for the judgment of training and tradition?"[109]

Ottilie Assing, familiar with the rich European literature celebrating the American Dream,[110] answered all these questions in the affirmative. For her America was not exile but a desirable place beyond the familiar here. She believed that the laboratory experiment in which the future of humanity was being tested would be successful, that universal human happiness could be achieved if only enough people contributed their skills, their imagination, and their enthusiasm. She, for one, was willing to give all. And she was sure enough of herself, her skills, and her ingenuity to believe that she could make important contributions to this New World. She would not be entering the country as a beggar. She saw herself as a woman whom experience and education had transformed into someone willing and able to help construct a glorious future for humankind. And in two realms especially she claimed special competence—race relations and the arts.

For more than thirty years Ottilie Assing had observed and even suffered from anti-Semitism in Germany, and she believed that her personal history prepared her for the encounter with a nation in whose history race played such a pivotal role. Like most German emigrants of her day and like many of her Young German friends, she dreamed the American Dream, yet unlike most of her contemporaries, she knew that she was departing for a country whose Declaration of Independence was written by a slaveholder, whose principles of freedom and equality clashed with the reality of slavery. From references in her letters and *Morgenblatt* articles we know that she was familiar with the contradictions between American principles and the impact of the "peculiar institution" and racism on everyday life which the well-traveled philosopher and expert on the Americas Alexander von Humboldt, one of Varnhagen's closest friends in Berlin, deplored in his writing.[111] The excitement over Harriet Beecher Stowe's *Uncle Tom's Cabin*, first published in 1851, was loud enough for the clamor to be heard even in Germany, and Assing was eager to read it. Like all educated Germans of her day, she had read Kleist's "Engagement in Santo-Domingo" (1811), and she shared the enthusiasm of German radicals for the Haitian Revolution and its hero, Toussaint L'Ouverture.[112] In 1849 liberal Germans welcomed the news that the University of Heidelberg had awarded an honorary degree to the fugitive slave James W. C. Pennington. The United States where Ottilie Assing hoped to make a new start was in the thralls of racism; it needed expert radicals like her to liberate itself from its self-imposed bondage, she believed.

Assing's knowledge of American slavery was taken from books, and so were the solutions she envisioned. It is possible that the glorification of Toussaint L'Ouverture among German radicals roused the hope in her that another great black liberator would arise in the United States. In 1848 Baison's precarious health had meant that she had watched from a distance as her friends marched for freedom in Germany; did she dream of an American revolution, so she could make up for the lost chance? Did she perceive herself as a potential witness of a black revolution? Is it even feasible that she was already imagining herself as more than just an observer? This speculation is not so far-fetched as it might appear. Visions of a black revolution, of a militant alliance transcending established boundaries of race and gender, were evoked in a novel she read during the year after Baison's death: Clara Mundt's *Aphra Behn* (1849). Ottilie liked all of Mundt's novels for the unconventional and powerful women in them, and for Mundt's courageous stand on women's rights and divorce, but the Aphra Behn story especially captivated her.

Published only one year after the Revolution of 1848, as its participants were persecuted and driven into exile, Mundt's text was a fierce indictment of European monarchies ruled by tyrants who were, her protagonist claimed, "blind, and [who] do not see their people's misery, or deaf, and do not hear their people's cries of pain."[113] The novel's villains are monarchs who despise the people they rule and exploit, hypocritical bishops and cardinals who ridicule religion and cynically misuse their power, colonial officers who brutalize, mutilate, and kill their slaves, men who rape and batter women—all observed from the perspective of the innocent young Aphra Behn, who, after witnessing the torture and murder of the black rebel hero Oronooko and after being raped by Oronooko's tormentor, transforms herself into "a passionate, revengeful woman, contemptible of the world."[114]

The heroine of Mundt's narrative is an actual historical figure, of course, the English novelist and dramatist Aphra Behn (1640–89), who became famous for her novel about a slave rebellion in Surinam, *Oroonoko, or, The Royal Slave* (1688). Behn's adventures in Surinam, her life at the English court, her career as a spy, and, finally, her success as a writer offered plenty of material for a three-decker novel. Yet Mundt's Aphra Behn was not only the biographer of the royal slave Oronooko. Although Mundt's Oronooko is married to the beautiful Imoinda, he and Aphra, in the novel's culminating scene, become lovers. When her lover hero incites his fellow slaves to rebel against their brutal master, Aphra stands by him, and she tries to save his life by sacrificing herself to his tormentor's lust, only to see her black prince die a terrifying death. In introducing the motif of the white woman offering her body to gain a black slave's freedom and failing, Mundt gave a tragic twist to the *Code noir** theme that had become popular among recent European antislavery writers. For example, claiming that the *Code noir* decreed that a slave became free when a white woman agreed to marry him, Madame Charles Reybaud celebrated the marriage of the noblewoman Cécile de Ratèl and the heroic mulatto slave Donatien in her short story "Les Epaves" in 1838. Two years later the Danish writer Hans Christian Andersen came out with his play *Mulatten*, an adaptation of Reybaud's tale, which was performed at the Royal Danish Theater in Copenhagen and translated into Swedish and German.[115] Clara Mundt had just experienced the terrors of the failed 1848 revolution when she wrote her novel, and she did not evoke images of successful defiance. Her black and white protagonists give all only to be destroyed and ravaged by forces beyond their control.[116] Though Ottilie Assing did not share Mundt's defeatist attitude toward revolution, the novel helped her to put the tragedy of her own life in a larger perspective, and it challenged her to free herself from the despondency into which she had descended. Perhaps America would be the land where Aphra and Oronooko could fight tyranny, where they would survive and triumph. Perhaps in America Aphra and Oronooko would claim the freedom to love.

Unknown to Ottilie Assing, the man with whom she was to attempt to create this interracial union and paradise only six years later had already succeeded

---

*The *Code noir*, or black code, was a body of laws that had regulated the institution of slavery in the French colonies.

in transforming himself from a slave into the United States' most powerful black leader. To authenticate the story he told so eloquently on the abolitionist lecture circuit, he had written his own memoir, the *Narrative of the Life of Frederick Douglass* (1845). The details he revealed about his life had forced him into exile; leaving behind his wife and their four children, he had escaped to England in 1845, where he spent two years mobilizing the British public against slavery; English subscribers raised £150 to purchase his freedom from Hugh Auld. When he returned to the United States in April 1847 he carried with him the determination to publish his own newspaper. The first edition of the weekly *North Star* appeared in his new hometown, Rochester, New York, in 1847. This venture, as well as changes in his abolitionist position, alienated him from the Garrisonians.

Douglass had begun his abolitionist career in the American Anti-Slavery Society under William Lloyd Garrison's intellectual guidance, and he had shared his mentor's doctrine of "No Union with Slaveholders" which argued that abolitionists should renounce their allegiance to a Constitution they regarded as proslavery. Yet he had grown increasingly dissatisfied with the Garrisonians' exclusive focus on moral suasion. When he began to demand that the battle against slavery be fought in the political arena, a position that was also taken by Garrison's rival and founder of the Liberty Party, Gerrit Smith, the rift between Douglass and the Garrisonians widened. A vicious warfare ensued.[117]* Then, when Julia Griffiths, a British abolitionist from Newcastle-on-Tyne, followed Douglass to Rochester to live with his family and help him with his paper, it seemed clear to many of his friends that a rupture in the Douglass marriage was final, and the Garrisonians spread rumors about the alleged affair in an attempt to ruin the "defector's" reputation. Frederick Douglass was the most powerful black American of the day, but he was also a deeply troubled man, a hero under siege. He could not know that a German woman had begun to dream of him without even knowing his name.

Racial reconciliation was one mission Ottilie Assing had on her mind as she

---

*Assing described the split between the abolitionists as follows: "One faction, represented by the American Anti-Slavery Society and Garrison, its founder, argue that the Constitution sanctions slavery and is, therefore, 'a covenant with death and an agreement with hell.' They see a solution only in the overthrow of the Constitution and a dissolution of the Union. . . . Opposed to them are the National Abolitionists, who defend the Constitution in word and spirit against the charge that it is proslavery; in that view, any tendency toward dissolving the Union is cowardly because it can only result in the exacerbation of the slaves' condition in the South. Douglass, who had once been an eager adherent of the Garrisonian theory, later became a supporter of the other view, thus bringing down on his head the most extreme enmity of his former collaborators."[118]

planned her American sojourn; to bring art to a beauty-starved nation was another. We have no reliable information as to who planted this idea in her mind, but Ottilie and Madame Baison were both convinced that the arts were so underdeveloped in the United States that Americans would recognize and embrace Ottilie's genius, and she would be able to make a good living by enriching the American cultural wasteland with her contributions. It is possible that the British traveler and novelist Frances Trollope can be blamed for this misconception, for Ottilie read her *Domestic Manners of the Americans* (1832), in which Trollope, who had been accompanied by a young portrait painter on her tour, deplored the absence of art in the New World. Anyway, she and Caroline Baison often joked that soon Ottilie would be so successful that she would be able "to buy a Negro to grind her colors."[119]

Ottilie Assing had not much cash when she left Germany, but she carried with her a verbal contract that promised a decent income for her first years in America. Carl Cotta, impressed by her intelligent and unconventionally subjective reports from conservative Hamburg, had promised to regard her as the *Morgenblatt*'s American correspondent. In addition, her friends from the *Hamburger Telegraph* signaled they would buy reports from her. That is why Ottilie Assing was among the few who could smile as the *Indian Queen* pulled out of Hamburg Harbor. She was thirty-three years old and eager to embrace the future. "You rave," Mundt's Aphra Behn answered when lectured on a woman's duty to make others happy. "I have another assignment before me! I want to make myself happy! This is Nature's first and most sacred law . . ."[120]

III

PILGRIM-FOOL

American Beginnings

I do not want to be a woman, but a free, feeling, thinking, and acting human being!
I want to have the right to live according to my own free will, I do not want to ask:
Is that proper? I no longer worry about the judgment of the world! Free and courageously I want to follow the call of my heart, the inspirations of my mind; I want to
serve truth, truth shall be my conscience and the only judge of my actions, and only
that which cannot stand before this inner truth shall I call sin, nothing else! . . . I
want to be a woman to love, and a man to think. I will have the heart of a Lais, and
the head of a Plato, and if the virtuous denounce me as a sinner, at least the sinners
shall call me virtuous! —CLARA MUNDT, *Aphra Behn*

Oh let us hope! Follow me, my friend!
Whosoever desires courageously has already conquered the world.
—KARL GUTZKOW, *Uriel Acosta*

*A*n Irish pub stood right across from the pier from which the boats departed that took
  tourists from Manhattan to the African-American Methodist camp meeting in Sing
Sing during the last week of August 1855.[1] Benches in front of the tavern invited the
passengers to rest and take refreshment while waiting for the boats in the simmering afternoon heat. The owner was patronizing and condescending as he served the ladies and
gentlemen, who, he knew, would never deign to look at his establishment at other times.
But today he was in control: not only could he charge them twice the regular price for his
watered-down lemonade but he could even make them feel grateful they got anything at
all.

  Ottilie Assing could barely keep from laughing at the comedy. Leaning against one of
the few trees that offered some shade there, she watched the New World gentry in their ex-

pensive holiday attire, crowded on rough wooden benches, jovially ridiculed by the bois-terous saloonkeeper, and surrounded by his usual ragamuffin customers, who, mugs in hand, were loafing about the premises, staring at the strangers from another world. Inside she heard the stomping of feet as a few indefatigable ones danced to the tunes of an Irish fiddler. Was she in the midst of an American Falstaffian revel or had she entered a Murillo painting?

Still no boat in sight. Two rather rough-looking gentlemen made their entrance: rep-resentatives of two rival boat companies. They each began to praise the speed, safety, and comfort of their own vessel and deride the shabbiness and unreliability of their competi-tor's. They raged, pleaded, tore their hair, and seemed almost to get at each other's throat—greatly to the amusement of their audience. When the boats finally pulled in, the warriors stormed down the pier and then faced the passengers in poses suggesting their willingness to throw into the water anybody who dared approach the rival boat. The travelers filed past them, and soon everyone was steaming up the river.

It was not Ottilie's first trip on the Hudson, but no matter how often she took it, the scenery never failed to enchant her. Fashionable European travel narratives about the Hudson tour, which, like visiting Niagara Falls, had become a "must" for Old World tourists, frequently complained about the aesthetic imbalance between the sublime and mighty river on the one hand and its soft banks on the other, but she was not influenced by these notions. In fact, she thought that the Hudson Valley might even be superior to the landscape canonized by the Romantics—the Rhine Valley. She was sure she was right as she sat on a comfortable deck chair and watched the mountains on the west, green to the very top, lined up before her like pearls on a necklace, the river snaking its way through them, the hills closest to her clothed in emerald abundance, the ones farthest away almost unreal in their blue mistiness. On the eastern side spacious mansions and idyllic cottages overlooked the river, and little towns like Hastings and Tarrytown seemed to signal to those who passed that it was a privilege to be there.

It was close to sunset when the boats reached Sing Sing after a three-hour trip. Ottilie climbed into one of the coaches waiting on the pier. The travelers were taken up a steep hill and along a bumpy road lined with pleasant painted wood houses. Eventually they came to a circle of almost eighty tents pitched in a beech forest. Most of the tents were open and brightly illuminated. Curiously Ottilie wandered among them, until the sound of singing tempted her to stumble along a barely lit path. This is how Hansel and Gretel must have felt that first night in the woods, she thought to herself, only she had no Hansel. But the scene she beheld when she finally emerged into a clearing was not out of the Grimm broth-ers' tales. On a high wooden platform six preachers—four black, one a rather dark-skinned mulatto, one with very light complexion—were competing for the audience's attention. In front, in a small fenced-in area strewn with straw, those who had already "experienced the light" were kneeling; behind were lines of benches on which sat those yet to be converted. One after another the preachers delivered their messages praising God for the chance for salvation He offered and warning sinners of the dire consequences if they continued to close their minds and hearts to His words. Time and again the same words, images, phrases were repeated rhythmically, interspersed with the congregation's "Amen!" and "Glory to God!" As one preacher's voice gave up, the next was ready to take over, castigating and exhorting, until the whole clearing seemed to soar with words and groans and cries.

    Ottilie found a mossy spot under a tree, and for two hours she watched the drama unfold. She was appalled by the speakers' performance—from her German perspective, they seemed to take hollering for rhetorical emphasis—and, ultimately, bored. Then one minister called a halt, asking the congregation to continue their efforts in the big tent in the middle of the camp. Everybody rushed to the tent, first and foremost among them a mulatto without legs seated in a little cart, pushing as hard as he could to be first. The hardness of his muscles showed through his shirt, and Ottilie could almost see the blood rushing to his head, his face contorted with exertion.

    The brightly illuminated tent was already packed, with people kneeling or lying on the straw floor, others in a circle around them. Exhorters, women and men, now began their work, and soon the tent seemed a mass of wringing and moaning bodies. Ottilie had been to Methodist meetings before, and she had been shocked; now she was almost nauseated. How could rational people submit to such a farce? How could they allow themselves to be carried away so shamelessly? There was only one explanation: their daily lives must be dreary beyond endurance and their thirst for entertainment, for something beyond the dark here and now, unbearable.

    All of a sudden a voice soared above the frenzy, manipulating and controlling it at the same time. A woman had begun to preach. She was tall and bony, with a calico bonnet whose long ribbons almost hid her face. Ottilie was struck by the color of her skin: she was dark, but not of the blackness of what Ottilie called "the real Negro" or the dark "yellow" of a mulatto; she was earthy gray. But the woman's most remarkable feature was her voice—deep and round, powerful and rich. Since her childhood Ottilie had been keyed to voices—they affected her likes and dislikes of people—and this tendency had only intensified during her life with Baison. Now she gave herself up to this woman's voice, allowing her to lift her up, shake her, throw her down, stomp on her, caress her, pinch her. In front of her a young woman lay on the straw, trembling and moaning uncontrollably as in an epileptic fit, and the light-skinned preacher she had heard before was bending over her, pleading with her softly to give herself to God and rise, while others prayed for her salvation. Singing began to replace exhortation—endless repetition of "God is my love!," stomping, clapping, wailing, with the indefatigable gray woman leading the chorus. Ottilie had never seen such a frenzy, had never heard such noises, and there seemed no end to it, only uncontrollable fluidity and growth. Then the light-skinned preacher stood up, reminding the congregation that it was past ten and they had done their duty before God. Ottilie was fascinated at the ease with which the people then calmly walked away. The young woman was picked up and carried outside.

The white spectators who had come from Manhattan now returned to the horse-drawn coaches to be taken back to the village where they planned to spend the night. They gazed in amazement when Ottilie got her leather satchel, which she had deposited with the driver, declaring that she intended "to go the whole hog!" Crazy Germans! Always pretending they were special! Ottilie bathed in their silent disapproval as she walked across the camp. Philistines all. Just like the Pepperbags in Hamburg. Not her kind of people.

An elderly black woman was cooking some kind of stew on a little camp stove, alternately stirring the soup and throwing bits of leftover bread to the chickens clucking around her. Ottilie entered her tent. "Excuse me, madam, could you perhaps put me up for the night?" The woman stared at her in disbelief. "I'll pay for it. And I would love a little soup, too. It smells good." Ottilie felt awkward. The woman pointed to the corner, where hay was stacked. "Put your thing over there." Ottilie put her bag down, and a few minutes later she was enjoying her stew. She couldn't chew the mutton, but the soup was spicy and felt good. Several people came in, among them the light-skinned preacher. They all looked at Ottilie in amazement, but once they had been served they forgot about her; the exhorter and his followers were ordinary people, chattering, laughing, exchanging gossip. Only when they got ready to leave did the preacher remember his role. He came over to Ottilie and took her hand in both of his: "My dear child, have you, too, come to be enlightened by the Bible?" How she despised this tone, had despised it since childhood! She laid her free hand on top of his. "No, I am only visiting and will leave tomorrow." She had always been good at freezing people.

The tent's owner began to prepare for the night. She pulled a curtain to divide the sleeping section from the cooking section, and the straw was spread so that two or more people could sleep on it. Ottilie was not enthusiastic, for it was clear the straw had hosted other guests before, and she looked for an alternative: putting wooden boards across two suitcases, she built a rough bed for herself and was about to retire when a large group of women and men, chanting hymns, began running through the camp. Together with her host she followed this joyous procession. The revel continued for hours, but Ottilie was exhausted and went back to the bed she had built and slept like a baby.

She was awakened by hymns. When she took a daylight look at the camp she saw that it had been transformed into a marketplace. Women were busy cooking breakfast on improvised stoves, and everywhere piles of fruit and vegetables had been stacked up; a milk cart was standing at the camp entrance. Soon a bell invited the believers to their morning prayer. Again the gray woman dominated the scene, yet to Ottilie's amazement and relief she now used her beautiful, rich voice not for religious exhortation but to convey a most powerful sermon on slavery, not only evoking the slaves' tribulations in the most moving words but conjuring up God's vengeance upon the slavemasters. She was succeeded by a light-skinned preacher well into his seventies, a former slave. He sang of God's grace in delivering him from slavery: "Yes," he shouted, "God has shown mercy for me. I was a slave, and He freed me, and then He gave me a family, a beautiful wife and dear children, so much, indeed, that I will never be able to thank Him enough. Come, stand up, dear wife, and show yourself, so that our brothers and sisters may judge for themselves whether I have reasons for being grateful to God!" A heavy black matron slowly rose from a bench, beaming with joy and pride. The black congregation looked on her and her children with happy approval, but the white onlookers snickered and nudged each other. Ottilie, too, felt she had never seen anything so ludicrous, and biting her handkerchief to keep herself from laughing out loud she left the gathering. It was time to return to Sing Sing and New York. What a great show!

D uring the months of preparation for her American venture, Ottilie Assing and her friends never used the word "emigration." It had a finality to it that none of them could bear. The transatlantic passage as such, the idea of an unchaperoned young woman traveling to a vast, unfamiliar territory somewhere out there beyond the ocean held terrors enough. Yet Ottilie made it clear that she was not just talking about a few months away from home. She longed to experience New York City; she was determined to see New England, all of it, traveling from city to city, to the Berkshires and the White Mountains; she would do the famous Hudson tour and go to Niagara Falls; the South was waiting to be discovered; friends somewhere out there in Wisconsin, the Rosenthals, were beckoning; she would encounter the American frontier. She wanted to see the grandiose landscapes of America and meet the people in all their diversity. It would be an adventure; it was bound to be fun. Ottilie was determined to follow her mother's advice to the last:

> Do you want to sail the broadest of streams profitably and joyfully?
> Then begin your journey full of courage! Chase the pearls![2]

And like Harriet Martineau, like Frances Trollope and Fredrika Bremer, like Tocqueville and Humboldt, she would write about the land, the people, their institutions, their cultures, the art they produced, the literature they wrote, and the songs they sang. Those back home would be fascinated by the new images, the radical readings she had to offer. She would make her name a household word, and her American reports would prove her intellectual independence and her professionalism. America promised autonomy.

Her situation was such that Ottilie could afford to open herself to the transformational process of travel. In her first reports about the transatlantic adventure, which she sent to the *Jahreszeiten* in Hamburg, the code of metamorphosis characteristic of her text shows that her gaze was directed exclusively toward the future. She was Rosa Maria's daughter to the core:

> Whatever you left behind,
> Do not look back upon it fearfully,
> Before you lie the blue mountains,
> And beyond them new happiness. . . .
> New happiness and new love,
> This is what each new place holds for you . . .[3]

Although she was among the few who escaped seasickness, Ottilie still called the voyage "a chain of misery and nastiness."[4] When the vessel was approaching the English coast, so fierce a storm struck that the passengers almost panicked. Unfavorable winds made the captain decide to take the dangerous northern route instead, and an enchanted Ottilie got to admire the stern sublimity of the Scottish coast, but weather was not what bothered her most. It was the people she was cast among. She loved company, but company she chose: intellectuals and artists willing and able to nourish her mind, individuals who were special in one sense or another. She liked the captain, "a small, cheerful American, full of joie de vivre, friendly, kind, and good-natured," but she had no good word for the eight fellow passengers with whom she shared the first-class cabin, people so dull that they could not even play a round of whist, preferring the infantile game Black Peter instead. Ottilie's intellectual arrogance, even rudeness showed: "Being compelled to live in such close quarters with strangers is unbearable for any educated person, and it becomes a perfect torture when you are unfortunate enough to fall into company that is boring and for the most part uneducated." Her problem was not class; she had her own individual ideas about education, political orientation, and, perhaps most important, personality. For she found among the second-class passengers what her first-class fellow travelers did not provide—"the positive elements of the German people from various classes . . . young scholars, honest farmers with their wives and children . . . craftsmen, an actor and—political fugitives, without whom no ship departs for America these days." It was with these people that she spent her evenings on deck, singing songs, telling stories, discussing politics. They were as close to familiar as you could get among strangers.

But worlds separated Ottilie Assing from those on the lower deck. "Completely separated from the other company were the steerage passengers," she reported, "but I was often entertained at noon, when lunch was distributed among them, to look down from the afterdeck upon the bustling activity." Typically, hers was a gaze from above, emphasizing distance and difference.[5] She evoked an exotic genre painting for her readers rather than sketching individual people—creatures she observed like beasts in a zoo, "others." The Young German radical betrayed how deeply she had internalized the social biases and anxieties of her class when she warned of the brute that lurked beneath the smooth surface of these domesticated creatures. Equality may have been a key word for Assing, but under the thin veneer of her liberal terminology she associated equality only with those whom she considered exceptional.

When the voyage was coming to an end, new passenger lists had to be prepared, and as one of the few people aboard who spoke German, English, and French, Assing volunteered as the captain's secretary and translator. The description she gave of her work attributes an almost symbolic quality to the metamorphosis of every passenger. "It was on the high seas that all these Saxons, Hessians, Hannoverians, and Mecklenburgians were given a common fatherland, and even the Prussians and Austrians, who usually look down haughtily on the rest of Germany, arrived as Germans," she wrote.[6] A united Germany was an American reality long before it happened in the Old World. "Social rank, too, was treated rather lightly, and all those farmhands, day laborers, and working people were raised to the level of farmers, for, as the captain said, it looks better!" She could not have agreed more. The Hessian and Bavarian, the Saxonian Serb and Jew from Bremen—America reinvented them as Germans; soon they would be German-Americans, and their children would call themselves Americans. The farmhand and the factory worker reemerged as farmers, the common soldier as captain.

What was true for all these others aboard also applied to Assing herself: she entered America not as a "half-Jew" from Hamburg but as a German woman;[7] the daughter of Rosa Maria and David Assing, governess of the Baison children, and occasional critic and columnist reemerged as the foreign correspondent Ottilie Assing. She could accept transformational American policies because the passage from one identity to another empowered her; she was confident she had reclaimed the right to self-definition. The category crisis that had burdened her all her life would cease. She was free to reinvent herself. Gradually she would begin to take on the perspective of the German-American reporter, using the identifying "us" and "we" as she delineated American events. Ottilie would become Ottilia. Could she have imagined on that 27 September 1852, as the vessel lay outside New York Harbor, that in less than four years she would proudly present her American citizenship certificate to the American man she loved?

Her first impression of the New World, written down while still aboard the *Indian Queen*, tells the whole story in the plainest of words: "In the most beautiful moonshine we dropped anchor near Staten Island, whose light towers extended their friendly glow to us. . . . The sight is enchanting, unforgettable, and when I saw a shooting star only a few moments ago, I quickly wished myself proprietor of one of the gorgeous mansions along the shoreline. If the star keeps his word, all my friends are invited to visit me here!" It had been night when the *Indian Queen* left Hamburg Harbor; the city had disappeared as if swallowed in fog that like a curtain cut her off from her old life. It was night again as she came to the gates to the New World. America, however, extended light and warmth to her—promise and prosperity, even in the night. Her delineation of this first encounter suggests that the prosperity of which Assing dreamed as America's lights illuminated the darkness and invited her in would not be used to take her back home; she would enjoy it in the land that offered it. She even planned to entice those left behind to join her rather than return to the Old World as a successful and triumphant Lady Bountiful. She was ready to embrace and love the New World that stretched out before her. "Ach! a deep breath, the first one on firm ground, and then into the city!"[8]

Ottilie Assing was an unusual "emigrant" in that she arrived in the United States as a single woman. Between 1820 and 1910 the ratio of male to female emigrants was 65 to 35, with the latter usually traveling as members of a family. As a rule, the emigration of single women began after their ethnic group had already established a place in the New World.[9] But although Assing knew that traveling by herself was unusual, it certainly did not bother her—to the contrary. Also, she was well prepared. Only a few days before leaving from Hamburg she had received a letter from Amalie Schoppe advising her on how to conduct herself upon her arrival in New York;[10] Schoppe also gave her addresses of decent boardinghouses and information about people she might approach for advice and help. Assing had almost unlimited confidence that she could cope with the challenges.

The records we have of Ottilie Assing's first years in the United States are sparse, and we have to rely almost exclusively on her public statements; even here the records are incomplete. Some of the articles she sent to the *Jahreszeiten*, the *Kompass*, and the *Morgenblatt*, to the *Gartenlaube* and *Westermann's Monatshefte* never made it to the publishers, though she never knew this. Also, many journals were not systematically archived and much of what was available was destroyed during the bombing of German cities during World War II. Ottilie wrote to Ludmilla only infrequently. "I am worried that again there was no letter from Ottilie," Ludmilla once wrote to Wehl. "It has now been many months since I have heard from her." The only other person with whom she corresponded was Caroline Baison.[11] But still, we know that Ottilie found America even more enchanting than she had dared to hope. There may have been days when she longed for her friends in Germany, nights full of homesickness, perhaps even tears. But she certainly did not communicate those feelings. In this, her response is strikingly similar to that which scholars have discovered in most of the transatlantic correspondence left behind by generations of immigrants from all nations and classes; for most of them, the decision to leave home had been too heartrending for them to admit failure.[12]

Ottilie was lucky to arrive in New York before drastic demographic changes in the immigrant population, nativistic upsurges in the United States, and radical restrictions in U.S. immigration policy put up barriers against newcomers that many were unable to surmount. The medical examination to which the passengers of the *Indian Queen* had to submit was a mere farce, and Ottilie, used to the officious and arrogant German bureaucracy, was pleasantly surprised at the friendly carelessness with which American customs officers treated her and her luggage. Hiring a porter and negotiating his pay in the chaos at the pier[13] was her first test of both her linguistic skills and her capacity for survival, and she bragged about her sagacity in escaping the typical emigrant's victimization at the hands of the notorious New York hotel runner system. She made it to the boardinghouse on Walther Street that Amalie Schoppe had recommended, and she liked the spacious, sunny, and well-furnished room to which Mrs. Schweizer, her landlady, conducted her.[14] She was too excited to unpack. New York City was waiting for her!

Within a few days she had made a first start at finding a place as a professional woman in this New World. Taking a few samples of her paintings with her, she toured the city's galleries, asking whether they were interested in exhibiting her work, offering the works on commission, hoping to sell a few pieces on the spot. It turned out that the American art scene was not panting for her: she was politely received wherever she went, but competition was fierce, and the dealers were not convinced of the superiority of her oeuvre. Portraits?

Didn't she know that "here each and every one can get a good daguerreotype of his ugly mug for only half a dollar"? Also, they were now painting daguerreotypes in oil—another blow. But would she be willing to learn that new technique? It did not take her long to realize that her European notions of art, art in America, and her need to find a job were three different things, but fortunately she was flexible enough to adapt to what was before her. When a German-American art dealer offered to commission her to paint copperplate engravings, she accepted. To her artist friend Remde from Hamburg, now in London and hoping to emigrate to the United States, she sent off a letter on 24 November warning him that American soil was not hospitable to art, though she was confident she would make it. "For a dilettante like me it [daguerreotypes in oil] is pretty convenient, for it is quickly done and easily learned; still, everybody tells me that I will need a little patience, for it takes time to penetrate such a large city and to acquire a reputation, and so, for the beginning, I am pleased to have found a job with a German art dealer who lets me paint copperplates and then takes care of the sales."[15] It was a beginning. Her new employer agreed to exhibit some of her work, and soon she reported to Rahel de Castro that she had sold her first painting—a genre picture called "The Moors' Washday."[16] Now she would try to find a position as an art instructor in a wealthy family. Her optimism was unlimited.

There were a few people in this New World Ottilie knew, but she did not reach out to them until after she had found decent lodging and regular employment, for she dreaded dependency on others, the feeling that others might regard her as a petitioner or even a burden.

Joseph de Castro, impatient at not hearing from her, paid her a visit at her boardinghouse. This black sheep of the de Castro family, who had emigrated to the United States more than fifteen years earlier, was now living with his family in New York, where he worked in the import-export business.[17] De Castro gave her a warm welcome and offered to show her the city, introduce her around, teach her about America. But Ottilie was not interested in the company he kept; she wanted to learn about America by doing, by trusting her own perceptions. Moreover, she saw that he was a troubled spirit; his business was doing poorly, he was torn by homesickness, yet he dreaded returning to Hamburg a failure. Ottilie continued to see him for politeness' sake and because she had promised Rahel she would, but her instinct proved right: in the fall of 1855, he gave up and returned to Germany.[18]

When she took leave of Ottilie, Rahel de Castro had been soothed by the conviction that Ottilie would stay in New York only briefly and then "seek refuge" in Amalie Schoppe's maternal embrace. Nothing could have been further from the truth. Her young friend enjoyed the metropolis too much to pine for the cozy college town of Schenectady, where Schoppe lived.[19] It was only when people told her that autumn was the best season to go, with the fall foliage in all its glory, that she deigned to see her mother's confidante. But seek refuge? Equipped with nothing but a light carryall, a token of her new American mobility, she boarded the steamboat to Albany on a Friday—and was back in New York on Tuesday morning. She was thrilled to embrace her old acquaintance once again and pleased to find her in such comfortable circumstances, and Schoppe, suffering from homesickness, gave a warm welcome to her. It poured with rain for two days, and so the women sat together exchanging memories of the past, gossiping about Hamburg, and discussing their American present and future. Schoppe had succeeded in establishing excellent relationships with the Schenectady community, and especially with several professors from Union College and their families; the president of the college, Eliphalet Nott, had taken a great liking to her, and she taught German and French at a girls' school run by Urania Sheldon Nott.[20] When the weather improved on Monday she introduced Ottilie to this society—"women so charming as to make them special even in Europe," Assing reported, "especially a woman president [Nott] . . ."[21] They went on long walks, and she was enchanted by the beauty of the countryside, the hills, the Mohawk River, the woods in the splendors of fall! Schoppe was sure that Ottilie had come to stay, that now she could be a mother to Rosa Maria's fallen daughter. She had already found her a position as governess in one of the town's most respectable families. Schenectady's polite society welcomed the niece of the famous Varnhagen, promising her a home, a family, a respectable position, an income, and all of that in a countryside which she described with metaphors of paradise. Yet Ottilie turned and ran—back to her strange isolation-without-privacy at her boardinghouse room in glorious New York City, to her painted copperplates, to the dangerous vitality of nineteenth-century New York's most notorious slum area, the Five Points. Schoppe would never understand. Nor would any friend of hers back home. "*We* cannot make her wise and prudent," Rahel de Castro sighed upon hearing of Ottilie's rejection; "her own experience has to do that, and this is always a struggle; may the struggle not be too fierce, though!"[22]

Only days before sailing from Hamburg, Ottilie had received a letter from Emilie Reihl, a poor cousin in Strasbourg, whom she had met in the 1830s, when Rosa Maria took her daughters to visit her mother's family,[23] and Emilie and her siblings had been taken with their cousins from Hamburg. But their enthusiasm was not returned. The Assing sisters hardly deigned to answer the letters from Strasbourg that started to pour in. So negligent were they in their responses that even Varnhagen asked them to be more charitable. Later, economic hardship forced Emilie to take up a teaching position in Pforzheim, but she became rheumatic there during her endless working hours in an unheated schoolhouse. In her letter of 8 August 1852 she announced that she had fallen in love with a teacher, Peter Nickert; in October they would marry, and they would emigrate to Buffalo, New York, if they could scrape together the money. Varnhagen helped them, but Ludmilla's comment was coldly haughty: "It seems, everything in this world turns around a few thalers!" she exclaimed in a mock-desperate letter to her uncle.[24] A few days after Ottilie returned from her excursion to Schenectady, she met with her poor relatives, who had just arrived in New York. Both Emilie and her husband were full of optimism. For the time being they planned to stay in New York, where he found work as a teacher and she as a governess, but both were already anticipating life in Buffalo, longing for the family and friends who would welcome them as soon as they were ready to move on.[25] They were so happy that they wanted to share this new prosperity with Ottilie, and invited her to join them. Yet another home, another family! Ottilie found it easy to decline. She would pay them a visit, perhaps . . .

There was one person left in New York, a woman from Germany who, for all she knew, might be a companion in her quest for personal autonomy. Therese Robinson, who was known as Talvj,[26] whom Ottilie had met briefly on the latter's trip to Berlin in 1850 and 1851 (the Assing sisters profiting from their uncle's fame), was an intellectual in her own right. She had been born Therese von Jakob in Halle, Germany, in 1797, but she spent most of her childhood and youth in Russia. When she returned to Germany in 1816 her poetry, novellas, and reviews began appearing in some of the most sophisticated journals of the day: she translated Walter Scott's novels into German, and in the mid-1820s she became famous for her translation of two volumes of Serbian folk songs. In 1828 she married an American theologian, Edward Robinson, and followed him to the United States. Therese experienced her American home as a cultural wasteland. Still, while her husband made an impressive career as a scholar, she wrote articles and books on Native American and Slavic languages, on the history of New England, on American culture. By the time Assing arrived in New York, the Robinsons' home at 9 University Place was known as one of New York's finest literary salons, despite the husband's aversion to social gatherings. Here writers, artists, philosophers, and politicians from the Old World and the New mingled, and when the German fugitives of 1848, among them Friedrich Kapp, began to arrive, Talvj threw her doors wide open for them.[27]

Perhaps Talvj saw her own intellectual curiosity and ambition in Ottilie; perhaps she admired her for her courage in coming to America by herself; perhaps she saw her as a potential friend or as a daughter that needed guidance; perhaps she needed to treat Varnhagen's niece decently. Whatever her motives, Therese Robinson extended a warm welcome. For years Ottilie was not only a regular guest at the Robinson salon but introduced to other aspiring women writers; and toward the end of her first New York winter acquaintances reported that Ottilie seemed happy and at home in this new circle.[28]

But Therese Robinson and Ottilie Assing never became close friends. It is possible that their age difference prevented intimacy, but it seems more likely that Robinson's devout religiosity and Assing's atheism made them unlikely partners. Also, they had very different attitudes toward America. Robinson thought of her life in the United States as exile, and she suffered from homesickness; when her husband died in 1863, she immediately returned to Germany.[29] But while Assing complained of the immaturity of American art, ridiculed the American stage, deplored the nation's racism, and railed at the scarcity of what she called refined company, she admired the United States as a nation on the road to perfection, and she was eager to participate in shaping its future.

Ottilie sold a number of her paintings at good prices, and when no money was to be made from the paintings, she was not too proud to take on needle-work[30] or teach. She had left the boardinghouse, with its lack of privacy,[31] and was now living in a minister's family, giving German and French lessons in exchange for room and board. It was the most respectable way of coping with high living costs in America. In May, Amalie Schoppe talked her into spending a few weeks in Schenectady. Her son was making enough money for her to retire, she claimed, and she had arranged for Ottilie to take over her job at Urania Sheldon Nott's school. "I offered her my local, very nicely paid position, where she would have had a secure livelihood teaching 1–2 hours daily, but a small town with 10,000 inhabitants was not to her liking, and she admitted she did not like teaching, either," she wrote to Ludmilla, regretting "that I can do nothing for my dearest friend's daughter. Her whole being is programmed for the great life in New York." Her desperation surfaced in the name she gave Ottilie—"our pilgrim-fool." "We have to wait and see patiently what Ottilie wants to do for herself. She will probably hold out over here for one or two more years, but then she will surely go home of her own accord."[32] But Schoppe misjudged her. There was no sign that Ottilie Assing ever thought of returning to Germany during those initial seasons. In less than a year she had found people she wanted to be with, and she was confident that eventually she could make a decent living.

Equally important, she had fallen in love with New York City.[33] Her reports
to the *Morgenblatt* and the *Jahreszeiten* show that she quickly became bored with
tourist America and was far more interested in what she considered the real, the
true America—New York street life, Chinese peddlers, the prison called the
Tombs, Little Germany, the Jewish neighborhoods. Time and again she distanced herself from the formulaic travel literature of her day, and insisted instead on the relevance of her own encounters. She herself decided what she
thought was worth seeing and reporting; she rapidly transformed her own perspective as protagonist and observer into that of participant observer. But in order to see for herself she had to defy two nineteenth-century conventions: that a
woman who could not avoid traveling must (1) never travel unchaperoned and
(2) use modalities of a quasi-domestic quality, such as coaches, which were private, closed spaces.[34] Ottilie, though, used New York's public transportation
system—streetcars, ferries, the omnibus, which were fast and cheap and threw
her into the company of people outside her social realm. More than that: she believed that a person can understand new places only by measuring them on foot.
Her reports for the *Morgenblatt* were rightly enough called "Rambles through
New York," and she committed the unladylike act of walking about the city all
by herself, with no guide or chaperone, talking to everybody she found interesting, from barkeeper to seamstress to artist to female prisoner, sticking her nose
into every alley, door, or window that promised a new sight, defying the warnings of those who depicted New York as a hotbed of vice, crime, and sin.

Her enjoyment of the city's worst quarters, the crime-ridden Five Points, illustrates the degree to which she freed herself from the conventions. Her report
opened by ridiculing German male journalists like E. Pelz who created their
hell imagery of New York while hiding in boring middle-class hotels, and she
suggested their emasculation by portraying herself in contrast as moving freely
in the realms they had declared taboo. "According to the stories of these pur-
veyors of blood and murder, it amounts to suicide just to show one's face
there—even in broad daylight. . . . This is obvious exaggeration, and in my capacity as curious traveler and dependable reporter who relies on observation, I
have personally walked around the Five Points on several occasions by myself."[35]

Though she digressed from the conventional tourist's path, she maintained
a tourist's attitude. Like Lady Bountiful, like any bourgeois traveler to the
working-class slum populating the social novels of the day, she descended into
the netherworld of the poor, pleasantly excited at the thought of "experimenting" with her own life, proud that the venture would give her reports the au-

thority of authenticity. After a few hours in this exotic territory she returned to her familiar realm to write about that other nation, about a world and people separate from her own.[36] There was no reformist angle to her reporting yet.

Ottilie Assing's journalism was a performance of continuous intellectual cross-dressing, one might say. Whenever she had to identify the speaker of her text, she used a male voice, a generic he, as she did in all generalizing references. Yet while assuming the guise of a man she never forgot that the person most important in shaping her personality had been a woman—her mother. The models Rosa Maria had given her were women: Rahel Levin Varnhagen, George Sand, Aphra Behn, Sabina von Steinbach, all of them exceptional, and Ottilie admired them and their achievements because they competed not just with men but with exceptional men. The norm of excellence to which she aspired was always that of the exceptional male. Here we have one reason why she demanded equal rights and equality of opportunity for women yet kept her distance from the women's movement; this is also why she adopted the male persona almost spontaneously. Yet on the other hand she realized that most of her readers knew that the American correspondent for the *Morgenblatt*, the *Jahreszeiten*, and the *Gartenlaube* was a woman, was in fact Ottilie Assing. So she crossed back and forth, passing and transgressing, inventing and performing in her quest for a self she would always define as a self in motion.

Her model was perhaps best expressed in her portrait of Ernestine Rose, whom Assing met in 1858 at a woman's rights convention in New York City. Ernestine Rose, a rabbi's daughter from Piotrków, Poland, and a disciple of Robert Owen, had emigrated to the United States in 1836, where she became involved in the women's abolitionist and trade union movements. Ottilie Assing admired her for her courage, her expertise, and her calm dignity, which enabled her to make exceptional contributions to the liberation struggle without displaying any signs of the eccentricity which appalled Ottilie in so many reformers. "Her opinions are based on a clear, liberal conception of all things and are not hemmed in by tradition. Her speeches . . . reveal a broadly educated, independent, and lucid mind; nothing is murky, nebulous, or illogical," she exclaimed. This was exactly what Assing herself aspired to, how she wanted to be seen: "Her knowledge of two continents has broadened her horizon; experience and understanding have matured her opinions."[37]

Not everything she saw was perfect. She was appalled at conditions in the Tombs; a minstrel show made her wince at the American sense of humor; she warned German workers of the high living costs in the United States; she commented on American violence and crime, on racism and the displacement of

Native Americans; she disliked the immaturity of American art and complained about the boorishness of German emigrants. The two aspects of American life that annoyed her most were the condition of its theater and the rule of religion. "I would feel even more comfortable here if there were more paintings, better drama, and less religion!" she wrote to Gutzkow. "This disgusting garlic smell and the stench of religion permeates all of life . . ."[38] She could and would not discard her European intellectual's way of seeing and evaluating, and especially her early reports suggest a certain naiveté, ignorance, European arrogance; but where many contemporary critics from the Old World proclaimed the failure of the American experiment, she used the dynamic metaphor of being as becoming, of caterpillars as the promise of butterflies. Beneath all her biases and criticism she sincerely wanted to understand the American way of life, enthusiastically to embrace what the New World offered.

Like most foreign correspondents she sent home reports on everything she thought of interest, a hodgepodge of information, gossip, rumors, and analysis, of the conventional and the unfamiliar, and she seems to have been uncomfortably aware of that. Perhaps that is why she decided to accept an invitation to visit German friends living in what Assing regarded as the frontier—Wisconsin. On 18 June 1853, after nine exciting months in New York, she left for the West, determined to see for herself that part of the New World about which the strangest rumors circulated in Germany. She had devoured Charles Sealsfield's novels and James Fenimore Cooper's *Leatherstocking Tales*, evoking the dangers of frontier life as well as glorying in the beauty and purity of a pristine wilderness, and she longed to encounter the real Natty Bumppos and Chingachgooks. We know that she wrote a short story on the West, sending copies to various German publishers, but no trace of the manuscript has been found.

Yet it was more than her romantic visions of the frontier and her love of traveling and adventure that motivated Assing to go and see for herself. It was also her skepticism. She knew dozens of German families, respectable, well-educated people who had been encouraged to seek a new beginning as farmers in America after reading Gottfried Duden's enthusiastic and popular *Bericht über eine Reise nach den westlichen Staaten Nordamerikas* (Report on a Trip to the Western States of North America). Written from the perspective of a wealthy traveler and published in 1829, during the height of Germany's first Leatherstocking craze, the book contributed, perhaps unintentionally, to a mania among educated Germans to emigrate to Missouri and other Western regions. As the daughter of Romantic poets Ottilie had been exposed to the idealization of rural life as a child, but experience in the countryside as well as exposure to the political discussions among the 48ers had made her aware of the discrepancies between romantic images of rural life and the dreary realities of brutalizing poverty, ignorance, and incessant hard toil. So she responded with a healthy skepticism to the myths about the West. She was a city person, an intellectual, as were all of her friends, and she could not imagine them transformed into contented farmers. She must go and see for herself—and send reports of the truth back to Germany. This could be her true mission, her American topic.

Friends of hers from Berlin, Adolph Rosenthal and his family, had moved to the little farming community of Sheboygan, on the western shore of Lake Michigan, a few years before. In letter after letter they invited her to visit them. Sheboygan, they claimed, was full of promise; despite the hardships of the frontier, settling there meant they participated in shaping its future, they lived out a dream. Ottilie's parting words to New York, however, suggest that she knew that her friends' hope of making a new convert to the agrarian ideal would be unfulfilled. "Farewell, New York, loveliest of cities, darling of the gods, rising from the sea!" she wrote in the *Morgenblatt*. "How I love you with your ever-beaming skies, with your colorful, turbulent street life!"[39]

She had already tried and celebrated American steamboats on her trips to Schenectady, so this time she decided to take the train. "How wrong those are who say that the poetry of travel has been destroyed by modern steam transportation!" she wrote. ". . . but what is such mail-coach romance compared to the greater poetry that lies in the lightning leaps from one country, from one people to another!" Far from uprooting our most cherished dreams, technology liberates us to achieve what was our parents' utopia: "The seven-league boots that our parents admired when they were children have been far surpassed, and yet they say that poetry is in decline. Whoever grasps the poetry of the present reality will always be richly rewarded and rarely will have to complain about disappointments and lost illusions."[40] Ottilie Assing certainly was far from sharing the skepticism of technology harbored by many of her contemporaries. She lauded the railroad and the steamboat, the telegraph that supported her work as a journalist, the sewing machine that gave her more leisure to read and write, the camera whose work kept loved ones close to her. Whereas critics warned of the bad effect material changes would have on one's mental state, she rejoiced at the greater mobility and freedom they provided for her.

Like all tourists before and after her, this woman who worshipped at the shrine of technology and progress was overwhelmed by the glorious gift nature offered at Niagara Falls. Assing could only express her awe at the greatest of

America's natural spectacles by quoting from Goethe. "There are brief moments in life, individual highlights of our being, in which a beautiful reality offers such perfect fulfillment that both the past and the future with all the pain we have survived and that threatens to be still ahead of us, that all shipwrecks suddenly seem as if wiped out and evaporated as we savor the present, in that sheer delight of living, and even at the risk of being bewitched by powers worse than those that are already poisoning our lives, we are enticed to exclaim the fatal 'Oh stay, you are so beautiful!' "[41]

For hours she walked from one island in the rapids to the next, gazing on the gorgeous scene all by herself, not struggling to control her emotions but inviting them to guide her. It was the only time in her American life that she tolerated an expression of her existential loneliness, of the suffering created by an individualism that chose to rely exclusively on her own precious self. "I could not sustain my emotion of full and perfect satisfaction for long, for I was all alone, forced to enjoy that splendor all by myself, without having one of you, whom I love, by my side to share the enjoyment of the view!" This exclamation was her final farewell to those she had left behind. At Niagara Falls, bathing in the sunshine and allowing the "indescribable cheerfulness" and "classic peace" of the falls to permeate her whole being, she made the decision to devote herself to the future only, and that was America for her. In the following decades she would revisit the falls regularly, as if to renew the pledge she made on that first enchanting encounter.

On her trip to Buffalo she had her first impressions of the land's newness the farther west she went. The sight of felled trees, burnt stumps, and rugged log cabins made her melancholy, and like Dickens on his first sojourn to this region she was appalled at the dreariness of the scene. "In general we can say that the beginnings of civilization are not beautiful, and where a higher civilization cannot yet be achieved, we would much rather encounter the horrors of the wilderness, for with the trees we cut down the poetics of the land, and neither the newly developing villages nor the towns can compensate the eye for that."[42] Cooper's glorious frontier was a mere slum with a few tree stumps.

From Buffalo she took the steamer *Lady Elgin* to Wisconsin. She was overwhelmed by the vastness of the Great Lakes, by the bleak wasteland quality that reminded her so much of her loneliness when crossing the Atlantic. But she enjoyed the company on board, the "curiosity devoid of obtrusiveness"[43] with which her American fellow passengers approached her, their almost childish interest in everything European, their warm advice and hospitality. The representative American she invented for her German readers was a good sport, indeed.

After three and a half days the *Lady Elgin* reached Sheboygan. Sheboygan County consisted of approximately 521 square miles, and it boasted five rivers that refreshed the eyes as you looked down into the valleys from the many soft rolling hills along the western shore of Lake Michigan. As Janice Hildebrand writes in a recent tribute to the area: "From the kettle moraine area in the western part of the county, known for its inland lakes, to the sand dunes and bluffs that border Lake Michigan, the countryside is a patchwork of rich Wisconsin farmland, small villages, scenic lakes, and streams."[44] Although fewer than 10,000 people actually lived in the county in the early 1850s, Sheboygan was a harbor of increasing importance for those planning to settle even farther west: 20,914 people disembarked there in 1854, and by 1855 the number had more than tripled. Immigration was the major incentive to growth; taverns and hotels were built along Pennsylvania Avenue and Center Street to accommodate the newcomers, livery stables and cartage companies were launched to move the crowds.[45]

Of all of that Assing was ignorant; she focused on the small group of people on the pier, eagerly looking for familiar faces. She was in for disappointment: nobody was there to welcome her. But as she stood waiting, an innkeeper addressed her who turned out to be from Berlin. He was so thrilled to discover her connection to this city that he gladly gave her a ride to her friends' home. Assing had expected to arrive in a booming frontier community, and she did; the problem was that her definition of "boom" and Sheboygan's were incompatible. Exhausted from her trip and worried by her friends' absence, she only saw a one-horse town, ambitious in layout but with little of substance to please the weary traveler and city person. "Such a town with its handful of inhabitants and long undeveloped streets gives the impression of a small child in a man's coat," she complained to her *Morgenblatt* readers. ". . . one is inclined to call the town merely a place for things that are still missing; there is still room for a neighborhood, room for a town, room for people and animals; and room in which to be happy."[46] She seems to have made up her mind that Sheboygan was not her kind of place even before reaching the Rosenthals' little farm on the outskirts of town. "Pictures of a swamp would be an appropriate title for any description of local conditions," she nagged in another article she sent home, "because, truthfully, this town, like so many around here, is nothing but a huge stagnating swamp, a small hamlet, compared to which many a German country village looks like an El Dorado. No trade, no industry, no factories: hence, neither life nor progressive conditions."[47]

Still, the warmth with which Jenny and Adolph Rosenthal and their children welcomed her compensated Assing abundantly for the strain of her long voyage and her lonely arrival. They were people of her own kind—German-Jewish educated bourgeoisie, people who had been at home in the intellectual elite of Berlin and Hamburg, Young Germans exiled from their country by anti-Semitism and the catastrophe of 1848. Rosenthal, who had been a physician in Germany, was now trying to make a new beginning as a farmer—"Latin farmers" his kind of people were called by those who ridiculed the discrepancy between their education and their conditions in the New World.

The Rosenthals' house stood on a low hill and was surrounded by trees past which one could see the lake like a dark blue band in the distance. Ottilie was thrilled at the abundance of butterflies and bullfrogs, insects of all kinds and snakes, birds, rabbits, and squirrels, and she went for long walks and horseback rides through the woods that stretched out behind the house. Her friends' hospitality, the intellectual nourishment they provided, the modest comfort of their home, the beauty of the surroundings appeased Ottilie, and her letters to Amalie Schoppe sparkled with happiness. But she expressed contempt and disgust at the larger setting in which this temporary home was embedded.

Approximately two-thirds of Sheboygan's population were of German descent. Ottilie complained that she hardly spoke a word of English in the eight months she spent there. There were German choirs, a German fire brigade, the turnverein; and the Rosenthals played a prominent role in all of these. Germans were beginning to be influential in local politics, and Assing cheered when Adolph ran successfully for public office. Yet she was not pleased to be living in a German setting. She was shocked to see that there was almost no communication between Americans and Germans in Sheboygan, and she blamed the Germans, most of whom never bothered to learn English, for this. In fact, she was appalled by the kind of Germany she encountered in the West:

> At least three-quarters of the population is German, and most of them are of the kind best described as riffraff and ne'er-do-wells. This is neither a united nor a divided, neither a young nor an old Germany: it is just a rabble of the worst kind. This riffraff—who of course do not have the deep republican roots of the American people; among whom a person of the lowest standing knows how to encounter the highest-ranking citizen as an equal without causing the least offense—avenge themselves here for everything of which they were deprived at home just because they are in the majority. They are mean-spirited and insulting toward the so-called aristocrats, among whom they include even the most honorable democrat if he has money and education; and he has to suffer their insults quietly for fear of physical assault.[48]

The underprivileged, pawns of fixed behavioral and cultural traits, not victims of socioeconomic factors, were being transformed into the dangerous underclasses. Assing's article represented them as Germans who had gone all the way to America only to ignore what the New World had to offer—material as well as intellectual and spiritual liberation—and it was for this blindness, not for their rank, not for their original ignorance, that she despised them. She thought they wallowed in Old World backwardness, in the stagnation and brutalization in which they had grown up, and they clung to the intellectual darkness as their only reliable possession. What had been mere backwardness in Germany became perverted, and showed itself as repulsive boorishness when it encountered a freedom they could not understand or cope with. If they refused self-elevation and progress and settled for stagnation, then, in a country defined by progress, that inevitably meant a downward spiral, even degeneration. Her report was a genuine mixture of social arrogance, disgust, and irony. She could not bear the idea that anyone might associate her with these Germans. To her they were almost a race apart, physically, mentally, and morally different. An advocate of the philosophy of free will and the principles of egalitarianism, Assing had recourse to popularized Lamarckian theorizing about evolution[49] when she emphasized *sentiment intérieur* and adaptation. It is important to keep her attitude toward these fellow Germans in mind as we encounter her representation of other immigrant groups and people from other ethnic backgrounds.

If Assing disliked the German "riffraff," as she chose to call these Germans, she was disgusted by the so-called respectable Germans she met—the "Honoratioren." They were "philistines," "Gothamites," "the solid, stolid, smug middle class from the German provinces, the most boring society I have ever come across."[50] These people were eager to welcome the niece of the famous Varnhagen von Ense in their midst; they were curious about this young woman who had come out West all by herself, who was a journalist. Several of them signaled their interest in her as a potential wife, and one went so far as to propose marriage. He was lucky: Assing had a cold shoulder for all of them. To Gutzkow she wrote: "A young German man even wanted to marry me, for all it is worth, but that was too much for me; I could have stayed in Europe had I wanted that! And a man from Hamburg on top of it!"[51] So deep was her—and obviously also her hosts'—aversion to these people "that, seeing them coming from afar, we locked the doors all around and threw ourselves on the floor to escape detection."[52]

Nonetheless, Assing reported that the American frontier was a perfect place for German farmers, farmhands, and workers, with its "cheap land, fertile soil, and a healthy climate." Even those arriving with little money but equipped with a will to work and some skills usually became "wealthy" in a few years' time. But she sent a dire warning to dispirited German intellectuals who believed this could also be their dream, their future. The examples were right before her eyes: the Rosenthals were bright people, eager to learn, industrious and sincere; their land was arable, and they made enough profit from it to hire help. Still, the former physician was now felling trees and plowing; his wife and daughters, used to domestic servants back home, now did most of the housework, milked the cows and fed the pigs, planted their own garden. Frost destroyed the first vegetables they had planted; they lost animals to thieves. The work was backbreaking, and when the back was breaking, how could the mind continue to soar? "Educated people coming from large cities, inveterate urbanites lacking agricultural experience and physical stamina, make a fatal mistake when they imagine they can succeed as farmers from one day to another in America . . . ; yet it is a mistake that thousands of educated and intelligent people have made. . . . [A] farm in a beautiful setting, perhaps surrounded by virgin forest—how poetic, how romantic!—but then they drop into the prosaic pothole of the most miserable reality."[53] No matter how much the free spirit of the frontier was celebrated, no matter how much the pioneer was glorified, Ottilie Assing trusted only her own eyes, and she would rather have walked back to New York City than become the mistress of even the most luxurious Sheboygan home.

Still, her friends persuaded her to spend the winter with them. Had Assing had any idea of what was ahead, she might have taken the last steamer back East. She was almost paralyzed by the cold, and when ice covered the lake and snow made the roads impassable, she felt entombed. She marveled at the activities the citizens of Sheboygan enjoyed during the long winter months, and she participated in the many dances, lectures, rallies (for and against prohibition legislation), but she thirsted for the kind of stimuli that only a metropolis could provide. "Farewell, friends of the West, who gave me a better home than I had in the Old World! Finally we must part!" she sang out as her boat pulled out of Sheboygan harbor on 20 April 1854. Metaphors of powerful movement, of electricity and fire, document her impatience to leave. "Mighty Lake Michigan is roaring, the steamer is rocking on the waves, red sparks flying from the smokestack compete with the lightning that now and then flashes on the horizon. The departure signal is given and the steamer takes off into the night. A long final look at the shore as it disappears from view; only the lighthouse provides a sense of direction until everything is swallowed up in the darkness." Good riddance, she seemed to exclaim, turning her back on an experience and lifestyle contrary to everything she wanted to be. She loved the friends she left behind, and she corresponded with them to the end of her days; she welcomed them to her home in Hoboken, reported on Adolph's career as a politician and diplomat, and cherished the Rosenthal children. But she never returned to Sheboygan. "Let me say it again: we who are educated and have certain expectations of nature, art, literature, and society have come too early to the American West by a hundred years."[54]

Chicago was, in contrast, "a picture of the most heartening progress,"[55] from where she took the train to Detroit. All the way back she celebrated city life. She made a brief detour to Lancaster, New York, where Emilie Nickert and her husband had now established themselves and where Peter was pastor of a small German-American church; there she seems to have run into the same kind of Germans she had so disliked in Sheboygan. There was another stop in Portage, New York, to admire the Genesee Falls, but then she rushed back to New York City. "Twelve hundred miles and a stage of my life lay behind me."[56]

Glorious, magnificent, buzzing New York! How good it felt to be back. Ottilie was thrilled at and invigorated by reimmersing herself in urban life, and her love of the city was not diminished even by her almost overwhelming financial problems. She still had not conquered her aversion to teaching and to the dependence—"slavery,"[57] she called it—that came with a job as governess or tutor; also, she was either unwilling or unable to reclaim her job with the art dealer who had commissioned her work during her first American year. There are many signs in the *Morgenblatt* columns she wrote during the following winter that her situation was at times desperate. When an extremely cold winter combined with inflation and economic crisis in 1854–55, unemployment rates skyrocketed, and for the first time in her life Ottilie Assing confronted actual need—hunger, cold, and the fear of homelessness. For months she worked between sixteen and seventeen hours daily as a seamstress, unable "to earn more than 3 to 3½ schillings or 15 silver groschen a day, which was just enough to pay for a simple one-dollar-a-week garret, a daily tallow candle, a cup of coffee in the morning, and the necessary clothing." Months later, when this personal crisis was over, she masked this terrifying experience in her *Morgenblatt* report as that of "a young lady who, though she had many talents and abilities, was forced to take this route by the unfortunate concatenation of circumstances that can so easily victimize the new immigrant." The article shows how hard she struggled to keep her despair from her friends. She had her "young lady" exclaim:

A noon meal was out of the question, and two cents for bread and two more for a quart of buttermilk was all that I could afford if I wanted to save a small amount for such unexpected expenses . . . and, above all, to keep my situation a secret from my friends. It is a hard misfortune that requires heroism, and only a sense of pride and the unshakable determination not to go into debt and not to accept charity made it possible for me to survive these four months.

Ottilie Assing had enjoyed those many tales of seamstress turned prostitute which the Industrial Revolution and its aftermath had made popular; all of a sudden she understood the brutal reality beneath the sentimental stories. Never again, she vowed while carefully distancing herself from them, would she condemn those poor women "for going astray and ending in ruin because they lack that heroism in the midst of privation that, with few exceptions, is a product of education. Who can fault them if they lack that higher mental development and have no other prospect than to work . . . under circumstances so destructive of body, mind, and youth?"[58] Her situation was so bad that she was tempted to accept the offer of a German-American professor to teach at a college near Cincinnati. She would be paid $400 annually in the beginning and later $1,000.[59] Instead, by early summer she found work as a tutor of French and German in a well-to-do family in New York City. Anything but return to the West; anything to stay in New York.

Of course none of these personal concerns made it into her family letters. The social problems she described so vividly and compassionately in her *Morgenblatt* articles were those of other people, while Ottilie Assing's life was happiness, adventure, free flight. She was not just pretending: there was Therese Robinson's exquisite salon, and every time she attended a party there she made new connections. She befriended Madame Löscher, a wealthy German-American woman who could afford to compete with Robinson in having a salon; it attracted freethinking Young Germans who were uncomfortable with Robinson's religiosity and nostalgia for the Germany of her aristocratic childhood.[60] Step by step Ottilie Assing made her way into an exclusive circle of German intellectuals who had been exiled by the Revolution of 1848 and who were beginning to carve out a community of their own in and around New York.[61] Many of them were making a home in Hoboken, a charming community on the New Jersey banks of the Hudson, from where "one can enjoy a splendid view of New York and of the reflecting river."[62] Life was cheaper in Hoboken than in New York, and ferries between New Jersey and Manhattan made commuting easy. Here people could enjoy the beauty and quiet of rural life with the city right at their doorstep. "The whole place and its environment give the impression of peace, happiness, and unspoiled nature that act like a balm after the dust and noise of New York streets," Assing chimed. "Tastefully designed houses with such modern comfort as gas and water lines do their part in making this a pleasant place to live."[63] There was the famous River Walk, the Elysian Fields, which William Cullen Bryant had lauded as "one of the most beautiful walks in the world"; even the pugnacious Frances Trollope had deigned to compare Hoboken to a Garden of Eden.[64] Thousands of New Yorkers crossed the Hudson each Sunday to enjoy the town's many beer gardens and restaurants. Though Americans did not consider it fashionable, the exiles from Germany thought it was fine, and by mid-1850 more than 1,500 of Hoboken's 7,000 inhabitants were German; it had become "one of New York's German sections."[65] They organized their own clubs, published their own newspapers, and soon opened a fine German-American school, the Hoboken Academy.[66]

In Hoboken, Ottilie Assing first met Dr. Hans Kudlich, from Lobenstein, Silesia, who had made his name as the liberator of the rural population there during the Revolution of 1848.[67] Together with his wife Luise, née Vogt, he came to Hoboken in 1854, and it was in the Kudlich home, in "that excellent family, well known and much beloved in Germany," that Assing spent the American national holiday in 1855. "There, high above the shallowness of America and the unruly masses, a small and select circle engaged in sparkling, witty conversation on the Fourth of July, as it is only possible among the elite of European civilization,"[68] she bragged to her German readers. Over the years she became good friends with the Kudlichs.

The weekend circle of Hoboken became even more attractive when Ottilie realized how many of her new acquaintances shared her atheism. First and foremost among them was Friedrich Kapp, a lawyer who had joined the Young German movement during his university years in Heidelberg, where, at his uncle's house, he had met the philosopher Ludwig Feuerbach, with whom he became lifelong friends. When Feuerbach's *The Essence of Christianity* was published in 1841, Kapp adopted it as his personal bible. Like a missionary, he preached Feuerbach's texts. He became so deeply involved in the revolutionary movement that he had to flee Germany when the revolution collapsed. He escaped to Paris and in 1850 emigrated to the United States, where he made a successful career as a lawyer and writer; he frequently invited Feuerbach to New York and advised him when he contemplated emigration.[69] He became one of the most influential figures among the German-American exiles in New York, and it is possible that he was the person who introduced Assing to Feuerbach's ideas.

Most of the 48ers in America saw themselves as exiles, living for the day when they would return to a liberated Germany. They were grateful for their American asylum, for they were disciples of the principles of democracy the nation represented, yet they disliked the New World culturally. They were willing to share their "superior" learning and cultural skills with these "materialistic" Yankees, and eager to participate in political reform movements, but many took the very suggestion that they assimilate as an insult. As one aggressive spokesperson, Karl Heinzen, declared: "To Americanize yourself means to give up yourself totally; to be true to yourself as a German means to love honor and education . . . Rather become an Indian than a German-American."[70] As for Kapp, he denounced Americans as "Protestant Jews," as "philistines among savages," as "serfs to ministers and prejudice."[71] These intellectuals approached America as missionaries of German culture. Ottilie Assing, too, was critical of American culture and politics, but she acted as appreciative guest rather than censor. For her, being able to live in the New World was a privilege, not a tragic fate. She ridiculed her friends' negativism and arrogance as intellectual shadowboxing: "He [the exile] cannot find anything here; neither materially nor intellectually, that might compensate him for what he left behind; he instinctively blames the country and its people rather than himself for his disgruntlement, thus falling into ridiculous extremes."[72] She would have liked Feuerbach's reply to one of Kapp's laments had she known of it:

> Consider yourself happy because you are in America. What are American spirits doing their table-rappings compared to the spirits in our country, who knock, not on tables and benches but from the pulpit, presidential chairs, and royal thrones? I think you do America an injustice in these matters; you make demands that are precocious, demands that it may be the duty of the German immigration to fulfill. But that's how it is: you feel the shadows in America and see only the bright sides of Europe, we the other way around.[73]

Still, Assing was enchanted with her new circle of friends, and in 1857 she moved to Hoboken to be closer to them. She was severing more and more ties with Europe, just as Europe seemed to be severing ties with her. She wrote to Gutzkow in 1855:

> It is strange . . . that the ocean, which seems so small to those who crossed it, remains such a barrier to correspondence, and that those who stay behind soon regard us as dead and give up upon us. I experience this on all sides, and things would be terrible for me if I were one of those people who always face backward and who try to turn the past into their present instead of trusting in the present and future, and

Ottilie Assing
In his memoirs the poet Heinrich Zeise remembered Ottilie Assing as "a beautiful girl with an opulent body." This photograph was probably taken during her early years in New York, when she was working for a German-American photographer and art dealer, coloring copper engravings.

Emilie Nickert, née Reihl
Emilie Nickert, Assing's cousin from Strasbourg, emigrated to the United States in 1852. She regularly reported to Ludmilla Assing on Ottilie's adventures. When Ottilie discovered this, she complained to Douglass: "From these letters it is quite evident that during the first years of her and my stay in this country . . . Mrs. Nickert, who was not remarkable for perspicacity and acuteness, . . . really played a little of the informer's part."

Luise and Dr. Hans Kudlich, together with their nine children
The Kudlichs, refugees of 1848, were among Assing and Douglass' best friends in Hoboken. Assing called the Kudlichs "that excellent family, well known and loved in Germany," and for her Luise Kudlich was "the only woman [in Hoboken] with whom you could make intelligent conversation." Douglass later appointed their son Hermann executor of Ottilie's will.

were it not for the many old and new friends I found over here I could imagine I was
all alone in this world.[74]

New York City had been love at first sight for Ottilie Assing; when she discovered Hoboken and its circle of radical Germans, the metropolis began to feel
like home. If dissatisfaction was still lingering in her, it was less with her social
realm than with her journalistic work. She still needed a central theme. But she
was fortunate. Indeed, she almost stumbled right into it when she returned
from her western trip: race relations, slavery, black America.

In May 1854, it was convention time in New York. Women's rights groups,
prison reformers, the temperance people, missionary and Bible associations,
abolitionists—thousands of people came to New York each May for their meetings. Many participants were members of several associations, rushing back and
forth between convention halls, eager not to miss out on anything and to meet
the lions of the day. This time around, convention week was more exciting than
ever, for 1854 was a hugely raucous, divided, and disputatious year for American politics, with slavery at the center of the debate: all eyes were on the abolitionists, for on 4 January Stephen A. Douglas, senator from Illinois, had
introduced the Kansas-Nebraska Bill. Douglas' original plan to organize the
Nebraska Territory and bring it under civil control had met with fierce Southern objection because Nebraska lay north of latitude 30° 30′ and, in accordance
with the Missouri Compromise of 1820 decreeing that slavery was banned in
the Louisiana Purchase land north of that line, would have to be admitted as a
free state. Douglas sought a compromise, suggesting that the two territories of
Kansas and Nebraska be defined and within them, on the principle of popular
sovereignty, the decision regarding slavery be left to the settlers. Of course his
opponents, and especially the abolitionists, immediately realized that the bill
was an attempt to repeal the Missouri Compromise, and they were promising to
put on a good fight. So intense was the outrage over the bill in the North that
the abolitionists were able to hold their convention in a New York church for
the first time. One faithful and attentive observer was Ottilie Assing, who listened that week to William Lloyd Garrison, Robert Purvis, Abby Kelley Foster,
and Wendell Phillips. She was deeply impressed by speeches that did not focus
only on the evils of slavery in the South; Wendell Phillips especially, whom she
almost worshipped for his rhetorical skills and analytical brilliance, left no
doubt that the "peculiar institution" could survive and prosper only with the
active complicity and moral support of the North. "It is the North that dominates the Union; the South merely supplies it with overseers of slaves," she

paraphrased Phillips, "the true merchants of slavery literally reside in the North."[75]

The one person absent from this impressive list of speakers was Frederick Douglass. His controversy with the Garrisonians over their rejection of political participation and what they perceived as his defection to the Gerrit Smith camp of political abolitionism, over the publication of *The North Star*, and especially over his relationship with Julia Griffiths had reached its ugliest stage. Douglass had become persona non grata on the Garrisonian agenda.

With a naiveté that bordered on willful blindness, Ottilie clung to the belief "that no enlightened European can honestly defend slavery," and she did so despite her own exposure to bigotry among even her Young German friends. Consequently she was aghast when German acquaintances with whom she tried to discuss her decision to focus on slavery and racism looked at her in utter disbelief. To many of them, slavery was not only an economic necessity in the South but also a blessing for the slaves, giving them discipline and guidance, work and food, a place in society compatible with their "nature." One German "gentleman," whom she had always respected for his refinement, even had "the nerve to make the absurd claim that . . . it is still an open question whether blacks did not really belong to a particular species of apes."[76] She decided to take on the abolitionist challenge, and to fight their battle where she, a German intellectual, would have the most impact—among Germans in the United States and Germany. Now her work as a foreign correspondent had a more clearly defined political focus. This was a new challenge she took on conscientiously, and an approach for which her own experience as a woman of Jewish descent in Germany had well prepared her. She did not need Wendell Phillips to instruct her that blacks existed, that slavery was an evil, that racism permeated American society; she had been aware of it even before she boarded the *Indian Queen*.

The New World, with its melting-pot dynamic, for Ottilie Assing was a laboratory where an abstract vision of a composite nationality could be tested and realized, a vision from which she was convinced her enlightened mind excluded no one, yet she seemed unaware that her idea of this composite nationality was averse to cultural pluralism. Her ideal was to be achieved as a process in which "the culturally backward"—and that included members of the underclass as well as women and men of various national, cultural, ethnic, and racial backgrounds—educated themselves into the mainstream. The key word was "assimilation"; the ideal American society she envisioned was raceless in that individual races would either disappear or no longer be an issue. On a personal level this meant that she discarded her dual identity as "half-Jew," as "both" and "neither." And what America had done for her and for other Europeans it must now do for everyone—Native Americans, Asians, and Africans. Her composite American nationality included these groups, too, both via education into the mainstream and, as she insisted in numerous articles, through physical assimilation, though this always translated into the "culturally backward" group's discarding its identity to become "like us." She wasted no time on those who would not or could not submit to this glorious metamorphosis.

If assimilation was Assing's panacea and vision, she was anything but naive when it came to confronting the reality of her American Dream. For Assing brought a kind of double consciousness to the antagonism that perverted relationships between those at the center and those at the margins, between "them" and "us." Imposing her personal experience on her reading of America life, she portrayed those at the margin—Jews in Germany, blacks, Chinese, and Native Americans in the United States—as both eager for and capable of assimilation. The impediment, according to her analysis, was always the social and racial arrogance of those who held the power to sign or withhold the admission ticket. Her uncritical adherence to upper-class cultural hegemony made her unable to see the irony of her antiracist, egalitarian discourse explicitly charging nonwhites to identify and blend biologically with whites.

Ottilie's sense of what the composite American nationality was or could be affected the images she constructed for her German audience. She was the adventurer who left no corner in New York unexplored, the explorer who traveled all over the free states, describing the landscape, people, customs, institutions; the art critic who took her readers to exhibits, the theater critic to Shakespeare performances, the music lover to concerts. Assing's attitude was one of empathy—that of someone determined to see, understand, and embrace the new, the newcomer intent on liking the country. When she encountered deficiency—especially in the realm of art and entertainment, but also in social and racial justice—she used caterpillar imagery, the optimism of being as becoming that spelled the promise of change and progress. What rendered her work exceptional from the start, however, was her keen awareness of the importance of race in the American experience. Her private letters to the Steinheims focused almost exclusively on this issue, so much, indeed, that Salomon Steinheim sent her his tract on Aristotle and slavery to help her position herself.[77] Almost every column she sent home during those initial years referred to racial incidents or to African-Americans.

American racism as she represented it in her first report for the *Morgenblatt* was not only vicious, backward, and dangerous but ridiculous to the point of absurdity. In the women's section of the Tombs, the notorious New York prison, in May 1853 she encountered a tragic mixture of victims of social injustice and what she regarded as the scum of the earth. And she knew how narrow was the line that separated her from the prisoners:

> Whoever is courageous enough to be honest with himself and the world must admit that, once we subtract everything we have become through education, knowledge, and beneficial influence, almost nothing remains; and no one can guarantee whether under exactly opposite circumstances he would be one iota better than the worst among those whom he is so ready to condemn. Once you have become what good fortune has made you, it is easy to predict the future and not to clash with the police; but it is presumptuous to consider it anything but good fortune.[78]

Her report is unconventional in its combination of liberal platitudes and Assing's peculiar sarcasm, and in its portrayal of the prisoners not as a homogeneous group but, in a tragicomic way, as a mirror of the community outside. Most of the women were white, and they had segregated the one black woman. What right, Assing asked, in the face of this human misery and degradation, have these white prostitutes, petty thieves, and murderers to look down on and refuse to socialize with the prison's only black female inmate—an old woman equal to them in every respect, "an old good-for-nothing who had been picked up for the third or fourth time."[79] Assing did not rely on the sentimental myth that the victim is morally superior to the victimizer. The black woman's equality lay in her ability to steal and lie like any other inmate, and she should have been an equal member of the company into which her peculiar skills had thrown her.

Assing needed relief after her descent into the Tombs, and she sought it at the Washington Exhibition, where, from the 160 paintings on display, she chose Emanuel Gottlieb Leutze's "Washington Crossing the Delaware" for special analysis. Her pride in Leutze as a German-American artist might explain her selection, and, knowing that the Rhine had served as Leutze's Delaware and colleagues from Düsseldorf as his models, we smile at her label "truth, simple truth, which—ennobled by beauty—is the highest and the only end of art" for it. What struck her as special in this, as well as in another painting of Washington as a boy hunting, was that Leutze always portrayed the Founder together with his "loyal black companion."[80] She did not write about the likelihood that the "companion" was, in fact, a slave.

Equally unnerving was the naiveté with which she reported on a minstrel show to which American friends dragged her. She wrote about this encounter to make a point about the immaturity of popular entertainment in the New World—the platitude of the jokes, the boisterous performances, the absurdity of the show, all the while wondering why the audience was so enormously satisfied by all this. Perhaps making jokes at the expense of the underclass, laughing at the dumb boorishness of the "German Michel," at the ridiculous poverty of the ghetto Jew, was so deeply ingrained in her own bourgeois worldview that the "darkie" in the minstrel show seemed as natural and benevolently condescending as the "German Michel."

When Assing traveled to the Midwest in the summer of 1853, she had proudly reported that the railroad cars from New York City to Albany were integrated. "In this regard alone republican equality rules: those who pay, whether white or black, travel in the same car." Yet she was aware of the racist tension beneath the apparently integrated surface: blacks and whites did not communicate, she complained, but sat apart. The black woman next to whom Assing seated herself responded with "friendly courtesy," but the white passengers were either annoyed at this "abolitionist demonstration"[81] or disgusted at her ignorance. It is impossible to ignore the condescension in Assing's attitude toward her black neighbor, her self-righteousness, her love of performance, her need to shock her white fellow travelers. But it is important that she saw beneath the surface of the integrationist pose. All was not right.

The most revealing expression of Assing's early approach to black-white relations was her report in the summer of 1855 on the visit she paid to an African-American revival meeting near Sing Sing, formerly Mount Pleasant, where the most famous Methodist camp meetings of the period took place.[82] The freethinker Ottilie Assing, who continually complained at how religion permeated American life and who had already written a number of scathingly critical commentaries on the Methodists and on Shaker communities, was appalled by what she observed—people who behaved "like lunatics"; a preacher who was "screaming and thumping himself into a passion as I had heretofore never seen it even among the Methodists"; women "who tried to outdo each other in uncontrollable wildness"; a preacher in whose eyes she perceived a "disgustingly sensual fire"[83]—and sexual innuendo was central to the images she evoked. Her article contained all the formulas of conventional nineteenth-century racialized discourse: ascribing uncontrolled passion, intellectual mimicry, and ugliness to blacks. And yet there were marked differences: Assing tried to suggest that the blame for what she could not help condemning as perversions lay with a vicious social environment that deprived these people of "healthy" expressions of their needs. What could have been mere racist slander became a lecture on the crimes of racism and the blessing of education:

> Every human being—especially with a lively imagination—longs . . . for something that lies outside the limitations of his daily life and that can elevate him . . . above life's sorrows and burdens. The educated person finds it in the enjoyment of art, travel, society, and literature—things from which these poor colored people have been excluded from the start. But since they are also unfamiliar with the entertainments, gatherings, and folk festivals with which the lower classes in Europe amuse themselves, such a camp meeting is for many the only diversion in their dreary lives.[84]

These blacks are not biologically inferior; they are victims of white racism. As she put it a few months later, after a visit to James W. C. Pennington's congregation in New York: "Hardly will you find another people who were so oppressed, mistreated and trampled upon, excluded from education and kept in ignorance by violent means, and who nonetheless possess so much natural delicacy, decency, and dignified civility."[85]

There are other signs that testify to Assing's struggle for meaning at this African-American revival. Although she spoke of black furies she did not feel threatened by them. She saw more than an anonymous black mass of religious fanatics. She was intrigued at the variety of complexions within this community, ranging from "pitch black" through yellow and gray to almost white; she identified social stratification and gender differences; she was enchanted by the melodious voice of a woman whose religious ecstasy repelled her; she had an eye for the comic and was moved by the beauty of youth. Beneath her racialized condescension there was an awareness of the complexity and individuality of these people, a sincere longing to understand them.

A few years before, Ottilie had protested against Karl Gutzkow's use of the formulaic "the Jew" in his *Uriel Acosta*, which failed to do justice to the heterogeneity of Jewish life in Germany; and her parents had deplored the narrow way that even enlightened Germans focused on "the Jewish problem" rather than Jewish achievement. Yet she was taking the same approach to African-American life. Like other European journalists with liberal leanings, she spoke of the suffering of millions; she saw ample proof of black deprivation, of past oppression, of discrimination; she did not write about black achievements that might raise hopes for a better tomorrow. However, in the fall of 1855, she told Rahel de Castro that she would "try whether she could not introduce her readers to highly educated darkies, a field which German writers [living in the United States] have totally neglected."[86] Everybody could write about black misery, and so many did that readers were bored. She would try to focus on individual black achievement, on the heroes of the race, on the exceptional. Ottilie Assing began to set herself up as Germany's "Negro expert."*

Again she was lucky. According to Nell Painter, New York City had "the largest concentration of African-Americans in the United States" as early as in the 1830s and 1840s. They were not sharply segregated though they suffered discrimination in the job market, in churches, schools, streetcars, and hotels. "In New York City, insult constantly fouled the lives of the black poor, and even educated and respectable colored gentlemen ran up against bigotry on a regular basis."[88] On a Monday in June 1855 one of these black gentlemen, Dr. James W. C. Pennington, minister of the Shiloh Presbyterian Church at 61 Prince Street, boarded a horse-drawn car of the South Avenue Railroad in violation of the company's segregation policy. He was arrested on charges of violent resistance and censured by the court for breach of the peace because he refused to leave the car when the conductor ordered him to.[89] Assing read about this racial incident in the newspapers, and evidently decided that Pennington was the kind of man whose story could launch her new project. She was delighted to discover his *The Fugitive Blacksmith*, first published in October 1849, the kind of success story she had been taught to cherish since her earliest childhood, the kind of story she herself had written when reinventing Baison's life. Born and raised in slavery, Pennington had in himself the willpower and ingenuity not only to liberate himself but also to educate himself, once he reached the free North. He was now the minister of the most influential African-American Presbyterian church as well as president of the National Negro Convention. Even more important, Assing realized that this man was no stranger to her and her German readers. In 1849 the theological faculty of the University of Heidelberg, a university proud to be first in conferring a doctorate on a Jew—the philosopher Baruch Spinoza—proud also to have endowed the first chair for natural rights and human rights, had given Pennington an honorary doctorate of divinity, an honor designed "to protest systematic educational discrimination against black people in the United States,"[90] but also an admission of Germany's historical complicity in the crime which Europe committed against

---

*A letter Assing wrote to William Lloyd Garrison in 1879 shows how proud she was of this role. She was, she wrote, "not exactly in need of instruction on the question since I have always stood on your side of it . . ."[87]

Africa and her people. "Europe has to atone for a terribly heavy guilt for the wretched sons of Africa who since centuries have been robbed of their sacred human rights,"[91] Pennington's certificate stated. Assing no longer hesitated to seek the personal acquaintance of this "highly educated darkie," introducing herself in a letter to Pennington as the American "correspondent of Mr. Cotta's *Morgenblatt*."[92] On 3 August she received a note in which Pennington, perhaps tongue in cheek, spoke of his pleasure "at your approval of my little tract on my slavery experience: which is every word true to the letter and to the spirit," and he expressed "hope for your pleasant company on Saturday the 4th . . . from 6 to 8 o'clock."[93]

Pennington was a black celebrity used to European travelers who included the slave blacksmith turned minister in their American tour to give it a touch of the exotic, just as today's tourists shiver happily when going to Harlem on their bus tours. Ottilie Assing received the politely noncommittal welcome that he, like other black celebrities, extended to such human rights tourists, but he quickly discovered something in this woman that went beyond curiosity. Not only had she read his autobiography, not only did she know about his doctorate; she knew Heidelberg, she belonged to a group of people who had acknowledged their guilt, who struggled for forgiveness and change. Assing was thrilled when he invited her to be his guest at a soiree in his church, and in the following months she became a regular visitor. The *Morgenblatt* carried her report on her first visit in March 1856,[94] and it shows she had learned one lesson: she had not yet discarded "darkie" from her vocabulary, but it appeared in quotation marks, and for the last time. After that Assing consistently used "Negro," "black," or "colored people."

More than a hundred members of Pennington's congregation attended this social event—"washerwomen, cooks, seamstresses, waiters, painters, barbers, hairdressers . . ." She saw them as working-class, unaware that the social hierarchy in the African-American community differed dramatically from the structures she knew from Germany and white America, and consequently she could only express amazement at the contrast between the dignified, calm mirth of these black people and the riotous behavior she had observed among lower-class Germans and Irish. "No loud words, no improper joke gave away that one was actually not in the most select, best-educated society, and the friendly, natural courtesy with which people treated each other would have done honor to the most fashionable salon."[95] Lower-class blacks who had danced through her text as furies only a few months ago reentered her columns as nature's ladies and gentlemen, doing the cakewalk!

She was not the only white observer at the dance: several other reporters attended, and two British families. Pennington assigned her a place at the "white" table, but this was not what she had come for. ". . . after a while I took the liberty of mixing with the 'darkies' to become acquainted with them. It seemed to embarrass them a little, but soon they overcame their reticence, and we were chatting amiably."[96] She wrote of them as if they were children, patiently approached and coaxed by the experienced adult; under her guidance they could relax enough for her to enjoy them.

They introduced her to a "handsome young mulatto from Pennsylvania," and Assing could barely believe her ears when this man addressed her in the purest Pennsylvania Dutch without even the slightest English accent. It had never occurred to her to associate blackness with German. Rhetorically and in the abstract she supported the mulatto's claim to social equality, yet her social response was to stare in wonder at a biracial man with "black features" who identified himself as German.[97] Assing could only describe the event thus: "It is impossible to convey how funny such an encounter with a black Swabian or Darmstadter is, and one is tempted to repeat the question that a German farmer once asked when he was addressed in German by a Negro: 'How's life treating you so far away from home, countryman, and what made you so black?' "[98] All she "could see was the ball on the seal's nose,"[99] to use McFeely's splendid metaphor for the white liberal gaze.

Not only did Ottilie Assing become a regular guest at Shiloh Church but the Penningtons welcomed her to their home on 26 Sixth Avenue. Assing admired Pennington for his struggle, for his physical and intellectual liberation, and she applauded his courage in his battle against segregation. She even sent his autograph to her uncle Varnhagen.[100] In turn, Dr. Pennington and his wife, Almira Way Pennington, a former teacher, seemed to have enjoyed the company of this lively young German who listened so carefully, who had so many stories of her own to tell. Assing was especially enchanted by the couple's son, "a handsome eleven-year-old brown boy with long glossy hair,"[101] and she began to give him German lessons.

During these months of a slowly developing friendship Assing wrote her most elaborate single report on African-American life in New York City, seventeen pages, filled with her filigree handwriting. She framed the article with a sharp indictment of American racism, the viciousness and backwardness of which she could only evoke by comparing it to the Indian caste system. It was a conventional piece of abolitionist discourse, with the usual condemnation of slavery, accusations against Northern racism and church complicity, but for the voice Assing adopted. She reduced her reporter's voice to that of the *rapporteur* introducing and recording the actual speaker of the day, the translator helping to build a bridge between James W. C. Pennington and the German readers. No doubt her text can also be read as putting the usual white stamp of authenticity on black narrative, which was conventional for the day, yet, more important, Assing seemed aware that it was her German audience rather than the black writer who needed guidance.

At some point in her relationship with the Penningtons, Ottilie Assing decided to translate major passages from *The Fugitive Blacksmith* into German, and with Pennington's permission she did so. They met frequently to select passages, discuss potential readings of events, the one explaining, the other struggling to delve below the surface of words. It was a gesture of respect, and a sign that her perceptual realm had matured and broadened; Ottilie had begun to progress from political theory to the individual human being. By insisting that Pennington speak for himself, by affirming his power of speech and authorship, Assing moved toward linguistically dissolving one of the major American boundaries between black and white.

The Pennington she introduced to her readers was a man of personal refinement and courage: "Pennington is not one of these saccharine personalities in whom a soft concept of Christianity has smothered the ability to hate and, along with it, the power of love and devotion, which alone provides the motive force for serving a great purpose. He speaks out with bitterness and passion against slavery." This warrior against slavery was also a loving father and husband, a man with whom she had good conversations, a man with a generous sense of humor and spontaneous kindness. She wanted her readers to meet in this exceptional man the promise of his race. "I do not know to what extent the Caucasian race is intellectually superior to the African," she argued, "but should, in the course of time, a happy turn of events sooner or later bring about the opportunity for developing their [Africans'] natural endowments, which—like the center of their hot homeland—still remain unexplored and unexploited, they will undoubtedly outstrip the expectations which people here and in Europe generally have of them."[102]

Ottilie Assing sent her introductory essay and her translation of Pennington to Cotta, confident that it would make a stir and knowing it was the beginning of a new professional orientation for herself. Reading Pennington's memoirs she had learned that there were dozens of slave narratives, and as she perused more of them, her determination grew to make them central to her work. She did not know that Cotta would refuse to publish the manuscript into which she had invested so much time and energy. As she mentioned in her dispatch, she had already taken up her next project—Frederick Douglass' *My Bondage and My Freedom*, which she promised to review.

Pennington's text had fascinated Ottilie, but *My Bondage and My Freedom* took her captive. And it was a blessing, for all of a sudden developments in Pennington's life put an end to their friendship. Assing had praised Pennington for his personal courage and for his devotion to black liberation; what she could not see was the price he paid for this constant struggle. Fellow abolitionists like William Wells Brown and Lewis Tappan indicated that he frequently sought escape in drinking; there were charges that he had incurred heavy debts. No doubt his challenge to the segregation in New York's public transit system was controversial in his congregation. By the end of 1855 Pennington was replaced as pastor of Shiloh. When he and his family left New York,[103] they also disappeared from Assing's life and letters, never to be mentioned again.

Assing selected her friends and acquaintances carefully, and she was loyal, sometimes to the point of self-denial, to those few she finally embraced—the Baisons, Karl Gutzkow, the Koehler family, Gustav Frauenstein, the Kudlichs, Frederick Douglass, to name only a few. Her absolute silence on the Penningtons arouses suspicion. As a belligerent atheist, Assing could not but notice keenly any incident of religious hypocrisy or examples of uncharitable behavior. Pennington's dismissal from his post would have made a wonderful story! Did she spare the Shiloh congregation because an assault on them would have undermined the images of African-American decency and integrity she had created in her *Morgenblatt* article? Or did she have more personal reasons? Is it possible that their friendship contributed to his fall? She had spent a lot of time with the Penningtons. The admiration she expressed was for the self-liberator and the liberator of others, for the kind and witty family man, for the good conversationalist. She never described his looks, his body, his features, or his complexion.[104] What was also absent was that glorification of the exceptional that had been central to her Baison biography and that would characterize her representations of Frederick Douglass. Pennington had no "magic" for her. There is no hint in Assing's public and private writing that she ever saw more than a respected friend in him; he had none of Oronooko's splendor, and, happy in his second marriage, he had neither need nor room for an Aphra in his life. If nothing else, his deep religiosity and her atheism must have served as a barrier between them.

Her characterization of Pennington suggests why it was not hard for her to give up "her" first African-American protagonist. Her enthusiasm for Pennington's narrative was controlled and condescending: while appreciating its plot and politics, she could not but deplore what she saw as the book's aesthetic weaknesses. She called *The Fugitive Blacksmith* a "brochure" that moved her in its "simplicity and brevity"; she characterized its style as "unadorned," its argumentation as "clear and to the point," its descriptions of slave life as "fresh and lively," and what she appreciated most was its "wild poetic strain."[105] Benevolent condescension probably best describes this attitude, a conscious determination to respect the writer for trying. Douglass' text, however, threw a magic spell over her. As Benjamin Quarles has put it, "Douglass' own writings are models of clarity and good literary form . . . Incapable of writing a dull line, Douglass invests his sentences with an almost poetic cadence, compelling the reader to turn the page."[106] His success story was one to which she could subscribe without reservation; his gift of rhetoric sparkled on every page, his power of analysis, courage of conviction, vulnerability, and nobility. Assing had heard of Douglass the orator and abolitionist; she had read issues of *Frederick Douglass' Paper*,[107] and she had hoped for a chance to hear him perform. After reading his autobiography she was determined to meet him personally.

In the months that followed she tried to get all the information on Frederick Douglass she could, plowing through newspapers to trace his itinerary, browsing through the journal he published, reading his *Narrative*, interviewing people who had met him. Even before she had seen him, she decided he was special. She would want to meet him well prepared. His portrait in *My Bondage and My Freedom* is of a dignified man in his forties, carefully dressed and groomed, with a stern look on his face that comes close to a frown. She remembered the black protagonists she had encountered in literature—Shakespeare's passionate Othello, the rebellious and ambitious George Harris in Stowe's soapy novel, Aphra Behn's noble Oroonoko, Clara Mundt's Oronooko, Haiti's Toussaint L'Ouverture. Douglass could not boast of the "polished jet" that distinguished Behn's hero, nor could he claim royal descent—but then, why would she, a self-proclaimed radical, want a prince anyway? Wasn't the slave transformed into a lion, wasn't this modern American Spartacus far more spectacular? As she looked at his features, Aphra Behn's words, which she almost knew by heart, all of a sudden made sense:

> [Oroonoko] was pretty tall, but of a shape the most exact that can be fancied; the most famous statuary could not form the figure of a man more admirably turned from head to foot. His face was not of that brown, rusty black which most of that nation are, but a perfect ebony, or polished jet. His eyes were the most awful that could be seen, and very piercing; the white of them being like snow, as were his

teeth. His nose was rising and Roman, instead of African and flat. His mouth, the finest shaped that could be seen; far from those great turned lips, which are so natural to the rest of the Negroes. The whole proportion and air of his face was so noble, and exactly formed, that, bating his colour, there could be nothing in nature more beautiful, agreeable and handsome. There was no one grace wanting, that bears the standard of true beauty. His hair came down to his shoulders, by the aids of art; which was, by pulling it out with a quill, and keeping it combed, of which he took particular care.[108]

Clara Mundt's Aphra Behn had looked down from her balcony upon her beloved black prince, barely able to conceal her arousal at the sight of him, his powerful eroticism, his glorious nakedness:

> Pride and majesty glowed from his forehead, and one was disposed to liken his bravely bright eye to that of the eagle, king of the air, while his tall body, only barely concealed by a short robe reaching from his belt to his knee, and the rare regularity of his limbs evoked associations with the much admired and adored statues of antiquity. He is the Apollo Belvedere, Aphra thought, lost in the admiration of her gaze, only that the burning sun has changed that matt whiteness of marble into shining ebony.[109]

Assing decided to make her encounter with Frederick Douglass the culmination point of her annual summer tour through New York State. In July, as the heat set in, she boarded the train to Schenectady to spend a few weeks with Amalie Schoppe; then she took a stagecoach to Schoharie County for a tour of Howe's Cavern and spent a few days in late August with the Nickerts in Lancaster. Emilie had given birth to a daughter, Mary, and Emilie's mother had come to live with them. The Nickerts were poor, and Emilie, always sickly, was finding it hard to recover from childbirth, but the family seemed happy, eager to share their abundance with the person they imagined was their lonely relative.[110] For the first time in her life Emilie Nickert felt rich, with a future worth embracing. Assing looked at this domestic bliss and moved on. Only a few days before, she had written: "Too often in my life I have been tortured by people who, in the most gorgeous surroundings, force their family stories on me, or, worse, serve me with their sentimental outpourings, not to prefer going out into the world all by myself, when I cannot have proper company."[111] Now, after three days, she took flight for Niagara. In 1853 she had spent only a short time at Niagara Falls; this summer she returned to pay more homage to what she admired as one of the Wonders of the World. She spent several days at Clifton House, took extended trips to see the falls from all perspectives in their full glory, measuring them by walking toward them and away from them, allowing free flow to her emotions, inviting her senses to soar. It was raining most of the time, yet as the train departed, "the sun came forth once again, and the most beautiful rainbow was displayed through the trees in the falls' drizzle."[112] She was on her way to Rochester, to Frederick Douglass.

IV

IRRESISTIBLE ATTRACTIVENESS AND DISTINCTION

Appropriating Frederick Douglass

Your beauty is of such a strange kind that we Europeans must first search for new words for it. When the men in my country want to praise us, they call us shining like the young day, sparkling like the young morning sun, white like the gleaming snow, soft like a young blooming rose . . . But all of that does not go with you. Your beauty had nothing in common with the day, nor with the sun. . . . I would love to liken you to the night, but the nights are not so beautiful as you!

—CLARA MUNDT, *Aphra Behn*

License my roving hands, and let them go,
Before, behind, between, above, below.
O my America, my new found land,
My kingdom . . .
My mine of precious stones, my empery,
How blessed I am in thus discovering thee!
—JOHN DONNE, "To His Mistress Going to Bed"

I could not separate the African from the man, nor prevent that disgust and horror which filled my mind every time I saw him touch the gentle Desdemona.

—ABIGAIL ADAMS, *Letters*

*O*ttilie Assing could have taken a coach to carry her to the Douglass residence, which was situated on a hillside almost two miles south of Rochester, near the city lines.[1] Despite her eagerness to meet the man whose autobiography had moved her so deeply, she chose to walk. After months of preparation for this encounter, she all of a sudden needed another hour of quiet reflection. Like her mother, she loved excursions in the country, and

like her mother, she was an indefatigable hiker. Whenever she had traveled to a new city,
village, or hamlet in the past she had insisted on walking its streets. The smells, the
sounds, drifting with the crowd—this was her way of appropriating a new environment.
She quickly realized that Rochester had nothing of New York City's metropolitan ele-
gance, its slum despondency, its aggressively buzzing street life, but to her great relief she
also saw nothing of that sleepy timelessness that seemed to freeze Amalie Schoppe's Sche-
nectady somewhere outside of history. As she walked down Buffalo Street toward the
Genesee River, the many businesses she passed, the people running errands, shopping, bend-
ing over paperwork, talking together, she sensed an almost restless vitality in this commu-
nity; she had entered one of those boomtowns rapidly transforming themselves into cities
bubbling over with life and enterprise. She had come prepared to like the town in which a
fugitive slave not only could build a home for himself and his family but could even
launch a career as an editor, prepared also to associate it with progress, mobility, openness,
in short with all the qualities of Americanness she embraced so eagerly. The businesslike
vitality of Buffalo Street confirmed her hopes.

As she crossed the bridge over the Genesee River, she gave herself a few minutes of rest.
How similar this town was to familiar communities in the Old World—and how utterly
different! Like the Elbe in Dresden, like the Neckar in the plains west of Heidelberg, like
the Rhine north of Bonn, this broad river flowed with powerful relaxed majesty along its
luxuriously wide bed, as if relieved that it was finally released from the straitjacket of
hills that had forced it to rush and tumble. As in Germany, people had built their facto-
ries and homes so close to the water that it seemed they regretted they could not live in it.
How strange in a country with so many unsettled territories! It almost seemed that people
huddled together to protect themselves against the vastness of the continent they had
claimed as theirs! Ottilie thought of Goethe's ode to America:

> *America, you are better off*
> *Than our continent, the old . . .*

As in Dresden, Cologne, Hamburg, Heidelberg, there were factories, banks, mansions,
schools, church spires—always in America too many churches for Ottilie—stores, a jail,
a courthouse, all crowding in on the river or, if they were farther off, claiming more space.
Yet here the likeness ceased: everything in Rochester was new, as if invented and built
only yesterday, in a single day, all at the same, glorious moment. True, some buildings
needed paint or were leaning dangerously to one side, as if exhausted after struggling
against a heavy storm, but they were not old, as buildings in Europe were old, just run-
down, dilapidated, like neglected children. There can be no youth, middle age, and old
age if history has barely fifty years to its name. But why sigh over something that cannot

be had? Wasn't it far more exciting to be involved in making history than touring it? Unlike Frances Trollope, who hated the country for its newness, who disliked its people for their boisterous pride in what they had built, and who ridiculed their attempts at developing a sense of history in the midst of newly constructed lives, Ottilie saw nothing offensive in the sense of achievement Rochesterians displayed. Only a few years later they were to describe their community of more than 50,000 as "a modern town, having risen from a wilderness in less than half a century . . . To see and appreciate the beauties of this really handsome city, one must drive through its broad, clean, well-paved and shady avenues—stroll through its parks—gaze upon its waterfalls—enter its elegant public and private buildings—visit its churches and schools—go among its flower mills and manufacturing establishments—walk in its nurseries and gardens, and then he may to some extent realize what an enterprising people can accomplish in half a century, upon a productive soil in a favorite clime and under the smiles of a bountiful Providence."[2] She felt these people needed no divine Providence to sustain them; they were enterprising enough to take on the future all by themselves. Eventually they would understand that freeing themselves from their self-imposed religious chains would be part of their growing up! Ottilie decided it was time to move on.

She sauntered down South Avenue at a leisurely pace, and she began to understand why people called Rochester "the Flower City." As houses became fewer, they were surrounded with large gardens abounding with fruit trees and ornamental shrubs. Their owners seemed almost in competition with each other. Ottilie remembered the hatbox garden in the Poolstrasse. How happy she had been there, in that diminutive Garden of Eden. But then, how she loved the open space that was America's gift to her, its abundance of trees and shrubs and flowers, the land people could afford to claim as theirs to cultivate, improve, farm according to their needs for sustenance and their notions of beauty!

Finally, as Ottilie began to walk up the hill—she could already see the Douglass home—she found herself surrounded by nurseries. "Ornamental trees are cultivated with care" in Rochester, the City Directory of 1863 boasted, "and the growth of fruit trees in the town and adjacent country is extensive. Here are the great nurseries of the American continent. Thousands of acres . . . are devoted to the culture of fruit trees and ornamental shrubs, and millions of trees are annually sent abroad to distant counties, States, and even to foreign countries. The annual product of these nurseries is valued at over $2,000,000."[3] Ottilie understood why these people were tempted to call themselves "blessed"—almost. She stopped once more to look back, and she was nearly overwhelmed by its abundance. So enchanted was she by the loveliness that her admiration for the man who had chosen this place, up on this hill, with this glorious view, increased by leaps and bounds. It did not occur to her that living out here, more than two miles from his business, *might not be a matter of choice, of taste, of love of nature, but a form of exile imposed by the hostility of the community, or self-imposed by pride, perhaps both.*

A few brisk steps brought her to Douglass' door, and only moments later he stood in front of her, a man much lighter in color than she had expected, even larger and more powerfully built than she had imagined, and with more gray streaks in his hair than his age required. They were almost the same age, weren't they? Assing felt very small all of a sudden, and very young.

And Douglass? Before him stood a white woman, probably in her early thirties, with a nervous smile on her face, introducing herself as a German journalist in faultless, yet somehow studied English. Obviously she had prepared a little speech, but she stumbled in her nervousness, and she seemed annoyed that her German accent showed, as it always did when she was insecure. Her gown, hat, and jewelry told him that she had exquisite taste. He liked the way she allowed her heavy blond curls to show against the confinement of the hat. She apologized for intruding on his privacy, explaining that she had tried the office first. He looked down the road. "You did not walk all that way, did you?" "I most certainly did." There was pride as well as defiance in her voice. "You must be tired," he suggested, his voice softer now, concerned, but a smile that had not been there before making its way into his eyes. She would have liked to explain that she enjoyed walking, was used to it, back home, in the old country, and in New York City. Instead, she turned back toward Rochester and laughed. "But this is so beautiful! I could have walked on for hours!" "You should try again in November or February," he replied somewhere between a frown and a smile.

A few minutes later they sat across from each other in the front parlor. It was sparsely furnished, not overstuffed like many in the homes she had visited. She was surprised to see a piano, with a violin lying on top of it, and many, many books, with book markers sticking out everywhere. One portrait on the wall she recognized as Wendell Phillips'. Douglass carefully studied her as her eyes quickly roamed the room, judging and evaluating, her face betraying her curiosity, her surprise. It was all so familiar to him, as was his response—a mixture of pride at being able to surprise her and anger that she had dared to expect less. "Wendell Phillips," they said almost simultaneously as her eyes rested on the picture, and for the first time they laughed together. "I need help with the other one, though," she admitted. "This is my dear friend Gerrit Smith, an . . ." "This is a man I must meet," she interrupted him, excited and nervous under her ladylike composure. "You would have to walk quite a few miles yet," he chuckled, as he rose, offering to get refreshments. "But perhaps I can introduce you to him."

She was explaining her reasons for coming to the United States and her professional background when the door was pushed open. A rather dark woman entered, carrying a tray with glasses and a tumbler of lemonade. She was tall, full-bodied, almost heavy, in her mid- or late forties, wearing a dark cotton dress with a white, meticulously starched apron over it. Her hair was hidden under a bandanna. Assing smiled at her, but there was only a slight nod of the head in return. Without a word, the woman opened two side tables for Assing and Douglass, then poured the lemonade, nodding to their "Thank you." Only after she was finished serving did she come up to Douglass, who rose and, taking her arm, formally introduced her: "My wife, Mrs. Frederick Douglass." Then, with a slight bow: "I want you to meet Miss Assing. Miss Assing is a correspondent from Germany." Assing needed the few moments in which Douglass looked at his wife to regain her composure. Douglass' wife! She had taken her for the maid! She jumped from her chair and extended her hand.

Douglass mentioned a wife in his autobiography, and when Ottilie had quizzed Pennington about her, he had spoken of Anna Murray with the highest respect. She knew that Mrs. Douglass was a freeborn woman who had helped Douglass to escape from slavery. Pennington had married them in New York in 1839. He had praised her qualities as a housewife and as a mother of five who managed the family business during Douglass' lecture tours. He described her as a deeply religious woman and a devoted abolitionist. He had never mentioned color or age. Assing had imagined Anna Murray as a perfect companion to the heroic Douglass of her dreams: as Oronooko's gentle Imoinda, as a woman with the natural refinement and gentility of Stowe's Eliza, light-skinned like her husband, and, like him, educated, intelligent, and heroic. The woman before her looked more like the illustrations she had seen of Aunt Cloe—minus the big smile and a few pounds. Her shock was to be expressed in the only public statement she ever made about Mrs. Douglass: "Douglass' wife is completely black . . ."[4]

Anna Murray Douglass shook hands, greeting Ottilie with a polite "How do you do," but the welcome smile around her lips never made it to her eyes. She knew exactly what was going on in the white woman's mind. It always happened when a white woman came to see Frederick. They had no control over their faces. Ottilie sensed that both her hostess and her host had observed her consternation and knew its cause. For the first time something deep inside told her that she might not be welcome.

Ottilie Assing had been nervous about this interview, insecure about how to address this black celebrity, but also confident that her social skills would enable her to handle any situation. She had been trained as a conversationalist in one of the best schools imaginable—in Rosa Maria's salon—and she had received her baptism of fire in Varnhagen's elitist circle. Therese Robinson had welcomed her to her parlor and had been proud to introduce her to her friends. In the past three years she had talked with America's leading abolitionists and feminists; she had interviewed Indians, Chinese peddlers, Irish musicians, prisoners in the Tombs, pioneers in Wisconsin, members of Pennington's congregation. Yet only thirty minutes into her conversation with Frederick Douglass this self-assertive German intellectual knew that she was not in control. She was shocked to see how ridiculously false her images of the Douglasses were, and she was almost annoyed to realize how eager she was to impress the man who sat across from her. She had assumed she would be doing this ex-slave an enormous favor by introducing him to German read-ers, by offering herself as his mouthpiece for the Old World. She began to comprehend that it was a privilege to enjoy his hospitality, to observe his struggle for meaning, to delve into ideas with him: it dawned on her that she must be on guard not to let him master her mind.

Douglass came to her rescue. He simply picked up their conversation where they had left off, and soon they were engaged in a lively exchange of ideas. He had just witnessed another Euro-American woman stumbling in that blinding maze of whiteness in which their culture raised them, and as always a hot flash of rage shot through him at the dead-ening repetitiveness of it all, but perhaps he sensed that he was facing a woman struggling for meaning, too. Assing had brought a list of questions she had meant to ask, but she forgot about them as she answered his inquiries about her past, as they discussed politics and laughed at the mishaps they both had had when lighting out for new territories. They realized during that first afternoon that they could talk together about philosophy, music, literature, religion, and yes, eventually even race. Assing discovered in Douglass a man for whose respect and perhaps even friendship she was willing to go a long way, and she made a decision she would never revise in the twenty-six years that followed: she would focus all her attention on Frederick Douglass. She would ignore his spouse to the utmost limits of common politeness.

We do not know how many hours Assing and Douglass spent in intense conversation on that first day, whether she was invited to join the fam-ily supper, whether he walked her back to town. As Assing was staying with Emilie Nickert's relatives, it is likely that she spent several days in Rochester, and it is possible that there were more conversations with Douglass. What we know, though, is that the impression they made upon one another was so favor-able and strong that both wanted to meet again. Very soon they would realize that there was enough substance, enough bite to keep them interested for more than two decades.

For our first glimpses at the slowly evolving Assing-Douglass relationship we have to rely entirely on Ottilie Assing's articles for the *Morgenblatt für gebildete Leser*. She later repeatedly referred to an introductory statement about her first visit to Rochester in the summer of 1856, obviously unaware that the

Morgenblatt had never published such a thing. The Deutsche Literaturarchiv in Marbach holds a number of long manuscripts from her that Cotta chose not to print; all of them dealt with slavery and abolition, so it is clear that Cotta felt that Assing's preoccupation with the African-American experience was not shared by his readers, or, as a few years later with her pieces on John Brown, he feared that her uncompromising radicalism would cause trouble with the German censors. He did not publish her columns, yet usually he preserved the manuscripts, but the Douglass article is not among them. We must assume that it was either lost in the mail or not forwarded by Caroline Baison, who served as a connecting link between Assing and Cotta in the 1850s. Fortunately for us, however, Assing must have kept a copy of it, for she integrated it into the introduction, the *Vorrede*, of her translation of Douglass' *My Bondage and My Freedom*.[5]

It is intriguing that the journalist who was so deeply interested in American politics and who was so anxious for her audience to respect her as a foreign correspondent rather than a society gossip decided to focus not on the public figure but on the private man, the individual Frederick Douglass, when introducing him. The text that was important enough for Assing to reprint three years later in a revised and enlarged form leaves little doubt that she was completely taken by Douglass' powerful male presence and determined to have her audience see him through her eyes. The word portrait she painted was designed to lure readers to identify with the hero of her story so that they could not only accept him as their equal in terms of a common humanity that transcends race and class, on the one hand, but adore him as an exceptional person in the hierarchy of human potentials, on the other. She tried to achieve this with two interdependent strategies of representation, bringing together the public message of the progressive journalist and the private text of the woman in love: her public discourse of equality and appropriation carefully elaborated on the three aspects that, according to nineteenth-century notions, constitute the human being—body, mind, and soul; her highly eroticized private discourse of enchantment stressed beauty and nobility, vitality and originality, willpower and strength. The article was the first and perhaps the most powerful and deeply felt of the many public love songs she was to compose for Frederick Douglass in the course of their many years together.

Assing knew her readers were used to stereotypical representations of blacks as the threatening, victimized, or ridiculous "other," as objects of white fear, tyranny, or pity. She also knew she was communicating with people who uncritically believed their own ethnic identity and culture to be the most highly developed in the world and the norm to which others should aspire, thus automatically associating difference with inferiority and demonizing it by creating what H. L. Malchow calls a "racial Gothic."[6] It was easy for her to respond to this mind-set because she had been—and in many ways still was—a member of this group, sharing their hierarchical concepts of culture, the arrogance with which they defined their culture as that magnet on the hilltop of human development to which others were attracted as through magic. She, too, was incapable of perceiving equality in terms other than sameness.

Assing shared this hierarchical creed, but without challenging its basic assumptions she had also begun to acknowledge the problematics. The educated bourgeoisie of Germany disliked "half-Jews" and ridiculed her aspirations as an art critic and journalist because she was a woman. Her years in America had taught her that static constructions of cultural superiority were used as apologies for excluding and even enslaving those defined as outsiders. Her concept of culture was hierarchical and hegemonic, a one-way street leading from the bottom to the top, but, as her notions of a magnet culture document, inclusive, open for those individuals who, independent of race, class, and gender, were willing and determined to join. Why not impose the familiar on the "other" and then, with luck, cajole her readers to support her efforts to extend the realm of that familiar? As Houston Baker, Jr., has shown, Frederick Douglass translated "an authentic, unwritten self . . . into a literary representation" in his *Narrative* by reconstructing "his 'authentic' self as a figure embodying the public virtues and values esteemed by his intended audience."[7] Assing's portrait seems to retrace and continue this road Douglass chose for himself, and it is possible that her approach to Douglass was shaped by strategic considerations. More likely, she herself needed to reinvent the black man in such terms in order to relate to him, to reach out to him, to love him. The images she created were intended to wipe out the blackness that was so firmly rooted in her and her readers' heads.

Assing's portrait carefully avoided any physical feature or character trait that might denote difference. Her depiction of Douglass was encoded exclusively in conventional Western notions of beauty, attributing to him the features of a Greek or Roman hero so beloved to a sophisticated German audience. "Douglass is a rather light mulatto of unusually tall, slender, and powerful stature,"[8] she began. Falling in with the nineteenth-century tradition of representing blacks by first inspecting their bodies,[9] she ran the gamut of neo-Petrarchian description: "His features are striking: the prominently domed forehead with a peculiarly deep cleft at the bridge of the nose, an aquiline nose, and the narrow,

beautifully carved lips betray more of his white than of his black origin. The
thick hair, already mixed here and there with gray, is curly and prominent
though not woolly."[10] The few, half-denied remnants of "blackness" were clearly
meant not as a means of racial identification but, as in Aphra Behn's and Clara
Mundt's narratives, as proof of his tragic descent, his authenticity, as markers
for her own sexual desire. Her image of the mulatto combined the best features
of both races, defying contemporary purist readings of the "mixed blood" as a
mongrel product of the worst qualities; she countered the popular argument of
the "natural" weakness of the "mulatto" by glorifying his manliness and vigor.
In her Douglass, two races, black and white, ceased to be antagonists, and the
energy that had been wasted in centuries of race warfare was finally used to create a new, powerful, beautiful race of many races, a composite American nationality. The images of "hybrid vigor" she evoked were directed toward a future of
promise, innovation, reinvigoration;[11] they extended the racialized definition of
"normal" beyond the traditional "black" and "white." Yet what she was depicting was a beauty and nobility that was recognizable as such because it had lost
its African assets. Her rhetoric of equality invited identification by affirming hierarchy, by enforcing difference.[12]

People of biracial descent ought to be free to choose the race with which
they wanted to be associated, if choose they must, her egalitarian creed decreed,
yet she did not doubt that the choice Douglass would make was whiteness,
though Douglass always insisted that the person of mixed race was equal in en-
dowment and potential to a person of "pure" origin.[13] Race crossing for her was
a means of liberating blacks from what she deplored as the curse of blackness.
Firmly anchored at the base of her formula was the conventional hierarchical
definition of "whites as the chosen people."[14] No matter how much she supported the unity of humankind, no matter how much she defended race mixing
as ennobling and perfecting humanity, when she insinuated that the benefit of
the encounter lay in whitening the black race, not the reverse, she implied the
superiority of whiteness. Hers was a description that deracinated Douglass, that
deprived him of his blackness; it appropriated his body, claimed him as one of
"us" by imposing on him a rhetoric of the white familiar.

The uncritical consistency with which she used these metaphors of sameness
and whiteness undermined the egalitarianism that was Assing's political creed.
She constructed sameness not as a ruse for her less enlightened readers; she
needed it for herself. No doubt romantic notions of the noble savage and of the
exotic conditioned her response to Frederick Douglass; his blackness and its
erotic associations may have aroused her, yet she needed to reimagine him as

one of "us." Still, we have to acknowledge that her studiously maintained discourse on "color blindness," sameness, absence of difference, was designed to expose the arbitrariness of exclusion and discrimination based on racialized notions of difference.[15] It undermined the purist myth of an "impassable gulf" separating the races, challenging established boundaries between "us" and the "other." That she clung to a neoclassical idiom, to the hierarchy of cultures, did not stop her from criticizing the sociopolitical practice of exclusion, from lashing out at slavery and racism.

Once she had defined Douglass' physical appearance, Assing, manipulating popular contemporary physiognomic doctrine which saw the body as the mirror of the soul, progressed to the next step: giving this body the qualities that metamorphosed it into a truly heroic, moral, and exceptional mode:

> His whole appearance, stamped with past storms and struggles, bespeaks great energy and a willpower that shuns no obstacle and has been the sole source of his success in reaching his present prominence in the face of all odds. One can easily see how, when little more than a boy, he stood up to his master (who wanted to beat him) and actually cowed him—as he related in his autobiography; or, when working in the shipyard at Baltimore and finding that the white workers refused to tolerate him, he lifted up his most ardent opponent and tossed him into the water.[16]

Assing carefully distanced Douglass from victimization imagery, from the pathology ascription that usually characterized both abolitionist and proslavery representations of African-Americans; equally, she avoided associating him with the popular stereotype of the noble savage. Her Frederick Douglass was an agent of progress and change, neither object of history nor helpless victim. He carried in him the knowledge of his humanity, the skill and the courage to effect his liberation, and the potentials to succeed as a free man. He was a self-liberator and thus also an ideal personification of that beloved nineteenth-century American stereotype, the self-made man.

In a third step Assing introduced her readers to the intellectual Frederick Douglass. One and a half centuries before, Aphra Behn had enticed her readers to condemn the enslavement of her African prince by glorifying his physical and intellectual superiority: "I have often seen and conversed with this great man, and . . . do assure my reader, the most illustrious courts could not have produced a braver man . . . for greatness of courage and mind, a judgment more solid, a wit more quick, and a conversation more sweet and diverting."[17] Assing, too, presented her black hero as an enlightened man, educated, knowledgeable, full of intellectual curiosity, flexible and determined, with a good sense of humor as well as joie de vivre, and, most important, a man who not only used these qualities and talents to elevate himself but devoted them to the elevation of others:

> Despite all vicissitudes, his whole being expresses a richly endowed, original, and happily matured nature. Everything about him is fresh, genuine, true, and good. Endowed with an exceptional talent for conversation, he knows how to inspire and elevate others, and in conversation proves to be cheerful, animated, witty, and knowledgeable. Glowing with passion for the cause to which he has dedicated his life, he is far too wide-ranging in his interests as not to engage other worthy causes with energy. We touched upon a wide variety of things—large and small, general and personal—in the course of our conversation, and everywhere I encountered understanding and sympathy.[18]

Assing anchored Douglass firmly in the realm of culture while insisting nature had not been banned from his unique self; culture and nature complemented each other, forming the sensuous intellectual.

Nothing in Assing's representation denoted difference. It is of special importance that she legitimized her appropriation of Douglass as one of "us" by stressing that his devotion was not just to the liberation of slaves but to any just and deserving cause. This man, discriminated against for his race, had the moral greatness to defend all people against violations of their human and civil rights; his eternal foe was injustice, not whiteness. The term "passion," with its potentially negative and racial connotations, was used exclusively in relation to the cause to which Douglass devoted his life.

In Assing's first introduction of Douglass, she encoded his portrait in metaphors of beauty, vitality, vigor; like Hans Christian Andersen in his *Mulatten*, she combined romantic images of the genius[19] with the concept of the natural gentleman; like Andersen's Horatio, her Douglass was a personification of human perfection, nobility of soul, and education in perfect harmony with his "Rousseauvian naturalness."[20] Exposed to her woman's gaze,[21] he became Genius and Eros in one. Falling in love with this man came naturally. In the expressions of personal enchantment which permeated this column and the ones that followed in the years to come, the public and the private became indistinguishable. It was no longer the journalist but the lover speaking when Assing portrayed Douglass as "the magnet" who "electrified" and "captivated"[22] anybody who entered his magic circle.

The private idiom almost explodes from the final sentence of the paragraph of her first *Morgenblatt* text—significantly separated from the discourse of sameness and equality by a dash: "Douglass' wife is completely black, and his five children, therefore, have more of the traits of the Negro than he."[23] After struggling over pages to explain away race where it did not suit her purposes, she immediately reinstated it and the hierarchy commonly associated with it when it was convenient for her.[24] No need to explain where she located Frederick Douglass in this "we"-"they" dichotomy.

As early as the fall of 1855 Ottilie Assing had confided to her old friend Rahel de Castro that she would "try whether she could not introduce her readers to highly educated darkies."[25] *My Bondage and My Freedom* offered everything it took to enlighten and entertain her audience, and Assing was confident that not only was she born to build this bridge between the Old World and the New, between black and white, but she possessed the skills to make it a perfect bridge. It is likely that she broached the idea of translating his text to Douglass during their first encounter. Douglass must have been pleased by her enthusiasm, and intrigued by the idea of spreading his political message beyond the English-speaking world. Is it possible that Assing's experience as a "half-Jew," the wisdom and the pain, the insecurity and the need to belong that came with it, made it easier for Douglass to confide in her? Jews, too, were seen as a race apart, marginalized, ostracized; there were even those who perceived them as black.[26]

They agreed that she would take up her work during the winter months. Were there other arrangements? We do not know. The work of translation, the struggle for meaning, the need to be understood and to understand, brought them closer. Perhaps it was in response to a letter from her that Douglass invited her for another visit to Rochester the following summer, suggesting that she enjoy his and his family's hospitality while working on their project. They would have time to talk, to ask and answer questions; she would better understand him by seeing him in his home, with his family; he would like to know more of the woman who spent so much time with his past.

We do not know whether they saw each other during the winter of 1856–57, but soon letters went back and forth on a regular, eventually weekly, basis. They exchanged gossip and family news, informed each other about their daily activities, discussed politics and their work, framing and interspersing news with formulas of endearment and intimacy as time went on, with a language that was all theirs. "Incendiary"[27] was the word Douglass used for this private discourse, and Assing's letters lived up to his expectations. To her contemporaries she may have seemed like a violation of everything that defined true womanhood:[28] where fragility, softness, and delicacy were celebrated, she boasted of indefatigability, vigor, strength, love of good food and delight in wine and even beer. In a society that worshipped chastity, she gloried in her role as a black and married man's lover. She ridiculed her contemporaries' notions of piety with her belligerent atheism. Her life as a professional woman appeared like a denial of woman's true destiny—wife- and motherhood. Douglass was enchanted by a rebelliousness that neither apologized nor explained.

Another development suggests that Ottilie Assing had begun to see Douglass as more than just a friend only months after their first encounter: it was that winter she decided to relocate from New York City to Hoboken. Once Douglass entered into her life, she needed a place that gave her the freedom to come and go as she pleased, and a privacy into which she could invite the man she was beginning to love.

In the past she had frequently taken the ferry at Barclay Street to spend Sundays in Hoboken. There she would promenade through the Elysian Fields, enjoy the many beer gardens run by enterprising German immigrants, and cultivate her friendship with the Kudlich and Loewenthal families. Her Hoboken friends rapidly came up with a solution to Assing's housing problems when she told them that not only was she tired of her makeshift arrangements; she also needed a place where Frederick Douglass could find a home away from home. From Assing's letters we can see that her confidence in their radicalism was strong enough to share her and Douglass' secret with them, and they did not disappoint her. The correspondence that survived[29] suggests that, at least on the surface, race was not an issue in the way Assing's acquaintances dealt with the liaison. It is possible that they welcomed it as yet another opportunity to prove their superiority as German radicals to the racism of their American neighbors. Nowhere in their letters was there a reference to race, and Assing gratefully interpreted their silence as approval. They introduced her to a Mrs. Marks, an elderly woman of German background who lived in a spacious and comfortable house on Washington Street. In the winter of 1856–57, Ottilie Assing rented two rooms from Mrs. Marks, with an option on a third, and they agreed that she would take her meals with the family. She did not hesitate to tell her landlady of her friendship with Frederick Douglass, knowing that surprise visits and hide-and-seek games would only cause embarrassment. From Douglass' autobiography we know that Mrs. Marks made it clear that Assing's friends would always be welcome to her home and to her table. Assing lived at Mrs. Marks's house until 1865, with Frederick Douglass a frequent guest.[30] Douglass and Mrs. Marks developed a keen liking for each other.

In May 1857 Douglass spent a week in New York City, addressing the American Abolitionist Society and speaking at the Shiloh Presbyterian Church. After his clash with the Garrisonians he had kept a low profile during the conventions; now he returned. His hibernation had never been complete; now, with Ottilie Assing waiting for him, it was over. In 1857 the abolitionists were up in arms over the Supreme Court's Dred Scott decision, ruling that no black person, slave or free, could be an American citizen, and Frederick Douglass, with his analytical skills and the passion of his words, was the man people wanted to hear. It was a good reason to return to the spotlight, and knowing that Assing was eager to see and hear him made duty a pleasure. Wherever he spoke, Assing was in the audience. "The lion of this season was Frederick Douglass, this excellent mulatto whom I have mentioned repeatedly in my reports," she wrote in June 1857. "Having hitherto known this talented, brilliant man only from his writings and from personal intercourse, I heard him for the first time as a public speaker, which gave me an appreciation of his great and general importance. Among the many great orators in this country he is one of the greatest." For two nights she heard him debate Beriah Green, Henry Highland Garnet, Austin Steward, and Charles Lenox Remond, stunned at the power of his logic, "the bright flashes of humor and wit."[31] As she turned the spotlight on him in her article, she transformed him into a secular preacher, lonely on the pedestal of his superiority, whose power enabled him to subdue and convert. In that, she affirmed what Richard Yarborough in his analysis of Douglass' manhood ideal has called "the white bourgeois paradigm of manhood."[32] Yet while portraying him as towering above his audience, almost superhuman in his exceptionality, she also represented him as a man who used his power exclusively to do his duty to fallen humanity. In a world of white male domination and competition Ottilie Assing's Frederick Douglass personified an alternative masculinity that was engendered as vigor of communal love and devotion. "Power over" as domination was replaced by "power to" as creation.

Assing was no longer a neutral observer; she was completely absorbed in Douglass' performance, enchanted by this "Rhetorical Man," this "black master of the verbal arts,"[33] as Henry Louis Gates, Jr., has characterized him. Clara Mundt had portrayed her Aphra Behn as "caught in a magic spell" when she listened to Oronooko's "vibrant, sonorous voice"[34] addressing his fellow slaves; Baison the actor had cast a spell over Ottilie Assing. But now a drama unfolded before her eyes with the protagonist not acting but reliving his suffering and fighting for human dignity, for justice, for recognition. She had loved Baison's voice, which, she thought, could express the whole gamut of human emotions.

That first night in New York she was captivated by the erotic vitality of Douglass' voice. She was not the only one: time and again women and men alike testified to its magnificent magnetism.

Ottilie Assing began to understand, for the first time in her American quest, the full meaning of racism for an individual human being. It was no longer something that happened somewhere else, to an anonymous other. It happened to a man to whom she could relate: "It is painful to think what high position such a man would hold, if only his skin were a few shades lighter. As it is, although he is one of the best, although he belongs to the true intellectual aristocracy, although he enjoys fame and reputation throughout the nation, and although he is gifted with a great mind and prodigious talent, with a commitment to action, personal charm, and a spotless character—so-called society shuns him because he is a 'nigger.' "[35]

In the spring of 1857 one of Caroline Baison's daughters, accompanied by a chaperone, arrived in New York to spend a few weeks with her former tutor and substitute mother. Josephine had tried to make a living as an actress after her father's death, and it is possible that she hoped Ottilie would help her launch an American career. But Assing, disappointed at Madame Baison's unreliability and probably still smarting from her financial loss, was no longer interested in her former charge and was rather eager for her to move on. Originally it had been agreed that the three women would spend the summer together in Sheboygan. Adolph Rosenthal,* whose business brought him to New York, would accompany them there, but Assing told the Rosenthals that professional obligations kept her from coming to Sheboygan. Her summer plans now focused on Douglass and Rochester; there was no room for anything else. Douglass was stumping western New York, and she heard that Lake Superior and Lake Erie still had ice.[36] It looked as if a wet and dreary summer would be succeeding an exceptionally cold winter and spring.

When the dog days set in, Assing and her two German guests escaped from New York and went directly to Quebec, where they met up with another friend, a man, as Assing wrote in two *Morgenblatt* accounts. She did not reveal the identities of her three traveling companions, but from Rahel de Castro's letters to Ludmilla Assing we know that the women were Josephine Baison and her chaperone; the man is still unknown. Is it possible that Frederick Douglass spent a

---

*It is possible that the Rosenthals were related to Mme. Baison, but the family connection cannot be established, since no family papers remain.

few precious days of this summer vacationing with Assing and her German friends? Assing, who consistently used the first person singular in her *Morgenblatt* reports, spoke only of "we" and "us" in the two Canadian articles; while she mentioned her female companions only in passing, her comments on the man's conduct, his every movement, indeed, signify special interest. Douglass' and Assing's secret honeymoon on the St. Lawrence would be a gem in our narrative of unfolding romance, but unfortunately our protagonists do not cooperate: Assing left Douglass' and her potential biographers in the dark.

The party met in Quebec, where they intended to take a boat down the St. Lawrence to Rivière du Loup, whence they were to go up the Saguenay River to Ha Ha Bay. When the vessel on which they were booked was delayed for several days, they took the train to Gorham, New Hampshire, in the White Mountains, instead. They found lodging in the spectacular Alpine House, which offered guided hikes up Mount Washington. Ottilie Assing had never been to this state, and she was enchanted by the raw beauty of the land. It was a cool summer, but they enjoyed the luscious green glory of New England's vast forests. What impressed her most was the tame bear which the hotel kept to amuse their guests. Thrice a day her party walked out to treat him to plates heaped with food. He gracefully took the meat out of their hands "and allowed us to caress his huge head."[37]

Despite the cool weather, they decided to rent horses for the famous Mount Washington tour. It was a weird party, indeed: only Ottilie Assing was an experienced rider; one of her female friends had never before been on a horse, and the other had suffered a fall in her childhood that left her in permanent fear of riding. But it was the male companion who attracted Assing's full attention. "Number three looked best, for although this was the first time on the back of a quadruped,"[38] he immediately showed a certain bravura, and "despite our guide's affirmation that we could leave free rein to the horses, he was determined to keep his under control, so that he was always ahead of me . . . Truly he took on the role of master with so much gusto and skill that the patient, careful animal finally came close to taking him down a precipice."

The excursion turned out to be a disaster. The trail ended at the tree line, and icy winds tore at them as their horses picked their way across the rocky terrain. One of the women gave up and insisted on walking back down to the valley. The others continued but were soon wet to the bone. Assing, who lost her shawl, was miserable, hating herself for suggesting the tour in the first place. "Only once in a while, when I saw travel companion number three at a distance, who now, where it mattered, left everything to his horse and had discarded all notions of mastery, something like a weak glimmer of humor came over me." After four hours they reached Tip Top House, but the travelers were too cold and tired to enjoy the gorgeous panorama. "A kind of tender love for the oven was the only emotion I could muster," Assing admitted. Before they could really warm up they were already on their way back, anxious to make it down to the valley before nightfall. Going up had been a challenge; descending became a nightmare. Yet once they reached the valley, Assing's usual joie de vivre quickly returned. "We were in the most joyful mood as we drove back to the Alpine House, and in passing we were greeted by the most beautiful glimmering shooting star." People say that a wish you make while seeing a shooting star comes true. She was, she suggested, a woman full of hopes, wishes, and dreams.

The boat trip down the St. Lawrence took place after this excursion to New Hampshire. Ottilie Assing loved the mixed company they encountered on board—British, Canadian, American, German, French —and her language skills enabled her to stay at the center of attention. Soon she found herself amusing passengers and crew with German fairy tales and legends. She had not entertained a group like this in years, and from the sheer joy expressed in her article we can see how much she must have missed this kind of public performance.

Assing was enchanted by the broad majesty of the St. Lawrence, but once the boat moved up the Saguenay, the dark beauty of the land almost overwhelmed her: the unbroken wilderness, the huge bluffs through which the river, so deep it appeared black, cut its way. For the first time in her life she understood the meaning of the term "pristine nature." The playful St. Lawrence tourist became more sober—with a sense of awe, of inner calm, of existential loneliness in the face of the sublime. She felt she had reached, if not the end of the world, a point of timelessness where values she believed in—civilization, progress—were irrelevant. It was almost with relief that she heard the whistle signaling their return from this place beyond the familiar to civilization and life.[39] No matter how much Cooper and Sealsfield, whose frontier novels she cherished, glorified the wilderness, no matter how much popular contemporary discourse praised the innocent and purifying qualities of rural life—Ottilie Assing was and would always remain happily addicted to city life. Back in Quebec Assing and her German friends parted, the women taking the boat to Sheboygan, their host traveling to Rochester to spend her summer with Frederick Douglass.

For two months, *Morgenblatt* readers had to do without reports from their American correspondent. We have neither letters nor diary entries to inform us what happened during this visit in Rochester. Douglass' memories of the vicious uproar caused by his friendship with Julia Griffiths were still painfully raw and fresh, and there are signs that he was eager not to expose himself and his family to another humiliation of that kind. And by this time Assing had thoroughly familiarized herself with his background, well beyond the information he provided in his autobiography. She knew of the Griffiths allegations and of Douglass' clashes with the Garrisonians, and she understood his motives for avoiding another scandal. She was happy to live removed from the public gaze, keeping a low profile for his sake.

Assing arrived at Rochester as a German journalist who was translating Douglass' autobiography. We can be almost certain that by the time this summer came to an end Assing and Douglass had become intimate friends and that they worked closely on the translation of *My Bondage and My Freedom*. In the course of the summer Assing's attitude toward the project changed dramatically. Her original approach had been determined by her political creed and her professional needs. She was annoyed at the paucity of sources from which the German public could learn about American slavery and racism. One choice was the political tract or scholarly treatise, many of them written by 48ers like Friedrich Kapp, Alfred Douai, Hans Kudlich, and Karl Heinzen,[40] but these were texts too abstract or sophisticated to attract and retain popular attention. Alternatively, there were Harriet Beecher Stowe's *Uncle Tom's Cabin* and other literary representations, which Assing disliked for what she considered their silly sentimentalism or equally sickening religiosity.[41] Douglass' *Narrative* and *My Bondage and My Freedom* were different. She would be the mediator between these texts and the German public. But her motives were not only idealistic: she needed money, a reliable income, if she wanted to continue her independent life in the United States. Teaching was one source, and up to a certain point she enjoyed tutoring children, yet this work had many drawbacks: a schedule that limited one's mobility, dependence on employers' whims, low pay. There was her contract with Cotta, to which she had added connections with the *Gartenlaube, Westermann's Monatshefte, Kompass*, and the *Hamburger Nachrichten*; but competition in journalism was fierce, with dozens of 48ers struggling to survive as foreign correspondents. In the slave narrative she had discovered a literary genre that had been neglected by her competitors. She could enhance her reputation as a translator and, even more desirable, would present herself as *the* authority on slavery and African-American life, as Germany's Negro expert.

For Assing, translating Douglass' autobiography was a gift of love she offered to the man whose magic realm she had begun to enter, and Douglass acknowledged and accepted it as such. "Her [Ottilie Assing's] interest in the Book and in the Cause it was designed to promote has led to an acquaintance and a friendship for which I have many reasons to be grateful,"[42] Douglass wrote a year later to her sister Ludmilla,* asking her help in soliciting a German publisher for the autobiography. He used both the neutral term "acquaintance" and the more intimate one "friendship," which Ludmilla would be sure to decipher in the proper way: she had written a biography of the German aristocrat Elisa von Ahlefeld, the title of which used "friend" to denote lover.[43] Translation was a transformational process, a joint venture, and that kind of professional and intellectual relationship for which one German scoffer had coined the term "double-gendered ink-beast."[44]

Ottilie had more to offer the Douglass household than her skills as a translator.[45] Ottilie Assing was a woman full of stories, and storytelling and performance came naturally to her. Her mother had left her with a legacy of German fairy tales and legends, with the Grimm tales, the Nibelungen, and the adventures of Rübezahl, the benevolent giant hero from Transylvania. There were stories about her family—the odyssey of her maternal family during the French Revolution, her father's war experience, his conversion, Rahel Levin's adventures, her own quest. There were ten years of age difference in the Douglasses' five children—in 1857 Rosetta was eighteen, Lewis seventeen, Frederick Jr. fifteen, Charles thirteen, and little Annie had just turned eight—but Ottilie would have stories for each of them. Like her mother, Ottilie did not just tell her stories: she performed them. She told her stories and begged for theirs, thus creating a choreography in which they learned to move toward each other and at times even together, each in her or his individual way. With her stories she sought to build a pathway into her hosts' hearts, inviting them to reimagine the white woman as the Miss Assing only they knew.

From storytelling it was only a small step to reading together. Assing was familiar with European literature, and thrilled to share it with anybody willing to listen. She and Douglass spent hours reading out loud together and discussing what they had read. And why not tap her knowledge of German? Playfully they took up their first lessons, their appetite increasing with every bite. Then there was music. Douglass loved to play the violin, but ever since Julia Griffiths' departure there had been nobody to accompany him. Assing not only was a tolerably good pianist, happily versed in the classics as well as in popular

---

*Ottilie resumed a more regular correspondence with her sister in the late 1850s. Possibly their long separation had softened her toward her sister; possibly she hoped Ludmilla would help her find a publisher for Douglass' autobiography. None of these letters was preserved.

tunes, but could even tune a piano. With her, music returned to the Douglass home. Storytelling, reading out loud, playing music—these were activities through which Assing reached out not just to Frederick Douglass but to his entire family.

She reached Douglass and the children, but Rosetta Douglass Sprague's memories of her mother suggest that Anna Murray remained aloof and reserved. In that summer of 1857 the wounds created by the Julia Griffiths scandal could not have yet healed, and now another European woman was invading her home. Anna Murray was suffering from bouts of rheumatism, from neuralgic attacks that distorted her face—and from bitter arguments with her husband. A letter of 17 April 1857 from Douglass to Mrs. Lydia Dennett, an acquaintance, amply documents the anger that erupted during this crucial period. Douglass obviously intended to strike a playfully ironic note, but the letter became a bitter, almost vicious diatribe against his wife.

> I am sad to say that she [Anna Murray] is by no means well—and if I should write down all her complaints there would be no room even to put my name at the bottom, although the world will have it that I am actually at the bottom of it all. She has the face . . . neuralgia. . . . She has suffered in every member except one. She still seems able to use with great ease and fluency her powers of speech, and by the time I am at home a week or two longer, I shall have pretty fully learned in how many points there are needs of improvement in my temper and disposition as a husband and father, the head of a family! Amid all the vicissitudes, however, I am happy to say that my wife gives me an excellent loaf of bread, and keeps a neat house, and has moments of marked amiability, of all of which good things, I do not fail to take due advantage.[46]

Small wonder if Anna Murray had to struggle to maintain even as much as a facade of politeness when Assing showed signs of settling on her territory.

In mid-August, Douglass left Rochester for an extensive lecture tour in Illinois and Wisconsin.[47] An article Assing wrote that fall suggests, however, that he made a brief detour to the Elgin Association in Buxton, Ontario, and that Ottilie Assing accompanied him.[48] During his stay in New York in May, Douglass had introduced Assing to Austin Steward, an ex-slave and businessman from Rochester, who had made his name as president of the all-black Wilberforce Colony in Ontario in the 1830s.[49] Steward had just written his account of the Wilberforce experience, and Assing may have felt that this might be another narrative she could translate; the history of this black colony might strengthen

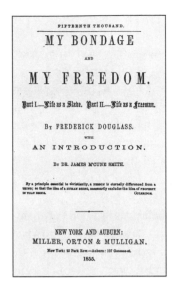

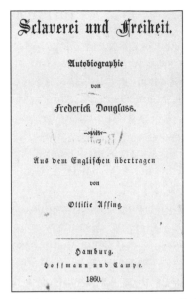

Frederick Douglass, *My Bondage and My Freedom* (1855), title page
In August 1856 Assing went to Rochester, New York, to interview Frederick Douglass, whose autobiography she had read. She hoped to interview the author and translate his text into German. Assing described his features as "striking": "the prominently domed forehead with a peculiarly deep cleft at the bridge of the nose, an aquiline nose, and the narrow, beautifully carved lips betray more of his white than of his black origins."

Frederick Douglass, *Sclaverei und Freiheit* (1860), title page of the German edition
Assing's translation of Douglass' book was published by the Hamburg publisher Hoffmann und Campe, together with a preface by Assing.

Rochester, New York
Rochester in the mid-1850s, as Ottilie Assing saw it when she arrived to interview Douglass. The Douglass mansion, she wrote, "located approximately half an hour away from the city on a hill and surrounded by a huge garden, has a peculiar poetic touch and is almost an island, a little world of its own . . ." No known picture of the house exists. The view in this picture is from the west.

her argument that free African-Americans, if only given a chance, were well able to fend for themselves. But Steward's *Twenty-two Years a Slave, and Forty Years a Freeman*, published in 1857, was a discourse on shattered hopes: for years the black pioneers of this colony, many of them people escaping from racial violence that had erupted in Cincinnati in 1829, had struggled to subdue the wilderness, but the odds against them—racism, corrupt agents, lack of farming experience, internal strife—could not be overcome. In 1838, Steward, who had joined this utopian venture in 1831, gave up and returned to Rochester a broken man.

Douglass knew that the Wilberforce experiment was only one of many similar ventures, some of which were more promising. Assing wanted to visit such a community, and Douglass may have suggested either that he arrange for such a visit or, since he was going west anyway, that he make a detour to Buxton, Ontario, if she was willing to join him. Buxton, situated in the peninsular area between Niagara and Detroit, was a village thirty miles southwest of Chatham, a terminal of the Underground Railroad in Canada[50] and only three miles from Lake Erie; it had been settled in the 1840s by fifteen ex-slaves brought from Louisiana to Canada by their former "master," a Presbyterian minister named William King, who had manumitted the slaves and bought a large tract of land which he divided up into parcels of fifty acres each. Each ex-slave received a parcel, the purchase price of which she or he had to pay on installment over ten years; they had to build their own houses, purchase their own farm implements, and provide for their families without further assistance. In 1857, the community consisted of 200 families and 2,000 people, each family living in a house they owned. It boasted two schools, a church, a post office, a potash factory, a sawmill, workshops, and stores. Most of the forest had been cleared and turned into farmland.[51]

Frederick Douglass had always been a fierce opponent of anything that smacked of colonization or of any kind of black separatism,[52] but he had been impressed with what he saw of Buxton when he first visited it in 1854. As the Chatham *Western Planet* paraphrased Douglass' remarks then, he

> was proud of his race to-day, when on visiting the Elgin Association, at Buxton, he saw men, women and children, who, but a short time ago, were under the rod of the slave driver, engaged in the peaceful and noble pursuit of agriculture, settled down on their own estates, administering to their own comforts, and growing in intelligence and wealth. The efficiency of their common school where the higher branches of education are taught, and eagerly acquired, did his heart good, and filled him with hopes for the future.[53]

In the fall of 1857, Assing published a detailed account of this trip in the German journal *Die Gartenlaube*. Assing frequently mentioned in letters to German friends and Ludmilla that she wrote for *Die Gartenlaube* and *Westermann's Monatshefte*, but as both journals published many articles anonymously and no author lists survived, it is difficult to authenticate them. Still, a stylistic analysis of "Eine Negerkolonie" and references to other Canadian trips that Assing made in later letters and articles point to her as the author of this text. As in her report on her Mount Washington and St. Lawrence excursions, she used "us" and "we" without identifying her traveling companion. A coachman of Irish descent, but, Assing remarked, curiously a Quaker, drove her and her escort thirty miles from Chatham to Buxton, over bumpy dirt roads in a dense forest. Then "well-kept farmhouses" appeared on both sides of the road, and they met people, "some in long carts, packed with men and women, some in one or two horse carriages, once a Negro woman on horseback with a boy of eleven or twelve sitting behind her." They were directed to the home of a Reverend King, who offered to show them the village. True, Assing later reported, the mastermind of this settlement was a white man, and its administration was still in the hands of the Elgin Association, a legally incorporated stock company, but, she continued, King gave advice only when asked for it. Regulations of daily life rested with the settlers, who elected representatives to community committees. The wilderness was subdued, the settlement prospered, it knew neither crime nor alcoholism nor illegitimate births. The ex-slaves themselves had made this miracle happen:

> Most of the settlers are fugitive slaves, and one-third of them are of pure African descent . . . those among them who were used to farming and had some money . . . quickly prospered; during the same time and under the same conditions they cultivated more land and made more improvements than the great majority of white settlers. Those who had neither skills nor money fared worse, but even those paid their installments promptly . . . Many already paid their debts in full and received their title deeds, others are about to do so next year, and Mr. King assured us that at the end of the ten years everybody will be owners of their land.[54]

The community that Assing wrote about was not an arcadia. The houses were "new, raw, and bulky," the roads rough and narrow, and everywhere traces of wilderness were still visible, but each house had a vegetable garden, and flowers and vines proved that proud owners were making efforts to beautify their property.

Assing wrote that she visited several homes: one owned by ex-slaves who had arrived in Buxton two years before; one belonging to a man who had escaped from Missouri fourteen years before, in 1843; and finally that of one of the first settlers; progress was described from the newly arrived pioneers, in their rough but clean log cabins, to the successful citizen whose spacious home boasted carpets, sofas, and even pictures on the walls. The emphasis of her report was on her own response to the encounters, not the feelings and thoughts of the objects of her gaze. Assing was enthusiastic, for again she could report black success: "We saw only a small, and, as we were told, the newest part of the settlement, which was not yet properly cultivated. Despite Mr. King's friendly invitation we could not extend our visit, and we left Buxton convinced that the colony is a brilliant refutation of the allegations which the friends of slavery make against the intellectual faculties of the black race." Buxton, she claimed, was definitely one "of the most interesting places a traveler can visit in North America."[55] Assing and her companion returned to Chatham that same day, where their roads parted.

The articles she sent to Germany document that the winter of 1857–58 was crucial for Ottilie Assing. The intensity with which she now reported on Douglass and his activities suggests not only that she was deeply and passionately in love with him but that her love was reciprocated. Even though she must have realized that his role as a race leader would make it almost impossible for him to desert his family to live with a white woman, she wanted to be with him and, she assumed, he with her. Eager and determined to commit herself to Frederick Douglass, she spent her long winter months reconsidering her relationship to the United States, thus initiating the long and tedious process of transforming herself from a European visitor into a German-American, and she struggled for definitions of self in her relationship to the man she loved. It was a process of transformation that did not come easy. She was still too full of European culture and class biases to perceive herself as an American, and the fact that her guide to America was black and married did not make things easier. An article in the *Morgenblatt* which she wrote in February 1858 illustrates that during the winter of 1857–58 the self she needed to construct began to take shape.

In early January 1858 the sophisticated New York public heard the announcement that Lola Montez would be lecturing on "beautiful women." Lola Montez was the stage name of Eliza Dolores Gilbert, daughter of a Creole woman and a Scottish officer, born in Limerick, Ireland, in 1818. Posing as a Spanish dancer and actress, this striking beauty had affairs with Franz Liszt and

Alexandre Dumas (*père*), and she achieved international notoriety when, in the 1840s, she became the mistress of King Ludwig I of Bavaria, a married man and father of nine children. She forced the king to acknowledge her as his lover, and she tried to use the power she had over him to push for political reforms in Bavaria and to curb the influence of the Catholic Church. When Ludwig made her Countess of Landsfeld in 1847, his cabinet resigned, and the scandal led to Montez' expulsion from Bavaria and Ludwig's abdication in 1848.[56] Montez then resumed her career as a dancer and launched a new one as a lecturer, cashing in on her fame as a royal concubine. In December 1851 she had come to New York for the first time, where she acted in plays that dramatized her European adventures, then took her show to Boston.

Assing went early to make sure she would get a seat in the front.[57] By the time Montez arrived, the lecture hall was packed, and many stood outside, hoping to at least catch a glimpse of the notorious femme fatale through the open door. Assing's report makes clear that mere journalistic curiosity had lured her, but she found a heroine. Writing for an audience familiar with the dancer's scandalous past, Assing had no need to refer to it. She simply represented Montez as a woman who united beauty, intelligence, rhetorical skills, rebelliousness, and a healthy sense of humor—that is, as a woman who, instead of denying her past, embraced it creatively.

Lola Montez, a notorious scarlet woman, may seem an unlikely choice of soul mate for the bourgeois intellectual and professional woman Ottilie Assing, yet a number of parallels between the two women's lives suggest the reasons for Assing's sympathy. Lola Montez was not a great actress, but she was quintessentially of the theater. And she challenged people to accept her on her own terms—shocking them with her aggressive display of her sexuality, carrying and using a whip, when necessary. It is obvious that Ottilie Assing was captivated by the performance quality of Montez' life, by the ease and brilliance with which this woman invented identity. Like Ottilie, she chose her man regardless of conventional notions of decency; she staged her liaison as a public performance with herself in the title role as the invincible lover, as Domina: when Montez began her affair with Ludwig I, she refused to be his secret mistress. She was there, for everybody to see, to admire, to fear; she forced the king to travel openly with her, to entertain guests with her as mistress of his table, to not only acknowledge her publicly as his concubine but to proclaim himself her lover and subject. She was more than the "other woman" in his life, more than a figure who ruled in the bed: while Germany drifted toward revolution in 1848, she enticed the monarch to revive progressive ideas on freedom of the press, on civil rights, on the emancipation of the farming population, on freedom of trade, which he had entertained as a young prince. Her opposition to the dominance of the Catholic Church and especially against the influence of Jesuits on Bavarian public life made her a heroine among liberals, and naturally also for Assing. Neither immorality nor scandal had forced this powerful woman out of Germany, Assing argued; like Ottilie Assing, it was the courage of her convictions, her integrity, on the one hand, and the hypocrisy of the establishment, a reactionary political system, the cowardice of her fellow citizens, on the other, that enticed her to seek new horizons. Lola Montez was not an exile, Assing maintained; she was a proud citizen of the world.

The first bridge that Assing built between herself and Montez in her report for the *Morgenblatt* was that of age. She had just celebrated her thirty-ninth birthday: a married woman her age would be called a matron; she was a spinster. Pretty soon it would be an old spinster, and she trembled in anger and fear at the thought of the ridicule that came with this title. Her body, her mind, the way she moved, the way people looked at her, Douglass' affection—all of these sent signals to her that being no longer young was not identical with being old. She had arrived at that precious and powerful stage in a woman's life when the insecurities, the not-yet-me adolescent, were left behind but the potential feebleness, the no-longer-me old woman, was still in the future. "There is much controversy over the actual age of this famous magician, but whatever it may be, one thing is certain: if she is no longer in the bloom of first youth, hers is the glow of youth's second being, which at times and for some tastes has an even greater fascination." "Magician" was a word usually reserved for Douglass. "The fire in her eyes, the lure of her smile, the graceful suppleness of her appearance amply compensate for whatever she may lack in conventional beauty; and one does not have to be a man to understand this whole 'Lola commotion,' especially because everything about her bears the stamp of intelligence and talent." Traces of the coquette, which Assing identified in a too short and too richly embroidered gown, far from appearing ridiculous, rather suggested a mature woman's eroticism, as her gentle reference to "the daintiest little foot that has ever been too vain to hide beneath the folds of a fashionable long robe" reveals.

Assing granted that Lola Montez' lecture contained nothing that was new, original, or relevant about "beautiful women," but what she said was offered "with such evident good humor, freshness, and wit, she seasoned with so much zest and imagination that she was amusing and fascinating from beginning to end. The audience expressed its gratification with loud applause and repeated demands for curtain calls." This woman of a "peculiar gracefulness" made the best use of charms that seemed naturally hers, but showed her intelligence by adding skills she had acquired through training—those of performer, orator—a knowledge of English* "which even the strictest hairsplitter cannot fault." The notorious femme fatale was *femme forte*.

Montez was notoriously ruthless in dealing with her enemies, and this was a quality that Assing, too, had been accused of, especially by her relatives. The kind of life Montez chose for herself had exposed her "to all manner of viciousness and evil," Assing wrote, to people surrounded by "an aura of notoriety":

> It is a peculiar thing, this aura of personality. To those who know something of character, personality is more revealing than all the descriptions and judgments of others put together; hence, this notorious beauty impressed me as being not only much better than her reputation but perhaps even superior to many of those virtuous souls who unctuously cross themselves whenever her name is mentioned.

Assing's representation neither denied Lola Montez' past nor tried to transform her into a victim of adverse social circumstances. Rather, it was a powerful plea to accept her on her own terms, to focus on her achievement rather than on scandalmongering and gossip, to appreciate her skills, the courage of her convictions, and her beauty rather than moralizing over her weaknesses, if weaknesses they were. She reinvented Lola Montez so she had company in her loneliness as "the other woman." She was in the process of transforming stigma into a badge of honor.

In June 1858, shortly before starting out on her third summer excursion to Rochester, Ottilie Assing eagerly availed herself of yet another opportunity to take on the controversial issue of extramarital relationships. An article headlined "An Excommunication"[58] cleverly manipulated her liberal readers' appetite for rituals commonly associated with medieval Catholicism, with the Gothic, with dark sensationalism. Beginning by reminding them that the remnants of medieval prejudices and rituals could still be found in remote hamlets all over Europe, belittled as curiosities by the more enlightened and romanticized by those unaware that the Middle Ages were "raw, naked, barbaric," Assing suddenly turned not to some Spanish abyss but to a Baptist church in Williamsburg, a Brooklyn district, where, a few days before, a well-known

---

*Like her contemporaries, and even King Ludwig, Ottilie Assing did not know that Lola Montez, the "Spanish" beauty, was in reality Eliza Gilbert, born in Limerick, Ireland.

judge had been expelled from the congregation for "immoral conduct": "[Judge] Culver's improper relationship with two ladies, whose names were mercilessly publicized on this occasion, was the cause given by church representatives after a pretense of an investigation, at which the accused had not even been present," Assing reported. After her lectures on the detrimental effect of religion in the New World, Assing's readers were prepared for yet another example of mass bigotry; instead, her narrative took another surprise turn: the congregation had rebelled; the elders' decision

> like a bolt of lightning . . . struck the peace and quiet of thousands of honorable and well-respected church members, who were horrified at the thought of having their own illicit affairs of the heart exposed. "If the church were to exert so much control over the life of each of its members," it was generally said, "the churches in New York would soon be empty; for can any man—including church elders and preachers—withstand such trial by fire?"[59]

Instead of portraying Judge Culver and his ladies as innocent victims of religious zeal, she celebrated them as members of a happily sinning crowd! She described Culver as a representative man, respectable, full of vitality, sensuous; his religious commitments healthy and natural enough to enjoy other natural human drives.

As her report continued, she made it clear that the elders' charges against Erastus Dean Culver's "immorality" were only a pretext to ostracize the man for a crime which they regarded as unforgivable—his abolitionism. This was not his first appearance on the pages of *Morgenblatt*; in December 1857, Assing had lauded him as "the judge with an antislavery disposition"[60] because he had freed a fugitive slave from a New York prison, enabling him to escape to Canada. Now he paid a terrible price for his convictions. All of a sudden the two issues that had become central to Assing's own life—extramarital relationships and abolitionism—fell together; the private and the public merged. She reconnected her narrative with the medieval images she had conjured up at the beginning of her report: "Should there still be disciples of the actual Middle Ages—the raw, naked, barbaric Middle Ages—they don't exist in the old, aristocratic Europe with its remnants of the past, but they do in the new democratic America, in the land where progress is driven by steam."[61] The slaveholding South, it would seem, had become her new Gothic realm, the proslavery forces her New World Inquisitors—devoid of the assets of greatness, however, that characterized the Old World originals:

The cowardice and cunning of this church are unparalleled, except perhaps for some of the other churches in this land of piety. Too cowardly to risk offending the party in power by tolerating an ardent opponent in its own ranks, the church is also too cowardly to acknowledge its wickedness and so resorts to scandal. There was something awesome in the wrath of the popes in the Middle Ages; they did not hesitate to hurl their sentences of excommunication at emperors and kings, and the lowliest priest had the courage, based on the authority of his superiors, to challenge the worldly powers. But the slaveholding church, currying favor with the slave owners, proves its courage and spirit of revenge by acting against individuals who cannot damage either its influence or its financial interests.[62]

Once again Assing used an event she witnessed from a distance to deal with issues that confronted her in her most intimate realm. She created a community of lovers for herself, in the midst of whom she could move as just another woman. Awakening in her readers an awareness for the vast difference that existed between public and private morality was one essential side of her new mission as a journalist. Imagining a world in which she could love Frederick Douglass, the married black man and father, and still remain a lady to others, a lover among lovers, was the other, equally important side of it.

In the second week of May 1858 Frederick Douglass was back in New York City for the annual meeting of the American Abolitionist Society, the National Woman's Rights Convention, as well as a meeting at the Shiloh Presbyterian Church to protest segregation on the city's public transportation system. Wherever he spoke, Assing was in the audience. Once again it was convention time in New York City. Since her arrival, she had looked forward to this spring week of reformers, preachers, fanatics, and enjoyed observing the celebrity performances. Her reports on these events ran the gamut of responses—deep respect for the courage of the feminist and abolitionist Quaker Lucretia Mott or Wendell Phillips, dislike of the moralizing cowardice of the American Tract Society, which wept over the country's moral degeneration while defending slavery, ridicule of the Bloomer costume. She listened carefully, and learned a great deal about the United States from that odd mixture of instruction and entertainment which the conventions provided. And now the convention season had a new quality: it was the time in which Frederick Douglass came to New York City. There were meetings, lectures, receptions. But there were also spaces which Douglass could and did claim for himself, time he could set aside to be with Ottilie Assing. What created this space where a man as visible as Douglass could become invisible, where the public orator could transform himself into a private man, even a lover?

Segregation made it possible for Douglass to embrace a life removed from the white gaze. On his travels, while attending abolitionist meetings, every white participant knew that Douglass usually could not stay in the same hotel with them. Thus it was taken for granted that he would walk off by himself, with hardly anybody asking where he would find lodging for the night. The mobility Douglass thus gained as a result of segregation was enhanced by the innate racism and moral indolence among his acquaintances. To ask Frederick Douglass at the end of a day's meeting "Where are you heading?" might have provoked an answer that would have forced the "friend" to offer a bed in his home or that necessitated new protests, additional struggle. Wasn't attending abolitionist meetings and conventions exhausting enough? It was so much easier to part from him with a friendly "Good night" and to greet him in the morning with a jovial "Hope you had a good night's sleep." There was space and privacy for Assing and Douglass in this philistine attitude.

During the convention week in May 1858 Douglass was in greater demand than ever, for this year the reformers were facing more than just another week of speechmaking. Pennington's case was still pending.[63] In 1855 Douglass had supported Pennington with a fervent denunciation of the American caste system: "What a commentary is this shameful outrage upon the institutions of free, humane, enlightened and Christian America!" he had thundered in his paper:

> Boasting and ranting about Freedom and Equality, the American people, as a whole, are the most inconsistent, and the most tyrannical people, the sunlight ever revealed to the gaze of men or of devils. Caste is the god the nation delights to honor. Caste is in their preaching, their singing and their praying. They talk about the caste of the Hindu, while they out-Hindu, in the development of this insatiate and malignant spirit, every nation under heaven. This spirit follows us by day and by night. It follows us at every step.[64]

Now, on 11 May, a protest meeting was scheduled at Pennington's former church, the Shiloh Presbyterian Church on Prince Street, and Douglass was invited to give the keynote address. As expected, he drew a large crowd.

Assing's report on this meeting shows that a new realism had made its way into her interpretation of race matters. Once, the big audience might have convinced her that more and more Americans were opening their eyes to the dangers of racism and slavery. Now she could see that many came not necessarily to support the abolitionist cause but to be entertained by the nation's most powerful orator, the black lion of the season. Curiosity rather than a sense of justice motivated them. In fact, the chances for victory in this campaign were almost nil, for the Supreme Court had just declared that African-Americans possessed no rights that whites were required to respect, Assing told her readers. It was the kind of argument against segregation, racial violence, slavery she had been making for years. Yet this time around she added a note that showed to what degree her relationship with Douglass had sharpened her perceptive faculties. In his article of 1855 on the Pennington case Douglass had bitterly attacked the Garrisonians, whose silence on the events he interpreted as approval of the segregation practices, and Assing now struck the same note: the situation is almost hopeless, she went on, "for even among the decided foes of slavery there are only few who would rise with lively interest on behalf of the free Negroes of the North; and whether blacks are allowed to ride in the cars on Sixth Avenue is, for most, a matter of such indifference that they would not bestir themselves."[65] The only solution she could envision—and she never stepped back from this position—lay within the African-American communities and the power they could muster under the leadership of the man whose exceptional qualities for her were a promise to the future of the race: "The magnet [which made so many people follow the rallying call] was Frederick Douglass," she wrote. "This excellent speaker knows how to electrify and captivate his audience. Something like a personal relationship develops between him and the listeners and elicits their undivided sympathy, letting them experience the magic of amiability that wins the heart of everyone who is fortunate enough to meet this vibrant and noble man."[66] The text that began as a report on a civil rights rally culminated in a public declaration of love for Frederick Douglass. In a public text Assing spoke of the magnetic eroticism that had pulled her into Douglass' magic circle, the charm and kindness that kept her there.

Yet "captivate" also implies captivity, bondage, finding yourself in a situation in which you are deprived of mobility. The term suggests that she sensed her precarious position. The metaphor associates maleness with power and activity, the listening woman as passive receiver, responding to his magnetism.

Once again, Ottilie Assing spent the summer in Rochester, not just four weeks, as in 1857, but more than two months. She made a brief stop in Schenectady in late June, visiting for a few days with Amalie Schoppe, who was suffering from a severe heart condition; her partial paralysis kept her housebound. As always, they talked literature, exchanged gossip and memories, chatted about Alphons' career and Assing's life in New York City—anything but that which Assing needed most urgently to articulate. For a few days Assing managed the conversation as a choreography of avoidance and silences, which made her sad as well as aggressive. It was with relief that she left Schenectady as soon as politeness permitted. When Amalie Schoppe died of heart failure on 30 September, Ottilie Assing wrote her obituary for the *Hamburger Nachrichten*.[67]

As she boarded the train for Rochester in August 1857, Ottilie Assing could still claim she had professional reasons for needing Douglass' help in the translation of his autobiography. Also, would any good journalist miss the chance of spending time with the country's most famous orator? Would any liberal European correspondent turn down an offer to observe black life from within a black family? This time around, however, everything was different. Ottilie Assing was taking this trip because above everything in the world she wanted to be with Frederick Douglass.

It turned out to be a quiet summer, with only a few guests stopping at the Douglass home, and with the exception of a brief trip to Pennsylvania in mid-September, Douglass stayed home. This year he seemed less anxious to avoid the public gaze. The articles Assing sent to the *Morgenblatt* in the fall of 1858 document that they walked Mount Hope together and along the banks of the Genesee River; they made excursions to the countryside and took boat trips. People may have stared at them, perhaps not bothering to veil their disgust. Still, Assing's and Douglass' conduct suggests that the respect they had for each other was not compatible with the isolation they had imposed upon themselves. Hiding their relationship from the public gaze was an avowal that it was objectionable. If there was anything Ottilie Assing learned from her encounter with Lola Montez, it was that. Somewhere in that summer of 1858 it apparently became clear to them that theirs was more than an exciting affair. They realized that what they felt for each other was worth cultivating and maturing, and they could not achieve this if they continued to stay in hiding. It was time to take that plunge from the top of the cliff; if they were lucky, they would grow wings on their way down!

On 19 August the streets of Rochester were packed with jubilant citizens celebrating the successful operation of the first transatlantic cable, which made it possible to exchange telegraph messages between the Old World and the New. People all over the United States had been tense with apprehension when Queen Victoria's cablegram to President Buchanan was delayed, but when it arrived strangers hugged each other in the streets, and stump orators sang the praises of the new technology. The Douglasses and Assing were in the crowd that cheered what Ottilie thought was a ludicrously small and bombastic parade down Main Street. A miniature cannon, placed on a bridge to fire salutes, blew up, which sent a wave of terror through the crowd, but nobody was hurt and the festivities continued into the night. Two tar barrels were set on fire and rolled down the street, and boys shot off firecrackers everywhere. Assing watched in amused fascination. "The American people certainly are anything but blasé," she wrote condescendingly, "and I have to admit that even children cannot be pleased and enthralled like these large masses."[68] It was late when the Douglasses got home. Then, in the middle of the night, strange noises from the city roused them: sparks from firecrackers had set straw on fire, and now the entire Minerva Block, the center of the business district, was going up in flames. Fierce rivalries between volunteer fire companies impeded the efforts to quench the fire, and the next morning the people of Rochester mourned destruction and damage amounting to almost $190,000, the most the city had ever suffered.[69] It was an anxious night in the house up on the hill, for Douglass feared that the flames might damage his office and precious printing press; they worried about the safety of friends. They were lucky: none of their friends was hurt, and Douglass' office and press remained unscathed.

Ottilie Assing had finished the translation of *My Bondage and My Freedom* during the winter of 1857–58; in mid-July she sent the manuscript off to Varnhagen and Ludmilla, accompanied by the letter from Douglass to her sister in which he asked for her support in finding a German publisher. Douglass' letter was deferential, but it was also remarkably candid in describing his relationship with Ottilie. In his references to their conversations and correspondence—which, he said, had long gone beyond the professional exchange of information—and by using the plural "we" ("what we want"), he suggested the intimacy that was theirs as a result of "her passionate interest" in him and his cause: "Through her kind and sisterly representation of you in letters and conversations, I feel it safe to approach you less as a stranger than as a friend,"[70] he wrote. This letter, along with the letters Ottilie Assing wrote to friends and family in Germany during this period, document that she began to speak openly about her liaison with Douglass in the summer of 1858.

During her summer in Rochester, Ottilie also put the finishing touches on the six-page preface, substantial passages of which she had written and sent off to Cotta as early as 1856. In this *Vorrede* and in an article of June 1858 for the *Morgenblatt*, Assing gave her readers her most elaborate Douglass portrait. She knew that the German public had been inundated with many sentimental renderings of slavery, with soapy Uncle Toms and ridiculous Topsy replicas flooding the European book market after the commercial success of *Uncle Tom's Cabin*. "Were this life story fiction, artistic invention, one would have to deplore that it was not published a few years earlier, before the interest in such narratives had been exhausted by the almost countless representations of slave life that now, since the publication of the famous *Uncle Tom*, have developed into a whole new branch of literature." But she believed that her readers "can stand the truth," "naked, unadorned, terrifying facts":

> Instead of an imagined hero, it is the author himself who is at the center of the events narrated: he actually lived these experiences, and he is now living among us, one of America's famous men . . . It is the whole human being—the noble self, the passionate, spirited, gifted, and dynamic man with the burning love of freedom and the virtuosity of implacable hatred of slavery and slavemasters—who steps from these pages in his irresistible attractiveness and distinction to meet the reader.[71]

Whereas her first (and unpublished) article on Douglass for the *Morgenblatt* had focused on the private individual, the preface introduced the reader to the public Frederick Douglass. Assing's respect for the author's intellectual autonomy showed in her refusal to play the role of mediator between the author and the reader. No commentary on the narrative was needed, she told her readers, for it was "the most faithful expression of his individuality." But she could and did speak of one of his qualities that could not be expressed in the autobiography and that she considered central—his skills as an orator:

> The reader will get to know all his qualities . . . except for his brilliance as an orator, which is the basis of his current renown. In this country of great orators, Frederick Douglass is one of the greatest. Perfect mastery of the subject, incisive and brilliant logic, and controlled moderation despite all passion are his hallmark. He often soars to tragic heights but then illuminates his subject with brilliant flashes of wit, speaks to his listener's heart, or provides comic relief with a joke. Everything is fresh, original, and compelling, and all these attributes are underscored by a perfect mastery of language and by so mellifluous, sonorous, flexible a voice speaking to the heart as I have ever heard.

The voice that emerged from these pages was the voice of seduction, a sexual signifier as well as an intellectual challenge.

For Ottilie Assing, Douglass was the perfect orator, uniting exceptional talent and exceptional skills with the power of a visionary. This harmonious interplay of talent, skill, and vision explained his enormous popularity everywhere:

> In every town and village of the northern United States the mere announcement of his name is enough to fill the halls to the last remaining seat. Although he addresses

it every year, I have seen the demanding public of New York thrilled and swept
away by him as if a new apostle had revealed to them for the first time a truth which
had lain unspoken in everyone's heart.

Like the apostles of old, Douglass knew the truth, and he had the gift of freeing
those who heard him from their moral paralysis, their comfortable intellectual
lethargy. The true leader may soar high above the crowd, she suggested, yet he
carries the masses forward and upward with him.

A few months later Assing elaborated on greatness and leadership when introducing her *Morgenblatt* readers to another famous orator of the day, Henry
Ward Beecher, pastor of Plymouth Church in Brooklyn. Every Sunday, hundreds made the pilgrimage to his church to hear him preach, and he was one of
the most highly paid speakers on the lecture circuit.[72] Are we surprised that
Ottilie Assing took a good look at him—and found him wanting? What she
deplored most was not, as might be expected, Beecher's religion but his "medi-
ocrity," for no matter how brilliant his rhetoric, he lacked vision and thus that
true quality of leadership which came so naturally to Douglass. "Beecher is not
a man who dominates and reforms his times and environment, as his admirers
claim," she observed. "Quite to the contrary, he is their product because he ac-
commodates himself to them, makes concessions and carefully avoids confronting them too harshly." A man firmly and comfortably rooted in a rather
lucrative here and now, the white minister of Assing's invention invited his audience to doze in the sun:

> Beecher knows the intellectual lethargy of the masses; he knows that they hate
> nothing more than to be shaken out of their mental torpor and asked to think for
> themselves. Thus he manages to offer his ideas attractively and tidily wrapped and
> packaged so that one can comfortably accept them without danger of being chal-
> lenged by some unpleasant truth forcing one into irksome reflection.[73]

In contrast, Douglass' skills were not self-serving. He exhorted and challenged
where Beecher titillated; he roused people so as to liberate them. Douglass' exceptionality did not isolate him from the less gifted and privileged; he used his
capability and courage to empower others. He passed on the light to the unen-
lightened, thus helping them to grow and rise. He was working toward that
day when the now exceptional would be the common good, when he, the superior mind, would be joined by the brother- and sisterhood of the enlightened.
She invented Douglass as the exceptional man struggling to transform the exceptional into the representative.

As she presented him, Frederick Douglass was an ideal personification of the classical Western orator. This implicitly dissociated him from the black cultural tradition, from African-American oratory, which we have seen she did not fully understand or appreciate. Douglass had turned away from "the bellowing repetition of the same phrases," the "raving" and "moaning"[74] she so disliked in black preachers, by using techniques that only a select few in Europe and white America mastered. Her representation automatically related him to a respected European intellectual tradition, with the art of classic oratory, and thus with the exceptional. In associating him with the universal and the exceptional on the one hand, and on the other linking his classic oratory and the power and eroticism of his voice, she could attribute to him the title of genius defined in romantic terms. She not only challenged her readers to apply the criteria of white bourgeois society to the evaluation of her black protagonist, but also subverted the traditional dichotomy between civilization and nature, between the intellectual and the sexual.

The general effect of Assing's introduction was to appropriate Frederick Douglass for what she called the "true elite" of the human race, defined by "intellect, personal amiability, and purest character."[75] This uncritical adherence to a Western cultural concept gave her representation of him a hierarchical and narrowly Eurocentric perspective. Her portrait excluded any notion of plurality, of difference, of "the other." Still, as we have seen, she was also subverting the racial myth of the "impassable gulf," and by portraying him as the leader whose magic power drew others to him, she attributed a transitional and dynamic quality to the exceptional. Like Douglass, she oscillated between an egalitarian creed and belief in human progress on the one hand and worship of the exceptional on the other.

On 1 October 1858 Frederick Douglass was to address the annual meeting of the American Abolitionist Society in Syracuse, New York. Ottilie Assing went with him to Syracuse and then proceeded to New York. Another summer was over, but despite that "old feeling of something like homesickness"[76] which Assing experienced when leaving Douglass after a considerable time with him, both were happy in the realization that they had established a relationship which was important and good. Her articles of 1858 show that she worshipped Frederick Douglass as a unique man, and she loved herself as an exceptional woman. They and their liaison were special in every way, and she gloried in this exceptionality. The discourse she constructed to justify their conduct was unassailable in its circularity: her and Douglass' exceptionality freed them for and justified their actions, while their actions manifested and validated their exceptionality.[77] They were aristocrats of the human race, and as such they had not only the right but the duty to defy those norms that confined their average fellow citizens, those too weak to be laws to themselves and consequently forced to settle for conventionality.

It was a relationship that violated the age's most important ideological icons; it was Ottilie and Frederick's delicious secret—and they performed in bright daylight. They must have known that it was a secret only because the world around them chose to treat it as such.

V

THE I AND THE OTHER

Ottilie Assing and the Douglasses

She had forgiven all men, had forgiven the entire world, because she had found the one she loved! She no longer demanded revenge for her trampled past, for her murdered youth, love reconciled her with the world. . . . She was a fallen angel, but the longing for Paradise was alive in her, and she still dreamed that she could reach it yet. —CLARA MUNDT, *Aphra Behn*

My mistress had taught me the precepts of God's word: "Thou shalt love thy neighbor as thyself." "Whatsoever ye would that men should do unto you, do ye even so unto them." But I was her slave, and I suppose she did not recognize me as her neighbor. —HARRIET JACOBS, *Incidents in the Life of a Slave Girl*

*T*he basket was filled with pears almost to the point of spilling over. Instead of putting another fruit on top of the precariously high heap, Ottilie Assing tore off its stem with her teeth and took a big bite. She ate with the greatest relish—core, seeds, and all. She looked at her morning's harvest with a triumphant smile. These were plump, almost perfect fruit. Not quite perfect, though, for she had collected them from the grass. She slowly carried her heavy load toward the circle of shrubs halfway to the house, where she sat down on a bench in the sun. For a few minutes she hardly moved, just leaned back and let her eyes feed on the luscious scenery before her.

The orchard was on a hill, and from where she sat she had a nice view of the town, about half an hour's walk away. It was still very early; the sun had been up for only an hour and had not quite finished licking away the fog that clung to the grass. The air was pleasantly cool and clear, and the town's white church steeples contrasted beautifully with the blue sky above and the abundance of dark green trees below. Some day I should bring *out my watercolors and paint this, she reminded herself, but then laughed at the thought, for it always came to her when she sat on this bench, and every time she was too happy just looking to disrupt the peace of the morning, to ridicule the skills of Nature by trying to copy her. She spread her arms and legs and lay back her head. She let the sun warm her body although it was in no need of this embrace; there was warmth and joy in her still, and she knew they would stay with her all day.*

After a long time she reached beneath the bench and pulled out two big metal bowls. She began peeling the pears, carefully looking for worm holes and cutting out the bruises, slicing the fruit into small pieces. She placed the fruit in the clean bowl and covered it with a cloth dampened with vinegar; that way the pears would not turn brown—a trick her mother had taught her. Rosa Maria was on Ottilie's mind every time she went on her early morning gathering sprees. They had had only one pear tree in their miniature garden in the Poolstrasse, and its fruit had been so precious that not one was ever left to rot on the ground. How different now! In the midst of abundance her morning exercise seemed almost ridiculous, but then she had been taught never to waste food, and it was a habit with her. Her American friends tolerated her Old World ways with a smile, and so she gathered what they scorned, and filled the pantry with spicy preserves they loved—pears and apples with cinnamon, cloves, lemon peel. Today she would surprise them with a recipe her father had brought into the family from Königsberg: pear dumplings with a rich vanilla sauce. It was a perfect dish for a hot August day, and Douglass would love it, as would the children.

"May I join you?" It was Rosetta. Ottilie had not heard her light step on the grass, but a broad smile betrayed her joy at the interruption. Rosetta was a tall, slim young woman in her early twenties; she had her mother's huge brown eyes—"rehbraun," brown as a deer's, Ottilie called them—and abundant hair framing her delicate features. It was a pleasure to look at her in her morning freshness. Patting the place next to her on the bench, Ottilie invited her to sit down, waiting for her to speak first. "I could not sleep any more. Too hot," Rosetta began, although she wore the light shawl Ottilie had given her around her shoulders, and she tucked her naked feet, cold from the dewy grass, underneath her skirt. Ottilie nodded and took up her work again. They had read a few chapters from Charles Dickens' David Copperfield *the night before, and for a while memories of David's infatuation with his child wife kept them chuckling about men's self-proclaimed superiority. "I wish I could write like that," Rosetta sighed. "I wish you would write, and write like yourself," Ottilie affirmed encouragingly. "You know I like your compositions. You just need more practice." The young woman looked pleased, and pulling out a few sheets of folded papers, handed them to her friend. "Would you read them for me?" With a big smile Ottilie signaled her to put them into the pocket of her skirt, holding up her sticky hands as an excuse for not touching them. Then they heard*

the kitchen door up in the house opening and closing, and, although he could not see them where they sat, Douglass came toward the bench behind the shrubs as if he knew what he would find there. He was pleased to see the two women together. Rosetta wanted to get up, but he bent low to give her his morning kiss, and he and Ottilie exchanged a warm smile that needed no words and no touch. "Feeding the Douglasses again?" He nodded toward the bowl of fruit. "What are you planning for today?" Ottilie laughed and shook her head in promise of something good. "I have to do some work on the trees today," he suggested, and with the frivolous generosity of proprietorship accepted her offer of help. It would be a good day!

It was time to get back into the house. Ottilie threw an almost sad parting glance at the orchard. "No melancholy yet," Douglass warned her, briefly putting his arm around her and pulling her toward him. "Not even halftime." They picked up the bowls and the basket and, with Rosetta in front of them, walked toward the house. Anna Murray was in the kitchen preparing breakfast. She was busy cooking and did not turn when the three came through the back door and put the pears on the table, but there was an amiable greeting. Only when she saw that Rosetta was with them did a frown briefly cross her face. "Would you mind if I prepared some pear dumplings for supper?" Ottilie suggested. "A recipe from Silesia, good for a hot day." Anna Murray filled the coffeepot from the kettle. "Since when do you ask?" The routine of the day had begun. They would fill it with sunshine and laughter.

It is striking that in all the images of harmony and union she used in writing about her life with Douglass, Assing never mentioned race. In introducing him to her German readers she had identified Douglass as a mulatto, his wife as black, and his children as darker than the father. After that she never again referred to his race or color when talking about their intimate relationship. It was as if the issue did not exist between them, and yet it was there, silenced perhaps, but irrepressible; race was one defining element in their relationship.

Frederick Douglass married a black woman, strong, independent, and devoted as his mother, Harriet Bailey, and grandmother, Betsy Bailey, had been. All the women with whom he was known or suspected to associate intimately in his adult life during his marriage—Julia Griffiths, Ottilie Assing, Helen Pitts—were white women who displayed the same qualities: strength, independence, and devotion. Douglass was not attracted to the Victorian ideal of the submissive child wife, the bloodless, languishing beauty; he embraced what he himself represented: vitality and power. Scholars have focused on the differences of class, race, and color among "his" women, but one must not lose sight of the equally important features those women shared. Yet in addition to these common characteristics the white women offered something only few black women would have been able to give in antebellum America: education and refinement according to white bourgeois norms, norms which Douglass affirmed as his personal ones. These were assets with an erotic magnetism for Douglass. The way these women moved, talked, thought, dressed, the letters they wrote, their professionalism, the sophisticated assurance with which they conducted themselves in public, their self-confidence seemed to arouse his interest. These qualities were so important for him that he hired a white woman, the Quaker Phebe Thayer,[1] as a tutor for his daughter, hoping that the social skills she taught would empower Rosetta to enter as a self-confident equal the social realm her mother shunned.

Douglass was surrounded with enamored white women of this class wherever he traveled, and his interest in them and their obvious enjoyment of his presence both fascinated and shocked his contemporaries, as it continues to occupy his biographers. The observations of the "white woman phenomenon" in Douglass' life which William S. McFeely offered in his biography of 1991 is typical. "There was, and is, much prurient speculation—not always devoid of racism—about the sexual component of Douglass' friendship with white women, and lurking within are fantastic images of a not-so-noble savage turned gleaming black beast and proving fatally attractive to pale virgins anxious to yield their chastity to some imagined hugeness." But, McFeely goes on,

> such damp reveries do not fit. Douglass was not black enough to gleam, even if he had wanted to, and it is exceedingly hard to imagine the resolutely dignified Victorian gentleman ever trying. What is at least as much to the point, all of the women in question were intellectuals living long before . . . Western science codified Africans as animals . . . swinging low on the human tree. When he had left the Freeland farm . . . Frederick Bailey had left behind a certain kind of physicality. . . . Douglass soon put on the proper clothes of the bourgeois gentleman he had elected to be. That these clothes made the body they hid more mysterious and compelling was no doubt true, but his attractiveness must be understood in terms of the mores of his world. If he was a man proud of his ability to draw emotional attention to what he had to say, he was also a man of discipline—a Darwin or a Palliser, rather than a Byron or a Heathcliff. The path of some of his friendships may have led to a bed, but it is difficult to imagine him springing upon it in wanton randiness. Douglass' undeniable sexuality was no less compelling for being made to smolder within well-tailored wool, tidied by crisp linen.[2]

The combination of gender and racial politics, of race, gender, and sexuality creates an explosive potion, indeed.[3] Memories of denunciations of black men as potential rapists of pure white women, of racist slurs, of lynchings,[4] on the one hand, celebrations of black womanhood that transform a black man's relationship with a white woman into an act of treason, on the other; racial phobias and nationalist affirmation; finally the legitimate fear that another black icon might be felled, another hero lost, another black narrative deconstructed are powerful, and it is difficult to approach our story in a direct line. They influence the way we perceive our subject, and we must face them as dynamic components of the narrative.

It is likely that Frederick Douglass' relationship to black and white women was influenced by his childhood experiences. He barely knew his mother, who worked on another plantation and came to see him only at infrequent intervals and at night. And then Harriet Bailey died before he was old enough to relate to her in a more substantial, knowing way. No matter what her predicaments were, the child could not help blaming her for what he may well have suffered as a desertion. His grandmother gave him the emotional nourishment and cultural knowledge his mother had been barred from giving, but Betsy Bailey, too, was forced to betray the boy's trust: when her master ordered her to deliver up his property to him, she had to obey. Was an unconscious resentment of these black mothers being expressed when, upon reaching the free North, he "self-consciously and ironically abandoned a strong matrilineal black heritage of five stable generations"?[5] Small wonder that a lonely boy, starved for affection, would not forget the pitiably few acts of kindness that his master-father's daughter, his half sister Lucretia Auld, extended to him; small wonder also that he loved Sophia Auld, his relatively benign mistress in Baltimore, as a surrogate mother. These white women figured prominently in a text characterized by the voicelessness of victimized black women.[6] When writing his *Narrative* only six years after his escape from slavery, Frederick Douglass' memories of these episodes were still raw, and his perspective fresh enough to express his emotions straightforwardly. In his rewriting of his life in the mid-1850s and as an elder statesman in the 1880s, his representations of Harriet and Betsy Bailey changed: he softened the edges of his first harsh account by celebrating love and loyalty in the midst of violence and violation. The mature Douglass began to understand the women's predicaments. But the new mother personae he created in his later works were also affected by his exposure to feminist discourse, his realization that his almost exclusive focus on the destruction of family bonds, the absence of filial affection, the pathology and deprivation of the slave family, which dominated the *Narrative*, potentially subverted his political mission. Reconceptualizing the black woman was an act of rational insight, of political expediency, of calculation, but did it soften the pain of desertion and betrayal that continued to linger beneath the surface? It seems not, for the mother he reinvented in *Life and Times of Frederick Douglass* was based on an illustration from Prichard's *Natural History of Man*—that is, as Peter Walker has suggested, on a picture of "a princely man" who "may have been white."[7] It seems not, when we consider the position in which he portrayed himself when describing his aunt Hester's flogging, as Jenny Franchot argues in her analysis of this scene, frozen in the "stasis of that observer, caught between the two 'races.' "[8]

In his second autobiography, *My Bondage and My Freedom*, Douglass maintained that by entering the abolitionist movement and becoming its most powerful orator he was finally able to emancipate himself from everything he associated with slavery: "For a time I was made to forget that my skin was dark and my hair crisped."[9] Many Douglass biographers like Quarles, Foner, and Huggins have accepted as truth his fiction of self that has him emerging from slavery unscathed and ready to take up the fight, piously translating this passage into an assertion that he donned his slave personality to assert his full manhood. As Walker argues, they "have all meant to portray the fugitive slave making his way in a white free society, either as the courageous paterfamilias of a race, showing American Negroes the way toward a secure and equal place in that society, or as revolutionary prophet carrying a message not only of racial equalitarianism but also of a militant racial class consciousness."[10] More recent readings, however, suggest that Douglass was haunted by slavery and racism, that his almost obsessive search for his lost paternity, the rewritten versions of his mother, his successive fictions of self reveal that he was torn between two races, tortured by his double consciousness of being both and neither. Seen from this perspective, his desire "to forget that my skin was dark and my hair crisped" can indeed be read as a denial of his mother's blackness and an expression—confirmed by the shedding of his mother's name in exchange for that of a fictional character who lost and regained his paternity—of his ultimate longing for an identification with his father's whiteness, and his love of white women as allowing him to claim as his the territory from which his father-master had exiled him. He reclaimed a manhood, a virility, a self which, given the "racist, sexist, and elitist assumptions upon which [this] Angle-American [sic] male ideal was constructed,"[11] he could only perceive as white, his rhetoric of black heroism notwithstanding.

Ottilie Assing's conduct in relation to Douglass and his family, the frankness with which she introduced him to her colleagues and friends in Hoboken, the enjoyment she drew out of public appearances with him, as well as her letters to Douglass, Ludmilla, and other acquaintances, suggest that she felt no compunctions at having a liaison with a married man. She believed that the Douglass marriage had been over long before she entered the scene, and in a way she was right. Douglass hinted at marital problems in letters to friends, describing himself in 1848, for example, as a "most unhappy man."[12] It was easy, almost natural for Assing to conclude this, for, much to the Douglasses' chagrin, the story of their marriage and their marital problems could have almost been called public property when Assing arrived in Rochester.

Anna Murray and Frederick Bailey met in Baltimore between 1836 and 1838, when Frederick was a slave in the service of Hugh Auld. He had talked his master into being allowed to provide for himself, and was relatively free with his leisure time. He liked to spend his evenings at the East Baltimore Mental Improvement Society, a benevolent association of free blacks devoted to education and self-elevation;[13] although slaves could not be members, they made special concessions to the ambitious and bright caulker, who had taught himself to read and write and who immediately impressed them by his rhetorical skills and his personal courage. It was here he met Anna Murray, the first of five freeborn children of Bambarra and Mary Murray (they had seven other children who had been born in slavery). Anna worked as a domestic servant in the home of Baltimore's postmaster, Mr. Wells, on South Carolina Street. She was seven years older than Frederick, a woman with a reputation as an excellent housekeeper and a passionate aversion to slavery, for both of which Frederick admired her. She was tall and strong, with features like her straight black hair that, some biographers claim, suggested a Native American ancestry. She was impressed by Frederick's hunger for learning, gave him books, and encouraged him to take violin lessons. The two fell in love, but Frederick, who had been determined to escape from slavery since his early childhood, decided that he would marry only as a free man.

On 3 September 1838 the twenty-year-old slave disguised himself as a sailor and, with Anna's assistance and the papers of a free seaman, boarded a ship that took him to the free North. A week after his arrival in New York, Anna joined him, and on 12 September they were married by the Reverend Pennington. The couple made their home in New Bedford, Massachusetts, living in two rented rooms on Elm Street, overlooking Buzzards Bay. Here their first four children, Rosetta (1839), Lewis Henry (1840), Frederick Jr. (1842), and Charles (1844) were born. As Houston Baker has shown, Douglass understood "the necessity for *individual* wage earning"[14] for a free married man, yet his attempts to make a living as a caulker were defeated when white shipyard workers refused to work with a black man. In desperation he took every job he could get, but the rapidly growing family could survive only because Anna Murray also worked for wages. She acquired such an excellent reputation as a domestic servant that families employed her despite her own family obligations, and when she could not leave the house she took in washing. She was a strong, determined partner, and there was all the loyalty and support imaginable, but little romance in their life together. Little in their past or present encouraged notions of romantic love—perhaps only a luxury for the leisured classes. The feelings that bound Anna Murray and Frederick together were defined by their daily struggle for bread, the demands of their growing family, their apprehensions of racial discrimination and violence, and their nagging fear of Frederick's reenslavement.

One difference between them, the significance of which only increased as time went on, was there from the beginning: Anna Murray was illiterate, and Douglass regarded their self-emancipation as incomplete so long as his wife had not freed herself from what he perceived as intellectual bondage. For Douglass, literacy had been the road to freedom, the means through which he intended to succeed as a free man, and he wanted and needed his wife to accompany him on this road. Like most people of the time, he equated illiteracy with ignorance, and took literacy to be the only reliable means of acquiring knowledge: "Education means emancipation," he would insist to the very end of his life. "It means light and liberty. It means the uplifting of the soul of man into the glorious light of truth, the only light by which men can be free. To deny education to any people is one of the greatest crimes against human nature. It is to deny them the means of freedom and the rightful pursuit of happiness, and to defeat the very end of their being."[15] For a while Anna was so busy that her reluctance to learn to read and write could be explained away. The problem, however, was that Douglass soon felt that he was leaving his wife behind. She seemed unwilling to participate in his intellectual pursuit. Communication between husband and wife became increasingly difficult.

The tension was exacerbated when in 1841 Douglass joined the Garrisonians and was hired as a lecturer. The abolitionists immediately recognized his oratorical gifts and the contribution he could make to the cause, and very soon they sent him on speaking tours throughout the North. As Douglass was "heroically ascending freedom's arc," Anna Murray stayed behind "taking care of the children," as Mary Helen Washington explains.[16] As he found his voice, his wife was locked into domesticity and silence. Within a year he was at the center of every abolitionist event, traveling to conventions, speaking at churches and private meetings, being lionized and reviled. He read voraciously; he met members of many classes of society, and found himself conversing with university professors and novelists, feminists and ministers, philosophers and bankers. When he came home, he was full of stories and new ideas, felt he had the world in the palm of his hand. Anna turned every homecoming into a special event, but she could talk only of the same old setting—children, work, neighbors. They had no way to communicate when he was away, sometimes for weeks; she could not tell him if she was lonely, if she felt alone in her bed at night, if the sole responsibility for their children and the need to earn money was too much for her, if she got discouraged; he could not write to her for advice or share his triumphs and tribulations.

The people with whom he associated on his travels admired Douglass for his brilliance, his learning, and it is possible that he began to be embarrassed by a wife who did not read. When was it that he started to apologize for her? Was he perhaps thinking of her when he made his notoriously patronizing remarks about Sojourner Truth, that "genuine specimen of the uncultured Negro," who, because she cared so "very little for elegance of speech or refinement of manners," mocked his endeavors to "speak and act like a person of cultivation and refinement" and took special pleasure "to trip me up in my speeches and to ridicule my efforts"?[17] As Jenny Franchot has said, his "heroic literacy—a sign of the black man's emancipation—rested upon an uneasy disaffiliation from black women."[18] His mother had been the only slave on the Lloyd plantation who could read. Now he was married to a woman who rejected this blessing though it was available to her. What kind of example was she giving to his children? What kind of mother was she? They began to live separate lives less than five years into their marriage.

Anna Murray supported his new mission unconditionally, with a diligence and self-sacrifice that enabled him to pursue it, although she was disappointed at his not having gone into the ministry. When still in slavery, Frederick's mentor, the slave Father Lawson, had insisted that God had equipped young Fred with his thirst for knowledge and the strength to steal it from his masters because he had been chosen to preach God's word. A deeply religious woman, Anna shared Lawson's conviction. She knew Douglass was skeptical of institutionalized religion, but also knew him to be a believer. She had been thrilled when he was licensed to preach in the African Methodist Episcopal Zion Church in New Bedford in 1839,[19] and worried when his association with the abolitionists, reviving his old hatred of slaveholding religion, drove a wedge between him and the church. It must have seemed to her that every time he tried to talk to God some written word forced its way between them, silencing the voice that should come from his own head and heart. Perhaps, like her contemporary Sojourner Truth, who disdained print culture and never learned to read and write, she shared a skepticism about literacy which many people raised in oral traditions will develop. Like Sojourner Truth, she may have preferred to heed the "voice of the Holy Spirit" rather than take her "cues from the public realm, from politics and business." According to Painter, "mental orientation as well as ideals of gender divided leading African Americans" from such women,[20] and it is possible that a similar dividing line was drawn between Frederick Douglass and Anna: Douglass associated literacy with freedom; she, with a silencing of God's voice.

In 1844 the Douglass family moved to Lynn, Massachusetts, a small town with a strong abolitionist reputation. Here Douglass wrote his *Narrative of the Life of Frederick Douglass*. The woman who paid for his heroic flight, who at times was the family's prime wage earner, who had given him four children, and whose devotion empowered him to make his glorious career, is almost absent from the text—"an afterthought," as David Leverenz notes.[21] A few years later, in his novella "The Heroic Slave" (1853), Douglass distanced himself even further from the kind of black womanhood he associated with slavery: in the story he kills off Susan, the wife of his slave protagonist, Madison Washington, whose support had enabled him to hide from slave catchers for five years, before his hero escapes to the North.[22]

The *Narrative*, published in 1845, became a best-seller almost immediately. In this book, Douglass revealed his whole background, including names, dates, and places that not only enabled his readers to identify his persecutors but invited his old master, Auld, to send slave catchers after him. Fearing for Douglass' safety, the abolitionists sent him on a speaking tour to Great Britain. Anna Murray and the children remained in Lynn, where she worked in a shoe bindery. The Massachusetts Society once gave her $20, but she preferred to be independent, managing instead to donate a fixed percentage of her income to the anti-slavery cause. Even the money Douglass sent from England and the royalties from his *Narrative* were not spent but put in a bank. This was Anna Murray's way of maintaining self-confidence, pride, and integrity, and despite Douglass' absence she was happy in Lynn.[23] For the first time since her departure from Baltimore she participated actively in community life, attended meetings of abolitionist women, and volunteered for the annual Anti-Slavery Fair in Boston's Faneuil Hall. She would never again find a circle of primarily white people with whom she felt so much at ease. She was legitimately proud of her achievements, her managerial skills, her progress in social relations, but how could she communicate this to her husband? The papers, especially Garrison's *Liberator*, were full of news of his triumphs in England, but she needed friends to read these reports to her. Strangers had to read his letters to her, and she could not write to him without their help. He could report only official versions of his success and use the expected polite formulas of concern for his family; there was no way to tell her of his self-doubts, his fear for his children's safety, of their growing away from him, his longing for her counsel and embrace. Intimacy was lost when the most private matters could only be articulated publicly. He became a celebrity even in his home, a persona created by the media, and there was no way of talking to the man; for him she became the woman left behind, a static, slowly dimming, and voiceless figure in the distance.

British friends purchased his freedom, and in 1847, after two years of absence, Douglass returned to Lynn a man transformed by his experience, to a woman matured by hers. But there was no time to restore the old intimacy, for he was more in demand than ever. Shortly thereafter, Julia Griffiths, the daughter of a friend of the British abolitionist William Wilberforce and a devoted abolitionist in her own right, whom Douglass had met in Newcastle-on-Tyne, arrived in the United States. She was to spend the next seven years with or near the Douglasses,[24] and she and Douglass promptly left for Albany and New York together; reporters published insinuating accounts. Julia seemed to have everything that Anna Murray was lacking. Although people ridiculed her for her unconventional dress, she was still deemed attractive, she was at home in the world, she was educated, she could accompany Douglass on the piano when he played the violin, and she helped Douglass write his lectures, set up his press, and raise money. The Douglass library at Cedar Hill, Washington, D.C., contains several dozen books with the insignia "Julia Griffiths / FD."[25] Meanwhile Anna Murray could only take care of his children, starch his shirts, and serve his meals. No matter how essential Anna Murray's contributions were to Douglass' success, within the gendered hierarchy of work hers was relegated to the realm of domestic service, to the inferior "only." There are no signs that she ever felt inferior to the woman who had invaded her home. Rosetta remembered that she "vigorously repelled" those "who presumed on the hospitality of the home and officiously insinuated themselves and their advice in a manner that was particularly disagreeable to her."[26]

Even the little that was left between husband and wife was severely undermined when, in May 1847, Douglass announced his intent to move his family to Rochester, where he planned to publish an abolitionist paper. His wife never forgave him for making these plans without consulting her, and she was bitter about having to leave Lynn. "She never forgot her old friends and delighted to speak of them to her last illness," Rosetta remembered about what she called her mother's "greatest trial." There was little solace in the fact that they eventually moved into a fine two-story brick house with nine rooms and a large garden, for Griffiths joined them there. Unable to find company to her liking in Rochester, where they lived far away from the African-American community, Anna (now thirty-seven) "drew around her a certain reserve . . . that forbade any very near approach to her," becoming "more distrustful."[27] She increasingly focused on her domestic realm, on her children, her husband, her gardening. All her energy and frustration went into turning the house into a perfect home and herself into the perfect housewife, yet the spirit was lacking, and often silence or angry words reigned. The children, fearing her morose ways and severity, began to withdraw. Douglass' letters spoke of her exhaustion and bouts of illness.

In a transformational process that extended over a decade, Anna Murray metamorphosed into the family housekeeper, admired for her cooking and immaculate household, her competency, her executive abilities, but challenged in the other roles of wife, lover, companion, even mother. Rosetta offered a perfect, though unconscious expression of her mother's displacement when she wrote, "Father was mother's honored guest."[28] Visitors to the Douglass homes, first in Rochester, later in Washington, reported that she behaved more like a domestic servant than mistress of the house. She prepared delicious meals, served the guests, and then retired to a rocking chair on the porch, leaving the more extrovert, charming Frederick to entertain his friends. Douglass biographers interpret this conduct as an expression of her dislike of small talk and her inability to communicate with sophisticated people, most of them white.[29] They fail to mention that the "cultured" white guests seemed unable or unwilling to talk to her—whether it was Gerrit Smith, Fredrika Bremer, Julia Griffiths, or Ottilie Assing; they fancied their racial tolerance as expressed in their "friendship" with the exceptional black leader, but did not extend it to his family. As Painter remarks, "Black families of any level of sophistication were too awkward for the admirers of well-known blacks to deal with on a footing of equality, and so family members disappear."[30] Much in Anna Murray's conduct indicates, and her daughter's memoirs confirm, that faced with the crumbling of a domestic structure on the model of a mainstream middle-class family, she began to reconfigure a household in which an independent and nonsubmissive woman like herself could maintain her dignity as a woman and mother despite her "absentee" husband. Her rules of personal conduct showed she had no need for approval from her spouse's guests and friends. External validation was neither warranted nor necessary.[31]

During 1848 Griffiths returned to England—officially to raise money for Douglass' *North Star*, but possibly also out of consideration for Anna Murray, who was pregnant. The Douglasses' last child, a daughter named Anna, was born in March 1849. But the situation became explosive when Julia Griffiths returned from England two months later and moved into the Douglass home. That same summer Douglass, over his wife's objections, hired a private tutor in a last desperate attempt to teach her to read and write after Griffiths' efforts had failed. But she "remained illiterate, able only to recognize the two words that spelled the name of her husband."[32] How do we explain her response? We do not know how to assess a personality who left neither correspondence nor personal notes.[33] How can we approach a woman whose self-representation may have been powerful at the moment it was displayed, but whose surviving representations lie in the silencing narratives of others, in their interpretations, in the outside gaze? Unlike Sojourner Truth, Anna Murray Douglass did not go on lecture tours or give speeches that others recorded; she had no photos that showed how she wanted to be seen and remembered. There are only a few photographs of her, the most popular one taken around 1865 when she was in her mid-fifties. It shows a dignified women who looks past the camera in what Susan Sontag calls the ennobling three-quarters gaze,[34] with an expression midway between pride and melancholy. Her hair is carefully done in the fashion of the day, and her well-tailored black dress, with a white collar held by a brooch, is of expensive material. Was this how she wanted to be seen, a woman who at home always wore a "dark cotton dress and a red bandanna on her head"?[35] There is no reliable way of knowing.

Some writers argue that Anna Douglass refused to respond positively to her husband's wishes that she be lettered because "she was totally indifferent to the world of ideas."[36] But this statement clashes with her daughter's claim not only that Anna Murray eventually learned "to read a little" but that her children read to her regularly, especially from books in which Douglass seemed interested. "She was a good listener, making comments on passing events, which were well worth consideration, altho' the manner of the presentation of them might provoke a smile."[37] After all, the Douglasses first met as members of a society devoted to the advancement of education and literacy among African-Americans. Why would a woman with no intellectual interests have gone to such a place? She was a keen, self-confident observer, and her experience may well have taught her to doubt Douglass' notions of cultural hierarchy, which accepted white American middle-class culture as the norm. Slaveholders knew how to read and write. Did it teach them to free their chattel? Douglass' abolitionist friends were highly sophisticated, yet they attacked the church. Douglass read voraciously and still drifted away from his God, then broke with Garrison and his Boston friends, then forced first one and then another woman on his wife. Julia Griffiths prided herself on her education, but none of her books seemed to tell her that the Douglass home was not hers. Did aspiring to this level really spell moral ascent, progress?

No matter what her motives, Anna Murray Douglass decided to remain illiterate and pay the price: alienation from her husband and children, and personal loneliness. In 1851 Griffiths complained in a letter to Gerrit Smith that Douglass was suffering from "a considerable increase of those home trials"[38] that were familiar to his friends. Did it ever occur to this enlightened abolitionist that she herself was a principal source of anguish?

The domestic tensions mounted after Douglass, like Henry Highland Garnet, Theodore S. Wright, William H. Day, Charles S. Langston, and other prominent African-Americans of the day, dissatisfied with Garrison's rejection of political participation, defected from the Garrisonian ranks. William Lloyd Garrison was deeply aggravated that the ex-slave to whom he had extended a helping hand should be so ungrateful as to publish his own paper, *The North Star*, and have his own political opinions. Not satisfied to question Douglass' new political position, he sought to destroy the character of the man who refused to be his creature. Douglass' domestic situation offered an opening which his opponents could not resist. The abolitionists had been alarmed at how excitedly women lionized and besieged Douglass on his tours; they feared lest these encounters throw a negative light on their movement: did they not confirm the allegation that abolition of slavery would expose white women to the sexual lust of black men? During Douglass' British sojourn, Dr. J. B. Estlin, a physician and Unitarian clergyman in Bristol, had written to his friend Samuel May, Jr., about Douglass' success especially with "the ladies," warning "that after having associated so much with women of education Douglass will feel a void when he returns to his own family."[39]

The arrival of Julia Griffiths in Rochester confirmed these fears. How, the Garrisonians insinuated in articles in *The Liberator* and the *National Anti-Slavery Standard*, can you entrust a man with the responsibilities of leadership who cheats on his wife, who violates all rules of propriety and decency? Worse, does not his conduct prove that he has become the tool of a ruthless woman who uses her power over him to alienate him from his true friends? Not only was Garrison exploiting the worst racial phobias when he wrote these lines; they also betray his own deep-seated racism in his inability to perceive an African-American as a free agent, a definer of his life: if Douglass claimed intellectual autonomy, a white woman, "a Jezebel whose capacity for making mischief between friends would be difficult to match," must have misled him. "For several years past, he has had one of the worst advisers in his printing-office," *The Liberator* charged, "whose influence over him has not only caused much unhappiness in his own household, but perniciously biased his own judgment."[40] Frederick Douglass was stunned by the viciousness of the assault, so shocked at what he deemed a betrayal that he literally lost his voice.[41]

Soon *The Liberator* published a reply from Anna Murray Douglass herself in which she denied the allegations: "It is not true, that the presence of a certain person in the office of Frederick Douglass causes unhappiness in his family."[42] This statement amazed everyone who knew the Douglasses enough to know of Anna Murray's illiteracy. An abolitionist from Rochester, Amy Post, reported to Susan B. Anthony that in conversation with her Anna Murray had denounced the letter as a forgery. Anthony wrote to Garrison:

> We were all surprised & shocked at the appearance of Anna Douglass' letter in the Liberator. *Anna did not*, to my certain knowledge, intend that letter to cover all the *essentials* of the Liberator's charge—for she declared to Amy Post, who happened to call there about the time, it was concocted by Frederic [sic] & Julia; that she would never *sign* a paper that said, Julia had not *made her trouble*. She said, *Garrison is right*—it is Julia that has made Frederic [sic] hate all his old friends. Said she, I don't care anything about her being in the *office*—but I won't have her in my house.[43]

Small wonder that visitors to Rochester regularly described Anna Murray's face as expressionless, which contemporary discourse automatically associated with an inability to feel, to suffer, or to enjoy (as popular renderings of "the Indian" document). But Rosetta saw Anna Murray's stoicism as one of control and pride. She understood her in radically different terms, as a representative of what modern historians have called "*the* black woman in American history . . . straight talking, authentic, unsentimental," in short the "sturdy binary opposite of the debilitated, artificial white lady."[44] Anna Murray Douglass' face, far from being expressionless, expressed all.

By the time Garrison's campaign ran out of steam, an insurmountable wall had risen in the Douglass family, and not even Julia Griffiths' return to England in 1855 and her subsequent marriage to the clergyman H. O. Crofts four years later enabled Douglass and his wife to reestablish a semblance of their original relationship. A reference to Griffiths in the "Prospectus of the Ninth Volume of Frederick Douglass' Paper," which Douglass published in February 1856, shows that even then he still refused to accept her departure as final.[45] And less than a year after Julia's departure Ottilie Assing knocked at the door.

Ottilie Assing was certain that she had not come between husband and wife. Anna Murray had lost Douglass long before, and as his lover, Ottilie absolved him from any guilt or blame. She described his marriage as a form of bondage, as a burden imposed upon him by his public roles as a race leader and a representative black man. She portrayed Douglass as a victim of inhumane social conventions that continued to stigmatize divorce. What, then, rendered the Douglass marriage inauthentic in Assing's eyes? As we have seen, Assing mentioned Anna Murray Douglass only with a single sentence in her public writings: "Douglass' wife is completely black."[46] She had no individuality, no name, no identity, no role, no place but that which her blackness prescribed. Never allowed to utter a single word in any of Assing's texts, she was rendered literally dumb. It is interesting that Assing's approach to the Douglasses was identical in this respect with one we find in the travelogue of the Swedish feminist Fredrika Bremer, who had visited their Rochester home in 1850. Bremer, too, appropriated Douglass as "a light mulatto . . . with an unusually handsome exterior, such as I imagine should belong to an Arab chief. Those beautiful eyes were full of a dark fire"—while dismissing Anna Murray as "very dark, stout and plain, but with a good expression."[47] Like many white feminists of her day who defied contemporary sexual ideology and its inherent value system, Ottilie's references to Anna Murray Douglass reveal that she had internalized their basic presumption, "that woman meant white"[48] and middle-class.

This attitude toward Anna Murray Douglass also permeated Ottilie's letters to Ludmilla. She usually did not mention her at all, and when she did, she used a neutral tone, avoided negative comments, while at the same time denying the woman's individuality by never even granting her a name. After her one public statement, she never again referred to her blackness. The adjectives she used to characterize Anna Murray all focused on class, age, and education. She was "the wife," "the old woman," one of "the uneducated and ignorant classes." And even the neutral pose collapses at close reading. "So far I was able to maintain the most friendly terms by means of diplomacy and feeding her with gifts,"[49] Ottilie assured her sister, suggesting her own superior diplomatic skills: Ottilie manipulated, Anna Murray was manipulated; the white subject acted, the black object reacted, or better: submitted. The relationship between the white woman and her lover's black mate here was almost a carbon copy of the Aphra Behn–Imoinda constellation in Clara Mundt's novel: there, too, the white woman's superior wisdom and strength enabled her to reach out in pity to Oronooko's childlike wife, duly grateful for the lady's generosity. What a model for Ottilie Assing! In her treatment of Anna Murray her whiteness sparkled.

Assing never considered that Anna Murray might be the one tolerating her out of a sense of inner strength and decency for which she had no words, out of a wisdom and a moral integrity that drew its strength from sources of which Assing was ignorant. Yet she was correct about one issue—that Anna Murray agreed to a truce with her. Mrs. Douglass had similarly treated Julia Griffiths with cold politeness several years before, even having a cup of tea and a chat with her when Griffiths deigned to visit her in the kitchen.[50] It could be argued that the legal situation of a married woman left her with no choice: Douglass was the owner of their house, and he determined who entered and lived in it. Anna Murray had no income of her own, and domestic service was her only choice if she should leave her spouse. The way she conducted herself suggests, however, that she was not just a passive chess figure, allowing her husband to move her around. By establishing a truce with the "other woman" she maintained at least a semblance of control and affirmed her sense of self. The inner struggle she fought must have been fierce, and her life story suggests that she paid an enormous price. Ottilie Assing, however, seemed to see nothing of that. Even two decades later, she was still confident that the peace was all her doing: "Border State is my smallest trouble," she assured Douglass. "I think I have shown my diplomatic tact by getting along with her nearly twenty years without any serious trouble."[51]

Step by step Assing unsexed and deindividualized Anna Murray, defining her out of the realm of a universal womanhood, banning her from the progress of humankind by reinventing her as the eternal "other." Her critique of Brontë's novel *Jane Eyre*, which Assing sent to her sister in the spring of 1850, can be seen as an eerie anticipation of her conduct. Assing was appalled when Brontë forced her protagonist Jane to leave her lover after finding out that Rochester was a married man. "How much greater and nobler, full of beautiful faith it would have been to remain at her friend's side, even if it were only to think things over calmly. . . . Concerning his strange wife, she is not even a real human being, and while reading I kept thinking that for many a modern writer this crazy woman would have been an invaluable figure to prove the nullity of many marriages."[52] Like the notorious madwoman in the attic, Anna Murray for Assing was a "nonwoman,"[53] and the bond between Douglass and his wife appeared like a violation and perversion of the institution of marriage. Assing's intervention became an act of heroism; the adulteress reinvented herself as liberator. The name which both Assing and Douglass coined for Anna Murray was indicative of the marginalization to which they exposed her—Border State. From the very beginning of her relationship with Douglass, Assing thus eliminated Anna Murray from the interracial love story she was about to construct. The romantic tales on which she had been nurtured had tears only for the beautifully suffering young lovers, not for the discarded elderly spouse deformed by pain. Assing's Anna Murray would forever be Aunt Cloe, relegated to the kitchen. The sense of selfhood her parents had instilled in her as disciples of Romanticism's egotistical sublime found a terrifying expression in the rationale of exclusion and liquidation she inscribed upon the black woman's body. Unable, or perhaps unwilling, to see Anna Murray as a fellow human being and as a woman, she walked right over her.

Ottilie Assing felt superior to Anna Murray Douglass, and she thought Douglass was superior to his wife. This sense of superiority was based less on notions of race than on a pronounced European sense of class as well as on her attitude toward education and her belief in cultural hierarchy. Anna Murray was a woman of authority and competence, but she rejected the gift of literacy. From Assing's point of view this was her "original sin." By wearing her "ignorance" as a badge of pride, she was violating a sacred obligation—to strive for perfection of the mind. Thus she was sinning against her husband by not joining him on his heroic intellectual quest. Refusing to adapt to her husband's intellectual growth, Anna Murray gave up her title as Douglass' wife—a place which Assing then claimed for herself. The original sin in the triangle Anna-Frederick-Ottilie thus lay with Anna Murray, not with Frederick and Ottilie! Anna Murray was a burden and a liability, maintaining her place only because the law and a perverted public morality decreed so.*

The opposition which Assing constructed between the Anna Murray–Frederick Douglass relation, on the one hand, and the Ottilie Assing–Frederick Douglass one, on the other, paralleled those of an intraracial marriage based on convenience or expedience and an interracial liaison based on love which the abolitionist Lydia Maria Child wrote of in *The Quadroons* (1842),[54] only with re-

*Assing also adopted this strategy in her comments on extramarital liaisons discussed in the American, British, and German press of the day: the allegations against Lord Byron, the Tilton-Beecher scandal, the relationships between George Eliot and G. H. Lewes and between her cousin Fanny Lewald and Adolf Stahr, the Lola Montez affair.

versed color patterns. So certain was Assing of her superiority, so sure of Anna Murray's unfitness to be Douglass' wife that, at least for the first decade of the liaison, she never doubted that her companion was only waiting for that blessed moment when the abolition of slavery and the end of his political mission would allow him to withdraw from the public gaze—when he would be free to marry her. All the plans for a life in Europe, in Haiti, in New York City she would draw up in the course of their unmarriage were based on this conviction.

She never understood that the Douglasses' attitude toward marriage and family differed fundamentally from hers. For her, as for Clara Mundt's Aphra Behn, "it means profaning marriage when you turn it into indissoluble fetters which may not even be shattered when it has chained us to a hell of pain."[55] The Douglasses, however, had experienced slavery, had seen women sold away from their husbands, husbands forced to suffer their wives' rape, children torn from their parents. Slavery, as Douglass put it in *My Bondage and My Freedom*, "made my brothers and sisters strangers to me; it converted the mother that bore me into a myth; it shrouded my father in mystery, and left me without an intelligible beginning in the world."[56] For people denied the right to institutionalized relationships in and about which they could feel secure, marriage was a goal they struggled for, a privilege associated with freedom.[57] For Ottilie Assing and members of her class it was a radical move to assault marriage, an expression of an emancipated mind; for American slaves it was a rebellious, seditious act to demand the right to marry. Frederick and Anna Murray Douglass had made too great an investment in claiming this privilege to be willing to discard it when things between them were no longer as good as they had been.

Douglass had suffered greatly to know that his white father-master, misusing his patriarchal power, had rejected his black son, disowned him, denied him protection, recognition, and love. His sense of deprivation and despair over this lost patrimony accompanied him through his life.[58] One reason he had run from slavery was that he did not want to father children he could not shield; he was determined that his daughters and sons should be secure in their father's love and that they should be proud of this father. It was essential that he fulfill the paternal responsibilities which his own father had scorned. So important was fatherhood for him that eventually he even took to adopting fatherless boys into his family. As Deborah McDowell convincingly argues, in defending the sanctity of the African-American family Douglass established a bond between abolitionism and the contemporary cult of domesticity; his definitions of manhood

and power largely depended on the rights of husband and father he claimed—
that is, on the ownership of wife and children.[59]

The Douglasses were surely aware that a failure of their marriage, made
public in a divorce, would not only undermine Douglass' position as a race
leader but give ammunition to those who claimed that African-Americans
lacked parental emotions and were unable to form lasting family relationships.
These were considerations that could not be put into words for outsiders like
Julia Griffiths and Ottilie Assing. Assing invented a different story. For her,
Frederick Douglass' decision not to divorce his wife was an act of self-sacrifice
for his political cause as well as a gesture of charity to the wife, just as
Oronooko's marriage to Imoinda could only be based on pity once he had discovered the glorious white Aphra. On this supposition all her plans for a future
with Frederick Douglass were based—and bound to founder.

In her sense of superiority Assing never tolerated the thought that anything
more than his visibility, his sense of responsibility as a race man, a political
leader, and unjust divorce regulations might bind Douglass to his wife: memories of better days, loyalty to the woman who had helped him escape and grow,
admiration for the wife whose service enabled him to soar, gratitude for the
daily contributions she made to his life, a common knowledge that he, the
black man, found only in his black woman, an affirmation of marriage and family in the midst of domestic strain, a love that defied romantic definitions. But
perhaps Ottilie knew all this deep inside, stifling any onset of insight and
doubt in her desperate efforts to survive. Perhaps she had to portray Douglass as
a victim of inhumane divorce laws, a martyr to his public role, for the alternative reading would have suggested that he stayed with his family because this
was what he really wanted, because he loved his public role, his property, himself more than her, that she was not in control, that she was being used, that the
black woman was stronger after all.

What did Ottilie Assing mean when she portrayed herself as Douglass' "natural" wife? The love she envisioned was what Ann duCille calls a "site of
utopian partnership,"[60] an eroticized union where sexual, political, and intellectual desire merge in a liberating single oneness. Assing's early public representations of Douglass spoke of the erotic magnetism that was centrally important
to her; she rejected any discourse of love that dissociated love and sexuality. Her
letters to Douglass, which she wrote as a lover of more than twenty years, celebrated a familiar rich sensuality. After one of Douglass' visits to Hoboken, she
described her return to the room they had shared in exclusively sensual terms:

Anna Murray Douglass
In her public writing Assing mentioned Anna Murray Douglass with one line only: "Douglass' wife is completely black, and his five children, therefore, have more of the traits of the Negro than he." In the Assing-Douglass letters Douglass' wife was referred to as Border State.

Rosetta Douglass
Assing embraced the Douglasses' eldest child, Rosetta, as a promising and ambitious young woman, and her feelings were reciprocated by Rosetta, whose letters to her father contain numerous references to "Miss Assing." This friendship between the two women survived the tension that came with Rosetta's unhappy marriage to the ex-slave Nathan Sprague.

"To be sure, one's room does not look as cheerful when entered after a dear guest has left it as it looked when he was in it, and yet there seemed to be left something in it as if it were in the very atmosphere—a little seasoned perhaps with the fragrance of cigars—that made it a better place than it would have been if that guest had not been in it. I feel rather inclined to enter on some details about that matter, but as I know that you would call them incendiary, I shall not say anything more except that I think it was a delightful time, admirably spent." Later, anticipating a visit in Washington, she promised "that I shall fly southward with the same feelings of longing as twenty years ago, intense as ever," and after it she found solace in the memory of the gratification both had enjoyed in the encounter: ". . . your company for me has such a charm and affords me a gratification the like of which I never feel elsewhere. Aside from other attractions it is such comfort to be allowed to communicate anything and everything to each other, to confide unconditionally without the least reserve or distrust. I might continue yet much longer in variations on this subject, were it not for the fear that you could accuse [me] of using incendiary language."[61] Everything in these reveries suggested satisfaction, peace; the word "incendiary" recurred frequently in her letters to Douglass.

Douglass' "natural" wife—this implies that Assing perceived herself as his ideal mate in his intellectual and professional quests. "I was lucky to find here a volume of Goethe in a good English translation, Faust, Egmont, Tasso, Iphigenie, and Goetz von Berlichingen, and you can imagine what pleasure it gives me to introduce Douglass to them," she wrote to Ludmilla. "I had already repeatedly talked to him about them, thus whetting his appetite for their acquaintance, and now I almost revel in the delight with which he listens. The hours which I thus spend with him and which I already experienced with other texts are like so many sparkling spots of light in the present as in my memories."[62] During his stays in Hoboken they regularly saw performances of Shakespeare and other classics; they enjoyed visits to the opera and waxed enthusiastic over traveling ballet companies. Intellectual exchange and enjoyment were central to their liaison. It was not a world to which Assing had to introduce Douglass; when she met him he already inhabited it, claimed his place in and right to it. Assing loved and admired him for that. But she offered greater variety than he had already encountered, and broadened her own horizon as she did so. There is no signal in her papers, however, that they were aware of the exclusiveness of their pursuit. Frederick Douglass spent countless hours in black churches, lecturing and discussing political issues with fellow African-Americans. He encountered America's black community and black culture every day; he edited a black newspaper and supported black enterprises. Yet it evidently never occurred to Douglass and Assing that she might find beauty, sensual pleasure, and intellectual stimulation in this culture. They went to the opera together because it was their cultural heritage and property, but they never went to a concert in an African-American church together. Did they discuss Phillis Wheatley's poetry or befriend black artists? It was not just that Douglass feared the attention and disapproval that Assing's presence at his side would attract. Her derogatory remarks about lower-class life may have given him second thoughts.

Also, Assing's fierce atheism, along with his liberalism, may have kept Douglass from introducing his friend to the realm where African-American culture found its most creative expression—the church. A letter to his daughter Rosetta shows how far he, too, had grown away from this: "I was in my carriage with Mother, Louisa,[63] Miss A[ssing], and Estelle[64] and off to camp meeting at a place called 'Good Hope' about three miles in the country. The sight of the people there assembled and their sayings and doings left me a great deal depressed for the future of my people. Stupidity, ignorance and and [sic] the darkest superstition were painfully present." He seemed to be observing "my people" from the perspective of an enlightened tourist, gazing from a distance and from above, finally turning away in disgust. "A sight of one of these camp meetings would impress you more vividly with the depths from which our people have come than anything I know of," he admitted. Then, using the distancing "he" and "one": "After seeing a camp meeting, one has need of seeing a colored school where the children are neat, clean and intelligent. This only will restore his lost hope."[65] If Douglass himself could not relate constructively to a camp meeting, how could he be expected to be Ottilie's guide to a world beyond the one familiar to them both? This one documented excursion and his response must have confirmed her biases rather than challenging them. Is it possible that Douglass, a man who had his own kind of double consciousness to struggle with, perceived Ottilie Assing as his alternative to this African-American world? In a letter of 1884 to Elizabeth Cady Stanton, he acknowledged, "Circumstances have during the last forty years thrown me much more into white society than in that of colored people. While true to the rights of the colored race my nearest personal friends owing to association and common sympathy and aims have been white people."[66]

European literature was one field which Assing and Douglass explored together, European philosophy another. Assing's social visions acknowledged the centrality of class to the human experience, and as the political radical she thought herself to be, she read Marx, Mazzini, Bakunin, Lassalle. She challenged Douglass, whose interest had already been roused during his trip to England—where he had read Carlyle's *Past and Present* and the industrial novels of the "Hungry Forties," encountered the Chartist ventures and the Irish question—to accompany her on these intellectual excursions, to open his eyes to the role of class in Western societies, to the intersections of race and class. The books to which she introduced him strengthened his awareness that racism was not just an American phenomenon, and she invited him to reimagine himself as a citizen of the world. One detects no condescension in her description of this—she used the egalitarian metaphor of the fellow traveler rather than the hierarchical image of the teacher—only an almost rapturous joy at the gift she could make, the satisfaction which his appreciation of the new gave her, the ecstasy of a common pursuit.

This intellectual harmony gilded the domestic realm they shared. Her letters are full of remarks about gardening together, playing games, preparing meals, and just loafing. Describing an average summer day in Rochester, she evoked for her sister images of harmony and peace that imposed a discourse of normalcy and pleasant triteness on the exceptional. "Also we read a lot together and play croquet, Douglass' great hobby," she wrote, "and feast on pears, of which we have an exceptionally rich harvest this year, and we bake in the marvelous summer warmth." In her letters she created a harmonious haven, "the green magic island," that excluded or ignored the people they moved among, the tensions which their display of belonging must have aroused. "I love to gather the fruit from under the trees in the morning, which, in a garden of this size, often means an extended tour."[67] With a proprietor's joy, she bragged of how many cherries "we" harvested, sold, dried, and canned—oblivious of Anna Murray's feelings about those realms of home, kitchen, and garden in which she invested so much pride and joy.

Ottilie Assing's notions of a perfect husband-wife relationship extended to professional pursuits. She and Douglass harmonized because she was not just his auxiliary but his partner. Rosa Maria had taught Ottilie to manage a small family budget, and the financial arrangements she made after her father's death show that she had a shrewd business potential. Years of fending for herself had made her familiar with investment and insurance issues. So now, just as he had welcomed Julia Griffiths' managerial talents, Douglass was pleased to have Assing advise him on his insurance as well as on his dealings with clients, colleagues, and debtors. In the 1870s her prudence saved him from financial ruin when his Rochester house burned to the ground: she had taken down the numbers of his $11,000 in securities, thus enabling him to effect recovery.[68] Several manuscripts in Assing's handwriting in the Douglass Papers show that she sometimes served as his secretary, and it is possible that she even drafted letters, speeches, and editorials for him.[69] He kept her informed about the details of his political work, discussed campaign strategies and editorial problems with her. Assing's intense interest in politics and her experience of both Old and New World sociopolitical settings made her a knowledgeable observer and commentator, and she encouraged Douglass to extend his perspective beyond the American horizon, while he introduced her to his, the African-American perspective of events. Her experience as a journalist had made her aware of the ways in which the public could be approached, while he taught her about the constraints on a political leader. They were partners, both teacher and both pupil, in a highly dynamic and productive professional relationship. Assing felt she understood Douglass' public role as a politician and social reformer to the fullest because as a teacher and journalist she had the same work ethic and sense of responsibility. For her, the reformer's and the journalist's obligations were identical. They both believed in a basic human goodness, in human perfectibility and progress, and both saw themselves as members of an enlightened vanguard whose duty it was to mold public opinion toward a perceptual and practical change that would contribute to achieving an ideal society.[70] Both strove to radicalize public sentiment so as to transform their vanguard perception into social and political reality, the exceptional into the representative. Where such accord prevailed, working together became an act of love, a sensuous encounter.

Assing must have been aware that the exclusiveness of this "ideal marriage" exposed them to the reproach of egotism. This is where Douglass' children came in: in her letters, it is clear that their approval, or at least toleration, of her relationship with their father purified and sanctified it.

Anna Murray Douglass had raised two daughters and three sons almost without her husband's help. Douglass was usually away when they came down with measles or the flu, when they needed a good spanking or were crying for a hug. Their mother taught them to pray, not to waste food, to exercise, to do their homework. The girls and boys were secure in her love, and they feared her wrath. For a long time, Anna Murray's authority as a mother went uncontested though her authority as a wife was already under siege. Still, Ottilie became something like a second mother to these girls and boys, in the one realm where Anna Murray, they all felt, could not compete: education. Racism notwith-

standing, the Douglass children were well educated; when the only decent public school in Rochester refused to accept Rosetta, Douglass sent her to a private
academy, and when they forced her to sit in a separate room from the white
girls even there, he hired a private tutor, the Quaker Phebe Thayer, to teach
her at home. The boys, too, were prepared for independent careers. Benjamin
Quarles claims that "the children inevitably developed a patronizing air toward
[their mother], an attitude regrettable in its failure to perceive her rugged
worth . . . but a reaction typical of surface-judging youth toward an adult of
unprepossessing appearance and no book-learning." And many passages in
Rosetta's short biography confirm this impression.[71]

Ottilie was a successful professional woman, at home in the world the adolescents were desirous to conquer, and she was willing to share her experience
with them; she could guide because she had been there. As we have seen, she
loved to tell stories of her past, her roving life; she was never too busy to play
games; she never tired of chasing the children around the garden; she filled the
house with her laughter, irreverent jokes, and funny comments on the sophisticated guests that made so many of their dinners boring and stiff. Her presence
radiated happiness when their mother was often morose. Assing read to them,
tutored them, encouraged their intellectual pursuits, and was familiar with
everything they learned. Even Annie, who had been a baby and thus still all her
mother's when Julia Griffiths lived with the family, seemed eager to fall under
Assing's spell. This youngest in the household was doted on by her parents and
spoiled by her siblings; she grew with a self-confidence that made her more intellectually ambitious than the other children. Hers was a nature Ottilie Assing
embraced spontaneously, and Annie found a willing guide in her new friend.
They worked at German lessons together, and Assing may even have been responsible for the Douglasses' decision to send Annie to a predominantly German school in Rochester, where, as the girl reported, the "German children like
me very much but I have gone a head [sic] of them and they have been there
longer than me too."[72]

Rosetta was Assing's favorite among the Douglass children. The young
woman was seventeen when Assing first came to Rochester, a shy, sensitive
teenager, eager to please, unhappy at the rift between her parents, and somehow
lost in adolescent loneliness. Her relationship to her mother was warped. The
oldest child and for a long time the only daughter, she had been expected to
take care of her siblings and help with household chores even in her earliest
childhood. And Anna Murray had been a demanding taskmistress, slow to
praise. Even as a grandmother, Rosetta could not really forgive her mother for

her lack of warmth. She was "a strict disciplinarian," she remembered; "her no meant no and yes, yes, but more frequently the no's had it, especially when I was the petitioner."[73] Then, as her education seemed to elevate Rosetta to a level above her mother's, the normal tensions between mother and teenage daughter intensified. In many ways their problems were similar to those which first- and second-generation immigrants or foreign workers in any new country encountered (and still encounter) as their children adapted to a new cultural setting. The years in which Rosetta began to move away from her mother were also the years when Anna Murray was confronted with Julia Griffiths' presence. Her own exhaustion perhaps made Anna Murray harsher in her dealings with Rosetta than the young girl could bear, and there were no explanations from the woman who withdrew into silence.

Like many daughters, Rosetta was emotionally closer to her father than to her mother. Douglass was easier to love not only because his long absences made him special, not only because, as an absentee parent, he could afford and perhaps also felt the need to be more lenient; she also perceived in him some of the lone-liness from which she herself suffered. When Julia Griffiths came to live with them Rosetta was old enough to be hurt by the domestic conflict that raged without being able to fully understand its causes. Douglass had been sad and withdrawn after Griffiths left. When Ottilie Assing began her extended visits, the smiles and the laughter returned with her, and now Rosetta was old enough to see that this woman gave something to her father which he needed to be himself. It was a painful dilemma: as Anna Murray's daughter, she hurt at her mother's suffering and anger; as Frederick's child, his joy made her happy. In a letter to Douglass which she wrote in 1869, fourteen years after Ottilie first entered their family, Rosetta tried to explain the war of loyalties that had torn her:

> You say you are a lonely man no one knows it better than myself and the causes. I have been in a measure lonely myself but would not allow myself to analyze my feelings as I was the daughter and had duties to fulfill in that relation. I knew where my sympathies were I do not know whether you ever thought about it having so many things to occupy your mind but my position at home was anything but pleasant. . . . I never dared to show much zeal about anything where you were concerned as I could never have ridicule and as jealousy is one of the leading traits in our family I could readily bring a storm about ears if I endorsed any of your sentiments about matters pertaining to the household.[74]

It is possible that she drew close to Ottilie because she realized this was a way of hurting her mother, on the one hand, and pleasing her father, on the other.

But it was more than that. Ottilie was as eager to make friends with Rosetta as Rosetta was to find a confidante. Miss Assing, as she called her, felt none of a mother's obligations to censure and punish; she could just listen and advise. She was almost like a sister in her happiness and vivacity, and a teacher and guide when that was needed. Between Anna Murray's harshness and silences, her brothers' roughness, and Douglass' prolonged absences, Rosetta was lonely; when Ottilie was in Rochester not only did she have a companion in her but her father was around, too, relaxed and happy. Anna Murray's moods darkened when the German woman arrived, but for Rosetta as for Douglass, Ottilie brought sunshine. And their relationship extended beyond these summer months. The two women wrote to each other regularly for many years, and Rosetta often sent her regards when Douglass wrote to Assing.

Through good relations with Douglass' daughters, Assing could prove that she possessed maternal potential. But she also saw these family constructions in terms of a give-and-take, a mutuality that characterized the other realms of their life together. While she befriended his offspring, she also tried to give him what he had never had: parents. She knew of the despair of deprivation that haunted him at the thought of his mother, his never-ending trauma at not being able to identify his father, his guilt at being unable to relate intimately to his half sisters and brothers. She tried to soften his pain by sharing her own family with him. They spent hours talking about her childhood experiences, her memories of her parents and grandparents. His white father denied him; she asserted that David Assing would have embraced him as a son. He barely remembered his mother; Ottilie gave him her rich memories of Rosa Maria's devotion and generosity. Time and again she asked her sister to send copies of her mother's and father's portraits so that she could give them to Douglass, who, she claimed, "really has a right to them . . . I also ask you to send one copy for Douglass, who would be so very close to [our mother] if everything were as it should be and unfortunately is not."[75] She tried to create a normal network signifying stability and continuity.

But along with her bliss on their "green magic island" ran endless months of absence when she wrangled with society and with fate for disapproving of what she thought should be accepted as natural and good: "Oh, what a home yours would be if only all the surroundings and conditions could be set right which actually are all wrong and out of joint,"[76] she wrote to Douglass. Far too often Assing had to seek solace in her work: ". . . the less time there is left for meditating and reflecting about our tragic fate, our hopes and disappointments and the exceptional, unparalleled injustice and cruelty practiced on us by nature itself, the better it is,"[77] she wrote. Fortunately she found great satisfaction in her work; fortunately also she was extroverted and interested in the world around her. She had many friends; she joined clubs and associations; she visited the opera and the theater, galleries and museums, she attended lectures and club meetings, she took Italian lessons and went horseback riding, she visited friends in Boston and took long walks all over New York City, she read voraciously and wrote hundreds of letters to friends in Europe. Still, no matter how much she internalized the role of the rebel, no matter how aggressively she wore the letter "A" as her badge of pride, no matter how much she gloried in thinking of herself as Douglass' "natural" wife, the desire for the calm security and pleasures of marriage was equally powerful. No matter how much she enjoyed her mobility and her independence, she also longed for a home. Above everything in the world she wanted to be Frederick Douglass' wife.

But then these tribulations provided the lovers' relationship with attributes that enabled Assing to define it as romantic love in the truest sense of the word—longing, adversity, devotion beyond death. The denial of ultimate consummation, the position of lovers on the edge of an abyss, the permanent sense of doom, the status of outcasts and rebels—all of this stood for a quality that prevented the liaison forever from becoming what Assing most abhorred: stale. Ottilie had read Goethe's *The Sorrows of Young Werther*, the famous epistolary novel in which a young intellectual, Werther, falls in love with a charming country girl, Lotte, betrothed to the honest but dull Albert. Werther is dazed with passion, but Lotte, though in love with him, rejects his advances in an act of heroic self-denial. They cannot stifle their love, but they deny themselves the triumph of consummation: Werther finally kills himself with a pistol which Lotte handed to his servant. Ottilie Assing, like hundreds of thousands of other readers, was fascinated with a hero destroyed by what distinguished him: imagination, emotion, love, passion, desire for harmony and social freedom; and she found solace in the parallels she saw between her and Werther's situation. They freed her personal narrative from the pariah's touch by associating it with the classics, the culturally refined. Yet her own needs and situation also demanded that she reconceptualize Goethe's tale, and in doing so she went to great lengths to affirm her intellectual autonomy. Of course she reversed Goethe's gender pattern—in her narrative the woman was the dynamic, free lover while the man wore the double shackles of marriage and a public life—but in her story the lovers also renounced renunciation. Her self-definition as Douglass' "natural wife," in combination with a romantic glorification of adversity and her decision to defy social convention, enabled her to distance herself from the femme fatale and libertine images which her contemporaries associated with extramarital liaisons and to transform herself and her lover into heroic and tragic figures. In claiming that she was giving herself where and how she chose, she invented the fiction of self as the ultimate denial of the conventional female role.

VI

OF EMERALD ISLANDS AND MAGIC GARDENS

The Antebellum Years

Two strong, voluptuous trees stood close, fresh and happily striving upward, their branches closely entwined. Beneath them the words were inscribed: "From the depth free and united up into the air!" —FANNY LEWALD, *Jenny*

"And wherefore would thou repulse my love, Maria? I am king, and my brow rises above all that are human. Thou art white, and I am black: but day must be wedded to night to give birth to the aurora and the sunset, which are more beautiful than either." —VICTOR HUGO, *Bug-Jargal*

The Legacy*

A light knock could be heard at the door. Aphra rose and sighed. "Even this solitude is no longer mine!" she exclaimed bitterly and went to open the door. Then she stepped back, frightened, her cheeks stained red. Oronooko stood before her. "May I come in?" he asked. Without a word Aphra gestured him in, and then she sat down on the sofa, overwhelmed.

Oronooko stood before her, his posture submissive, his look beseeching. "Will the white virgin forgive the slave for daring to come to her?" he asked softly, and Aphra felt her heart contract at the tone of his gentle, melodious voice. "Oronooko is welcome!" she said, and pointed to a chair next to her. The slave shook his head and remained in his submissive posture. "I should have come sooner, to thank you for your generosity!" he said. "Why!" Aphra exclaimed with a bitter smile. "You had forgotten me! That is natural! Happiness makes people egotistic."

The slave said nothing, but as he looked at Aphra, his eyes bespoke such deep, painful

*This italicized passage is from Clara Mundt's novel *Aphra Behn* (1849), 1:137–51.

sadness that Aphra was moved. "The white dove is angry at me!" he finally whispered slowly and lowered his head to his breast. Aphra felt tears in her eyes, but her pride kept them back, and so as not to soften she became sarcastic and cruel. "What do you care about the dove?" she said. "Doves are not gold-feathered birds, and Oronooko thinks only of his gold-feathered bird!"

"It was Oronooko's sacred duty!" the Negro said solemnly. "In his homeland the noble Oronooko swore to the gold-feathered bird, You will be my wife, and I shall devote my life to you! This is what he told her, and what a man promises he has promised, and he must keep his word to his dying day! Oronooko became a slave, but his soul is free, and what it has recognized as its duty it must fulfill! The gold-feathered bird became a slave for Oronooko's sake, she sacrificed her freedom and her glory for Oronooko, and for that Oronooko gives her what he has to offer—himself, his whole life, his poor naked being!" "And his noble, great heart, which is worth more than a king's crown!" Aphra cried, blushing. "Oronooko gives what he can give!" he repeated simply, gazing at her.

There was something magic, irresistible in Oronooko's eyes for Aphra. When they rested on her, she felt transformed, humble, subdued. But what was it in his eyes that spoke to her today? What did she read in those eyes that rested so steadfastly on her? It was a voiceless language, but Aphra understood it. She trembled from head to foot, and her face lit up with a celestial light. She paled. The blood left her cheeks and rushed to her heart, which pounded stormily, taking her breath away. . . .

"Imoinda will be angry if her beloved husband stays away too long," she said lightly. "And your longing will return you to her. I understand that! Lovers are always full of longing when separated! Why then did you not bring Imoinda, my cherished friend, with you?" "Because I wanted to talk with you alone," the Negro said firmly. Aphra laughed. "I don't think we have any secrets to discuss!" she said with forced cheer. "I for my part have no secrets to tell, for I have none!"

"But I do!" Oronooko whispered. "Hear then, beautiful white dove. Oronooko trusts nobody in this world but you, nobody but you to whom he can entrust the precious treasure of his secret! Tell me, white girl with the proud soul and the sunlit eyes, tell me: if one of your white brothers feels death approaching, what does he do? Does he avert his eyes from everything that is his, and leave to fate whatever he possesses?" "No, he makes his will and appoints heirs!" "And to whom does he give what is most precious to him?" "To the one he loves most!" "Imagine," said Oronooko, "just imagine I am one of your white brothers who feels death approaching! The most precious thing I own I will deed to you!" "Oronooko!" Aphra cried, trembling.

"Hear me! I will entrust you with a secret!" And kneeling, he bent toward Aphra's ear and whispered, "This night all Negroes will leave their huts and go to the woods. Not to sit in council but to act! The decisive hour is here! The Negroes no longer want to

be dogs, they want to be men! They will meet in the woods, and from the woods they will march together, like liberated men! They will come and revenge themselves on these white tyrants, who treat human beings like dogs and who call the black people their domestic animals! The hour of revenge has arrived! The black men will no longer be brutes! They want to die as men or live as victors!" "But do you not realize that one word of this terrible secret will bring death to all of you?" Aphra said, trembling. "If I drop only a hint to the governor that you plan to rise, you are lost!" "You will not drop that hint!" said Oronooko. "You want to murder my fellow countrymen, my white brothers!" "Those bloodthirsty barbarians are not the white dove's brothers. Vultures and doves have nothing in common." "But you will be defeated!" Aphra exclaimed, wringing her hands. "You have no weapons, no firearms. Oh God, they will capture you and punish you terribly!" "You say we have no weapons? Don't we have our arms, and the long knives with which we cut sugarcane?" "Of what good are the knives? You can only use them at close hand. Firearms strike from a distance." "Finally they will run out of powder, but the knives stay sharp!" "Reconsider!" Aphra begged. "Don't act, at least not tonight! Think again whether you want to take this great risk!" "What has been decided is decided!" the Negro said solemnly. "The Great Spirit may judge between the black men and their white tormentors." "And if you are defeated?" "Then we die! Death is preferable to slavery!"

"And your women, your children? Will they go with you?" "No! Women and children do not belong on the battle lines. They remain in their huts and sleep. Once victory is ours, we shall rouse them with our victory songs; if we are defeated, they, too, shall die!" "Does Imoinda know of your plan?" "No! We have sworn not to tell any woman. Their fear and wailing is like a fire that tries to warm and soften men's steely hearts! Imoinda knows nothing, for she is a woman!" "And I?" Aphra asked with a happy smile, "you swore to tell your secret to no woman, and you tell me?" "Oh you! You are no woman! Oronooko bows before you and worships you, for you are his good angel!"

The still kneeling Negro bent and kissed her feet. "You are Oronooko's angel!" he repeated. Aphra's heart vibrated with joy. She sat silently, motionless. He had embraced her feet with his arms, his head rested on her knees. Mechanically her hand played in his long, wonderful hair, which came down over his proud neck and his white robe like a lion's mane. It was a beautiful, enchanting picture, this gorgeous woman, tender and voluptuous, from whose translucent white face joy and passion glowed, and this Negro who knelt before her, whose face could not be seen, but whose body with its perfect beauty and harmony one could say was an Indian Hercules. Both were silent, as if any movement might destroy the magic of this moment.

Suddenly a soft, trembling song could be heard outside, underneath Aphra's window, a woman's voice, singing the Negroes' sorrow song with a tender voice. Slowly Oronooko looked up. Aphra bowed her head to her breast and sighed. Both awakened from their dream, and the moment of happiness was over. "Imoinda!" Oronooko said gently. "Imoinda!" Aphra repeated, her voice trailing away in a sigh of pain. Oronooko stood up. "I must leave," he said. "What did you say, you beautiful white angel? When one of your brothers dies, he makes his will, and the most precious thing he owns he gives to the one he loves most? Wasn't that what you said?" Aphra nodded and her eyes filled with tears. "You will not die!" she whispered, giving him her hand, which Oronooko took and pressed to his heart. Then both were silent.

Imoinda's voice could still be heard below, singing the Negroes' sorrow song. It struck Aphra's ear like a threnody. Overwhelmed by dark foreboding, she pressed Oronooko's hand and whispered, "Don't go, Oronooko! Stay here! Out there death awaits you!" "I must leave!" the Negro said firmly. "Oronooko is no longer a slave but a man, and he wishes once again to be a hero! If death lurks, Oronooko must defeat it! But before dying he wants to make his will! The most precious thing he owns he gives to the one he loves! Hear, you white dove! I leave you my wife, I give you Imoinda, the gold-feathered bird, who unfolded her wings for love's sake and flew to be in the sad cage of slavery with me! I leave you Imoinda! If I die, she will be my legacy to you, and you will honor it and protect it, you will never forget that Imoinda was a heroine for love for Oronooko! You will protect her as widow of a poor slave who was once a king!" Imoinda still sang the Negroes' sorrow song. Her voice accompanied Oronooko's words and enhanced the moment's melancholic solemnity. "Will the white dove swear that she will hold this legacy sacred," Oronooko asked, "that she will protect Oronooko's wife against the brutality of the white tyrant?" "I swear it by my father's spirit!" the young woman exclaimed solemnly. "At this very hour I will call Imoinda to me, and I shall never leave her side. Should you win, your wife will greet the victor, and should you be defeated, she will be my sister!" "I thank you," the Negro said tenderly. "The will has been made, now Oronooko can go!" "Not yet! Not yet!" Aphra whispered breathlessly. "Oh God, if you should not win, if they defeat you, if they kill you! No, stay, stay, Oronooko! This hour belongs to life, don't walk toward death, Oronooko!" And the young woman, trembling, leaned against Oronooko.

"Beautiful white dove, do you tremble for the poor Negro slave?" Oronooko asked, his voice trembling. "If they kill you!" Aphra repeated, resting her head against his breast. Oronooko gently pressed her to him and directed his eyes, sparkling with happiness and emotion, heavenward. His lips moved softly, perhaps he was praying. A wonderful radiance lightened his noble, expressive features. It was like the last flickering of the evening sun. Then the radiance expired, and night was on his dark face. Oronooko bowed his head and lightly kissed Aphra's hair. "Goodbye," he whispered, "goodbye!" Aphra looked up at him, her large eyes brimming with tears. "Goodbye!" she said with the courage of innermost despair. They held hands and stood silently together.

Suddenly the song stopped, the Negro lamentation was over, and Oronooko remembered Imoinda. "She is my legacy!" he said. "Yes! Be it!" Aphra said solemnly. Then Oronooko crossed the room to leave. Aphra said nothing, did not try to stop him. She was no longer the trembling young girl but the courageous, determined woman. At the door Oronooko stopped again and turned. Aphra stood where he left her, unmoving, hardly breathing. Her arms were firmly crossed, her head was raised courageously, around her voluptuous half-open lips a disdainful smile was playing, and her eyes, which she held on Oronooko, sparkled with brilliant fire. She was a heroine, bravely standing up to fate instead of allowing fate to conquer her, who would rather thrust the dagger into her own breast than to beg for mercy!

Oronooko bowed his head and greeted her with his eyes. "Goodbye!" she said firmly. The door closed behind him.

After a long summer together Ottilie Assing and Frederick Douglass left Rochester on 29 or 30 September 1858, traveling to Syracuse, where Douglass addressed the annual meeting of the American Abolition Society. Assing returned to Hoboken. A few days later, a note from Alphons Schoppe informed her that his mother had passed away on 29 September. Assing had spent years defending her independent lifestyle against Amalie Schoppe's efforts to remodel her according to more conventional notions of womanhood, respectability, and decency; she had fled from the maternal embraces, and a certain cold distance had come to separate the two women. Yet with Schoppe's death, Ottilie had lost the only woman in America who, despite the advice she used to force upon Ottilie, had always been willing to take her in unconditionally. Whatever had alienated her from the older woman, Assing would always respect and remember her as Rosa Maria's most intimate friend. Now she had lost them both.

Very soon thereafter, more news came: Karl Varnhagen von Ense had died in Berlin on 10 October. Assing did not even pretend to mourn a man whom she had came to dislike, although her feelings for him had softened when she heard that he was sincerely impressed with Douglass' *My Bondage and My Freedom*, which she had sent him as a Christmas present the year before. He had found the text fascinating,[1] and he and Ludmilla had supported Ottilie's search for a German publisher.

Varnhagen left his voluminous archives and private papers, as well as most of his considerable estate, to Ludmilla, his devoted companion and secretary for the past years. Ludmilla was devastated at his death; in a letter to her friend the Swiss novelist Gottfried Keller, she wrote, "my life with my beloved uncle was all my happiness . . . At first I could not believe that he had been torn from me . . . He looked so beautiful, so enviably content, as if sleeping sweetly and happily. During that night . . . I locked myself in, alone with him, and often approached him. Ach, he did not awaken! You cannot see from this letter how immeasurably unhappy I am, and will ever be!"[2]

Like Varnhagen at Rahel's, like her father at Rosa Maria's, like Ottilie at Baison's death, Ludmilla now tried to cope with her loss by making Varnhagen's writing available to the German public. When she began to assemble the correspondence between Varnhagen and his friend Alexander von Humboldt for publication in 1860, readers were outraged at disrespectful remarks about the Prussian monarch and the royal household; Ludmilla was threatened with arrest and saved only by the intervention of an influential friend, Prince Hermann von Pückler-Muskau. But even his power failed to protect her when the first volume of Varnhagen's diaries appeared in 1861. Sentenced to two years of confinement in a Prussian fortress for lèse-majesté, she escaped to Italy to avoid arrest; there she spent the remainder of her life.[3]

Varnhagen's death, the subsequent dissolution of his household, and her sister's flight to Italy severed another vital link between Ottilie Assing and Germany. If anything had prevented her from ceasing all communication with Varnhagen, it had been the memory of her mother's love for this man—her admiration for his genius, her affection for his wife—and his death took away the part of her mother that had continued to be alive through him. An association that might have kept her from leaving her German past behind for good had dissolved. Yet her response shows that she experienced this in terms of liberation rather than loss.

There was a good reason for this: though Varnhagen had bequeathed his archives and papers and most of his estate to Ludmilla, he also left a substantial sum of money to Ottilie. This windfall, if invested wisely, would free her from worry about economic crises or periods of sickness; from the interest she could now afford to subscribe to all the American newspapers and journals she needed for her work, to travel, to add personal touches to the rooms she rented, to purchase books, to entertain her friends more liberally and buy gifts for their children; she took up horseback riding again, and she hired tutors to polish her Italian and Spanish. Douglass loved cigars; from now on, she regularly had boxes of the finest Havanas sent to him. The money gave her security and new mobility, but most important, should she and Douglass ever decide to begin a new life together, whether in the Americas or in Europe, she now had capital to put their venture on a sound financial footing. Still, she was angry that the bulk of the Varnhagen estate went to Ludmilla, and added "legacy hunting" and "greed" to her sister's long list of crimes, though she accepted her own bequest graciously.

Between October 1858 and July 1859, when another vacation began in Rochester, Ottilie Assing sent off eleven major articles to the *Morgenblatt*; these were published in fourteen installments. In addition, her correspondence suggests that she also wrote for *Westermann's Illustrierte Monatshefte*, Cotta's *Augsburger Allgemeine Zeitung*, and *Die Gartenlaube*. As in the years before, her pieces were medleys of news reports, analysis, comment, and gossip—on the transcontinental railroad, on Broadway as a glorious example of American enterprise, on German prejudice in understanding crime in New York City, on the craze for spirit rapping, on parades. Her readers learned about the mob that destroyed the quarantine wards on Staten Island and of the fire that burned the Crystal Palace. She took them to picture galleries, and told them of what she thought of the deplorable quality of the American theater.

As Ottilie Assing became increasingly involved in the most important political controversy of the day, the slavery debate, the articles she wrote showed a strong shift of emphasis. From the beginning she had displayed a keen awareness of black-white relations in the American North, but now, under the influence of Frederick Douglass, a new attitude took shape. She was spending months each year living with an African-American family, sharing their daily routine, witnessing Douglass' struggle to keep his paper going and to make a decent livelihood; with Anna Murray and Frederick Douglass she met travelers of the Underground Railroad when they arrived at the Douglass home late at night, exhausted, anxious about friends and family they had left behind, and fearful of the future; she listened to their stories and bowed in respect before their courage and determination. She subscribed to Douglass' journal, prepared lectures with him, and attended abolitionist meetings. She was beginning to understand how radically different American history looked from an African-American perspective.

Ottilie Assing still knew—and always would know—only a few African-Americans well: Douglass, his family, a small group of friends, the Penningtons, usually highly educated black people. She knew nothing, beyond what Douglass told her, of the lives of black domestics, field laborers, sailors, of those struggling to make a living off the land or survive in the cities. Her interest in them, as in the lower classes in general, was a philanthropic mixture of curiosity, pity, condescension, and the will to assist. Like most people of her class, she took it for granted that those socially beneath them needed help and advice.

They might have stories to tell, yet she doubted not that they required the educated to speak for them.[4] But she was truly roused only by the suffering of those who were sincerely struggling to become "like us" or who, like Douglass, had "arrived." Still, despite her perceptual limitations, which she did not recognize and would never really overcome, Assing was willing, even eager to learn, and she did.

Racism for her became a definer of American life. With the Douglasses she learned to see slavery as the root from which all other evils that perverted the country's social fabric sprang and grew. Slavery and race moved center stage in her commentaries, which became part of a unified abolitionist discourse. The Dred Scott decision, the Kansas-Nebraska Act, proslavery churches, antiabolition mobs, John Brown's raid on Harpers Ferry, Southern violence, racial prejudice among abolitionists—Ottilie Assing's articles reported on the turmoil of a nation divided over slavery. The European observer transformed herself into a participant. Her American images changed, became darker, at times almost forbidding, as she discarded the we-they dichotomy of her early reports. She learned to perceive and embrace the United States as her country, and with that came the desire to contribute to the perfection of that home; she began to perceive herself as a German-American; there came a point when she would reinvent herself as an African-American *honoris causa*.

In the first week of July 1859 Ottilie Assing was once again on her way to Rochester. These summers with Douglass, which began in 1857 with the translation of *My Bondage and My Freedom*, became a habit: for the next twenty-two years she regularly moved into the Douglass home in June or July and lived with the family till October or November. She now talked and wrote proudly and openly of the association, and Douglass, too, spoke to friends about their summers together. Martha Greene, an old confidante of Douglass', wondered regularly in her letters to him "if your German fr. is with you?"[5] Assing's friends, business partners, and relatives automatically addressed their letters to Rochester and later Washington during the summer months, and she not only wrote in great detail about her life with the Douglasses in her letters but included this information in her commentaries for the *Morgenblatt*. Her first description of the Douglasses' Rochester residence appeared in November 1859, in an article in which public and private matters were indistinguishable:

> This house, located approximately half an hour away from the city on a hill and surrounded by a huge garden, has a peculiar poetic touch and is almost an island, a little world of its own, in which the individual courageous enough to challenge vile

prejudice and enter this magic circle will be embraced by such a rich intellectual life, so much kindness, sympathy and an un-American warmth, coming directly from the heart, that he is inclined to think this distance from the rest of the world as a charm rather than a flaw.

Douglass' home, Assing's discourse suggested, was more than just another house somewhere out there in America, on the outskirts of a booming town. Boldly signifying on America's sacred metaphors, on the country's civic religion, she associated it with the nation's founding myth, the City upon the Hill, the New World Garden that offered humanity a chance for regeneration and a new beginning in innocence. She not only affirmed the validity of the original American Dream but moved the black family's home from the periphery to its center. But the Douglass house was also an island in a stormy sea. The center, the living black reality of the American Dream she portrayed, was a place under siege, and racism had perverted what should be representative of America—a haven where black and white, women and men mingled freely and happily— into the exceptional, the endangered. The island metaphor is ambivalent in that it invites association both with utopia, on the one hand, and with an isolated piece of land threatened by a violent sea, on the other.

Hers was a discourse on the essential Americanness of the American blacks as against the un-Americanness of white racism. It was a strange song she sang—full of contradictions and unresolved tensions. The multiracial haven which the Douglass residence represented in her columns was an America Ottilie Assing could embrace. It was home, a place where she recovered those childhood dreams, that childhood magic she had thought irrevocably lost. Entering Douglass' magic circle, she maintained, was like stepping "back to the times of magicians and fairies, when a traveler might sometimes find himself within a magic mountain, a moated castle, or a magic garden. Intercourse with the inhabitants would make time fly so incredibly fast that, upon returning to the quotidian world, the traveler would realize that he had spent a century instead of a month inside the magic circle."[6]

Island of bliss, paradise under siege, magic circle—Ottilie Assing invented these images to document that she had arrived at the heart of the true America, was one of the elect—the Pilgrims would have used the term "Saints." Was she aware that the signs she sent out also betrayed a kind of isolation, even ostracism that came with her new sense of belonging as black? No matter how much her self-created public persona gloried in the perfect company she enjoyed in this emerald garden, the private woman must at times have felt caged. Since her earliest childhood she had been used to a vibrant social life of constant intellectual challenge and stimulation. But loving and living with Frederick Douglass meant moving within a very limited circle of the converted, and staying in his house in Rochester reduced even this small circle further. Most of Douglass' white abolitionist friends associated with him during conventions or when he lectured in their cities, and some even were liberal enough to invite him to their homes for receptions. Very few ever visited him in his home, for this implied an intimacy with his family they found difficult to imagine.[7]

To be sure, there was a regular flow of visitors to the Douglass residence—many of these travelers white women—but Assing was appalled by, and no doubt also jealous of, the celebrity tourism to which Douglass was exposed. The Douglasses were friends with other black abolitionist activists like Sojourner Truth, Harriet Jacobs, and William Nell, and Ottilie Assing may have become acquainted with them, but she never mentioned them in her writing. Amy and Isaac Post, prominent members of Rochester society who had founded the Western New York Anti-Slavery Society in 1843 and were active in the women's rights movement, were among those white abolitionists who had stood unwaveringly by Douglass during the uproar over his relationship with Julia Griffiths, and they were among those whose embrace also included his wife and children. Nell I. Painter calls them "extraordinary among nineteenth-century white Americans for their lack of racial prejudice."[8] Ottilie Assing must have met them, but their names appear in neither her private nor her public writings, and she is not mentioned in any Post family letters that have survived. Again, religious orientation might explain this absence of social intercourse. The Posts were Quakers who were also deeply immersed in spiritualism. They "attended séances, heeded spirit voices, and formed new religious organizations"[9]—an enthusiasm for the supernatural that even alienated Frederick Douglass. In a letter to Mrs. Post he wrote half jokingly: "I am always so happy to agree with you generally that I almost regret that I am not a spiritualist and the same feeling makes me regret that you are one."[10]

Assing also never mentioned Susan and Samuel Porter, prominent Rochester abolitionists and philanthropists whom Frederick Douglass regarded as special friends, and they never wrote about her.[11] Susan Porter, an active member of the Rochester Ladies Anti-Slavery Society, had worked side by side with Julia Griffiths in publishing the *Autographs for Freedom* in 1853 and 1854, and it may be that the Porters' view of Douglass' companionship with Griffiths explains why Assing, so far as we know, never encountered them. Early in 1852 Samuel sent a warning note to Douglass in which he, as a friend, advised him on the course he should take to avoid public scandal about the rumors circulating about him and Griffiths. In a long reply Douglass not only insisted on his right to privacy but suggested that class difference had led to a lack of frankness and loyalty:

> Individuals have rights no less than Society—and while I do not wish to trench upon the rights of Society—I am as little disposed to admit any unjust claims, which any individual may set up in the name of Society. You and I have been friends during the last two or three years—and on as intimate terms as can well Subsist between the Rich and the Poor. . . . It seems to me that a friendly word might have been, ere this, whispered to me—apprising me of the "Scandalous reports"—and advising me how to allay them. In not doing this you have acted more delicately than faithfully.[12]

And then there was Susan B. Anthony, a friend of both the Post and Douglass families. Douglass, who was an enthusiastic supporter of the American women's movement,[13] introduced the two women during one of the convention weeks in New York City; they exchanged a few letters; but there is no evidence the women sought each other out during Assing's summers in Rochester. Assing believed women should be enfranchised, should receive equal education and equal opportunities in the professions; she did not believe marriage and motherhood were a woman's sole destiny, and she favored more liberal divorce laws. In all this she not only shared the central demands of the women's rights movement but in some ways was even more radical than Anthony. Still, her *Morgenblatt* articles suggest that she had little respect for the movement and its main protagonists—indeed, she seemed embarrassed by many of their activities, by their speechmaking, and especially by their advocacy of the Bloomer costume, which, she feared, only exposed women to ridicule. "It takes women like Ernestine Rose, a woman of education, experience, dignity, i.e., professional women with expertise and devoid of the eccentric, to lead the way to a free womanhood," she claimed. Only then would the "baroque appearance [of the women's movement] . . . give way to more substantial accomplishments than any refusal to pay taxes or any penchant for sermonizing can ever achieve."[14] Assing's conduct shows that for her equality meant emulating the professionalism of exceptional men; it was the company of exceptional men she sought. The assumptions of the American women's movement, with its belief in the moral superiority of women, in a special women's realm, were incompatible with her notions of individual self-liberation. Under Douglass' influence Assing became more supportive of Anthony and her movement, only to revert to antagonism in the controversy over the Fourteenth and Fifteenth amendments.

Rochester boasted a large German-American community. It had its own churches and schools, newspapers and theaters, choirs and turnvereins, debating clubs, and a militia, even a churchyard of its own. Its impact on local politics was considerable.[15] Yet nothing in the public or private archives suggests that Assing ever associated with German Rochester. Given her response to Sheboygan and Lancaster, we must conclude she had little interest in and even less patience with German-American communities, and the fact that most of Rochester's Germans associated with Democrats would have made them political opponents in her eyes.

The relative isolation of Ottilie Assing during her Rochester summers was in a way self-created and self-imposed. At the same time there can be little doubt that even unconventional Rochesterians would have had little interest in better getting to know that German woman who unashamedly disrupted the Douglasses' already difficult family life. Even those who forgave Frederick Douglass for forming the liaison—after all, he was a man, and married to a wife who would or could not join him in his new world—were less willing to justify the "other woman." Douglass could not really be blamed for taking what was offered so shamelessly, but for an educated white woman from the upper strata of society to so degrade herself as to throw herself into black arms—there was no excuse for that.

Douglass must have sensed her loneliness, for in the course of this summer he made good on a promise he had made earlier in their friendship: he introduced her to Gerrit Smith and his wife Ann. Gerrit Smith,[16] one of the richest men in New York State, a generous philanthropist and dedicated abolitionist, had first reached out to Frederick Douglass during that difficult year when he launched *The North Star*, settled in Rochester, and moved away from the Garrisonians. Douglass was grateful for a man who promised financial support for his editorial schemes and respected him in his own right as a business partner and fellow politician. As David Blight points out, Douglass embraced Smith as his mentor after breaking with a surrogate father who had begun to stifle his growth.[17] The Smiths stood by him when Douglass was assaulted by the Garrisonians for his relationship with Julia Griffiths, and their home in Peterboro was a haven to which Griffiths withdrew when the situation in Rochester seemed unbearable; Ann Smith was the person to whom Griffiths wrote to unburden herself. Douglass thus knew that the Smith mansion was one place in the white abolitionist world where he need not disguise his feelings for Ottilie

Assing. The friendship that developed between the Smiths and Ottilie Assing shows that his expectation was not misplaced.

We know about this developing friendship from a report Assing wrote for the *Morgenblatt* in the fall of 1859 that was never published. Assing described Smith as a tall man with regular, noble features. "His fresh and healthy complexion as well as his supple and lively movements make him appear younger than his sixty-two years despite a long gray beard. His voice, an unusually deep, sonorous bass, must have a mighty effect in large halls filled with listeners." They seem to have liked each other, for Smith invited Assing to make a detour to Peterboro on her way back to New York City. She gladly accepted. In Canastota she was met by an attractive young woman wearing bloomers—Mrs. Elizabeth Miller, Smith's daughter—and long before they arrived at the Smith residence Assing knew that she was about to be introduced to people she could embrace almost without reservation. "Surrounded by old trees and bounteous gardens as one finds them only in the older, well-established areas, Gerrit Smith's palatial house is animated by the most generous hospitality, as it is home not only to a large family of children, grandchildren, and other family members. Mrs. Smith, still an attractive woman with traces of her former beauty, radiates that friendliness that comes from the heart and shines like a sunbeam in anyone who possesses it; the sons, nieces, and grandchildren glory in their easygoing youth and vitality. An agreeable sense of enjoying life energizes the whole house, and the freethinking German visitor is bothered only by a certain aura of religious orthodoxy that unfortunately infects even the best of men over here."[18] Here she met the German emigrant Wilhelm Zecher, whose life Smith had saved when, a few years earlier, he had been falsely accused of robbing and killing his employer. Among the houseguests were Sarah Grimké, the abolitionist activist from South Carolina, and Dr. Harriet K. Hunt, a physician from Boston. Joie de vivre, love of the arts, style, and with all of that a republican simplicity and a firm political commitment to causes to which she subscribed. Ottilie Assing was perfectly happy.

In subsequent years she visited the Smiths whenever she could, sometimes with Douglass, sometimes by herself; many of these visits occurred during summer days when Douglass was away from Rochester. Douglass frequently included references to Assing in his letters to Gerrit Smith.[19]

By the summer of 1859 Ottilie Assing, foreign correspondent and translator, was no longer just a privileged guest in the Douglass residence. She found herself able to call it a home, to move beyond the visitors' parlor. Douglass had had enough confidence in her to let her translate his autobiography into a language he did not understand; he was pleased by her interest in his work, and he enjoyed discussing it with her. Now he also invited her to involve herself in the part of it that had to be done under cover—the family's activities in the Underground Railroad.

In her mother's biography Rosetta Douglass Sprague described her parents as dedicated agents and untiring workers in the Underground Railroad. "To be able to accommodate in a comfortable manner the fugitives that passed our way, father enlarged his home where a suite of rooms could be made ready for those fleeing to Canada," she remembered. It was a busy station, close to the Canadian border, and unannounced fugitives arrived frequently—sometimes as many as forty a month—usually under cover of night. "It was no unusual occurrence for mother to be called up at all hours of the night . . . to prepare supper for a hungry lot of fleeing humanity."[20] Now Ottilie was asked to participate in this liberation work. She wrote that the Douglass home was a place of refuge not just for her but also for those who ran for their lives. In this "modern magic castle" guests appeared regularly "who underscore with dramatic vividness a less than ideal but very American part of reality," she reported. "They are passengers on the Underground Railroad, fugitive slaves, who avail themselves of Frederick Douglass' hospitality for one night on the way out of slavery to freedom and then proceed to Canada."[21]

Not all the fugitives who came to this house on the hill were black. In the early autumn of 1859 John Brown, Jr., knocked at Douglass' door.[22] He was the son of John Brown, the militant abolitionist, whose killing of three proslavery men in Pottawatomie, Kansas, in May 1856 had made him and his sons outlaws. Just before arriving in Rochester, the younger Brown had used violent means to release a fugitive slave who had been held in a Northern prison pending his forced return to his master, but he came to Douglass not only because he needed to hide from the U.S. marshals but to recruit Douglass to Brown's guerrilla army. That same summer Jeremiah G. Anderson, one of John Brown's African-American followers, called on Douglass with the same message.[23] John Brown was making preparations for Harpers Ferry.

Ottilie Assing was present at these meetings. She described young Brown as a freedom fighter, "determined to offer the utmost resistance" and equipped "with a whole arsenal of pistols, revolvers, and daggers." Later, in a talk in 1868, she would admit that she had underestimated Anderson, taking him for "an indolent man of very limited intellect, whom nobody would have thought capable of such enthusiasm for an idea as to stake his life and liberty."[24] She never met the older Brown,[25] but she considered him a hero. There would be an insurrection, perhaps the beginning of a revolution, and she and Douglass would be in the midst of it all—Douglass as the liberator and leader of the African-American people, and she as his faithful companion. White America had created a wall of scorn around the Douglass home; history might someday celebrate it as the place where the second American Revolution was launched!

Small wonder, then, that Ottilie Assing thought of the Douglass residence as a Garden of Eden surrounded by a hostile world, yet also as an island of hope and promise. "American color prejudice is the demon that surrounds [it] like a Chinese Wall, which only initiates—that is, the most determined and dedicated abolitionists—dare to scale."[26] In depicting this home as a magic realm, a source of liberty and liberation, an island of happiness and freedom under siege, Assing had begun to reverse established racial hierarchies: Douglass was apotheosized as morally and intellectually superior to the white world. Should the true American Dream ever be reclaimed, it would have to come from within this magic garden, and the regeneration would be masterminded by a black man.

The Rochester summer had come to an end, though, and Assing left for Peterboro for her first of many visits to Gerrit and Ann Smith. A few days later Frederick Douglass and Shield Green, an ex-slave who had escaped from Charleston, South Carolina, and was now living "free and without cares in Rochester,"[27] left the city by train. It is possible that Assing joined them in Canastota and that they went to New York City together; they certainly spent time together in the city, where Douglass tried to raise funds for Brown in the black churches. Douglass' biographers agree that it was only with the greatest reluctance that Douglass had promised Brown Jr. to meet with his father in Chambersburg, Pennsylvania.[28] Only then, after getting the details of the campaign from him, would he decide about his involvement.

Ottilie was an untiring optimist, with her eyes always directed toward tomorrow, and the pictures she conjured up usually were those of promise and light. Yet all of a sudden everything was blurred. She may have wanted Douglass to share her vision of a glorious revolution, tried to make him see himself as that modern Oronooko, waging a bloody war against slaveholders, but he thought differently. "The fact is, I never see much use in fighting, unless there is a reasonable probability of whipping somebody," he had written only four years before, and hadn't she translated that? The hero of Kansas, he cautioned, had hacked three men to death with a broadsword—was that heroism, progress,

sanity? Douglass had spent a lifetime proving that blacks were not barbarians—only to be associated with this? Could she imagine the form which white
retaliation—North and South spontaneously reunited against black self-
liberation—would take? The dread and rage were still with him that had almost stifled him that day in 1835 when, after his first attempt to escape from
slavery, white men had dragged him and a group of fellow slaves down the road
toward St. Michael to try them for conspiracy. It was unlikely that he would be
willing to risk all for a plan that seemed pure madness to him, for a road he
knew would lead to "a perfect steel-trap."[29]

In many ways, Douglass' life had been defined by violence, and even in the
years when he supported moral suasion he had not denied that in certain situations violent resistance must be accepted.[30] He was ready to listen to anyone
willing to act against slavery, but listening was far from supporting or even
joining. He was deeply impressed by John Brown's sincerity, his personal
courage, the daily sacrifices he was making to the cause; he was intrigued by the
respect Brown accorded his own achievements and work, and perhaps he was
flattered by the importance Brown assigned him in his various schemes—flattered, perhaps, but most certainly also aware that beneath the militant rhetoric
one could sniff the stench of white superiority. Black liberation, Brown's every
move insisted, could only be effected by a white mastermind, with Douglass in
the role of aide-de-camp. The old hierarchy was left untouched. "Give us the
facts," his white abolitionist superiors had admonished Douglass many years
before, "we will take care of the philosophy."[31] He had rebelled then against
this arrogance, and there was no reason why he should submit now. And the
other black abolitionists approached by Brown no doubt agreed: Martin Delany,
Henry Highland Garnet, Jermain Wesley Loguen, Harriet Tubman all adopted
a wait-and-see policy, and silence.[32]

Meanwhile Brown and his schemes were supported by many whites, most
prominent among them the later notorious Secret Six: Julia Ward and Samuel
Gridley Howe, Mary and George Luther Stearns, Theodore Parker, Franklin
Sanborn, Thomas Wentworth Higginson, and Gerrit Smith.* The difference
between Assing and the Six was that she could not imagine a black liberation
movement without Douglass as one of its masterminds, if not its leader and ultimate hero. Still, Douglass must have been shaken by the blindness to the potential consequences of Brown's scheme which characterized her rocking chair
radicalism, her bay window militancy. It appears Assing was convinced that

---

*Contemporary representations as a matter of course counted only the men.

Douglass would cherish her enthusiasm for Brown's plans as a token of her devotion, sincerity, and love. But he must have been aware of the perceptual incompatibility, the gap between black and white that separated them.

In Brooklyn, Douglass lectured before a predominantly black audience, and John Brown was omnipresent. The twenty-five-dollar contribution to Brown's campaign collected that evening[33] was ample testimony that there were black people hoping, even praying for his success, even if they had little money to spare, but there was no volunteer to join Brown. Douglass understood, but Ottilie?

The next morning Douglass and Green took the train for Philadelphia, where Douglass spoke to an all-black congregation. His listeners did not hesitate to warn him in the strongest possible terms of the potential consequences of Brown's actions, yet they also raised money for his support. Then the two men moved on to Chambersburg, a little community about eighty miles west of Philadelphia, close to the Maryland border, where in an abandoned stone quarry they met Brown, accompanied by his Swiss-American "secretary of war," John Henry Kagi. Only now could Douglass and Brown discuss the issues openly and unreservedly. Douglass learned with a shock that Brown had discarded his "Appalachian scheme" for a separate black mountain nation, a haven for fugitive slaves, from which assaults against the slave states and raids to liberate bondspeople could be launched, and instead had decided to lead his small band of less than two dozen men against the federal arsenal at Harpers Ferry. "I looked at him with some astonishment, that he could rest on a reed so weak and broken, and told him that Virginia would blow him and his hostages sky-high rather than that he should hold Harper's Ferry an hour,"[34] Douglass later wrote. For two days they struggled, and then they parted. Shield Green (who also called himself Emperor[35]) stayed with Brown; he was among the men who raided the arsenal—and one of those who died. Douglass meanwhile returned to Rochester, though one of Brown's daughters later claimed that Brown and Kagi told their men that Douglass "had promised that he would follow Brown 'even into death' "[36] and would join them as soon as possible. Did Douglass really make this promise?

For Frederick Douglass, these were days of anxiety, terror, self-doubt, fear. But he had Green with him in Chambersburg; he was always in motion, met with people, lectured; back in Rochester he had his family, his friends, and his paper. Ottilie Assing was alone with her fears and anticipation. These were days when the awareness of what it meant to be the "other woman" must have struck her forcefully and painfully. Douglass' wife, a disgusted Ottilie charged, had not been ashamed to accept board from John Brown when he wrote his "constitu-tion" in the Douglass home,[37] but she, not Ottilie, was now at her husband's side. It was unbearable.

As always when her inner tensions threatened to overwhelm her, Ottilie Assing escaped into activity. During the next days and weeks she wrote about her visit with the Smiths at Peterboro, and invented her magic garden on that emerald island in the midst of a sea of violence and hatred. Then, on 16 Octo-ber, John Brown led his army on Harpers Ferry. On 17 October paper boys were bellowing out the news all over New York City, and Ottilie bought every paper and flyer she could. " 'Dreadful and exciting news! Negro insurrection at Harper's Ferry! Extensive conspiracy among the negroes in Virginia and Mary-land! The arsenal seized by the insurrectionists! Arms taken and carried in the interior! The bridge fortified and defended by cannon! Railroad trains stopped and fired at! Several men killed! The telegraph wires cut! A contribution laid on the citizens! Troops from Baltimore and Washington sent against the insurrec-tionists!' "[38]—Assing would never forget these phrases that rang through the streets and screamed from every paper. It was a day full of anxiety, followed by a sleepless night, succeeded by a day defined by news of the catastrophe: John Brown had been defeated and captured; most of his men were dead. And the newsboys not only yelled out the gruesome details of the slaughter but soon screamed the names of "co-conspirators" whose letters had been found in Brown's carpetbag: Joshua R. Giddings, Samuel G. Howe, Franklin Sanborn, Gerrit Smith—and Frederick Douglass. Assing needed no one to tell her what this meant. The hunt was on. Virginia's governor, Henry Wise, requested Pres-ident Buchanan's assistance in arresting the conspirators, and he left no doubt that the one he wanted above all was "Frederick Douglass, a negro man . . . charged with . . . inciting servile insurrection."[39]

Ottilie Assing, at this dramatic moment, had no way of getting in touch with Douglass. This very day he was scheduled to give one of his most popular lectures, "Self-Made Man," at Philadelphia's National Hall. "The announce-ment [of the capture of Brown] came upon us with the startling effect of an earthquake," Douglass later remembered. "It was something to make the bold-est hold his breath."[40] But he acted as if he had nothing to fear: he gave his lec-ture, added comments about Harpers Ferry, and defended Brown's action as the legitimate response to slavery.[41] The next morning he accepted an invitation from Amanda Auld Sears, daughter of his former mistress (and probably half sister) Lucretia Aaron Auld, who was now married to the coal merchant John Sears; a member of the family that had once owned him as a slave and disowned him as a brother and son reached out to him.

Assing could not know that street urchins were calling Douglass' name while this reunion took place in Amanda Sears's parlor. She was unaware that a telegraph message from Washington ordered the sheriff of Philadelphia County to arrest Douglass and that, had it not been for James Hern, a local telegraph operator and devout antislavery man, who delayed delivery long enough to warn Douglass of the danger, Douglass would have been on his way to Virginia. Late that night Mrs. Marks's house in Hoboken was roused by a knock at the door: Frederick Douglass was seeking shelter. Once again he was a fugitive, and this time he was running for his life.

Douglass had spent too many days and nights in Mrs. Marks's house on Washington Street for the neighbors not to know him, not to be aware of the special relationship that brought him there; fear of betrayal therefore was their companion as they sat in Assing's parlor, going over the events of the past days, and trying to make plans for the next. Douglass was shaken to the core at the realization of his utter loneliness in this new battle. When a warning of his imminent arrest came, he had beseeched white friends in Philadelphia to accompany him to the ferry from Walnut Street, hoping that if U.S. marshals awaited him there, his friends might protect him against violence, "but, upon one ground or another, they all thought it best not to be found in my company at such a time . . ." (Only one, Franklin Turner, stayed with him until he was finally able to leave.) But Assing did not hesitate to take him in, and he would never forget that. Twenty years before, Anna Murray's love and strength had helped him make his escape from slavery, and her unconditional support established a bond between them he would never sever. Now, Assing's unquestioning loyalty, strength, and ingenuity tied a knot between them more powerful than any legal bond.

That night, Assing proved to him that she was a woman willing to risk all and give all. In the midst of chaos she was able to think clearly and precisely, to make suggestions for his escape and to effect it, to be a reliable source of strength and support. Her prominence in Douglass' reminiscences of this "*anxious* night" shows his recognition of her love and devotion. She had chosen Douglass because he was an exceptional man; now she proved to him that she was an exceptional woman.

It was Douglass' greatest fear that marshals would search his home in Rochester before he could discard the papers locked in his desk—several letters as well as that "constitution" in John Brown's hand. At the earliest hour Assing hastened to the telegraph office to send an encoded message asking Douglass' son Lewis to take care of this issue. The morning newspapers, which she brought back from her errand, made clear that every effort was being made to round up Brown's allies and hand them over to Governor Wise, and the name of "that yellow Negro" Frederick Douglass was on the top of the list. Assing almost begged Douglass not to return to Rochester, for they both were sure that marshals were waiting for him there, but Douglass was adamant. He would have to go to Rochester, if only for a few hours, and he claimed that people there would protect him against extradition to the South. But could he really be sure? People seemed almost unanimous in their condemnation of Brown's act. Anxious not to do anything that would bring upon them allegations of approval or even conspiracy, might not most Rochesterians choose not to be there when he needed them most? They decided he had only one choice: to cross the border to Canada, then move on to England if necessary.

They both knew that Douglass could not risk taking the train from New York City, for, as Douglass later remembered, "that city was not less incensed against John Brown conspirators than many parts of the South."[42] Assing finally decided to take some of her German friends into their confidence, and together they came up with a solution. As night set in, a carriage stopped in front of Mrs. Marks's door. It belonged to a Mr. Johnston, who had volunteered to drive Assing and Douglass to Paterson—more than twenty miles in darkness, time for Assing and Douglass to hold on to each other, to speak those words that had to be said before parting, perhaps to look beyond those next few hours. Even if he was fortunate enough to escape, a long separation was ahead of them—certainly several months. It was possible that Douglass might have to go into exile. Did they discuss the possibility of Ottilie following him to Europe? In Paterson they parted; Douglass took the Erie Railroad north, and Assing returned to Hoboken.

Only later did Ottilie hear that Douglass was forced to run from his home only moments after entering it; friends (among them the Posts) helped him get to a boat bound for Canada. The man who had been one of the most important conductors on the Underground Railroad was now a passenger on it. In Canada he moved from town to town, fearful of being kidnapped, yet also unable to decide whether to return to the States. Amy Post, with whom he corresponded regularly, warned him against returning. Only after a last-minute escape from a trap set by false "friends" did he finally acknowledge that there would be no easy way back.[43] From Canada West Douglass went east to the province of New Brunswick, and on 12 November he boarded the steamer *Scotia* for England. "I could but feel that I was going into exile, perhaps for life," he later wrote. "Slavery seemed to be at the very top of its power . . . No one who has not himself been compelled to leave his home and country and go into permanent banishment can well imagine the state of mind and heart which such a condition brings." Fourteen days later he found himself "upon the soil of Great Britain, beyond the reach of Buchanan's power and Virginia's prisons."[44] Behind him he left Anna Murray and their five children, who faced the possibility of police harassment, perhaps even confiscation of their home.[45] Would they be able to survive without him? Would he ever return? Would they, too, have to leave the United States, and where would they go? Was Anna Murray aware that Ottilie had contributed to Douglass' escape? No matter how much the Posts and other friends tried to help, Douglass' wife was as if suspended in midair.

As was Ottilie Assing. The letters and articles she wrote during these first weeks of Douglass' exile show that he had found ways of informing her of his whereabouts, yet the situation was still unbearable. Since her earliest childhood Assing had been encouraged to see herself as the architect of her own life, but now her life seemed to be shaped by forces over which she had no control. She could only wait and respond to developments she could neither prevent nor direct.

As always in periods of extreme pain and agitation, Ottilie Assing sought solace in writing. While Douglass was still in Canada, she composed a detailed report on John Brown and Harpers Ferry for the *Morgenblatt*—twelve pages in October, ten in November, and twelve pages in December. But the material was so uncompromising in tone, so militant in purpose, that Cotta did not publish it.[46]

"The Insurrection at Harpers Ferry," the manuscript written in October, shows beyond doubt that she had knowledge of Brown's venture possessed only by members of the inner circle. Some of her biographical information on Brown was inaccurate, and many of the details reported on Harpers Ferry differ from the historical accounts of these events; still, she had information of which the general American public learned only months or years later. She wrote of Brown's underground life as Isaac Smith in the period between the Kansas campaign and Harpers Ferry; she described his recruitment efforts, the alias he adopted, the arsenal of weapons he collected. And she was quite detailed about Brown's most ambitious dream—the Appalachian state. "Brown intended to launch raids, as he had done in Kansas, abduct masses of slaves from their plantations, and on occasion raid and capture the slaveholders themselves at night so as to have them purchase their freedom by freeing one or two of their slaves. Brown hoped that the slaves of Virginia would rally to his side in a great mass as soon as they received news of the presence of his force, and that the revolt would gradually spread throughout the state."[47]

In describing the way Northern supporters of slavery denounced John Brown as a vile terrorist, she mentioned a series of letters by an English "political adventurer" by the name of Hugh Forbes that had been published in the *New York Herald* in an attempt to besmirch prominent Republicans. Colonel Forbes, as he chose to call himself, allegedly had fought with Garibaldi in 1848. Claiming military expertise, he had approached John Brown during the Kansas campaign, and Brown had made him his military strategist and confidant. In November 1858 Forbes visited Frederick Douglass in Rochester, equipped with a letter of introduction from Brown. Douglass claimed that he was uneasy about this man from the start, "but I 'conquered my prejudice,' took him to a hotel and paid his board while he remained." He did more than that: he gave Forbes money for his family in exile, and an address where he knew his reminiscences of Garibaldi and John Brown's Kansas would be sympathetically received—Ottilie Assing's. Douglass' moves show he knew Ottilie's radical biases; it also shows how much he trusted her and "my German friends in New York,"[48] as he called them. Assing opened many a door and many a purse to Forbes, yet she was too alert not to see that something was terribly wrong with this new friend. Forbes's fund-raising activities, his whining about his family in Paris, his demands that were gradually transformed into threats left no doubt they were dealing with a crook. When she heard rumors that he had betrayed Brown's schemes to Horace Greeley of the *Tribune* and to government officials in Washington, she warned Douglass, who informed John Brown. Brown immediately postponed the enterprise another year. In her report of November 1859 she carefully avoided any wording that would suggest acquaintance with Forbes, but her characterization of him could only have been written by a participant observer.

Assing knew that German readers would get the basic information on Harpers Ferry from other foreign correspondents like her friend Friedrich Kapp, but she believed she was the one who could and would provide the proper reading of the events. She never hesitated to suppress information if she wished, and she feared neither contradiction nor inconsistency. She had begun to tailor facts to her political agenda—a technique she soon perfected. Her John Brown, "the hero of Kansas," was a superman without blemishes, his "religious fanaticism" excepted. "He has always shown himself to be of unselfish, noble, and honest character, unsullied by the least blemish. Yet he has a will of iron, an unparalleled decisiveness, quickness of mind, and personal courage." She portrayed him as a fearless antagonist of slavery and as a "terrible avenger" of the dispossessed without depriving him of his innocence. Barbarity and violence for her were prerogatives of Southern "knights." The man who had chopped up his Kansas enemies with a broadsword emerged from her pages bloody but unsullied: "Stern and implacable like death itself, if necessary, he was never guilty of needless cruelty; to the contrary, he often proved his innate kindness and humanity." Only a society that perverted law to justify its transgressions against humanity could persecute this man as a criminal, she charged; only a corrupt world, only a debased law could denounce him as a terrorist. A certain ambivalence surfaced only in the line she drew between the individual John Brown, the hero without blemish, and the actual raid, for which she used the terms "incomprehensible," "blindness," and "folly."[49] In this her analysis resembled that of other abolitionist women of her day, of Harriet Tubman, Lydia Maria Child, Julia Ward Howe, Abigail Hopper Gibbons.[50] Like Child, she transformed John Brown into a martyr, even using this very term, long before most Northern abolitionists began to discover the propagandistic potential in Brown's death.

The unblinking and untainted heroism of Assing's John Brown and his men stood in sharp contrast to the cowardice she associated with the Southern response. The determination and courage of five black and fourteen white men sufficed to put the whole South, that land of chivalry and bravado, into a state of panic, transforming them into a nation under siege by an omnipotent foe. Governor Wise was ridiculed as "a veritable Don Quixote of slavery," a commander of an army of Sancho Panzas who in panic "kept shooting at anyone who did not immediately respond to their 'Who's there?' No distinction was being made between biped and quadruped, putting cows and pigs in imminent danger."[51]

Ever since 1848 Assing had been tired of lost causes and dead heroes; she was a woman whose every drive was directed toward a future she could anticipate in terms of hope and progress, and to achieve that, to revive the dream of a better tomorrow, she needed a hero who was alive, who could personify this dream. At the center of her text, right between her analysis of Brown's defeat and his execution, she therefore directed the spotlight on Frederick Douglass. At a time when even the most courageous abolitionists did what they could to

cleanse themselves of any suspicion of co-conspiracy, one man stood up to acknowledge frankly his participation in the conspiracy, even though the consequences for him are more dangerous and pernicious than for most others. It is the famous orator Frederick Douglass. Immediately following the events at Harpers Ferry he was identified as one of the secret leaders of the conspiracy, and only by his hasty flight to Canada did he escape the clutches of the United States marshals, those henchmen of [the] government.[52]

The man who in his autobiography would claim he was unsure whether it was "my discretion or my cowardice" that made him "proof against the dear old man's eloquence,"[53] who had been prudent and realistic enough to avoid an unsought martyrdom, in Assing's narrative is the mastermind and true leader of this liberation army, the very group she had decried as self-delusive only a month before.

On 31 October 1859, before departing for England, Douglass had written a letter to the *Rochester Democrat and Observer* in which he expressed his deep respect for "John Brown—the noble hero" as well as his firm belief that "it can never be wrong for the imbruted and whip-scarred slaves, or their friends, to hunt, harass, and even strike down the traffickers in human flesh." Yet he also denied in the strongest possible words that he had ever given his consent to the Harpers Ferry raid: "I have always been more distinguished for running than fighting, and tried by the Harper's-Ferry-insurrectionists, I am most miserably deficient in courage . . . The taking of Harper's Ferry was a measure never encouraged by my word or by my vote."[54] In Ottilie Assing's narrative this conciliatory letter becomes "a magnificent, brilliant manifesto dictated by that implacable hatred for slavery and that dedication to liberating the oppressed which knows no consequences, no matter how devastating their effect on his life."[55] Of course she never mentioned that the African-American press was criticizing Douglass for escaping to Europe. Douglass declined to perform according to her notions of heroism, but for Assing this was no problem. She simply reimagined the man who preferred to be an African-American Cicero as a black Spartacus, as her Oronooko. After all, she was a writer, and like Aphra Behn, she used the power of the word, her free imagination to invent the Douglass that was all hers.

Her glorification of Douglass as Brown's legitimate heir and as the revolutionary upon whom the nation's hope for moral regeneration rested culminated in the portrayal of the freedom fighter as a fugitive from American injustice: "Whether and when [Douglass] can return, and whether his effectiveness as an orator will not be at an end, only time will tell,"[56] she concluded. Yet what was an expression of resignation on the public, the political level at the same time contained a subtext of personal hope. Assing knew that her translation of *My Bondage and My Freedom* would be out in January or February, and she was convinced that it would be a success. This autobiography in combination with her articles about John Brown and Douglass might be the beginning of a European career for Douglass.

There are many signs that Assing's plans were more than an infatuated woman's pipe dream. Material in the Frederick Douglass Papers shows that Douglass had begun to study German and even to learn the complicated traditional German script.[57] His determination so inspired his youngest child, little Annie, that she joined him in his efforts. "Annie attends school regularly, she is the favorite of her German teacher he says. She is the best scholar he has,"[58] a proud Rosetta wrote to her absent father in December. In one of the last letters she ever sent him, Annie, too, claimed: "I am proceeding in my German lessons very well for my teacher says so. I am in the first reader and I can read." Her father and fellow student better prepare for a big surprise, the little girl bragged happily: "I expect that you will have a German letter from me in a very short time."[59] Assing's fluency in English made conversation in English unproblematic for them, so Douglass may indeed have been contemplating a German sojourn. Perhaps he was thinking of a lecture tour in connection with the publication of his autobiography; perhaps he was looking for a new place, and with Ottilie Assing by his side Germany had become a tangible alternative. Whatever his motives, he was able to read and write German texts by the time he went into exile.

In letters to her old friend Rahel de Castro at about this time, Assing let it be known that she was planning a return to Europe.[60] Meanwhile she learned that Douglass was spending his Christmas in exile, as well as all of January, with Julia Griffiths Crofts and her husband in Halifax, England. In January 1860 Castro wrote to Ludmilla Assing, "Ottilie told me everything about Douglass and hopes he has landed in Europe. This could bring Ottilie to Europe, I think. You know that I was the one who once predicted her emigration to America?" In her next letter she was triumphant: "Ottilie's letter made me so glad, it confirms my speculation, but I think there will be some delay, though not for long." By the end of February, she was reading *My Bondage and My Freedom*, which had just been published by Hoffmann und Campe. "He must be a glorious man, and this is a stronger argument for the abolition of slavery than anything one can justifiably say against it."[61]

As spring approached, Douglass was traveling in England and Scotland, lecturing and visiting with friends. Harpers Ferry had added to the British interest in American slavery, and his association with John Brown greatly increased his demand as a speaker. Then he told his British friends that he intended to fulfill a dream he had long cherished—a trip to France; he did not mention that he expected to be joined there by Ottilie Assing. It seems that he and Assing decided to launch their European venture on neutral ground. Douglass was too prominent in England for them to meet without attracting public attention, without jeopardizing his reputation, for the British public had not forgotten that their money had bought his freedom in 1846 so he could be reunited with his family. France, however, posed none of these problems. There Douglass was virtually unknown, as was Ottilie Assing. She had a few acquaintances in Paris, the European city she loved most, and she spoke French well. Emigration was a popular theme in antebellum American interracial literature—in Richard Hildreth's *The Slave; or, Memoirs of a Fugitive* (1836), William Wells Brown's *Clotel, or, The President's Daughter* (1853), Frank Webb's *The Garies and Their Friends* (1857)—and Assing and Douglass may not have been immune to the message.[62]

The delays about which Ottilie complained in her letter to Rahel de Castro were caused by problems Douglass encountered with the American embassy in England when applying for an American passport. A recent assassination attempt on Napoleon III had roused French suspicion of British conspiracy, and Douglass was eager to acquire valid papers to avoid difficulty with the French authorities. He was shocked when the minister, a Democrat named George Dallas, denied his request "on the ground that I was not a citizen of the United States."[63] Once again Douglass was the victim of the Dred Scott decision. The United States was, it seemed, working to ease his mind about turning his back on rather than embracing his native country. But Douglass asked the French minister in London for a visa, and his request was quickly granted. He was ready to depart on what would perhaps be a completely new life.

Douglass was enjoying a final visit with friends in Glasgow when news reached him that his bright, impish daughter Annie, his youngest child, had died on 13 March, nine days before her eleventh birthday, succumbing to an illness that had kept her in and out of bed since December. He decided immediately to return to Rochester. In January, a Senate inquiry had implicated him directly in John Brown's raid,[64] but all he wanted now was to be with his family. In his memoir, he mentioned his response to Annie's death only in two rather formulaic and syntactically subordinate half-sentences, saying he was "deeply distressed by this bereavement," but from letters his daughter Rosetta wrote to relatives we know that his pain was excruciating. Not only had he lost his youngest child, "the light and life of my house," but he was torn by guilt. William McFeely suggests that "Douglass's anguish was intense, not the less so, no doubt, for being mixed with remorse and anger that he had not been on hand when the illness struck—he, the self-made man who could accomplish everything, could surely have prevented this tragedy. But he had not been there."[65] Not only had he not been there; he had been about to depart on a plea-

John Brown

Assing never met John Brown personally, but she glorified him in her *Morgenblatt* articles as a liberator and martyr, a man "stern and implacable like death itself, if necessary," but characterized by "innate kindness and humanity."

Ludwig Feuerbach

After reading Feuerbach's *Essence of Christianity* with Douglass, Assing wrote to the German philosopher: "For the satisfaction . . . of seeing a superior man won over for atheism, and through that to have gained a faithful, valuable friend for myself, I feel obliged to you . . ."

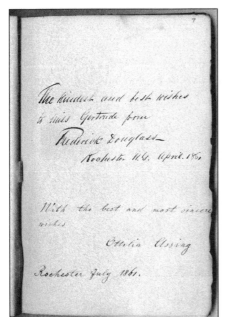

Autographs of Frederick Douglass and Ottilie Assing

These signatures grace the autograph book of Lucy Coleman, a prominent abolitionist from Rochester (never mentioned by Assing in her correspondence). The album was compiled by Coleman's daughter.

sure trip with Ottilie Assing. He could talk about the blame he heaped on himself for not returning when he heard of Annie's sickness. That other truth, however, had to be hidden deep inside. For weeks he stayed on, reclusively, in Rochester. Of course he was keeping a low profile in order to escape persecution, but he was also dealing with emotions more powerful than any legal difficulty could cause.

We do not know how and when Assing was informed of Annie's death. She and Rosetta corresponded regularly during Douglass' exile,[66] and so it is possible that Rosetta told her, or perhaps Douglass himself. On 24 April, Rahel de Castro received a letter from Ottilie reporting "that she would very likely not come to Europe this year."[67] In early July she arrived in Rochester instead. Then, on 20 July 1860, she took her oath of allegiance to the Constitution of the United States and signed the declaration of intention to become an American citizen. The document, in which she renounced "forever all allegiance and fidelity to any and every foreign Prince, Potentate, State or Sovereignty whatsoever, and *particularly* all allegiance and fidelity to the King of Prussia," described her as "a resident of the City of Rochester."

We have almost no information about the summer that followed Annie's death, but mourning and anger, sadness and frustration must have been nagging guests at the Douglass home. From Rosetta's letters to her aunt Harriet we know that Anna Murray was "not very well now being quite feeble though about the house."[68] Anna Murray was thirty-six or thirty-seven when Annie was born, and she was approaching the age when women were said to lose their sexual attraction and become "matrons." And little Annie was not only her namesake but closest to her mother of all the children. Anger, resentment, and sadness must have mingled in Anna Murray at a husband who was not there when she needed him most, and an undercurrent of suspicion that he blamed her, his illiterate wife, for the child's death. And then a shock for which there were no words, that utter disbelief when he, only weeks after his return, invited this German woman into their house of mourning.

For Ottilie Assing, too, these were difficult months. The deluge of letters she had sent off to German friends during Douglass' exile ebbed away, and she did no writing for the *Morgenblatt* or any other journal. Her focus seems to have been entirely on Douglass' tragedy. It is likely that she, too, grieved at Annie's death, for she cherished children, and this little girl was the kind of child she loved spontaneously—impish, bright, eager to learn, loving. Anna Murray, too, was a presence she had to cope with, but her return to the Douglass residence that summer proves that Assing either considered Anna Murray incapable of harboring deep emotions like pain,[69] love, humiliation or chose to ignore them.

Ottilie Assing had been so close to her goal of having Douglass all to herself that she must have been raging at a fate that betrayed her so. Her translation of his autobiography and her promotional columns had prepared the stage for a new European career for Douglass, and she was certain that her friends would have been fascinated by that gorgeous mulatto at her side—by the exotic eroticism of his presence, his oratorical skills, his intellectual brilliance. It never seemed to occur to her how much of Douglass' magnetism as an orator would be lost if he depended on her voice for translation or if he spoke in a language not his own. Assing's romantic definition of genius contributed to her belief that Douglass' brilliance would sparkle anywhere; she was determined to see him as a citizen of the world. She did not understand that the man who had struggled so hard to make it in America would experience as exile what she extolled as freedom of flight. He could not become a citizen of the world before he had become what he most desired to be—a citizen of the United States! But all of that was unimportant now anyway. There would be no European future for them. All of these dreams had evaporated. Douglass' response to Annie's death showed that there was a level on which she could not compete with his wife and children.

There was one beam of light in this summer of mourning, and that was a book that interested both Assing and Douglass: Ludwig Feuerbach's *The Essence of Christianity*. For years Ottilie Assing had heard about Feuerbach's radical critique of Christian dogma, and she had attended lectures about his philosophy; then, in the fall of 1859, in a New York bookstore, she had discovered it in an English translation by the British novelist George Eliot. Perhaps Feuerbach's eloquence would help her achieve what her missionary zeal had failed to do— convert Douglass to atheism. They felt deeply about each other; they agreed on political and social issues; they shared their fascination with books, their abolitionist commitment, their belief in education and progress. The bone of contention between them was Christianity. As Assing would admit to Feuerbach himself twelve years later: "Personal sympathy and concordance in many central issues brought [Douglass and me] together; but there was *one* obstacle to a loving and lasting friendship—namely, the personal Christian God."[70] Harpers Ferry and Douglass' subsequent exile came between Assing and her missionary errand, but she brought the book with her to Rochester that summer.[71]

In *The Essence of Christianity*, Feuerbach argued that religion was based on what he described as "simple natural realities." The secret of theology, he proclaimed, was anthropology. God is a projection of the human imagination, of human needs and desires; the substance of religious dogma is human. Man, Feuerbach declared, created God in his own image, and then God returned the favor. This analysis abolished the opposition between the divine and the human and defined religion as a first step toward self-knowledge.

The Essence of Christianity became an intellectual challenge Assing and Douglass tried to meet through long evenings of reading, questioning, debate. "The book . . . resulted in a total reversal of his attitudes," Assing claimed in her letter to Feuerbach. "Douglass has become your enthusiastic admirer, and the result is a remarkable progress, an expansion of his horizon, of all his attitudes."[72] The effect on Douglass was probably far less dramatic than this, for he had already gone a long way toward what his intellectual biographer, Waldo E. Martin, Jr., defines as "religious liberalism," a "liberal religious belief in the human determination of human affairs."[73] Liberal religion and religious pragmatism came with the chains he wore, with the whippings that accompanied the sermons when he got religion as a slave. Douglass always insisted that it was Charles Lawson, a slave in Baltimore, who was his "spiritual father" during his adolescent search for God, who put the notion into his mind that the Lord, wanting him to preach the gospel, "had a great work for me to do."[74] Yet from the start, the young slave was torn between the need to believe and his hatred of the proslavery religion practiced by Southern whites. Slavery taught him every day that he could not wait for the Lord to deliver him; his freedom depended upon himself, and he translated this insight into action when escaping from the South. Years later he put this in the clearest possible way during a controversy with Henry Ward Beecher. When Beecher said that he preferred to wait for God to abolish slavery, Douglass retorted that "if the Reverend gentleman had worked on plantations where I have been, he would have met overseers who would have whipped him in five minutes out of his willingness to wait for liberty."[75]

As we have seen, in the North, Douglass became a member of and licensed preacher in New Bedford's African Methodist Episcopal Zion Church after he was "jim-crowed at the altar of a white Methodist church,"[76] and his abolitionist struggle soon drew fierce opposition from conservative Christians in both North and South. To his friend the Reverend Thomas James he wrote that he felt forced to "cut loose" from a church that had been perverted into becoming a "bulwark of American slavery."[77] He struggled to differentiate between Christian doctrine and Christian institutions, between Christian belief and practice. Ottilie Assing herself characterized the Douglass of this period as an individual tortured by the hypocrisy of the church while still unwilling to part with a faith that had guided him since his childhood days. "He was in this respect in about the same position as those who denounce the Pope and Priesthood and hold them responsible for all the abuses in the Church, yet cling to the 'only true faith,' and do not see that Pope and Priesthood are merely the necessary results of that faith, that in fact they cannot be different from what they are, as long as that faith and church are existing."[78] But the gap between Douglass and his faith widened with every new encounter with proslavery religion. "For my part, I would say, welcome infidelity! welcome atheism! welcome anything! in preference to the gospel, as preached by the Divines!"[79] he cried out in frustration and anger in his famous Fourth of July speech of 1852. His skepticism found many backers among the abolitionists, and his belief in human perfectibility and the need for human moral action was strengthened when he encountered Theodore Parker's Transcendental Unitarianism. He concluded that God was a minimalist, an instrument in the hands of whoever had the power to claim that He was on their side. Slavery and racism demystified religion for Douglass, and he shifted emphasis from a determination of human life to the human will long before he read Feuerbach with Ottilie Assing.

Feuerbach's text did not ask Douglass to bend his knees and close his eyes in prayer; it challenged him to continue what he was already doing: stand upright, look unblinkingly at the world, and do what needed to be done. *The Essence of Christianity* was important for providing sound philosophical foundations for a free spirit. Still, Assing would always celebrate Douglass' encounter with Feuerbach as a conversion experience:

> They [Feuerbach's ideas] struck him like a ray of light, and accomplished a complete revolution of his opinions. I add with great satisfaction that it was German radicalism that worked that revolution, and that to our great, venerated Feuerbach above all others our thanks are due for having pointed out the path to intellectual liberty to the distinguished man, after he had freed himself of the fetters of slavery.[80]

For her, it was a liberation as important as his escape from slavery, and friends in Hoboken reported that she bragged about being an agent in this second emancipation.[81] Eventually, busts of Ludwig Feuerbach and David Friedrich Strauss adorned his study,[82] together with portraits of his abolitionist friends Wendell Phillips, Charles Sumner, and John Brown, of Toussaint L'Ouverture and Abraham Lincoln. Yet Douglass continued to use religious terminology and biblical images in his speeches and lectures.

In the summer of 1860 Ottilie Assing finally understood that Douglass was more thoroughly American than she perhaps had acknowledged, that if they were to have a future, she would have to transform not him into a reluctant European but herself into a devoted American. Their future would have to be forged here and now, in the presence of American racism, in the face of Anna Murray and the children. Applying for American citizenship was Ottilie Assing's pledge of faith to Frederick Douglass, a sign that she was willing to give herself unconditionally and without qualification, a promise that she would be his, married or not. Her signature on the citizenship certificate was like a marriage vow, given freely and voluntarily. His gift to her was a little red kitten, which she named Fox.[83]

VII

THE IRON ARM OF THE BLACK MAN

The Civil War Years

"It is too late!" Aphra screamed, throwing her arms around Oronooko's neck. All the Negroes had thrown themselves upon the ground, crying and whining; they were nothing but a trembling, moving mass. Oronooko alone stood in their midst, straight like a rock; the mortal Hercules, against whom the white dove leaned with fluttering dread. —CLARA MUNDT, *Aphra Behn*

> We will invite Hell itself to be our guest;
> Plantations all ablaze in celebration,
> The white day has carried the crown for too long;
> Soon black night will sit on his throne.
> —HANS CHRISTIAN ANDERSEN, *Mulatten*

Ottilie Assing shook like a leaf in the Newark railway station, waiting for the train from Philadelphia. It was one of those bright, warm summer evenings she loved, with a pleasant light breeze from the east. Pretty soon the dog days would set in, and swarms of mosquitoes would force people to withdraw into their stifling parlors. But today was perfect. Still, she could not stop the tremor, and she thought she looked ashen and old with anxiety. Yet it was a moment when it was so important that she be beautiful.

Her friends had begged her to stay home, but she had to see for herself, see what people do to each other, so she could testify to it. For three days New York City had been terrorized by the mob. They were protesting the draft, they claimed, but when they were finally stopped, black men were hanging from lampposts, black women had been raped and butchered, and black children were lying dead. The houses of black people had been attacked and set on fire, stores looted. For three days Assing had read every newspaper she could, devouring every report, every flyer, greedy for every piece of information, rumor, gossip. Last night she had woken suddenly, crying with horror, wet with perspiration from a terrifyingly familiar "Hep Hep" dream. Jews over there, blacks here—would it never end?

She walked the blocks where the mob had raged for three days. Cobblestones, shattered glass, pieces of wood, bricks, signs of fire, broken furniture and china discarded by the looters—how familiar this looked! No black faces anywhere, only a few whites hastening through dirty, empty streets, looking at no one. The mob might still be out there, in some new streets. "My friends," Governor Seymour had addressed them. Friends indeed!

Assing went down Fifth Avenue, slowly, almost hesitantly, so that nothing would escape her, and came to the black orphan asylum. The windowpanes were smashed, broken furniture and toys were strewn all over the sidewalk, torn curtains hung from the branches of a tree. She walked through the open gate. No sign of life. A few years earlier she had sat in this yard, surrounded by children, the little ones clowning to attract her attention or shyly cuddling up to her, a courageous one touching her earring, adolescents watching from a distance, most pretending not to be interested, a few smiling at her. All gone. Even the bench on which she sat was in splinters. She almost choked when she saw that someone must have tried to set it on fire, and she wept—wept for those who sat trembling in their basements, with "Hep Hep" cries ringing in their ears; wept for Rosetta, sitting in a classroom by herself; wept for the poor souls who were forced to watch their synagogue burn to the ground; wept for the baby who would never learn to speak; wept for the men hanging from lampposts; wept for Douglass, facing the mob at Boston's Tremont Temple; wept for the woman who could not fight off these dirty white drunkards; wept for her father's humiliation; wept for a dream without soil to take root, now that even this new paradise was forever contaminated.

She expected Douglass in New York that night, on 16 July 1863. What a target he would make for Seymour's "friends"! There was no way he could get safely to Hoboken. Fortunately she had his address in Philadelphia, and so she had telegraphed him the day before, offering to pick him up in Newark. It had taken her several hours and a lot of money to convince a hackman to bring her to Newark.

Douglass looked tired as he came toward her, and they hurried to their coach without even exchanging greetings. "We're becoming experts in doing those night rides through New York!" He tried to cheer her up, but it did not sound right. Nothing did, as they struggled to speak of events that threatened to shatter everything they believed in, needed to believe in. "Rebel force, without rebel uniform," Douglass called them. "Irish rebels" was her reading. "Hating us seems to be the first thing every immigrant learns when he enters the country," he muttered. "First thing they teach them, and everybody so eager to learn, just for once."

The next morning they took another coach to the Chambers Street station of the Hudson River Railroad and boarded the train to Rochester. It was time to escape to their emerald island, if only for a few days. Douglass had to prepare for his meeting with the President. He was in the proper mood for it.[1]

In May 1861 the readers of *Douglass' Monthly* were startled by Frederick Douglass' announcement that he was about to take an extended tour of Haiti.[2] "A dream, fondly indulged, a desire, long cherished, and a purpose, long meditated, are now quite likely to be realized," he wrote, describing the trip in terms of pleasure and joy—rare in a paper so dedicated to the abolitionist cause—portraying himself as a man who, after years of incessant toil, treats himself to a vacation. "At this writing, we are on the eve of starting . . . and before the announcement can reach all of our readers and friends . . . we shall probably be well on our ocean-way to the shores of *la Republic de l'Haiti*." Using a pseudo-French name for his dream island was not just a reference to the language spoken there; that a man so eager not to expose himself to ridicule heaped on pretenses to education did not bother with the right spelling shows that he was happily playing with the popular images of the French way of life— ease and beauty, elegance and eroticism, joie de vivre.

But this opening sentence reached beyond pleasure to something more serious. He also talked of "a purpose, long meditated." Douglass was a man deprived of the first years of leisurely growth and maturation in which the freeborn form themselves in study and travel, he wrote, and even the life of freedom that followed his escape was one of struggle, of "clouds and storms, ice and snow, moral as well as physical." He toyed with the popular notion that blacks were creatures of the tropics, and spoke of his longing for "the beams of a tropical sun, . . . the luminous stars of the tropical sky, . . . the sweet warblings of tropical birds, . . . the fragrance of tropical breezes, . . . the endless wealth of a tropical soil." Finally, he was "going to a land where nature is in full dress, and unfolds her charms in all their loveliness." With these eroticized images of a luscious Southern nature, it was as if he was admitting that the purpose of his trip was to see if there was really a place more congenial to his nature than the North where he had been making his home.

Also, Haiti was "a refutation of the slanders and disparagements of our race," and he pointed out that he was eager to enter "the theater of many stirring events and heroic achievements, the work of a people, bone of our bone, and flesh of our flesh." He wanted to see for himself; he hoped to vindicate in his representations a nation to which he felt a special affinity and which the racialized politics of white nations had perverted into "the bugbear and scarecrow of the cause of freedom."

Before the events at Harpers Ferry, Douglass had been fierce in his denunciations of the "peculiar institution," but his lectures had always balanced warning and hope. The witch hunt following John Brown's defeat had forced him to flee the United States for a second time; it had taken him to a country where he was treated as a fellow human being, respected for his skills, lionized as a heroic freedom fighter, and loved as a friend. Upon returning in April 1860, he was less willing than ever to tolerate the daily humiliations to which he was exposed in America. The situation was deteriorating dramatically: in December 1860 a mob in Boston harassed and spit on him, denied him the right to speak, called him "nigger"[3] and pushed him off the podium. The newly elected President, Abraham Lincoln, in whom he had never invested much hope, began, he thought, to bend "the knees to slavery as readily as any of his infamous predecessors."[4] In July 1860 Ottilie had made him the gift of her American citizenship, and he was moved by this gesture of love and loyalty, but it was a gift that reminded him that America regarded him as a bastard. For her, the "half-Jew" from Germany, embracing America was indeed a free choice, but America offered neither place nor choice for its black son.

As David Blight has convincingly argued, "beneath the surface of the symbolic leader . . . dwelled an increasingly frustrated man."[5] Douglass came to realize that he was not the only African-American who felt overwhelmed and stifled, who was exhausted by years of struggle. More and more of his fellow blacks were seriously considering emigration. In April 1861, Douglass finally admitted that he and his people might face another exodus: "The apprehension is general, that proscription, persecution and hardships are to wax more and more rigorous and more and more grievous with every year; and for this reason they are now, as never before, looking out into the world for a place of retreat, an asylum for the apprehended storm which is about to beat pitilessly upon them." He still spoke of potential emigrants as "they," distancing himself from them at least rhetorically. He could not yet bring himself to look to Africa; he had no affinities for South America. But there was a black republic, right across from America's doorstep. It was a black "city set on a hill" to which they could escape and find a home among people of their own kind, now that the American "City upon a Hill" had been perverted. He had kind words for twelve African-American families from Rochester who followed their minister, a Baptist, to

Haiti.[6] It seems that Douglass, realizing he was powerless to stop this movement, decided he would rather be at its helm than a latecomer,[7] and he offered himself as a volunteer scout. "For the next six or eight weeks, therefore, we know of no better use to which we can put ourselves, than in a tour of observation in this modern land of Canaan, where so many of our people are journeying from the rigorous bondage and oppression of our modern Egypt."[8]

Douglass' readers were informed that he would travel on a steamer which the Haitian Bureau at Boston had chartered. His friend James Redpath, the Haitian consul in Philadelphia (and an early supporter of John Brown), had offered to pay passage for Douglass and his daughter, a gift he gratefully accepted. Douglass did not of course mention that he and Rosetta would be accompanied by Ottilie Assing. But in her article for the *Morgenblatt*, published the same month as Douglass' "Trip to Haiti," Assing, too, told her readers she was planning "to make an excursion to Haiti, in order to learn by direct encounter about the conditions in this Negro republic."[9] This was not the first time Assing had thought about Haiti: in 1855, before she met either Pennington or Douglass, she told Rahel de Castro and Karl Gutzkow she was taking Spanish lessons because she wanted to visit Cuba and the black republic, fulfilling a childhood dream.[10] In Germany, Enlightenment and Romantic sources, as well as the Young Germany movement, had appreciated the Haitian Revolution as well as the American one, and their enthusiasm for Toussaint L'Ouverture was strengthened by anti-Napoleonic feelings after the German wars of liberation. As a child Ottilie had read Heinrich von Kleist's "The Engagement in Santo Domingo" (1811), a tragic tale of interracial love during the Haitian Revolution, and she was familiar with other histories of this revolution and of the black liberator.

Other reasons besides political disillusionment and a need for a temporary escape may have been behind Assing and Douglass' plans to go to Haiti together. It is possible that they now hoped that Haiti might be a place for a radical new beginning for both of them together. Douglass was reluctant to envision a future for himself in continental Europe. Haiti, however, was different: his skills as a politician and orator, as a writer and editor, his history as a black freedom fighter, and his friendship with Redpath promised a respectable place and a career as a black man among blacks. Haiti had not been on his original personal itinerary, but if what he most desired could not be had where he wanted it, the island became an alternative he could bring himself to embrace.

Ottilie Assing prided herself on her cosmopolitanism, and she bragged she could be at home anywhere in the world where her talents, her skills, and her need for autonomy were recognized. She was certain that German journals would compete for her reports from Toussaint's republic, and she knew that her linguistic competence would enable her to make a living wherever she went. More than that: she could not imagine Douglass in anything but a lustrous role. Was she envisioning herself as his Haitian mate, empowered by his power? The years since their first encounter in Rochester in the summer of 1856 had been emotional roller-coaster rides for both of them, years of joy and anticipation, of loss and strife. They gratefully embraced every event that signaled an increase of abolitionist sentiment in the country, and were distressed by the compromises made even by their allies. Is it difficult to believe that Assing and Douglass, both in their mid-forties—young enough to long for a new start and too old not to feel the exhaustion of years of struggle—might want to escape from it all, to an island that promised sunshine, warmth, leisure, beauty? "If we are going away," Douglass had admonished his readers in 1859, "let us go without noise, and be done with it."[11]

The steamer taking Assing, Douglass, and Rosetta was to sail from New Haven, Connecticut, on 25 April, and they hoped to arrive in Port-au-Prince on 1 May. On 12 April news of the bombardment of Fort Sumter by Confederate troops shattered their dreams. From the moment those shots were fired, both Assing and Douglass realized that the plans must be postponed. "Since this article upon Haiti was put in type, we find ourselves in circumstances which induce us to forgo our much desired trip to Haiti, for the present," he informed his readers in a paragraph added to the end of "A Trip to Haiti." Violence had come between him and his plans, he stated, but the kind of eruption he greeted with a heartfelt "God be praised!"[12]

> The last ten days have made a tremendous revolution in all things pertaining to the possible future of the colored people of the United States. We shall stay here and watch the current of events, and serve the cause of freedom and humanity in any way that shall be open to us during the struggle now going on between the slave power and the government. When the Northern people have been made to experience a little more of the savage barbarism of slavery, they may be willing to make war upon it, and in that case we stand ready to lend a hand in any way we can be of service. At any rate, this is no time for us to leave the country.[13]

For the duration of the war Ottilie Assing and Frederick Douglass devoted their skills as journalists and political agitators to two ends: to redefine the Northern mission—that is, to transform the Civil War from a war to save the Union into

a war on slavery—and to create a counterdiscourse to the white misrepresenta-
tions of the black experience during the war. They would rewrite the Civil War
as a war of black self-liberation. They decided to make one more investment in
the American Dream.

Assing and Douglass knew that their work as journalists and agitators was
political praxis, situated within political power structures, participating in and
shaping them. They had few allies in opposing the strategies and images the
danger and viciousness of which only they seemed to perceive, as long as the
Lincoln administration clung to the Union paradigm and did not immediately
address the abolition issue. Assing's papers document that they worked closely
together, discussing strategies, selecting topics, writing articles and speeches
together, exchanging ideas, information, material. This cooperation, as well as a
degree of intellectual isolation, forged a new tie between them. Anna Murray
had accompanied Douglass out of slavery and on the precarious road to freedom;
Ottilie Assing fought the Civil War with him.

The articles Assing wrote for the *Morgenblatt* ran parallel to the pieces Douglass published in his *Douglass' Monthly*, she took up the same topics and con-
veyed the same message, at times coming dangerously close to plagiarism.
Assing perceived herself and Douglass as partners and equals, as a "bisexual ink
animal," but what she lauded as a working symbiosis was asymmetrical as she
subjected her own radical critiques to his more pragmatic and reformist approach, transforming herself into a kind of auxiliary lieutenant to Douglass, a
role she later named "pigtail."[14]

There was only one major difference between his articles and hers. Douglass,
despite his increasing religious skepticism, firmly encoded his messages with
apocalyptic metaphors, balancing prophecies of doom with promises of regeneration and salvation. "Men have their choice in this world. They can be angels, or they may be demons," he said in an address entitled "The American
Apocalypse," delivered at the Spring Street AME Zion Church in Rochester on
16 June 1861. Paraphrasing Revelations 12:7–9 as well as Milton's *Paradise
Lost*, he continued:

> In the apocalyptic vision, John describes a war in heaven. . . . Michael and his angels
> are still contending against the infernal host of bad passions, and excitement will
> last while the fight continues, and the fight will continue till one or the other is
> subdued. Just what takes place in individual human hearts, often takes place be-
> tween nations, and between individuals of the same nation. Such is the struggle now
> going on in the United States. The slaveholders had rather reign in hell than serve
> in heaven.[15]

A belligerent atheist, Assing abstained from biblical references and used exclusively secular terms. She clung to nature imagery, calling upon thunderstorms, hurricanes, and earthquakes, epidemics and cancerous growths, to threaten doom and destruction to the guilty, while promising eternal sunshine to the enlightened and the reformed.

Assing's delineation of African-American life and suffering, and her proposed solution to the race problem, had always been conventional from an abolitionist point of view: she deplored black victimization and wanted the abolition of slavery as well as the cultural absorption of African-Americans into white America. For her as for other abolitionists, there was no black culture; remnants of Africa's cultures had been destroyed by slavery, and racism left no room for new cultural developments. Her columns show how pity and contempt were intertwined and belief in black inferiority triumphed even among the most enlightened white liberals of the day. As late as 1861 she would write against the Southern mob in standard terms, describing these poor whites as a class "who in their ignorance and coarseness are barely half a step above the slaves,"[16] but that half step was important. She perceived African America as an emergent culture on which Americanness was to be imprinted; liberation from a cultural wasteland could only mean education into the mainstream culture, which she considered superior. Her creed was progressive in that she discarded biologist theories and never doubted the ability of blacks to adopt Western norms. On the other hand, her uncritical insistence on a white cultural hegemony blinded her to the unconscious ironies in an antiracist and egalitarian discourse that defined a culture nurturing slavery as superior to that of its victims.

Even after she met Douglass, Assing did not discard these views. There was no need to do so, for Douglass, like her, combined a firm belief in egalitarian humanism with notions of cultural hierarchy; he, too, saw the absorption of African-Americans into the mainstream as the ultimate and only viable solution to American racism. What began to change was less her social and political creed than the quality of her images: after 1856 she wrote of African-Americans as subjects of history, as agents of progress and change, as self-liberators.

With Douglass, Assing unconditionally welcomed the war, celebrating it as a revolution that, by inevitably "leading to the total . . . abolition of the curse to which we own this present disaster,"[17] would purify the nation and put it on the road to progress, to the American Millennium. Douglass had cried out as early as 1852, "For it is not light that is needed, but fire; it is not the gentle shower, but thunder. We need the storm, the whirlwind, and the earthquake."[18] Now he embraced the war as a means of breaking with the past, of repairing the damage which the misguided sons of the Founding Fathers had done to the nation.[19] The effect would be like that of a thunderstorm in summer, she echoed—"fertile and salutary": "Everyone whose sense of humanity and justice has not been poisoned by the national epidemic of slavery must admit that the bloodiest war is preferable to the so-called peace that we 'enjoyed' under the rule of the Democrats and slaveholders; he has to admit that this war must be seen as the salvation and deliverance of the nation if—as seems to be evident now—slavery will be dealt its final blow."[20] The war was more than a conflict between good and evil; it represented the transition from one age to another.

For more than a year Ottilie Assing had prepared her German readers for this apocalyptic encounter, "the inevitable struggle between slavery and freedom, which," she predicted in March 1860, "approaches slowly but inevitably,"[21] by evoking images of Southern moral deterioration and unbridled bestiality, of Northern compromises and complicity with the Southern evil. In March 1859 she had used the Sickles scandal—Daniel S. Sickle, a New York congressman, shot his wife's lover, Philipp Barton Key, district attorney for the District of Columbia, in front of the White House—as an example of this moral deterioration. Preston S. Brooks of South Carolina assaulting Charles Sumner, Philemon T. Herbert of California gunning down a hotel manager, Joseph Chambers McKibbon of California, shooting with pistols into a packed railroad car in which his sister's seducer was traveling, brawls during congressional sessions—the violence emanating from these individuals, all of them members of Congress, were, in Assing's reports, truly representative. All of them "either are members of the Southern slavocracy or their even more abominable shield bearers and allies, the Northern Democrats."[22] She cited the flight of thirty-six antislavery farmers from Kentucky as proof that "neither life and freedom nor the property of the most peaceful, innocent citizen are safe beyond Mason and Dixon's line if he dares to believe in the injustice of slavery."[23] "The brutality, licentiousness, and violence of these savage gangs [in the South] are beyond all comprehension."[24] Gambling slavemasters, Southern students rioting on Northern campuses, tobacco-chewing Southern women, censored mail, antiabolitionist violence, the collapse of Southern education, the stagnation of Southern literature, an expanding transatlantic slave trade—in article after article Assing had given instances of a nation on the brink of self-destruction.

During her first months of war reporting Assing left no doubt of her certainty that the inevitable outcome of the struggle would be the destruction of the "peculiar institution":

> The circumstances that have led to the outbreak of this revolution at this time are accidental; however, the deeper, seminal cause existed already at the inception of the republic and has grown along with the country until it assumed its present dominance: it is the eternal conflict between slavery and freedom that no power in the world can resolve. It will continue until the last slave on this continent has gained his freedom. Until then it is beyond the power of the warring parties to make peace even if they would, for the principles they represent are stronger than they and will always lead to new battles. Only a devastating blow against slavery itself can assure peace for the future.[25]

In "The American Apocalypse," an address delivered a month later, Douglass took the same position, declaring that the administration and the Union officers "are woefully mistaken if they think this country can ever have peace while slavery is allowed to live . . . for the statesman of this hour to permit any settlement of the present war between slavery and freedom, which will leave untouched and undestroyed the relation of master and slave, would not only be a great crime, but a great mistake, the bitter fruits of which would poison the life blood of unborn generations."[26] Those who want peace must fight, they both insisted.

Like many abolitionists and most of her fellow German journalists reporting on the war, Assing vigorously criticized the conciliatory gestures and wavering attitude which the Lincoln administration displayed toward the Southern rebels. She railed against Lincoln's "narrowness and his dependence on the prejudices of his environment."[27] How right Douglass had been when, in his open letter of May 1860 "To My British Anti-Slavery Friends," he charged that the "Republican party is . . . only negatively anti-slavery. It is opposed to the political power of slavery, rather than to slavery itself."[28] No solution would be achieved, she thought, as long "as the President and his cabinet are decidedly opposed to any measure that might threaten the sacrosanct institution."[29] The government "continues to make all sorts of efforts to suppress the rebellion of the slaveholders, except for the one measure that would surely and inevitably lead to the desired goal—the liberation of the slaves," she charged. She condemned Lincoln's colonization plans as products of "obtuse minds filled with prejudices."[30]

She even doubted the President's trustworthiness after the Emancipation Proclamation. In October 1862 she wrote:

> One realizes that its effectiveness will be largely destroyed because it is now a necessary measure of war rather than an act of justice and humanitarianism. It comes too late, the President having resisted far too long everything that resembles an act

of emancipation in the hope that nobler motives might prevail. His hand was finally forced by desperate circumstances resulting from a series of bloody defeats in which nearly all gains of the previous six months were lost.

Slaveholders and their Northern friends were enraged by the measure, she reported, yet no one dared rejoice, given "the doubts—hanging over them like a black cloud—that this proclamation was indeed intended to bring about the unconditional abolition of slavery; they fear that instead of the solid gold of emancipation they may be paid in paper notes of dubious value."[31] She, for one, would not have been surprised had she heard of Lincoln's secret meeting with the Confederacy's Vice President, Alexander H. Stephens, aboard the *River Queen* in Hampton Road on 3 February 1865, and Lincoln's deliberate vagueness about the fate of slavery after the war even on the eve of his victory would not have astounded her. She agreed with Douglass that "our Government is still deluded with the idea of conquering by conviction, and are for healing the wounds of the Union by new drafts upon the Negro's blood."[32]

She did not stop there: she needed to censure, to accuse, to expose. During a Fourth of July meeting in 1861 in New York, which she attended, Douglass accused the administration of treason, denouncing Union generals as traitors and impostors. Assing could not have agreed more. From beginning to end her coverage of the war concerned not just white failure and corruption but deceit: she thought Union generals, especially George B. McClellan, were actively sabotaging the war effort. This "Napoleon of Defeats," as she called him, missed chances for victory, and "his mistakes, his lack of courage, and his failure to act have led to all those terrible defeats that are endangering the overall success of the war, have threatened the total annihilation of the army, and resulted in the most pointless bloodshed."[33] What, if not treason, was behind the replacement of the charismatic General John C. Frémont (whom the German 48ers had taken to their hearts) or the slanderous campaign against Franz Sigel? To Assing, Northern racism showed its ugly face as Union officers offered to suppress slave risings, and when slaves seeking Union Army protection were returned in chains to their masters.

The rumor of a slave insurrection was recently going around in Maryland, and General Butler, commander of the United States troops in that state, offered to suppress it . . . In Pensacola, Florida, several slaves took refuge at Fort Pickens in the belief that they would find protection under the Union flag. But the commander returned them in chains to their owners so that they might flog them to death. Colonel Dimmick, commander of Fort Munroe, Virginia, is mean and cowardly enough to assure the rebels that there is not a single abolitionist under his command and that he would not tolerate any tampering with the system of slavery.[34]

The President and his cabinet, as represented in Assing's *Morgenblatt* pieces, were possessed of that same treacherous spirit when they expressed their reluctance to organize black regiments and later in their discrimination against black soldiers.[35] So permeated by images of cowardice, treason, and racism were Assing's representations of the Northern war efforts that the draft riots that erupted in New York City in the summer of 1863 appeared only as another natural expression of this national inadequacy. This was not the people's outcry for peace, she charged, but a mob that had been formed and manipulated by proslavery forces: "It was not mere coincidence but the result of collusion between the Democratic Party leaders of the North and those of the South that the murders and mayhem in New York occurred almost simultaneously with the rebels' invasion of Pennsylvania and Maryland." She named New York's governor, Horatio Seymour, as a ringleader, and charged, "They hoped . . . that a frightened, terrified public would let itself be tempted by the governor and his allies to assume a hostile attitude against the government, thereby forcing the administration to accept a disgraceful peace that would, in fact, put the free North under the rule of the slavemasters."[36]

For Assing it was the treasonous conduct of the Lincoln administration that explained why the slaves were reluctant to support the Union effort with a rising that would end the masters' rebellion. In January 1861 she asserted:

> Should the dreaded Negro uprising actually erupt, it would squelch all rebellious movements more quickly and more surely than all repressive measures of the government would do, for none of the slave states has the means to fight a superior black force. At the first news of the destruction of a few plantations and the killing of some slaveholders and overseers, these very loudmouths and ruffians who today are only too eager to curse the North would come crawling for its protection and assistance.[37]

In 1863, however, she cautioned: "Since the beginning of the rebellion, the slaves have been treated too hypocritically, insidiously, and cruelly by the federal government and particularly by the Democratic generals, and their hopes have been too often dashed for them to rise up against their masters in the expectation of protection and assistance." Even after the Emancipation Proclamation, she thought that there was a time when such an edict would have been sufficient to join the entire black race into an army of active allies; yet, how can the slaves . . . of Louisiana not remember their thirty companions who arrived in New Orleans, unarmed . . . hoping to find protection, but who instead were shot and killed in cold blood by our own troops? . . . How can the slaves of Alabama forget four hundred of their companions whom General Mitchell had promised their freedom in return for their loyal services, but who—upon his transfer—were turned over the very next day to their so-called owners by his successor, General Buell . . . ? The history of this war is replete with such shameful actions: they are the monuments of a moral condition that is beyond expression.[38]

Northern treason, far from being an exception, thus was the rule in Ottilie Assing's war reports.

In this perspective, the Northern reluctance to recruit, train, and put black troops into action was no longer simply an expression of racism but a calculated sabotage of the war effort. Her final evaluation, published in August 1865, bespoke her disillusionment: ". . . the abolition of slavery was not a measure arising from the nation's sense of humanity and justice but simply an act necessitated by circumstances," she thought, and she predicted that "the task of emancipation will for the near future remain little more than a fragmentary patchwork."[39] For her, the postwar rhetoric of reconciliation between North and South signified one thing only—renewed black suffering.

Only when focusing on the African-American contribution to the war could Ottilie Assing reimagine the war in terms of heroism, liberation, and progress. Parallel to her discourse on white failure thus ran a discourse on black bravery, skill, and expertise, which transformed the Civil War from a white man's war into a black people's revolution, from a war in which white soldiers liberated helpless black slaves into a process of black self-liberation. In August 1861 Assing proudly told the story of the free black steward William Tillman, whose schooner, the *S. J. Waring*, was kidnapped by the Southern privateer *Jefferson Davis*. The *Waring*'s captain and first mate were sent back to New York, but two seamen, a passenger, and Tillman were retained as the vessel, now manned with a Southern crew of five, continued toward Charleston. When Tillman overheard the Southerners chuckling over their good luck at capturing a "Nigger," whom they intended to sell for at least $1,000, he "determined to maintain his freedom at whatever cost and asked two sailors, his fellow prisoners, for assistance. One of them refused to go along; the other one, however, a German by the name of Stedding, promised to assist him in his dangerous undertaking," Assing wrote. It was yet another fine African-American–German alliance.

The schooner was within fifty miles of Charleston when Stedding finally passed word to Tillman that the crew were asleep and the black steward could begin what Assing defined as liberation work: "He dashed down to the cabin with a hatchet, the only weapon he had been able to obtain, split open the heads of all three with terrifically accurate aim, and then, with Stedding's help, fed the twitching bodies to the sharks. It was the deed of just a few minutes and happened so quietly that it did not awaken the other two pirates."[40] Assing's sensationalist account treated her readers to every gory detail, yet carefully avoided any formulation that would enable them to interpret it in racist terms. Her black protagonist united physical force and restraint; his aggression was controlled. Assing's Tillman was like Douglass' Madison Washington, with "the head to conceive, and the hand to execute"; he was "one to be sought as a friend, but to be dreaded as an enemy."[41] And the participation of a white man, a German whom her audience would not associate with savagery, authenticated the deed as well as cleansing it of negative racial implications. Assing's heroes plotted and observed; they had the patience to wait for the right moment, thus maintaining the intelligent, rational posture of men who control their fate. Rather than massacring all of the whites, they executed only three of their tormentors, for they knew they would need help in getting the *Waring* back to New York, and they refused to take more lives than absolutely necessary. This was neither an act of revenge nor of passion, Assing explained; the two brave men were acting in self-defense, on the basis of the most basic of natural rights—the right to life. Although neither Tillman nor Stedding was a navigator, they made it back to New York. There Tillman arrived in triumph—"as captain of the vessel on which he had shipped as a steward," Assing quoted him as saying.

Assing's account of the Tillman episode was written while she was staying with the Douglasses in Rochester, and in the same month Douglass published his Tillman story in *Douglass' Monthly*. The two articles illustrate how closely Assing and Douglass worked together: except for the fact that one was written in German, the other in English, the narratives were almost identical in wording, structure, and message. They deviated in one passage only—in the sentences describing the pirates' execution: Douglass named the fact of the execution but remained silent on the details. "Tillman," he wrote, ". . . began his fearful work—killing the pirate captain, mate and second mate, and thus making himself master of the ship with no other weapon than a common hatchet . . ."[42] No mention of blows and split heads that featured so prominently at the center of Assing's text. Writing for a German audience in German, Assing was free to satisfy, though in a controlled way, her readers' thirst for the sensational, but it is revealing that she did not rely on her own dramatic skills. Her delineation of the killing was an almost verbatim translation of central passages from Douglass' only venture into fiction—the story "The Heroic Slave," first published in 1853, in which he had dramatized the self-liberation of blacks on the slave vessel *Creole* in 1841.[43]

The awareness of black individuality, of the heterogeneity of black life, made Assing's war reports radically different from those of fellow German abolitionist journalists. German-American liberals like Friedrich Kapp, Alfred Douai, and Hans Kudlich wrote sophisticated and abstract tracts on slavery, arguing on the level of political and social theory. African-Americans as a race appeared as objects of learned discussion, as victims to be liberated by enlightened whites, especially by heroic German-Americans. But nowhere in their texts do we encounter an individual black person; in vain do we look for the free black agent, the autonomous black voice. Ottilie Assing was the only German-American journalist of the day who perceived and represented the African-American experience as both the history of a people and the history of individuals; in her work, African-Americans speak for themselves.

In an article published in May 1862 Assing made sure her German readers understood what Douglass had stated so clearly in his *Narrative* and in *My Bondage and My Freedom*: the longing for freedom was ingrained in every human being, in fact constituted humanity; it thus also defined the existence of those who had never had the privilege of experiencing it. The hero of this story was Robert Smalls, a slave serving as a pilot in Charleston, South Carolina. He was to steer the steamer *Planter*, loaded with weapons and ammunition worth a million dollars, and manned with slaves, out to sea early in the morning. Consequently he aroused no suspicion when he began preparing the vessel the evening before its scheduled departure. At night, he smuggled his family on board, and the *Planter* sailed with the rising sun, "in full view of the cannons of Forts Sumter and Moultrie, where no one had the least doubt that the commanding officer was on board and nothing was amiss." Upon reaching the Northern blockade, Smalls hoisted the Union flag and handed over the vessel. "Congress awarded Smalls and his companions a third of the value of the cargo, to which they were legally entitled, so that the heroic slave is now a free and wealthy man,"[44] Assing reported triumphantly. Though raised a slave, Assing's black protagonist needed no white mentor to teach him the value of freedom; he needed no white liberator to guide him to freedom land. His intelligence, shrewdness, and skills empowered him to liberate not only himself but his family and fellow slaves. Smalls was her refutation of the myth of hapless black chattel waiting for white saviors, as well as her answer to one of the most frequently articulated questions of the day: "What shall we do with the free Negro?" She placed this ex-slave in a line with Pennington, Douglass, and Tillman, as another personification of the African-American's ability to live up to the privileges, duties, and responsibilities of American citizenship.

Assing was careful not to dissociate her individual black heroes from the anonymous masses of slaves. She knew that whenever contributions and achievements by members of a minority were considered exceptional, apologists of the status quo misused this to legitimize and perpetuate conventional hierarchies and power structures. Consequently she developed discursive strategies designed to protect her reporting against such manipulations. How could Union troops succeed, she asked, but for the thousands of slaves, the North's "natural allies," who supplied them with important information, who volunteered as their spies and scouts? "The Negroes prove to be hardworking laborers and faithful, reliable allies wherever you go, and they often provide valuable information about the movements of the enemy."[45] It was slaves, she continued, "who, in enemy territory, where the population either has the most intense hatred of the Union troops or is intimidated by the system of terror that reigns throughout the South, often provide the most useful information about the enemy's movements and numbers, thereby having brought about many a victory and prevented many defeats."[46] Only the ingenuity of slaves had enabled fifty Northern prisoners of war to escape from a Southern prison camp in Richmond in 1864. "These Negroes helped them to find the right route, they taught them how to avoid rebel ports, they hosted them and provided them with food."[47] Once liberated, the ex-slaves supported the war effort. "Meanwhile, on the island of Port Royal off South Carolina, which was taken by our troops a few months ago, Negroes who had been abandoned by their masters and thus obtained their freedom are busy planting cotton and other crops," she wrote in May 1862. "Reports from that region are very positive and encouraging; they convincingly contradict the silly, base, and ignorant fairy tale that the Negro will work only under duress."[48] Blacks in Assing's articles were portrayed as sustainers of life, as nurturers; she gendered their war contribution by evoking associations with traditional nineteenth-century female virtues and obligations, thus empowering her slave protagonists without evoking conventional notions of black ferocity or incompetence.

Yet Assing knew that the accepted hierarchy that elevated a man's work above a woman's tasks extended to the realities of the Civil War; fighting and killing were considered superior to providing for the family, nurturing, healing, keeping the economy running. If African-Americans were to stand a chance of being respected as citizens, they must avoid being associated exclusively with female qualities. It was essential that they prove their valor in both female and male realms, in nurturing and fighting. "If this conflict shall expand to the grand dimensions which events seem to indicate, the iron arm of the black man may be called into service,"[49] Douglass had prophesied during the opening month of the conflict. In a speech in Philadelphia on 14 January 1862 he charged: "We are fighting the rebels with only one hand, when we ought to be fighting them with both. We are recruiting our troops in the towns and villages of the North, when we ought to be recruiting them on the plantations of the South. We are striking the guilty rebels with our soft, white hand, when we should be striking with the iron hand of the black man, which we keep chained behind us. We have been catching slaves instead of arming them."[50] Assing faithfully reported on Douglass' struggle for black participation in the conflict, and with Douglass she believed that black enlistment in the Union Army would guarantee rights of citizenship after the war, that loyalty in a period of national distress might be the chance for African-Americans to end their marginalization—an illusion German Jews like her father had harbored during the Napoleonic Wars and would revive during World War I, a vision to which African-Americans had subscribed during the War of Independence and to which they returned during World War I.

In February 1863 Douglass began a vigorous recruitment campaign, traveling thousands of miles and giving his famous "Men of Color, to Arms" address. African-American men responded, and on 28 March 1863 he witnessed the dress parade on Boston Common of the black Massachusetts 54th Regiment, among them his son Lewis, before they boarded the *DeMolay* at Battery Wharf.[51] The African-American soldiers were cheered and celebrated by friends, family, and abolitionist bystanders as they marched to the harbor, but they were also beaten (Lewis Douglass was one of the victims) and spat upon, their weapons torn from their hands. Douglass was silent about these outrages, fearful lest the information endanger his recruitment campaign. A year later, he and Assing were among the New Yorkers who cheered a regiment of black volunteers as they marched down Broadway to board a steamer for New Orleans. "The soldiers looked splendid, presented themselves nobly, and were admired by all," Assing wrote, listing the assets her readers would expect of a disciplined, well-trained German militia. "Many are of tall, powerful stature, and these children of the South inspired confidence in their strength, their endurance, and their courage."[52] Subverting the presumption that military valor was a white man's asset, she asserted, "Most of them were genuine Negroes."

Clearly she was relieved that thousands of whites were cheering African-American soldiers on the same Broadway where a mob had terrorized and killed Blacks only a few months before, during the draft riots. What pleased her most, however, was that New York's African-Americans were there in droves: "most of them in their Sunday best, their dark faces beaming with pleasure at seeing their brothers so honored and recognized rather than despised, mistreated, or at best tolerated as an unavoidable evil . . . In spite of the crowd there was perfect order: everywhere you looked people were friendly and full of good spirits; no loud or rude word and no argument disrupted the overall good feeling."[53] Black and white remained separate—Broadway was white, Canal Street black—but Assing's city basked in goodwill.

Although during the final two years of the war one-tenth of the Union Army was black, these African-American soldiers received second-class treatment.[54] For months, the Massachusetts 54th remained without uniforms or proper shoes; their weapons were ridiculously outmoded; black soldiers received less pay than whites; and since the administration refused to commission African-American officers, their leaders were white men who often faced their men's initial distrust as well as ostracism and ridicule by their fellow officers. In December 1862 Jefferson Davis declared that the Southern slave code would be used against African-American soldiers caught by the Confederates—that is, they would be treated as insurrectionists. As a result of this proclamation, black prisoners of war were executed in the South, the wounded were refused medical treatment or murdered on the spot, exchange of black prisoners was ruled out. The Lincoln administration remained silent on this challenge for months.[55] Douglass was caught in a frightful dilemma: after years of struggling for the establishment of black regiments, of claiming the black community's willingness to fight for its people's liberation, Lincoln's policy was resulting in what came close to an African-American boycott. Douglass could not help sympathizing with this aggressive display of black pride and solidarity, yet he was too shrewd a politician not to realize that a low black turnout would be detrimental to black claims in a civil rights debate after the war. On the one hand, he continued to lecture on the necessity of black participation despite harassment, and on the other, he protested vigorously and loudly against discrimination, as well as against the Confederate treatment of black war prisoners. He finally declared that he would cease his recruitment efforts until the black regiments were guaranteed equal treatment and rights. In July 1863 the administration relented, and in a meeting between Lincoln and Douglass not only did the President promise to end discrimination in the Union Army but Secretary of War Stanton

Charles Douglass
Ottilie Assing sent a copy of this photo of
Charles wearing the Union uniform to her
sister in February 1865. She was proud of
Charles' military career but ridiculed the photo
as a "veritable Rochester product."

Lewis Douglass
In 1868 Lewis Douglass, then a secretary in a
Colorado mining company, spent two weeks at
Ottilie Assing's place in Hoboken. In a letter
to Ludmilla she praised him as "an educated
and pleasant young man."

Frederick Douglass, Jr.
Frederick was only fourteen when Ottilie Assing first came to Rochester. He always maintained friendly relations with her. After his
marriage, his parents and Ottilie Assing were
frequent dinner guests at his home in Washington, D.C.

offered Douglass a commission as brigadier general to General Lorenzo Thomas, then stationed in Vicksburg, Mississippi. Douglass was to raise regiments of freed slaves in the liberated territories.[56]

Frederick Douglass returned to Rochester, impressed by the President's predicaments and sincerity, and hoping that he had achieved a major break-through. If he harbored doubts after this encounter, he never spoke of them in public, and perhaps he even dismissed them from his own mind out of a des-perate need for a perspective, for allies, for individuals in whom he could be-lieve. Determined that he could "better serve my poor bleeding country-men whose great opportunity has now come, by going South and summoning them to assert their just liberty, than I can do by staying here," he decided to cease the publication of his *Douglass' Monthly*, explaining in his "Valedictory" leader of 16 August 1863 that he was "going South to assist Adjutant General Thomas, in the organization of colored troops, who shall win for the millions in bondage the inestimable blessings of liberty and country."[57]

Ottilie Assing had helped Douglass prepare for his encounter with the Pres-ident, and she had been by his side after his return from Washington. An en-thusiastic supporter of Frémont, she was reluctant to believe in Lincoln's sincerity, and she trembled at the thought of Douglass entering enemy territory, but she was thrilled at the respect which the President had paid him, and an-ticipated Douglass' military distinctions and heroism. But the letter from Washington never arrived. In the fall, a now publicly humiliated Frederick Douglass resumed his abolition work, denouncing the administration for its "absence of all moral feeling."[58]

So exclusively did Ottilie focus on Douglass' hopes and disappointments that she totally neglected her own work. From May until October 1863 the *Morgenblatt* received not a single line from her. When she resumed her commu-nication in November, however, she allowed her pent-up disgust and bitterness full expression. Reporting on the extraordinary bravery and skill which the 54th Massachusetts Regiment (in which Lewis Douglass served as sergeant ma-jor) had displayed at Fort Wagner in July 1863, she called the battle, "though not crowned by success . . . one of the most magnificent military episodes of the entire war."[59] But she contrasted this valor with the administration's treatment of Douglass:

> This past summer, the Secretary of War suggested to the famous orator Frederick Douglas [sic], a colored man, who had probably captivated him by his imposing and congenial personality, to act as a recruiting officer and to organize colored regiments

in the South. The news of this appointment caused a considerable stir and was reported in every newspaper. As far as I know, there was no word of criticism, yet the Secretary of War did not have the courage to act on his own freely conceived and proposed idea. He tried to back off by means of petty excuses and intentional misunderstandings, so that Douglas [sic], fully aware of the game that was being played, broke off the discussions in complete disgust and dismay.

Assing made sure her readers understood that a superior African American man—his nobility and power expressed by the word "majestic"—had been humiliated by white officials unfit to hold a candle to him. For her, Lincoln was responsible for Douglass' humiliation, and she never forgave the President. Only after his assassination did she find words of sympathy, but even those seemed forced.

In July 1862 Douglass had declared in his *Monthly* that the "true history of this war will show that the loyal army found no friends at the South so faithful, active, and daring in their efforts to sustain the Government as the Negroes."[60] Assing's descriptions of the black regiments supported this reading. In each military encounter she described, unloved black regiments distinguished themselves by discipline, bravery, and skill:

When the government, forced by necessity, decided to arm the free Negroes and the slaves in the face of American color prejudice, all the friends of the rebels—the secret as well as the openly declared friends—shouted: "But the Negroes don't want to fight!" It was a silly objection, behind which lurked the fear that the Negroes would be all too serious in battle, that they would prove to be the slaveholders' all too bitter enemy and thus deal slavery its final blow. . . . Wherever blacks have stood face to face with the enemy they have displayed a courage and discipline that would have done honor to the best-trained white troops.[61]

Douglass had always argued that African-Americans were America's conscience;[62] during the Civil War they became, for Assing, America's liberation army.

The terms she used to describe all this almost comically betrayed her German upbringing: "Those [colored people] who . . . cultivate the land or construct canals or entrenchments are as industrious, orderly, and reliable as one might wish. The black regiments are the most useful and have proven their courage under fire during the few opportunities that they have had; they have developed a fortitude and discipline that would do honor to the best army in the world."[63] Assing knew only too well that her contemporaries' Eurocentrism, combined with a deeply rooted belief in racial hierarchies, automatically associated difference with inferiority. She tried to cater to her audience's sympathies by clothing the "other" in images of the familiar, reimagining African-American laborers and soldiers as perfect German laborers and soldiers with dark skin. They could become her heroes because she reimagined them as conforming to the norms she had internalized. Still, fifty years before W. E. B. Du Bois protested against the exclusion of African-Americans from American Civil War historiography, almost a century before Benjamin Quarles and James M. McPherson drew our attention to the African-American contribution to the Civil War, more than a century before African-American historians and novelists finally welcomed the chance to rewrite this war from an African-American perspective, Ottilie Assing's Civil War was a war of black self-liberation. "But we are not to be saved by the captain this time, but by the crew," Douglass had announced to his abolitionist audience on 4 December 1863[64]—by a black crew at that, Assing's writing insisted. She focused on the marginalized, invited the silenced to speak up, and subverted contemporary notions of how history would be written.

The outbreak of the Civil War was like an injection of new hope for Ottilie Assing and Frederick Douglass at a point when they had been ready to turn their backs on the nation that rejected its African-American daughters and sons. The war years, however, threatened to deprive them of the last vestiges of respect for a country that seemed composed of Southern barbarians and Northern traitors. From the first day of the war they joined forces to redirect this erring nation to the path of justice and honor, but though the abolition of slavery was finally achieved, they both knew that political expediency and military necessity, rather than a moral awakening, had brought about this important transformation. For strategic reasons they continued to balance, in their public statements, images of apocalypse with those of hope, threats of doom with promises of salvation and regeneration. It was a performance in the service of their political creed and mission that exhausted them, drained their strength. For the ex-slave Frederick Douglass this war had a meaning that it would never have for any white American, not even for a woman as passionately in love with him as Ottilie Assing. The war forced him to deal with that deeply personal hatred of slaveholders he had struggled to control by transforming it into words; it now flared up with new vigor, including those Northerners who conspired with his former tormentors.[65] It seems likely that he at times had to cope with feelings, especially in his relationships with his white acquaintances, which he could not possibly communicate outside the African-American realm, with the exception of, perhaps, Ottilie. Her exposure to anti-Semitism had familiarized her with the humiliation, anger, and hatred, the bitterness and sadness of the rejected "other." For the duration of the war she stood by his side, served as his secretary, ghostwriter, and inspiration, unconditionally and unwaveringly. Her European upbringing no doubt made it difficult for her to grasp many of Douglass' feelings, but her absolute loyalty as well as her sincerity in trying to understand won her an unprecedented degree of respect and devotion from Douglass.

Although his obligations required that Douglass travel extensively during the war years, the relationship between him and Assing intensified as they spent more time together than ever before. Assing's summers in Rochester began as early as June and often lasted into late October and early November. Pressing invitations from her relatives in Wisconsin received friendly but firm rejections; after Amalie Schoppe's death she discontinued her correspondence with Amalie's son; she canceled the extensive travel plans she had made before meeting Douglass. She realized how much she could contribute to Douglass' mission, how much he valued the professional partnership she offered, how much he needed a person who shared his beliefs. As a woman who never stood in the spotlight of public life, there was no need for her to make the kind of political compromises Douglass could not avoid, and her radicalism and stubbornness kept him from relaxing into any of these compromises, urged him on, reminded him of what was at stake. She, in turn, learned to accept realism, pragmatism, even opportunism from Douglass, and she began to understand the role of what Vincent Harding calls "self-inflicted amnesia"[66] in political life. Douglass taught her about strategy, about the need for compromises, about the power of words as well as of silences.

These Rochester summers during the Civil War had a special quality also because they were all theirs. European tourists of abolitionist leanings, who used to visit the Douglass home as a historic landmark, a conveniently political stop between the Hudson tour and Niagara Falls, observed and commented on the war from a safe transatlantic distance. Many American abolitionists who had continued to befriend Douglass after his clash with the Garrisonians had fallen away with the rumors of Douglass' involvement with Harpers Ferry and his exile in England; the few who stood by him now mostly felt that the war spelled the end of their abolitionist endeavors. The Douglass home had almost ceased to be a stop for the Underground Railroad; there were few black guests. The Douglass social circle in Rochester was small—the Posts, the Anthonys, the Porters, members of the Spring Street AME Zion Church; they visited only irregularly. Annie was dead; in 1862 Rosetta, twenty-three years old and still of a "quarrelsome disposition towards my mother,"[67] left for Philadelphia to become a teacher; before the war was over she was married to the ex-slave Nathan Sprague and had a daughter (called Annie); in 1863 Lewis and Charles joined the army. With her children gone, with few friends and no fugitives, Anna Murray withdrew to the kitchen and the garden.

But even during the winter months, in which Assing lived and worked in Hoboken, Douglass and Assing saw more of each other than ever before. Douglass lectured frequently in the area, and there were numerous occasions for excursions to or stopovers at Hoboken, always special and precious because not a single moment could be taken for granted.

In August 1863 the Douglasses received the news that their son Lewis was seriously ill. After weeks of anxiety, his condition improved and he was put in a military hospital in New York City. Douglass immediately came to be with his son, and for three weeks he spent as much time at Lewis' bedside as he could.[68] We do not know why, but Anna Murray stayed in Rochester, and it was Ottilie who often accompanied Douglass on his daily trips to the hospital; to her he returned in the evenings, to talk about his anxiety, to share his sense of relief when Lewis began to regain his strength. For Assing these weeks of care and fear were an invaluable chance to prove to Douglass that her love was not limited to him alone, was not purely self-centered, but extended to his family. For three precious weeks of extreme emotional challenge, in which his son's life was at stake, Assing could slip into all the roles of mother and nurse, adviser and listener, friend and lover. By reaching out to his son, by embracing him as her charge, as her concern, she dramatically expanded the roles she played in Douglass' life, thus adding new substance to the relationship.

When the war ended, Assing and Douglass realized that years of fierce work and considerable humiliation, of traveling, writing, lecturing, and waiting, had taken a heavy toll on Frederick Douglass. By 1865, once the shock of Lincoln's assassination and the excitement of victory parades abated, the extent of his exhaustion became visible. The abolition of slavery also abolished his occupation. No wonder that he was torn by what he later called "a strange and, perhaps, perverse feeling." "My great and exceeding joy over these stupendous achievements, especially over the abolition of slavery [. . .] was slightly tinged with a feeling of sadness. I felt that I had reached the end of the noblest and best part of my life; my school was broken up, my church disbanded, and the beloved congregation dispersed, never to come together again. The anti-slavery platform had performed its work, and my voice was no longer needed. 'Othello's occupation was gone.' "[69] At the age of forty-seven, he had to decide all over again how he wanted to and could shape his life in the years ahead, and it was not easy. On the one hand, he knew that the success of his public life and the personal satisfaction he drew from it would make it hard for him to return to the menial jobs he had held decades before; on the other hand, he doubted that the skills he had acquired in the antebellum decade would enable him to find the "more congenial and higher employment"[70] to which he aspired.

Ottilie Assing was aware of these anxieties and doubts. But whereas the end of the war left Douglass suspended in midair, she was full of happy anticipation. Nine years ago she had agreed to be the "other woman" in Douglass' life, knowing that his role as a prominent public figure made it impossible for him to divorce his wife; knowing that his work and responsibility might last a lifetime; knowing that American society ostracized the adulteress; knowing that it spat on the woman who violated the color line; knowing that she was denying herself children, a home. She had exposed herself to this because the physical, emotional, and intellectual rewards, the sense of belonging she found in her relationship with Douglass by far outweighed the liabilities of the situation. But there can be no doubt that underneath the defiant pose there was also a longing for stability, normalcy, and respectability.

And then, after nine years under the shadow of Douglass' public life, his mission came to an end. As much as she had admired and glorified him as a black freedom fighter, she could not be sad that history abolished this role. Not only had he freed the slaves; their emancipation also freed him. Finally he could withdraw from the limelight and begin a new life, removed from the cruelty of the public gaze. No longer observed and watched, he would finally be empowered to solve his domestic problems, and her letters to her sister Ludmilla document that there was not the slightest doubt in Assing that this could only mean separation from Anna Murray and a legalization of their liaison. Frederick Douglass had liberated his race; it was time for him to liberate himself—for Ottilie Assing and their love. At the age of forty-six, a woman on the eve of menopause, about to enter a phase of a woman's life which her contemporaries associated with the end of sexual desire and desirability, the end of erotic vitality and luster in women, the changes that so frightened Douglass must have appeared like bright rays of hope to Assing. This was her chance for a new beginning, for personal satisfaction, for an almost normal domestic life. Perhaps her last chance for personal happiness.

She began to cherish hopes for her and Douglass' future, and when it became clear that the Northern victory was inevitable, these hopes surfaced in her *Morgenblatt* articles. Time and again she wrote of attempts to define an American future without slavery, of race relations in a liberated, regenerate America. She revived her old hope for a composite American nationality, of people of various races and nations living together peacefully. To this familiar notion she added a suggestion that was a product of her most intimate experience: an article on race crossing. Submitted to the *Morgenblatt* in January 1864, it was more than yet another unconventional political vision; it was also a personal programmatic statement.

Her article was based on a seventy-two-page pamphlet entitled "Miscegenation: The Theory of the Blending of the Races Applied to the American White Man and Negro," which first circulated in some Eastern cities late in December 1863. The anonymous author, the first to use the term "miscegenation," recommended race crossing as a panacea not only for America's racial dilemmas but for the much debated physical degeneration of what was commonly called "the American race." If Americans wanted to become "the finest race on earth" they must blend "all that is passionate and emotional in the darker races, all that is imaginative and spiritual in the Asiatic races, and all that is intellectual and perceptive in the white race," the pamphlet argued, claiming that it was a well-established fact "that the miscegenetic or mixed races are much superior mentally, physically, and morally, to those pure or unmixed."[71] Most people assumed that the booklet's author was an abolitionist fanatic, but in fact the publication was launched by allies of the Democratic Party as part of their campaign of racist demagoguery. "Fathers, save us from nigger husbands" was the young women's slogan in Democratic Party parades of the day,[72] and the pamphlet fell in line with the party's attempt to implicate the Republicans. It was written by David Goodman Croly and George Wakeman, both working for the conservative *New York World*.[73]

Ottilie Assing had not the slightest suspicion that this text was a vicious political hoax. She took its statements at face value, yet hers was too acute a mind to ignore its weaknesses. She criticized it for appearing anonymously; she noted its stylistic errors and lack of sophistication: "The piece is obviously well-meaning and based on honest conviction, but it is written with neither brilliance nor originality. The moral, physiological, and historical reasons adduced by the author have in large part been accepted by people of enlightened thinking; but some of his other reasons are either superfluous or lack a sound foundation." But she was grateful that finally somebody had the stamina to speak up on an issue on which silence reigned: "Its significance . . . lies in the fact that there is someone today who dares to champion a cause that hitherto has been considered to be the most contemptible, offensive, disgraceful, even immoral idea banished from society. A woman who left her husband with another man has a greater chance of being graciously readmitted into this society than she who marries the most respectable and educated colored man out of love and by respecting all legal formalities."[74]

In his essay "The Question of Amalgamation" (1860), Douglass had spoken of the equality of "pure" and "mixed" races.[75] But Assing knew of the detrimental effects of the pseudoscientific discourse that denounced all forms of race mixing as unnatural. In *Types of Mankind* (1854) Josiah Clark Nott and George R. Gliddon argued that blacks and whites were members of different species, warning that "the superior races must be kept free from all adulterations, otherwise the world will retrograde . . . in civilization,"[76] and in 1863 Louis Agassiz declared that race mixing was as immoral and perverse as incest: "Viewed from a high moral point of view the production of half-breeds is as much a sin against nature, as incest in a civilized community is a sin against purity of character."[77] The abolitionists, whom Assing usually portrayed as friends of the black cause, not only abstained from tackling this taboo, she noted, but internalized it:

> As little as two years ago any word in favor of mingling the races would have caused a unanimous outcry of shock and horror. It was the very issue on which even abolitionists, who called for complete civil equality of the Negro, could not overcome their prejudice. Many who treated the colored man socially as an equal and who did not hesitate to go against public opinion by showing themselves in public with him or even treating him as a friend would have revolted against the thought of darkening their Anglo-Saxon blood by mixing it with the African. And those who perhaps had no personal objections were loath to incur the rejection and contempt of the masses.[78]

One can easily discern here the autobiographical subtext of pain and anger, of personal vulnerability and humiliation. It is one of the few passages in Assing's writing—whether public or private—in which she allowed us a glimpse of the ostracism, disgust, and rejection which she experienced as Douglass' companion. She noted that famous abolitionists were either tardy in defending or silent about actual love between blacks and whites: "Even Wendell Phillips, one of the most courageous leaders in the struggle for the cause of the Negro, came out only last year in favor of the intermingling of the races; and Harriet Beecher Stowe, in all her descriptions of Southern life and relations between the races, did not give a single instance of true love between their representatives." Yet, she suggested, such love matches occurred. "Though rare, they occur in spite of all prejudice and ostracism." And, she went on, in a celebration of hope and promise, "now that someone has made a start, the issue will not be allowed to rest."[79]

Now that slavery was abolished, leaving the United States was no longer an option for Frederick Douglass, but withdrawal from the public gaze certainly was. As early as the fall of 1862, when the Emancipation Proclamation became a historical reality, he began toying with the idea of "following the noble example of my old friends Stephen and Abby Kelley Foster, purchase a little farm and settle myself down to earn an honest living by tilling the soil."[80] No matter how committed Assing was to Douglass, no matter how much she shared his longing for privacy and a new start, this rural dream was hard for her to swallow. She was a city woman, enchanted by Paris, enthusiastic about Berlin, in love with New York City. Thus the warning that Julia Griffiths Crofts sent off to Douglass upon learning of his plans could have been dictated by Assing: "No, my dear friend, do not be led astray. You know nothing about farming yourself and would be like a fish out of water without mental *labors* & public work!"[81]

The Civil War ended Frederick Douglass' mission; the Northern victory forced him to reimagine himself. For the first time since they met, Douglass and Assing had a realistic chance to make a new start. Ottilie Assing believed that their personal fulfillment could and would be achieved if they joined their fates. Did it occur to her that her and Douglass' visions might not be compatible? Did it strike her that she might be the only one dreaming of that perfect union?

VIII

A DELIGHTFUL TIME, ADMIRABLY SPENT

The Reconstruction Years

The world is constituted so that we can only laugh about it! . . . Let us be jolly . . . together we will forever invent new festivities, and then, whenever they allow us to go unnoticed, we will weep together! People shall only see us laughing, but perhaps God will see our tears, and He will forgive us!

—CLARA MUNDT, *Aphra Behn*

I have done the state some service and they know it . . .

—WILLIAM SHAKESPEARE, *Othello*

New York, 15 May 1871[1]

My Dear Sir!

You may be amazed to be addressed from so great a distance by a person unknown to you. I might not have had the courage did I not believe that any success in your endeavors for the intellectual liberation of the human race must give you something of the satisfaction which the Christian missionary experiences when he, from his point of view, has saved souls. I had always hoped to pay a visit to Germany, after a long period of absence, and to meet you personally, and although I have not abandoned this hope, so many obstacles are momentarily in the way of fulfillment that I prefer to tell you in the form of a letter what I had planned to talk to you about.

A number of years ago I met Frederick Douglass, a man whose name has possibly reached you. He is a mulatto, was born a slave in the South, and gained his freedom through flight to the North. Thanks to his exceptional talent, his skills as a writer, and his brilliant rhetoric he worked his way out of obscurity within a few years and became one of the most famous men in America. He was one of the most superior among the anti-

slavery agitators, and since the abolition of slavery he excels no less by his discourse on political and social questions. Personal sympathy and concordance in many central issues brought us together; but there was one *obstacle to a loving and lasting friendship— namely, the personal Christian God. Early impressions, environments, and the beliefs still dominating this entire nation held sway over Douglass. The ray of light of German atheism had never reached him, while I, thanks to natural inclination, training, and the whole influence of German education and literature, had overcome the belief in God at an early age. I experienced this dualism as an unbearable dissonance, and since I not only saw in Douglass the ability to recognize intellectual shackles but also credited him with the courage and integrity to discard at once the old errors and, in this one respect, his entire past, his lifelong beliefs, I sought refuge with you. In the English translation by Mary Anne Evans we read the* Essence of Christianity *together, which I, too, encountered for the first time on that occasion. This book—for me one of the greatest manifestations of the human spirit—resulted in a total reversal of his attitudes. Douglass has become your enthusiastic admirer, and the result is a remarkable progress, an expansion of his horizon, of all his attitudes as expressed especially in his lectures and essays, which are intellectually much more rich, deep, and logical than before. While most of his former companions in the struggle against slavery have disappeared from the public stage since the abolition, and, in a way, have become anachronisms because they lack fertile ideas, Douglass now has reached the zenith of his development. For the satisfaction of seeing a superior man won over for atheism, and through that to have gained a faithful, valuable friend for myself, I feel obliged to you, and I cannot deny myself the pleasure of expressing my gratitude as well as my heartfelt veneration.*

Finally, I venture with typical American audacity to importune you with a request. Would you be so kind as to grant me the pleasure of receiving a photograph of you? I would ask you for two copies, one for me and one for Douglass. We as atheists, who create no god to worship according to our image of ourselves, are all the more attached in deep and ardent veneration to those human beings in whom we recognize the representatives and translators of the highest ideas of our age.

Your devoted

Ottilie Assing

A fter years of living in boardinghouses Ottilie Assing was tired of makeshift arrangements and borrowed places. Since 1857 she had been more or less satisfied with the rooms she rented in Mrs. Marks's home, not only because Mrs. Marks respected her need for solitude and independence but especially because

Douglass had always been welcome, no eyebrows raised, no questions asked. But in the summer of 1865, while staying in Rochester, she learned she had to move.[2] Under normal circumstances this would not have been a big issue, but Assing's circumstances were anything but normal. The problem was not to find new lodgings; it was to find a place that would also keep its door open for Frederick Douglass.

The German-American community in Hoboken—her "gang,"[3] as she called it—had given her a sense of belonging and stability for eight years. The German aristocrat and professional revolutionary Carlos von Gagern, who made himself a name as an officer in the Mexican Revolution and who visited New York in 1865 and again in 1870–71, remembered Ottilie Assing as an active member of a dynamic community of radical freethinkers: "She was then already a lady in her more mature years. Like her mother, the poet of charming songs, she had educated herself to become a teacher. The only spinsterly aspect I found in her was her love of cats, of which she had several fine specimens. Otherwise she had remained young in heart and spirit, enthusiastically embracing any sign of progress, especially in the religious realm." Her love of Douglass and her devotion to his cause was central to the impression she made on Gagern. He was deeply moved that she, as he put it,

> had, in order to prove her lack of prejudice, entered into an intimate friendship with a full-blooded Negro, who, ever since he escaped from slavery, had, by educating himself, worked his way up and become the eloquent champion of his race's equality which, after the victorious Civil War, has been realized only in theory but not in actual social life; and in addition she fulfilled with untiring enthusiasm her duties as a board member of the "Free Community" in Hoboken. I have scarcely met any other woman so marked by deep emotions as well as active charity and a rational mind, who never hesitated to take the logical consequences from premises she realized as truth.[4]

The German-Americans of Hoboken, radical fellow travelers in the beginning, became dear friends as they incorporated abolitionism in their American agenda; Ottilie loved them as her family when they accepted Frederick Douglass as her companion. There had been no wavering among them during the Civil War, and Assing read the friendship they extended toward Douglass as a promise that they would be allies in the postwar era. And in many ways they were. When Gagern tried to introduce racial discord into the group by reminding them of the impropriety of befriending a member of an "inferior race," they formed a protective circle around the couple. Johannes Lange, even though he was tiring of Assing's hero worship of Douglass,[5] took a stand against this "adventurer devoid of principles." "He declared he would never stoop to associate with inferior races, the colored people, and could not understand how our closest friends and acquaintances, especially you, Miss Assing, Frauenstein, and I can bring ourselves to befriend Fred Douglass, especially since it is a well-known and indisputable fact that all colored people stink . . . In my polite way I threw out this baron." The association of freethinkers responded likewise. When the "revolutionary" offered to entertain them with his lectures they declined.[6]

Hoboken thus might have been an ideal place for Ottilie Assing to build a house of her own: near a big city, at the center of events, in the midst of friends. Rumors circulated among Douglass' acquaintances that he was planning to move to New Jersey.[7] But it would be years before Assing was able to realize at least part of her dream.

Meanwhile Douglass began to consider other options, including moving to the South! In early spring 1865 he confided to Julia Griffiths Crofts that he was hoping to make his home in Baltimore; but a few weeks after Douglass wrote this letter, Lincoln was dead and Secretary of State William Henry Seward severely hurt in another assassination attempt. Crofts, shocked by this eruption of violence, warned him: "Pray, my dear old friend . . . do not throw your valuable life away by venturing near the *old home*—think of *realities* and let those romantic visions remain in abeyance . . . Dreadful murders are never anticipated by the sufferers."[8] Crofts's warning did not go unheard. A year later, at a convention in Philadelphia in September 1866, John Curtis Underwood, an influential planter and abolitionist from Virginia, and Chief Justice Salmon P. Chase invited Douglass to move to Alexandria, Virginia, to edit a paper there. Douglass declined almost immediately, insisting that his place was in the North and West, where the fate of Reconstruction America would be determined, but he admitted that he feared Southern violence: "It is not my duty to court violence or Martyrdom or to act in any manner which can be construed into a spirit of bravado."[9]

Douglass was no doubt influenced by a belief that "high office would come to him not through a new job or an appointment, but through election, in upstate New York,"[10] as one of his biographers contends. He was also swayed by Crofts's warnings, but the fiercest opposition to his Southern leanings was probably put up by Ottilie Assing.[11] For more than a decade she had evoked images of the South as the black people's hell, had written of black slaughter, mutilation, humiliation, and if anybody was converted by her sermons on Southern perversity it was first and foremost Ottilie Assing herself. Adventuresome as she was, she had never traveled beyond northern Virginia, and she was always worried whenever Douglass dropped a hint of going to a Southern state. At one point she gave away his plans to Horace Greeley and other journalists, hoping that the publication of his intentions might force him to desist, and begged a mutual friend, Sylvester Rosa Koehler, to warn her friend. Douglass' reply shows how he felt about her meddling: "I thank you for your note of advice not the less because I did not ask it. In a matter of this kind it is well to know the opinion of others." He acknowledged he was "in the habit of regarding myself as extremely obnoxious to the whites of the South," and he feared his travel might result in violent acts against "Colored people generally," but he insisted on his right "to pursue my own course":

> My good friend—Miss Assing, is wise in many things—but is sometimes disposed to look at "Mole Hills" as Mountains. She has herself to thank for your assistance in this Southern business for I only mentioned to her that I thought of going to Georgia, when lo and behold! my thought is magnified into a purpose, and my purpose is trumpeted to the world. I must be a little more careful how I whisper my thoughts to my dear Miss Assing. The vehemence of her opposition sometimes makes necessary a just sense of Independence to go straight forward.[12]

While all this was going on, Ottilie Assing unexpectedly lost her place as one of Germany's most unusual and outspoken American correspondents and journalists. On 24 December 1865 the last edition of the *Morgenblatt für gebildete Leser* appeared. For fifty-nine years this journal had entertained, informed, enlightened its educated German audience; now changes in the house of Cotta in response to a changing market, new concepts of journalism, and the transformation of the German social and political landscape, spelled the end of this influential paper.[13] Assing was shocked. So much had she relied on her excellent relations with Cotta that she had neglected to cultivate relationships with other German publishers, and by now the American connections of major journals like *Die Gartenlaube* and *Westermann's Monatshefte* were firmly entrenched; there could be only occasional openings for her. It was another five years before the *Zeitschrift für bildende Kunst*, a journal for the fine arts in Leipzig, gave her another chance to contribute, and they were not interested in her political reporting. The death of the *Morgenblatt* silenced Ottilie Assing as a political correspondent.

It is almost impossible to measure the effect Assing's articles had on the

German reading public's perception of the United States. The paper's reader-ship was quite small, though influential. Still, through her, Douglass' voice could cross the boundaries of the English-speaking world and be heard in the German-speaking realm. Ottilie Assing deserves a respectable place among those liberal journalists and travel writers who created an awareness of the race issue in American history. So the failure of the *Morgenblatt* was a severe loss for German readers: they lost a woman reporter who was aware that American destiny was not white, a writer who moved beyond the master narrative by listening to and representing the polyphony of American life.

We do not have Assing's response to these events, for none of her correspondence of these initial postwar years survived. But it seems that she found ways of compensating for her loss of income. German acquaintances claimed, many years later, that she made a career as a teacher in, possibly even as principal of, a German-American school in New York City, but her name does not appear in New York or New Jersey school records, and she never referred to school or academy activities in her surviving letters. Also, the freedom with which she extended her visits to the Douglass residence and changed her schedule is not compatible with a regular job, much less an administrative position. Perhaps she accepted freelance teaching positions, for certainly she was an excellent teacher; well-to-do families in New York and Hoboken competed for her services, and her German-American friends in Hoboken, anxious lest their children might forget their German, hired her as a language tutor. But she disliked being dependent on the parents' whims, and balked at the restrictions the work placed on her mobility. Above all, she wanted to be free for Douglass—go to Rochester whenever he wanted her there, take time off whenever he came to Hoboken.

There are signs that she was employed by Hallgarten & Co., a banking and brokerage house in New York. She asked European friends to send their letters to their address, and she often used the Hallgarten stationery for her correspondence. The Hallgartens, a German-American family, lived in Hoboken. Assing's secretarial skills and especially her fluency in several languages were important assets to this firm, which focused on international trade; they, in turn, seem to have offered Assing what she needed: a reliable income, flexible working hours, the freedom to take time off. This was also why she was pleased to receive more and more offers to translate texts from English into German or French and vice versa—business letters, art catalogues, literary texts. Freelance work she could do anywhere, anytime, but it had its drawbacks: where once she had created texts, initiated reflections, she now had to submit to the words and thoughts of others. In her childhood her mother had taught her to write by challenging her to retrace the letters she had copied out for her; her translation work seemed to reduce her to a state of intellectual childhood. But then it gave her freedom to come and go, as well as money to afford a decent lifestyle, and that's all she wanted during this difficult, this tumultuous and enchanting time of her life.

"What shall be done with the free Negro?" was a question often raised, not only in white America but also in Europe. Assing answered that question for Germans by giving them Douglass, Tillman, and Smalls, black farmers, scouts, and soldiers. "Do nothing with us!" Douglass cried out:

> Your doing with us had already played the mischief with us. Do nothing with us! If the apples will not remain on the tree of their own strength, if they are worm-eaten at the core, if they are early ripe and disposed to fall, let them fall! I am not for tying and fastening them on the tree in any way, except by nature's plan, and if they will not stay there, let them fall. And if the Negro cannot stand on his own legs, let him fall also. All I ask is, give him a chance to stand on his own legs! Let him alone![14]

Was Douglass really overlooking "the damage slavery had done to many of [the freedpeople]—damage he had escaped,"[15] as has been charged? As others have argued, he did not escape unscathed. In fact, he was deeply scarred. Still, he was a man who had invented himself, proving to the world that the victim could still be the agent of her or his personal history. He liked to see himself not only as an exceptional, as a self-made man, but also as a personification of all his race could achieve, of the potential of his race. An attitude combining egalitarian humanism with elitism, belief in human potential with disgust at human failure, had characterized Douglass' public statements since the beginning of his career, and it became even more pronounced as he entered into an intellectual companionship with Ottilie Assing. She, too, was eager to embrace as her equal and extol as model the chimney sweeper reinventing himself as magistrate, the drunkard's son transforming himself into the successful actor, the slave metamorphosing into the orator, the seamstress taking on the responsibilities of a union leader. She, too, turned in disgust from those who preferred the workbench to the school, the beer hall to the lecture hall; human beings they were, but only theoretically—that is, potentially—equal. Substantial equality could come only with education, she believed. Education was "the uncontested criterion for being human," so that it could "be identified with emancipation."[16] She had moved beyond the position of German liberalism in that she no longer considered education the precondition for emancipation, for through Douglass she learned to assert freedom as a human right independent of class, race, gender, or merit. Still, education and regeneration were linked, as they were for Douglass. Emancipation was moral regeneration within a supportive environment. Freedom as such was ennobling, they argued, but also required freedpeople to refashion themselves in exchange for their rights. There was no difference between the rabble, the mob, the Irish loafer, the Kraut in the beer halls of Little Germany whom Ottilie conjured up in her *Morgenblatt* reports, and the "ignorance and servility of the ex-slave"[17] Douglass deplored in his speeches.

And yet those speeches expressed more than a simple self-help ideology. They were the products of humiliation Douglass had suffered at the hands of his abolitionist friends when they admonished him to "Give us the facts, we will take care of the philosophy"[18]; of his disgust at the Lady Bountiful pose struck by the freedpeople's aid societies; of his anger at the ways in which the black contribution to the Civil War was denied by self-styled white liberators. To be sure, the ex-slaves need education above everything, he wrote to J. Miller McKim, who suggested that his missionaries open schools for blacks in the South, but the black pupils should be considered "in common with all other ignorant and destitute (white as well as colored) of the South."[19] What the freedpeople needed was not charity but justice, he preached, not "fancied or artificial elevation" but "fair play."[20] It was a political philosophy coined in terms of conflict and contradiction, for he lived in a historical situation of conflict and contradiction.

"Fair play" as Douglass evoked it in his "hands-off" lectures was not in the agenda when in 1865 the notorious Black Codes were adopted in the former Confederate states (except Tennessee), which deprived the freedpeople of mobility and denied them the right to buy land; when teachers were killed for the crime of teaching black children; when black laborers working without contracts were threatened with vagrancy charges by the Freedmen's Bureau; when hooded night riders burned, crucified, raped, and hanged black women and men; when Andrew Johnson's administration restored "home rule" in the South and ignored the virtual reenslavement of the freedpeople. Douglass sounded as if he and Assing had just come from a lecture by Karl Marx when he described the freedom Southern blacks suffered rather than enjoyed: ". . . the world has never seen any people turned loose to such destitution as were the four million slaves of the South," he said:

> The old roof was pulled down over their heads before they could make for themselves a shelter. They were free! free to hunger; free to the winds and rains of heaven; free to the pitiless wrath of enraged masters . . . They were free, without roofs to

cover them, or bread to eat, or land to cultivate, and as a consequence died in such numbers as to awaken the hope of their enemies that they would soon disappear. We gave them freedom and famine at the same time.[21]

This was why he forged a new alliance with Wendell Phillips and opposed William Lloyd Garrison when he proposed disbanding the American Anti-Slavery Society. "Slavery . . . has been called by a great many names," Douglass remarked at the thirty-second annual meeting of the society on 9 May 1865, "and it will call itself by yet another name; and you and I and all of us had better wait and see what new form this old monster will assume, in what new skin this old snake will come forth next." That day he announced the goal that would define his mission for the rest of the decade: "Slavery is not abolished until the black man has the ballot."[22] Only the ballot would protect African-Americans against reenslavement and racism; only the ballot would empower them to raise themselves to the cultural level they deserved. "They gave us the bullet to save themselves," he contended a few months later; "they will yet give the ballot to save themselves."[23]

Ottilie Assing was in the audience when Frederick Douglass gave this speech, and she gave him all the support and the enthusiasm she could muster: "Truly, it seems incomprehensible that any person, at least halfway accessible to truth and reason, should not see the justice in a demand when it is advocated by a man who in his very person, talent, and conduct so brilliantly contradicts all those hackneyed sophistries and phrases of Negro hatred about the 'Negro's incompetence' and an 'inferior race.' "[24] As many others before, her report was a public text with a powerful private subtext: our struggle will continue, she announced, and we will need all the support we can get. Yet the enthusiastic battle cry was also a song of renunciation of personal fulfillment and a declaration of love and loyalty. Subordinating her own desires for a man's, agreeing to play "second fiddle," behind the veil, to Douglass' public career, left her in a female dependency that stood in stark contradiction to the kind of womanhood she sought to live for herself. Yet when forced to choose between that self and her liaison with Douglass, she followed Douglass. Ottilie Assing's transformation into Douglass' "pigtail" was taking shape.

Assing pledged her support to Douglass—as Douglass pledged his devotion to the civil rights struggle—and she never recanted. She was not only one of his most reliable and faithful, her experience as a "half-Jew" also made her one of his most knowledgeable companions. For Assing the postbellum fate of African-Americans was déjà vu, for in many ways she recognized in these events a tragic repetition of the fate to which the Jewish community in Germany had been forced to submit during the Restoration period: incomplete emancipation combined with only partial social integration, the forces of reaction eagerly grabbing every chance to reimpose the old pariah definitions.

Assing knew from experience what Douglass was talking about when he spoke of the need "to protect the results and preserve the meaning of the war as it receded into memory,"[25] and she vowed that she would do everything she could to save "her" successful American revolution from falling into the hands of the enemy. The lesson of 1848, deeply implanted in Assing's mind, could never be erased. The revolution in Germany had not just been defeated by military forces but had also fallen by a process of self-deconstruction—undermined by political wavering and bickering, by lack of courage, by cheap compromises, by a betrayal of radical commitments. "In the past days I was in a state of ecstasy at Congress passing the constitutional amendment which abolishes slavery forever in the entire nation," she wrote triumphantly to Ludmilla about the Thirteenth Amendment in early 1865. "At times reality outdoes everything even the most voluble fantasy can imagine. Five years ago none of us believed we would live to see the day of liberation, and now we stand a good chance of experiencing many other good things on top of it all." Yet her remarks reveal that she was an impatient believer: "The regular development of nations is a slow process, so that one century in that respect changes less than five years in an individual life, but let a revolution erupt, and within the shortest period progress will be made by the people that could not be effected by fifty, even one hundred years of peace. By taking this step the nation has decided its fate, and there is a great future ahead."[26] To her *Morgenblatt* readers she wrote: "31 January [1865] was the great day, the greatest, the most important in the nation's history since the Declaration of Independence, the day on which the American people, through a decision of its Congress, forever shook off the curse of slavery, and only by doing that did they truly enter the ranks of the civilized, educated nations of the world."[27]

Yet affirmation was anything but calm resignation. When Northern liberals grew increasingly restless at the conciliatory policy toward the South and the contempt for African-Americans which Lincoln's successor displayed, Assing shared their anxiety, while at the same time refusing to accept their placatory interpretation of the President's position. "In the meantime sultriness reigns, and in lower and louder voices they whisper to each other in pain and disgust: Johnson has betrayed us to the South," she commented in September 1865. The analysis she offered implicated white America as a whole in this perversion of the American Dream and the betrayal of the nation's black citizens: "Half of the guilt is on those unprincipled and unscrupulous party leaders, who nominated Johnson as Vice President . . . Johnson's nomination was by no means an error, but a well-calculated unscrupulousness, a political and moral crime."[28]

The war was still raging and the enemies of progress would not give up. "The only counterweight against this destructive influence lies with the Negroes," Ottilie continued; as before, for her, African-Americans were the only true Americans. "Without exception they are loyal and patriotic, the most faithful friends and most reliable disciples of the administration who gave them freedom, and they would always vote for the right party and thus defeat all onslaughts of former slaveholders and rebels."[29] She seemed to be whistling in the dark: "Slavery has received its deathblow and will never again grow into a dominating power, and civil equality is the logical and inevitable consequence of this initial great step. Despite all opposition it will sooner or later be the law of the land, for the spirit of the century, of civilization, and of progress demands this imperiously, and it is the precondition for the republic's greatness, stability, and survival."[30]

Of equal importance was the emotional support Assing provided for Douglass in those difficult first years of Reconstruction. They both knew that emancipation could not abolish racial prejudice and violence; they suffered harassment and discrimination and were prepared for years of struggle, pain, and humiliation, as their writing of the period shows. Yet whenever prejudice, arrogance, and even physical violence struck, they, who had been hurt so often that they felt they were beyond pain, hurt with a pain so intense that they were terror-struck. For a woman and a man with few illusions left, the first postbellum year was almost paralyzing in the disillusionment it held in store for them. The moment the new President, Andrew Johnson, entered his office after Lincoln's assassination, it was clear to Assing and Douglass that African-Americans were fighting an uphill battle.

The Convention of Colored Men, with Henry Highland Garnet as their presiding officer, gathered in Washington in February 1866. Alarmed by the implementation of the Black Codes, they chose a delegation to confront President Johnson with their grievances.[31] As head of the delegation they appointed George T. Downing, who, as manager of the dining room in the House of Representatives, had inside knowledge; Frederick Douglass and his son Lewis were included too. When the group met with Johnson on 7 February, it was Douglass whom the President singled out as a special target of his spite. When Douglass demanded that blacks be given the ballot so that they could protect and "save ourselves," not only did Johnson make it clear that he was unwilling to imperil his reputation by supporting this, to him, irrational claim, predicting a race war should blacks and poor whites meet at the ballot box, but he also insisted to Douglass that colonization was the nation's only viable solution to the "Negro problem." He ended his harangue by boasting of his skills in handling slaves: "I have owned slaves and bought slaves, but I never sold one. I might say, however, that practically . . . I have been their slave instead of their being mine." We can only guess how Douglass felt when the President denounced him as a dealer "in rhetoric . . . who never periled life, liberty, or property."[32] After the delegation left, he raged against them as "those d——d sons of b——s [who] thought they had me in a trap," and it became clear that it was "that damned Douglass" who had roused his special ire. He was, Johnson declared, "just like any nigger," who "would sooner cut a white man's throat as not."[33]

Douglass, so frequently exposed to racial harassment, had grown to expect it, but he was unprepared for such open, undisguised and unashamed racism in the White House. Not even in his nightmares would he have imagined the President, once an indentured servant and runaway tailor's apprentice, humiliating him in front of his son. He was in a cold rage, but stronger even than his anger was his sense of shame that a man like Johnson should be America's leader at this crucial juncture. The *National Anti-Slavery Standard* of 17 February decried Johnson as a blot on the entire nation and lauded Douglass as a personification of the best the country had to offer:

> One of the speakers in this dialogue is President of the United States, representing by his official position what there is best in the civilization of the Anglo-Saxon race. The other is Frederick Douglass, a Negro, with nothing to back him but his own manhood and talent. Yet, if we are compelled to accept Andrew Johnson as our representative, we blush for the white race. Dignity, force of speech, modesty, manliness, simple faith in justice, weight of character, are all on the side of the Negro.[34]

After his onslaught on Douglass, Johnson became a new villain of Gothic dimensions in Ottilie's letters to her sister. Her hatred of the President was exacerbated when, a year after this disastrous White House meeting, Johnson tried to use Douglass as a pawn in his game against his political opponents by scheming to appoint him director of the Freedmen's Bureau. In June 1867, Douglass received a letter from William Slade, steward of the White House, in effect asking him to replace the bureau's present director, Commissioner O. O. Howard. "There was no job, short of president or pope, that Frederick Douglass would have liked better,"[35] his biographer suggests; still, in less than two weeks Douglass declined the offer. As Nathan Huggins has argued, there was no way in which Douglass could claim the position and not lose out: "Had Douglass accepted, he could hardly expect support from a president who had vetoed the legislation establishing the bureau. Without his support, Douglass would have been at the mercy of a staff of white men . . . Furthermore, to accept such a post from Johnson and place himself under the president's aegis would have compromised Douglass' alliance to the radical Republicans."[36] Douglass turned down the offer because he knew a trap when he saw it; however, his decision was also influenced by the fact that he believed he would make his political career not via appointment but through election. He was confident that some day soon New York State would send him to Washington as a representative, and he did not want his reputation tainted by association with a tainted President. It is revealing that Douglass never mentioned this incident in his autobiography, but he stumped tirelessly against the President, whose policy was a ridicule and denial of everything Douglass stood and fought for.

In the spring of 1866 Johnson's supporters, worried at the resistance that radical Republicans had successfully begun to put up against him, decided to rally behind him in a convention to be held in Philadelphia in mid-August. The radicals immediately set up a counterconvention, to meet in Philadelphia's Independence Hall in early September. Yet when Republicans in Rochester appointed Douglass as a delegate and Douglass proudly accepted, they were dismayed. One Rochester delegate refused to serve with a black person, and during his stay in New York and on the train to Philadelphia, fellow travelers spoke frankly to Douglass of the "undesirableness"[37] of his participation. "They dreaded the clamor of social equality and amalgamation which would be raised against the party, in consequence of this startling innovation," was Douglass' sarcastic comment sixteen years later. "They, dear fellows, found it much more agreeable to talk of principles of liberty as glittering generalities, than to reduce those principles to practice."[38] He refused to turn back, only to find himself ostracized upon his arrival in Philadelphia. At this moment of utter isolation Theodore Tilton, editor of the New York *Independent*, came up to him and seized his hand; the two men walked away arm in arm, amidst cheers and scowls. "I have in my life been in many awkward and disagreeable positions . . . but I think I never appreciated an act of courage and generous sentiment more highly than I did that of this brave young man,"[39] Douglass later remembered.

With the support of Tilton and the young women's rights advocate Anna

Dickinson, Douglass was able not only to make his presence felt among men who did not want him, but to transform what began as humiliation into a very personal triumph. The belligerent trio persuaded the convention to give its support to the black ballot! Douglass had forced an alliance, and the radical Republicans had found a powerful and loyal companion who would campaign well for them and the policy on race relations they represented—however reluctantly. His autobiography documents that Douglass neither forgot nor forgave the pain his "friends" inflicted upon him, but in his public response he chose to focus on his triumph rather than on his disillusionment. How else could he maintain his personal dignity; how else could he wield political influence; how else could he continue the civil rights battles that needed to be fought? It was a tactic of survival for a man who knew that the battle could not be fought by African-Americans alone.

For Ottilie Assing, the American party system, with its emphasis on interest groups and pragmatism, was at odds with her German definition of political party as an ideologically and theoretically consistent structure;[40] events such as these alienated her even more. Like Douglass, she would continue to support the party, at times with great rhetorical aplomb, but her letters to Ludmilla show that the old enthusiasm was forever gone. From now on Republicans for her were only the lesser of two evils. As time went on and Douglass became deeply enmeshed in party politics, her skeptical pragmatism became a source of contention between them.

The summer of 1866 was full of tension for the people who lived together in the Douglasses' house on the hill. The struggles of the past years, the relentless oscillation between hope and disillusionment, between triumph, rage, and humiliation, left everybody exhausted, and yet there was no prospect of rest. During the war years, hardly any visitors had been around and most of the children were gone, but now the house buzzed with life like a beehive. Rosetta had returned to be with her parents during her first pregnancy, and after the war her husband, Nathan Sprague, joined his wife and daughter; they were expecting another baby and could not yet afford a place of their own. Charles, too, came back from the war, and he and his young wife Libbie (Mary Elizabeth Murphy) were depending on their parents' hospitality. Lewis and Frederick Jr. had just moved west, to Colorado, where they worked for the Red, White, and Blue Mining Company, but a new son had been adopted into the family: while stationed in Washington in the summer of 1865, Charles met a thirteen-year-old ex-slave, Henry Strothers, from Georgia. Uprooted by the war, the boy had drifted into the city in the wake of Sherman's army, and he was now one of those half-starved, desperate street urchins who slept under bridges and in abandoned buildings like stray cats. He was lucky to stumble upon Charles who, overcome with pity, asked his father's permission to send him to Rochester. Henry was the first to seek and find shelter in a place that had, less than five years before, been a haven for fugitive slaves. He, too, was living proof that Douglass' work was far from accomplished.

No, the house which Ottilie Assing entered was anything but a quiet retreat. Not only was it full of people but the Douglass children were now adults, and she had to renegotiate her relationship with them. The newcomers—Libbie, Nathan—must have been shocked to realize the role she, a white woman, played in their venerated father-in-law's life. It is unlikely that they were used to living in such close proximity with any white person, and they may have been uncomfortable with her. Also, her presence complicated their relationship with Anna Murray. Living with a mother-in-law who could be so harsh was difficult in itself; could they get along with Assing without drawing upon themselves Anna Murray's wrath? Eventually the new family members learned to cope with Ottilie's presence, and during the summers invitations to the Douglasses' automatically included "Miss Assing."[41]

Beyond that, there were stresses within the family itself. When Rosetta's husband returned from the war, it seemed he had a hard time finding and holding any job. Charles, also without work, was tending the family farm, but he, too, had no income and was starting a family. Lewis and Fred were in the West, but they needed financial support at least for a while, and the Douglasses were taking care of Henry. One could blame the children's problems on the postwar economy and other structural issues, and the happiness and gratitude the Douglasses felt that all their boys had survived the war left little room for darker moods. Still, clouds on the horizon signaled heavy weather ahead. However, for the time being Ottilie refused to see the storm that was brewing in her beloved Emerald Island.

Anna Murray was once again mistress of a household buzzing with life; there were more mouths to feed than ever, and the laundry took on dimensions of a medium-sized hotel. She must have been gratified at having all her sons with her when so many mothers in Rochester wept over children sacrificed, and Rosetta's little Annie warmed her heart with memories of the girl taken from her. But she was tired, exhausted after years of futile struggle to shape the kind of family she desired, to receive the kind of respect from her husband and children she knew she deserved. Her relationship with Rosetta had improved slightly after the birth of Annie, but it was and would always remain precarious. Her children still were embarrassed at their illiterate mother, at the way she talked and dressed, and Anna Murray must have been wary to discover those familiar signs that told her in the cruelest way possible that Nathan and Libbie, too, were catching on. There was no end to it.

Anna Murray had been prone to bouts of sickness ever since she came to Rochester; she seemed now to have less and less strength to fight back, and various neurological problems, perhaps exacerbated by emotional stress, slowly gained the upper hand. In April 1867 Rosetta described the doctor's diagnosis: "Mother has been quite sick ailing for a week and last Saturday while at the sink she fell across it . . . after which she seemed stupid . . . she had a vomiting spell and . . . complained mostly of her head,"[42] she wrote to her father. It was the first of many bouts of sickness to which Anna Murray would eventually succumb.

Exhausted as Douglass and Assing were when they began their summer in Rochester, there was no chance for them to recuperate. The nation's situation was too precarious for Douglass to sit back and relax. His speaking assignments and meetings with potential allies for his civil rights struggle interrupted their summer, and his nomination as a delegate to the Republican Convention required careful preparation. He returned from Philadelphia exhilarated by his success and deeply wounded by his fellow politicians' hypocrisy. Ottilie Assing had to focus on Douglass' needs, on the challenges he encountered as a black leader, on his career, on his emotional problems, on the new domestic situation. But this was happening at a time when her professional life had suffered a deadly blow with the end of the *Morgenblatt* and her private life was faced with the realization that there would be no quiet domesticity for her and Douglass in the near future. The pet names she used—"Big Bird" for Douglass, "Pigtail" for herself—illustrate to perfection the conventional gendered roles of male determination and female submission that were displacing the former symmetry of their relationship. Did she realize that she was beginning to stifle a vital element of that precious inner self, that she was transforming herself from Ottilie Assing into Douglass' auxiliary? Perhaps she did, and perhaps it did not bother her, for that was what she wanted. Perhaps she was aware of the transformation and suppressed doubts, for only if she succeeded in internalizing her compliance as an act of choice and free will could she muster the strength to go down the road she was on. Determined blindness, willful deafness as means of survival.

Thus Assing was in good spirits and full of plans as she sat on the train back to New York City in late October 1866. She knew that the winter ahead would be hard on Douglass: he had already accepted many lecture assignments, and the battle for the Fifteenth Amendment and for civil rights would dominate his schedule, but these activities also made it possible for him to come to Hoboken more frequently than ever. She had been desperate when she lost her rooms at Mrs. Marks's the year before, but it had turned out a blessing in disguise. Dr. Loewenthal, whom she asked to find a place for her—anywhere, anything, she wrote, so long as Douglass was welcome—had been a reliable friend, and had found rooms for her with the Koehlers, a young German-American family. Assing had seen Sylvester Rosa Koehler only once, and she did not know his wife. Now, after nine months of boarding with them, and for the first time in America and away from Rochester, she cherished the feeling of going home to her Hoboken family.

Amalie and Sylvester Rosa Koehler[43] were much younger than Assing; he was in his late twenties, Amalie in her early twenties. Born in Leipzig in 1837, Koehler had come as a child to the United States with his parents, artists who emigrated in the late 1840s; Sylvester Rosa inherited his parents' love of art, but the family's financial situation did not allow him to acquire the education he craved or to launch a career in the arts. After his marriage to Amalie Susanne Jaeger in 1859 and the birth of their three children, he made a living as a clerk, hating every moment of it. Amalie tried to improve their meager income by renting part of their house to boarders.

Ottilie Assing had been anything but thrilled when she first saw the Koehlers' shabby little house and her small rooms, yet all that was forgotten as she became acquainted with the couple. "Not only did I find them to be highly respectable, charming, and friendly people who possess an education that is rare even among the local Germans, but our opinions, likings, and taste match in all things that are relevant," she reported to Ludmilla. The young family could barely make ends meet, but their house boasted a fine library, and if the furniture was simple, the conversation around the dinner table was everything Assing could wish for. The two boarders who were living with the family were also good friends: Dr. Johannes D. Lange, an attorney; Dr. Gustav Frauenstein, son of a Jewish family, a physician. All of them were freethinkers; they shared a passionate love of art; and once Assing made their acquaintance she never again lacked companionship for the theater or opera. Assing was pleased when she discovered that they were fellow travelers in their radical Republicanism, and she was thrilled when she realized that they shared her belligerent atheism. Most important, however, "Mr. Koehler and Douglass have taken a real liking to each other, and it is always a treat for the young home when he comes to stay for one or several days."[44] Assing's new domestic arrangements were perfect.

Almost. No matter how enjoyable the company, the house they rented was inferior and much too small. The Koehlers had bought a lot in Hoboken where they hoped to build a house of their own someday, but there was simply no money. In the winter of 1865–66, in long conversations with Douglass, Assing had come up with a plan that, they hoped, would solve both the Koehlers' and their problem: Assing would loan money for the new house, and in exchange she would get the kind of apartment and boarding arrangement that suited hers and Douglass' needs. She would continue to pay room and board, and the Koehlers would pay her a 7 percent interest on their loan.[45] In the fall of 1867 "the gang"—the Koehlers, Frauenstein, Lange, and Assing—took possession of a beautiful new house on Bloomfield Street.

With Douglass visiting frequently, and in a domestic setting to her liking, the winter of 1866–67 flew by, and the clouds on the horizon during the previous summer in Rochester seemed gone when Ottilie returned in 1867. Republicans had won the midterm elections in 1866, and President Johnson's power was now curtailed by a solid congressional majority. There were many occasions for triumph that year: Douglass, Anna Dickinson, and Wendell Phillips were launching a vigorous campaign for the Fifteenth Amendment, and they had little doubt that they would be victorious.

On the domestic side, too, things seemed to improve in the Douglass family. Rosetta gave birth to her second child, Harriet, and she and her young family now lived in their own home on Pearl Street. Nathan bought "a handsome span of grays" and a hack, "the finest that can be found on either stand,"[46] as the proud wife reported to her father in April 1867. True, he had to contend with the racism of the white hackmen, but for a while at least the Spragues were on their feet. Lewis and Frederick Jr. were still in Denver, working for the mining company, Lewis as secretary, Frederick in the printing office. And in the spring of 1867 the family's youngest, Charles, was hired by the Freedmen's Bureau in Washington. As a matter of course, he left Libbie, pregnant with their first child, with his mother. So quickly did he take off for the capital that he did not even bother to make arrangements for the Rochester livestock he cared for, and one cow starved to death. Anna Murray, severely ill at the time, was enraged. But Charles was happy: "I am the second colored man in the Government that has been given a first class clerkship," he sang out in his first letter from Washington. (Commissioner Howard, Charles' superior, had to warn furious white clerks protesting against a black colleague that "if they did not like it they might leave and he would fill their places with colored men.") At $100 a month he felt rich—but he asked his father for a loan of $1,800 for "a small good house," although he knew "too that there are too many outlets to your purse."[47]

Douglass declined, gently suggesting that his youngest wait with the house until he could pay for it with his own earnings.

Assing was surely relieved at these developments, for she took an almost
maternal pride in the achievements of the Douglass children. In 1865, she had
sent Ludmilla a photo of Charles in uniform, apologizing for the bad quality of
this "veritable Rochester product" which "does him no justice at all."[48] And she
proudly introduced Lewis to her friends in Hoboken when he spent two weeks
with her in February 1868, lauding him as "an educated and pleasant young
man."[49] What was equally important for her, however, was that independent
children meant additional mobility for Douglass. She worried about his health
as he went on his extended lecture tours to the West, still his main source of income, and she hoped that with fewer mouths to feed he would be able to relax
into a less demanding schedule. Perhaps there would even be enough money to
go on the European tour they had been postponing since 1860.

The children had barely left the Douglass home when their place was filled with
newcomers, people for whom Ottilie Assing—and perhaps even Frederick Douglass—was unprepared: in July 1867 Douglass' elder half brother Perry Downs,
his wife, and four children arrived in Rochester. In late 1864, during his first
sojourn to Baltimore after the war, Douglass had embraced his half sister Eliza
Mitchell; now another member of the family he thought lost forever reemerged.
"The meeting of my brother after nearly forty years of separation is an event altogether too affecting for words to describe," he wrote to J. J. Spelman, whose
generosity made this family reunion possible. "How utterly accursed is slavery,
and how unspeakably joyful are the results of the overthrow!"[50] Douglass and
Perry spent the summer building a cottage for the Downs family on the Douglass property. "I have now completed for him a snug little cottage on my own
grounds, where my dear old slavery-scarred and long-lost brother may spend in
peace, with his family, the remainder of his days. Though no longer young, he
is no sluggard. Slavery got the best of his life, but he is still strong and hopeful.
I wish his old master could see him now—cheerful, helpful and 'taking care of
himself.' "[51] They worked together, but were they, the powerful, educated orator and the freedman "deeply marked by the hardships and sorrows of that hate-
ful condition," still able to communicate? Was it possible for the Downses and
the Douglasses to live as one family? The metaphors Douglass used in his letter
to Spelman after all were those of speechlessness, and they denoted more than
pathos. Perry had been a slave for fifty-six years; in him Douglass saw in the
most heartrending way what might have become of him had he not escaped.

Perry personified everything he had struggled and was still struggling to leave behind, to forget. "I would write a narrative of my brother Perry's bondage," he admitted to Tilton. "But let the old system go! I would not call its guilty ghosts from the depths into which its crimes have cast it. I turn gladly from the darkness of the past to the new better dispensation now dawning." The orator refused to provide his brother with a voice; the politician fighting against national amnesia closed his eyes and ears to that personalized past he could not bear to take on.

Thomas Carlyle, with whose writing Douglass was thoroughly familiar, when writing of the barriers to communication between the working classes and the bourgeoisie in England, used the image of two nations. "As if he had lived on another planet," was what Douglass said about the distance between himself and his brother. It is revealing that Perry had only a first name in Douglass' letter to Tilton, and he was called "Uncle Perry" in the Douglass-Assing correspondence, while his wife and children remained anonymous.

Douglass's children did not seem to understand the situation. "I dont [sic] understand in what way those people you have at home are related to you," Charles wrote, avoiding an inclusionary "us." "Is it that Mr. Downs is your half brother? For what I have heard of their conduct I should be afraid even to have them in the same neighborhood, and more especially when you are away in the winter months."[52] As for Ottilie Assing, she never mentioned them in any of the letters of the 1860s that survive. But then, they are also absent from Douglass' autobiography, a text in which the reunion with the *white* part of his family is crucial. Barely a year after helping build the cottage where the "slavery-scarred and long-lost brother" was to spend "the remainder of his days," Perry Downs and his family returned to Maryland's Eastern Shore.

On her way back to New York City in the fall of 1867 Ottilie Assing made her habitual stop at the Gerrit Smiths' for a few days,[53] but she was eager to see her new home in Hoboken and her "gang"; the winter months, with her long separation from Douglass and the extreme cold she so abhorred, would be more endurable now that she lived with people she loved in a house that her own ingenuity and generosity had made possible. She was not disappointed. Her rooms were custom-tailored for her—spacious, quiet, with big windows to catch as much sunshine as possible and huge American stoves to keep out the cold. Douglass managed to drop in so often that he almost seemed to be one of this extended family. "This morning I was greatly surprised to find F. Douglass at the breakfast table," Assing's fellow boarder Lange wrote to Koehler in 1868. "Douglass arrived yesterday in the middle of the night, and he left by 10 this morning to continue to Philadelphia via train. He will lecture there and in various New Jersey towns, and he hopes to return to Hoboken at the end of this month, at least stop over . . ."[54] Douglass was here; Douglass was expected; Douglass is with us—references to Douglass popped up in nearly every letter that members of the "gang" wrote to each other during these years.[55] In February 1868 his Denver company sent Lewis Douglass on a business trip to New York, and as a matter of course he stayed at the Koehlers'.[56] Assing was thrilled not only because the young man and his personal success story were living proof of her gospel of black potential, but because his being there legitimated her relationship to Douglass.

The satisfactions Ottilie Assing experienced in her personal life were boosted by developments in the political arena. President Johnson was finding himself totally caught up in a self-fabricated political crisis, and his defiance of the Tenure of Office Act led the House of Representatives to pass a resolution of impeachment. "All these events are an irrefutable illustration of the excellence of republican institutions," Ottilie observed. "There are plenty of corrupt generals, Democrats and former rebels who would love to support Johnson's *coup d'état* and to scatter Congress by force of arms, but so strong is the belief in the power of a sovereign people and the absolute futility of such an enterprise that nobody wants to have anything to do with it. The worst of republics is still a thousand times better than the best of monarchies."[57] She became fascinated with the impeachment proceedings, following developments in Washington "with sheer delight."[58]

Then, unexpectedly, she was dealt a stunning blow: in March 1868 Sylvester Rosa Koehler, desperately unhappy with his professional situation in New York City, received a tempting offer from the chromolithograph publishing house of L. Prang in Boston; he left New York on 3 April, and his wife and children followed him in May. They decided to put the house up for rent. Only five months into her communal dream the bubble had burst. Ottilie Assing was "thunderstruck," she admitted to her sister, for she had made an enormous emotional and financial investment in this family, but her response is a powerful testimony to her generosity, loyalty, and strength. The autonomy she claimed for herself was an autonomy she would never withhold from others. The Koehlers deserved a better life, and it was their right and duty to go for the best. "The improvement is so obvious, the work itself, requiring a specialist, is so fully to his liking that we can only regard this as a stroke of fortune,"[59] she wrote, using the identifying "we" to underline the consensus. Her love of the Koehlers remained intact. They visited regularly, wrote to each other; Assing supported Sylvester's business and publication ventures, and she even remembered them generously in her will. (And her extensive correspondence with the Koehler family is the most reliable documentation we have of her final years.)

The change in Hoboken came in the very month when Ludmilla announced to her sister that she was building a fancy house of her own in Florence, her place of refuge since her escape from Prussia. She had always contended that Italy was exile for her, no matter how much she loved the country and how deeply she became involved in revolutionary politics,[60] but now she was putting down roots, while Ottilie, a proud citizen of the United States, was still unsettled:

> Happiness, joy, and good company in your new house! It must be a wonderful feeling to be thus settled within your own four walls, and since years it has been my burning desire to at least have my own household, no matter who owns the house, but I do not see the slightest chance of attaining it, as I'm working in New York all day and thus would be totally exposed to a maid's despotism, and if I were to give up my job for that I would lack the most important thing . . . , money, and so I will just have to continue my old ways and feel fortunate that I live among educated people and kindred spirits, where all my guests are welcome and where especially Douglass finds a hospitable welcome anytime.[61]

Assing's composure at the collapse of her domestic utopia was helped by the spontaneous generosity of her friends in Hoboken, especially the Kudlichs and Loewenthals, who all invited her to board in their homes—and this despite her liaison with Douglass, her unconventional lifestyle, her strong political and religious convictions. Assing was deeply gratified.

The most tempting proposition came from Gustav Frauenstein, who considered Ottilie one of his dearest friends. He suggested that Assing, Lange, and he "establish a little ménage together." Assing was tempted, "for we know each other well and get along fabulously." Still, she declined, explaining to her sister "that all three of us are still too much like gypsies, too unstable."[62] The Koehlers' mobility had left scars after all. It is unlikely that she feared a public outcry about her living with two unmarried men, but sharing a house with two bachelors would put much of the responsibility of managing the household in her hands, which she did not want. Instead, she moved in with her neighbors at 219 Hudson Street, the Loewenthals. Loewenthal was so pleased with his new houseguest that he even made efforts to purchase the Koehler residence, espe-

Sylvester Rosa Koehler

Amalie Koehler

Hedwig and Walter Koehler

Ottilie Assing and Frederick Douglass liked the young Koehlers enough for Assing to lend them money for their house in Hoboken. "Mr. Koehler and Douglass have taken a real liking to each other," Assing wrote to her sister in 1868, "and it is always a treat for the young home when he comes to stay for one or several days."

Karl Heinzen
The 48er Karl Heinzen and Ottilie Assing became friends during Assing's frequent trips to Boston in the 1870s. Although Assing disliked his fierce German chauvinism, their mutual admiration for Ludwig Feuerbach and their shared position on American race relations made them fellow travelers.

Ottilie Assing
In 1871 Ottilie Assing sent this photo to her sister with the following comment: "Of course my eyes are still wide with the fear with which I always gaze into nothing on occasions such as this . . . I have gained a little weight, especially in the upper parts, but the waist is still the same. I do my hair myself, and I wear a large chignon . . . as I have plenty of hair for it I cannot bring myself to parade with false hair, as so many people do. The earrings are the old blue ones: I did not make the collar myself . . . The dress is black . . ."

cially "since Miss Assing would have been able to move in with them and live in her former quarters."[63]

Her new home turned out to be disappointing. "The apartment is not half so nice and friendly and the domestic arrangement not so comfortable, as he [Loewenthal] is not very happy with his wife, who unfortunately is rather uneducated," she told Ludmilla. It was the old story—Assing's lack of sympathy for women with less intellectual ambition and opportunity. Like her aunt Rahel and her mother, she enjoyed the company of intellectuals, mostly male, while merely tolerating their wives. Her attitude toward Anna Murray had many parallels in her treatment of women she knew in Hoboken. Yet all of these issues were of little importance as long as these people accepted Douglass. ". . . he [Loewenthal] is a witty, educated man, and, what is most important, a kindred spirit, a close acquaintance of Douglass', so that he will be as warmly received as here, and so I must give it a try."[64] Douglass made his first visit to her new home in May, spending "a few days" with her, and after "a very animated, cheerful party"[65] together with the Loewenthals, Kudlichs, Frauenstein, Lange, and the German-American diplomat C. N. Riotte, she felt she had made the right decision after all.

With her domestic problems solved for the time being, Ottilie decided she needed to treat herself to something special. For months she had devoured every report on the Johnson impeachment; now she would travel to Washington, to the stage where this drama was being performed. She was in such high spirits that she invited her poor cousin Emilie Nickert, widowed since 1853 and desperately struggling to make a living in Wilmington, to join her.[66] A report she later sent her sister shows that she designed her tour as both a trip into Douglass' past in Baltimore and his predicted future in the nation's capital. But the first plan was a failure. She wanted to see the Baltimore in which Douglass had spent much of his childhood, and she knew only a black person and an ex-slave could give her the information and guidance she wanted. When she could not find such a person, she dropped the plan.[67]

Washington made up for the disappointment of Baltimore, and Charles and Libbie Douglass were eager to prove to her that they belonged. "We also went to the Capitol last night," Charles wrote to his father, "and I devoted my time in pointing out the different members to Miss Assing."[68] Her other guide was her old friend Riotte, the former minister resident in Costa Rica, who was in town waiting for a new appointment.[69] You do not truly understand American public life until you have seen the capital, Ottilie told Ludmilla. "You can spend a whole life in New York without being directly touched by politics; here every step forces upon you the awareness that you are in the midst of a great republic . . . In the White House, in the Capitol, in all public buildings people walk with the free, proud ease and confidence that obviously springs from the knowledge of being an equal, active part of the great whole, of moving within your own property." Frances Trollope had been appalled at the sight of civil servants in the Capitol, sitting with their feet propped up on the tables; Assing smiled at people feeling so at home! She was enchanted with the Capitol, raving about its "infinite magic": "I could spend many hours there every day, without tiring," she exclaimed. There could not possibly be a better place for Douglass to unfold the magic of his voice! She had to walk the city, the Navy Yard, Arlington Heights, to feel the city's slavery past and triumph over it, so that she could take possession of it for the future. "What a triumph it is to enter the former slave states as free soil!"[70] she exclaimed.

Assing painted Washington in a good light: there was not a word in her letter, for example, that the streetcars, though officially desegregated immediately after the war, "seldom stopped for blacks,"[71] She never mentioned the abominable conditions in which most of the city's blacks were living—the homeless, the starving, the omnipresent beggars. It is possible that Charles designed an itinerary for her that avoided troublesome locations, or perhaps she was unwilling to taint her narrative of progress; perhaps the people she saw were not the kind of deserving poor to whom she was always sympathetic.

Ottilie was disappointed when the Republicans were unable to obtain the necessary majority for Johnson's conviction, and the President was acquitted by one vote. "Had there been a decent President, nothing could have prevented me from enjoying one of the receptions at the White House," she confided to Ludmilla, "but to pay my respect to Johnson, to shake paws with him and to be grinned at by him, would have been just too sordid . . ."[72]

One of the highlights of her trip was an excursion to Mount Vernon that she took with Emilie Nickert and the Douglasses. "Miss Assing treated us to a visit to Mt. Vernon yesterday and we had a very nice time,"[73] Charles reported to his father. In her first American column for the *Morgenblatt* Assing had praised George Washington as a paragon of republicanism; now, fifteen years later, she made this excursion into a celebration of her heroically enlightened self in the midst of racial bigotry. "Our companionship with Charles and his wife attracted considerable attention, and I was addressed on the subject very curiously," Ottilie bragged, "for although Negroes in the District of Columbia enjoy all civil rights, including the ballot, and although people are used to seeing them in the company of whites in a subordinate position, social prejudice is not at all gone, and a mixed party making a pleasure trip as equals still is conspicuous."[74] At Mount Vernon she encountered a black gardener who claimed to have been a teenager at Washington's death. Assing took a close look and felt that this was rather far-fetched, but she decided that a man who had endured slavery had every right to make a little money by fooling a few credulous whites. She, one of the innocents and a woman of higher insight, could afford to be generous and let him have his fun. Her sense of superiority and righteousness was unshakable.

They were in the midst of a lively conversation when a lady approached them. "I must shake hands with you!" she said to the gardener, who, so Assing claims, immediately put on a mask of neutrality—for which, of course, there had been no need while chatting with Ottilie! "I think there is no position more venerable and honorable in the country than to have been the slave of General Washington." It was a chance to deliver a lesson in tolerance and solidarity Assing could not pass up. Grabbing the poor fellow's hand, she exclaimed: "And I will shake hands with you because we are so lucky to meet here on free soil." Naturally "the poor gardener smiled in approval"[75] at our heroine.

Ottilie Assing was delighted by Washington and would have liked to spend more time, but she "became so impatient to be with Douglass" that she decided to leave for Rochester, where she arrived on 2 July, after a beautiful train ride through the hills of Pennsylvania and along the valley of the Susquehanna River. Douglass welcomed her at the station, and as they walked toward the house her cat, "my dear yellow Fox,"[76] ran up to greet his mistress.

The summer she and Douglass spent together in 1868 was one of almost uninterrupted happiness. Douglass' children were living their own lives now, and although they still occasionally needed financial assistance, it appeared they were on the right track. Anna Murray seemed to enjoy the quiet and was happy in her garden. There were hardly any visitors. Assing had brought a copy of John Motley's three-volume *Rise of the Dutch Republic* (1863), and they spent hours reading to each other, discussing a history far removed from Douglass' experience and yet familiar to Assing. Douglass loved to study history, troubled by what he called "my ignorance of the past,"[77] and Assing was only too glad to accompany him on these intellectual excursions. Dickens' *Hard Times* was another book they shared this summer, and this time it was Douglass, who had seen the working-class slums of Manchester, Liverpool, and London, who had been to the mining districts of Wales and in the industrial north of England, who could invite Assing into a world unknown to her.

They spent a lot of time going through Douglass' manuscripts, revising and editing. He still needed income from his lectures, but his audience now wanted different kinds of messages from him. Also, he had to prepare for work in the upcoming presidential campaign. Assing was skeptical about the Republican candidate, Ulysses Grant, admitting to her sister that she had "not much confidence in him,"[78] but Douglass had decided to campaign for him, and so she worked with him as he drafted his speeches. "I see little of the world, and I am so completely satisfied with the garden life I live here that I have not the slightest desire for change, especially since this garden holds a whole universe for me. The summer on the green magic island passes with incomprehensible speed,"[79] she wrote. From the relaxed tone of Assing's letters to her sister we can see that the summer of 1868, like the two that followed, were probably the happiest periods in Ottilie Assing's life with Frederick Douglass.

It was a happiness that invigorated and inspired her, and it showed in her work. She no longer had the *Morgenblatt* to write for, but she managed to create a new public space where her voice would be heard when she launched a lecture series for the association of freethinkers in Hoboken for which she was secretary. Her letters to her sister show that she was extremely nervous about speaking before a large audience. After all, she had spent years criticizing other orators, especially women, yet the praise that was heaped upon her after her first lecture in February or March 1869[80] encouraged her to continue. The first talk she gave was on John Brown,[81] and though she used material from her original *Morgenblatt* manuscripts, the text of 1868 shows how much the Civil War and its aftermath had changed her attitude toward the United States. Her earlier text portrayed a nation caught in a maelstrom of slavery and corruption, a country that perverted its most faithful children into terrorists, and drove its most courageous defender of the American Dream into exile. Now, nine years later, she read the John Brown raid on Harpers Ferry as a cataclysmic upheaval which, despite its failure, forced upon Northerners an awareness of the political and ideological bondage in which the Southern slave states kept them. In her retrospective analysis President Buchanan still conspired with the South, and politicians and the press denounced Brown as a madman and an insurrectionist, yet these were rearguard actions in a changing political climate. John Brown's martyrdom, she claimed, eventually inspired the North to reclaim America.

The hero of her first text was Frederick Douglass; the heroes of her postwar text were the "radical Abolitionists, who always were several generations in advance of the rest of the people"—and at their center those uncompromising 48ers among whom she made her home. Having themselves suffered persecution, this European elite now stepped forth to help the people who had to escape Buchanan's bloodhounds. "For the first time we saw political fugitives in this country"—the "we" is significant—"and we went again through experiences with which we had thought to have done forever when we left Europe and its monarchies. There were arrests and persecutions." Their reward was that they were able to participate in a revolution that resurrected the American Dream: "*One* great revolution will educate a nation more rapidly than a century of peace. Less than ten years have elapsed since we sheltered in our houses the fugitives from Harpers Ferry and their allies, since we helped them across the borders, and only four years later our volunteers entered the conquered Southern cities and fortresses with the sounds of the hymn: John Brown's body lies moldering in his grave; his soul is marching on!"[82]

In her lecture, John Brown's true errand was not the bloody raid but the peaceful mountain republic he planned for fugitive slaves. Nation building and liberation rather than warfare moved center stage. And Frederick Douglass, mastermind of her *Morgenblatt* manuscripts, was completely absent. How much she was really aware of Douglass' political transformation can be seen from the second major talk she gave in Hoboken, on 11 December 1870:[83] "Frederick Douglass,"[84] whom she introduced as a friend "well known to all of you," "the equal of the best of the nation," "the self-made man." She invited her audience to review with her his tribulations as a slave and his heroic self-liberation, yet despite her reliance on Douglass' autobiographies the emphasis of her talk was not on the past; the past became a gateway to the future. She talked about slavery because she needed her audience to understand what equipped Douglass to be their guide into the nation's future. "It is evident that D. must possess more than ordinary perseverance and power of will, more than ordinary abilities in order to rise to his present height under circumstances so hostile," she said. Her reassessment of Douglass' association with John Brown pointed into the same direction. True, Douglass had aided Brown in the past, but she also said that from the beginning he was too prudent to join a venture that was bound to fail, giving him a place of honor in the event while at the same time distancing him from its seedy, gory side. "I keep still a letter from John Brown to FD, written a few weeks before the attack on Harpers Ferry: He warmly advocated his demand, and even represented it as FD's duty to comply with it. If FD could have been persuaded, he would in all probability have shared the fate of the others, who were either killed, or executed as high traitors."

The Douglass she depicted for her German-American audience was a heroic liberator, but his powers were healing, nurturing, and building ones. Once a free man, he had courageously followed the path to intellectual emancipation, and "he now is endeavoring to lift his audience to that atmosphere of intellectual liberty that he has reached."[85] The qualities she attributed to him were not just those of a liberator of his race; he was a man equipped to lead a purified America into a glorious future, and she exhorted her friends to embrace him as their guide.

For the first time in years life seemed so full of promise that Assing dared to once again bring up the idea of an European tour. How eager she was to show Douglass the places she loved—Paris, Berlin, Hamburg, Prague, Dresden, Strasbourg, Heidelberg; how eager she was to explore with him the sights she longed to see—Rome, Naples, Switzerland, Vienna! How proud she would be to parade Douglass before her friends! Assing was so certain they would go that she discussed her plans in great detail with her friends, and she resumed her Italian lessons.[86] But Douglass was still reluctant to make that kind of commitment. "I would give everything to get Douglass to move next spring. Then I could go in peace and with an undivided heart, and enjoy," Ottilie wrote to Ludmilla immediately upon her return to New York City. "Should I not succeed, however, I once again will be in a terrible dilemma. He does not try to detain me and even advises me to take the trip, but first of all I know only too well how lonely he would feel . . . during that long summer, and then I cannot see how I could bear being separated by an ocean. The five months he spent in England after the John Brown affair were terrifying enough."[87] From now on, announcements of their trip, followed by cancellations on account of Douglass' responsibilities and declarations that she could not bring herself to go without him became fixtures in Assing's letters to her sister. They show how desperately she longed for a gesture of acknowledgment and a commitment from Douglass; also how much she had delegated the power of decision making to him.

As with all their aborted trips, she seemed to make the plans, which Douglass, pleading demands of the hour, then frustrated. He was not willing to desert his family, nor would he leave his country at this special period of American history. A vigorous man full of plans and ambition, he was convinced that the United States was now entering an era of hope, promise, and progress—for the nation as a whole, and for him as an individual. It was time to collect his rewards. He lectured all over the country; he campaigned for Grant; he attended Republican, women's rights, labor union, and civil rights conventions; he fought for the Fifteenth Amendment and for improved race relations; he struggled to achieve justice for African-Americans, to create a better America—and to make a career for himself. How could Assing expect him to take a year off? He would not leave after Grant's inauguration, for he needed to be there when the spoils were distributed. He could not leave after all the positions were filled and he had been passed by, for might not Grant reconsider? Later it would be the *New National Era*, his position at the Freedman's Savings Bank, then Grant's reelection campaign, then the Hayes campaign. It is obvious that Douglass cared deeply about Ottilie Assing. Twelve years into their relationship, he still welcomed every chance to spend a night, perhaps a few days, with her in Hoboken, and he treasured their summers in Rochester. She was an attractive woman, strong, irreverent, courageous, sincere, with a wonderful sense of humor and an inspiring joie de vivre. She was soul mate and companion in the best sense of the word. Yes, he cared deeply about her. But he would not give up his self for her. And going to Europe with her would be just that.

At the end of this summer Ottilie Assing initiated what would become a routine pattern: instead of returning directly to New York City, she traveled to Boston, to spend two weeks with the Koehlers. They had rented a comfortable house in Roxbury, but they were lonely, too shy to make friends easily in their new community. Ottilie Assing became their virtual social relations officer. During her first stay in Boston, she sought out Karl Heinzen, one of the most famous and politically active German 48ers, notorious for his militancy as well as for his choleric nature.[88] He and Assing got along famously; they developed a productive working relationship and later cooperated closely on a fund-raising drive they initiated for Ludwig Feuerbach in the 1870s; Heinzen also introduced Assing to his neighbor, the physician Dr. Maria Zakrzewska, who took her all over Boston as she visited her patients and invited her to meet other female physicians.[89] Ottilie had long wanted to make the acquaintance of Fanny Garrison Villard, William Lloyd Garrison's daughter, who was married to another German 48er, Henry Villard, and in that, too, she was successful. She spent a delightful evening at the Villard home, enjoying a long conversation with William Lloyd Garrison, whom she admired as "the veteran apostle of liberty, whose country is the world and whose countrymen all mankind," and meeting a former friend of Douglass', the black Garrisonian abolitionist Charles Lenox Remond, "who made the impression of a half-dead man to me."[90] During one visit to Boston she also befriended Caroline Remond Putnam and Sarah Remond, Charles Remond's sisters, thus establishing a relationship that would even accompany her on her European tours. The Koehlers offered Assing their hospitality; she, in turn, made them the gift of an enlarged social arena.

•   •   •

Frederick Douglass spent the fall of 1868 campaigning for Ulysses Grant and, he was convinced, for black suffrage. Then, all of a sudden, he found himself in the midst of a storm that he would later remember as one of the most painful of his life—a controversy with Susan B. Anthony, Elizabeth Cady Stanton, and the American women's rights movement. It was "one of the saddest divorces in American history,"[91] as one historian has put it, the scars of which are visible to this day. Douglass' relationships to the women in his private life—his mother and grandmother, the misses Auld, Anna Murray, Julia Griffiths, Ottilie Assing—were complex and full of contradictions, as we have seen, but from the very beginning of his public career he was an unwavering supporter of women's rights. His activities were in part motivated by gratitude for the contributions women had made to the abolitionist struggle; more significant, however, was his firm belief in human equality. Women had been his most reliable allies in the past, and Douglass took it for granted that they would work hand in hand for black suffrage. He was shocked rather than appalled when, almost immediately after the war, more and more women's rights activists vowed to fight any extension of the vote that did not include women. Now that the blacks were free, Elizabeth Stanton argued in 1868, "it becomes a serious question whether we had better stand aside and see 'Sambo' walk into the kingdom first."[92] When Douglass and Theodore Tilton, one of the founders of the American Equal Rights Association, appealed to the women's solidarity in what Tilton called "the Negro's hour," Anthony bluntly charged that she would "sooner cut off my right hand than ask the ballot for the black man and not for woman."[93] No matter how hard Douglass tried to argue that the ballot for black men would be a first step to universal suffrage, Anthony and her disciples could not condone this kind of male-imposed gradualism. They, too, saw the era as a time of transformation and hope, and they were determined to go for the here and now. The clearer it became during the midterm campaign of 1866 and the presidential campaign of 1868 that even radical Republicans would not support the women, the more aggressive was their response. Class entered the controversy, then nativist biases, and then, ultimately and unavoidably, race: educated white ladies would not stand back while illiterate ex-slaves walked to the ballot box, they contended. In the fall of 1868 the controversy became so heated that Douglass declined to attend a women's rights meeting in Washington. Black suffrage—he should have said black male suffrage—was his priority, not, he explained in a letter to "my dear Friend" Josephine Sophie White Griffing, because it was "more sacred," but because it was "more urgent," because it was "life and death to the long enslaved people," who faced race riots and the Ku

Klux Klan, who were "mobbed, beaten, shot, stabbed, hanged, burnt" as well as exposed to "all that is malignant in the North and all that is murderous in the South."[94] The women saw this as an act of hostility. The greater the opposition they faced, the more violently the women's rights activists lashed out. In January 1869 Stanton railed against the "dregs of China, Germany, England, Ireland, and Africa," against "Patrick and Sambo and Hans and Yung Tung."[95]

Assing was in the audience when, in May 1869, Douglass addressed the Equal Rights Association in New York City in a last desperate effort to reunite the forces that were moving in opposite directions. His resolution in favor of the Fifteenth Amendment was rejected because, as an infuriated Johannes Lange commented, the women "could not accept that savage, uneducated Negroes be given the right to vote before the gentle women had received it."[96] Lange well expresses the frustration and indignation that permeated "the gang" as they met with Assing and Douglass in her parlor, going over the events of the day.

As we have seen, Assing preferred the company of educated men to that of women. For her, the women married to the men she knew were simply too uneducated, too conventional, and the more sophisticated independent women she befriended—Clara Mundt, Fanny Lewald, Therese Robinson, Susan B. Anthony—she scrutinized more harshly than she did her male friends. It had been Douglass' steadfast commitment rather than her own experience that gradually improved her attitude toward Anthony and her followers, but with the first signs of black-baiting, Assing was up in arms. Her old reservations and biases resurfaced with this onslaught of racism and nativism. To her sister she confided that she thought the women's struggle superfluous because their enfranchisement was just around the corner anyway, an inevitable result of America's progress. "The issue of women's suffrage has gained such priority of late that I would not be the least amazed if women will exercise the right as well as men in only a few years." The most persuasive proof for her was that even German men were beginning to get the message. Anthony's struggle thus was one more of "vanity and egotism than genuine principle," she thought; she would have nothing to do with women who, co-conspiring with power for power's sake, "want to push the women's vote through at the Negroes' expense and thus agree to become the Democrats' ploys, who in turn only use them to beat up the radicals."[97]

This matter of personal preference became an open declaration of war after Douglass' defeat at the New York convention. "At their anniversary meeting the behavior of the emancipated women was so stupid, tactless, and vulgar that a cry of outrage went even through those papers which usually support them, and they themselves have thus dealt a harsh blow to their cause," she wrote. "The most ridiculous aspect is their bragging . . . that they are women, as if that were a merit that makes them superior to men. . . . Fortunately nobody cares about their opinion," she claimed, "and the Fifteenth Amendment will pass despite their opposition."[98] Ottilie Assing's breach with the women's movement was permanent. Douglass, too, was distressed by these developments, but he possessed a rare gift for differentiation as well as a pragmatic nature: he could fight vigorously over political issues and still remain on friendly terms with his opponents. His relationship with Anthony changed after these events, but they continued to reach out to each other. Assing, however, knew only friend or foe. Once she had crossed a line, there was no turning back for her.

Still, she did not let politics ruin a precious week with Douglass. "The anniversaries brought Douglass to New York, who stayed with me from Monday through Friday," she reported. "Although he was busy with the antislavery and Equal Rights Association meetings every day, there was many a quiet moment in it too, and we made the best use of our time. Together with Frauenstein and Riotte we had a marvelous night out at Edwin Booth's new theater, where we saw a superb performance of *Othello*." Nothing could diminish her optimism, not even the fact that Mrs. Loewenthal's dislike of her presence had forced her to move again in Hoboken—this time to the home of an elderly widow, Mrs. Werpup, like Assing a lover of animals. Since Mrs. Werpup immediately fell for Douglass, Assing was happy. To celebrate this new beginning and the stability and rootedness it promised, Douglass made Assing the present of a green macaw. "These are golden times," Assing reported a few months later, after Grant's victory in the presidential election. "Finally we have a genuinely Republican administration, even more radical than the majority of the people. This is a blessing none of you over there in Europe can imagine . . . There is truly no greater happiness for a people than to belong to this republic." She even became expansionist in her joy: "If only we had Cuba!"[99]

Douglass had enough influence in Washington to secure positions for his sons, but President Grant was not interested in having him there. For a while there were rumors that Douglass would be appointed minister resident to Haiti, as Charles immediately reported to his father, and Ottilie Assing to her sister,[100] but then the honor went to another, less controversial black leader, Ebenezer D. Bassett of New Haven. The draft of a letter to George Downing that Douglass sent in response to this development is in Ottilie Assing's handwriting—perhaps an indication that Douglass left it to Assing to defend his pride.[101] Still, there were moments of triumph: on 30 March 1870 President Grant announced the adoption of the Fifteenth Amendment, granting suffrage rights to all citizens regardless of "race, color, or previous condition of servitude"—for Douglass a day of jubilation, and the foundation stone of his unswerving loyalty to Grant; in that he was joined by Assing, who had been skeptical at his nomination. "From a political perspective there can be no greater happiness than belonging to the United States,"[102] she affirmed.

In April the American Anti-Slavery Society gathered in New York's Apollo Hall to celebrate the ratification of the amendment: Frederick Douglass, Abby Kelley Foster, Henry Highland Garnett, Julia Ward Howe, Lucretia Mott, Wendell Phillips, Robert Purvis, et al. Every one of them had given the best years of their lives to abolitionism and the civil rights campaigns. It was hard to believe that the moment they had spent decades fighting for had arrived. "I seem to myself to be living in a new world. The sun does not shine as it used to,"[103] said a deeply moved Frederick Douglass. Ottilie Assing, sitting next to Caroline Putnam, accompanied Frederick Douglass on that glorious evening,[104] and to her he made a special gift that night, an acknowledgment of the spiritual guidance and companionship she had given him: "I want to express my love to God and gratitude to God, by thanking those faithful men and women, who have devoted the great energies of their souls to the welfare of mankind. It is only through such men and such women that I can get a glimpse of God anywhere."

At yet another ratification celebration in Philadelphia's Horticultural Hall a week later, Douglass said he did not want to dwell on "hackneyed cant about thanking God for this deliverance," and he fiercely attacked the churches which "led everything against the abolition of slavery, always holding us back by telling us that God would abolish slavery in his own good time":

> God has given to man certain great powers, and man, in the exercise of these great powers, is to work out his own salvation—the salvation of society—eternal justice, goodness, mercy, wisdom, knowledge, with these gospels of God to reform mankind, and my thanks to-night are to willing hearts and the willing hands that labored in the beginning, amid loss of reputation, amid insult and martyrdom, and at imminent peril of life and limb. My thanks are to those brave spirits who in the evil hour had the courage and devotion to remember and stand by the cause of liberty, and to demand the emancipation of the bondsman.[105]

The black clergy were scandalized. In a mass meeting the Reverend James Williams spoke for many when he declared: "While we love Frederick Douglass, we love truth more. We admire Frederick Douglass, but we love God more."[106] Douglass' reply, published in the *New National Era*, might almost have come from Ottilie Assing's pen: associating his critics with the Inquisition of old, he painted them as forces of regression and death that misused the power they held over people's minds and hearts. "Thanks not to faith, but to the enlightenment of the age, and the growth of rational ideas among men, to differ with the Church today does not bring torture and physical death,"[107] he commented.

Ottilie's letter to Ludmilla in which she recounted this dispute bubbled with excitement. The relevant passage deserves to be quoted in full:

> Finally Douglass is in open battle with the pious party, after they had long ceased to know what to make of him. On the occasion of the ratification celebration for the Fifteenth Amendment in Philadelphia he spoke up against the silly drivel about "divine Providence" and the resolutions "to thank God for this miracle," saying: "I deal here in no hackneyed cant about thanking God for this great deliverance; I look upon this great revolution as having been brought about by man, rather than by any special intervention of divine Providence." Upon that, some sanctimonious individuals have started a terrible howl and have attacked him fiercely. He wrote to me: "The bloodhounds of Zion are now hot on my tracks. Bethel Church in Philadelphia has taken me under its special care, and arraigned, tried, and condemned me for the utterance of dangerous sentiments." He struck back, and of course the "pious bloodhounds," as he calls them in another passage, will lose out with their stupid belief in the struggle against reason, as always. These events give me the greatest pleasure, for first of all his attitude toward these things becomes clear to anyone, and then, as the orthodox turn away from him with pious shudder, he will find even more friends and disciples among the freethinkers and the enlightened.

She was so eager to claim Douglass for her camp that she imposed her notion of atheism on a position that in fact stood in the tradition of many reform-minded Christians who denounced the church as an institution.[108] And she seemed unaware that a more radically atheist position would alienate him from most African-Americans—or if she was, it posed no problem for her. Ottilie Assing had never felt closer to Frederick Douglass, at one with him, body, mind, and soul soaring! She asked Ludmilla to send their mother's portrait to "Douglass, to whom Mother would be ever so close, if everything was as it should be, and unfortunately is not."[109] And only now, after what she celebrated as his outing, did Assing compose her long letter to Ludwig Feuerbach, lauding him as Douglass' spiritual liberator.

President Grant's Washington had no place for Frederick Douglass, and so Frederick Douglass began to invent a place for himself. In the fall of 1868, after extensive negotiations, months of complicated financial maneuvering, and a difficult personal decision-making process, Douglass agreed to join his son Lewis, the Reverend J. Sella Martin (a former slave who was pastor of a black Presbyterian church in Washington), George Downing, and others in launching a weekly journal for black Americans, a journal that, as Douglass put it in his "Salutatory of the Corresponding Editor" of 27 January 1870, would be "proudly and joyfully sustained by every intelligent and patriotic colored man in the land." The journal was to be an all-black enterprise, with Martin as editor, Douglass as corresponding editor, and Lewis Douglass in charge of the print shop. The first *New Era* was published on 13 January 1870. By the summer of 1870 it was all but dead; Martin had resigned; the type and press were seized by creditors. On 8 September the paper resurfaced as the *New National Era* with Frederick Douglass as editor-in-chief. He had purchased a half interest in both the journal and the printing plant; in December he invested another $8,000, which made him sole proprietor. Liberation of the mind, he explained to his readers, was the most important struggle of his own life; he was now ready to make an investment in the intellectual liberation and improvement of the entire race. "From the time I learned to read, and learned the value of knowledge, it was among the deepest and sincerest wishes of my soul, to assist in the deliverance of my people, not only from the terrible bondage of slavery, but from the more terrible bondage of ignorance and vice."[110] And he moved to Washington.

"The news of the day is that Douglass has decided to become editor of a radical journal in Washington, the *New National Era*," Assing wrote to Ludmilla. She was relieved that this would spell an end to his tedious lecture tours, but for once she could not fully share his optimism. She warned Douglass of the financial risks, but when she realized how important the enterprise was for him she promised unconditional professional support. "He approaches this venture full of zeal and optimism, and I fear he is a little too sanguine about it." She tried hard to see the advantages—the erring nation needed Douglass' enlightened mind and voice; he would spend the dreary winter months in a more congenial Southern clime; they would still retreat to their emerald island during the summers; Douglass would "keep the house with everything in it, peacock, deer, etc., and the wife, too, will stay." Most significant, however, "Of course I will be an active contributor,"[111] the journal's European correspondent and one of its invisible masterminds!

Ottilie's first article was on the relations between the Prussian king and Louis Napoleon; later she contributed a number of comments on the Franco-Prussian War; she also wrote a "Letter from New York." Structured like her former *Morgenblatt* reports, her articles usually appeared on the front page, signed "R." In an editorial note of 1873 she was praised as "our welcome lady correspondent 'R' from New York City."[112] So invigorated was she by her new involvement with journalism that she was only too happy to accept an offer by the German *Zeitschrift für Bildende Kunst* to submit regular opinion pieces on the American art scene.[113]

By December it again seemed as if Douglass' business would falter; months later Assing reported to her sister that she spent "the most miserable Christmas, for I had predicted this outcome to a point." She noted that Douglass had already lost $7,000 and was about to give up.[114] They toiled on, however, and although the *New National Era* was always on the brink of bankruptcy, their close cooperation as journalists became another inspiring link between them. "During the week we write our editorials for the *New Era*, which, when done as the most beautiful teamwork, is a great pleasure and keeps me busy enough,"[115] Assing wrote from Rochester in August. She was not just reporting on European issues, she claimed; she was writing together with Douglass and, even more important, said that many of the articles on American political and educational issues that were identified as Douglass' actually came from her pen. "On his way to Washington, Douglass spent one day and two nights with me. I have the satisfaction of hearing that my pieces are taken note of in Washington and are often reprinted by local papers. Once Douglass begins his winter tour I will again have to do most of the work,"[116] she reported in October. On 16 April 1872 she told her sister that the series of articles on the split between the Republican Party and the Liberal Republican movement was entirely written by her, and in August she reported from Washington about the thrill of once again meddling in politics. "The campaign is in full swing and Douglass is one of the most influential and outstanding leaders on the Republican side. All of a sudden the *Era* has become powerful, and you will imagine that I absolutely delight in not only being led into all the depths of political maneuvering but, as a journalist, in having my paws in everything and moreover knowing that my columns are read and acknowledged."[117]

Douglass claimed that he wanted to devote the paper to the elevation of his race, and this is what he did, just as he had with *The North Star*, *Frederick Douglass' Paper*, and *Douglass' Monthly*. But he also had very personal motives: he wanted to set up his sons as independent businessmen. Lewis' and Frederick Jr.'s Western venture had failed, and so they had come back East and followed Charles to Washington, but the government positions Douglass secured for them were precarious at best: Charles lost his in the spring of 1869 when budget cuts forced the Freedmen's Bureau to reduce its staff.[118] When Lewis found work in the Government Printing Office, the Printers' Union accused him of being an untrained scab—though the union itself excluded blacks. "Douglass is made a transgressor for working at a low rate of wages by the very men who prevented his getting a high rate," his father cried out in desperation. "He is denounced for not being a member of the Printers' Union by the very men who would not permit him to join such Union. . . . There is no disguising the fact—his crime was his color." He could not bear to see his sons thus humiliated. "I had felt the iron of Negro hate before, but the case of this young man gave it a deeper entrance into my soul than ever before."[119] So his acquisition of the journal was also an effort to give his sons, whom he himself had trained as printers, economic independence, to infuse them with entrepreneurial spirit. Charles became one of the journal's correspondents; Lewis was in charge of editorials and Frederick Jr. of business management.[120] "I have bought the entire printing establishment of the *New National Era* . . . and have given it to my three sons in the hope that they may be able to serve themselves as well as their people," he wrote to Gerrit Smith. "I am sure, you will say this is pretty well for a fugitive slave. It is just thirty-three years tomorrow, since I ran away from Master Tommy Auld, and it seems but yesterday, though a world of change has taken place since then."[121] The plan failed. In October 1874 Frederick Douglass had to close the *New National Era*. Assing never mentioned this defeat in her letters to Ludmilla.

As we have seen, Assing was dubious about the enterprise from the start, and no matter how much she enjoyed her reentry into journalism and her teamwork with Douglass, she was painfully aware of the journal's problems. Her letters to her sister were filled with hints: there was not sufficient funding in the first place; Douglass miscalculated the ability and willingness of the black community to support this kind of journal; his long absences were detrimental to the administration and quality of the paper. Assing understood all this, but, as always, she refused to indict Douglass. Instead, she turned on his sons and the staff of the *New National Era*. A letter of 16 April 1872 was representative of the position: Douglass had been on the lecture circuit all winter, she reported, while she had struggled to cover his back by writing about the defection within the Republican Party; she was lonely, frustrated at these political developments, disgusted by the paper's shabby, unattractive layout. "I wrote several articles about these things [the party's problems], of which I will send you two," she said, but cautioned: "Incidentally, don't take too close a look at the paper, for during Douglass' absence . . . and in the hands of his sons and of an incompetent, ignorant, and malicious assistant editor it has become pretty bad."[122] For years she had observed the younger Douglasses moving in and out of jobs, launching little businesses and failing at them, landing government jobs and being fired, starting families, building houses—and it always meant their parents investing money to get them started, their parents paying off creditors to avoid scandal, their parents covering their bills when they were unemployed. It meant there was no money left for Douglass to have a European tour; it meant another winter of lecturing. Assing was fully aware of the discrimination these young men had to contend with,[123] but her anger about that paled before the effect of these setbacks on Douglass, and also on her. Unwilling to blame Douglass or herself for their makeshift arrangements, their canceled travel plans, and a growing sense of stagnation, she began to blame his children.

It was easy to do so, for Frederick Douglass was not only angry about the racist slander his children had to endure but incensed at their inability to cope, frustrated at the never-ending and increasing demands they made on his financial resources. Despite his enormous energy and physical vigor, he tired of the annual lecture circuit and was unnerved by his own inability to secure the kind of position he deserved. His awareness of the forces they faced allowed him to rationalize their defeats, yet it could not stifle his growing resentment of his children. Assing was evidently oblivious to the fact that it was one thing for a father to censure and complain, but quite another when the complaints came from the outside, especially from a white person; in that event, he would spontaneously become protective. When Ottilie Assing joined Douglass in his tirades against his offspring, she was unwittingly undermining their relationship. It happened slowly, one step at a time, imperceptibly to both.

In the winter of 1870 President Grant appointed a commission to Santo Domingo and made Douglass its secretary. Having first requested to be annexed by Spain in 1861, then, after a nationalist revolution, having persuaded Spain to relinquish control, and now fearful of an invasion by the Haitian Army, the government of Santo Domingo had made a formal request to be annexed by the United States. Grant gave support to this plan, not only influenced by real estate pressure groups but also intrigued by the idea that the country could become a safety valve for relieving the pressures of the American race problem. But there was fierce opposition, headed by Senator Charles Sumner, a former abolitionist and now chairman of the Senate Committee on Foreign Relations, who accused Grant of wanting to dump African-Americans on a foreign shore rather than securing their rights at home. Grant decided to dispatch an investigative commission and invited Douglass to join it—a clever move, since it secured public support from a black leader renowned for his opposition to African-American colonization. Douglass saw this mission as his long-sought chance to receive the public recognition and, though through the servants' entrance, also the government position he desired. He was so eager for a federal post that he betrayed his former position and defied Sumner, his ally in the abolition and civil rights causes.[124]

Assing rejoiced at this appointment, certain that it would lead to greater honors. The house that Douglass had bought on A Street on Capitol Hill, only steps away from the Supreme Court, suggests that his move to the nation's capital for good was just a matter of time; there are signs indicating that Ottilie Assing planned to join him there, as mistress of his new home.[125] "The final days of the old year and the first of the new passed in an unusually pleasant way," she wrote to Ludmilla. She and Douglass had their own pre-Christmas when he came to spend a few days with her on 22–24 December on his way to Rochester, and he returned on New Year's Eve; while German-American Hoboken was welcoming the New Year at the opera and with fancy balls, they sat at home "in the most beautiful peacefulness." Yet Assing wanted to give public expression to her pride, to show that Douglass' success was also hers, and she took care to spread word of his appointment and his visit to Hoboken. "But so many friends had already invited themselves in anticipation of Douglass' visit that I had to have the whole party over for the next night, although he had asked to avoid all 'lionizing,' " she confided to her sister. "Even people whom I hardly knew or knew not at all used the occasion to see him and begged to be introduced just for that reason, so that it was 'lionizing' in the fullest sense of the word, which everybody, and Douglass no less than the others, enjoyed to the utmost."[126] On 16 January, Douglass came again to Hoboken to have breakfast with her before embarking for Santo Domingo. Ottilie was jubilant. There was only one drawback: "I would have loved to join him, but *only* men were going, and so it was impossible."[127]

Frederick Douglass faced discrimination aboard the Caribbean-bound vessel, and he later admitted that his role on the commission was "inconsiderable and unimportant."[128] Assing, however, reported only success. "He is enchanted with the tropical clime, the country, and seems generally very satisfied with this tour," she told Ludmilla after Douglass' return visit in Hoboken. (We do not know whether Douglass made up a success story for his friend, or she could not admit defeat to her sister.) "As there can be no greater blessing, politically, than to belong to the United States, I feel we should grant this blessing to a people who plead for it so urgently," she went on, hinting that great things might be in store for him, as "the President thinks so highly of him."[129] But when Grant gave a dinner party for the Santo Domingo commission, Douglass was absent from the guest list. In Assing's letters silence reigned about this slight and the subsequent defeat of Grant's annexation plan in the Senate. More clouds on the horizon. Whistling in the dark became a habit with Ottilie Assing.

IX

LA DONNA È MOBILE?

Years of Suspense

She was a free woman, yet she lay bound in fetters she could not tear, for she was unhappy! She had freed herself from all prejudice, and therefore she drifted in the universe, the world unable to understand her ideas and ridiculing them.

—CLARA MUNDT, *Aphra Behn*

Should there be a leader of blacks and whites,
Then let him be of the middling color!
The mulatto must be chosen as king,
Then nobody could complain!

—HANS CHRISTIAN ANDERSEN, *Mulatten*

ATTEMPT TO LYNCH A NEGRO AT ROCHESTER[1]
RIOT AT ROCHESTER
ATTEMPT OF A MOB TO BREAK INTO A JAIL AND LYNCH A NEGRO—THEY ARE FIRED UPON BY THE MILITARY—TWO PERSONS KILLED

Rochester, N.Y., Jan. 2 — The excitement over the outrage committed upon a little white girl by a negro named HOWARD is very great. A mob of four or five hundred people went to the jail and attempted to break in and kill the prisoner. They were foiled by the Sheriff and the Police. There is now an immense crowd about the jail, and they are frantic over the report that the little girl has died of her injuries. The evening papers are out with the evidence against HOWARD. It is conclusive, and leaves no doubt that he is the man who committed the dreadful outrage. The Police are at the jail and the military are assembling at the arsenal. Attacks are made by roughs and others on unoffending negroes who appear in the streets. It is feared that there will be an outbreak to-night. The Sheriff and his side stand firm, and are determined to uphold the laws.

8 P.M. — The Police have made another raid on the crowd . . . and dispersed it. There is more quietness just now, but all is speculation as to whether there will be another mob to-night or not. The repulse of the one this morning, it is hoped, has had the effect to prevent another assemblage to-night. The Police and military are on duty. The Grand Jury are in session, and they will indict HOWARD tomorrow forenoon, and he will be brought into Court to plead to the indictment. Efforts have been made this P.M. to have him plead guilty, but he refuses, and maybe he is innocent. The evidence against him accumulates. It would seem almost criminal to take HOWARD from the jail at present, as the mob would rescue him from the authorities and kill him.

There are about a hundred of the military guarding the jail this evening. There is a mob there yelling and shouting, and there have been several stones thrown at the military. The Police, who had been relieved, are again ordered to the jail.

Midnight — About 9 o'clock, while the crowd was yelling at the corner of Court and Exchange streets, the military fired a volley, killing two men and wounding one man and one boy. The names of the killed are JOHN ELTER, a railroad worker, and HENRY MERLAU. JOHN HILRECHT was shot through the calf of the leg. The name of the boy has not been learned. He was hit in the shoulder. The excitement is great, and people are hurrying to the scene of the conflict. The crowd said it was not necessary to fire, while the military say that they were compelled to fire to protect themselves as they were being pelted with stones.

An account of the difficulty is thus given by an eyewitness, Policeman BRANCH. The squad of military were lined across the west end of the bridge facing Exchange-street. A man stepped up to Policeman BRANCH and said that some boys a few feet off were picking up stones. The officer drove them away. At the same moment the word "forward" was given by the officer in command of the squad, and he pushed the policeman aside. The shots were fired at this time. The men shot were standing in Exchange-street, and had not participated with the mob. ELTER was a highly respectable and influential German citizen. He lived but a few moments after being taken into a saloon near by. It is reported that a woman was shot, but it is not yet confirmed. The feeling against the military is intense. The Police are being drawn in from the outer districts of the city and dispatched to the vicinity of the jail. It is feared that more blood will be shed before morning. The colored people are fleeing to their homes to hide, as it is not deemed safe for them to be seen in the streets.

On 16 May 1872 Frederick Douglass arrived in Hoboken: it was convention month again. But this time he came with no speaking assignments, no meetings. "We had the most exquisite time together and made our plans for the summer,"[2] Assing reported to her sister. He and Assing agreed to meet in

Rochester in mid-June. Four days later Douglass went on to Rochester to spend a few days with his family, and returned to Washington on 29 May. Then terrible news struck. Assing had already made her travel plans when she learned that the Douglass residence had burned to the ground on 2 June. The members of the Douglass household—Anna Murray and the Sprague family—had escaped unscathed, and most of Douglass' books, furniture, pictures, even the piano, were saved, but "the only existing complete run of *The North Star, Frederick Douglass' Paper,* and *Douglass' Monthly* as well as hundreds of personal letters,"[3] which probably included hundreds of letters from Ottilie Assing, went up in flames. There was no way to replace this "beautiful residence, which holds so many memories, a 'historic' place which I regarded as my home and which was most intimately connected with my past and my present," Ottilie wrote nine days later. The tension of the week, her sadness and her fear, exploded: "The ground has been pulled from under my feet!"[4]

"One of the city's most beautiful ornaments, Frederick Douglas' [sic] elegant residence, including outbuildings, on Douglas Hill on the southern end of South Avenue burnt down completely at 12 o'clock last night," Rochester's German newspaper *Täglicher Beobachter* reported on 3 June 1872. "It was a frame house, but elegantly built and furnished, and surrounded by very beautiful gardens." "The fire is attributed to an incendiary," the *Rochester Daily Union and Advertiser* reported the morning after the catastrophe. The police investigated, but nobody seemed surprised when the arsonist was never identified. In a fierce indictment of Rochester's "Ku Klux spirit which makes anything owned by a colored man a little less respected and secure than when owned by a white citizen," Douglass tried to express the pain of his loss. "It is the spirit of hate, the spirit of murder, the spirit which would burn a family in their beds,"[5] he charged. On 17 June the *Rochester Daily Union and Advertiser* reported large passages from this "Letter," expressing disgust at its "bad temper" and conveniently forgetting to comment on Douglass' gratitude to those who had stepped forward to help in the hour of loss. "Every effort possible was made by the police and fire department to save property, and the neighbors (all white) did everything in their power to afford relief to the shelterless family," he had said. It also disputed Douglass' Klan indictment by reporting that the investigations seemed to be implicating "colored persons as the guilty party," insinuating that the arsonist might even be a member of the family.

Ottilie Assing never used the term "arson" in reference to the loss of Douglass' home, and her letters to Ludmilla contained no hint that the Douglasses had been victims of a criminal assault. She wrote about her feelings: her sadness at having lost a beloved home; her anger at Anna Murray's failure to save Douglass' bonds and papers; but racially motivated violence was conspicuously absent from her report. A close look at events in the first half of 1872 in Rochester suggests that Ottilie Assing may have been protecting more than Douglass' reputation.

On New Year's Eve 1871 a ten-year-old German-American girl, Cäcilia Ochs, was raped. The African-American William Howard, whom local newspapers described as a twenty-two-year-old notorious loafer and dandy, was accused of this crime. He was caught, identified by Cäcilia, and locked up in the local jail. "If Howard had lost his life for this heinous crime, the people would say it was just retribution," the *Rochester Daily Union and Advertiser* commented, lamenting that the suspect was safely locked up rather than hanging from a lamppost.[6] When rumors spread that the girl had died of her injuries, a mob of more than a thousand men—many of them of German descent and led by Cäcilia's father, Nicholas Ochs—attacked the jail. "Cries of 'Give us the nigger,' and 'Hang the villain,' were freely made," reported *The New York Times*; the militia was called, and in the ensuing riot two men were killed and several others wounded. One of the casualties was John Elter, "an influential and highly respected, able German citizen, a member of the Mannerchor [sic]" and father of seven; the other was Henry Merlau, a young man who, said *The New York Times*, "took no part in the disturbances."[7] For days a civil war raged in the city; African-Americans were attacked in the streets, and there were clashes between citizens and the militia. So horrified were the authorities by the mob that the accused man's face was disguised under a layer of chalk when he was led to the courthouse under cover of darkness, and his trial took place at night, with the courtroom windows carefully boarded up, so that nobody on the street would suspect what was going on. Tried for rape, Howard pleaded guilty and was sentenced to twenty years. As he entered Auburn State Prison, he reportedly turned and, "placing his thumb on his nose, waved his fingers tauntingly at the crowd."[8]

The city's German-American population was especially outraged at these events. Memories of abolitionist agitations and the personal losses many of them had suffered during the Civil War were still vivid, and together with anger at Cäcilia's injuries and the death of two respected citizens, they formed a dangerous potion. Most of Rochester's German-Americans were conservative people with a strong leaning toward the Democrats; for them, abolitionists had been rabble-rousers at best, and yet they had had to send their sons, brothers, and husbands off to fight, as they saw it, for the slaves. The widows and orphans in their midst were a constant reminder of what black emancipation had cost them. What were their feelings when Douglass, whose activities as an agitator they blamed for inciting the bloodshed (rather than the slave owners), was able to embrace his soldier sons after the war?

Worse, Douglass was known to be an unwavering supporter of President Grant—the president who had supported France and Napoleon III in the Franco-Prussian War. Douglass' *New National Era* covered the war, and though it took a more neutral position than the Grant administration, German America—in the thralls of what one German historian characterized as "boisterous nationalism"[9]—grouped anybody with the enemy who did not share their patriotic frenzy. A few months later, the *Rochester Daily Union and Advertiser* published a series of articles accusing the Republican administration of providing France with arms and ammunition. "The German Indignation Against Grant and the Republican Party" on 24 February discussed the details of this trade, and on 23 March the paper waved a red flag in front of its German readers when uncovering "How a Republican Federal Administration Armed Frenchmen with U.S. Muskets to Shoot Down Germans." Even though Douglass never spoke up in favor of France, his support of Grant and the Republican Party told the story for the German patriots in Rochester.

The situation was further exacerbated when, in March 1872, disenchanted Republicans left Grant's party to form the Liberal Republican Party. Among the leaders of this rebellion was Carl Schurz, a 48er who had come to the United States in 1852. A prominent figure in the young Republican Party and a successful officer during the Civil War, he was the uncontested hero of German America. When he accused Grant of boycotting reconciliation and thus true reforms in the South and, together with Horace Greeley, became one of the instigators of inner-party rebellion, Germans defected from the party in droves. Assing, however, denounced him as a traitor to republican ideals. "Germans seem to follow Schurz blindly," she lamented, "and they either do not see or do not want to see all the contradictions and falseness of which he has been guilty during the past year, no matter how obvious."[10] The *New National Era* carried commentaries condemning the Liberals, articles which the German-American community, like almost everybody else, attributed to Douglass, never divining that a fellow German, and a woman at that, was the one who was vilifying their icon. Though Douglass was in Santo Domingo during the height of the controversy, after the Liberal Republican Convention in Cincinnati the *Rochester Daily Union and Advertiser*'s headline read: "Fred Douglass and His Whitewashing Brigade at New Orleans."[11] Even radical German-American papers in Rochester joined the campaign against Douglass, and tried to undermine his authority as a political leader by airing rumors about his immoral private life. The parallel to the Garrisonian assault on Douglass and his liaison with Julia Griffiths was remarkable. The attacks became so vicious that even the *Advertiser*, which had been writing for months against Douglass, protested the slander. "As best friend and only sincere champion of Fred. Douglass, we desire to enter our protest against the efforts of the Radical party here and elsewhere to bring him into ridicule by parading his board and bedding matters before the public," they charged. Of course, they were less interested in protecting the black leader and his family than in vilifying the radicals: "The meddling of the Rochester Radical prints with Mr. Douglass's private affairs is a piece of the grossest impertinence, and it should be severely rebuked."[12]

No, there was no love lost between Frederick Douglass and the German-American community of Rochester. And it did not help that this German woman came to live with the Douglasses every summer, lodging and fraternizing with a black family, riding with Douglass in his buggy, promenading down Buffalo Street on his arm, a woman who did not attend their meetings, who was not interested in their clubs.

Yet there is no evidence that Germans were involved in the burning of the Douglass residence. Neither Assing nor Douglass ever even insinuated this, but their very silence about this accumulation of tension between the German-Americans and Douglass in Rochester is itself interesting. Douglass and Assing surely knew of the rape and the riots. Why did they not mention these events in their private or public writings?

Douglass lashed out at an anonymous white adversary; Assing, however, vented her rage on Anna Murray, the woman who had in fact suffered most from the flames. "Eleven thousand dollars in U.S. bonds burnt, probably because this stupid old hag totally lost her head, as it usually happens with uneducated people, for she had plenty of time to save them, and as they were deposited in a light tin box in her bedroom, and it had been forcefully drummed into her head what to save first in case of an accident, no other explanation is possible. She probably thought more of her wig and some dozen silver spoons." Assing portrayed Anna Murray as a creature that had to be trained for proper performance, and who forgot her instructions under stress. Like a panicky child she had grabbed what was important to her. Saving silver spoons rather than the bonds in a cheap, ugly tin box associated her with the magpie, the bird notorious for going for glitter. The woman who should have been Douglass' reliable helpmate was a useless creature, a burden, even a liability, Assing insisted.

This harangue was exacerbated by insult. Assing spoke of an "old hag," associating Anna Murray with senility and ugliness, the wig symbolizing the baldness of old age as well as an old woman's futile struggle to defy age by purchasing beauty. Her outburst reveals how much she disliked the woman who, from her perspective, lacked everything that defined true womanhood, yet whom she could not dislodge.

The burning of the Douglass residence was the last straw for Ottilie Assing, perhaps. When Douglass was appointed to the Santo Domingo Commission, they had celebrated it as a sure sign that public recognition in Washington was just a matter of months away, and he had bought the house on A Street to be ready. Douglass told everyone that his wife would stay in Rochester, and Assing may well have envisioned herself as mistress of his Washington residence. Then an arsonist destroyed the dream.

So Anna Murray was the dark villain of Assing's Gothic tale, and she made herself its angel heroine: "Fortunately Douglass will receive a replacement [of the bonds] from the government, because Congress passed a resolution for cases such as this, and because—thanks to my circumspection!—he has the numbers, which I had copied for him a long time ago."[13] The story of the fire was transformed into a eulogy about Assing's superiority and wisdom, a story of black failure and white success.

But Douglass described it very differently. "I have lost five or six thousand dollars by my fire, and many things to which I can attach no money value, but if I get my Government Securities all right, as I have no doubt I shall, I can stand the loss. It is very hard to give up my old home. Mrs. Douglass is here [in Washington] with me,"[14] he wrote to Gerrit Smith in July. The Douglasses and some of the Spragues moved into the new house on A Street, and while they settled in, Douglass left for a campaign tour of the South. When he returned, he telegraphed Assing, who was staying with the Koehlers in Boston, to join him. "I left Boston on the 9th [of August], arrived the following morning in New York, after a beautiful water trip on one of the magnificent floating palaces which daily ply Long Island Sound; from the steamer I went directly to the train, and arrived here that same afternoon."[15] She arrived in a house full of too many people, and she took up a comfortable room, which only made things worse. She seems to have been ruthless in her conduct toward the Douglass family, her ruthlessness matched only by Douglass', who sent for her regardless of his wife's wishes or condition.

Though her dream of having Douglass to herself in Washington had been ruined, Assing was a city person, and she seems to have enjoyed the new situation in at least some respects. Washington was in the midst of a fierce presidential campaign, with Douglass active in it; she enjoyed being at the center of things, one of the insiders; and the *New National Era* with its offices right on the spot was there for her to wield her pen, to once again make and shape opinion; she made almost daily excursions to the Capitol, sticking her nose in the campaign offices, working closely with Douglass, writing articles. It was almost as exciting as her involvement in the John Brown affair! A letter of 15 August to Ludmilla shows that she saw herself no longer simply as an observer but as a participant; then she was so busy that she did not even take time off to write to her sister until December. She stayed in Washington through election day, and returned to Hoboken only on 6 November.

Her two letters to Ludmilla in which she described these months with Douglass used terms of pleasure, activity, power; they contained not the slightest hint of domestic tension. Indeed, Douglass' family was not even mentioned. And yet on 30 December her words suggested tremendous stress; she seemed near breakdown:

> As beautiful and rich this summer turned out for me, so bad has been my winter so far. During the final days of my stay in Washington I caught a terrible cold, as a result of the abrupt change from burning heat to cold fall weather, and it affected my ears, in the form of incessant ringing, which has not stopped in weeks; this makes it almost impossible to do any kind of intellectual work and often almost drives me to despair. I had no idea that one could be exposed to such torture, and that while free from pain, fever, and in perfectly good health.[16]

Her friend Dr. Frauenstein reassured her that she need not fear deafness, and prescribed rest rather than drugs. Her letter spoke of a bad cold, but both the symptoms she described and the cure the doctor recommended point to a different direction: she suffered from acute hearing loss brought on by extreme stress. He wrote a cautionary letter to "My Dear Friend" Douglass a few months later: "Miss Assing is improving in a ration of a late spring. It is to be expected, that she will recover her philosophical calmness within the cranial cavities of her auditory system for—at least—the warm summer months," he stated, yet he cautioned that the inflammation might flare up again any time. "I am afraid, the cold winter season, will make her aware, that she has . . . an Achilles' heel in her body." Frauenstein used a physician's language to keep the incalculable at bay, yet he was careful to include specifics that Douglass, if he cared for Assing, would be sure to understand. Frauenstein's account of Assing's dramatic response to changes of season was not just a reference to the weather but to Assing's and Douglass' pattern of life. He knew that for Assing the winters, when

Douglass was often absent for months, were long and dreary, months of mounting frustration and even depression. He also saw that it was becoming harder for her to cope with this depression; perhaps this was worsened by her going through menopause. "Her self-slaughterous tendencies remain unabated, notwithstanding her improvement, and it is useless, to reason with her on that nonsense; for, it is nonsense in itself, to reason on nonsense."[17]

Ottilie had been ready to move to Washington not only because she wanted to be with Douglass but because her social life in Hoboken was rapidly losing its luster. Also, her circle of friends was shrinking. What had brought and held "the gang" together for more than two decades was their memories of 1848, their hope for a united and free Germany, their devotion to abolitionism, their enthusiasm as freethinkers, and their Republican commitments. But when in 1870 war broke out between France and Prussia, Assing—though she decried the French aggression and denounced French war atrocities, as well as their stalling tactics during the later peace negotiations—was shocked at the blind nationalism and fierce jingoism that took hold of even the most radical of her friends. As Friedrich Sorge, a German-American socialist then living in Hoboken, put it when he wrote to Wilhelm Liebknecht on 25 September 1870: "Our local German citizens have gone rabid as a result of the Prussian war, and it took the greatest efforts on our side to at least keep a small group of ideologically sound workers together."[18] The peace rallies the German-American community organized sickened Assing with their boisterous patriotism, and meanwhile her friends regarded her with dismay when she reminded them that the king they were glorifying as their German savior was the very tyrant who had driven them into exile. "Revolution or war against a tyrant is good and necessary, but when these tyrant-vermin wage war against each other, the people must bleed, and that without liberty gaining ground," she wrote to her sister, and in September she reported from Washington: "The enthusiasm among the Germans is unbelievable, but they make the mistake of transferring it from the *cause* to the *king*, whom *fortune* rather than *merit* appointed representative of this circle. Even the old revolutionaries of 1848 like Schurz, Sigel, Loewenthal, and Kudlich are said to be caught in this ruse, and they all cheer William, the King by God's Grace, the lifelong representative of conservatism, the buckshot prince of 1848, and the outspoken enemy of free institutions."[19]

With attitudes like these, and a voice that needed to be heard, she could not help alienating her German friends, especially when they knew she was the European correspondent behind the *New National Era*'s critical commentaries on the war. In 1872 a disgusted Johannes Lange wrote to Sylvester Rosa Koehler in Boston: "The *New Era* has deteriorated into one of the most vulgar campaign papers, and its denunciations and defamations of its antagonists can hardly be surpassed by any other paper";[20] the letter arrived when Assing was with the Koehlers—which only heightened the tension. The alienation was increased when she opposed the Liberals and Carl Schurz and sided with Grant. "This lady seems totally wrapped up in politics," Lange wrote. Two years later he remarked, "She still believes in the Republican Party as the only road to salvation and goes through fire for them, though rarely through water."[21] They continued to work together in their freethinkers' association; Assing tutored their children, and she was invited to their social events, but the old spontaneity and ease was gone. In a letter to Koehler, Hans Kudlich complained in the mid-1870s: "Life in our old circle offers little. Everybody lives only for himself and his family. That circle which stuck together during your days in Hoboken no longer exists."[22] The harmonious choir turned into a array of competing voices. Also, several of Assing's friends, among them Friedrich Kapp, the Riottes, and, for a while, Hans Kudlich and his family, returned to Germany after Bismarck established the German Reich.[23] "So many are drawn back to Germany, and when they are rich enough to live comfortably they sail away, never to be seen again,"[24] she lamented.

The workload she took on to compensate for the loss and disappointment was enormous: teaching, translations, writing, her work at the Hallgartens' and for the *New National Era*. Also, she had become deeply interested in the American Society for the Prevention of Cruelty to Animals (ASPCA), which Henry Bergh, a philanthropist of German descent, had founded in January 1866.[25] She was a strong woman, stronger perhaps than most of the women she knew, and these activities kept her busy, but too many hopes had been roused in the past years only to be crushed; too many new problems were emerging.

We have no information, except Frauenstein's letter, on how Ottilie Assing fared during the next year after the frightening winter of 1872–73, for either she ceased to write to Ludmilla or her sister discarded her letters. It was a year, however, that can hardly have contributed to her peace of mind. Meanwhile President Grant was inaugurated and showered his supporters with offices; Douglass was not among them. He continued his struggle to keep the *New National Era* in print; the lecture circuit was still his most reliable source of income. He became irritable, discouraged, and withdrew even from friends and family. ". . . really I was little fit to visit any body and did well to hide myself at Old Orchard Beach," he admitted to Rosetta in August 1873. He began to dread approaching old age as a threat to his vigor and health. "I find my continuous working power, in some measure failing me," Rosetta read, "and my health rather uncertain as I grow older."[26] To his friend Henry O. Waggoner he complained of the "want of the feeling . . . in our people," and Waggoner's response shows that he understood Douglass was not discussing African-Americans in general; he was talking about his most intimate realm, about his desire for "a congeniality of Natures and dispositions," about "a decent and proper affinity for each other."[27] The domestic situation in Washington, too, remained unchanged, with the Douglasses, Louisa Sprague, and sometimes children and grandchildren living together in the rather small house. Assing's late summer visit in 1873 was very brief: she came to Washington in August and returned to Hoboken in late October.[28] Douglass was desperate enough to even contemplate a temporary escape to Europe. When he shared these escapist dreams with Waggoner, his friend replied: "I wish my matters should so come around as to allow me to accompany you to Europe. What a pleasure that would be to me."[29]

At this moment Ludmilla Assing told her sister of her approaching marriage. Ludmilla had carved out a most successful career as a writer and journalist after her uncle's death. She first made a name for herself as the biographer of the Countess Elisa von Ahlefeld in 1857 and of the novelist Sophie de la Roche in 1859; in the 1860s she began to edit and publish her uncle's papers, approximately sixty volumes in all, as well as the correspondence of Count Pückler; she translated Mazzini into German and wrote a biography of the Italian revolutionary Piero Cironi while also working as a foreign correspondent for several German journals. Her success translated into money, and she was justifiably proud of the fine mansion she built in Florence. Here she held court, as Rahel Levin had in Berlin, and intellectuals from all over Europe and America vied for an invitation to her salon.[30] Ludmilla Assing was exceptionally successful, much more so than her American sister, but her private life was one of disruption, failure, tragedy. Her first love, Theodor Mundt, was happily married; Feodor Wehl was infatuated with an actress and unaware of Ludmilla's feelings for him; Varnhagen had come between her and a young poet in Berlin; and the Swiss novelist Gottfried Keller, to whom she wrote inviting letters, remained untouched by her charms. "Every woman . . . is happiest when she can live exclusively for her lover, lose herself in him, wear herself out for him, give herself up," Ludmilla confided to Wehl as early as 1848. "But when their humiliated and abused hearts—for that's what you do to them, not only the evil ones, but even the best of men—finally stop beating, then you wonder why your 'kiss, the look of your eye, the smile of your lips' have lost their power."[31] She had fallen in love with the revolutionary Piero Cironi in Italy, and for the first time her feelings were reciprocated, but after only two years Cironi died, in 1862, and Ludmilla found solace in the traditional Assing-Varnhagen way: she wrote his biography.[32] Later she became intimate with an Italian officer, and was pregnant with his child when she discovered that he was a family man; she immediately ended the relationship, and the baby, a boy, died after only three months.[33] In the midst of her parties, her travels, and her writing she was a lonely woman. Then, at the age of fifty-one, she met the officer Gino Grimelli, an attractive and charming man almost twenty years her junior. One year later they announced their engagement.

Most of Ludmilla's friends and relatives were scandalized at the thought that a woman of fifty-two would dare to marry a man so much younger than herself, and an Italian of dubious reputation at that. Her old confidante Johanna Steinheim, then living in Zurich, warned Ludmilla: "A few days ago I received your letter, but you do not answer the highly important question of age," she scolded. "You have *decided*, while I am approached with questions by our acquaintances whether it is true that you will marry a very young man. May God grant that you have not touched too hot an iron." She expressed her strong hope, formulated like an order, "that my questions relating to your engagement will help to calm you down,"[34] which for her could only mean to end this foolishness.

For seventeen years Ottilie Assing had written herself a narrative of perfect interracial love, of love under assault, of love defined as illegitimate but empowered by adversity—a countertext of happiness and promise to Ludmilla's story of pain and betrayal. Ottilie could not quite compete with Ludmilla's professional acclaim, but she did have her romance. And then all of a sudden Ludmilla had a story and a lover almost as exceptional as her own—one of Mazzini's officers, a revolutionary, a beautiful young man, brilliant and radical—and wedding bells ringing! We can only guess at her emotional state on 30 December 1873, reflecting on her sister's happiness, with a lonely New Year's Eve ahead and Douglass on his Western tour. "Every day I think that this might be your wedding day, and I keep repeating my hope that Grimelli will prove as true, as faithful, and as thoroughly good and noble as Douglass," she wrote. But she sounded exhausted and bitter when she claimed: "Seventeen years, in defiance of all external adversity, with people and prejudices of all kinds against us, this is what must be called a true ordeal by fire."[35]

When a letter about Ludmilla's wedding—which in fact had taken place on 1 December—arrived, Ottilie replied gracefully. "Really married then! My warmest, heartfelt congratulations!" she exlaimed. "How lucky you are that no external conditions are in the way of following your inclinations. The mere will is enough to transform the wish into reality." But in the face of Ludmilla's happiness she could no longer deny her own yearning. "How differently have I fared. Unmarried for seventeen years and yet united in a deeper love than many who are married, without the slightest perspective that it will ever be different," she lamented. And then, lest it might choke her, rage exploded out of her: ". . . and, what is worse, separated from each other by a true monster, who herself can neither give love nor appreciate it; what a terrible fate! If I were superstitious I would believe that my name is somehow fatal." Then she ended her letter with a warm gesture of love, wrapped in old childhood memories. "Adieu, dear Ludmilla, I wish that you may be 'happier than one can be'! You will not have forgotten this saying from our childhood."[36]

Two months later a letter from Ludmilla told Ottilie of her separation from Grimelli: apparently the young man had abused and cheated on her; she had kicked him out rather than bear the humiliation of an unhappy marriage, however much the world around her would gloat over her fate. A year later the couple were divorced; rumor had it that Ludmilla paid a lump sum of 20,000 thalers as well as a monthly allowance to get rid of the man. "It was my fate to be alone, although I would surely have been suitable for companionship," she confessed to Feodor Wehl. "Everybody must submit to conditions as they are; this is what I do, and I try to make as much out of every day and make it as fruitful as my strength allows."[37] And the world did gloat. A letter written by her old "friend" Gottfried Keller was sadly representative: "Yesterday Mrs. Steinheim . . . had Dilthey ask me whether I knew that her niece . . . has been deserted by her young husband, the rifleman-lieutenant, who made off with her money and estate. Looks like Sappho and Phaon! And so promptly! I had counted on it that she would get a good beating someday, because she is so ugly. Still, I cannot enjoy stoning her. I'm not sure I, too, would not have fallen, had I been an old maid and my money had attracted a lieutenant."[38] Friends were scarce in Ludmilla's world, it seems.

Ottilie's response was a curious medley of genuine sympathy, the I-knew-it-all-along of the expert in human relations, and a sigh of relief. The balance was reestablished between the sisters! Ludmilla's letter "confirmed my apprehensions," and she could "read much worse between the lines . . . Won't you trust me with your sorrows? You know that you are safe with me, and I understand *everything*," Ottilie wrote, offering solidarity while promising that she would "not even inform Douglass, if you forbid me to do so, although we usually tell each other everything." Love makes women vulnerable in ways only women can understand, she suggested, offering female bonding in sorrow as a means of coping with betrayal: "I do have certain presentiments and usually see sharply when looking into the distance as well as into the future. When you are so intimately connected with *one* man as I am with Douglass, you will get to know men as well as women from a perspective that would never be revealed to you otherwise, especially if it is a man who has seen so much of the world and who was loved by so many women!"

Yet the text claiming to establish equality between the sisters as love's victims contained a subtext that reaffirmed the hierarchy Ottilie had been struggling to solidify between the sisters since her relationship with Douglass began. She underlined "*one* man," thus insinuating that Ludmilla's relationships with men had been a series of failures and subtly reminding her that the problem might be Ludmilla herself rather than the men in her life. Ludmilla's experience, she suggested, was one of passion and thus of the irrational, the blindly physical, which carried the seeds of destruction within itself, while Ottilie was speaking of love, of a physical, emotional, and spiritual communion between woman and man that would only be strengthened by adversity—adversity, at that, which could only come from the outside, while a relationship based exclusively on passion was of necessity self-destructive. In addition to that, Ottilie drew a sharp line between the philandering *papagallo* who trapped Ludmilla and Douglass by describing Douglass as "a man who was loved by so many women"—that is, as an extremely attractive man, of course surrounded by a mob of admiring women, but who chose her alone from this seductive crowd! The letter offering sympathy and solidarity became a fierce assault on what Ottilie took to be Ludmilla's emotional incompetence and sterility.

Ottilie then proceeded to tell her sister in great detail about proofs of his love with which Douglass was showering her. "Douglass, who is just adding a large wing to his house, which means he will gain six spacious rooms, feels that I should move in with him for good. You will imagine how happy it would make me to be together with him always." The Douglasses were indeed building an extension to their house, yet there is no evidence other than this letter to confirm Ottilie's claim. Was she only bragging, just as Ludmilla's household was in a state of disarray? Or was Douglass as tired of their makeshift arrangements as Assing was? Was this invitation his response to Frauenstein's warning? It would be purest happiness to live with Douglass, she went on, "yet I must consider seriously whether it would be prudent to live continually in proximity to his charming wife. So far I have been able to maintain the most friendly terms by means of diplomacy and feeding her with gifts, but with people so ignorant and uneducated you never know what weird notions hit them. What would you say, for example, if you were accused of having bewitched someone?"[39] Ottilie seemed to establish a common bond between herself and her sister by arguing that she, too, had to cope with disappointment, yet what a difference she made between Ludmilla's suffering and hers! Ludmilla's empty house was a sign of failure, of a pipe dream exploded; if Ottilie's dream did not materialize it was Ottilie making this decision. The failure was not the lovers'; it was again brought upon by external circumstances, and Ottilie responded to this adversity beyond her control as any rational human being ought: with calm resolution, wisdom, prudence, and foresight. Equally significant: Ottilie implicitly claimed that she, the elder of the two siblings, was indeed still able to bewitch a man, while her younger sister had bought love and was dumped. Like the "old hag" with her wig of the arson narrative, Ludmilla was ridiculed for her attempt to claim a woman's prerogatives.

Ottilie's letters in the following months combined a flood of sisterly advice with proofs of her own foresight. Time and again Ottilie repeated that she and Douglass were not in the least surprised by Ludmilla's catastrophe, which they had to observe from a distance, unable to help yet suffering with the victim. "Just as the one who stands directly under a tower or at the foot of a mountain has a less exact measurement for its height than the one who looks upon it from a free spot in the distance, so the outsider, the one at a distance can often evaluate human conditions more clearly than the one in the midst of them," she wrote. "Douglass wrote to me as early as April: 'Oh, if I could have saved her from the terrible fate I imagine for her! But no power could have done that. When once she was in the upside, there was nothing left but to go over.' "[40] (In fact, the letter Douglass wrote to Ottilie about her sister shows that his assessment was almost identical with Gottfried Keller's—an old woman fooled by a young buck! "I have my own views of the sad affair of your sister, and am no less sympathetic on that account," he cautioned. "The man's character must have been well known before the marriage and the trouble came *after* marriage and so soon as to leave no doubt on my mind as to the cause."[41]) There was no need, no justification even, for a betrayed woman to mourn over something that should never have claimed the title of love, Ottilie admonished; Ludmilla's attitude should be one of gratitude at having escaped from this emotional maze she created for herself. "As it is, you can almost look upon it as a dream which began beautifully but had an ugly ending, yet which allows you to breathe freely after awakening from it."[42] A year later, when the divorce went through, Ottilie wrote, "My heartfelt, sincere congratulations at your complete separation from this vermin."[43]

Ottilie Assing needed Ludmilla's catastrophe to maintain her sanity and strength in the emotional turmoil she now was caught in. Focusing on her sister's pain enabled her to approach her own uncertain condition as if she were in control of it, and Ludmilla's shipwreck served as an emotional safety valve, during a year, 1874, that was a succession of catastrophes. It began full of hope: in early 1874 the trustees of the Freedman's Savings and Trust Company made Douglass its president. Douglass made considerably less as bank president than as a lecturer, but it was a highly respectable position, with a fine office, and it might become a stepping-stone to something better. Still, it is interesting that Assing did not mention Douglass' new position in her letters to Ludmilla. To Douglass himself she wrote encouragingly: "I acknowledge that above all others I am influenced by personal motives. I thought it such a pleasant and easy occupation for you, and the difference between the income derived from it and that earned by lecturing more than balanced by the gain in comfort and health."[44] Apparently neither Assing nor Douglass ever imagined that running a bank might require special skills, and Assing's faith in Douglass' genius was boundless.

Douglass would always claim that he was "ignorant of [the bank's] real condition till elected as its president,"[45] but there were rumors to which he might have listened and documents he should have checked. Perhaps his desire for a respectable position was stronger than his common sense:

> So I waked up one morning to find myself seated in a comfortable arm chair, with gold spectacles on my nose, and to hear myself addressed as President of the Freedmen's [sic] bank. I could not help reflecting on the contrast between Frederick the slave boy, running about at Col. Lloyd's with only a tow linen shirt to cover him, and Frederick—President of a bank counting its assets by millions. I had heard of golden dreams, but such dreams had no comparison with this reality.[46]

They turned out to be pipe dreams, and they exploded in his face.

The bank was chartered by Congress in March 1865, and its name promised African-Americans a safe place to invest their money, in an institution that belonged to them; it promised to be a means toward that great American Dream—financial independence. Branches were opened across the nation, and tens of thousands of people made deposits—more than $57 million in all.[47] Yet by late 1873 the bank was on the brink of ruin, the result of mismanagement and speculation, incompetence and fraud. Most white trustees had deserted the enterprise, and those who remained, African-Americans with no banking experience, very likely chose Douglass in a last effort to claim the institution as truly theirs, hoping that the venerated orator and liberator would inspire new confidence in their customers, who were beginning to withdraw their savings in response to the rumors about the bank's insolvency. The idea was bound to fail. Douglass had neither the financial acumen nor the staff nor the backing from the Grant administration it would have taken to save the faltering institution. "My dear Friend: You will believe me when I tell you that all these days I have been reading all the news about the bank with the greatest anxiety," Assing wrote to him. "Certainly, there are many reasons for wishing that the institution would stand the shock and prove able to brave the storm . . . Your name may yet achieve great things, however."[48]

Once he realized that the bank was insolvent, Douglass, with the support of John Sherman, chairman of the Senate Finance Committee, made vigorous last-minute attempts to reorganize it. But to no avail. Only three months after his appointment he was ready to admit defeat. "I have neither taste nor talent for the place," he confessed, "and when I add as I must that the condition of the bank is not prosperous and possibly not sound, you will appreciate my ill fortune."[49] To his son-in-law Nathan Sprague he wrote in late May: "I have got myself in a hard place in this Freedman's Bank and shall consider myself fortunate if I get out of it as easily as I got into it."[50] His isolation and loneliness were clear in a letter written to Assing the next day: "Is it still your purpose to go to Boston before coming here on the 21st June?"[51] he asked. On 1 July he was forced to vote for closing the bank. Thousands of sharecroppers, laborers, and domestics lost their deposits. His enemies celebrated, for what better proof of black incompetence could be given than this black icon leading his black institution directly into bankruptcy! Douglass was angry at yet another betrayal of black people's hopes, and personally humiliated. "It has been the black man's cow, but the white man's milk,"[52] he wrote to Gerrit Smith.

One day later Ottilie Assing arrived in Washington. From her letters to her sister, we learn that at the vital moment she sought help and strength in literature, inviting Douglass to escape into romance. Her choice was the letters of Abelard and Héloïse, of which she found the Latin original with a French translation in the Library of Congress. "It is one of the strongest, most moving and beautiful books you can read," she told Ludmilla. "Nearly 800 years have passed, yet how close these two are to us not only emotionally, but in many ways in their beliefs, their thoughts and their style! How pure, how tender was their mode of expression for so rough an age, and then this triumph of the highest human emotion over the religious doctrine of the century."[53] She continued to make no mention of the bank.

She was silent on yet another defeat that September, when the last issue of the *New National Era* appeared. As one of Douglass' biographers has put it: "The newspaper, designed as a beacon for a reformed, racially integrated nation, had found few white readers. For it to become a journal read only by the African American community in Washington would have defeated its original purpose and, in the absence of a shift to a more parochial focus, would have doomed it to unprofitability as well."[54] Douglass lost heavily in this venture, though he later claimed he never regretted the investment and commitment he made. "A misadventure though it was, which cost me from nine to ten thousand dollars, over it I have no tears to shed. The journal was valuable while it lasted, and the experiment was to me full of instruction, which has to some extent been heeded, for I have kept well out of newspaper undertakings since."[55] But at the time he could hardly have been cheerful. "The moral atmosphere [in Washington] is more than tainted, it is rotten. Avarice, duplicity, falsehood, corruption, servility, fawning and trickery of all kinds, confront us at every turn," he complained to Gerrit Smith. "There is little here but distrust and suspicion."[56] Ottilie Assing, still with Douglass during these difficult months, offered what support she could muster. Small wonder that her ear problems returned with a vengeance: "I hear again as well as ever, but this dreadful ringing in my ears will not cease and decreases with a reluctance that drives me to despair," she wrote to Ludmilla. "This is the only thing which prevents me from taking my often postponed European tour next spring."[57]

The new wing to the Douglasses' house was finished in the spring of 1874, but the family situation that summer was hardly calm. Douglass' professional shipwreck was not just a personal disaster but also the end to the dream of self-reliance and success for his sons Lewis and Frederick Jr. Both were married, with growing families, when they closed down the *New National Era*, and experience had taught them what they would face on Washington's labor market. Once again they depended on their parents for support. For a while Charles, the youngest, was the only Douglass child to be employed. He worked in the Treasury Department and was proud of the house he had built for himself and Libbie. Yet his was a troubled marriage, with Libbie accusing him of philandering while he complained of her jealousy; unable to cope with their marital tensions, they displayed them before the Douglasses. Low wages forced Charles to borrow money from his parents; soon creditors were threatening legal action against both father and son.[58] Like Lewis, he had even taken to borrowing money from Assing. Creditors were also haunting Rosetta, who had gone back to Rochester with her family; her husband had taken to drink and displayed an exhausting talent for losing jobs and failing in business.[59] In the fall of 1876 creditors would haul their miserable little household out into the street. In a letter to Rosetta of 30 June 1875 an extremely agitated Douglass claimed that he had "been nearly ruined financially by coming [to Washington]. I have things to tell you concerning my affairs which trouble me very much and lead me to fear the worst. Age and want are an ill matched pair."[60]

Ottilie sought refuge from these family difficulties in the Library of Congress, which became her haven. In late August she escaped for a few days to Vienna, a little hamlet in Virginia, where "I reveled in the Southern sunshine, the rich Southern vegetation, the abundance of peaches and milk"[61] and enjoyed rural life as one would a genre painting. Back in Washington, she and Douglass swayed between amusement and disgust as swarms of American journalists fell on the Beecher-Tilton scandal* that summer.[62] They spent considerable time reading and playing music together, and they took excursions together into the countryside. Assing extended her visit till November, but by the time Douglass left for a lecture tour in the West she had made up her mind that it would be better for both of them if she returned to Hoboken rather than live permanently with the Douglasses in Washington.

"I have once again moved in with my dear old housewife," she reported to Ludmilla on 9 November. "The day after tomorrow Douglass will start his lecture tour, and then it would have become unbearable for me in the company of his charming wife and a not more agreeable daughter-in-law."[63] One can infer that either Lewis' or Frederick Jr.'s wife had decided to side with Anna Murray against Ottilie Assing as a female ally for Anna Murray, which tormented Rosetta would or could not be. Never again would Assing mention Douglass' invitation to live with him. The photograph of Douglass in the travel attire he wore on his Western tour, which she sent to Ludmilla on 6 September 1874, was thus a token of defeat rather than pride. "He could be doing so well were it

---

*In an interview of December 1870 Theodore Tilton had accused Henry Ward Beecher of improper relations with his wife Elizabeth, a member of Beecher's congregation. Beecher denied the allegations, and in 1874 a church committee acquitted him; Tilton then filed a complaint, demanding damages of $100,000, but the trial resulted in a hung jury. The Council of Congregational Churches also held Beecher innocent. The scandal attracted enormous public attention.

not for his dear family," she wrote a year later; "it is certainly not their merit that they have not yet devoured him or teased him to death."[64]

In the winter of 1875–76 Ottilie Assing finally decided to go on her long-postponed European trip. Several of her German acquaintances had died in the past two years; her friend Gutzkow had barely survived a suicide attempt; Douglass was resuming his tedious lecture circuit. "Miss Assing is fighting her way here as usual," a rather wary Douglass had reported half jokingly to Rosetta in August. "Every body seems to hit the blue ball on the Croquet ground. As usual I fight on the side of my old friend."[65] But Assing had had enough. Frauenstein urged her to go, as did the Koehlers, all of them concerned about her precarious emotional state. In addition, she received several letters from Johanna Steinheim, now widowed and in her eighties, who insisted that it was her duty as a sister to stand by Ludmilla during this arduous period. She had always had a meddling nature, and it was too much even for Ottilie: "It seems she still has not discovered that we are really mature enough to know what we are up to without needing a mentor," she wrote to Ludmilla.[66]

Ludmilla must have hinted to Steinheim that she intended to change her will, not only so that her young gigolo husband's hope for an inheritance would be dashed but also to suggest that she intended to give the bulk of her estate to the Italian revolutionary movement, thus disinheriting her sister Ottilie. Steinheim was stunned; she virtually begged her "not to deprive your only sister totally of her inheritance." She reminded her, "Your parents loved you so tenderly; therefore repay their love by showing leniency toward your sister, the only person who belongs to you." If sisters fail to get along, "*both* are usually at fault," she warned. "Follow my well-meant advice: invite Ottilie to come to you . . . and give her the rooms *downstairs* . . . That way you will be reunited yet still separate."[67]

All through the spring of 1876 Assing was torn between her reluctance to part with Douglass and her resolution and longing to go. She grabbed every excuse to postpone her departure, still hoping that Douglass might join her after all—health problems, cold weather, the Centennial Exhibition in Philadelphia, anything came handy. Douglass was at the center of everything she felt and did. "Of course it is a huge decision to tear myself away from here, and especially the long separation from Douglass and from my faithful green macaw will almost kill me, so that I am already homesick while I'm still here."[68] Only after Douglass vowed he would try to meet her in Paris the following spring did she book passage on the *Frisia* for 13 July.

Frederick Douglass in his travel outfit
Assing sent this photo of Douglass in the clothes he usually wore on his lecture tours to the West to her sister in September 1874. She blamed his family for his frequent absences: "He could be doing so well were it not for his dear family . . ."

Ludmilla Assing
Ludmilla Assing, always notorious for her biting sarcasm, became a bitter woman after her marriage to Grimelli. The Swiss novelist Gottfried Keller commented: "I had counted on it that she would get a good beating some day, because she is so ugly . . . still, I cannot enjoy stoning her."

Gino Grimelli
Ludmilla Assing met Gino Grimelli, almost twenty years her junior, in the early 1870s. They were married on 1 December 1873. In her greetings to the newlyweds Ottilie Assing wrote: "I keep repeating my hope that Grimelli will prove as true, as faithful, and as thoroughly good and noble as Douglass." Only a few months later, Ludmilla filed for divorce.

Douglass made good on his promise to join Assing for what they expected to be their last meeting before Assing's departure. They had agreed not to spend these final days in Washington, and for once they would treat themselves to a few days alone: they chose Philadelphia and its Centennial Exhibition. J. M. Mundy's bust of Douglass was on display there, which surely must have pleased both of them, but Ottilie did not mention it to Ludmilla; instead, she focused exclusively on her happiness at having Douglass all to herself. "When I tell you that I met with Douglass there and saw all this glory with him alone, as it were, you will imagine how perfect this trip became." Perhaps this brief excursion gave Douglass a foretaste of the happiness that would be theirs on an extended European sojourn; perhaps he was tired of her pleading; perhaps her sadness roused his compassion—but whatever the reason, Ottilie Assing left Philadelphia with his promise in her heart that he would try to follow her next spring. "Douglass plans to also come over next spring and is especially eager to see Paris," she exulted. Now she was ready to depart. "The results of the experiment [the excursion to Philadelphia] are so perfect in every respect, and I feel so much better ever since, that I have finally made up my mind and booked my stateroom on the *Frisia* to Hamburg, where I shall arrive around the 25th or 26th, provided the water and wind gods are favorable."[69]

By 3 July in Boston, however, where Ottilie spent a few quiet days with the Koehlers, the optimism which had inspired her in Philadelphia was quickly undermined by doubts. "I think I should look forward to the trip with some expectation if I only could rely that my large bird would follow me in due time," she wrote to Douglass. "Without this confidence it is just one degree above going into exile."[70] Her anxiety was well grounded, for Douglass was sick of traveling, especially after spending all his winters on the tedious lecture circuit. "I am beginning to look upon a journey as a positive misfortune," he told his daughter. "My long public career of traveling has cured my desire for change of location—and I now like to remain in the same place, dine at the same table, sleep in the same bed, bath in the same tub, and do an [sic] hundred other same things."[71] But as if to calm her fears, Douglass made a last-minute decision to go to Hoboken and see her off on her "world tour," as she chose to call it. Another few days that were all theirs. Then she was off. On 25 July she wrote him that after a pleasant passage, the *Frisia* was safely in Plymouth, signing her note with "Yours on land or water, Ottilia."[72]

Ottilie Assing reentered the Old World at the same port from which she had departed: Hamburg—"like cats, of whom it is said that, after a prolonged absence from the house, they always return through the same door, the same window, or the same skylight through which they departed."[73] As she had hoped, Ludmilla met her there, but it was a cold reunion. The sisters had resumed their feud even before they stood face to face again after twenty-three years of separation. Ottilie had suggested to Ludmilla that, rather than proceeding directly from Munich to Florence, they enjoy an excursion to Switzerland. Since her childhood days she had dreamed of seeing Switzerland, especially the Alps; Johanna Steinheim was in Zurich, and she had letters of introduction to relatives of the Kudlichs in Bern and Geneva. Ludmilla had balked, but Ottilie was adamant. "I am determined to see Switzerland this summer," she had written. "It would truly be absurd if I let slip my only chance to see this magic land only because I might spend an additional one or two thalers daily for two or three weeks, so that, when I die, I will leave 100 thalers more and enjoy seven thalers interest annually during my lifetime." Aware of Ludmilla's irascibility, she suggested a compromise: "Should this tour inconvenience you, I will not talk you into it; we can separate for a short period, and then meet again at a more convenient place."[74] But it was already too late: their European tour was a catastrophe even before it began.

Still, they did travel in Germany together. They spent more than a week in Hamburg, then took the romantic Rhine tour, stopping in Cologne and Bonn, treating themselves to an excursion to Frankfurt and a few days in romantic Heidelberg—following the itinerary of the memorable trip their mother had taken with them in the 1830s. How many of their relatives and acquaintances were gone! Yet there were new people to meet, new relationships to establish. Ottilie sought out German-American friends who had returned to Europe, and she readily embraced people Ludmilla had befriended in the past years. "Time passes in a succession of enjoyment and pleasant excitement," she wrote to Karl Gutzkow. She almost wept when she saw the once so promising dramatist and novelist, the vigorous and manly ideal of her youth, in his home in Heidelberg. He was an old man, embittered, depressive, unable to recover from his suicide attempt. A note she sent him to thank him for his hospitality was clearly designed to cheer up a man who had lost his sense of self. "It happens so often that moments, long anticipated and imagined innumerable times in advance, fall short of these hopes in the face of a reality that is pale and colorless. I am truly happy to tell you that our reunion amply fulfilled, if not surpassed, all my dreams and hopes, and my visit is definitely a culmination point in my trip with its profusion of delights."[75] It was their last meeting. Karl Gutzkow died in 1878.*

The sisters' next stop was Strasbourg, the old city their mother had never ceased to love as her home. Ottilie knew that the city had been severely damaged during the Franco-Prussian War, but what shocked her more was her own inability to reclaim the childhood spirit in which she had loved this place so many years before. Not only was Strasbourg "extremely narrow and old-fashioned" and "remarkably Germanized" but it was defined by Roman Catholicism: "priests, monks, and choirboys with their rough and dumb faces pursue their humbug with a cold business manner, scratch . . . their noses and ears so diligently that the whole thing would be ridiculous were it not so overwhelmingly repulsive. Only a Methodist camp meeting is worse."[77] Her dogmatism rendered her blind to the beauty around her; it barred her from the spontaneous recovery of childhood memories.

In Strasbourg, Ottilie and Ludmilla parted, Ludmilla to return to Florence, Ottilie to go on to Switzerland.† By October she was in Florence, eager to see her sister's house and orchard, to meet her sister's friends; they had agreed to spend the winter in Florence; around Easter they would begin an Italian tour and then go to Paris to meet Douglass. But on 8 December Ottilie was in Rome, all by herself. The feud between the sisters had become so violent that she had departed.

At first she had been delighted with Ludmilla's property in Florence, on Via Luigi Alamanni, behind the old Dominican chapel of Santa Maria, near the northern railway station. Stairs led from a magnificent library, filled with Varnhagen's books and manuscripts, to a vast and pretty garden.[78] Ottilie praised everything generously: the tastefully designed and furnished house, the garden, the marvelous panorama, the friendly servants, Ludmilla's large circle of fascinating friends, Florence with its museums and galleries. Yet it took the sisters only a few days to turn this paradise into a battlefield. Letters they sent to relatives and friends contained only generalizing statements and promises to give the details in their next tête-à-têtes, but some of the problems can at least be sketched. Ludmilla still disliked Ottilie's independence, which clashed with her

---

*On the news of his death, Ottilie wrote to Sylvester Rosa Koehler: "For me Gutzkow's death is an end to a whole series of the most beautiful memories of my youth, and I am glad that I went over in time to see him once more, although the impression was rather painful, for I found only the ruin of his former self, though still an important and impressive ruin."[76]

†As Ottilie's letters from this period are missing, we cannot trace her steps, but we know that she spent several days with Johanna Steinheim in Zurich.

imperious nature. Despite the notables who lined up to gain access to her salon, she was a lonely woman, her imperious ways masking her insecurity. The disappointment of her marriage had embittered this already troubled nature, and she alienated even old friends. From Gottfried Keller we have a detailed account of the ways in which her struggle with Grimelli over her independence and dignity had transformed her: "I saw Mrs. Ludmilla Assing. . . . One thing is for sure, it will be the last time I go, for the impression she made on me is unbearable. She had gold-rimmed glasses on her nose, bragged that she was studying Latin, threw utensils around the table with her harsh, manly movements, started to cry, made advances, always talking about herself, etc."[79] And Ottilie's letters suggest that Ludmilla's disillusionment found release in accusations she heaped on her sister. She demanded that Ottilie break her American ties and start anew in Europe.

Life in Florence could have been heaven for the art lover Ottilie Assing, but Ludmilla's lifestyle was ascetic: rising at sunrise, cold-water baths, no heating even in winter. Sensuous Ottilie loved to indulge herself: sleeping until mid morning, a warm room, the comfort of hot water and stoves. After shivering through a cold and rainy November, Ottilie knew it was time to leave. Ludmilla must have written to Johanna Steinheim about this, and the old lady made a last attempt at reconciliation between the two. "I would not want to make *my* opinion a criterion respecting the impression Ottilie makes on strangers, were it not that those who saw her when she was here with me confirm my evaluations, and they all saw deep furrows of grief," she cautioned. "There was no bitterness; on the contrary, that pleasant impression of an upright character. Never ever has she expressed toward me even the slightest criticism against you; exactly the opposite." She begged Ludmilla not to push her sister from her embrace and force her back into what Steinheim perceived as American exile: "Dear Ludmilla, none of us are angels, and the saying ' 'tis human to err' is *true* and to the point. Let us show patience and mildness, leniency and compliance."[80] Her words remained unheard.

In Rome, Assing rented two comfortable warm rooms and spent the next three months "feasting and reveling in its marvels,"[81] as she told Douglass. Although an acquaintance from Boston, Caroline Remond Putnam, invited her to stay with her, she declined; she wanted to live among Italians while in Italy.[82] She continued to send regular reports to Ludmilla, in which she bragged of the beauty she had discovered, the company she kept, the cheap and comfortable lodging she had found—every word showing she could easily fend for herself. Her sole complaint was about the weather, which was out of anybody's control.

The only letter in which she mentioned anything like loneliness was written in early January 1877, with Christmas and New Year's Eve fresh on her mind, a holiday season during which the museums were closed. ". . . what I miss are those old friends together with whom I have experienced and enjoyed everything for so many years," she wrote, stressing that she was speaking of American friends, and of friends, not family. "I feel the more you see, enjoy, experience, the greater and overwhelming the impressions, the more you wish to talk about it . . . and the more splendid the world . . . the more you want to share your delight with those you love . . . What a world would not open up before Douglass or Koehler . . . I thought you would be able to read that between the lines."[83] It was essential for her that everybody—especially Douglass, who had failed to travel with her, and Ludmilla, whose anger isolated her—understand that she was surrounded by people who cherished her company. "It is quite gratifying for me to notice that wherever I go I make friends, and whom I once have won I hold," she told Douglass, saying that Ludmilla was "the only exception . . . She is actually hostile to me and is doing her best to poison other people against me."[84]

Yet Ottilie Assing was lonely. "I am rather a little isolated here," she wrote to Douglass, "and of course should like to have some good friend with whom to enjoy in common and exchange thoughts about the impressions received, yet I don't complain and feel comparatively happy since I can again move about freely, without having constantly to endure those outbreaks of temper, of great rudeness and all the petty malice, of the kind that only a woman is capable of." To her most intimate friend she admitted that the conflict with her sister "has left a shadow and [that] I can't help thinking it over again and again . . ."[85] In her letters to Ludmilla, though, Ottilie stressed the joys of traveling, the fact that she could do it all on her own, and the opposition between Ludmilla's isolation and the community that was hers.

But there are many signs suggesting that the anger directed at Ludmilla was indicative of a frustration that lay much deeper—the sense of betrayal that simmered in her ever since Douglass had told her she would have to go to Europe without him. Her letters to him were more than ecstatic accounts of a pleasure trip; she was punishing him with detailed accounts of the joys he was missing. She contrasted Douglass' lecture tours with the pure and sensuous pleasures of her sojourn: ice, snow, blizzards, a landscape covered by a white sheet, nature in a state of frozen stupor—the images of the America he traveled in were those of death and paralysis, while she was enjoying the "glorious climate," "the warm sun of noon," nature in a state of perpetual growth and bloom. In great detail she wrote of Douglass' suffering during "your trying and fatiguing winter trip," on "the state of your health and the terrible strain on your constitution," on the problems with his eyes. Despite his "excellent constitution" he was slowly coming apart, a victim of the social burden he refused to cast off. The man who ran from slavery, the man who fought the slave-breaker, now allowed his kin to enslave and break him. That was what her letters insinuated. In contrast, she was a woman in free flight, a woman soaring, a woman rejuvenated. ". . . you will be glad to learn it, [I] am as indefatigable as ever. Up and down mountains, to the spires and domes of the highest churches, nothing seems too much for me, and frequently I find in the evening that I was five or six hours or even more in constant motion." Too often had Douglass seen a tired, dispirited Ottilie Assing in the past years. Every line was designed to make him understand that she was experiencing rejuvenation:

> May I hope yet to see you in spring? If you only let me know exactly the time when you expect to touch this continent, I shall be ready to start and receive you at the landing. You can form no adequate idea of the enjoyment in store for you . . . Impressions so grandiose, truly tending to enlarge one's mental horizon that they may truly be called experiences of life. I should be delighted of course to have you here.[86]

Douglass did not join Ottilie Assing in Europe. After months of dispute an electoral commission declared that the Republican candidate, Rutherford B. Hayes, for whom Douglass campaigned tirelessly, was the nation's nineteenth President, and on 17 March 1877 the Senate confirmed Frederick Douglass as Marshal of the District of Columbia. His relief and pride as well as his awareness of the historical significance of this moment were nicely expressed in the reply he sent to his friend Samuel D. Porter's note of congratulation: "Only men like yourself—men born in advance of their time, men who saw and comprehended the dignity of human nature under one complexion or another, long before these sunny days—can now fully comprehend the significance of this appointment and confirmation."[87] Ottilie Assing was in Naples when Douglass' telegram reached her. Once again, his public triumph was defeat for her private ambitions; as always in their relationship, her dream had to be retailored to accommodate his needs. We can only imagine the sense of deprivation and disappointment, the sadness that swept through her as the full implication of Douglass' appointment for their future struck home—and the joy and jubilation that was hers at his recognition, his success, the financial security his position provided, the stability it would give to his life. We do not have the correspondence they exchanged during these weeks, but the playful tone of the letter she wrote him from Munich in July 1877 shows that she did not allow any negative feelings to mar her relationship to him. She was determined that she would never be in his way, never be a burden; she would always be his companion, supportive and strong, no matter what the cost. The announcement she made to Ludmilla flatly denied even the remotest possibility of disappointment, yet the meticulous list of advantages betrays her inner struggle, her overwhelming need to convince herself: "All of a sudden the prospect of Douglass following me is over. The event, however, that keeps him over there is one so desirable and so welcome that I do not feel the least disappointed, and it is with the greatest pleasure that I cross out our common travel plans." Douglass' appointment was not only "honorable and lucrative" but well deserved, after twenty years of service to the Republican Party. "Since he will now be in the closest proximity of the President, there is hope he will win his way to a beneficent influence."[88]

The itinerary Ottilie Assing designed for her final months in Europe illustrates that, as always in times of trouble, she sought to stifle her depression by incessant activity, movement, physical exertion to the point of collapse. Although she had promised Ludmilla to return to Florence on 12 April, she stayed in Naples till the end of April, joining a caravan on horseback to the crater of Vesuvius, and spent days wandering through the ruins of Pompeii; in defiance of Italian friends' warning her not to enter the town's forbidden quarters, she roamed all over Naples, though children kept snatching at her purse; she went to Capri. Nor could she resist the charms of Rome, either, and said a prolonged goodbye to it and its treasures. She arrived in Florence during the first week of May, but barely a week later she was already admiring the architecture of Parma and Bologna. After a brief stop at Milan she treated herself to a week in Venice, the city her mother had so longed to see. "How fortunate we plants of the nineteenth century are that with relatively small effort we can enjoy all those miracles which in former times could only be reached by the most favored,"[89] she wrote to Ludmilla. She had fallen in love with Italy.

From Venice she went directly to Vienna, where she indulged in a week of theater days and theater nights such as she had not experienced since Baison's death. Then off to Dresden, Berlin, Potsdam, and back to Hamburg, "which felt as homelike as ever and tearing myself away was very difficult."[90] After that she turned south again, to the Harz Mountains and up to the top of Mount Brocken, to Eisenach to see Luther's Wartburg, to Nuremberg and Munich, where she met with Feuerbach's widow and daughter, and off to Switzerland again and a parting visit with Johanna Steinheim. She spent a few days with the Riottes, her old friends from New York, now living in the beautiful Alsatian town of Münster, and paid a final visit to her relatives in Strasbourg. She did go to Paris, even though the City of Light seemed dreary, now that she was deprived of the pleasure of rediscovering its beauty arm in arm with Douglass.

Ottilie Assing had spent more than a decade planning and postponing her grand European tour—taking on extra work, saving every penny, studying Italian, drafting her itinerary, devouring literature about the places she hoped to visit. She started out shaken at Douglass' refusal to join her; her reunion with her sister led to an explosion; and she had to cope with the disappointment of Douglass' canceled visit. Yet at no point did she allow anyone to see this journey as anything but a smashing success. She had the talent of enjoying beauty when it was before her, love when it was there to be grabbed, laughter that invited her to join in—even in the midst of gloom. There was a carpe diem quality about her that was an enormous source of strength, keeping her going as it attracted others to her. She was determined to savor her European tour, and she did, for there was so much to delight in, all that magic nobody and nothing could take away from her. Her sojourn liberated her in that it showed her that she was strong enough to tear herself away from Frederick Douglass. She relearned that there was a world out there worth exploring and enjoying, even if she had to do so without the man she loved. And at the end of her excursion away from him, she knew what she wanted above everything: return to Frederick Douglass.

Assing had never planned her tour as anything but a pleasure trip; at no point had she conceived it as an experiment in returning to the Old World, as a potential homecoming. Hers was too radical a nature to share her German-American friends' enthusiasm about a united Germany under Bismarck, and her sojourn strengthened her conviction that unity under monarchic rule would inevitably lead to tyranny. This Germany could not be her political home. Parallel to her disenchantment with German politics ran her awareness that she could not really reconnect in the private realm. She was exhilarated at once again walking the streets of Hamburg; there was a trip to Oevelgoenne, to Rahel de Castro's summer place, a visit to the theater in which Baison had celebrated his greatest triumphs. Her German itinerary was defined by friends and relatives eager to host her. Yet there were also all those old acquaintances who could no longer be traced. Those she found had aged with her; giggling girls suddenly were grandmothers, young gallants respectable burghers; the revolutionary of old was a mere ruin of his former explosive self. After twenty-four years they had many stories to tell, yet how often did they discover that there was really nothing to say. She traveled from person to person, delighting in the moments they shared, yet it was no longer her community in which she moved. She was lionized as a tourist. Most of Ottilie's old acquaintances could not understand this determination to return to the United States, especially as she seemed bewitched by the beauty of Italy. "I wrote a birthday letter to your sister in Rome," Johanna Steinheim reported to Ludmilla a few months before Ottilie's departure, "begging her not to go back to America. I explained to her that Rome for her would be the ideal place where even the elite of travelers love to linger. Rome is unique, like no other city in the whole world."[91] Steinheim even invited Ottilie to live with her in Zurich, hoping to change her mind. But there was really nothing in Europe to hold her. A sense of family was not in the blood, Ottilie Assing learned during her painful encounters with her sister; it was not a haven into which we are born and which is ours forever. No, the better community was the one we create by reaching out to others, by giving of ourselves. We invent it, and it will be ours only so long as we work at it, creating and recreating, constructing and reconstructing.

On 1 September 1877 Ottilie Assing boarded the *Lessing* in Le Havre, not going off into the unknown, as twenty-five years ago, but returning home.

X

HAGAR'S SHADOW

Separation and Suicide

So it was: her thoughts were strong and powerful, with a male grasp and precision, her feelings chaste and pure and imbued with a high, noble enthusiasm; but her heart often glowed with a consuming fire that scorched everything, even her mind; and while she cursed love, she longed for it, searched for it everywhere, never found it; and finally she would fold her hands over her heart, filled with despair, bidding it quiet or the sleep of death, and try to seek solace in her mind. Her two natures, enclosed in her being, never united, remained clear and separate, side by side, a demon and an angel both residing in her breast.   —CLARA MUNDT, *Aphra Behn*

One of the most moving characters in the Bible is Hagar. In her we have the first conflict between love and marriage, between human liberty and the rigid legitimacy of marriage—and the latter was victorious even then.

—FANNY LEWALD, *Meine Lebensgeschichte*

Miss Ottilie Assing, formerly a regular contributor to the Süddeutsche Post, *has given no sign of life for so long that we are seriously concerned about her, especially since the paper deliveries she ordered poste restante have been returned unclaimed for quite some time now. Miss Assing, who long worked in America for liberty, and lately rendered notably outstanding service in the struggle for the emancipation of the slaves, lived in Hoboken, near New York, until two years ago. Responding to problems related to the inheritance of her sister Ludmilla (the famous editor of the diaries of her uncle Varnhagen v. Ense, recently married to Major Grimelli, as we all know), she came to Florence, whence she traveled all over Italy. She last wrote to us from Naples at the beginning of this summer . . . As Miss Assing was already of advanced age and was all alone in a foreign country, our concern about her well-being seems justified. We beseech anyone who*

might have information on her condition to send it as soon as possible, and we urgently re-
quest our colleagues in the press to help wherever possible.[1]

"Since he will now be in the closest proximity to the President, there is hope she will win his way to a beneficent influence," a triumphant Ottilie Assing predicted to Ludmilla when she had the news of Frederick Douglass' appointment as Marshal of the District of Columbia. But she erred grievously. Not only did the Hayes administration see to it that there would be no proximity whatsoever, generously "relieving . . . 'the *insolent* Negro' "[2] of the arduous duty of standing next to the President during formal receptions; Douglass, who observed to his son Lewis in 1883 that "places of honor and responsibility are as pleasant to me as to most men," though "to be acceptable they must come freely and without harm to any,"[3] recognized that the position of marshal came with the condition that he swallow his tongue. All too often he complied. He was silent when, in February 1877, before his confirmation, Hayes informed him of his plans "to pursue conciliatory policy toward the South"[4] while continuing to protect the constitutional rights of African-Americans; his voice remained unheard when federal troops were recalled from the South and Southern Redeemers were given free reign.[5] The position did not come "without harm to any," either. To hold it, he had to accept the end of Reconstruction, and in that he wounded the African-American community, he wounded his nation, and he wounded himself. Douglass biographers agree that "the stances on various issues that Douglass was to take between 1877 and 1881 were the least honorable and least helpful to his fellow former slaves of any in his long life. They were, in fact, entirely consonant with the betrayal of promises that ended Reconstruction."[6]

When Ottilie Assing spelled out her proud prophecy about Douglass' beneficent power she could not yet know of the public humiliation of exclusion that came with the appointment, nor was she aware of the dismay which these events caused among African-Americans. Douglass, who was very sensitive to slights, eager for respect and recognition, and concerned about his personal dignity, cannot have been happy about his situation, but he was relieved finally to be in a lucrative and respectable government position, and he refused to listen to fellow blacks who demanded loudly that he protect his dignity by resigning. In words that came dangerously close to the Supreme Court decision against the constitutionality of the Civil Rights Act of 1875, he defended the President's right to treat him as he wished: "Because the choice as to who shall have the honor and privilege of such attendance upon the President belongs exclusively and reasonably to the President himself, and that therefore no one, however distinguished, or in whatever office, has any just cause to complain of the exercise by the President of his right of choice, or because he is not himself chosen." He insisted that he "should have presented to the country a most foolish and ridiculous figure had I, as absurdly counseled by some of my colored friends, resigned the office of Marshal of the District of Columbia, because President Rutherford B. Hayes, for reasons that must have been satisfactory to his judgment, preferred some person other than myself to attend upon him at the Executive Mansion and perform the ceremony of introducing on state occasions."[7]

Also, Assing could not have predicted that only two months after taking office Frederick Douglass would be struggling for his political survival. On 8 May 1877 he gave a lecture, "Our National Capital," at Baltimore's Douglass Institute, in which he predicted a glorious future for a city purged of the evil of slavery, while at the same time evoking its history as a den of slaveholders and describing its present state as "a most disgraceful and scandalous contradiction to the march of civilization."[8] The speech, written months before he took office, ignited a storm of indignation. Douglass' appointment had been controversial in the first place; now his enemies pounced on the chance to oust him. Washington's *Evening Star* and the *National Republican* proclaimed his unfitness, and a petition circulated demanding his removal from office; more than 20,000 were said to have signed it. President Hayes rode out the storm in absolute silence, and a grateful Douglass stayed in office. Assing, a subscriber to "our good and faithful ally" *The New York Times*, observed the controversy from afar: "Of course I am delighted that the malignant pro-slavery element of Washington has failed in the attempt to oust you from your position," she wrote, "once for the sake of principle and the precedent established for the first time, and further because I want you to keep the office as long as possible on account of its pecuniary advantages, and just as much because I cannot bear the thought of your going on lecturing trips any more . . ."[9] But the shock was greater for Douglass than Assing could imagine. The promptness of his enemies' response, the fierceness of the assault and its broad public support were frightening proof of his vulnerability. President Hayes had backed him, but he might not be able or willing to do so in the future. So while federal troops returned to their barracks, while the Democrats "redeemed" the South, while the Ku Klux Klan terrorized the South and African-Americans were disenfranchised, dispossessed, and exploited, he preached the gospel of self-improvement and progress. At least to the public world, he was unwavering in his stalwart Republicanism.

Yet he seems to have taken this position even privately. "It is great comfort to me that you take a hopeful view of the situation," was Ottilie's reply to a letter in which he had obviously tried to quell her criticism of Hayes's conciliatory policies. "At a distance matters look terrible, and I should give up Republicanism not exactly for dead but for paralyzed at least for many years, thanks to Hayes, Schurz, and others of the same tendency, if it were not for your hopefulness. Every number of the paper records new deeds of crime and violence." They had been writing to each other for too long for Douglass to miss her subtext of doubt and warning. Assing always cautioned against the loss of perspective entailed in proximity while extolling the need for the perspective only distance can provide. For her it was essential that Douglass see the attack on him as well as the events in the South not in isolation but as warning signals about the direction the nation was drifting in. She advised him, for example, to take a close look at "Judge Hilton's dastardly attempt against the equal rights of the Jews." It was minority against minority, the powerless turning against each other. "It is an ugly feature in human nature that the lower the stage of development which either a race or an individual has reached, the more it is oppressed, the more it will yearn to oppress some one more humble in its turn. The Jews and the Irish, so long downtrodden in their own country, are foremost among the Negro haters, and the slaves used to vent their superiority on poor defenseless animals." Assing had lost the empowering idealism of her early years, which assumed that the victim was morally superior to the victimizer, that suffering ennobled. She no longer believed that the underdogs' struggle for equal rights was necessarily directed toward an improvement of social and political conditions for humanity in general; it seemed to her that all they desired was to join those who wielded power, the victimizers. Assing's pessimism was more than a mature and disillusioned woman's reluctant concession to Darwinian readings; it was intended to warn Douglass to beware.

Her implicit criticism of Douglass becomes clearer when we look at the framework in which she placed it. Douglass had told her about a rather pleasant conversation with Carl Schurz, Assing's onetime hero who had fallen from grace when he put himself at the helm of the Liberal Republican movement, and she must have been shocked to hear that Douglass had taken a liking to a person she disliked as an opportunist. "Your encounter with Schurz too is rather a pleasant affair, if—as I think it quite natural—you like each other's society, why not do so!" she flattered him, using the carrot-and-stick tactics of an experienced teacher. "I do not object either to associate superficially once in a while with people of whose character and fidelity to principle I have not exactly the highest estimate, provided they are interesting company." Again she abstained from reproaching him, knowing that after the storm of criticism he had just sustained he needed sympathy rather than further demolition, but she made sure that he not forget that he was courting a reputation for lack of character. Stressing that such an encounter was superficial and exceptional, she again manipulated the metaphor of distance. Socialize, yes, she admonished, but never forget what the other represents. The Republicans were no longer her party; they were only a lesser evil, and she supported them because she trembled at the thought of a Democratic victory. They were no longer "we" but "they," and she struggled desperately against her Douglass becoming "one of them."

Ottilie Assing's love of Douglass did not blind her to his weak spots. But in her public representations as well as in letters to her friends and to Ludmilla, she maintained the image she had invented in the 1850s of the unblemished hero, the genius, the superman. She still gloried in Douglass' courage to defy the white power structure, to challenge white claims of superiority.

During the early summer of 1877, while Assing enjoyed a parting visit to her native town of Hamburg, Douglass, too, went "home" for the first time in more than forty years. Taking the *Matilda* from Baltimore, he traveled to Talbot County, on the Eastern Shore of Chesapeake Bay, where he had spent his early childhood. On this sojourn he met with his half sister Eliza Mitchell's nine children and their families for the first time in his life, addressed the mostly African-American welcome crowd at St. Michaels, toured the countryside, and visited with the Auld family. Four years later, in his memoirs, Douglass devoted an unusual amount of space to this homecoming, presenting it almost exclusively as a quest of reconciliation with the whites who once had held power over him: Thomas Auld and the former sheriff of Talbot County. Douglass saw the abominable living conditions of the Southern Blacks, the poverty of his own family; he memorialized only his reconciliation with the master. Choosing to close his eyes to the ragged crowd at the landing, he reminisced that the

conditions were favorable for remembrance of all his [Auld's] good deeds, and generous extenuation of all his evil ones. He was to me no longer a slaveholder either in fact or in spirit, and I regarded him as I did myself, a victim of the circumstances of birth, education, law, and custom. We addressed each other simultaneously, he calling me "Marshal Douglass," and I, as I had always called him, "Captain Auld." Hearing myself called by him "Marshal Douglass," I instantly broke up the formal nature of the meeting by saying, "*Not* Marshal, but Frederick to you as formerly."[10]

Did the Captain become Thomas for Frederick? It is unlikely.

The letter in which Douglass described this homecoming to Ottilie Assing seems to have been written in a spirit of gratitude and relief. "If only for once I could see the Eastern Shore in your company!" she responded. She was as eager to encounter the place and the people that formed him as she was for him to know where she came from. The memories of her days in Hamburg were fresh in her mind, the joy and sweet pain of seeing familiar places, of listening to the voices of old, of remembering things she had forgotten, of pictures discarded flashing back to her mind. And yet she could not help reminding him that something was unequal in the give-and-take, in the mutuality of forgiveness he evoked. "The meeting with your old master naturally was one of the chief points of interest and under the circumstances you met him, loaded with honor, one of the most prominent men in the country, it must have been quite gratifying to you and rather an act of condescension on your part than otherwise."[11]

This entire long letter, written to Douglass from Munich on 12 July 1877, was complimentary and grateful. Yet while every word she wrote was designed to bolster his morale, she did so not by denying the position at which she had arrived, but by adding it to his narrative, in a continuous process of critique and redefinition. During her European months, traveling by herself, with distance to see anew and time to think and feel clearly, she had recovered her voice and decided to make it heard. She spoke up, with acumen and determination, as a companion and friend of the mind should.

Assing arrived in New York in mid-September. She had told only her closest friends of her schedule, and she gave herself only a few days of rest; then she was off to Washington. After all, she had to make up for two summers without Douglass. There was so much to look forward to! However, a long letter which she wrote to him from Boston on 21 August 1878, a full year later, indicates that considerable tension characterized their reunion. The letter does not inform us about the nature of the problems, but if we combine what we know of the previous summers with what we know of events that succeeded the summer of 1877, it is at least possible to identify some of the conflicts. The Douglasses were still living in their house on A Street. They had added a wing to accommodate their extended family, yet the new space had filled quickly. In September 1877 the Spragues, who had returned to Rochester after the fire of 1874, were ousted from their home by creditors, who dumped their household goods into the street;[12] Rosetta and her children found shelter with her parents, while Nathan went off to Omaha, where he launched his own business as a baker. Charles and his family also lived with the Douglasses that summer, for Libbie was desperately ill and Charles had lost his job. Also, Nathan Sprague's sister

Louisa was there, relieving the often ailing Anna Murray of household chores and serving as her nurse. Ottilie Assing's presence may simply have been too much for this overcrowded household. Her attitude toward the Douglasses transforming their home into a shelter, the uneasiness she expressed about their children's repeated failings, and her constant reminders that he save for his retirement rather than spread himself too thin financially certainly did nothing to ease the tension that existed.

Assing's letter of 21 August 1878 was written while she was staying with the Koehlers in Boston, postponing her trip to Washington until the Douglasses had managed their move to a new home in Anacostia, in the southern part of the capital. But more than this family relocation was behind the delay. "I don't fully understand your apprehensions," she wrote to Douglass; "if they refer to me I have only to remind you of all which I wrote you months ago and which then you thought quite satisfactory." It is interesting that she flatly denied that Anna Murray (usually the scapegoat in her correspondence with Ludmilla) was to blame for the tension. "Border State is my smallest trouble. I think I have shown my diplomatic tact by getting along with her nearly twenty years without any serious trouble," she protested, calling her "amiable compared to Ludmilla." The source of conflict lay rather with other members of the household and between Ottilie and Frederick themselves. "My *feelings* for you can never change," she pleaded, "but if all this, after all, is nothing to you, a [sic] if *you* anticipate for yourself more pain than pleasure, you know that you may shake me off whenever you please." The old partnership between equals that had always been Assing's ideal was evaporating. For the first time she allowed the possibility of separation, of a life without Douglass, but it was not a decision made by both of them. Overwhelmed "by unmitigated sorrow," Assing could envision a Frederick Douglass who was discarding her.

Douglass had promised to spend a week with her and the Koehlers, but then a telegram came in which he canceled his visit, pleading ill health. Assing had looked forward to this time together in a beneficial and soothing setting. The Koehlers were good friends, their three children well behaved and loving, and their house in Roxbury promised peace and quiet. "So many excursions had been planned and your presence was looked forward to as the great event, the culminating point of the season," she wrote to Douglass. She was not only expressing her concern over his health problems, however; she also suggested that he was seeking refuge in the anonymous world of Washington, while shunning the company of friends and a setting where sincerity and commitment were required. "I think you hardly realize how devoted the Koehlers are to you, none are more genuine, more free from any selfish motives though they are less noisy in their demonstrations than many others."[13]

The reply which Douglass sent to her, "your last good note," was so conciliatory in tone that it calmed her fear of an impending separation. He suggested an "experiment," the nature of which it is impossible to decipher. Was it that he asked her to end their sexual liaison, to transform love into friendship? The many references to longing and restraint in her letters point in this direction, while the calm sensuousness in which she wrapped the reminiscences of the summer that followed tell a different story. Her immediate comment shows, however, that she was deeply upset at being forced to choose between submitting to the "experiment" and canceling her visit. She chose the "experiment." "I have no fear of the 'experiment' as far as I am concerned, and the question is only whether and how *you* will stand it?" Assing replied, insisting that her commitment to Douglass was independent of external circumstances, independent even of his feelings for her. It was her way of redefining the vulnerability to which their liaison exposed her in terms of strength and free choice. "I know exactly my own feelings, but from all which you have told me about yourself and others I have come to the conclusion that in some respects I am so entirely unlike the majority of men [sic] that I cannot well consider myself at all a standard by which to measure the feelings and sensations of others."[14]

In mid-September Ottilie left Boston to spend a week with the Huntingtons in Stamford, Connecticut. She had met the elderly Mrs. Huntington in Naples, at the introduction of Anna de Castro, a relative of Assing's friend Rahel, who served as Mrs. Huntington's travel companion and nurse.[15] The women had many intellectual interests in common and became close friends, and Assing had gladly accepted the invitation to spend time with her family. But it was a detour, not the place she wanted to be, and she was burning to receive a telegram ordering her to Washington. "After that I shall fly southward with the same feeling of longing as twenty years ago, intense as ever, the old pigtail that hangs behind him, but perfectly reliable as to self-control,"[16] she wrote to Douglass.

It was the last week in September when Assing left New York for Washington: her first visit to Cedar Hill. The new Douglass residence surpassed her highest expectations: it lay in Uniontown, an integrated community across the Potomac River in the Anacostia Hills—an elegant, spacious white mansion with a spectacular view over the capital. With nine acres of land, to which the Douglasses soon added another fifteen, the property boasted a fine garden, an orchard, and even a barn. Purchasing this house had been a personal triumph for Douglass, in that he had succeeded in overturning a restrictive covenant against African-Americans' buying it.[17] The Douglasses had arrived! Assing was enchanted by Cedar Hill, a residence that amply reflected the importance as a historic figure, as an American mastermind she attributed to Douglass, and her irreverent nature no doubt made her chuckle at the way Washington now lay literally at his feet, exposed to his commanding gaze. The house upon the hill was a symbol of his self-empowerment.

There are many signs that Assing and Douglass experienced a sense of healing and rejuvenation in their relationship during the two months they spent together at Cedar Hill that fall. The spaciousness of the house allowed the kind of intimacy that had been stifled in the crowded town house. They could play their music in the front parlor while others sat around the dining table; they had a library to retreat to. Upstairs, the bedrooms were arranged in an unusual way, with the master bedroom separated from one guest room only by a velvet curtain, while Anna Murray had her own room on the opposite side of the corridor. Had Douglass finally been able to design a truly private space for himself and Ottilie? Was this the "experiment" they had discussed? When Assing returned to Hoboken in mid-November, the thank-you note she sent to Douglass displayed the calm confidence, gratitude and relief of a person who had reembraced life after a long bout of sickness. "It is with the old feeling of something like homesickness which I always experience when leaving you after spending a considerable time with you, that I am thinking of you now. Whatever there may be distressing about the conditions under which we only can meet, yet your company for me has such a charm and affords me a gratification the like of which I never feel else where," she wrote. Even her old playfulness returned. "I might continue yet much longer in variations on this subject, were it not for the fear that you would accuse [me] of using incendiary language in spite of honest intentions and promises to the contrary." So secure was she in her love that she embraced not only the man who rekindled it but his entire world: "My love to your glorious place and all who walk on it on either two or four legs, to its trees, hills and valleys!"

She could once again look into the future, make plans, launch new projects. She was aware of the snares of representation, the pitfalls of historiography; observing the degree to which Douglass was already under attack even within African America and among his political allies, she therefore wanted him to be the architect of his reputation in history, his own voice and paintbrush. During the first months in Cedar Hill she began to implant in Douglass' mind the need to write his memoirs. "I should much rejoice if you would employ your leisure in writing the sequel of your autobiography," she urged him. "I have no doubt you could make it a highly attractive book. John Brown, political and abolitionist reminiscences, intercourse with prominent men, such as Lincoln, Sumner, Grant, etc., deliverance from religious bondage and so many other interesting topics you might treat. The long winter evenings are just favorable for such work . . ."[18] Douglass' *My Bondage and My Freedom* had brought and joined them together twenty-two years ago. Was she hoping to reclaim the spirit of their young love, to strengthen their bond by working together once again on a text by Douglass about his life? "There is but *one* animal in the world with whom I could live even on a desert island without ever missing other company,"[19] she wrote ten days later, signaling her eagerness for free flight by reviving her old endearment of her "big bird."

Ottilie had no idea, as she indulged in these sweet reveries, that her two months of happiness were about to give way to a winter in which she would have to muster all her strength and courage. The problems started piling up as soon as she was back in Hoboken. Before leaving for Europe, Ottilie Assing had made a major loan to Julius Fehr, Mrs. Werpup's son-in-law, who wanted to establish his own business as a druggist. The venture had failed, and Assing ended up as owner of the rather decrepit two-story house with a store at 128 Bloomfield Street.[20] Friends talked her into accepting this arrangement, arguing that even though she had no intentions of occupying the place, it made an excellent retirement investment. This was a terrible miscalculation: the economic instability of the late 1870s, to which Fehr's enterprise had succumbed, massively augmented her own financial crisis. The businessman who rented the store and first floor, a Mr. Hake, could barely make ends meet and did not pay his rent for months; nor did her tenants on the second floor. A storm damaged the roof, and the water pipes leaked. It was a catastrophe. To Sylvester Rosa Koehler she admitted: "The knowledge of carrying this millstone is like a poison that gives me no rest, and it will lead to my ruin, for that cursed box not only brings no revenue but is a greedy pest that only costs money." It took her until March 1880 to sell the property; she lost more than $4,000 in the process and, with it, her self-confidence as a shrewd businesswoman.[21]

What was especially annoying was that financial straits forced her to do without the little comforts and luxuries that were so important for her. She canceled her subscription to various newspapers; she gave up horseback riding; at one point she could not even afford to buy Douglass his traditional Christmas gift of cigars: "It has always been endless gratification to me to see you smoke and enjoy them and I feel the deprivation most keenly."[22] Most unsettling, however, was that she could not support her cousin Emilie Nickert, Emilie's daughter Mary, and her ninety-year-old mother. Emilie Nickert had never been able to make a decent living as a teacher after her husband's death. A self-educated woman, she spoke German and French with a delightful but heavy Alsatian accent; since her English was far from perfect, it was almost impossible for her to get or keep a teaching position. Ottilie, who after all had worked as a seamstress and at various other jobs when she needed to, advised her to seek other kinds of employment, but Nickert balked; her class consciousness kept her in poverty. So for years Assing had supported this little family of women, buying their clothes, paying their fuel bills and sometimes even the rent, helping with Mary's tuition. "Mrs. Nickert's earnings fall shorter every year, and all which I can do for the present is to give them a few articles of clothing," she told Douglass. "Need everywhere!"[23] The problem became acute when, in March 1879, Emilie became seriously ill. "In such emergency I feel the strait doubly painfully in which I am placed,"[24] Assing wrote. Emilie Nickert died a few months later. Assing had always patronized her, sneered at her lack of education and her naiveté, ridiculed her religiosity, disliked her sentimentality. But she had never hesitated to extend a helping hand, and she continued to provide for Emilie's aged mother, Mrs. Reihl. It hurt to lose another tie to her former, European self.

Yet another one of her friends was also in trouble, Sylvester Rosa Koehler. After ten years of working for the Prang Company and in the midst of an economic slump Koehler gave up his job to devote all his energies to the fulfillment of a lifelong dream: to edit and publish an art journal. He succeeded in launching the *Art Review* in 1879, but it was a journal under financial siege from day one. He hoped to find a job that would give him a reliable income and time to work on the journal, but he miscalculated. There were no openings for which he qualified; the family had very little savings and three children in school. The day came when he was willing to take anything to keep the wolf from the door. He even started borrowing money from his friends in Hoboken. Assing was desperate about the Koehlers' fate as well as about her inability to help; it did not help much when Douglass reminded her that Koehler's recklessness had brought on this situation. She even asked Douglass whether he could not get a position for Koehler in Washington.[25] Nothing came of these efforts, and it took Koehler years to recover from his rash move.

On top of all this, during the hard winter of 1878–79 Ottilie's difficulties with Linn Fehr, the woman with whom she had been boarding since returning from Europe, became so acute that she had to find new lodgings. She had chosen Mrs. Fehr after her former landlady, Mrs. Werpup, with whom she had developed such a warm relationship over the nine years she lived with her, had retired, and she had hoped that Mrs. Werpup's daughter would be a reliable substitute. She was wrong. Linn Fehr did not respect her privacy; she exploited and battered an orphan girl who lived with her, and used up a whole squad of maids; most important of all, she disliked Assing for her friendship with Frauenstein—according to Assing's version of the conflict. But Ottilie conveniently forgot to mention her own arrogance and sharp tongue. Johannes Lange, who dined frequently at the Fehrs' during this period, told Koehler, "Miss A. was anything but popular among the inhabitants. I cannot say whether her eccentricity has increased lately and thus caused this general dislike."[26] By May 1880 the entire Fehr household moved to New York, and Assing returned to her dear old Mrs. Werpup, who now also lived in New York.

So Ottilie Assing left Hoboken, where she had lived for twenty-three years, exhausted and angry. How frustrating it must have been for her to see Anna Murray so firmly ensconced with Douglass in her gorgeous house in Anacostia. Her exclamation, "Oh, what a home yours would be if only all the surroundings and conditions could be set right which actually are all wrong and out of joint,"[27] expressed her desperation. She had left Europe knowing she no longer belonged in the Old World; on returning to the United States she had realized with a shock that post-Reconstruction America violated her most sacred political and social beliefs. She was left with no place she could proudly love as her home, as her *Heimat*. Acknowledging this fate gave a new quality to her relationship to the man who personified her American Dream: Frederick Douglass.

"Aside from other attractions it is such comfort to be allowed to communicate anything and everything to each other, to confide unconditionally without the least reserve or distrust,"[28] Assing had written to Douglass after her first vacation at Cedar Hill. She seemed blind to the dangers in unreserved communication, and she had no antenna for the taboo zones in his life. He was grateful for having someone with whom he could share the sadness, the anxiety, the anger, even the embarrassment he felt about his children's precarious situations, but she did not realize that the last thing he needed was an amplifying echo of his distress. It was one thing for him as a father to call Nathan shiftless and Charles untrustworthy, quite another if she did. Yet she could not but see the tragic way in which more and more people came to depend on the aging Douglass as their sole provider. In February 1879 she described the situation as follows in a letter to the Koehlers:

> The useless son-in-law, who starts and tries just about anything except the one thing where he might succeed, namely honest physical work, is again stranded with the bakery he started, as could be expected, and he has now traded it in for a farm six or eight miles outside of Washington. However, as there is no school nearby, Douglass will be lumbered with the three eldest children for at least a year, also Charles's two children, the youngest of whom is not gaining weight and is a mere shadow, yet alive and a torment to those around; moreover his half brother with his daughter, for whom he has provided a little cabin on his premises; this means he has seven mouths to feed, five children to clothe in addition to those for whom he has to provide anyway. Worst of all is the burden of Charles, who has been drifting about New York, without work, for a year.[29]

Assing was especially distressed by the tragedy of Rosetta, who had been coming apart ever since she married Sprague, "a lazy scoundrel, bound for the workhouse at best, and very likely for a worse place." Assing called him "a scamp . . . absolutely destitute of moral feelings and perceptions, who will not shrink from any crime," vowing to Douglass that she would rather "undertake the task to teach a cat or even Border State grammar than to impress him with a sense of truthfulness and honesty."[30] During Rosetta's adolescent years, Assing had been proud of her intellectual progress, supportive of her ambitions; the Rosetta of 1878 was a defeated woman, prematurely aged, dependent on her father's charity. Her letters were now barely legible; the spelling, punctuation, and even grammar erratic at best. Her husband not only failed to provide for her and their six children, not only incurred debts, swindled, stole, and drank heavily, but also cheated on her. Assing was greatly relieved when Rosetta separated from him, applauding this as a sign of strength and dignity, and shocked when Rosetta agreed to return to Nathan only a few months later. To give them yet another chance, Douglass sold them a farm he had bought as an investment. "Rose too unfortunately shows traces of the long demoralizing contact with him," Assing warned Douglass, "otherwise she could not have consented to live with him again, for even if she could have forgiven his rascality, his treachery towards her must have opened her eyes."[31] What a strange letter to write to a man whose relationship to his wife was precarious at best, for a woman who had spent two decades clinging to a dream deferred!

If Ottilie Assing was distressed about Rosetta, she had only contempt for the Douglasses' youngest son, Charles. After losing his government job he had practically dumped his family on his parents. Libbie was fatally ill, wasting away rapidly; Anna Murray and Louisa Sprague took turns at her sickbed, and for once Assing could not suppress a grudging admiration for Anna Murray's devotion and skill. "If the poor little piece of humanity should live, it will be chiefly owing to Madame's and Louisa's care,"[32] she acknowledged to Douglass. Libbie died in the spring of 1879, and the Douglasses took charge of her children. Assing liked them and sent them fancy silhouettes and clothes she made for Christmas, but, like Douglass, she had lost patience with Charles, who had literally abandoned his family.

Then, at virtually the same time, Douglass returned from another trip to the Eastern Shore with his brother, Perry Downs, and Perry's daughter. Douglass knew he had brought the "dear old fellow" home with him to die. To Amy Post he wrote: "I do not think he will ever be able to make his own living again. Slavery got about all the work there was in him and he has come to me to spend his last days."[33] Assing applauded his decision as "just like you and natural enough under the circumstances," but the next sentence reveals her brutality: "Among all the leeches that feed on you he is one of the most harmless and least expensive, and since you are wisely going to put him in the little house you will not be greatly troubled by his presence."[34] It was the most vicious remark she ever made about the Douglasses and their dependents.

"You know that frequently, when speaking of the demands and exactions of your children, I reminded you of King Lear and told you how the story never would become antiquated," Assing wrote to Douglass after yet another failure of Charles to find a job. " 'Put money in your purse,' Iago says to Rodrigo; 'Hold your own purse strings firmly,' I say to you."[35] The Shakespearean references show that Ottilie Assing was no longer thinking of unions banning African-Americans from their ranks, of the lower wages black workers received if they were employed at all, of the ease with which they were fired. She saw only the opportunities Douglass had created for his children, not the psychological burden his strength and success might have been for them, let alone the discrimination they faced on the job market. They were a liability where they should have been his glory and pride, models of black achievement he could display in his civil rights struggle. She could and would not forgive them, and she was increasingly impatient with the leniency Douglass continued to display. In contrast, he could never forget, would never deny the meaning of his children's blackness, the way "the presumption of incompetence confronts him [a black man], and he must either run, fight, or fall before it."[36] Also, he himself had failed more than once; his experiences with the *New National Era* and the

Freedman's Bank were fresh in his mind. Many years ago only Julia Griffiths' intervention had saved him from bankruptcy, and all too often he depended on the expertise of experts. Most important, his father had disclaimed paternal responsibilities and prerogatives; Frederick Douglass would never discard his children. He was determined to embrace fatherhood as a privilege and a vocation, even in the midst of failure. This was something Anna Murray saw and acted upon without words, while Assing challenged him to kick his children out and forget them. He was struggling for solutions that would allow them to live decently, while Assing worried about the next presidential elections and their implications for his career. Time and again she warned him to lay aside money for his retirement. "Provided you have enough through life, I shall neither worry about the rest, since I too feel convinced that all that you have acquired by your labor will be squandered without benefit to anybody,"[37] she told him.

The deceptive confidence which Assing regained in the fall of 1878 also extended to Douglass' performance in the public arena. She was stunned at Douglass' refusal to admit that the nation was in the process of reversing all the progress it had made. After his experience with his Baltimore address she understood why he had become more careful in articulating any kind of critique, yet she was shocked when he defended Hayes's policy even in their private conversations. The voices of protest from within the African-American community against many of his positions and statements were loud enough even for her to overhear, and she listened carefully.

She had encouraged the difficult, often contradictory and double-edged policy of hands-off and support, of laissez-faire individualism and social justice that Douglass advocated during these early Reconstruction years; she backed on the one hand his assaults on discrimination, his demands for educational programs, his suffrage campaign, and on the other his stern appeals to the freedpeople for self-improvement. With Douglass she shared a firm belief in human equality, in the blessings of education, in progress. Now, his personal success, the physical and intellectual self-liberation he had achieved made him increasingly impatient with those who would or could not follow his steps. He recoiled at being associated with illiterate black field workers; he was ashamed of the "noise," the "shouting, singing, and stomping"[38] that characterized so many black gatherings, appalled at the ways black people lived rather than enraged at those who kept them in poverty. By now he had adopted a lifestyle that had nothing in common with most African-Americans, North and South, rural and urban, and a fierce social Darwinism crept into his rhetoric as he exhorted his stunned black admirers on his lecture trips. "We must not talk about equality until we can do what the white people can do. As long as they can build vessels and we can not, we are their inferiors," he said to the farmhands and domestic servants, among them his own relatives, in St. Michaels. They were a "doomed race,"[39] and rightly so if they failed to catch up with white America, he proclaimed—this to people whose school shacks were going up in flames, whose teachers were terrorized by night riders, whose children had to pick cotton.

In 1878, when he returned to the Eastern Shore to deliver a version of his "Self-Made Man" lecture at the African Methodist Episcopal Church in Easton, he sent a glowing report to Assing, accompanied by a laudatory column from the *Easton Gazette*, which went into great detail about his bootstraps message and the dressing-down he had given his black audience. But Ottilie's response was not what he expected. "Anything in the line of success or praise and acknowledgment you win, very naturally gives me pleasure and consequently I felt gratified in reading the article of the *Easton Gazette*," she commented drily. She had told him so often and in so many words how much she longed to accompany him to the region where he grew up. The letter shows that she could barely contain her anger at having been left behind again. Perhaps it was this anger and disappointment that finally made her perceive Douglass as a man who came dangerously close to forgetting, if not betraying, the principles they both stood for, a man also whose self-reliance and Darwinian rhetoric was unconsciously playing into the hands of white supremacists. Assing did not attack Douglass directly; she accused the *Gazette* rather than Douglass of taking "a view by far too sanguine and rosy of the condition of the South and the prospects for the future." Yet there can be no doubt that the object of her criticism was Douglass:

> True, we are rid of slavery but that is about all and no likelihood [sic] of any progress for many years to come. A solid South, the Republic party there virtually dead, the Blacks virtually disfranchised even where they form the majority, ku-kluxed, defrauded, really without any rights which white men are bound to respect, there is indeed no cause to boast and crow over. Your own position is entirely an exceptional one, owing to your exceptional gifts, to your being a unique specimen of mankind, a.g.m. in short.[40]

Assing's acute assessment forced Douglass into a self-defensive reply, but Assing did not back down. "I am glad to learn that notwithstanding the election frauds and outrages in the South, notwithstanding the disfranchisement of the Blacks you are yet capable of taking a hopeful view of the political situation, since thus far I have always found you a trustworthy barometer," but, she protested, "I cannot entirely share it."[41] A letter she had written to Garrison the year before shows how worried she was about American politics at this period, "when principles are unscrupulously compromised away and sacrificing our friends to our mortal enemies is called reconciliation and mistaken for magnanimity." Not surprisingly, Douglass was not among the figures to whom she looked for guidance. "One might almost despair of the future but for the knowledge that such men as yourself and Wendell Phillips, who once awakened the nation to a sense of their wrongs, are still there, ready to fight the enemy in the future as well as in the past and to raise the people to a higher standard."[42] To Koehler in 1878 she confided: "Douglass is fairly optimistic, but it seems to me as if in the atmosphere of Washington, which is not at all a yardstick for the nation's mood and circumstances, these cronies are only too willing to affirm each other's hopes and to take possibilities and wishes for reality. Yet it is possible that he is right and of course it will give me the greatest pleasure to admit that I saw things in too dismal a light."[43] The fact that she openly discussed Douglass' political weaknesses—this was the only instance I could find in twenty-eight years of correspondence—shows how deeply concerned she had become. Was her Douglass on the way to becoming "one of them," one of the "cronies"? Had he joined the ranks of the men she abhorred as "speculators, soldiers of fortune and salary grabbers . . . weather-vanes," driven by "egotism, personal enmity, injured vanity and love of self, frustrated ambition and especially by their craving for Uncle Sam's fat salaries"?[44] Ottilie Assing could not bear the thought. Douglass clung to his belief in the "ultimate rule of moral law," to the idea that "Justice, honor, liberty and fidelity to the Constitution and Laws may seem to sleep, but they are not dead."[45] Assing reminded him that they were in great danger of either self-destructing or being throttled in their sleep. Justice cannot afford to sleep, ever, she cried out.

"Suffering and hardship made the Anglo-Saxon strong—and suffering and hardship will make the Anglo-African strong,"[46] Douglass exhorted an increasingly restless African-American community in 1879. But thousands of blacks in Mississippi, Louisiana, Texas, and Tennessee had begun to respond to Hayes's rollback policy, to their disfranchisement and their exposure to violence and exploitation, by packing their belongings and getting out of the South—by voting with their feet. Most black leaders, among them George T. Downing, Henry Highland Garnet, Richard T. Greener, John M. Langston, and Sojourner Truth, as well as abolitionists like Garrison and Phillips, supported what came to be known as the Exodusters. Douglass was almost alone when warning, as he had during the colonization controversy, that any kind of black separation, any form of black emigration was "an abandonment of the great and paramount principle of protection to person and property in every State of the Union . . . The business of this nation is to protect its citizens where they are, not to transfer them where they will not need protection."[47] He did not concede that he was serving an administration proud to have withdrawn this kind of protection, and he seemed sadly unaware of the frightful conditions in the Deep South, strangely oblivious that his appeal to black self-sacrifice in the name of the common good, his cast-down-your-bucket philosophy was ridicule in the ears of an abused people. Forty years after his escape from slavery the man in the house up on the hill seemed to have forgotten that desperate people want nothing more than to get out, principle or no principle.

Douglass may have forgotten, but Ottilie Assing, even though her knowledge of the situation was more abstract, had not. Douglass might reiterate the old myth that oppression made the Anglo-Saxon strong; Assing's father, her exposure to Jewish ghetto life in Hamburg, her excursion into the slums of New York taught her that it made people miserable, that it degraded and brutalized, and the information she had about the Deep South confirmed this belief. Hayes's post-Reconstruction policy exceeded the worst apprehension she had articulated in the final months of the Civil War, and her disillusionment now reached a point where she felt only another war could abolish the new cancers growing in the Redeemer South.[48] "I think that in principle you are perfectly right in opposing the stampede of the negroes [sic], but what shall men do when their lives are in jeopardy?" she challenged Douglass:

> It is one thing to recommend and advise a measure on general grounds and quite another to resort to it as the only means of escape from a violent death. Formerly it was a question of liberty and slavery, now it is one of life and death, and besides, what do those poor, ignorant men know of the political situation, whether it is only temporary or permanent? A man will jump right into the sea to escape from a burning steamer. It is a terrible state of things to which we have come and I yet can look in the future only with feelings far from confident.[49]

Douglass himself understood that his views exposed him to severe criticism from other African-American leaders. "In all my forty years of thought and labor to promote the freedom and welfare of my race, I never found myself more widely and painfully at variance with leading colored men of the country than when I opposed the effort to set in motion a wholesale exodus of colored people of the South to the Northern States,"[50] he wrote in his autobiography. But Assing's awareness of this black opposition only strengthened her determination to help him see the direction he was drifting in. She saw herself as a friend of his mind, to use Toni Morrison's phrase. He began to dodge her. Their exchange of letters on the situation of Southern blacks and on Republican politics shows that her political acumen made her keenly aware of the corrupting influence of power and privilege. "For five years the great Republican Party has ruled," she had written in November 1865 in the *Morgenblatt*, and warned: "With the sweet habit of ruling it has also learned the fear and the timidity of the propertied, who see ghosts of bankruptcy and ruin in any major change, any revolution."[51] Now, fourteen years later, she was shocked to see similar tendencies in the man who had been her lodestar, and just as she had refused to be silenced by the general clamor of victory in the postwar euphoria, she now refused to be silenced out of a false sense of loyalty. Speaking up was her way of loving.

Ottilie Assing had come a long way since those early days when she and her friends discussed the blessings of revolution, the glory of political martyrdom in her little smoke-filled parlor in Hamburg's Poolstrasse. Frederick Douglass had taught her the need to differentiate between theory and political practice, and she had been an eager, though always recalcitrant pupil who, while accepting his pragmatism, insisted on lecturing him on her radical principles. Now she sat across from the freedom fighter turned staunch Republican, reminding him that even in the midst of political warfare it was essential to remember theory and principle, cautioning him about the danger in allowing the pressures of political practice to stifle principle. And when he clung to principle, she called out to him to take a look at the reality of people's lives. She was like a sting in his flesh when he expected her to caress his wounded soul. Douglass had spent a lifetime fighting; he needed a period of rest. It is unlikely that he was unaware of the terror and poverty that surrounded him; it seems more likely that he chose, at least for the time being, to close his eyes and ears because these issues were so overwhelming. It was self-protection, an effort to survive by an aging man who, to use Cornel West's beautiful metaphor, was looking down from the mountain and saw Egypt on all sides! What he wanted most of all, now that he was entering the seventh decade of his life, was to enjoy the respect paid to an elder statesman, the glory of the lion. It must have seemed to him as if Assing had joined the swelling ranks of those who were out to deny him that right to his earnings. Her analysis of the Exodusters was the last letter of hers he filed.

The chasm that opened between Ottilie Assing and Frederick Douglass seemed to widen with every step they took, with every letter they exchanged. Assing sounded tired in the New Year's message she sent to Douglass on the day after

Christmas in 1878: "May the stars grant us a tolerable year, since anything better is denied to us."[52] By mid-February 1879 this sadness had developed into another full-blown depression, Assing once again trying to escape from its spell by burying herself in work: ". . . the more work I have, the more I can accomplish, and the less time there is left for meditation and reflecting about our tragic fate, our hopes and disappointments and the exceptional, unparalleled injustice and cruelty practiced on us by nature itself, the better it is."[53] And now the problems she was trying to cope with were not just Douglass' domestic situation, their ideological differences, her financial anxieties. Twenty-two years into her relationship with Douglass it began to dawn on her that what she had to fear most was not Anna Murray, not his children, not his career, but other, younger women. Ottilie Assing and Frederick Douglass had been in their late thirties when they met. Now she had to realize that, at the age of fifty-nine, he was dreaming of rejuvenation. The problem had become acute in late 1878, when Helen Pitts first came to Cedar Hill.

Helen Pitts was born in Honeoye, New York, in 1838, the eldest daughter of parents of strong abolitionist and feminist leanings. She was a well-educated woman who had graduated from Mount Holyoke Seminary in 1857 and had taught at Hampton Institute. In the summer of 1878 she visited her uncle Hiram Pitts in Washington, and she quickly became involved with the local feminists around Caroline B. Winslow, with the Moral Education Society, and with their journal *Alpha*.[54] This slim, vivacious woman with her gold-rimmed glasses took a spontaneous liking to Douglass and he to her; their common interest in women's rights provided abundant material for conversation. Pitts loved music; she was well read, unconventional and outspoken in her opinions, with a good sense of humor. Assing could not overlook the eroticism in the air. The more she saw of the younger woman, the more she feared her. She was enormously relieved when Douglass wrote her in December 1878 that Pitts's visits had ceased. What he did not tell her was that he continued to correspond with Pitts and even to visit her when possible.[55] "There is a distressing lack of genuineness about her, which I imagine even to notice in her face," Assing commented acidly, and warned that Pitts was only scheming to use his good name to bolster the standing of a project which, to Assing, was a disgusting hodgepodge of radical feminist rhetoric and religious hypocrisy. "I should rejoice anyhow to see you keep aloof from anybody and anything at all connected with that infamous *Alpha*," she went on. "If you had read it as I have, notwithstanding my disgust, just for the sake of having a right to denounce it, you would agree with me that no good and pure minded woman can advocate those monstrous doctrines, allow her imagination to run always in that same channel, read all that obscene stuff hidden under religious cant without being shocked unless she is so incurably and irredeemably stupid as to be considered altogether irresponsible."[56] As always when she was under stress, there were no limits to the ferocity of her tongue.

In January 1879 Douglass attended a lecture given by two Mormon women who gave an enthusiastic justification of polygamy. Assing's response to his—perhaps tongue-in-cheek—report was a passionate defense of monogamy! "Whatever may be a man's views and inclinations on the subject—and I readily believe that one does not need to go round with a lantern to find many who would prefer a score of wives to monogamy—the institution goes too diametrically against woman's feelings and instincts as to make it at all credible that any should advocate [polygamy] in good faith. On this point the stupid and the intelligent, the refined and the ignorant women are all alike." Her sermon culminated on a poignant note: "Anything may be shared and enjoyed in common, save a man's affection!"[57] It was an almost pitiful appeal for Douglass to remember what they had sought and found in each other, to rescue and reclaim their ideal.

Two weeks later (and two weeks before her sixtieth birthday) Assing found a chance to elaborate on yet another theme that she favored at this time: the eroticism of mature women. Her reveries were prompted by her first encounter with Helene von Racowitza, a former actress who had became famous when her lover, the German Socialist Ferdinand Lassalle, was killed in a duel with her fiancé, Janko von Racowitz. Spectacular love affairs and several marriages as well as a sensational divorce played a much larger role in making her name a household word in Germany than her skills as an actress. Twenty years before, Ottilie Assing had been intrigued by the life of the notorious Lola Montez; now, on the brink of what most of her contemporaries would describe as old age, she welcomed another femme fatale, the notorious "Red Countess." Racowitza and her husband, Baron Serge von Schewitsch, who had decided to make a new beginning in the United States, called on Ottilie Assing, and their friendship came easily once the two women discovered how much they had in common: there was their fascination with the stage, with acting; both were atheists; both were radical Republicans, and both loved animals. Even more important, Helene von Racowitza, like Ottilie Assing, was of mixed parentage. Her mother came from an old Jewish family in Berlin and had befriended the famous salonnières Rahel Levin Varnhagen and Henriette Hertz; her father, a professor of history, was Swedish-Norwegian, claiming Viking ancestry. In an age that despised the hybrid, Racowitza proudly claimed that she was of "pure Semitic and Aryan blood"![58]

Assing was enchanted with her new friend, and told Douglass she was "a highly attractive woman, well known in literary and artistic circles, who once was the cause of a duel in which a former lover of hers was killed." All the assets of Assing's model woman were listed: she was a famous writer and artist; she had creativity, intelligence, erotic magnetism. More, she "is now at her third husband, and although no longer young still turns the heads of old and young men."[59] Eros is ageless, she proclaimed in aggressive defiance of the familiar numbers game. So inspired was she by her discovery, so certain that Douglass would not resist her message that she could even signify on her own situation: Racowitza's reputation was "a little bit tainted," she warned him, but "you know however that such people are frequently the most amiable companions."[60] Soon Assing was busy translating Racowitza's succès de scandale into English: *My Relationship with Ferdinand Lassalle*.[61]

From letters she wrote to the Koehler family during those months we know that the aggressively unconventional baroness caused Assing many a headache, but the friendship was too important for her to give it up. Though there were many women in the social circles she moved in, Assing had not formed a deep or intimate friendship with any woman in America; even her male friends were few in number. So exclusively had she focused on Douglass that her interest in relationships that went beyond superficial socializing was limited. When she awoke from her Douglass dream she must have realized with a shock how utterly alone she was. For the first time in decades Ottilie Assing reached out to another woman, acknowledging her need for sisterhood and female bonding.

Racowitza seemed like a perfect confidante because she came from outside, and Ottilie Assing could talk with her about what was still central to her life—Frederick Douglass—as she could talk to none of her friends in Boston, Hoboken, or New York. For years and years she had told them her narrative of perfect interracial love, of romance thriving in the face of adversity. How could she reveal to them her dread that her fabulous lover was attracted to another woman? Racowitza knew only the bare outline of the story, but she knew men; she knew passion; she knew the temptation of youth, the exotic, the new; she had betrayed and was betrayed, had been victim and victimizer. Perhaps her friendship, the ability to talk simply gave Assing a new sense of self and calmed her down. When she returned to Cedar Hill for her next visit, the change in her conduct was remarkable: the critical eye was there, but the vicious aggressiveness was under control.

Robert Ingersoll
Ottilie Assing and Frederick Douglass befriended the notorious religious skeptic Ingersoll after Douglass moved to Washington. "A little while ago Douglass and I spent a lovely evening at Robert Ingersoll's," she wrote to Koehler in 1880. "We were really in our element, and it was like being among old friends."

The Douglass house on Washington's A Street
After the fire that destroyed their home in Rochester, the Douglasses moved to a house on Washington's A Street. In March 1874 Assing confided to her sister, "Douglass, who is adding a large wing to his house . . . feels that I should move in with him for good."

Cedar Hill
The Douglasses moved into the mansion they called Cedar Hill in the summer of 1878. Assing loved it. "My love to your glorious place and all who walk on it on either two or four legs, to its trees, hills and valleys!" she wrote to Douglass in November 1878.

In her autobiography, published several years later, Helene von Racowitza claimed an intimacy with Ottilie Assing that gave her an insider's perspective on the tragedy that ensued. Did Assing really open her heart to her new friend? Or was the story as she told it to Racowitza yet another version of her life's invention, that fiction of self and other? We have no way of knowing. What we know, however, is that she was eager for Douglass and Racowitza to meet when Douglass came to New York.

Ottilie Assing and Frederick Douglass faced many challenges after Assing's return from Europe, yet each held on to the other. Their weekly correspondence continued uninterrupted, obviously a challenge and source of inspiration to both of them. Douglass still liked to visit her in New York, to spend a few days with her and her interesting circle of friends, and in 1878 he came to Boston while she was with the Koehlers, making up for the lost opportunity the year before. Ottilie Assing took on additional translation projects to ease her financial problems; there was no hyperactivity, as in the winter before, no harangues against the Douglass family. Douglass was optimistic that if the Republicans won the presidential election in 1880, even greater honors were in store for him—perhaps a cabinet post. Assing's views were less rosy. She anticipated a Democratic victory and, with it, the end of Douglass' government career, but it was useless to create tension over this difference of opinions.

During the last days of March 1880 Ottilie Assing received a telegram from Florence telling her that her sister Ludmilla had died there on 25 March. It took Assing weeks to get all the facts about the cause of her sister's death: Ludmilla had suffered from meningitis; the physician called to examine the raging woman diagnosed insanity and had her transferred to a mental asylum, where she fell into a coma from which she never recovered. She was buried at Agli Allori, a cemetery halfway between Florence and Certosa.[62] The Swiss novelist Gottfried Keller, upon hearing the news, wrote to a friend: "Ludmilla! now it is over with all that fooling; she has closed her eyes and lips very unexpectedly. It is likely that she was already sick last fall, as her conduct struck many of her friends as strange. Men just did not favor her, and to this day I have not read one obituary that did her justice, not even halfway."[63]

There is no sign that Ottilie mourned over her sister; she was too honest to pretend. Their rupture was too brutal not to have left scars. And after Emilie Nickert died and Nickert's daughter let Ottilie go through her mother's papers, she had found a whole stack of letters from Ludmilla which had deeply hurt her. "They are a real curiosity, overflowing with empty, sentimental gush, yet bristling with malignant hints and falsehoods about me," she had told Douglass. "It is truly disgusting reading, a mixture of molasses for Mrs. Nickert and rat's poison for me."[64] Ottilie could only perceive and revile Ludmilla as her archenemy, and would not weep over her grave.

Then worse information came. Ludmilla had willed the entire collection of Varnhagen papers, as well as her own, to the Royal Library in Berlin; these included Rosa Maria's diaries, her precious silhouettes, the family portraits, her parents' manuscripts and letters—personal items that were as much Ottilie's as hers and many of which were of little value for a library. Meanwhile Ludmilla's estate—her house, her money, and her security bonds—went to her Italian political friends, the Battaglias; she had decreed that the money be used to transform her mansion into a model school in which German was to be obligatory.[65] Assing knew that there was a considerable amount of money involved: only a few years earlier, Ludmilla had transferred 50,000 thalers, probably her Varnhagen inheritance, from Germany to Italy, and she had made good money from her writing.

Soon Ottilie heard that she was not the only one who had been left nothing; Ludmilla's servants, Assunta and Eugenio, who had been promised a pension, received not a penny. They claimed the Battaglias had so harassed Ludmilla during her last year of life that she had not only changed her will in their favor but succumbed to nervous spells that eventually killed her. These rumors were confirmed by the American consul in Florence, whom Assing authorized to investigate the matter for her, and further evidence was provided by an Italian acquaintance, Rinaldo Kientzel, an attorney who offered to take on her case free of charge. Ottilie decided she would pursue the issue herself: she was determined to recover her family papers and portraits, and she hoped to reclaim at least some of the money; even a few thousand dollars would help her.* Aware that her only chance of contesting the will lay in declaring that Ludmilla had been mentally incapacitated, she asked several of her sister's acquaintances to testify to her insanity. To Feodor Wehl she wrote: "I know that Ludmilla spent some time in Stuttgart during her last trip, and I also know . . . that there were already strong signs of insanity, that she returned from the trip distraught and disturbed, and consequently I beg you to inform me . . . of the impression she made on you."[66] With the help of the American consulate in Florence she commissioned two Italian lawyers, a Mr. Sannini and his partner, to plead her case.[67]

---

*In her righteous anger Ottilie conveniently forgot that the will she had written as early as 1871 had disinherited Ludmilla.

Frederick Douglass in his library at Cedar Hill
The library was Ottilie Assing's favorite place in the Douglass residence. She gave Douglass the busts of Feuerbach and Strauss.

Helen Pitts
Ottilie Assing and Helen Pitts met during Assing's first visit to Cedar Hill, and Assing immediately recognized her as a rival. "There is a distressing lack of genuineness about her," she warned an obviously intrigued Douglass, "which I imagine even to notice in her face."

Frederick Douglass
Douglass liked to distribute this photo among his admirers.

Ottilie Assing
This last picture of Ottilie Assing was probably done in Florence. Helene von Racowitza, who befriended Assing and Douglass shortly before Assing left for Italy, remembered: "The aging heart of our good Ottilie was . . . entwined in passionate love with the beautiful dark Fred—this creature of her mind."

Assing was not alone in her indignation. German journals, which had vilified Ludmilla for years, spread the word, and soon Assing was flooded with letters from friends and relatives urging her to come back to Europe and fight for her rights. She answered every one of these letters, eager for sympathy, eager to let people know how she had been betrayed and wronged. "German and Italian papers comment on this, and all my close and distant acquaintances cry out in indignation," she told the Koehlers, "and many of our mutual friends, who still used to have a good opinion of her [Ludmilla], are appalled and letters come in from Europe from friends who all articulate their amazement and their anger." She was honest enough to admit that this gave her "great satisfaction."[68] All the emotional tension that for years had been building in her could now be channeled onto this substitute battlefield.

But many of her European spectator-friends were less supportive than she assumed they would be. Another letter from Gottfried Keller was representative:

> Your rule *de mortuis nil nisi bene*, which you pronounced on the occasion of Ludmilla Assing's death, has been respected only halfheartedly, and least of all by the deceased's own sister. One of our local families has received a letter from this lady, who is living in Neuyork [sic], which reveals a dreadful insight into the lives of an educated sisterhood of literary fame. Nothing but condemnations and vituperations about the almost total disinheritance that Ludmilla committed against the dear sister, not only in her last, but also in another will of an earlier date which surfaced on this occasion. She herself, i.e., Ludmilla, had always been a legacy hunter and liar, a fury possessed by vanity and megalomania and worse, and it was about time the truth be known, etc.[69]

During the months after her return from Europe in 1878 Assing had told everybody that she was determined to go on another extended tour as soon as she had saved enough money, and now, when she learned of Ludmilla's testament, she declared she would leave as soon as possible. Yet weeks and months passed, and Ottilie Assing stayed in New York. It was an election year again, with Douglass campaigning for the Republican candidate, James A. Garfield, and consequently Assing had postponed her summer trip to Washington. In August she spent a few weeks with the Koehlers in Boston, then visited with Mrs. Huntington in Stamford. In mid-September she arrived at Cedar Hill and she stayed through December, even attending the opening session of the new Congress. She was tense about the outcome of the election, but the letter she wrote to Koehler a week after Garfield's victory shows how thrilled she was at having been wrong. Yet the Republican success did not relieve her of her anxiety regarding Douglass' fate. "If only Garfield had the courage to leave Douglass in his position!"[70] She was too aware of the fierce opposition to Douglass' reappointment among Democrats and Republicans alike.

"My fall pleasure" was the phrase she used to describe her stay in Washington. Douglass' house was still an asylum for those who had nowhere to go—Rosetta's eldest children, Charles' children, Louisa Sprague. Charles had finally landed a job and was about to marry again. "Uncle Perry," as Assing called Douglass' brother, had died, but his place was immediately taken by "Aunt Kitty," a half sister, with her son and his wife. So the domestic situation was more or less unchanged, but Ottilie evidently had accepted it; she seemed to have taken a real liking to the eleven-year-old orphaned grandson of yet another Douglass half sister. "Douglass, in his unlimited generosity, immediately agreed [to take him in], and as he is a very bright boy who can read and write and of course will continue to attend school, he stands a good chance of enjoying him." She had learned to resort to humor or sarcasm instead of anger: "These little boys of forty are a greater burden than they were at four or fourteen,"[71] she sighed after Charles' marriage.

She also enjoyed a rich social life with Douglass during these months. There was no hiding in the attic, no withdrawal to the back row for her. "A little while ago Douglass and I spent a lovely evening at Robert Ingersoll's," she told the Koehlers in November. "We were really in our element, and it was like being among old friends."[72] And when Rutherford Hayes, accompanied by his son and Secretary John Sherman, paid a visit to the Douglass home, he was welcomed by Frederick Douglass, Anna Murray—and Ottilie Assing. The visit was "a demonstration of Hayes's respect and his friendly intention, which gave us not little satisfaction."[73] Douglass was obviously making no attempt to hide the white woman in his life, and as in all those years before, Assing was only too proud to be seen with him and as his. People were aware of the Douglasses' unconventional domestic arrangements, and they gossiped. Assing claimed that several women associated with *Alpha* even addressed letters to Lucretia Garfield, smearing Douglass' reputation in an attempt to oust him from his position.[74] But none of Douglass' opponents made these rumors public. As far as we can see from the happy and relaxed tone of Assing's letters, nothing of this kind happened to spoil her visit. She knew these might well be the last "quiet weeks"[75] she and Douglass would share for a long time to come, and she was determined to make the most of them.

Thus one year after Ludmilla's death Ottilie Assing was still in the United States, talking of having to go and take charge of her affairs in Europe—her "sensation novel," as she now called it half jokingly[76]—but reluctant to leave. She continued to roam New York's galleries and museums, so that she could enlighten her German readers about the state of American art. Her comments were softer now, more optimistic that American artists were catching up with their European colleagues, and she still lashed out fiercely at expressions of negative racial stereotyping. Most American painters were either unwilling or unable "to represent the beautiful, the higher type of the black race," she argued, reviewing one of Edgar E. Ward's plantation idylls: "Instead, they prefer to dish up, time and again, the caricature of the Negro, the ridiculous Negro as he appears in the black-faced minstrel shows. Do these painters not take the time to look for more noble models, or are they infected with American color prejudice, which needs to see the Negro as disgusting and apelike, to justify the discrimination he still suffers in the South?"[77]

She acted as if nothing had changed, and nothing was about to change. The winter storms, Douglass' precarious position after the elections, her domestic situation, letters from her attorneys—everything helped to postpone what to her appeared as "this dreadful trip." "If only one could get to Europe without having to leave here," was her lament. "Douglass entertains great—and it seems to me, sanguine—hopes for the moral effect of my presence, and urges me on in every letter,"[78] she told the Koehlers, but she hesitated. Was she aware that her relationship with Douglass had become precarious? Her letters to friends contain no hint that anything might be amiss.

In May 1881 one problem which had kept Assing in suspense all winter was solved, at least on the surface: President Garfield gave an old friend of his the highly visible position of Marshal of the District of Columbia, and he appointed Frederick Douglass Recorder of Deeds. This was an insult to Douglass, banning him, as it were, from the atrium to the basement of Washington politics, but "Douglass swallowed his pride, and with bitter disingenuousness claimed that the new job was better suited to his tastes."[79] Assing was quick to support him, fearful of friends who might interpret his attitude as weakness or opportunism. "Of course you know that Douglass was re-appointed as recorder, and you will imagine how pleased we are at that," she affirmed, using that reassuring "we." "Yesterday I received my first letter from him since he took up his new office, and it sounds as satisfying as I could hope. There will be no major difference in income, and as for the rest, his new environment and everything attached to it are much more to his liking, so that everything is à merveille! Also, that he was confirmed almost unanimously . . . is a great triumph he had not anticipated."[80]

As summer approached, her lawyers' letters became more insistent that her presence was needed in Florence. Assing finally booked passage to Hamburg for early August. Before she left, however, she made a point of seeing all the people to whom she had developed close relationships in the past years. There were goodbye parties in Hoboken; she spent a few days with her friends in Stamford, and she went to Boston for a final visit with the Koehlers, "to take in a deep breath of homey impressions and homey American air."[81] As she had no idea how long she would be absent, she arranged with Mrs. Werpup's daughter, a Mrs. Hymer, to leave all her effects with her in Hoboken,[82] including her cat, her birds, her turtle.

Four days before her departure Douglass came to Ottilie Assing, and they revisited many of the sights they had enjoyed together in the past years. Assing later reported that their days were filled with pleasant excursions[83]—attempts to recover the old intimacy and joy, perhaps; parting from something that was no longer theirs. Why did Douglass join Assing during these final days in New York? Was it a reassuring gesture, a sign of his commitment to their relationship? Did he come because he felt pity for her, because he felt guilty about the way he had begun to look at her? Was this a parting of old lovers, or of two people who decided to treat each other decently and kindly even after love had died? Was she still clinging to her construct of perfect love as she sat beside him aboard her boat during that final hour before departure? Or were they already strangers, living in distant, different worlds, performing intimacy? Sometime during this period Frederick Douglass wrote a poem entitled "The Meeting of Two Friends After Long Separation." In it he evoked memories

> Of trusted and truest friends,
> With pulses responsively beating
> To noblest aims and ends.

The poem spoke of dreams of a life together and of the pain of separation:

> Could they live in light of each other,
> All trouble would pass as a dream,
> More they, than sister and brother
> In friendship, love and esteem.
> Hard fate has decreed separation
> As fate has decreed such before
> But the sacred cords of affection
> Are bonds that live evermore.

The poem was about separation, but it also celebrated a spirit of love that conquered distance and fate:

> And doth not the spirit linger still
> Around the volumes thy hand has bless'd?
> And is it not upon Cedar Hill
>   Thy spirit finds sweetest rest?
> Come freely then, thou spirit of love
> Defying the bans of space and time
> Over these fair hills divinely rove,
>   Wreath them with beauty and grace sublime!

Was this poem dedicated to Ottilie Assing, whom Douglass would later call "one of my most precious friends,"[84] or was he already composing love songs to Helen Pitts? This time there were no promises to Ottilie that they would meet somewhere in the Old World to renew their relationship.

"I left home with a heavy heart," Ottilie Assing wrote to the Koehlers from Hamburg. She had hated every moment of her transatlantic passage—its boredom, all the "over-salted and over-peppered muck, tacky brown sauces, undrinkable tea and coffee, rancid butter, annoying noises and even worse smells," the "insipid" company. This was not a pleasure trip; this was an angry, unhappy woman, forced by unfavorable circumstances to make a trip for an uncertain and lonely future. The only person who sought her acquaintance was a beautiful but emotionally disturbed young woman who, after confiding all her most intimate problems, asked Assing whether it would not be best for her to commit suicide. An unhappy soul seeking companionship with another doomed soul—Assing balked while at the same time acknowledging that she knew what attracted the woman to her. "Of course I had a hundred reasons to prove to her that she had neither the right nor a cause for doing this, but is it not alarming that semi-lunatics generally feel I understand them?"[85] Deeply wounded herself, she had no strength to sympathize with other sufferers.

From Hamburg, Ottilie Assing traveled directly to Florence, where she boarded with Ludmilla's former maid Assunta. The two women had taken a liking to each other before; now, as fellow victims of Ludmilla's malice, they determined to take on the Italian legal system together. "Ludmilla may have disinherited me and done everything to poison my friends against me; she could not, however, prevent my inheriting Assunta. As to all the other riches out there on the moon, they look rather lunatic for the time being, and I am quite prepared to see them dissolve like moonshine,"[86] she wrote to her friend Bertha

Gutzkow, Karl Gutzkow's widow. Ludmilla's riches had indeed evaporated by the time Ottilie arrived in Florence, though her diaries were still in her study.

After her last meeting with Ludmilla, after her conversations with German friends, and after reading her sister's letters to Emilie Nickert, Ottilie must have had few illusions left about Ludmilla's emotional state. Yet the ferocity of hatred she encountered in the diaries was overwhelming. Self-hatred, envy, and hatred of her older sister tainted even the young teenage entries.[87] "It is a story gruesome, painful, and pathetic beyond description," Ottilie wrote to Bertha Gutzkow, "and I feel as if an abyss had opened before me, full of evil, lies, unnaturalness, and make-believe on the one hand and brutality and ingratitude on the other."[88]

Fighting a legal battle in a foreign land and in a language not her own, Assing depended on others as never before in her life. The American consulate was of great help, but her most reliable support came from former acquaintances of Ludmilla's and from Sannini and his partner. She knew that only Italians could open the doors of city councilors to her, and for that she was willing to make unconventional alliances. "I did some lobbying," she wrote to the Koehlers in May 1882, "and thanks to the good recommendation I received from the excellent Countess Gabardi, the aunt of poor Gino Grimelli, I was promised . . . that the government would take charge of things."[89] Assing obviously found common ground with the Grimellis. She was so impressed with their side of the story that she readily transformed Ludmilla's husband from "vermin" to "poor Gino Grimelli." "You cannot even dream *how* evil and completely contemptible Ludmilla was," she wrote to Amalie Koehler. "There never was a more malicious person."[90]

However, Assing quickly came to realize that hers was an almost hopeless case, no matter how eager her acquaintances were to assist her: Ludmilla's mansion was lost irrevocably. The local administration approved Ludmilla's plans for a school, but it would take months to appoint a trustworthy committee to whom the Battaglias would be answerable, and it was almost impossible to trace the money that had fallen into the Battaglias' hands. Nobody knew how much Ludmilla had willed them in the first place; there were no traces of bank accounts, bonds, or other papers, for the two rogues had had access to her home and desk, and had cleared out the place. After six months in Italy, Assing knew she was on the losing side again. She now redirected her energy to see to it that at least Assunta and Eugenio would get their 40,000 lire, and to get the administration to sue the Battaglias for fraud. "This whole story is only the smallest particle of the kind of bad luck that has been the red thread in my life,"[91] Assing admitted.

Once she accepted the situation, however, she decided to do what had always been her guiding principle: transform a catastrophe into an adventure. She had loved Italy the first time around, and had complained about the haste with which she had had to rush through places where she wanted to dawdle, her spirit to soar. Now, in the spring of 1882 she was off to Rome, then Sicily. "It is a magic land," she wrote to the Koehlers, "a beautiful landscape, with almost tropical vegetation . . . and a brilliance of color and sun as I did not even see it in Italy. It is the South in all its splendor, but also with its ugly sides, a people going to seed through dirt, ignorance, superstition, poverty, and lethargy." She was finally driven from this paradise manqué by its true monarch, the flea— "the hopping Capuchin."[92] In Pompeii, she spent a week roaming the ruins, reimagining the life that had been wiped out, the laughter, the flowers, the voices. She was in high spirits and, as always when feeling good, she longed to share her abundance with others. Friends were flooded with happy letters; in June, Dr. Loewenthal informed Douglass, "Miss Assing wrote to me from Italy to procure 500 Regalia Segars and send them to You [sic]."[93]

Assing was in southern Italy when Anna Murray Douglass, at the age of sixty-nine, suffered a paralytic stroke in mid-July. The children joined Douglass and Louisa Sprague in nursing their mother, but she died on 4 August, and Douglass, Rosetta, and Rosetta's daughter Annie accompanied the body to Rochester.[94] After the funeral Douglass returned to Washington, where on 7 August he received a remarkable letter of condolence from Sylvester Rosa Koehler. "Death is a sad visitor, under whatever circumstances he may come to us. If our sympathies are of any value to you, you may rest assured that they are with you."[95] We have no clue as to how Assing responded to the news of Anna Murray's demise. From references in other papers we know that Douglass and Assing were still writing to each other regularly over this summer, but the letters are lost. Assing did not mention it in her correspondence with the Koehler family. In fact, she seemed to disappear completely for months after Anna Murray's death, telling nobody where she was and where she planned to go. The German publisher Viereck, to whose *Süddeutsche Post* she sometimes contributed, became so anxious about his friend's well-being that he published a search inquiry. "They were worried that something had happened to me, and they finally asked German newspapers to track me down!" Assing reported to the Koehlers several months later, then "a day later, carried a notice with the heading 'She is safe!' " Assing was pleased that people cared this much about her, and she wanted the Koehlers to know that she was not lost and alone. "I greatly enjoyed this venture," she wrote. "I would not have believed that the appearance or disappearance of a straying mouse . . . would have even been no-ticed . . ."[96] Meanwhile her friends in Hoboken, too, were worried about her silence, and Dr. Loewenthal begged information from Douglass. "As I may sup-pose that You are in frequent correspondence with Miss Assing, please let me know, when You heard of her the last time."[97] But we do not know how Doug-lass responded to his wife's death, or whether and when he told Ottilie about it. The fact remains, however, that Assing chose to withdraw from the world. Per-haps she needed time to think and feel honestly. The moment for which she had longed for more than twenty years had finally arrived: Frederick Douglass was a free man. The most powerful external barrier between them no longer existed. It was just Frederick Douglass and Ottilie Assing now. She must have trembled at the thought.

Assing did not rush back to the United States, but in December 1882, in a long letter to Amalie Koehler, she made it clear that America was the home to which she intended to return as soon as possible. "What do you think of me! That I could give up the friends and community with whom I spent half my life and stay away just like that, without thinking of returning! . . . the longer I am in Europe, the greater is my longing for my friends and for the country in which I am so deeply rooted." Her attitude toward Europe was that of a tourist, she claimed: she enjoyed the beauty it had to offer, and she rejoiced in meeting new people, but she did so as an outsider, and she was lonely. There was no way in which she could have with strangers the immediacy and sense of community she shared with her American "gang." In order not to offend "people among whom I live only temporarily, I steer clear of politically or religiously compro-mising issues. I would certainly fly back next summer were I not so absolutely sure that I will certainly not go on another world tour, and would like to see my friends in Germany for a last time."[98]

Assing left for the German trip, but first for two weeks she gave herself up to the spell of Venice—"this miraculous city, which I saw only in great haste six years ago." For thirty cents a day she rented a room in a palace on the Grand Canal, spending hours just sitting on her tiny balcony and enjoying the beauty and the sunshine. The pleasure she felt in galleries, architecture, canals, even churches was expressed in almost erotic terms. "I could scream out loud with joy at this miracle."[99]

Her first stop in Germany was Munich, where she was the guest of the Viereck family. She had planned to stay for two weeks, but they kept her for six, and she loved every day of it. Viereck was said to be an illegitimate son of the German emperor, but he was an unruly son, indeed, not only publishing the socialist paper *Süddeutsche Post* but hiring radical intellectuals as reporters and journalists. Assing was thrilled to have a publisher eager to publish her unconventional assessments of American life and politics,[100] and she could not have been happier with the circles to which the Job introduced her: "Atheists, Socialists, dyed in the wool Republicans, all of them, many of whom have won their spurs either in prison or in exile."[101] These were not young hotheads, as many of her friends had been in the 1840s; these were men in their forties and fifties, with a long history of political commitment and persecution, undefeated, unwilling to compromise. She had forgotten that Germany still had people like that. Still, there was no remark that suggested a desire to stay.

That Germany could never again be her home was to become crystal clear when, later that year during a last visit in Munich, German police knocked at her door early one morning, took her to the police station, where they carefully scrutinized her papers, and quizzed her about her relationship to Munich's Social Democrats and her public criticism of an international art exhibition. Her fierce response in an article for publication shows that she saw the incident as more than an attempt to intimidate a foreign radical; in bringing up her Jewish background the police committed an act of racial harassment, she charged. How could freedom blossom in a land where "Jew-baiting" was normal and "antiSemitic vermin"[102] claimed the authority of public office?

But even before this racial incident she was determined to remain a traveler, as long as she "could not tempt a small circle of friends to join me permanently"[103] in her sightseeing. She explored the German and Austrian Alps; there were two weeks in Potsdam, at Mrs. Loescher's, and four weeks in Berlin, now a booming city. In Hamburg she was entertained by a childhood friend, possibly Maria Birkenstock, and then she turned south again, to Frankfurt, Heidelberg, and Switzerland. Friends in Zurich helped her gain access to the papers of Johanna Steinheim, who had died in 1878, and Assing was able to reclaim her and Ludmilla's letters to her "aunt." All the old hatred and bitterness of the sibling relationship erupted as she went through these letters. "These are again lovely revelations of the nature I find everywhere, and these are once again true rarities of lies, hypocrisy, malignity, and raging hatred against me," she complained to Koehler. "Her own ugly characteristics, her unlimited egotism, her arrogance, her infallibility, dogmatism, cantankerousness, her brutal tantrums which she associates with me and complains about in her hypocritical sentimentality!"[104] The hatred for her sister poisoned her travels, her associations, herself.

Assing had once seemed ready, even eager to go back to the United States. "I will be so happy to be over there again," she had declared in late 1882. "Actually, I am homesick."[105] But was this still true two years later? Was she still hoping to return to Frederick Douglass? Or did she know that the process of replacement had begun, that Douglass had hired Helen Pitts as a clerk in his recorder's office in 1882? Assing never mentioned Douglass in her letter of December 1882, but it is possible that her schedule was open-ended because she still hoped that Douglass might join her. Frederick Douglass himself had confided to his old friend Grace Greenwood, then in Paris, that his first response to Anna Murray's death in the summer of 1882 had been to seek solace in travel, to "break up my home and possibly go to Europe—but upon reflection—I felt it too late in life to . . . become a wanderer."[106] It was a sensible idea, but implausible given the actual issues he faced. Douglass was a troubled man during these months, struggling with severe bouts of depression, as his biographers confirm. And his problem went beyond old age and the loss of his spouse.

Douglass' feelings at Anna Murray's death must have been highly ambivalent. He and his wife had been too different in nature to create a harmonious marriage. But with Anna irrevocably gone Douglass could not avoid remembering how much he owed Anna: for the encouragement she had offered to the slave Frederick Bailey; for the unconditional support she had provided when he decided to escape from slavery; for all the work she had done, the problems she had tackled silently, so he could focus on his mission. When was it that the frustration, the annoyance had begun to stifle that knowledge of what she was for him? When had he started to see the woman at his side, his helpmate, merely as a burden, as a liability, as an embarrassment? He must have come face to face with the humiliation and agony he imposed upon his wife not only when he forced her to tolerate his relationships with other women but when he brought these women, white women at that, into their home. He must have known that her anger, her bouts of sickness, her harshness with her children were partly his doing. He must have ached over his inability to apologize, to explain, to express the gratitude she deserved, to make good. There must also have been a sense of relief that finally these trials were over, that he need no longer feel ashamed at what some called the "mistake of his youth," that there would be no further embarrassment—and a wave of shame and denial at these feelings. He was talking about so much more than the sobering effect of death when he wrote to Grace Greenwood: "There is not much room for pride or self-importance in the presence of this event."[107]

He agonized over the past, and he agonized over the future. He and Assing had been together for twenty-six years, and all those years she had been made to believe, had made herself believe, that only his obligations to Anna Murray and the children as well as his responsibilities as a public leader deterred him from deserting his family to live with her. He knew that she was waiting for him to make the commitment he had avoided for more than two decades. It was a commitment he was no longer willing to make. The fact that he visited with her to the last moment before her departure, that he continued to write to her, indicates that after twenty-six years he was still comfortable in her company, but it seems he was no longer excited; perhaps there was something of the boredom of long marriage in the way he saw her. She talked about the eroticism of mature women; he saw that they had grown old together. Like Assing, Helen Pitts was a strong woman, intelligent, well educated, political, independent; she was vivacious and full of laughter and wit; it was all there, without the bitterness, without the obsession that kept breaking through Assing's amiable surface. Helen Pitts was twenty years younger.

The relationship between Ottilie Assing and Frederick Douglass was not the victim of a hostile environment, of racist slander, of social ostracism, of Victorian philistines. They doubtless encountered all of this, yet they were individuals who thrived on adversity. A relationship defined as illegitimate, even unnatural, took much longer to succumb to the pitfalls of normalcy that marriage entailed—boredom. On the other hand, this, perhaps unconscious, desire to make the utmost of every hour that was theirs created a new kind of tension, a choreography of almost obsessive happiness and avoidance. Rather than marvel why this relationship deteriorated after more than twenty years we should acknowledge the intellectual freshness and the erotic vitality that kept it intact and prospering for so long. Still, upon entering its third decade the narrative of perfect love under siege lost its glamour as the soul mates began to take off their rose-colored glasses.

So Douglass did not go to Europe, and he did not invite Ottilie Assing to come to his side. By the summer of 1883 the conflict between inclination and obligation had become so fierce that he was "depressed almost to the point of a breakdown,"[108] as one biographer acknowledges. In a poem called "What Am I to You," probably written during this period of turmoil and rupture, he compared his desire for "thou greatly honored Maid" to man's longing for the forbidden fruit from the Garden of Eden:

> An apple swinging light and free
> High pendent on a brave old tree
> Flung a sweet fragrance down to me
> That thrilled all my senses.

> In size and form and hue divine,
> Perfect in beauty's every line
> Lock framed to pierce a soul like mine
>   Though fortified by reason.

He wrote of a desire regarded as transgressive—as a black son's yearning to gain entry into his white father's forbidden garden:

> Amazed I stood in wonder sound
> Till then such fruit I'd never found,
> I needed help and looked around
>   For means to gain possession.
> But none was there to give a hand
> And I could scarcely understand
> Why I such treasure should command
>   As that so far above me.
> But there it was and there was I
> With face upturned to tree and sky
> With will to do, but not to try
>   Held to the spot enchanted.[109]

Was it right to discard this dream of a perfect relationship with Helen Pitts for the sake of pity and gratitude, for the sake of moral obligation, for the sake of friendship—the only feelings he apparently could still muster for Ottilie Assing? He had to choose between hurting Ottilie Assing or himself; he chose to hurt Ottilie.

The inner pressure and turmoil which Douglass experienced during the first year after Anna Murray's death made his physical and psychological state precarious. The physician he consulted prescribed rest; Douglass knew he needed time and space to think and feel honestly. This he could not get at Cedar Hill, with his children worrying over him, with friends and colleagues calling, with Helen Pitts around. He had to break away from it all. He withdrew to Poland Springs, a resort in Maine, accompanied by his old friends Martha Greene and her husband. And then, on 24 January 1884, Helen Pitts and Frederick Douglass were married by the Reverend Francis Grimké at Washington's Fifteenth Street Presbyterian Church.

Douglass' second marriage was neither so simple nor so direct as he claimed. His children were distressed—a well-known response to a parent's remarriage after a spouse's death. Neither Rosetta nor her brothers came to the wedding. Louisa Sprague left the house in cold rage, even threatening to sue Douglass for back wages for the domestic work she had done—which tempted Charles Douglass to speak of "the Sprague conspiracy."[110] The children's opposition has usually been attributed to their feeling that in marrying a white woman Douglass was sullying the memory of their black mother and disinheriting his dark children, yet this might not have been the only concern. Perhaps they also resented that their father after losing their mother now also displaced a woman they—especially Rosetta—had learned to cherish as their second mother. Very likely it was not so much the new wife's whiteness that appalled them as the fact that this white woman was Helen Pitts rather than Ottilie Assing.

Did Douglass write to Ottilie Assing about his impending marriage? Or did Douglass prefer silence, as he did with his children, his closest friends, even Julia Griffiths Crofts?[111] Did Assing read the news in *The New York Times*? Although they apparently corresponded to the last, it seems Douglass chose silence. One day before Douglass' marriage, Ottilie Assing, spending another winter with Assunta in Florence, wrote a long letter to Mrs. Koehler full of travel plans and gossip, relaxed in tone.[112] If Douglass had informed her about his marriage, this composure was remarkable, indeed. Douglass was absent from all her extant letters after Anna Murray's death, just as he ceased to be written about in her columns. Ottilie Assing withdrew into complete silence after Douglass' marriage. Even as a child she had been reluctant to discuss her feelings;[113] and for twenty-seven years she had created images of perfect love, of lovers under siege, of lovers kept apart by adversity, of a martyrdom for abolitionism and civil rights for her family and her friends and, above everything, for herself. Anna Murray stood between them and perfect bliss; political obligations prevented the ideal marriage. Thus Assing and Douglass had comforted each other and explained to others. Adversity had defined the fiction, and it had always been adversity from outside; never in all those years had she even as much as hinted to anybody other than Douglass that it could be located within the relationship. Now Anna Murray was dead, and Douglass had married another woman. And not only had he married a younger woman; they were married by a minister!* It was perhaps the worst blow he could deal, her ultimate defeat. It was as if she had never happened.

Twenty-eight years were wiped out without a trace. What was there for her to say? She had not been willing or able to communicate her anxieties, her fear

---

*"Mr. Lange has forfeited his claim to atheistic saintship by consenting to be married by a clergyman. Queer that a sensible man should allow himself to be thus henpecked by such an inferior woman!"[114] she had joked with Douglass only a few years earlier. Now he had taken the same road.

and anger about this collapse of her dream with anybody as long as its surface was intact; what could she say now? That she had been wrong all along? That she had been blind, willfully blind? That her hero had used and deceived her, as he had used and deceived his wife? All those phrases must have raced through her mind, questions she had banned from her heart all those years. When had he started to drift away from her? When had he started to pretend? What had been real, genuine, ever? Was there a memory she could trust, when the end tainted even the beginning? Oronooko discarding Aphra Behn—it was unthinkable. There must have been sadness, rage, self-hatred, shame at having allowed this to happen to her. How could she relate to anybody after that when she had been so terribly wrong in the most important, the most intimate relationship in her life? And where should she go? How could she face those friends who had known and embraced her as Douglass' mate? She knew she could not stay in the Old World, and she did not know how to return to the New. With Douglass she lost the home, that precious borrowed place that had never really been hers. There were no words, for there was neither center nor direction, only a roaring, deafening silence.

As always, she sought solace in almost aggressive traveling, socializing, writing; the ongoing battle over Ludmilla's estate became her safety valve. She was triumphant when Assunta's and Eugenio's suit was finally successful, only to learn that there was no money left to be distributed and the victors were empty-handed. Corruption, lies, treason wherever she looked. In July 1884 she left Florence for Turin and then an ancient monastery in Savoy, where she spent a week with an English family she had met the winter before. During the first week in August she arrived in Paris. The letter she wrote to the Koehlers on 2 August was the first in which she did not mention plans for return. It reflected her sadness at the death of an old acquaintance, Luise Kudlich, in whose home in Hoboken she had spent many pleasant evenings, Christmas holidays, precious hours with the children; she admitted that she could not imagine living in Hoboken without Mrs. Kudlich's company, she being "the only woman [in Hoboken] with whom you could make intelligent conversation." But she wasted little time on musing over the past; the letter was directed toward the future. "But my plans don't end here," she promised in the exhilarated tone she always adopted when coming out with a big surprise, "for I actually intend— and you will be amazed—to make a tour through Spain this fall, for which I was told you can buy a first class ticket for about 230 francs. I spent all winter recapturing my Spanish, which had rusted a little." The only obstacle was the quarantine the Spanish government had imposed out of fear of cholera, "and the prospect of spending two weeks in a village in the Pyrenees, living in a tent, is not at all attractive. *Nous verrons!* And now kind greetings to young and old and whom it ever may concern, humans and animals!"[115] She had always signed her letters to "the gang" not with her name but with a drawing of a cat, her favorite animal. This time she drew a snake.

Vigorous, active, indefatigable, full of plans and joie de vivre—nothing in this final letter and her representation of self reflected the earthquake that had shattered her life. Ottilie Assing would not allow anything or anybody to question the image of the strong, independent, unconventional woman she had created for herself. Nothing, not even an incurable illness, not even cancer. It is possible that she consulted a physician in Paris about lumps she discovered in her breast.[116]

Certainly, growing up as the daughter of a physician, Ottilie Assing was familiar with sickness, suffering, and death. As a young woman she had sat at her mother's bed, witnessing in helpless horror the physical pain that distorted her every feature, the emptiness that took over with morphine. There were the weeks in which her father had depended on his daughters feeding and washing him—the final helplessness and humiliation of a fiercely proud man. She feared dying, not death. As Frederick Douglass put it in a letter to Martha Greene: "She has always maintained her right in case of being afflicted with an incurable disease to save her self the pain of a lingering death and her friends the trouble of caring for her."[117] Perhaps there were no friends willing to be burdened with a dying woman; it is more likely that she could not bear the thought of dependence. Her mother had struggled for life surrounded by her husband and daughters, with friends and maids helping her. Her father had willed himself to die, but his daughters and friends had been with him, all the way to the end. Ottilie Assing was alone, and she had no home to withdraw to. The loneliness, indignity, humiliation of sickness and dying—Ottilie Assing knew them too well to expose herself to them.

All the documents we have of Ottilie Assing's suicide refer to breast cancer or incurable illness as her motive to end a life that no longer made sense to her, yet there is no reliable documentation of this medical diagnosis. It is possible that Assing suffered from cancer, but we should also consider the possibility that this, like so many other events and relationships in her life, was an invention. It might have been a final gesture of love and generosity to Douglass, to protect him against the charge of being responsible for her death, or a gentle lie, a parting kiss of absolution for the man she still loved, or an invention she needed to maintain her pride and integrity, an act of defiance against the man who had betrayed her.

Many years earlier, shortly after her father's death, the return of the Steinheims to Hamburg after a long trip all over Europe had moved the twenty-five-year-old Ottilie Assing to a deeply emotional profession of loyalty to the notion of home, or *Heimat*, "that old battered thing, as Heinrich Laube called his '*Heimath*' ": "How uncomfortable a thought it must be not to have a *Heimat*, especially when you exchange such a well-furnished and cozy domesticity for such a roving life," she wrote to her friend Gutzkow. And yet this same letter already showed her awareness that with her father's death there was no longer a definite place she could justifiably call home.[118] She had challenged fate by calling the world her home, had claimed that home was where she related to people, where she gave and received love, and she had thrived in the openness, the mobility that was hers. But in her hotel room in Paris during her final days, she must have understood her essential rootlessness, her ultimate homelessness. There had been rooms in New York and Hoboken, sunny, warm, cluttered with her things, but she had been drifting from one lodging to the next, the victim of her own arrogance and explosive temper, and exposed to the whims of landladies, a dweller in borrowed places. She had called it freedom, and in many ways she loved it, avoided by all means a situation where she would have been in charge, tied down by responsibilities—yet she always longed for a place that was all hers. There was the house upon the hill, the emerald island she embraced as hers, but she was never more than a guest, tolerated, on the edge of a bed, at best. She had loved her freedom, had gloried in the role of the lover, of the woman who defied morality, religion, notions of race, class, and hierarchy, and yet she raged at a fate that denied her the stability of marriage, a family. If her life had been anything, it had been contradiction, conflict, and she loved and hated it at the same time. But now it was time to let go, and to do so with decency and dignity.

As a young woman Ottilie Assing had banned God from her life; there was no God to whom she would or could entrust her dying. For her, to be mistress of her life was also to be mistress of her death. She had been raised in a cultural environment that not only celebrated life but also cultivated the *ars moriendi*, that differentiated between suicide and a life that no longer made sense. For generations of Germans Goethe's *Werther* had idealized suicide as a legitimate alternative to life without love; the Romantics sang hymns to lovers choosing death over separation. The novellas and ballads Rosa Maria Assing wrote for her young daughters featured beautiful countesses seeking ecstasy in the arms of the river god rather than facing loveless marriages; she read to them the poetry of Karoline von Güderode, who stabbed herself to death on a little peninsula on the Rhine when her married lover discarded her. Beautiful death and suicide were vital components in Ottilie Assing's images of life and love. Only seven years earlier Ottilie Assing's cousin Fanny Lewald had written: "It is very easy to say that suicide is a crime, not the least because it throws a dark, lasting shadow on the lives of those who survive; but not to end a life you no longer enjoy, of which you have to say with full, honest conviction that it is no longer useful for substantial acts of creation, that nobody suffers a real loss by its ceasing, and very many make many small or large desirable profits by it—not to end such a life, whose end is close anyway; and with the continuation of which you cannot connect the slightest hope—from that only our cowardice detains us."[119]

There was nothing unusual about Ottilie Assing when she left the Hotel d'Espagne on Cité Bergère on that sunny afternoon of 21 August. She was dressed elegantly, as always, wearing a tightly corseted summer dress held at the neck by a brooch decorated with oak leaves. A light coat was draped over her shoulders. She never went out without a hat, and she never walked out of the hotel without waving a friendly goodbye to the servants in attendance. Today her goal was the Bois de Boulogne, where she had spent so many pleasant afternoons enjoying the park's beauty, couples promenading arm in arm, nurses pushing strollers, children playing hide-and-seek. It was one of those gorgeous days she delighted in—sunny, warm but not too hot, with a little breeze.[120] Did she think of that lovely afternoon, twenty-eight years ago, almost to a day—possibly their anniversary—when she had walked up the slope to Douglass' mansion, to her emerald island, for the first time? It was a good day, a good place from which to depart. Paris. This was where they had hoped to meet when Douglass was exiled. This is where he had promised to join her during her first European tour. Paris. The City of Light. A perfect place of departure for a woman who willed herself a citizen of the world and yet was without a home, for a woman so fiercely in love with life and yet so happy to die. Seating herself on a bench somewhat removed from the park's main walks, she carefully uncorked the little vial she took from her purse and swallowed the potassium cyanide it contained.

That evening Ottilie Assing's body was delivered to the Paris morgue. There was no need for an autopsy; the vial they found told all. "Poison," the officer filled in next to "cause of death"; "suicide" he marked, as opposed to homicide; "incurable illness" was the motive indicated. They carefully listed Assing's possessions: "a shirt marked O.A., knickers, 2 petticoats, corset dress, coat, hat, stockings, boots, leggings, a red leather purse containing 70 francs, a yellow metal brooch with oak-leaf insignia, a small key, a set of false teeth in a red canvas case."[121] The "body of the unfortunate deceased lay during two weeks at the morgue of Paris awaiting identification," her former pupil Hermann C. Kudlich reported to Frederick Douglass months later,[122] for she had carried no identification papers with her. However, when the body was about to be delivered to the medical school for dissection, a friend of Assing's from Florence, Rinaldo Kientzel, heard of her death and hastened to make decent funeral arrangements with the help of the American consul in Paris, George Walker. Ottilie Assing was interred in the Cimetière de la Morgue in Ivry,[123] and her file was closed on 13 September.

We know that Ottilie Assing, in a final letter to Frederick Douglass, "spoke of incurable cancer," but Douglass claimed that she had said "nothing of her intention to shorten her days." Yet he admitted he had sensed what might be coming: "When I heard of this ailment I felt and have felt afraid that she would do precisely as she is reported to have done."[124] Apparently his response to her cry of pain was silence, and it seems she wrote no parting note to any of her friends or family. The American "gang" heard about her death from German-American newspapers. On 20 September her old friend Johannes D. Lange (to whom she had denied atheist sainthood when he was married by a clergyman) inquired of Sylvester Rosa Koehler: "Have you heard that Miss O. Assing has been dead since 21 August? According to a report in today's *Handels Zeitung* they found her body on the day mentioned above in the Bois de Boulogne in Paris. She is said to have poisoned herself with potassium cyanide because she was suffering from an incurable breast ailment. I had never heard of anything like that before. Might not the issues around her relationship have caused this suicide? A sad end to an all in all rather gruesome refrain."[125] They had been friends for too long for Lange not to spontaneously point to Douglass' marriage as the motive of Assing's suicide. Three days later, in response to vague information he received from the Koehlers, Lange was still worried and concerned: "My deepest thanks for the information on Miss Assing. I am afraid we have little hope that the news reports were not authentic. Should you hear from Florence, please be so kind and write to me."[126]

Carlos von Gagern, who had met Ottilie Assing in New York in 1865 and had been deeply impressed by her unconventionality, the courage of her convictions, and her vivaciousness, heard of her death while working on his memoirs.

He was one of her few acquaintances who did not relate her suicide to Douglass but exclusively to her unwillingness to allow cancer to become her tyrant: "While writing these lines, I receive the sad news that Miss Ottilia Assing has voluntarily ended her life by poisoning herself with potassium cyanide. A breast ailment, which she considered incurable, made her close the door which leads into eternal nothingness. Coming from Florence, where she had been living after years dedicated to her literary and journalistic tasks, she was on a trip to Spain and committed suicide in the Bois de Boulogne in Paris on 21 August 1884. One noble woman less in this world!"[127]

And Frederick Douglass? "I have been made inexpressibly sad . . . by confirmatory news of the death of my dear friend Miss Assing," he wrote to his old confidante Martha Greene, and hastened to add that the cause of Assing's suicide was "an incurable cancer on her left breast." If anybody knew of his most intimate feelings and relationships, it must have been this long-standing friend. "You will easily believe that this is a distressing stroke for me—for I ever held her as one of my most precious friends. I never had one more sincere."[120] He spoke exclusively of *his* distress and *his* sadness: there was not a word on the pain Ottilie Assing must have suffered during her final months. He carefully avoided anything that might implicate him in this "precious friend's" suicide. To the contrary: his private obituary combined incurable sickness and Assing's rationalism into a perfect formula of absolution for himself.

In November, Henry Bergh forwarded to him a letter from Assing's Italian friend Rinaldo Kientzel with details on her death and funeral. The correspondence that ensued dealt exclusively with the will "our dear friend"[129] had made.

CONCLUDING REMARKS

Aequanimitas

❦

No, Aphra said, lost in thought. Love is never a catastrophe. It redeems us by chaining us; it liberates us by putting us in bonds; it gives us perfect happiness by filling our eyes with tears and our heart with blissful despair. Love is a divine catastrophe, and when it kills you, you die a blessed death.   —CLARA MUNDT, *Aphra Behn*

Yet we know that nothing is perfect,
Least of all a man.
—ROSA MARIA ASSING, "On the Morning of the Wedding"

❦

Of Others and Me[1]

Two names are ringing in my ears—Ottilie Assing and Fred Douglas [sic]. She, the sister of Ludmilla Assing, well known in Europe, was raised in her uncle Varnhagen von Ense's home, and she was the more outstanding of the sisters, though the less noisy. The influence of the great scientists of the day, especially of the two brothers Alexander and Wilhelm von Humboldt, found expression in her excellent education, as did Rahel's and that of the whole "aesthetic" salon of Varnhagen in her exquisite manners. She had come to North America out of her passionate, compassionate love of poor Southern slaves and had offered her services to the "abolitionists."

After all kinds of adventures to which she was exposed when saving Negro slaves, and persecuted by the enraged governments of the Southern states, she became one of the leaders of the New York society supporting and rescuing Negro slaves who had succeeded in escaping bondage but who, hunted and totally without means, would have perished miserably, had not members of the society hidden them in their homes.

This is how Ottilie met Fred Douglas, who had also escaped from slavery, and in him she found an exceptionally gifted human being.

His mother, an ebony black Negress, had given birth to him on a plantation of the rich white American Lloyd—who was rumored to be little Fred's father—during the first half of the nineteenth century. Even as a little boy, when he saw the plantation owner's children read and discuss what they had read, he cried bitterly because he did not possess this skill. Against his "master's" will he found a way of learning arithmetic, reading, and writing. He was not on good terms with his "owner"—or, as they whispered, his father. He did not want an educated slave and finally sold him to another state.

Fred always tried to increase his knowledge, and despite the greatest difficulties, he succeeded in acquiring an excellent schooling. When, after his successful flight, which he described in a picturesque way in "my bondage and my freedom" [sic], he came to Ottilie, she continued to tutor him, kept him hidden at her place for—I think—two years, and had the great pleasure to see him become one of the leading men in the United States, excelling equally in war and peace.

When my husband and I met him in 1878, he held one of the highest positions in the country, United States Marshal in Washington. Carl Schurz, our great compatriot, counted Fred Douglas among his most intimate friends. Every child in America knows "Fred"!

We found him a strikingly attractive, tall, glorious type of man, built like a lion, in whom race mixing—for he thinks he also has Indian blood in his veins—has created the most fortunate potion. Of an enticing charm, he had—despite his extraordinary, universal learning, which was especially striking in America, where a very rudimentary school education usually prevails—lost nothing of the gentleness of character that characterizes the Negro in his folk songs and that makes men and women of this race such popular domestics. Our old friend Ottilie Assing had taught him perfectly polished manners. In short, we found in him one of the most interesting and agreeable people among our acquaintances. Wit and a humorous approach to life were as much in his command as deep seriousness and erudition.

As a young slave, long before his liberation, he had married a pitch-black Negress, had fathered coal-black children with her, and despite the excellent education he provided for her as well as for the children, they remained just ordinary "niggers." But he had this black family come to him and lived in a very good marriage with his wife until she died.

The aging heart of our good Ottilie was, as was only human and natural, entwined in passionate love with the beautiful dark Fred—this creature of her mind. But she honored his marriage bond—and probably hoped that, once his black wife's death had liberated him, he would lay this freedom at her feet.

The poor woman was bitterly disappointed. Death indeed came as a liberator, for Fred Douglas, whose snowy white hair now contrasted with his dark complexion, gave his hand to a younger white woman who had been his secretary in his government office.

Ottilie—my friend who had been so brave to this moment—was so desperate that she killed herself. In the Bois de Boulogne in Paris, to where she had traveled in her soul's pain, she poisoned herself with cyanide on a lonely bench, thus ending in a wretched way a life that had been so rich in significant action.

Except for me, only very few people knew the cause of her tragic end.

On 9 November 1871 Ottilie Assing wrote her last will and testament, naming Henry Bergh, president of the American Society for the Prevention of Cruelty to Animals, as its executor:

> I give and bequeath to my executor . . . the sum of Thirteen Thousand ($13,000) dollars to have and to hold the same, in trust, nevertheless, to and for the following uses and purposes to wit: to invest and keep the same safely invested at interest for and during the term of the natural life of Hon. Frederick Douglass . . . to pay over the net interest and income therefrom by equal semi-annual payments to the said Frederick Douglass for and during the term of his natural life, in recognition of his noble labors in the antislavery cause; and upon and after his decease, to pay over unto the American Society for the Prevention of Cruelty to Animals . . . the whole of said principal sum of Thirteen Thousand ($13,000) dollars.

Douglass was also to receive her gold pens as well as the books he had chosen from her library. She left this will in the care of Henry Bergh and informed Frederick Douglass of its provisions.[2]

The will was drafted during a period when Assing and Douglass' relationship was, despite its perennial problems, loving and full of promise and hope. Douglass was in a precarious professional and financial position, having launched the *New National Era*, and his hopes for an appointment in the Grant administration were frustrated. The arrangement Assing made for him was typical of her circumspection: it would give him a small but reliable income for the rest of his life. She wanted him to profit from it during his lifetime; she saw to it that her money would not be part of the estate his children, she firmly believed, were sure to ruin after his demise. Her need to protect and control him extended beyond the grave.

Assing also established a trust fund for her cousin Emilie Nickert and her dependents, to whom she also bequeathed her clothing; her books went to friends. She virtually disinherited "my dear sister Ludmilla Assing," decreeing that she receive only "all my Jewelry, Thread and Guipure Lace, my black Lama Shawl, my Lace Pockethandkerchief and my Album."[3]

On 7 April 1883, nine months after Anna Murray Douglass' death, Ottilie Assing met with William L. Welsh, the American consul in Florence, to change her will. Several beneficiaries—Ludmilla Assing, Emilie Nickert, and Anna Maria Reihl—were deceased, and she now arranged for lump sums to be paid to Mary Nickert Walpuski and the Koehlers. The financial arrangement she had made for Douglass remained unchanged. The most personal item in her belongings, "my large album," was now to go to Douglass; it was as if he was the only family she had left. The most important provision she made, however, related to the papers, letters and diaries she had collected throughout her life, following the good Varnhagen tradition: "All the letters which will be found in my possession, are to be destroyed immediately."[4]

Assing was in Florence when the news of Douglass' marriage to Helen Pitts reached her. There was plenty of time for her to change her will again. She did not. What kind of final message was this to Frederick Douglass? The arrangement she had indicated would remind him twice a year that she had been, and still was, a part of his life. He would have to remember Ottilie, what she had been to him, what he had given up, what he had done to her. Every six months the man who devoted his life to humanity would know that he was responsible for a life devoted to him. In an age when a mistress was usually kept by a man, she had turned things upside down by paying the lover for services performed in the past. Ottilie Assing always refused to believe in ghosts; perhaps she simply devised a more substantial way of haunting Frederick Douglass.

In November 1884 Frederick Douglass received a curious letter from Bertha Hirschfeld, a distant relative of Assing's. She had heard of Assing's death only a day before and expressed her amazement that Ottilie should have committed suicide "after her last letter so full of life and plans for the future." Hirschfeld had also heard that Assing had bequeathed him a substantial amount of money and did not hesitate to request that he share his new abundance with "an aged lady and such near relative of the departed." She reported that Ludmilla had promised to provide for her and her invalid son, but had not kept her promise. Now she appealed to the man in Ottilie Assing's life for help: "She called you her noble friend. This thought gives me courage and hope."[5] We do not know whether Douglass ever responded to this strange letter. On 26 January 1885 Henry Bergh sent a copy of Assing's will to Douglass. Bergh declined to act as executor, but he did not hesitate to claim the property to which his association was "entitled."[6] Other letters document that Sylvester Rosa Koehler could not wait to lay his hands on the money Assing had bequeathed him.[7]

Ottilie Assing obviously was not lacking in friends and kin eager to cash in on her death; they were less willing to perform the service for which she had asked. Douglass, too, was not at all reluctant to accept the money allotted to him by "our late respected and lamented friend, Ottilia Assing."[8] In fact, the letters exchanged between him and Henry Bergh in September and October 1884 show that upon news of her death he immediately made inquiries about her will, even before knowing what exactly had happened to her.[9] Together with Koehler, Douglass appointed her former pupil, the young attorney Dr. Hermann C. Kudlich, as executor. From the correspondence between Douglass, Bergh, and Kudlich we know that Douglass went to New York in February 1885[10] to go through Assing's belongings, which were stored at Mrs. Hymer's. He did not take time to choose books, as Assing had requested; he was not interested in the photo album.* This all suggests that there were no sentimental motives behind his visit; it is more probable that he wanted simply to reclaim his letters to Ottilie Assing, possibly also her diaries, before the executor could read them.

Kudlich was unable to find the gold pens of which Assing spoke in her will, or her jewelry; they probably disappeared in Paris, together with her trunks. In a letter of 18 July 1885 Kudlich told Douglass that he had executed Assing's will and "destroyed a large number of carefully preserved packages of letters arranged according to date from the year 1830. They constituted a treasure in themselves and bore the signatures of eminent men and women and I was reluctant to permit these precious documents to disappear in smoke."[12] Ottilie Assing's life had been words, letters, narrative. By instructing that these documents "be destroyed immediately" upon her death, she erased herself from memory. A clean slate.

On 15 September 1886 Dr. Gustav Frauenstein went aboard the steamer *City of Rome* to pay a parting visit to Helen and Frederick Douglass, who were about to leave New York for a trip to Europe and Egypt. That night Helen Douglass noted in her diary: "We talked of Miss Assing & as the genial Dr. left he threw his arms around Frederick's neck in a good old fashioned hug & kissed him, kissed me, and ran off the steamer."[13] Frauenstein had been sincerely devoted to Ottilie Assing for more than fifteen years, a friend who had laughed with her in her happiness and who had always been there to catch her when she threatened

---

*The book selection was later made by Dr. Loewenthal, who shipped it to him together with the photo album and a complete run of the *New National Era*.[11]

to succumb to depression. Frauenstein knew the meaning European trips had had in her life; he knew, and remembered.

What were Douglass' feelings during this meeting? What went through his mind as he saw the dignified gentleman run away from him? His diary contains no entry on Frauenstein's visit.

The Douglasses first went to England, spending several days in animated conversation with Julia Griffiths Crofts, widowed since 1880. Then Helen and Frederick Douglass paid their first and only visit to continental Europe. For twenty-six years the City of Light had been like a dream deferred for Douglass, and the woman who had planted this dream in his mind must surely in some sense have been strolling with him as he and his wife promenaded down the boulevards and ventured into side streets, sat in sidewalk cafés, and roamed the city's galleries and museums. Paris, Rome, Naples, Pompeii—it seemed as if he had been there before, through all the grandiose word pictures Ottilie had conjured up for him. Yet in his diary silence still reigned. In the spring of 1887, after an exhilarating excursion in Egypt and Greece, the Douglasses went to Florence. Douglass was eager to see the mansion which Ludmilla Assing, "the sister of my friend of many years Miss Ottilia Assing," had built for herself, but he failed to find it. "Alas!" he exclaimed that night. "How soon are the dead forgotten."[14] Not quite.

Notes

ABBREVIATIONS

AAA	By permission and courtesy of the Archives of American Art
AKP	Amy Kirby Post
AMD	Anna Murray Douglass
BJK	By permission and courtesy of the Biblioteka Jagiellonska Krakowa
BPL	By permission and courtesy of the Trustees of the Boston Public Library
CA	By permission and courtesy of the Cotta Archive, Schiller National-museum/Deutsches Literaturarchiv
CRD	Charles R. Douglass
DA	David Assing
DLA	By permission and courtesy of the Schiller-Nationalmuseum/Deutsches Literatur-archiv
DM	*Douglass' Monthly*
FD(P)	Frederick Douglass (Papers)
FW	Feodor Wehl
GS(P)	Gerrit Smith (Papers)
HLHU	By permission and courtesy of the Houghton Library, Harvard University
JDL	Johannes D. Lange
JG(C)	Julia Griffiths (Crofts)
JSt	Johanna Steinheim
LA	Ludmilla Assing
LTFD	*The Life and Times of Frederick Douglass*
LC	By permission and courtesy of the Library of Congress
KG(P)	Karl Gutzkow (Papers)
MARS	By permission and courtesy of the Museum and Archeology Research and Sup-plies
Mb	*Morgenblatt für gebildete Leser*
MBMF	*My Bondage and My Freedom*
NFD	*Narrative of the Life of Frederick Douglass*
NNE	*New National Era*
NJHS	By permission and courtesy of the New Jersey Historical Society
NYHS	By permission and courtesy of the New-York Historical Society
NYPL	By permission and courtesy of the New York Public Library
OA	Ottilie Assing
PFP	Post Family Papers

PP	Porter Papers
RdC	Rahel de Castro
RD(S)	Rosetta Douglass (Sprague)
RMA	Rosa Maria Assing
RDUA	*Rochester Daily Union and Advertiser*
RTB	*Rochester Täglicher Beobachter*
SBB	By permission and courtesy of the Staatsbibliothek zu Berlin—Stiftung Preussischer Kulturbesitz
SDP	Samuel D. Post
SPost	*Süddeutsche Post*
SRK(P)	Sylvester Rosa Koehler (Papers)
SSt	Salomon Ludwig Steinheim
SU	By permission and courtesy of the Syracuse University
SUBF	By permission and courtesy of the Stadt- und Universitätsbibliothek Frankfurt
UR	By permission and courtesy of the University of Rochester
VvE	Karl Varnhagen von Ense
VC	Varnhagen Collection
WLG(P)	William Lloyd Garrison (Papers)

INTRODUCTORY REMARKS

1 Gagern, *Todte und Lebende*, 2:271. All translations from German material are mine unless otherwise indicated.

2 Zeise, *Aus dem Leben und den Erinnerungen eines norddeutschen Poeten*, p. 50. Zeise went on to quote Gagern's delineation of the Assing-Douglass relationship in full.

3 Racowitza, *Von Anderen und Mir*, pp. 273–75.

4 FD, "The Anti-Slavery Movement," January 1855, in *Life and Writings of FD*, ed. Foner, 2:354. See also Martin, *The Mind of FD*, p. 168; Rafia Zafir, "Franklinian Douglass: The Afro-American as Representative Man," in *FD*, ed. Sundquist, pp. 99–117.

5 Assing contributed 125 articles to the *Morgenblatt für gebildete Leser*, copies of which are in the Cotta Archive at the Schiller-Nationalmuseum/Deutsches Literaturarchiv, Cotta-Archiv (Stiftung der Stuttgarter Zeitung), in Marbach am Neckar, Germany. The *Morgenblatt* copies there were collected by the publisher himself: "Redaktionsexemplare der Zeitung." They contain handwritten notes in which individual journalists and contributors are identified and their royalties listed. In addition there are three lengthy manuscripts of articles the *Morgenblatt* did not publish, probably out of fear of German censorship regulations; these manuscripts are also at the Schiller-Nationalmuseum/Deutsches Literaturarchiv, Nachlass Hauff-Kölle. As marked, most translations of Assing's *Morgenblatt* articles and manuscripts are by Christoph Lohmann.

6 OA to FD. 14 September 1878. FDP. LC.

7 OA, "Last Will and Testament," 7 April 1883. Surrogate's Office, County of Hudson, New Jersey. FDP. LC.

8 See Hermann C. Kudlich to FD. 18 July 1885. FDP. LC.

9 Gates, Jr., *Figures in Black*, p. 116. See also De Pietro, "Vision and Revision in the Autobiographies of FD," pp. 384 ff; Matlack, "The Autobiographies of FD," pp. 15 ff.; and Tuttleton, "The Many Lives of FD," pp. 16 ff.

10 Walker, *Moral Choices*, p. 212.

11 Gay, *Education of the Senses*, p. 415.

12 See Favret, *Romantic Correspondence: Women, Politics and the Fiction of Letters*. See also Altman, *Epistolarity: Approaches to Form*; and Kaufman, *Discourse of Desire: Gender, Genre, and Epistolary Fiction*.

13 As Amanda Gilroy and W. M. Verhoeven write: "In any correspondence, each writer is also a reader, and every reader is a writer; to read and write about letter writing is to join the process of deciphering that goes on *within* the correspondence, and to (re)construct the subjectivities that are in circulation." A. Gilroy and W. M. Verhoeven, "Introduction," in *Correspondence: A Special Issue on Letters. Prose Studies* 19:2 (August 1997), p. 126.

14 See Gay, *The Naked Heart*

15 On constructions of the "self," see Benstock, ed., *The Private Self: Theory and Practice of Women's Autobiographical Writings*.

16 On the concept of the "other" see Said, *Orientalism*.

17 OA to LA. 27 January, 26 March 1874. VC. BJK.

18 See Johnson, "Twisted Trust," p. 40.

19 Mehegan, "Scenes from the Lives: the Seductions of Biography," p. N34.

20 *Mb* 263, October 1851, p. 1051. CA. DLA. Trans. Chr. Lohmann.

21 Walker, *Moral Choices*, p. 254.

22 See OA, "Last Will and Testament," 9 November 1871. Surrogate's Office, County of Hudson, New Jersey. FDP. LC.

23 FD quoted in McFeely, *FD*, p. 319.

24 "Fred Douglass," *RDUA*, 7 June 1872, p. 3.

25 Reports even spoke of thirty years! See McFeely, *FD*, p. 319.

26 See Homberger and Charmley, eds., *The Troubled Face of Biography*; Machann, *The Genre of Autobiography in Victorian Literature*; and Nadel, *Biography: Fiction, Fact and Form*.

27 Walker, *Moral Choices*, p. 222.

28 See Hahn, "Suche alle meine Briefe: Die wiederaufgefundene Sammlung Varnhagen"; Hertz, "Die Varnhagen Collection ist in Krakow."

29 See Stern, *Die Varnhagen von Ensesche Sammlung in der Königlichen Bibliothek zu Berlin*.

30 Hertz, p. 224. The music collection contained manuscripts by Mozart, Beethoven, Bruckner, Brahms, Mendelssohn, Haydn, and Schubert.

31 See Pickett, "The Friendship of FD with the German OA," *Georgia Historical Quarterly* 7:3 (Spring 1989), pp. 88–105; "Perspectives on a National Crisis: A German Correspondent Reports on America, 1853–1865," *Tamkang Journal of American Studies* 4:3 (Spring 1988), pp. 5–15; and *The Unseasonable Democrat K. A. Varnhagen von Ense* (1985).

32 See Dick, "Eine geistreiche Plauderin: OA," in *Deutsch-jüdische Geschichte im 19. und 20. Jahrhundert*, eds. Heid and Knoll, pp. 463–86; Dick and Hahn, eds., *Von einer Welt in die andere: Jüdinnen im 19. und 20. Jahrhundert*; Dick, "Freundinnen: Rahel de Castro,

Ludmilla Assing, Ottilie Assing"; and "Wie Sie sicher von Fräulein Rahel de Castro wissen . . . ," in *Die Sefarden in Hamburg*, ed. Studemund-Halévy and Koj, pp. 383–414; Felden, *Frauen Reisen*; and Wagner, ed., *Was die Deutschen aus Amerika berichten*.

33 See Garvey and Ignatiev, eds., *Race Traitor*. McFeely, *FD*, p. 320.

34 Lorimer, "Race, Science and Culture: Historical Continuities and Discontinuities, 1850–1919," in *The Victorians and Race*, ed. West, p. 12.

35 Walker, *Moral Choices*, p. 224.

36 Golden, "Introduction," in *Skin Deep*, eds. Golden and Shreve, p. 3.

I. A MOUNT CALVARY OF JOY:
Ottilie Assing's Childhood and Youth

1 The following information on Rosa Maria Assing's final months is taken from the Assing family letters, VC, BJK, and from KG, "Rosa Maria."

2 Rosa Maria Varnhagen, "Frühling," *Musenalmanach auf das Jahr 1806*, p. 81.

3 KG, "Rosa Maria," p. 291.

4 In his autobiographies Douglass gave 1818 as his birth year; later he claimed 1817. Dickinson J. Preston, relying on Aaron Anthony's slave records, lists February 1818. Other Douglass biographers have accepted this date. See Preston, *Young FD*, p. 31.

5 FD, *LTFD*, p. 481.

6 FD, *MBMF*, p. 155.

7 McFeely speculates that either Aaron Anthony, his son-in-law Thomas, or Mr. Stewart could have fathered Frederick. *FD*, p. 13.

8 FD, *MBMF*, p. 172.

9 For information on Varnhagen von Ense and the Varnhagen family see VvE, *Denkwürdigkeiten*, 1: ch. 1; Pickett, *The Unseasonable Democrat*, ch. 1.

10 VvE, *Denkwürdigkeiten*, 1:41.

11 On the French Revolution and its effect on concepts of womanhood, see Schmidt-Linsenhoff, ed., *Sklavin oder Bürgerin: Französische Revolution und neue Weiblichkeit*.

12 See Hebbel, *Tagebücher*, 4:293.

13 See Kopitzsch, *Grundzüge einer Sozialgeschichte der Aufklärung in Hamburg und Altona*; Kaplan, *The Making of the Jewish Middle Class*.

14 See VvE, *Denkwürdigkeiten*, 1; Pickett, *The Unseasonable Democrat*, p. 14.

15 In the decades after the Revolution, approximately 40,000 French refugees lived in Hamburg, among them Madame de Genlis, Countess Flahout, the Duc de Rochefoucauld, General Valenze, the Duc d'Aiguillon, and the Comtesse Sopie Tott. See Wehl, *Hamburgs Literaturleben*, pp. 280 ff.

16 On Amalie Schoppe, see Schleucher, *Das Leben der Amalie Schoppe*.

17 Amalie Schoppe to Justinus Kerner, 5 January 1811, in *Kerners Briefwechsel*, ed. Kerner, 1:173.

18 Justinus Kerner wrote to Ludwig Uhland in April 1810: "Amalie . . . is the girl who once fell so deeply in love, she has now deserted her groom and has returned to Rosa," *Kerners Briefwechsel*, 1:125.

19 Kerner quoted in Schleucher, *Das Leben der Amalie Schoppe*, p. 26. The "we" are Kerner, Rosa Maria, her brother Varnhagen von Ense, Uhland, and Chamisso.

20 Rosa Maria Varnhagen, "Romanze," in *Rosa Maria's poetischer Nachlass*, p. 5.

21 *Rosa Maria's poetischer Nachlass*, p. 1.

22 Rosa Maria Varnhagen, "Frühlingslied," in *Rosa Maria's poetischer Nachlass*, pp. 23–24.

23 Rosa Maria Varnhagen, "Meinem Bruder den 21 Februar 1806," in *Rosa Maria's poetischer Nachlass*, p. 11.

24 Rosa Maria Varnhagen, "Verluste," in *Rosa Maria's poetischer Nachlass*, p. 15.

25 For information on Jews in Preussen and Königsberg, see Bruer, *Geschichte der Juden in Preussen*; Jolowicz, *Geschichte der Juden in Königsberg*.

26 Lewald, *The Education of Fanny Lewald*, pp. 3–4.

27 Lewald, *Education*, p. 3.

28 Lewald, *Education*, p. 4.

29 Some sources also name the University of Göttingen. His dissertation was published in Göttingen. *Lexikon deutsch-jüdischer Autoren* 1:216. *Lexikon der hamburgischen Schriftsteller*, 1:105.

30 See Sorkin, *Transformation*, pp. 60 ff.

31 Meyer, *Origins of the Modern Jew*, p. 55. See also Breuer, *The Limits of Enlightenment*.

32 Meyer, *Origins of the Modern Jew*, p. 87.

33 RMA, "Der Schornsteinfeger," in *Rosa Maria's poetischer Nachlass*, p. 230.

34 On Rahel Levin Varnhagen, see Arendt, *Rahel Varnhagen*; Stern, *Der Text meines Herzens*; Tewarson, *Rahel Varnhagen*; Lowenstein, *The Berlin Jewish Community*.

35 See Gallois, *Geschichte der Stadt Hamburg*, p. 594.

36 Ludwig Uhland to Justinus Kerner, 24 August 1811; Ludwig Uhland to August Mayer, 16 August 1812, in *Uhlands Briefwechsel*, ed. Hartmann, pp. 259, 325. See Gilman, *Rasse, Sexualität und Seuche*, pp. 181 ff.

37 See Lewald, *Education*, p. 10.

38 Wehl, *Hamburgs Literaturleben*, pp. 21–22. See also Zimmermann, *Hamburgischer Patriotismus*, pp. 15 ff.

39 The community included Jews of the city of Hamburg with those in the towns of Altona and Wandsbek. See Herzig, "Die Juden in Hamburg, 1780–1860," in *Juden in Hamburg*, ed. Herzig, p. 62. See also Davis, *Women on the Margins*, p. 9; Freimark, *Juden in Preussen, Juden in Hamburg*; Freimark, Lorenz, and Merwedel, *Judentore, Kuggel, Steuerkonten*; Krohn, *Die Juden in Hamburg*; Whaley, *Religious Toleration and Social Change in Hamburg*, pp. 70 ff. See Marwedel, "Die aschkenasischen Juden in Hamburg, 1780–1860," in *Juden in Hamburg*, ed. Herzig, pp. 45 ff.; and Marwedel, ed., *Die Privilegien der Juden in Altona*.

40 RMA to Justinus Kerner, in *Kerners Briefwechsel*, ed. Kerner, 1:271–72.

41 Rosa Maria Varnhagen, "Abschied und Bündniss," in *Rosa Maria's poetischer Nachlass*, p. 43.

42 See Zlocisti, *Mitwirkung der Juden an der freiwilligen Krankenpflege*, pp. 17 f.

43 See Lange, "Die christlich-jüdische Ehe. Ein deutscher Streit im 19. Jahrhundert."

44 See Tewarson, *Rahel Varnhagen*, pp. 105 ff.

45 Gustav Schwab to Justinus Kerner, 25 November 1815, in *Kerners Briefwechsel*, ed. Kerner, 1:415.

46 RMA, "Auf mein früh gestorbenes Kind," in *Rosa Maria's poetischer Nachlass*, p. 49.

47 Amalie Schoppe to Justinus Kerner, July 1819, in *Kerners Briefwechsel*, ed. Kerner, 1:487.

48 See Hipp, *Freie und Hansestadt Hamburg*, pp. 196 ff.

49 RMA, "An Assing. Den 12. December 1824," in *Rosa Maria's poetischer Nachlass*, p. 50.

50 RMA, "An Assing. Den 5. April 1825," in *Rosa Maria's poetischer Nachlass*, p. 51.

51 OA to VvE. 10 February 1840. VC. BJK.

52 RMA's diaries are in the Varnhagen Collection in Krakow (BJK).

53 RMA in her diary, 1 January 1827. VC. BJK. In nineteenth-century literature and painting a woman's open hair was read as a sign of seductiveness, abandonment, and unruliness. See Westhoff-Krummacher, *Als die Frauen noch sanft und engelsgleich waren*, pp. 322 ff.

54 These diaries are in the Varnhagen Collection in Krakow (BJK). It is likely that Ottilie, too, kept a diary. Her personal reminiscences were probably part of the papers which the executor of her will, Dr. Kudlich, destroyed after her death.

55 KG, "J. D. Assing," in *Gesammelte Werke*, p. 306.

56 See Sollors, *Neither Black Nor White*, pp. 133 ff.

57 Gay, *Education of the Senses*, p. 444.

58 KG, "J. D. Assing," p. 315.

59 See H. L. Malchow, "The half-breed as Gothic unnatural," in *The Victorians and Race*, ed. West, p. 104.

60 See Gallois, *Geschichte der Stadt Hamburg*, p. 598.

61 KG, "Rosa Maria," pp. 292, 300, 299.

62 KG, "J. D. Assing," p. 310.

63 Lewald, *The Education*, p. 256.

64 See de Castro, *Grundrisse der Geschichte der Familie de Castro*; Studemundt-Halévy and Koj, eds., *Die Sefarden in Hamburg*; Dick, "Rahel de Castro"; Schoeps et al., eds., *Salomon Ludwig Steinheim*; Dick and Schoeps, eds., *Salomon Ludwig Steinheim und Johanna Steinheim: Briefe*, pp. 7–19.

65 See Davis, *Women on the Margins*, p. 204.

66 Wehl, *Zeit und Menschen*, 2:3.

67 OA to VvE. 12 September 1835. VC. BJK.

68 "I think that we really were not at all long enough in Paris," she wrote. OA to VvE. 12 September 1835. VC. BJK.

69 RMA, "Die Wahrsagerin," in *Rosa Maria's poetischer Nachlass*, p. 108.

70 KG, "Rosa Maria," pp. 297–98.

71 RMA, "Fahrt auf dem Rhein," in *Rosa Maria's poetischer Nachlass*, p. 62.

72 See Christiansen, *Romantic Affinities*, p. 58.

73 RMA, "Das Fräulein und der Fischer," in *Rosa Maria's poetischer Nachlass*, p. 76.

74 Wehl, *Zeit und Menschen*, 2:5. See Hertz, *Jewish High Society in Old Regime Berlin*.

75 See KG, *Rückblicke*, pp. 115 ff. See also Tiggemann, "Familiensolidarität, Leistung und

Luxus: Familien der Hamburger jüdischen Oberschicht im 19. Jahrhundert," in *Juden in Hamburg*, ed. Herzig, p. 425.

76 Quoted in Zimmermann, *Hamburgischer Patriotismus*, pp. 23 f.

77 On the relationship between place and space, see Tuan, *Space and Place*, p. 3.

78 See Wehl, *Zeit und Menschen*, 2:2.

79 KG, "J. D. Assing," p. 307.

80 See Harris, *David Friedrich Strauss and His Theology*; Steven Gillies, "Strauss, David Friedrich," in *Metzler Philosophen Lexikon*, pp. 757–60.

81 KG, *Rückblicke*, p. 140.

82 See Werner Jung, "Ruge, Arnold," in *Metzler Philosophen Lexikon*, pp. 670–72.

83 SSt to LA and OA. 26 April 1843, in *Steinheim Briefe*, eds. Dick and Schoeps, pp. 203–4.

84 KG, "J. D. Assing," p. 311.

85 These letters are in the Varnhagen Collection in Krakow (BJK).

86 See Herzig, *Die Juden in Hamburg*, p. 71; Zimmermann, *Hamburgischer Patriotismus*, pp. 33 ff.

87 Quoted in *Steinheim zum Gedenken*, ed. Schoeps, p. 13 n. 30. See also Meyer, *German Political Pressure and Jewish Religious Response*.

88 KG, *Rückblicke*, p. 115

89 See Houben, ed., *Gutzkow-Funde*, p. 263; and Zimmermann, *Hamburgischer Patriotismus*, pp. 36 ff.

90 KG, *Uriel Acosta*, in Houben, ed., *Gutzkow-Funde*, p. 311.

91 RMA, "Distichen," in *Rosa Maria's poetischer Nachlass*, p. 135.

92 RMA, "Rückblick," in *Rosa Maria's poetischer Nachlass*, p. 132.

93 OA to VvE. 10 February 1840. VC. BJK.

94 See LA to VvE. 4 April 1840. VC. BJK.

95 Zeise, *Leben und Erinnerungen eines norddeutschen Poeten*, p. 48.

96 Zeise, *Leben und Erinnerungen*, p. 50.

97 DA to VvE. 10 February [no year]. VC. BJK.

98 *Rosa Maria's poetischer Nachlass*, unpaginated.

99 LA to VvE. 11 April 1842. VC. BJK.

100 See LA to VvE. 25 April 1842. VC. BJK.

101 OA to VvE. 30 April 1842. VC. BJK.

II. IF ONLY I WERE A BIRD: Vagrant Years

1 OA, "Transatlantische Briefe: Von Hamburg nach New York," *Jahreszeiten*, November 1852, p. 1596.

2 See Zimmermann, *Hamburgischer Patriotismus*, p. 79.

3 OA to VvE. 12 May 1842. VC. BJK.

4 OA to VvE. 12 May 1842. VC. BJK.

5 See SSt's letters to OA and LA, in *Steinheim Briefe*, ed. Dick and Schoeps, pp. 176–266.

6 OA to VvE. 12 May 1842. VC. BJK.

7 OA to VvE. 21 May 1842. VC. BJK.

8 OA to VvE. 27 June 1842. VC. BJK.

9 See OA to VvE. 27 August 1842. VC. BJK.

10 Alexander von Sternberg, *Erinnerungsblätter*, ed. Kühn, pp. 186 ff.

11 VvE to Justinus Kerner, summer of 1842, in *Kerners Briefwechsel*, ed. Kerner, 2:220.

12 OA to VvE. 25 June 1842. VC. BJK.

13 Theodore Mundt's anti-Semitism surfaced especially in his correspondence with his wife. Thus the self-professed liberal preferred to be lonely during a vacation in Paris rather than to associate with old friends who "have teamed up with another Jewish clan . . . , which makes it impossible for me to join them." Theodor Mundt to Clara Mundt, 14 August 1851, in Ebersberger, ed., *Erinnerungblätter*, p. 290.

14 See Mackowsky, "Rahels Haus Mauerstrasse 36."

15 Lewald, *Lebensgeschichte*, 3:200–2.

16 Quoted in Dick, "OAs Aufbruch in die Neue Welt," p. 126.

17 OA to KG. 11 January 1847, quoted in Dick, "Eine geistreiche Plauderin: OA," p. 481.

18 Wehl, *Zeit und Menschen*, 2:1.

19 Julius Rodenberg, quoted in Bebler, *Keller und Assing*, p. 30.

20 When Varnhagen spent an evening with Dore and his dog, Bello, Ludmilla noted in her diary: "A hundred times I ask myself whether I am really so evil to deserve that he prefers this old woman to me; my self-confidence oscillates continuously, and I am often desperate." LA in her diary, entry of 29 April 1843. VC. BJK. See also Dick, "Freundinnen," pp. 189 ff.

21 Pickett, *The Unseasonable Democrat*, p. 8.

22 Lewald, *Lebensgeschichte*, 3:206.

23 Clara and Theodor Mundt, quoted in Wehl, *Zeit und Menschen*, 2:193.

24 Engels quoted in Pickett, *The Unseasonable Democrat*, p. 10.

25 Lewald, *Gefühltes und Gedachtes*, pp. 44–45.

26 OA to KG. 6 August 1843. VC. BJK.

27 OA to KG. 21 September 1842. KGP. SUBF.

28 LA to FW. 6 August 1853. VC. BJK.

29 Riehl, quoted in Gay, *Education of the Senses*, p. 435.

30 OA to KG. 6 August 1843. VC. BJK.

31 See Lewald, *The Education of Fanny Lewald*; Möhrmann, *Die andere Frau*, pp. 118–40. See also Lewis, "Fanny Lewald and George Sand"; Steinhauer, *Fanny Lewald, die deutsche George Sand*.

32 See Möhrmann, *Die andere Frau*, pp. 60–84.

33 Clara Mundt to LA. 10 June 1845. VC. BJK.

34 See Varnhagen's letters of 7 November 1843 and 5 November 1846 to Justinus Kerner, in *Justinus Kerners Briefwechsel*, ed. Kerner. See also Cocalis, "Der Vormund will Vormund sein: Zur Problematik der weiblichen Unmündigkeit im 18. Jahrhundert."

35 Detailed, though secondhand, reports can be found in Hebbel, *Tagebücher*, 5:81–82, and Wehl, *Zeit und Menschen*, 1:99. Hebbel's information came from Amalie Schoppe; it is likely that Wehl heard the story from either the Mundts or Ludmilla.

36 *Mb* 30 June 1857, p. 720. CA. DLA.

37 Hebbel, *Tagebücher*, 5:82.

38 LA to SSt. 12 October 1843. VC. BJK.

39 Georg Schirges to OA and LA. 29 January 1843. VC. BJK.

40 Georg Schirges to LA. 19 February 1843. VC. BJK.

41 SSt to OA and LA. 26 April 1843, in *Steinheim Briefe*, ed. Dick and Schoeps, pp. 203, 204.

42 LA to FW. 9 June 1845. VC. BJK.

43 LA to FW. 24 August 1846. VC. BJK.

44 LA to VvE. 24 August 1846. VC. BJK.

45 LA to FW. 24 August 1846. VC. BJK.

46 OA to KG. 14 November 1846. KGP. SUBF.

47 LA to FW. 7 September 1846. VC. BJK.

48 SSt to LA and OA. 16 August 1843, in *Steinheim Briefe*, ed. Dick and Schoeps, p. 209.

49 Emilie Nickert to LA. 7 May 1857. VC. BJK.

50 For an analysis of the nineteenth-century fascination with hypocrisy, see Gay, *Education of the Senses*, ch. 6.

51 Wehl, *Hamburgs Literaturleben*, pp. 192–94.

52 OA, *Baison*, p. 85.

53 OA, *Baison*, p. 32.

54 Amalie Schoppe to LA. 27 February 1848. VC. BJK.

55 KG quoted in Wehl, *Das Junge Deutschland*, p. 176.

56 LA to FW. Undated (but 1846). VC. BJK.

57 OA, *Baison*, p. 101.

58 OA, *Baison*, p. 1.

59 OA, *Baison*, p. 2.

60 OA, *Baison*, p. 54.

61 LA to FW. 24 August 1846. VC. BJK.

62 OA to KG. 28 January 1847. KGP. SUBF.

63 Rahel Varnhagen in her diary in 1803, quoted in Tewarson, *Rahel Varnhagen*, p. 62.

64 See Möhrmann, *Die andere Frau*, pp. 10 ff.

65 See Vordtriede, ed., *Therese von Bacheracht und Karl Gutzkow: Unveröffentlichte Briefe*.

66 See Janssen, *Die Frauen rings um Friedrich Hebbel*.

67 Lewald, *Clementine* (1843), p. 24, quoted in Lewald, *The Education*, p. 225.

68 Lewald, *Römisches Tagebuch 1845–46*; also *Gefühltes und Gedachtes* (1900).

69 Lewald, *The Education*, pp. 127–28.

70 Gay, *Education of the Senses*, p. 410.

71 Amalie Schoppe to LA. 27 February 1848. VC. BJK.

72 Clara de Castro to LA. 20 February 1847. VC. BJK.

73 LA to VvE. 18 August 1847. VC. BJK.

74 For an analysis of this tradition see Lea, *Emancipation, Assimilation and Stereotype: The Image of the Jew in German and Austrian Drama*.

75 See LA to FW. 28 February 1847. VC. BJK.

76 OA, *Baison*, p. 69.

77 See LA to FW. 26 April 1848. VC. BJK.

78 This information was set forth by Ottilie's cousin Emilie Nickert, then living in Brooklyn, to LA. 10 October 1853. VC. BJK.

79 See Uhde, *Das Stadttheater in Hamburg*, pp. 235 ff. In a letter of 25 January 1849 Rahel de Castro wrote to Ludmilla Assing: "So far I know nothing—Ottilie has confessed nothing to me, and that the whole world insists that Baison had her money and it is now lost—that is an old city gossip, now revived, but nobody can know the real truth in it." VC. BJK. Dick, "Rahel de Castro," p. 407.

80 See Wittke, *Refugees of Revolution*, pp. 18 ff.

81 See Grab and Schoeps, eds., *Juden im Vormärz und in der Revolution von 1848*, and Tatlock, "The Young Germans in Praise of Famous Women: Ambivalent Advocates."

82 OA, *Baison*, pp. 97–98.

83 See LA to FW. Undated. VC. BJK.

84 Amalie Schoppe to LA. 28 January 1849. VC. BJK.

85 See LA to FW. 27 March 1849. VC. BJK.

86 LA to VvE. 10 July 1849. VC. BJK.

87 OA to KG. 10 April 1849. KGP. SUBF.

88 See Uhde, *Das Stadttheater*, p. 98: "The author was Ottilie Assing . . . an elder sister of the notorious Ludmilla."

89 Ludmilla's maternal friend Johanna Steinheim, who had known about the relationship and who was familiar with the Assing-Varnhagen tradition, wrote to her: "You have lost a reliable friend, and your obituary proves how much you loved him. When I heard of his death, I immediately assumed that you would honor his memory in that way." JSt to LA. 16 June 1868. VC. BJK.

90 LA to JSt. 20 May 1850, in *Salomon Ludwig Steinheim*, ed. Dick and Schoeps, p. 304. See also LA to FW. 12 February 1850. VC. BJK.

91 LA to VvE. 17 June 1852. VC. BJK.

92 LA to VvE. 16 July 1852. VC. BJK.

93 See Höfle, *Cottas Morgenblatt für gebildete Stände*; Lohrer, *Cotta: Geschichte eines Verlags*.

94 OA to Carl Cotta. Nachlass Hauff-Kölle. DLA.

95 The journalism which the Cottas claimed to encourage was, as they stated in one of their programmatic remarks, "pure, manly." Lohrer, *Cotta*, p. 79.

96 This information was provided by Dr. Bernhard Fischer from the Schiller Nationalmuseum in Marbach, Germany.

97 See Geiger and Weigel, *Sind das noch Damen?*, p. 8.

98 See Amalie Schoppe to LA. 27 October 1850. VC. BJK.

99 See *Mb* 195, July 1851, pp. 783–85. CA. DLA.

100 *Mb* 4, January 1852, p. 91. CA. DLA.

101 See Grab and Schoeps, eds., *Juden im Vormärz und in der Revolution von 1848*.

102 KG quoted in *Gutzkow-Funde*, ed. Houben, pp. 279–80.

103 JSt to LA. January 1855. VC. BJK.

104 LA to VvE. 16 July 1852. VC. BJK.

105 See LA to VvE. 6 August 1852. VC. BJK.

106 See LA to VvE. 31 July 1852 and 14 August 1852. VC. BJK.

107 See Stout, *The Journey Narrative*, pp. 30, 91.

108 See Tocqueville, *Democracy in America*, 2:404.

109 Commager, "Introduction," to Tocqueville, *Democracy*, 1:xiv.

110 See Bauschinger, Denkler, and Malsch, eds., *Amerika in der deutschen Literatur*; Meyer, *Nordamerika im Urteil des deutschen Schrifttums*; Mikoletzky, *Die deutsche Amerika-Auswanderung des 19. Jahrhunderts in der zeitgenössischen fiktionalen Literatur*; Schüppen, ed., *Neue Sealsfield Studien*; Weber, *America in Imaginative German Literature*; Barba, "Emigration to America as Reflected in German Fiction"; Bausch, "America in German Fiction."

111 Humboldt had defined his position on natural rights as early as 1845 in his major work, *Kosmos*. See Foner, ed., *Alexander von Humboldt über die Sklaverei in den USA*. The Douglass Library contains several volumes of Humboldt's writings.

112 From Rahel de Castro's letters to Ludmilla we know that she and her friends read and discussed Stowe's novel in English only months after its publication, and Assing discussed her response to it retrospectively in letters to Ludmilla of 15 October 1869 and 5 January 1870. The travel plans for Haiti which she made in the mid- and late 1850s reflect on her fascination with the Haitian revolution. See *Mb* 23, May 1861, p. 548. CA. DLA. Also OA to KG. 27 April 1855. KGP. SUBF; RdC to LA. 5 May 1855 and 11 December 1855. VC. BJK.

113 Mundt, *Aphra Behn*, 1:55.

114 Mundt, *Aphra Behn*, 1:245. Mundt's male protagonist is called Oronooko, while the black protagonist of Aphra Behn's novel of 1688 is Oroonoko. I will follow these spellings, using "Oroonoko" when I refer to Aphra Behn's text and "Oronooko" when I speak of Mundt's text.

115 See Sollors, *Neither Black Nor White*, ch. 6.

116 See Möhrmann, *Die andere Frau*, pp. 79 ff.; Joeres, "1848 from a Distance: German Women Writers on the Revolution."

117 See McFeely, *FD*, ch. 13.

118 *Mb* 51. June 1857, p. 718. Trans. Chr. Lohmann.

119 LA to VvE. 22 June 1852. VC. BJK.

120 Mundt, *Aphra Behn*, 1:244.

III. PILGRIM-FOOL: American Beginnings

1 Ottilie Assing recorded the following events in *Mb* 46, August 1855, pp. 1212–17.

2 RMA, "Die Flüsse," in *Rosa Maria's poetischer Nachlass*, p. 133.

3 RMA, "Wanderlied," in *Rosa Maria's poetischer Nachlass*, p. 80.

4 Assing's following comments on this trip are from her "Transatlantische Briefe I," *Jahreszeiten*, November 1852, 1505–12.

5 On the construction of difference, see Scott, "The Evidence of Experience," pp. 773–97.

6 On the phenomenon of moving from one identity to another, see Stonequist, *Marginal Man*, pp. 97 ff.; Sollors, *Neither Black Nor White*, ch. 9.

7 On the relationship between German Jews in the United States and other German immigrants, see Cohen, *Encounter with Emancipation*, pp. 58 ff.; Nadel, "Jewish Race and German Soul in Nineteenth-Century America."

8 OA, "Transatlantische Briefe I," *Jahreszeiten*, November 1852, 1505–12.

9 See Bretting, "Die Konfrontation der deutschen Einwanderer mit der amerikanischen Wirklichkeit," p. 320; Gabaccia, *From the Other Side: Women, Gender and Immigrant Life*; Seller, *Immigrant Women*; Bergland, "Immigrant History and the Gendered Subject."

10 See LA to VvE. 14 August 1852. VC. BJK.

11 LA to FW. 25 August 1853. VC. BJK. In the nineteenth century letters were usually not regarded as the strictly private property of the person to whom they were addressed but as property of the community within which that person moved. Letter writers thus often attached confidential "private" notes to their "public" letters. Ottilie's friends and relatives expected Madame Baison to circulate her letters among them, but the actress was still too hurt by the haughtiness and outright disrespect with which they had treated her to comply; when she did, she requested the recipients to return them to her. (See Caroline Baison to LA. 18 October 1852. VC. BJK.) It also appears that she was careless with the articles Ottilie sent her; manuscripts might have been discarded, or they simply disappeared in the chaos for which the Baison household was notorious. Another woman to whom Ottilie occasionally wrote was Rahel de Castro, who also received reports on Ottilie through her brother Joseph, then living in New York. And as Rahel was also on good terms with Ludmilla, we derive some secondhand information on Ottilie's adventures from her letters to Ludmilla; Rahel also forwarded the few letters Ottilie addressed to her sister, but Ludmilla must either have discarded them or returned them to Rahel. None was preserved. Neither Caroline Baison's nor Rahel de Castro's descendants collected or preserved their papers. Another fairly reliable source of information on Ottilie's first American years is letters which her cousin from Strasbourg, Emilie Nickert, who also emigrated to the United States in 1852, wrote regularly to Ludmilla Assing.

12 See Helbich, *Alle Menschen sind dort gleich*.

13 See Kapp, *Immigration and the Commissioners of Emigration in the State of New York*, pp. 5 ff.

14 See Emilie Nickert to LA. 7 May 1857. VC. BJK.

15 OA to ? Remde. 24 November 1852. VC. BJK.

16 RdC to LA. 23 November 1852. VC. BJK.

17 See New York City Directories 1851 to 1853–54. Reel A14.

18 See RdC to LA. 11 December 1855. VC. BJK.

19 OA described Schoppe and her American home in *Mb* 51, October 1853, pp. 1221–22. CA. DLA.

20 See Danton, "Amalie Weise Schoppe," pp. 428 ff.; Schleucher, *Das Leben der Amalie Schoppe*, pp. 409 ff. From Schoppe's letters to Ludmilla we know that Ottilie wrote regularly to her, but none of these letters survives. Alphons Schoppe destroyed some of her papers at his mother's death; others burned in 1874. The records of Union College contain no Schoppe items relating to Assing.

21 OA, "Transatlantische Briefe II," *Jahreszeiten* 1:4. 20 January 1853, p. 106.

22 RdC to LA. 8 September 1854. VC. BJK.

23 Rosa Maria described these visits in great detail in letters to David Assing. See VC. BJK.

24 LA to VvE. 14 August 1852. VC. BJK.

25 See Emilie Nickert to LA. 10 October 1853. VC. BJK.

26 See Löher, "Talvj: Ein deutsches Frauenleben." Voigt, "The Life and Works of Mrs. Therese Robinson." Smith and Hitchcock, *The Life, Writing and Character of Edward Robinson.*

27 See Therese Robinson to VvE. 23 March 1854. VC. BJK.

28 See RdC to LA. 24 April and 20 June 1853. VC. BJK.

29 See Robinson, *Fünfzehn Jahre* (1868).

30 See Amalie Schoppe to LA. 6 October 1853. VC. BJK.

31 The criticism of the American boardinghouse Ottilie gave in the *Morgenblatt* was scathing. See *Mb* 19, 1855, pp. 448–51. CA. DLA.

32 Amalie Schoppe to LA. 6 October 1853. VC. BJK.

33 For a description of nineteenth-century New York City, see Pye, *Maximum City: The Biography of New York.*

34 See Pelz, *Reisen durch die eigene Fremde*; Russell, *The Blessings of a Good Thick Skirt.*

35 *Mb* 45, 1855, p. 1071. CA. DLA. Trans. Chr. Lohmann.

36 See Dorah Epstein Nord, "The Social Explorer as Anthropologist: Victorian Travellers Among the Urban Poor," in *Visions of the Modern City*, ed. Sharpe and Wallock, pp. 118–30; Blumin, "Explaining the New Metropolis," pp. 18 ff. For an analysis of this approach, see Pittenger, "A World of Difference: Constructing the 'Underclass' in Progressive America," pp. 26 ff.

37 *Mb* 17, March 1858, pp. 404–5. CA. DLA. Trans. Chr. Lohmann. See also Suhl, *Eloquent Crusader: Ernestine Rose*; Eiseman, *Rebels and Reformers.*

38 OA to KG. 27 April 1855. KGP. SUBF.

39 *Mb* 51, October 1853, p. 1221. CA. DLA. Trans. Chr. Lohmann.

40 *Mb* 51, October 1853, p. 1221. CA. DLA. Trans. Chr. Lohmann.

41 On Niagara Falls, *Mb* 52, October 1853, p. 1244. CA. DLA.

42 *Mb* 52, October 1853, p. 1244. CA. DLA.

43 *Mb* 52, October 1853, p. 1245. CA. DLA.

44 Hildebrand, *Sheboygan County*, p. 9. See also Leberman, *One Hundred Years of Sheboygan.*

45 See Hildebrand, *Sheboygan County*, p. 29.

46 *Mb* 2, December 1853, p. 48. CA. DLA. Trans. Chr. Lohmann.

47 *Mb* 3, December 1853, p. 71. CA. DLA. Trans. Chr. Lohmann.

48 *Mb* 3, December 1853, p. 71. CA. DLA. Trans. Chr. Lohmann.

49 On the impact of Lamarckianism, see Stocking, *Race, Culture, and Evolution*, pp. 234–69.

50 *Mb* 3, December 1853, p. 71. CA. DLA. Trans. Chr. Lohmann.

51 OA to KG. Undated, but 1854. KGP. SUBF.

52 *Mb* 3, December 1853, p. 71. CA. DLA. Trans. Chr. Lohmann.

53 *Mb* 3, December 1853, p. 71. CA. DLA. Trans. Chr. Lohmann.

54 *Mb* 29, June 1854, p. 692. CA. DLA. Trans. Chr. Lohmann.

55 *Mb* 29, June 1854, p. 693. CA. DLA. Trans. Chr. Lohmann.

56 *Mb* 30, June 1854, p. 720. CA. DLA. Trans. Chr. Lohmann.

57 Emilie Nickert to LA. 10 October 1853. VC. BJK.

58 *Mb* 45, 1855, pp. 1070, 1071. CA. DLA. Trans. Chr. Lohmann. Letters from Schoppe and Nickert to Ludmilla Assing confirm that Ottilie indeed worked as a seamstress in the winter of 1854–55. Assing frequently used the persona of "a young lady" to describe adventures with which she did not want to be associated.

59 See RdC to LA. 20 February 1855. VC. BJK.

60 See RdC to LA. 20 February 1855. VC. BJK.

61 See Bruncken, "German Political Refugees in the United States"; Dobert, *Deutsche Demokraten in America*; Levine, *The Spirit of 1848*; Moltmann, ed., *Deutsche Amerikaauswanderung im 19. Jahrhundert*; Nadel, *Little Germany*; Wittke, *Refugees of Revolution*; Wust, *Guardians on the Hudson*; Zucker, ed., *The Forty-Eighters*; Lapham, "The German-Americans of New York City, 1860–1890"; Nadel, "From the Barricades of Paris to the Sidewalks of New York."

62 *Mb* 46, 1855, p. 1096. CA. DLA. Trans. Chr. Lohmann. See also Foster and Clark, eds. *Hoboken*; Cahalan, *Hoboken—A City in Transition*; Pelz, *New York und seine Umgebung*; Chambers, *The Early Germans of New Jersey*.

63 *Mb* 25, May 1857, p. 599. CA. DLA. Trans. Chr. Lohmann.

64 Bryant, *The American Landscape*, p. 7; Trollope, *Domestic Manners*, pp. 343 ff.

65 *Mb* 25, May 1857, p. 599. CA. DLA. Trans. Chr. Lohmann. See also Wilhelm F. Kroupa, "Hans Kudlich und seine Zeit," in *Festschrift zum 160. Geburtstag von Hans Kudlich*, p. 24.

66 See Dulon, *Aus Amerika: Über Schule*, pp. 170 ff.; Harris, "German Reform in American Education"; Arndt and Olsen, *Die deutschsprachige Presse der Amerikas*, vol. 1.

67 See Kudlich, *Rückblicke und Erinnerungen*; Prinz, *Hans Kudlich*, pp. 156 ff.; Seifert, *Der Bauernbefreier Hans Kudlich*, pp. 80 ff.; *Festschrift zum 160. Geburtstag*, pp. 24 ff. Dobert, *Die Schriften der deutsch-amerikanischen Achtundvierziger*, pp. 142–47.

68 *Mb* 46, 1855, p. 1096. CA. DLA. Trans. Chr. Lohmann.

69 See Kapp, *Aus und über Amerika; Geschichte der Sklaverei in den Vereinigten Staaten von Amerika; Geschichte der Deutschen im Staate New York;* Dobert, *Die Schriften der deutsch-amerikanischen Achtundvierziger*, pp. 120–30. See also the Kapp-Feuerbach correspondence in *Ludwig Feuerbach: Ausgewählte Briefe*, ed. Bolin, pp. 142 ff., 184, 187, 204; Bolin, *Ludwig Feuerbach: Sein Wirken und seine Zeitgenossen*.

70 Quoted in Bretting, "Die Konfrontation der deutschen Einwanderer mit der amerikanischen Wirklichkeit," p. 256.

71 Kapp quoted in Bolin, *Ludwig Feuerbach*, p. 190.

72 *Mb* 28, June 1859, p. 672. CA. DLA. Trans. Chr. Lohmann.

73 Feuerbach to Kapp, 31 March 1853, in *Feuerbach Briefe*, ed. Bolin, p. 204.

74 OA to KG. 27 April 1855. KGP. SUBF.

75 *Mb* 32, June 1854, p. 762. CA. DLA. Trans. Chr. Lohmann.

76 *Mb* 32, June 1854, p. 763. CA. DLA. Trans. Chr. Lohmann.

77 See RdC to LA. 25 May 1854. VC. BJK.

78 *Mb* 27, May 1853, p. 643. CA. DLA. Trans. Chr. Lohmann.

79 *Mb* 24, May 1853, p. 644. CA. DLA. Trans. Chr. Lohmann.

80 *Mb* 24, May 1853, pp. 644–45. CA. DLA. Trans. Chr. Lohmann.

81 *Mb* 51, October 1853, p. 1221. CA. DLA. Trans. Chr. Lohmann.

82 See Clyde, " 'A People Called Methodists,' " pp. 51–56.

83 *Mb* 49, August 1855, pp. 1214–15. CA. DLA. Trans. Chr. Lohmann.

84 *Mb* 49, August 1855, p. 1216. CA. DLA. Trans. Chr. Lohmann.

85 *Mb* 18, March 1856, p. 432. CA. DLA. Trans. Chr. Lohmann.

86 RdC to LA. 3 November 1855. VC. BJK.

87 OA to WLG. 8 March 1879. WLGP. BPL.

88 Painter, *Sojourner Truth*, p. 63. See also Freeman, "The Free Negro in New York City";
Walker, "The Afro-American in New York City."

89 See Thomas, *Pennington*, pp. 57 f.; Washington, *The First Fugitive Foreign and Domestic
Doctor of Divinity;* Swift, *Black Prophets of Justice*, pp. 204–43.

90 Thomas, *Pennington*, p. 180.

91 "Ehrenpromotion James W. C. Pennington" (trans.) in Thomas, *Pennington*, Appendix,
p. 185.

92 OA, "Die Farbigen in New York," unpublished ms. Nachlass Hauff-Kölle. DLA. [Unpaginated]

93 Pennington to OA. 3 August 1855. VC. BJK.

94 See *Mb* 18, March 1856, p. 432. CA. DLA.

95 *Mb* 18, March 1856, p. 432. CA. DLA. Trans. Chr. Lohmann.

96 *Mb* 18, March 1856, p. 432. CA. DLA. Trans. Chr. Lohmann.

97 Mary Waters offers a possible reading of this encounter when she writes: "Certain ancestries take precedence over others in the societal rules on descent and ancestry reckoning. If one believes one is part English and part German and identifies as German, one is not in danger of being accused of trying to 'pass' as non-English and of being 'redefined' English. . . . But if one were part African and part German, one's self-identification as German would be highly suspect and probably not accepted . . ." Waters, *Ethnic Options*, pp. 18–19.

98 *Mb* 18, March 1856, p. 432. CA. DLA. Trans. Chr. Lohmann.

99 McFeely, *FD*, p. 180.

100 RdC to LA. 3 November 1855. VC. BJK. Varnhagen included it in his collection of autographs, and it is still in the Varnhagen Collection.

101 OA, "Die Farbigen in New York." Nachlass Hauff-Kölle. DLA. Trans. Chr. Lohmann.

102 OA, "Die Farbigen in New York." Nachlass Hauff-Kölle. DLA. Trans. Chr. Lohmann.

103 See Thomas, *Pennington*, p. 58.

104 David Smith contends that Pennington was "evidently of pure African blood." Smith,
Black Prophets of Justice, p. 204.

105 OA, "Die Farbigen in New York." Nachlass Hauff-Kölle. DLA. Trans. Chr. Lohmann.

106 Quarles, "FD," p. 161.

107 See OA, "Die Farbigen in New York." Nachlass Hauff-Kölle. DLA.

108 Behn, *Oroonoko*, pp. 80–81.

109 Mundt, *Aphra Behn*, 1:14.

110 See Emilie Nickert to LA. 12 March 1856. VC. BJK.

111 *Mb* 46, 1856, p. 1097. CA. DLA. Trans. Chr. Lohmann.

112 *Mb* 46, 1856, p. 1167. CA. DLA. Trans. Chr. Lohmann.

IV. IRRESISTIBLE ATTRACTIVENESS AND DISTINCTION:
Appropriating Frederick Douglass

1 On the location of Douglass' home, see U.S. City Directory, Rochester, New York, 1861–81, Reel 1-1: Rochester 1861–65.

2 U.S. City Directory, Rochester, 1863, p. 36.

3 U.S. City Directory, Rochester, 1863, p. 36.

4 OA, "Vorrede," in FD, Sclaverei und Freiheit. Autobiographie von Frederick Douglass, p. xii. Trans. Chr. Lohmann.

5 The page numbers in the quotations following refer to this published "Vorrede."

6 Malchow, "The half-breed as Gothic unnatural," p. 101.

7 Baker, Jr., The Journey Back, p. 39.

8 OA, "Vorrede," p. xii. Trans. Chr. Lohmann. For an analysis of the mulatto as a literary stereotype, see Brown, "Negro Characters as Seen by White Authors," in The Negro Caravan, ed. Brown, Davis, and Lee, pp. 5 ff.; for a critique of Brown's position, see Sollors, Neither Black Nor White, ch. 8; Hortense Spillers, "Notes on an Alternative Model—Neither/Nor," in The Difference Within, ed. Meese and Parker, pp. 165–87.

9 See Painter, Sojourner Truth, p. 154.

10 OA, "Vorrede," p. xii. Trans. Chr. Lohmann.

11 In a dissertation on representations of the "mulatto" in Latin American literature, Carol Anne Beane distinguishes between the conservative model of the mulatto, associated with the past, and a more dynamic model that associated the mulatto with the future. See Beane, "The Characterization of Blacks and Mulattoes in Selected Novels from Colombia, Venezuela, Ecuador, and Peru," pp. 81 ff.

12 For a sophisticated analysis of this technique in abolitionist discourse, see Jenny Franchot, "The Punishment of Esther. FD and the Construction of the Feminine," in FD, ed. Sundquist, pp. 146 ff.

13 See FD, "The Question of Amalgamation," DM, December 1860, pp. 371–72.

14 Sollors, Neither Black Nor White, p. 102.

15 Ruth Frankenberg's The Social Construction of Whiteness: White Women, Race Matters suggests that "race blindness . . . camouflages socially significant differences of color in a welter of meaningless sameness" (p. 149) and averts issues of power. For new readings of the literary mulatto, see Simone Vauthier, "Textualité et Stéréotypes: Of African Queens and Afro-American Princes and Princesses: Miscegenation in Old Hepsy," in Regards sur la littérature noire américaine, ed. Fabre, pp. 88 ff.

16 OA, "Vorrede," p. xii. Trans. Chr. Lohmann.

17 Behn, Oroonoko, p. 80.

18 OA, "Vorrede," p. xii. Trans. Chr. Lohmann.

19 See Peters, Der zerrissene Engel: Genieästhetik.

20 Sollors, Neither Black Nor White, p. 178.

21 For a discussion of the racialized gaze, see Mary Hamer, "Black and White? Viewing Cleopatra in 1862," in The Victorians and Race, ed. West, pp. 53–67.

22 Mb 27, June 1858, p. 644. CA. DLA. Trans. Chr. Lohmann.

23 OA, "Vorrede," p. xii. Trans. Chr. Lohmann.

24 For an analysis of this attitude, characteristic of abolitionist discourse of the time, see

Toni Morrison, "Unspeakable Things Unspoken: The Afro-American Presence in American Literature," in *Modern Critical Views: Toni Morrison*, ed. Harold Bloom, p. 203.

25 RdC to LA. 3 November 1855. VC. BJK.

26 See Gilman, *The Jew's Body*.

27 OA to FD. 18 November 1878. FDP. LC.

28 For an analysis of the nineteenth-century concept of true womanhood, see Welter, *Dimity Convictions*.

29 I am referring to comments on Assing and Douglass in the letters in the Sylvester Rosa Koehler Papers. See also OA to LA. 19 January 1868. VC. BJK.

30 See FD, *LTFD*, p. 749.

31 *Mb* 29, June 1857, p. 696. CA. DLA. Trans. Chr. Lohmann. For an analysis of Douglass' rhetorical skills, see Blassingame's introduction to *The FD Papers*, 1; Gregory, *FD: Orator*.

32 Richard Yarborough, "Race, Violence, and Manhood," in *FD*, ed. Sundquist, p. 182.

33 Gates, Jr., *Figures in Black*, p. 108.

34 Mundt, *Aphra Behn*, 1:18.

35 *Mb* 30, June 1857, p. 718. CA. DLA. Trans. Chr. Lohmann.

36 See *Mb* 32, July 1857, p. 768. CA. DLA.

37 *Mb* 51, November 1857, p. 1215. CA. DLA. Trans. Chr. Lohmann.

38 For this and subsequent quotations from this report, see *Mb* 51, November 1857, pp. 1215–17. CA. DLA. Trans. Chr. Lohmann. This remark proves the male companion was not Adolph Rosenthal, who loved horses, and with whom Assing had often ridden in Sheboygan.

39 See *Mb* 51, November 1857, pp. 1217–18. CA. DLA.

40 See Cronholm, *Die Nordamerikanische Sklavenfrage im deutschen Schrifttum des 19. Jahrhunderts;* Woodson, *American Negro Slavery in the Works of Friedrich Strubberg, Friedrich Gerstäcker and Otto Ruppius.*

41 In her letters to Ludmilla, Ottilie repeatedly complained about Stowe's "sickly sweet, sanctimonious, hypocritical style." OA to LA. 5 January 1870. VC. BJK. See also letters of 15 October 1869 and 6 September 1874.

42 FD to LA. 14 July 1858. VC. BJK.

43 See LA, *Gräfin Elisa von Ahlefeld, die Gattin Adolfs von Lützow, die Freundin Karl Immermanns* (1857).

44 Assing's friend Gottfried Keller coined this phrase, *"zweigeschlechtiges Tintentier,"* to ridicule the professional symbiosis between Fanny Lewald and her lover, Adolf Stahr. See Schneider, *Fanny Lewald*, p. 8.

45 References to these domestic activities permeate the letters which Assing wrote to her sister Ludmilla from Rochester in the 1860s and 1870s. They are also central to her description of the Douglass home she wrote for the *Morgenblatt* 51, November 1859, pp. 1223–24. CA. DLA. See Chapter VI.

46 FD to Lydia Dennett, 17 April 1857, in *Life and Writings of FD*, ed. Foner, 5:392.

47 See Blassingame and McKirigan, eds. *FD Papers*, 3:xxvii.

48 "Eine Negerkolonie in Canada," *Die Gartenlaube*, 1857, pp. 687–89.

49 See *Mb* 29, June 1857, pp. 695–96, and *Mb* 30, June 1857, pp. 718–20.

50 Nearly one-third of Chatham's citizens were African-Americans, among them Martin R. Delany, who moved to Chatham from Pittsburgh in 1856. See Quarles, *Allies for Freedom*, pp. 42 ff.

51 See Pease and Pease, *Black Utopia*, ch. 5; Winks, *The Blacks in Canada*, pp. 152 ff.; Tanser, *The Settlement of Negroes in Kent County, Ontario*, pp. 34 ff.

52 As an example for this attitude, see his exchange with Horace Greeley from the *New York Tribune* in 1852, in *Life and Writings of FD*, ed. Foner, 2:172 f.

53 *Western Planet*, 9 August 1854, quoted in Pease and Pease, *Black Utopia*, p. 177 n.

54 [OA], "Eine Negerkolonie," p. 688.

55 [OA], "Eine Negerkolonie," pp. 689, 687.

56 See Rauh and Seymour. *Ludwig I. und Lola Montez*, pp. 10 ff.; Seymour, *Lola Montez: A Life;* Wintersteiner, *Lola Montez*, pp. 7 ff.

57 See *Mb* 13, February 1858, pp. 308–9. CA. DLA.

58 *Mb* 31, June 1858, pp. 738–39. CA. DLA. Trans. Chr. Lohmann.

59 *Mb* 31, June 1858, p. 738. CA. DLA. Trans. Chr. Lohmann.

60 *Mb* 4, December 1857, p. 96. CA. DLA. Trans. Chr. Lohmann.

61 *Mb* 31, June 1858, p. 738. Trans. Chr. Lohmann.

62 *Mb* 31, June 1858, pp. 738–39. CA. DLA. Trans. Chr. Lohmann.

63 See Thomas, *Pennington*, pp. 57 ff.

64 FD, "The Case of Rev. Dr. Pennington," 8 June 1855, in *Life and Writings of FD*, ed. Foner, 5:352.

65 *Mb* 27, June 1858, p. 644. CA. DLA. Trans. Chr. Lohmann.

66 *Mb* 27, June 1858, p. 644. CA. DLA. Trans. Chr. Lohmann.

67 OA, "Amalie Schoppe, geb. Weise. Ein Nekrolog." *Hamburger Nachrichten*, 18 December 1858.

68 *Mb* 45, October 1858, p. 1073. CA. DLA. Trans. Chr. Lohmann.

69 McKelvey, *Rochester: The Flower City*, p. 31.

70 FD to LA. 14 July 1858. VC. BJK.

71 This and the following quotations are taken from OA, "Vorrede," pp. x ff. Trans. Chr. Lohmann. I thank Mr. Lohmann for the point concerning the male voice as sexual signifier.

72 See Shaplen, *Free Love and Heavenly Sinners*, especially chs. 4 and 5.

73 *Mb* 22, April 1859, p. 527. CA. DLA. Trans. Chr. Lohmann.

74 *Mb* 51, 1855, p. 1214. CA. DLA. Trans. Chr. Lohmann.

75 OA, "Vorrede," p. xiv. Trans. Chr. Lohmann.

76 OA to FD. 18 November 1878. FDP. LC.

77 For an analysis of this logic, see Gay, *Education of the Senses*, pp. 95 ff.

V. THE I AND THE OTHER: Ottilie Assing and the Douglasses

1 See Quarles, *FD*, p. 108.

2 McFeely, *FD*, pp. 125–26.

3 See Martha Hodes, "Romantic Love Across the Color Line: White Women and Black

Men in Nineteenth-Century America," in *New Viewpoints in Women's History*, ed. Ware, pp. 81–98.

4 See Robyn Weigman, "The Anatomy of Lynching," in *American Sexual Politics*, ed. Fout and Tantillo, pp. 223–45.

5 Gates, Jr., *Figures in Black*, p. 114.

6 See Deborah McDowell, "In the First Place: Making FD and the Afro-American Narrative Tradition," in *Critical Essays on FD*, ed. Andrews, pp. 192–214.

7 Walker, *Moral Choices*, p. 254.

8 Franchot, "The Punishment of Esther," in *FD*, ed. Sundquist, p. 148.

9 FD, *MBMF*, p. 366.

10 Walker, *Moral Choices*, p. 212.

11 Richard Yarborough, "Race, Violence, and Manhood: The Masculine Ideal in FD's 'The Heroic Slave,'" in *FD*, ed. Sundquist, p. 182.

12 FD to Abigail and Lydia Mott, 21 February 1848, quoted in McFeely, *FD*, p. 154.

13 Towers, "African-American Baltimore in the Era of FD," pp. 165 ff.

14 Baker, *Blues, Ideology and Afro-American Literature*, p. 49. For a discussion of Northern racism and Jim Crowism, see Litwack, *North of Slavery*.

15 FD, "Speech, Dedication of Manassas (Virginia) Industrial School," 3 September 1894, p. 13. FDP. LC.

16 Washington, "These Self-Invented Women: A Theoretical Framework for a Literary History of Black Women," p. 4.

17 FD, "What I Found at the Northampton Association," in *History of Florence, Massachusetts*, ed. Sheffield, pp. 131–32.

18 Franchot, "The Punishment of Esther," p. 163n.

19 Douglass claimed this in a letter written in 1894 to James W. Hood, historian of the AME Zion Church. See Andrews, "FD, Preacher," p. 596.

20 I thank Professor Painter for making me aware of the parallels between Anna Murray Douglass' and Sojourner Truth's experiences. See Nell Irvin Painter, "Representing Truth: Sojourner Truth's Knowing and Known," pp. 72, 465 ff.; Mabee, *Sojourner Truth: Slave, Prophet, Legend*, pp. 66 ff.; Ong, *Orality and Literacy*, pp. 78–116.

21 Leverenz, *Manhood and the American Renaissance*, p. 128.

22 See FD, "The Heroic Slave," in *Life and Writings of FD*, ed. Foner, 5:496. See also Yarborough, "Race, Violence, and Manhood," p. 176.

23 See RDS, *AMD*, pp. 12–13. FDP. LC.

24 See Quarles, *FD*, p. 103. FD in *The Liberator*, 11 June 1847.

25 See Petrie and Stover, eds., *Bibliography of the FD Library at Cedar Hill*.

26 RDS, *AMD*, pp. 20–21. FDP. LC.

27 RDS, *AMD*, p. 14, p. 16. FDP. LC.

28 RDS, *AMD*, p. 18. FDP. LC.

29 See Quarles, *FD*, pp. 101 f.

30 Painter, *Sojourner Truth*, p. 252.

31 For a discussion of the alternative concept of womanhood developed by nineteenth-century African-American women, see Carby, *Reconstructing Womanhood*, pp. 38 ff.; and Jones, *Labor of Love, Labor of Sorrow*.

32 Quarles, *FD*, pp. 101, 103.

33 Painter observes that her exposure to Sojourner Truth's life taught her that "if we are to write thoughtful biographies of people who were not highly educated and who did not leave generous caches of personal papers in the archives where historians have traditionally done their work, we will need to develop means of knowing our subjects' way of making themselves known, that look beyond the written word." Painter, "Representing Truth," p. 462.

34 See Sontag, *On Photography*, p. 38.

35 Minnie Blackall Bishop to Charles H. Wiltsie, 25 February 1929, quoted in Quarles, *FD*, p. 101.

36 Quarles, *FD*, p. 101.

37 RDS, *AMD*, p. 21. FDP. LC.

38 JG quoted in Martin, *The Mind of FD*, p. 42.

39 Quoted in Quarles, *FD*, p. 103.

40 "May we not well ask, 'On what meat hath this our Caesar fed, that he hath grown so great?'" the *National Anti-Slavery Standard* asked. *National Anti-Slavery Standard*, 14:18 (24 September 1853), p. 70. The *Liberator*, 18 November 1853.

41 See Walker, *Moral Choices*, p. 258; Martin, *The Mind of FD*, pp. 42 ff.

42 *The Liberator*, 2 December 1853.

43 Susan B. Anthony to WLG, 13 December 1853, quoted in Foner, *FD*, p. 401 n. 34.

44 Painter, "Representing Truth," pp. 4, 464.

45 "Mrs. Julia Griffiths, now on a visit to her native land, will, upon her return, continue to write the Literary Notices for the Paper." (FD, "Prospectus," *FDP*, 1 February 1856, in *Life and Writings of FD*, ed. Foner, 5:381.) The same holds true for those around him. As late as August 1857 William Cooper Nell inquired of Amy Kirby Post whether she knew when (not whether) Griffiths was expected back. See William Cooper Nell to AKP. 23 August 1857. PFP. UR.

46 OA, "Vorrede," p. xii. Trans. Chr. Lohmann.

47 Bremer, *The Homes of the New World*, 1:585.

48 Carby, *Reconstructing Womanhood*, p. 34.

49 OA to LA. 26 March 1874. VC. BJK.

50 See McFeely, *FD*, p. 171.

51 OA to FD. 21 August 1878. FDP. LC.

52 OA to LA. 19 March 1850. VC. BJK.

53 Carby, *Reconstructing Womanhood*, p. 36.

54 See Sollors, *Neither Black Nor White*, p. 205.

55 Mundt, *Aphra Behn*, 2:121.

56 FD, *MBMF*, p. 157.

57 See Gutman, *The Black Family in Slavery and Freedom;* Sundquist, *To Wake the Nations*, pp. 93 ff.

58 On the impact of the father-master connection, see Henry Louis Gates, Jr., "Binary Oppositions in Chapter One of *Narrative of the Life of FD, an American Slave, Written by Himself*," in *Critical Essays on FD*, ed. Andrews, pp. 79–93. See also Davis, *Leadership, Love, and Aggression*, pp. 17–101. Walker, *Moral Choices*, pp. 209–61.

59 See McDowell, "In the First Place," in Andrews, ed., *Critical Essays on Frederick Douglass*, pp. 199 ff.

60 duCille, *The Coupling Convention*, p. 112.

61 OA to FD. 14 April 1870; 14 September 1878; 18 November 1878, FDP. LC.

62 OA to LA. 10 August 1869. VC. BJK.

63 Louisa Sprague was the sister of the Douglasses' son-in-law Nathan Sprague.

64 Estelle was Rosetta's daughter.

65 FD to RDS. 23 August 1875. FDP. LC.

66 FD to Elizabeth Cady Stanton. 30 May 1884, in *Life and Writings of FD*, ed. Foner, 4:410.

67 OA to LA. 24 August 1871; 24 August 1868; VC. BJK.

68 See OA to LA. 15 August 1872. VC. BJK.

69 Drafts of letters to George T. Downing on Ebenezer Bassett's appointment as minister to Haiti (FD to G. T. Downing. Undated but 1869. FDP. LC) and to Senator Henry Wilson of Massachusetts (FD to H. Wilson. 12 September 1866. FDP. LC) are in Assing's handwriting.

70 See Martin, *The Mind of FD*, pp. ix f.

71 Quarles, *FD*, pp. 109 f.; RDS, *AMD*, p. 21. FDP. LC.

72 Annie Douglass to FD. 7 December 1859. FDP. LC.

73 RDS, *AMD*, p. 18. FDP. LC.

74 RDS to FD. 15 March 1869. FDP. LC.

75 OA to LA. 10 February, 5 June 1870. VC. BJK.

76 OA to FD. 1 April 1879. FDP. LC.

77 OA to FD. 12 February 1879. FDP. LC.

VI. OF EMERALD ISLANDS AND MAGIC GARDENS:
The Antebellum Years

1 Varnhagen's diary entry on Wednesday, 20 January 1858, read: "Read in Frederick Douglass until one a.m." *Tagebücher: Aus dem Nachlass Varnhagen von Ense*, ed. K. Feilchenfeldt, 14 (1870), p. 186.

2 LA to Gottfried Keller. 6 November 1858, in Gottfried Keller, *Gesammelte Briefe*, ed. Helbling, pp. 79–80.

3 See Müller, "Vermittlungsversuche zwischen deutscher und italienischer Kultur: LA in Florenz (1862–1880)," in *Deutsch-jüdische Geschichte im 19. und 20. Jahrhundert*, ed. Heid and Knoll, pp. 452 ff. See also Pickett, *Unseasonable Democrat*, p. 89.

4 A letter she sent to William Lloyd Garrison is indicative. Thanking Garrison for the initiative he had taken against the spread of anti-Chinese sentiment, she wrote: "I, for one, not exactly in need of instruction on the question since I have always stood on your side of it, have a feeling of personal gratitude toward you, such as the persecuted Chinese would entertain for you if they perfectly understood your efforts on their behalf." OA to WLG. 8 March 1879. WLGP. BPL.

5 Martha Greene to FD. 7 July 1870. FDP. LC. See also 16 October 1869. FDP. LC.

6 *Mb* 51, November 1859, p. 1224. CA. DLA. Trans. Chr. Lohmann.

7 See Painter, *Sojourner Truth*, p. 252.

8 Painter, *Sojourner Truth*, p. 118.

9 Painter, *Sojourner Truth*, p. 144.

10 FD to AKP. 15 January 1877. PFP. UR.

11 In the Porter Family Papers at the University of Rochester no reference to Ottilie Assing could be found.

12 FD to Samuel D. Porter. 12 January 1852. PP. UR.

13 See Foner, ed., *FD on Women's Rights*; Giddings, *When and Where I Enter: The Impact of Black Women on Race and Sex in America*, pp. 55–74; Martin, *The Mind of FD*, pp. 136 ff.; Quarles, "FD and the Women's Rights Movement."

14 *Mb* 17, March 1858, pp. 404–5. CA. DLA. Trans. Chr. Lohmann.

15 See McKelvey, "The Germans of Rochester"; Pfaefflin, *Hundertjährige Geschichte des Deutschtums von Rochester.*

16 See Friedman, *Gregarious Saints*, pp. 96–126; Harlow, *Gerrit Smith*; Renehan, Jr., *The Secret Six*, pp. 11 ff.; McKivigan, "The FD-Gerrit Smith Friendship and Political Abolitionism in the 1850s," in *FD*, ed. Sundquist, pp. 205–32.

17 See Blight, *FD's Civil War*, p. 30; Sundquist, *To Wake the Nations*, pp. 93 ff.

18 OA, "Ein Besuch bei Gerrit Smith" (A Visit at Gerrit Smith's). Unpublished manuscript. Nachlass Hauff-Kölle. DLA. Trans. Chr. Lohmann. [Unpaginated]

19 See FD to GS. 9 August, 19 September 1867. GSP. SU.

20 RDS, *AMD*, p. 16. FDP. LC; see Blassingame, *FD*, p. 21.

21 *Mb* 51, November 1859, p. 1224. CA. DLA. Trans. Chr. Lohmann.

22 See McFeely, *FD*, p. 195.

23 See Quarles, *Allies for Freedom*, p. 78.

24 *Mb* 51, November 1859, p. 1224. CA. DLA. Trans. Chr. Lohmann; OA, "John Brown" (1868), p. 18, FDP. LC.

25 To her sister Ludmilla she wrote ten years later: ". . . I was very busy writing an article on John Brown. Even here I am amazed at how many people have insufficient information on him, and I therefore believe that in Germany an article on him would be appropriate in any journal, and, even though I never saw him, I was so deeply let into his venture that I have plenty of interesting things to report." OA to LA. 6 February 1869. VC. BJK.

26 *Mb* 51, November 1859, pp. 1223–24. CA. DLA. Trans. Chr. Lohmann.

27 OA, "John Brown" (1868), p. 18, FDP. LC. Assing claimed that she "knew two of the colored men, Anderson, who made his escape from Harpers Ferry, and Emperor, called there Shield Green, who was taken with John Brown and hanged afterwards."

28 See McFeely, *FD*, pp. 198 ff.; Martin, *The Mind of FD*, pp. 267 ff.; Huggins, *Slave and Citizen*, pp. 61 ff.; Quarles, *FD*, 170 ff.; Foner, *FD*, pp. 176 ff.

29 FD, *MBMF*, p. 318; *LTFD*, p. 753.

30 See Takaki, *Violence in the Black Imagination*, pp. 17–35. Goldstein, "Violence as an Instrument for Social Change."

31 FD, *MBMF*, p. 367.

32 See Quarles, ed., *Blacks on John Brown.*

33 For an excellent account of these events, and the trip to Chambersburg and the meeting with John Brown, see McFeely, *FD*, pp. 186 ff.

34 FD, *LTFD*, p. 759.

35 FD, *LTFD*, p. 757.

36 Annie Brown Adams quoted in Quarles, *Allies for Freedom*, p. 78.

37 See McFeely, *FD*, p. 192.

38 OA, "John Brown" (1868), p. 19. FDP. LC.

39 Cited in McFeely, *FD*, p. 198.

40 FD, *LTFD*, p. 748.

41 See Quarles, *Allies for Freedom*, p. 114.

42 See FD, *LTFD*, pp. 748–50, for his account of his time en route from Philadelphia to Rochester.

43 See FD to AKP. 27 October 1859. PFP. UR.

44 FD, *LTFD*, pp. 761–62.

45 Douglass' friends saw confiscation of property as an imminent threat, but Douglass did not share their fear. "I am about convinced that nothing is to be feared at this point," he wrote to Amy Post. "It cannot be lost unless I am convicted. I cannot be convicted, if I am not tried. I cannot be tried, unless I am arrested; I cannot be arrested unless caught; I cannot be caught while I keep out of the way—and just this thing it is my purpose to do." FD to AKP. 27 October 1859. PFP. UR.

46 See OA, "Der Aufstand bei Harpers Ferry" (The Insurrection at Harpers Ferry). Unpublished manuscript. October/November/December 1859. [Unpaginated] Fortunately Cotta saw to it that the manuscripts were preserved. Nachlass Hauff-Kölle. DLA.

47 OA, "Der Aufstand bei Harpers Ferry," October 1859.

48 FD, *LTFD*, p. 757.

49 OA, "Der Aufstand bei Harpers Ferry," October 1859.

50 See Wendy Hamand Venet. " 'Cry Aloud and Spare Not': Northern Antislavery Women and John Brown's Raid," in *His Soul Goes Marching On*, ed. Finkelmann, pp. 98–115.

51 OA, "Der Aufstand bei Harpers Ferry," December 1859. Trans. Chr. Lohmann.

52 OA, "Der Aufstand bei Harpers Ferry," November 1859. Trans. Chr. Lohmann.

53 FD, *LTFD*, p. 760.

54 Douglass quoted this letter in full in his autobiography. FD, *LTFD*, p. 753.

55 OA, "Der Aufstand bei Harpers Ferry," November 1859. Trans. Chr. Lohmann.

56 OA, "Der Aufstand bei Harpers Ferry," November 1859. Trans. Chr. Lohmann.

57 See "German Lessons," FDP. LC. Reel 11, Container 17.

58 RD to FD. 6 December 1859. FDP. LC.

59 Annie Douglass to FD. 7 December 1859. FDP. LC.

60 As stated before, Ottilie Assing's letters to Rahel de Castro are lost, but we have about two hundred letters from Castro is to Ludmilla Assing, in which Castro regularly reported on what she learned from Ottilie. See also McFeely, *FD*, p. 203.

61 RdC to LA. 8 January 1860. Undated, but January or February 1860, and 20 February 1860. VC. BJK.

62 See Sollors, *Neither Black Nor White*, pp. 336–59; for a reading of Paris as a Mecca for African-Americans, see Stonequist, *Marginal Man*, p. 187.

63 FD, *LTFD*, p. 762.

64 See McFeely, *FD*, pp. 207 ff.

65 FD, *LTFD*, p. 763; McFeely, *FD*, p. 207.

66 In December 1859 Rosetta wrote to her father: "I have just written a letter to Miss Assing in reply to one I received from her dated November 26th." 6 December 1859. FDP. LC.

67 RdC to LA. 24 April 1860. VC. BJK.

68 RD quoted in McFeely, *FD*, p. 207.

69 In letters to her sister, which Ottilie wrote during the 1870s, she frequently denounced Anna Murray as a woman devoid of feeling, as "a true monster, who herself can neither give love nor appreciate it." OA to LA. 30 December 1873. VC. BJK.

70 OA to Ludwig Feuerbach, 15 May 1871, in *Ausgewählte Briefe von und an Ludwig Feuerbach*, ed. Sass, 12/13:365.

71 See Petrie and Stover, *Bibliography of the FD Library at Cedar Hill*, p. 266.

72 OA to Ludwig Feuerbach, 15 May 1871.

73 Martin, *The Mind of FD*, p. 175; see also Van Deburg, "FD: Maryland Slave to Religious Liberal."

74 FD, *NFD*, p. 232.

75 Quoted in Martin, *The Mind of FD*, pp. 127 f.

76 Quoted in Andrews, "FD, Preacher," p. 593.

77 Quoted in McFeely, *FD*, p. 85.

78 OA, "FD" (1870), FDP. LC. [Mostly unpaginated]

79 FD, "The Meaning of the Fourth of July for the Negro," in *Life and Writings of FD*, ed. Foner, 2:197.

80 OA, "FD" (1870).

81 "Of course Miss Assing is jubilant and attributes Douglass' position to German radicalism, i.e., herself, a glory I certainly will not deny to her." Johannes D. Lange to Sylvester Rosa Koehler. 11 June 1870. SRKP. AAA.

82 In 1874 the German freethinkers' association of Hoboken commissioned a German-American artist to sculpt busts of Feuerbach and Strauss, and members could buy copies of them. It is possible that the busts in Douglass' library were from these series and were gifts by Ottilie Assing. See JDL to SRK. 10 December 1874. SRKP. AAA.

83 See OA to LA. 16 July 1868. VC. BJK.

VII. THE IRON ARM OF THE BLACK MAN: The Civil War Years

1 Ottilie Assing reported on the New York draft riots of July 1863 in the *Morgenblatt* of November 1863, pp. 1194–96; Douglass in *LTFD*, pp. 793–95.

2 FD, "A Trip to Haiti," *DM*, May 1861, in *Life and Writings of FD*, ed. Foner, 3:85–87.

3 FD, "The Legacy of John Brown," 3 December 1860, in *FD Papers*, ed. Blassingame and McKivigan, 3:401.

4 FD, "The Inaugural Address," *DM*, April 1861, in *Life and Times of FD*, ed. Foner, 3:74.

5 Blight, *FD's Civil War*, p. 2.

6 See McKelvey, "Lights and Shadows in Local Negro History," p. 11.

7 An open letter of 17 September 1858 to Benjamin Coates, a prominent supporter of African colonization and especially of Martin R. Delany's mission in 1858, which Douglass published in *Frederick Douglass' Paper*, had already signaled a shift of position on the colonization/emigration issue. "If free colored men, self-moved, wish to go to Africa or elsewhere, as individuals or as masses, and choose to form themselves into emigration societies or committees, preparatory to final removal from the United States, however much we might regret their determination on other grounds, we should be saved from the mortifications of those whose pride and prejudice were the cause of their removal. Let colored men go to Africa, and go to St. Domingo, to Jamaica, Mexico, or elsewhere, just as they list, but let them be self-moved in migratory qualities." FD, "The Letter of Benjamin Coates, Esq.," *FD's Paper*, 17 September 1858, in *Life and Writings of FD*, ed. Foner, 5:416.

8 FD, "Haiti," p. 88.

9 *Mb* 23, May 1861, p. 548. CA. DLA. Trans. Chr. Lohmann.

10 See OA to KG. 27 April 1855. KGP. SUBF; RdC to LA. 5 May 1855 and 11 December 1855. VC. BJK.

11 FD, "All Going to Haiti," *DM*, May 1859.

12 FD quoted in Foner, Fort Sumter to the Emancipation Proclamation," in *Life and Writings of FD*, ed. Foner, 3:11.

13 FD, "Haiti," p. 88.

14 OA to FD. 14 September 1878. FDP. LC.

15 FD, "The American Apocalypse," 16 June 1861, in *FD Papers*, ed. Blassingame and McKivigan, 3:437–38.

16 *Mb* 9, January 1861, p. 209. CA. DLA. Trans. Chr. Lohmann.

17 *Mb* 23, May 1861, p. 550. CA. DLA. Trans. Chr. Lohmann.

18 FD, "What to the Slave Is the Fourth of July?" in FD, *MBMF*, p. 434.

19 See FD, "The Slaveholders' Rebellion," 4 July 1862, in *Life and Writings of FD*, ed. Foner, 3:242–39.

20 *Mb* 24, May 1862, p. 572. CA. DLA. Trans. Chr. Lohmann.

21 *Mb* 18, March 1860, p. 430. CA. DLA. Trans. Chr. Lohmann.

22 *Mb* 17, March 1859, p. 408. CA. DLA. Trans. Chr. Lohmann.

23 *Mb* 9, January 1860, p. 216. CA. DLA. Trans. Chr. Lohmann.

24 *Mb* 9, January 1861, p. 209. CA. DLA. Trans. Chr. Lohmann.

25 *Mb* 27, May 1861, pp. 645–46. CA. DLA. Trans. Chr. Lohmann.

26 FD, "American Apocalypse," pp. 441–42.

27 *Mb* 28, May 1862, p. 666. CA. DLA. Trans. Chr. Lohmann.

28 FD, "To My British Anti-Slavery Friends," in *Life and Writings of FD*, ed. Foner, 2:482.

29 *Mb* 13, February 1862, p. 311. CA. DLA. Trans. Chr. Lohmann.

30 *Mb* 48, October 1861, p. 1147; *Mb* 24, May 1862, p. 573. CA. DLA. Trans. Chr. Lohmann.

31 *Mb* 47, October 1862, p. 1126. CA. DLA. Trans. Chr. Lohmann.

32 FD, "Our Army Still Slave-Catching," *DM*, September 1861, in *Life and Writings of FD*, ed. Foner, 3:151.

33 *Mb* 22, April 1863, p. 525. CA. DLA. Trans. Chr. Lohmann.

34 *Mb* 27, May 1861, p. 646. CA. DLA. Trans. Chr. Lohmann. See also *Mb* 9, January 1863, p. 215; *Mb* 44, September 1864, p. 1052.

35 *Mb* 37, August 1861; *Mb* 52, November 1863, p. 1242. CA. DLA. Trans. Chr. Lohmann.

36 *Mb* 50, November 1863, p. 1194. CA. DLA. Trans. Chr. Lohmann. See also *Mb* 17, March 1864, pp. 406 f.

37 *Mb* 9, January 1861, p. 210. CA. DLA. Trans. Chr. Lohmann.

38 *Mb* 9, January 1863, p. 215. CA. DLA. Trans. Chr. Lohmann.

39 *Mb* 39, August 1865, p. 930. CA. DLA. Trans. Chr. Lohmann. See also *Mb* 5, December 1862, p. 116. *Mb* 11, January 1865, p. 263.

40 *Mb* 37, August 1861, p. 885. CA. DLA. Trans. Chr. Lohmann.

41 FD, "The Heroic Slave," in *Life and Writings of FD*, ed. Foner, 5:476.

42 FD, "A Black Hero," in *Life and Writings of FD*, ed. Foner, 3:133.

43 "The Heroic Slave" was first published in *Autographs for Freedom*, edited by Julia Griffiths in 1853, pp. 174–238. See Sundquist, *To Wake the Nations*, pp. 115 ff.; Yarborough, "Race, Violence, and Manhood," in *FD*, ed. Sundquist, pp. 166–88.

44 *Mb* 28, May 1862, p. 667. CA. DLA. Trans. Chr. Lohmann.

45 *Mb* 7, January 1862, p. 164. CA. DLA. Trans. Chr. Lohmann.

46 *Mb* 28, May 1862, p. 667. CA. DLA. Trans. Chr. Lohmann.

47 *Mb* 15, February 1864, p. 356. CA. DLA. Trans. Chr. Lohmann.

48 *Mb* 24, May 1862, p. 573. CA. DLA. Trans. Chr. Lohmann.

49 FD, "Revolutions Never Go Backward," 5 May 1861, in *FD Papers*, ed. Blassingame and McKivigan, 3:435.

50 FD, "The Reasons for Our Troubles," 14 January 1862, in *Life and Writings of FD*, ed. Foner, 3:204.

51 See Foner, "FD: Fort Sumter to the Emancipation Proclamation," in *Life and Writings of FD*, ed. Foner, 3:32–33; McFeely, *FD*, pp. 224–25.

52 *Mb* 17, March 1864, p. 407. CA. DLA. Trans. Chr. Lohmann.

53 *Mb* 17, March 1864, p. 407. CA. DLA. Trans. Chr. Lohmann.

54 See McPherson, *The Negro's Civil War*, pp. 193–203; Belz, "Law, Politics, and Race in the Struggle for Equal Pay During the Civil War."

55 See Quarles, *Lincoln and the Negro*, pp. 173 ff.

56 See Blassingame, *FD*, p. 32.

57 FD, "Valedictory," 16 August 1863, in *Life and Writings of FD*, ed. Foner, 3:376.

58 FD, "The Mission of the War," 13 February 1864, in *Life and Writings of FD*, ed. Foner, 3:394.

59 *Mb* 50, November 1863, p. 1242. CA. DLA. Trans. Chr. Lohmann.

60 FD, "Services of the Colored Man," *DM* July 1862, in *Life and Writings of FD*, ed. Foner, 3:234.

61 *Mb* 50, November 1863, p. 1241. CA. DLA. Trans. Chr. Lohmann.

62 See Blight, *FD's Civil War*, p. 39.

63 *Mb* 17, March 1863, p. 334. CA. DLA. Trans. Chr. Lohmann. See also *Mb* 45, September 1865, p. 1072.

64 FD, "Emancipation, Racism, and the Work Before Us," 4 December 1863, in *FD Papers*, ed. Blassingame and McKivigan, 3:608.

65 See Davis, *Leadership, Love, and Aggression*, pp. 35 ff, 52 f.

66 Harding, *There Is a River*, p. 239.

67 RD to FD. 2 December 1862. FDP. LC.

68 See FD to GS. 10 October 1863. GSP. SU. *Mb* 50, November 1863, pp. 1194 ff. OA to LA. 22 February 1868. VC. BJK.

69 FD, *LTFD*, p. 811.

70 FD, *LTFD*, p. 812.

71 "Miscegenation," quoted in Wood, *Black Scare*, p. 55.

72 See Sollors, *Neither Black Nor White*, p. 323.

73 See Wood, *Black Scare*, pp. 53–79; Kaplan, "The Miscegenation Issue in the Election of 1864"; Aaron, "The 'Inky Curse': Miscegenation in the White Literary Imagination"; Bloch, *Miscegenation, Melaleukation, and Lincoln's Day*.

74 *Mb* 11, January 1864, p. 264. CA. DLA. Trans. Chr. Lohmann.

75 FD, "The Question of Amalgamation," *DM* (December 1860), pp. 371–72.

76 Nott and Gliddon, *Types of Mankind*, p. 405.

77 Louis Agassiz quoted in Sollors, *Neither Black Nor White*, p. 298.

78 *Mb* 11, January 1864, p. 264. CA. DLA. Trans. Chr. Lohmann.

79 *Mb* 11, January 1864, p. 264. CA. DLA. Trans. Chr. Lohmann.

80 FD, *LTFD*, p. 812.

81 JGC to FD, 5 December 1862, in *Life and Writings of FD*, ed. Foner, 3:38. See Blight, *FD's Civil War*, pp. 171 ff.

VIII. A DELIGHTFUL TIME, ADMIRABLY SPENT:
The Reconstruction Years

1 OA to Ludwig Feuerbach, 15 May 1871, in *Ausgewählte Briefe von und an Ludwig Feuerbach*, ed. Sass, 12/13:365–66.

2 Information on these events can be found in a letter Ottilie wrote to Ludmilla more than two years later. It does not mention why the Marks home was no longer available. See OA to LA. 19 January 1868. VC. BJK.

3 Assing regularly used the term "Bande" in her letters to German friends. See her letters in the SRKP. AAA.

4 Gagern, *Todte und Lebende*, 2:271.

5 "Miss Assing will really lecture on Fred Douglass tomorrow. I am really curious how this glorification will turn out." JDL to SRK. 10 December 1870. SRKP. AAA.

6 JDL to SRK. 11 September 1871. SRKP. AAA.

7 Phebe Dean, an abolitionist from New Jersey, wrote to Amy Post: "I heard yesterday that Mr. Douglass was going to move to Newark, N.J., in May." Phebe Dean to AKP. 27 February 1868. PFP. UR.

8 JGC to FD. 28 April 1865. FDP. LC.

9 FD quoted in McFeely, *FD*, p. 254.

10 McFeely, *FD*, p. 254.

11 See FD to SRK. Rochester, June 9 (no year given). FDP. SU.

12 FD to SRK. Rochester, June 9. FDP. SU.

13 See *Mb* 52, 24 December 1865, pp. 1–2. CA. DLA. Lohrer, *Cotta*; Höfle, *Cottas Morgenblatt für gebildete Stände.*

14 FD, "What the Black Man Wants," April 1865, in *Life and Writings of FD*, ed. Foner, 4:164.

15 McFeely, *FD*, pp. 241 f.

16 Sorkin, *The Transformation of German Jewry*, p. 25.

17 FD, "Reconstruction," *Atlantic Monthly* 18 (December 1866), p. 762.

18 FD, *MBMF*, p. 367.

19 FD quoted in McFeely, *FD*, p. 242.

20 FD quoted in Martin, *The Mind of FD*, p. 68.

21 FD quoted in Foner, *FD*, p. 318.

22 FD, "The Need for Continuing Anti-Slavery Work," in *Life and Writings of FD*, ed. Foner, 4:169.

23 FD, "The Douglass Institute," October 1865, in *Life and Writings of FD*, ed. Foner, 4:177.

24 *Mb* 27, May 1865, p. 647. CA. DLA. Trans. Chr. Lohmann.

25 Blight, *FD's Civil War*, pp. 189 f.

26 OA to LA. 3 February 1865. VC. BJK.

27 *Mb* 15, March 1865, p. 356. CA. DLA. Trans. Chr. Lohmann.

28 *Mb* 45, September 1865, p. 1073. CA. DLA. Trans. Chr. Lohmann.

29 *Mb* 27, May 1865, p. 647. CA. DLA. Trans. Chr. Lohmann.

30 *Mb* 39, August 1865, p. 931. CA. DLA. Trans. Chr. Lohmann.

31 See Foner, *FD*, p. 242.

32 "Interview with President Andrew Johnson," in *Life and Writings of FD*, ed. Foner, 4:184–85.

33 A first report of this meeting was published in the *New York Tribune* of 12 February 1866. See also FD, *LTFD*, pp. 820 ff. Green, *The Secret City*, p. 79; Painter, *Sojourner Truth*, p. 208; Huggins, *Slave and Citizen*, p. 113.

34 Quoted in Foner, "FD," in *Life and Writings of FD*, ed. Foner, 4:23–24.

35 McFeely, *FD*, p. 260.

36 Huggins, *Slave and Citizen*, p. 116.

37 Blight, *FD's Civil War*, p. 192.

38 FD, *LTFD*, p. 825.

39 FD, *LTFD*, p. 828.

40 See Nagler, *Fremont contra Lincoln*, p. 4.

41 Thus Douglass wrote to Rosetta: "Mother, Louisa and Miss Assing and myself took dinner at Fred's yesterday." FD to RDS. 4 November 1872. PFP. UR.

42 RDS to FD. 24 April 1867. FDP. LC.

43 See *Who's Who in America*, 1899–1900.

44 OA to LA. 19 January 1868. VC. BJK.

45 See OA to LA. 19 January 1868. VC. BJK.

46 RDS to FD. 11 April 1867. FDP. LC.

47 CRD to FD. 30 April, 14 July, 9 May, 19 May 1867. FDP. LC.

48 OA to LA. 3 February 1865. VC. BJK.

49 OA to LA. 22 February 1868. VC. BJK.

50 FD quoted in Blight, *FD's Civil War,* p. 197.

51 FD to Theodore Tilton. September 1867, in *Life and Writings of FD,* ed. Foner, 4:205.

52 CRD to FD. 16 August 1867. FDP. LC.

53 See FD to GS. 19 September 1867. FDP. LC.

54 JDL to SRK. 8 April 1868. SRKP. AAA.

55 See JDL to SRK. 3 January 1870, 1 April 1870, 9 April 1870, 14 May 1870. SRKP. AAA.

56 See OA to LA. 22 February 1868. VC. BJK.

57 OA to LA. 22 February 1868. VC. BJK.

58 OA to LA. 3 April 1868. VC. BJK.

59 OA to LA. 3 April 1868. VC. BJK.

60 See Müller, "Vermittlungsversuche zwischen deutscher und italienischer Kultur," p. 454.

61 OA to LA. 2 January 1869. VC. BJK.

62 OA to LA. 3 April 1868. VC. BJK.

63 JDL to SRK. 3 September 1869. SRKP. AAA.

64 OA to LA. 3 April 1868. VC. BJK.

65 OA to LA. 29 May 1868. VC. BJK.

66 Her travel companion was not, as McFeely suggests, Lewis' wife, Amalia Loguen Douglass, but Assing's cousin Emilie Nickert. Lewis did not marry Amalia Loguen until 1869. See McFeely, *FD,* p. 262; OA to LA. 16 July 1868. VC. BJK; CRD to FD. 1 September 1869. FDP. LC. See also Emilie Nickert to LA. 5 May 1857. VC. BJK; Louise Garcin to LA. 31 October 1858. VC. BJK.

67 See OA to LA. 16 July 1868. VC. BJK.

68 CRD to FD. 25 June 1868. FDP. LC.

69 In April 1869 Riotte was appointed minister resident to Nicaragua, where he stayed till January 1873. See U.S. Department of State, *Principal Officers of the Department of State and U.S. Chiefs of Mission, 1778–1990,* p. 125.

70 OA to LA. 16 July 1868. VC. BJK.

71 Painter, *Sojourner Truth,* p. 210. See also Green, *The Secret City.*

72 OA to LA. 16 June 1868. VC. BJK.

73 CRD to FD. 25 June 1868. FDP. LC.

74 OA to LA. 16 July 1868. VC. BJK.

75 OA to LA. 16 July 1868. VC. BJK.

76 OA to LA. 16 July 1868. VC. BJK.

77 FD to GS. 24 August 1868. FDP. LC.

78 OA to LA. 16 July 1868. VC. BJK.

79 OA to LA. 24 August 1868. VC. BJK.

80 See OA to LA. 28 March 1869. VC. BJK.

81 This lecture was probably written in Rochester in the summer of 1868. A fragment of this lecture is in the FDP. LC.

82 OA, "John Brown" (1868), pp. 24–26. FDP. LC.

83 See OA to LA. 3 December 1870. VC. BJK and JDL to SRK. 10 December 1870. SRKP. AAA.

84 A fragment of this talk is in the FDP. LC. As not all pages of the manuscript were numbered, some quotes will be without page numbering.

85 OA, "FD" (1870), FDP. LC.

86 See JDL to SRK. 26 November 1868. SRKP. AAA; and OA to LA. 29 May 1868. VC. BJK.

87 OA to LA. 10 October 1868. VC. BJK.

88 See Heinzen, *Communism and Socialism* (1881); Dobert, *Die Schriften der deutsch-amerikanischen Achtundvierziger*, pp. 105–17; Wittke, *Against the Current: The Life of Karl Heinzen*; Schinnerer, *Karl Heinzen: Reformer, Poet and Literary Critic.*

89 See OA to Karl Heinzen. 29 January 1872. Karl Heinzen Papers. University of Michigan: Special Collections Library; Zakrzewska, *A Woman's Quest: The Life of Maria E. Zakrzewska.*

90 OA to WLG. 8 March 1879. WLGP. BPL; OA to LA. 10 October 1868. VC. BJK. Remond died in 1873.

91 McFeely, *FD*, p. 266.

92 Elizabeth Cady Stanton quoted in *FD on Women's Rights*, ed. Foner, p. 26.

93 Tilton quoted in Quarles, *FD*, p. 246; Anthony in McFeely, *FD*, p. 266.

94 FD to Josephine Sophie White Griffing. 27 September 1868, in *Life and Writings of FD*, ed. Foner, 4:212.

95 See Stanton et al., eds., *History of Woman Suffrage*, 2:353–55; Painter, *Sojourner Truth*, p. 230.

96 JDL to SRK. May 1869. SRKP. AAA.

97 OA to LA. 6 February 1869. VC. BJK.

98 OA to LA. 23 May 1869. VC. BJK.

99 OA to LA. 23 May 1869. VC. BJK.

100 CRD to FD. 21 March 1869. FDP. LC: "Should that happen, what I do not wish at all, I would have to visit the Negro republic, which I would really like to see." OA to LA. 28 March 1869. VC. BJK.

101 See FD to George T. Downing. Undated draft, but 1869. FDP. LC.

102 OA to LA. 15 October 1869. VC. BJK.

103 Quoted in Blight, *FD's Civil War*, p. 207. Foner, *FD*, p. 267.

104 See OA to LA. 11 April 1870. VC. BJK.

105 Quoted in Foner, *FD*, p. 269.

106 Quoted in Martin, *The Mind of FD*, p. 179.

107 *NNE*, 14 July 1870. LC.

108 I thank Lois and Jim Horton for this reading of Douglass' position.

109 OA to LA. 5 June 1870. VC. BJK.

110 FD, "Salutatory of the Corresponding Editor," in *Life and Writings of FD*, ed. Foner, 4:222.

111 OA to LA. 17 September 1870. VC. BJK.

112 See "The Death of Napoleon III," *NNE*, 16 January 1873. "Bismarck's Resignation,"

NNE, 30 January 1873. "Three Great Battles: Königsgraz, Gravelotte, and Sedan," *NNE*, 13 February 1873. "The Spanish Republic," *NNE*, 20 February 1873. "Losses in the Franco-Prussian War," *NNE*, 10 April 1873. LC. She reported on concerts in New York of the black singers Emma Louisa and Anna Madah Hyers, on the Hampton Singers from Virginia, and on the German "Liederkranz," 27 March 1873, and on 26 June 1873 about a meeting of the School Teachers' Association at New York's Grand Opera House. The "Editorial Note" is from the issue of 27 May 1873. LC.

113　See OA to LA. 10 February 1870. VC. BJK.

114　OA to LA. 20 June 1871. VC. BJK.

115　OA to LA. 24 August 1871. VC. BJK.

116　OA to LA. 29 October 1871. VC. BJK.

117　OA to LA. 15 August 1872. VC. BJK.

118　See McFeely, *FD*, p. 272.

119　FD, "My Son, Lewis Douglass," August 1869, in *Life and Writings of FD*, ed. Foner, 4:219–20.

120　See FD Jr. to AKP. 20 January 1871. PFP. UR.

121　FD to GS. 2 September 1871. GSP. SU.

122　OA to LA. 16 April 1872. VC. BJK.

123　In one of her Hoboken lectures she said: "I have heard of putting men in tight places, and have sometimes felt the pinch of circumstances myself, but I know of few places more trying than that in which the Negro stands to-day. If he steals, we send him to prison; if he begs, we spurn him from our doors as a good-for-nothing; if he goes to work at a respectable trade we combine to cast him out and even to threaten his life. I know the grounds upon which it is attempted to excuse this base and infamous conduct towards Lewis H. Douglass and others in Washington." OA, fragment. FDP. LC.

124　See McFeely, *FD*, pp. 276 ff. Douglass had made up his mind on the annexation issue before his departure, as a later article he wrote for the *New National Era* of 12 January 1871 amply documents. See FD, "Annexation of Santo Domingo," *NNE*, 12 January 1871. LC.

125　See OA to LA. 26 March 1874. VC. BJK.

126　OA to LA. 8 January 1871. VC. BJK.

127　OA to LA. 3 March 1871. VC. BJK.

128　FD quoted in Blight, *FD's Civil War*, p. 209. See also Brantley, "Black Diplomacy and FD," pp. 197 ff.

129　OA to LA. 5 May 1871. VC. BJK.

IX. LA DONNA È MOBILE?: Years of Suspense

1　*The New York Times*, 3 January 1872.

2　OA to LA. 11 June 1872. VC. BJK.

3　On the fire, see McFeely, *FD*, pp. 274 ff.

4　OA to LA. 11 June 1872. VC. BJK.

5　FD, "Letter from the Editor," *NNE*, 13 June 1872. LC.

6　See *RDUA*, 2 January 1872; *RTB*, 2 January 1872. I thank Richard H. White of Port

Crane, N.Y., director of the African-American History Project, for sharing his research on the potential link between the burning of the Douglass home and the rape case of January 1872. For information on the Howard case, see McKelvey, "Lights and Shadows in Local Negro History," p. 13. The day before Cäcilia identified Howard, the police had arrested another African-American, but the girl declared that he was not the culprit.

7 *The New York Times*, 4 January 1872. The *RDUA* heard cries only of "Hang him." 3 January 1872. The *Rochester Demokrat und Chronicle* claimed on 3 January that the militia had been inebriated.

8 *RTB*, 5 January 1872. *RDUA*, 6 January 1872.

9 Doerries, "Organization and Ethnicity: The German-American Experience," p. 309.

10 OA to LA. 16 April 1872. VC. BJK.

11 *RDUA*, 15 April 1872.

12 Unfortunately an extensive search in the archives of the Rochester Public Library, the Rochester Historical Society, and the library of the University of Rochester for these radical press articles was unsuccessful. We can only infer that Douglass' relationship with Assing and Griffiths was targeted, as the *Advertiser* intimated.

13 OA to LA. 11 June 1872. VC. BJK.

14 FD to GS. 1 July 1872. GSP. SU.

15 OA to LA. 15 August 1872. VC. BJK.

16 OA to LA. 30 December 1872. VC. BJK.

17 Gustav Frauenstein to FD. 4 May 1873. FDP. LC.

18 Quoted in Doerries, "Organization and Ethnicity," p. 310.

19 OA to LA. 15 June 1870, 17 September 1870. VC. BJK.

20 JDL to SRK. 19 July 1872. SRKP. AAA.

21 JDL to SRK. 10 October 1874. SRKP. AAA.

22 Hans Kudlich to SRK. 13 August 1875. SRKP. LC.

23 See Krommer and Raimann, eds., *"Verlass das deutsche Narrenschiff!" Hans Kudlichs politisches Testament;* Hinners, *Exil und Rückkehr;* Vagts, *Deutsch-amerikanische Rückwanderung.*

24 OA to LA. 3 March 1872. VC. BJK.

25 See Noble, "Christian and Henry Bergh: A Biographical Sketch." NYHS.

26 FD to RDS. 28 August 1873. FDP. LC.

27 Henry O. Waggoner to FD. 28 February 1874. FDP. LC.

28 See FD to RDS. 28 August 1873 and 16 October (1873?). FDP. LC.

29 Henry O. Waggoner to FD. 28 February 1874. FDP. LC.

30 See Müller, "Vermittlungsversuche zwischen italienischer und deutscher Kultur," pp. 458 ff.

31 LA to FW. 21 March 1848. VC. BJK.

32 LA, *Piero Cironi, ein Beitrag zur Geschichte der Revolution in Italien* (1867); *Vita di Piero Cironi* (1865).

33 Biographical sketches of Ludmilla Assing usually assume that Cironi was the father of her boy. (See Dick, "Freundinnen," p. 196.) But her most recent biographer, Marion Brandt, has suggested to me that another relationship after Cironi's death resulted in the pregnancy.

34 JSt to LA. 18 May 1873. VC. BJK.

35 OA to LA. 30 December 1873. VC. BJK.

36 OA to LA. 27 January 1874. VC. BJK.

37 Quoted in Wehl, *Zeit und Menschen,* 2:86.

38 Gottfried Keller to Marie Exner, 17 June 1874, in *Kellers Gesammelte Briefe,* ed. Helbling, 4:226.

39 OA to LA. 26 March 1874. VC. BJK.

40 OA to LA. 30 May 1874. VC. BJK.

41 FD to OA. 1 June 1874. FDP. LC. This epistolary fragment is the only letter from Frederick Douglass to Ottilie Assing that has survived.

42 OA to LA. 30 May 1874. VC. BJK.

43 OA to LA. 23 December 1875. VC. BJK.

44 OA to FD. 1 May 1874. FDP. LC.

45 FD to GS. 3 July 1874. GSP. SU.

46 FD, *LTFD,* p. 839.

47 See Blassingame, *FD,* p. 38; also Osthaus, *Freedmen, Philanthropy, and Fraud.*

48 OA to FD. 1 May 1874. FDP. LC.

49 Quoted in Blight, *FD's Civil War,* p. 209 n.

50 FD to Nathan Sprague. 30 May 1874. FDP. LC.

51 FD to OA. 1 June 1874. FDP. LC.

52 FD to GS. 3 July 1874. GSP. SU.

53 OA to LA. 13 July 1874. VC. BJK.

54 McFeely, *FD,* p. 286.

55 FD, *LTFD,* p. 837.

56 FD to GS. 24 September 1874. GSP. SU.

57 OA to LA. 6 September 1874. VC. BJK.

58 See Blight, *FD's Civil War,* p. 205.

59 See McFeely, *FD,* p. 287.

60 FD to RDS. 30 June (1875). FDP. LC.

61 OA to LA. 6 September 1874. VC. BJK.

62 See OA to LA. 6 September 1874. VC. BJK.

63 OA to LA. 9 November 1874. VC. BJK.

64 OA to LA. 13 December 1875. VC. BJK.

65 FD to RDS. 2 August 1875. FDP. LC.

66 OA to LA. 30 December 1873. VC. BJK.

67 JSt to LA. 19 and 20 February 1876. VC. BJK.

68 OA to LA. 11 June 1876. VC. BJK.

69 OA to LA. 11 June 1876. VC. BJK.

70 OA to FD. 3 July 1876. FDP. LC.

71 FD to RDS. 30 June 1875. FDP. LC.

72 OA to FD. 25 July 1876. FDP. LC.

73 OA to LA. 21 February 1876. VC. BJK.

74 OA to LA. 11 June 1876. VC. BJK.

75 OA to KG. 21 August 1876. KGP. SUBF.

76 OA to SRK. 26 December 1878. SRKP. AAA.

77 OA to KG. 21 August 1876. KGP. SUBF.

78 For a description of Ludmilla Assing's mansion, see Gottschall, "Erinnerungen an LA," p. 298.

79 Gottfried Keller to Marie Melos. 26 December 1879, in *Kellers Gesammelte Briefe,* ed. Helbling, 4:272–73.

80 JSt to LA. 18 February 1877. VC. BJK.

81 OA to FD. 5 January 1877. FDP. LC.

82 See OA to LA. 11 December 1876. VC. BJK.

83 OA to LA. 10 January 1877. VC. BJK.

84 OA to FD. 11 February 1877. FDP. LC.

85 OA to FD. 5 January 1877. FDP. LC.

86 OA to FD. 11 February 1877. FDP. LC.

87 FD to SDP. 21 March 1877. PP. UR.

88 OA to LA. 26 March 1877. VC. BJK.

89 OA to LA. 20 May 1877. VC. BJK.

90 OA to SRK. 20 July 1877. SRKP. AAA.

91 JSt to LA. 18 February 1877. VC. BJK.

X. HAGAR'S SHADOW: Separation and Suicide

1 Translation of the search notice which the *Süddeutsche Post* published in 1882. *SPost,* 11 October 1882.

2 Quoted in McFeely, *FD,* p. 292.

3 FD to Lewis Douglass. 18 July 1883. FDP. LC.

4 "Chronology," in FD, *Autobiographies,* p. 1069.

5 See Ayers, *The Promise of the New South: Life After Reconstruction,* esp. chs. 1–5.

6 McFeely, *FD,* p. 291.

7 Douglass, *LTFD,* pp. 860 f.

8 FD, "Our National Capital," in *FD Papers,* ed. Blassingame and McKivigan, 4:454.

9 This and following quotations from OA to FD. 12 July 1877. FDP. LC.

10 FD, *LTFD,* pp. 875–76. See also Andrews, "Reunion in the Postbellum Slave Narrative: FD and Elizabeth Keckley," pp. 5 ff.

11 OA to FD. 12 July 1877. FDP. LC.

12 McFeely, *FD,* p. 287.

13 OA to FD. 21 August 1878. FDP. LC.

14 OA to FD. 14 September 1878. FDP. LC.

15 See OA to LA. 5 March 1877. VC. BJK.

16 OA to FD. 14 September 1878. FDP. LC.

17 See Blassingame, *FD,* p. 41.

18 OA to FD. 18 November 1878. FDP. LC.

19 OA to FD. 28 November 1878. FDP. LC.

20 See City Directories, Jersey City, NJ, 1861–1881. Reel 7: 1878/9 through 1881/2.

21 OA to SRK. 16 February 1879; and see OA to SRK. 13 March 1880. SRKP. AAA.

22 OA to FD. 2 December 1878. FDP. LC.

23 OA to FD. 2 December 1878. FDP. LC.

24 OA to FD. 1 April 1879. FDP. LC.

25 See OA to FD. 14 September 1878, 28 November 1878, 15 January 1879, 29 January 1879, 17 February 1879. FDP. LC.

26 JDL to SRK. 15 September 1880. SRKP. AAA.

27 OA to FD. 1 April 1879. FDP. LC.

28 OA to FD. 18 November 1878. FDP. LC.

29 OA to SRK. 11 February 1879. SRKP. AAA.

30 OA to FD. 15 January 1879, 5 January 1877. FDP. LC.

31 OA to FD. 5 January 1877. FDP. LC.

32 OA to FD. 10 December 1878. FDP. LC.

33 FD to AKP. 14 April 1879. PFP. UR.

34 OA to FD. 2 December 1878. FDP. LC.

35 OA to FD. 12 February 1879. FDP. LC.

36 FD quoted in Blight, *FD's Civil War*, p. 231.

37 OA to FD. 18 December 1878. FDP. LC.

38 FD quoted in McFeely, *FD*, p. 293.

39 FD quoted in McFeely, *FD*, p. 293.

40 OA to FD. 10 December 1878. FDP. LC.

41 OA to FD. 18 December 1878. FDP. LC.

42 OA to WLG. 30 October 1877. WLGP. BPL.

43 OA to SRK. 20 June 1878. SRKP. AAA.

44 OA, "Die amerikanischen Wahlen" (The American Elections), *SPost*, 26 November 1882. Assing was not the only one of his white friends who feared for Douglass' political integrity. Samuel D. Porter, too, sent a note of warning during this period, to which Douglass replied: "Thanks for your gentle warning. It was like you to give it and I honor your fidelity. The perils are abundant in every part of the voyage of life—and are as abundant when nearing the shore as when in mid ocean. I can only promise to keep a man at the 'mast head' and a sharp look out and a firm hand upon the helm. Some degree of safety is assured by a knowledge of danger at hand." FD to SDP. 30 June 1879. PP. UR.

45 FD quoted in Martin, *The Mind of FD*, p. 73.

46 FD, "The Negro Exodus from the Gulf States," 12 September 1879, in *FD Papers*, ed. Blassingame and McKivigan, 4:519.

47 FD, "The Negro Exodus from the Gulf States," p. 526.

48 See OA to FD. 19 March 1879. FDP. LC.

49 OA to FD. 22 April 1879. FDP. LC.

50 FD, *LTFD*, p. 863.

51 *Mb* 51, November 1865, p. 1221. CA. DLA.

52 OA to FD. 26 December 1878. FDP. LC.

53 OA to FD. 12 February 1879. FDP. LC.

54 Among other things, this society tried to gain influence in the field of public education, "so that pure thoughts, elevated tastes, refined feelings, and healthful habits may

raise the standard of social purity, and lift future generations above the sensuality which is only restrained by fear of discovery." It sought "the enactment and enforcement of laws which tend to the removal of vice and the promotion of morality." *Alpha*, 7:6 (February 1882), p. 4. The society also promoted sexual education and birth control via continence.

55 References to the meetings between Douglass and Pitts can be found in Martha Greene's letters to Douglass. See Martha Greene to FD. 27 May 1880 and 31 July 1880. FDP. LC.

56 OA to FD. 10 December 1878. FDP. LC.

57 OA to FD. 15 January 1879. FDP. LC.

58 Racowitza, *Von Anderen und Mir*, p. 5.

59 Racowitza, born in Munich in 1845, was twenty-six years younger than Assing and seven years younger than Helen Pitts, but Assing chose not to elaborate on details.

60 OA to FD. 29 January 1879. FDP. LC.

61 See OA to SRK. 13 November 1879. SRKP. AAA. Racowitza's *Meine Beziehungen zu Ferdinand Lassalle* was published in 1879.

62 See Gottschall, "Erinnerungen an LA," p. 299. Müller, "Vermittlungsversuche zwischen deutscher und italienischer Kultur," p. 460.

63 Gottfried Keller to Ida Freiligrath. 6 April 1880, in *Kellers Gesammelte Briefe*, ed. Helbling, 4:356.

64 OA to FD. 22 April 1879. FDP. LC.

65 See Müller, "Vermittlungsversuche zwischen deutscher und italienischer Kultur," p. 460.

66 OA to FW, quoted in Wehl, *Zeit und Menschen*, 2:97.

67 Assing gave detailed reports on these events in her letters to the Koehler family. See OA to SRK. SRKP. 1880–84.

68 OA to SRK. 18 May 1880. SRKP. AAA.

69 Gottfried Keller to Ida Freiligrath. 20 December 1880, in *Kellers Gesammelte Briefe*, ed. Helbling, 4:357–58.

70 OA to SRK. 19 December 1880. SRKP. AAA.

71 OA to SRK. 13 November 1880; 22 February 1881. SRKP. AAA.

72 OA to SRK. 13 November 1880. SRKP. AAA. Assing was enchanted with Ingersoll, a leading spokesman of religious liberalism in the United States, and paid tribute to him in an article for the *Süddeutsche Post*. See OA, "Amerikanische Freidenker" (American Freethinkers), *SPost*, 24 December 1882.

73 OA to SRK. 19 December 1880. SRKP. AAA.

74 See OA to SRK. 24 May 1881. SRKP. AAA. Her letters did not mention that Helen Pitts had moved to Washington in 1880, living with her uncle and working in a government office. But that she explicitly identified the *Alpha* group as the most hypocritical and vicious among those opposed to Garfield's intentions to appoint Douglass to another government office could be a sign that she anticipated trouble from anybody associated with the *Alphaweiberbande*, as she called them: the "*Alpha* female gang." See also McFeely, *FD*, p. 310. Neither President Garfield's diary nor his correspondence

with his wife contains references to this intervention. Garfield never mentioned Douglass in his diary. See Garfield Papers. Series 1 and 3. LC. Also no article pertaining to Douglass' lifestyle was published by *Alpha* during these months.

75 OA to SRK. 13 November 1880. SRKP. AAA.

76 OA to SRK. 22 February 1881. SRKP. AAA.

77 *Beiblatt zur Zeitschrift für bildende Kunst*, 16:36, May 1881, p. 586.

78 OA to SRK. 24 May 1881, 13 November 1880, 22 February 1881. SRKP. AAA.

79 McFeely, *FD*, p. 306.

80 OA to SRK. 24 May 1881. SRKP. AAA.

81 OA to SRK. 24 May 1881. SRKP. AAA.

82 See Rinaldo Kientzel to Henry Bergh. 27 October 1884. FDP. LC.

83 See OA to SRK. 22 August 1881. SRKP. AAA.

84 FD to Martha Greene. 4 November 1884. FDP. LC.

85 OA to SRK. 22 August 1881. SRKP. AAA.

86 OA to Bertha Gutzkow. 21 October 1881. KGP. SUBF.

87 And she repeatedly accused Ottilie of intellectual theft. See entry of 26 March 1838. VC. BJK.

88 OA to Bertha Gutzkow. 21 October 1881. KGP. SUBF.

89 OA to SRK. 30 May 1882. SRKP. AAA.

90 OA to Amalie Koehler. 17 December 1882. SRKP. AAA.

91 OA to Amalie Koehler. 17 December 1882. SRKP. AAA.

92 OA to SRK. 30 May 1882. SRKP. AAA.

93 E. J. Loewenthal to FD. 6 June 1882. FDP. LC.

94 See FD to AKP. 21 August 1882. PFP. UR.

95 SRK to FD. 7 August 1882. FDP. LC.

96 OA to Amalie Koehler. 17 December 1882. SRKP AAA.

97 E. J. Loewenthal to FD. 17 December 1882. FDP. LC.

98 OA to Amalie Koehler. 17 December 1882. SRKP. AAA.

99 OA to SRK. 30 June 1883. SRKP. AAA.

100 See OA, "Die amerikanischen Wahlen" (The American Elections), *SPost*, 26 November 1882; "Amerikanische Freidenker" (American Freethinkers), *SPost*, 22 and 24 December 1882; and "Zur Rassenhetze in Amerika" (On Race Baiting in America), *SPost*, 13 November 1883.

101 OA to SRK. 10 August 1883. SRKP. AAA.

102 OA, "Von Deutschland nach Italien" (From Germany to Italy), *SPost*, 22 December 1883.

103 OA to SRK. 10 August 1883. SRKP. AAA.

104 OA to SRK. 24 November 1884. SRKP. AAA.

105 OA to Amalie Koehler. 17 December 1882. SRKP. AAA.

106 Cited in McFeely, *FD*, p. 312.

107 Cited in McFeely, *FD*, pp. 312 f.

108 McFeely, *FD*, p. 313.

109 FD, "What Am I to You," FDP. LC.

110 CRD to FD. 17 February 1884. FDP. LC.

111 Crofts wrote to him: "I have this morning received, from the kind hand of our mutual friend, Mrs. Charles Miller, a copy of the *Rochester Democrat* which makes mention of your marriage—and I, as one of your truest and warmest friends, hasten to send you (and Mrs. Douglass) my most sincere congratulations, and to express the hope that the steps you have now taken may tend to promote your true happiness in the evening of your days. I shall be glad to hear from your own hand a few particulars regarding the lady." JGC to FD. 11 February 1884. FDP. LC.

112 See OA to Amalie Koehler. 23 January 1884. SRKP. AAA.

113 In 1831 Assing's mother recorded in her diary that her husband "does not like to talk about it when he is feeling badly, and this is a quality which also characterizes Ottilie." RMA in her diary. 24 October 1831. VC. BJK.

114 OA to FD. 10 December 1878. FDP. LC.

115 OA to SRK. 2 August 1884. SRKP. AAA.

116 "Miss Assing was suffering from a cancer in the breast." Rinaldo Kientzel to Henry Bergh. 27 October 1884. FDP. LC.

117 FD to Martha Greene. 4 November 1884. FDP. LC.

118 OA to KG. 3 November [1842]. VC. BJK.

119 Lewald, *Gefühltes und Gedachtes*, p. 271.

120 According to *Le Figaro* of 21 August 1884, the temperature that day was 24.5 C.

121 Paris Morgue Register #64, 1884, p. 111. Archives of the Préfecture de Police, Département de Seine, Paris. Trans. Tessa C. Spargo.

122 H. C. Kudlich to FD. 18 July 1885. FDP. LC.

123 See Rinaldo Kientzel to Henry Bergh. 27 October 1884. FDP. LC.

124 FD to Martha Greene. 4 November 1884. FDP. LC.

125 JDL to SRK. 20 September 1884. SRKP. AAA.

126 JDL to SRK. 23 September 1884. SRKP. AAA.

127 Gagern, *Todte und Lebende*, pp. 271–72.

128 FD to Martha Greene. 4 November 1884. FDP. LC.

129 Rinaldo Kientzel to Henry Bergh. 27 October 1884. FDP. LC.

CONCLUDING REMARKS

1 Helene von Racowitza, *Von Anderen und Mir*, pp. 273–75.

2 See Henry Bergh to FD. 5 October 1884. FDP. LC. See FD to Martha Greene. 4 November 1884. FDP. LC.

3 OA, "Last Will and Testament." 9 November 1871. Surrogate's Office, County of Hudson, New Jersey. FDP. LC.

4 OA, "Last Will and Testament." 7 April 1883. Surrogate's Office, County of Hudson, New Jersey. FDP. LC.

5 Bertha Hirschfeld to FD. 15 November 1884. FDP. LC.

6 Henry Bergh to FD. 26 January 1885. FDP. LC.

7 Kudlich wrote to Koehler: "If you are very anxious to receive part of the sum coming to you before the lapse of that time—May 19th 1886—I can perhaps accommodate you, although I frankly confess that I would rather not do so . . . before my account is

settled and the Court grants the usual order that I pay the money to the legatus." Hermann C. Kudlich to SRK. 5 August 1885. SRKP. AAA.

8 FD to SRK. 31 January 1885. FDP. LC.

9 Henry Bergh's letters to FD are in FDP. LC.

10 See FD to Henry Bergh. 31 January 1885. FDP. LC.

11 See Hermann C. Kudlich to FD. 5 August 1886. FDP. LC.

12 Hermann C. Kudlich to FD. 18 July 1885. FDP. LC.

13 Helen Pitts Douglass, Diary, 15 September 1886. FDP. LC.

14 FD, Diary, 19 March 1887. FDP. LC.

Bibliography

I. ARCHIVES AND MANUSCRIPT COLLECTIONS

The Amistad Research Center
Tulane University
New Orleans, La.

Archiv Bibliographia Judaica
Frankfurt/Main, Germany

Archives of American Art
Washington, D.C.
  Sylvester Rosa Koehler Papers

Bayrische Staatsbibliothek
Munich, Germany

Biblioteka Jagiellonska Krakowa
Uniwersytet Jagiellonski, Krakow, Poland
  Varnhagen von Ense Collection

Bibliothek der Jüdischen Gemeinde Hamburg
Hamburg, Germany

Boston Public Library
Boston, Mass.
  William Lloyd Garrison Papers
  Weston Family Papers

Connecticut Conference of the United Church of Christ
Hartford, Conn.

Département de Seine (Archive)
Paris, France

Deutsches Literaturarchiv
Schiller-Nationalmuseum, Bibliothek
Marbach, Germany
      Morgenblatt für gebildete Leser

Ferguson Library
Stamford, Conn.

Frederick Douglass National Historic Site
Washington, D.C.

German Society of the City of New York
New York, N.Y.

Harvard University
Cambridge, Mass.
Houghton Library
      New National Era
      The Liberator
      Fanny Garrison Villard Papers
      Garrison Family Papers
      Henry Villard Papers
      Wendell Phillips Papers
Widener Library

Hayes Memorial Library
Spiegel Grove State Park, Fremont, Ohio
      Letters and Papers of Rutherford Birchard Hayes

Herzog August Bibliothek Wolfenbüttel
Wolfenbüttel, Germany

Hoboken Public Library
Hoboken, N.J.

Leo Baeck Institute Library
New York, N.Y.

Library of Congress
Washington, D.C.
      New National Era
      Frederick Douglass Papers (Microfilm Copy in Widener, Harvard University)
      Friedrich Kapp Papers
      Carl Schurz Papers (Microfilm Copy in Widener, Harvard University)
      James A. Garfield Papers (Microfilm Copy in Widener, Harvard University)
      Sylvester Rosa Koehler Papers

Missouri Historical Society
St. Louis, MO.
        Franz Sigel Papers

Moorland-Springarn Research Center
Howard University, Washington, D.C.
        Frederick Douglass Collection

Museum and Archeology Research and Supplies
Glen Dale, Md.

Museum für Hamburgische Geschichte
Hamburg, Germany

New Jersey Historical Society
Trenton, N.J.

New-York Historical Society
New York, N.Y.

New York Public Library
New York, N.Y.

Paris Morgue Register, 4th Arrondissement
Paris, France

Philadelphia Jewish Archives Center
Philadelphia, Penn.

Préfecture de Police (Archive)
Paris, France

Presbyterian Historical Society
Philadelphia, Penn.
        Shiloh Presbyterian Church Records

Rochester Historical Society Library
Rochester, N.Y.

Rochester Public Library
Rochester, N.Y.

Salomon Ludwig Steinheim-Institut für deutsch-jüdische Geschichte e. V.
Duisburg, Germany

Schaffer Library, Union College
Schenectady, N.Y.

Schlesinger Library, Radcliffe College
Cambridge, Mass.
        Susan B. Anthony Papers, 1815–1961 (Microfilm)

The Schomburg Center for Research in Black Culture
New York, N.Y.

Staatsarchiv Hamburg
Hamburg, Germany

Staatsbibliothek zu Berlin—Stiftung Preussischer Kulturbesitz
Berlin, Germany

Stadt- und Universitätsbibliothek Frankfurt/M.
Frankfurt/Main, Germany
        Karl Gutzkow Papers
        Georg Schirges Papers

State Historical Society of Wisconsin
Madison, Wis.

Sudetendeutsches Archiv
Munich, Bavaria

Syracuse University Library
Syracuse, N.Y.
        Gerrit Smith Papers (Microform)
        Sylvester Rosa Koehler Papers

The University of Michigan Library
Ann Arbor, Mich.
Special Collections Library
        Karl Heinzen Papers

The University of Rochester Library
Rochester, N.Y.
        Frederick Douglass Letters 1850s–1890s
        Post Family Papers
        Porter Family Papers

West Virginia University
        Frederick Douglass Papers

Yale University Library
Sterling Memorial Library
New Haven, Conn.

II. BIBLIOGRAPHIES

Arndt, Karl J. R., and May E. Olsen. *Die deutschsprachige Presse der Amerikas.* Vol. 1. *Geschichte und Bibliographie 1/32–1955.* Munich: Verlag Dokumentation, 1976.

Cahalan, Brigid A. *Hoboken—A City in Transition: An Annotated Selective Listing of Source Materials. 1855–1983.* Research Paper (MLS), Queens College, CUNY, 1983. NYPL.

Calendar of the Gerrit Smith Papers in the Syracuse University Library. Albany: The Survey, 1941–42.

Deutsches Biographisches Jahrbuch 1914–1916. Vol 1. Stuttgart: Deutsche Verlagsanstalt, 1914.

Frels, Wilhelm. *Deutsche Dichterhandschriften von 1400 bis 1900: Gesamtkatalog der eigenhändigen Handschriften deutscher Dichter in den Bibliotheken und Archiven Deutschlands, Österreichs, der Schweiz und der CSR.* Leipzig: Karl W. Hiersemann, 1934.

Gabaccia, Donna. *Immigrant Women in the United States: A Selective Annotated Multidisciplinary Bibliography.* New York: Greenwood, 1989.

Hope, Ann, and Jörg Nagler. *Guide to German Historical Sources in North American Libraries and Archives.* Washington, DC: German Historical Institute, 1991.

Index to Personal Names in the National Union Catalog of Manuscript Collections, 1959–1984. Alexandria: Chadwick-Healey, 1988.

Jüdisches Biographisches Archiv. Munich: K. G. Saur, 1994.

Kloss, Heinz. *Research Possibilities in the German-American Field.* Hamburg: Buske, 1980.

Litoff, Judy Barett. *European Immigrant Women in the United States. A Bibliographical Dictionary.* New York: Garland, 1994.

Lülfing, Hans, and Horst Wolf, eds. *Gelehrten- und Schriftstellernachlässe in den Bibliotheken der Deutschen Demokratischen Republik: Nachträge, Ergänzungen, Register.* Vol. 3. Berlin: Deutsche Staatsbibliothek, 1971.

National Union Catalogue of Manuscript Collections. Alexandria, Va.: Chadwick-Healey, 1959–84.

Petrie, William L., and Douglass E. Stover. *Bibliography of the Frederick Douglass Library at Cedar Hill.* Fort Washington, Mass.: Silesia, 1995.

Pochmann, Henry A. *Bibliography of German Culture in America to 1940, revised and corrected.* Millwood, N.Y.: Kraus International, 1982.

Schlawe, Fritz. *Die Briefesammlungen des 19. Jahrhunderts: Bibliographie der Briefausgaben und Gesamtregister der Briefschreiber und Briefempfänger 1815–1915.* Stuttgart: Metzler, 1969.

Schramm, Percy E., and Ascan W. Lutteroth. *Verzeichnis gedruckter Quellen zur Geschichte Hamburgischer Familien.* Hamburg: Zentralstelle für Niedersächsische Familiengeschichte, 1921.

Stern, Ludwig. *Die Varnhagen von Ensesche Sammlung in der Königlichen Bibliothek zu Berlin.* Berlin: Behrend, 1911.

Studemund-Halévy, Michael. *Bibliographie zur Geschichte der Juden in Hamburg.* Munich: K. G. Saur, 1994.

Ward, Robert Elmer. *A Bio-Bibliography of German-American Writers, 1670–1970*. White Plains, N.Y.: Kraus International, 1985.

III. ENCYCLOPEDIAS

Adams, Oskar F. *A Dictionary of American Authors*. Boston: Houghton, 1897.

Allgemeine Deutsche Biographie. 32 vols. 1875–1912. Ed. Historische Kommission der bayerischen Akademie der Wissenschaften zu München. Berlin: Duncker & Humblot, 1967–71.

Appleton's Cyclopaedia of American Biography. New York: Appleton, 1887–89.

Bettelheim, Anton, ed. *Biographisches Jahrbuch und deutsches Nekrolog*. Boston: Deutsches Biographisches Archiv, 1903.

Bindewald, Karl Wilhelm, ed. *Deutschlands Dichterinnen. Blüthen deutscher Frauenpoesie aus den Werken deutscher Dichterinnen der Vergangenheit und Gegenwart ausgewählt und mit einem biographischen Dichterinnenverzeichnisse versehen*. Osterwieck/Harz: Zickfeldt, 1895.

Bornmüller, Franz, ed. *Biographisches Schriftsteller-Lexikon der Gegenwart*. Leipzig: Bibliographisches Institut, 1882.

Brinker-Gabler, Gisela, ed. *Deutsche Literatur von Frauen*. Munich: C. H. Beck, 1988.

Brümmer, Franz, ed. *Lexikon der deutschen Dichter und Prosaisten des neunzehnten Jahrhunderts*. 4 vols. Leipzig: Reclam, 1884.

Brümmer, Franz, ed. *Deutsches Dichter-Lexikon. Biographische und bibliographische Mittheilungen über deutsche Dichter aller Zeiten: Unter besonderer Berücksichtigung der Gegenwart für Freunde der Literatur zusammengestellt*. 2 vols. Eichstätt, Stuttgart: Krüll, 1876.

Chamberlain, J. S, ed. *Universities and Their Sons*. Boston: R. Herndon, 1899.

Doderer, Klaus, Hannelore Daubert, et al. *Lexikon der Kinder- und Jugendliteratur* Weinheim: Beltz, 1979.

Eckart, Rudolf. *Lexikon der niedersächsischen Schriftsteller von den ältesten Zeiten bis zur Gegenwart*. Osterwieck/Harz: Zickfeldt, 1891.

Encyclopaedia Judaica. 16 vols. Jerusalem: Macmillan, 1972.

Fielding, M. *Dictionary of American Painters, Sculptors and Engravers*. New York: Carr, 1965.

Goetze, Edmund, ed. *Grundriss zur Geschichte der deutschen Dichtung*. Leipzig: L. Ehlermann, 1848.

Gross, Heinrich, ed. *Deutsche Dichterinnen und Schriftstellerinnen in Wort und Bild*. Berlin: Fr. Thiel, 1885.

Herlitz, Georg, and Bruno Kirschner, eds. *Jüdisches Lexikon*. 4 vols. Berlin: Jüdischer Verlag, 1982.

Herringshaw, Thomas W. *Herringshaw's National Library of American Biography*. Chicago: American Publishers Assoc., 1909–14.

Heuer, Renate, ed. *Lexikon deutsch-jüdischer Autoren*. 5 vols. Munich: K. G. Saur, 1992.

Hyamson, Albert M., and A. M. Silbermann, eds. *Valentine's Jewish Encyclopaedia*. London: Shapiro, Valentine, 1938.

The Jewish Encyclopedia. 12 vols. London: Funk, 1907.

Kosch, Wilhelm, ed. *Deutsches Literatur-Lexikon. Biographisches und Bibliographisches Handbuch*. 2 vols. 1928. Halle (Saale): Max Niemeyer, 1930.

Krüger, Hermann Anders, ed. *Deutsches Literatur-Lexikon*. Munich: C. H. Beck, 1914.

Lexikon der Frau in zwei Bänden. Zürich: Encylios, 1954.

Lexikon der Niedersächsischen Schriftsteller von den ältesten Zeiten bis zur Gegenwart. Hildesheim: Georg Olms, 1974.

Lutz, Berndt. *Metzler Philosophisches Lexikon: Dreihundert biographisch werkgeschichtliche Porträts von den Vorsokratikern bis zu den neuen Philosophen*. Stuttgart: Metzler, 1989.

Neue Deutsche Biographie. Berlin: Duncker & Humblot, 1953–87.

Schem, Alexander. *Deutsch-amerikanisches Conversations-Lexikon*. 11 vols. New York, 1869.

Singer, Isidore, ed. *The Jewish Encyclopedia*. New York: Funk, 1926.

Schröder, Hans. *Lexikon der hamburgischen Schriftsteller bis zur Gegenwart*. Hamburg: Perthes-Besser und Mauke, 1851–83.

Schütze, Karl. *Deutschlands Dichter und Schriftsteller von den ältesten Zeiten bis auf die Gegenwart*. Berlin: Bach, 1862.

Schwab, Gustav. *Fünf Bücher deutscher Lieder und Gedichte von A. Haller bis auf die neuste Zeit*. Leipzig: Weidmann'sche Buchhandlung, 1835.

Stauff, Philipp, ed. *Semi-Kürschner oder Literarisches Lexikon*. Berlin: Selbstverlag, 1913.

Stern, Adolf. *Lexikon der deutschen Nationalliteratur: Die deutschen Dichter und Prosaiker aller Zeiten, mit Berücksichtigung der hervorragendsten dichterisch behandelten Stoffe und Motive*. Leipzig: Verlag des Bibliographischen Instituts, 1882.

Who's Who in America, 1899–1900. Chicago: A. N. Marquis, 1899–1900.

Winninger, Salomon, ed. *Gross Jüdische National-Biographie mit mehr als 8000 Lebensbeschreibungen namhafter Männer und Frauen aller Zeiten und Länder: Ein Nachschlagewerk für das jüdische Volk und dessen Freunde von Salomon Winninger*. Czernowitz: Orient, 1925–36.

IV. PRIMARY SOURCES

1. Ottilie Assing

(a) PUBLISHED WORKS

"Uriel Acosta." *Privilegierte wöchentlich gemeinnützige Nachrichten von und für Hamburg* 8, 09. 1847.

Jean Baptiste Baison: Ein Lebensbild. Hg. von einem Schauspieler. Hamburg: Meissner & Schirges, 1851.

"Transatlantische Briefe. I. Von Hamburg nach New-York, 27 September 1852." *Jahreszeiten* (undated but probably November 1852): 1505–12.

"Transatlantische Briefe II." *Jahreszeiten* 4 (20 Jan. 1853): 105–12.

"Eine Negercolonie in Canada." *Die Gartenlaube* (1857): 687–89.

"Amalie Schoppe, geb. Weise. Ein Nekrolog." *Hamburger Nachrichten*, 18 Dec. 1858.

"Vorrede." *Frederick Douglass, Sclaverei und Freiheit: Autobiographie von Frederick Douglass—aus dem Englischen*. Trans. Ottilie Assing. Hamburg: Hoffmann und Campe, 1860. 9–14.

"John Brown." *Deutsch-amerikanisches Conversations-Lexikon*. Ed. Alexander Schem. New York. 1869. 2.639–40.

"Frederick Douglass." *Deutsch-amerikanisches Conversations-Lexikon.* Ed. Alexander Schem. New York. 1870. 3. 750.

Ottilie Assing's articles in *Morgenblatt für gebildete Leser* 1851–65:

1851

Hamburg, July 1851. 195. 783–85.
Ein Auswandererschiff—Amalie Schoppe—Eine Mutter im Irrenhause—Die österreichische Besatzung.
Hamburg, August 1851. 214. 853–55.
Äusserer Charakter der Stadt—Quartiee—Frauenverein—Theater.
Hamburg, September 1851. 232. 927–29.
Die Besatzung—Amicitia und Fidelitas—Volksvergnügen—Theater—das Weiss'sche Kinderballett.
Hamburg, October 1851. 262. 1051–52.
Victoria regia—Die Ehe zwischen Christen und Juden—Bürgermilitär—Ein Altarblatt.
Hamburg, November 1851. 280. 1117–20.
Die Thorsperre—Die Börsensperre—Auch ein Kassendieb—Hamburger Militär—Der fire-annihilator—Die Schröderstiftung—Auswanderungswesen—Das alte Theater im Opernhof.

1852

Hamburg, January 1852. 4. 90–91.
Winter und Überschwemmung—Bloomercostüm—Aus der Gesellschaft.
Hamburg, March 1852. 15. 256–358.
Der Abmarsch der Österreicher—Kastengeist—"Die Mutter im Irrenhause"—Bankerott—Theater.
Hamburg, April 1852. 20. 478–80.
Die Sonntag—Bankerotte—Alterthümer.
Hamburg, May 1852. 24. 575–76.
Theater—Der erste Mai—Der Bündelabend—Kunstausstellung.
Hamburg, June 1852. 29. 688–89.
St. Pauli—Die Bürgerwehr—Nachtwächter—Der fire-annihilator.
Hamburg, July 1852. 33. 792.
Das Waisengrün—Der Electro-Biolog.
Hamburg, July 1852. 34. 815–16.
Réunions de beau monde—Thierbändigung.

1853

Newyork, May 1853. 27. 643–46.
Die Tombs—Die Washington Exhibition—Die Minstrels.
Aus dem Norden der Vereinigten Staaten, October 1853. 51. 1221–24.
Von Newyork nach Schenectady—Die Shakerkolonie.
Aus dem Norden der Vereinigten Staaten, October 1853. 52. 1244–45.
Die Niagarafälle und die Reise auf den Seen.

Aus dem Norden der Vereinigten Staaten, December 1853. 2. 48.
Eine kleine Stadt im Westen.
Aus dem Norden der Vereinigten Staaten, December 1853. 3. 71–72.
Eine kleine Stadt im Westen (Schluss).

1854
Ein Winterbild aus einer kleinen Stadt im Westen, April 1854. 19. 445–47.
Newyork, June 1854. 29. 692–93.
Von Westen nach Osten, Teil I.
Newyork, June 1854. 30. 719–20.
Von Westen nach Osten, Teil II.
Correspondenz-Nachrichten: Newyork, June 1854. 32. 761–64.
Ein Antisklaverei-Meeting und die schiffbrüchigen Auswanderer.

1855
Newyork 1855.19. 448–451.
Schnellmalereien aus Amerika: Ein Boardinghaus.
Newyork 1855. 38. 902–6.
Gesellschaftsleben in Newyork.
Newyork 1855. 39. 926–29.
Gesellschaftsleben in Newyork (Schluss).
Newyork 1855. 45. 1069–72.
Spaziergänge durch Newyork.
Newyork 1855. 46. 1093–96.
Spaziergänge durch Newyork (Schluss).
Newyork 1855. 51. 1212–17.
Ein Ausflug nach Sing-Sing im Staate Newyork.
Ein Campmeeting—Das Staatsgefängnis.

1856
Newyork 1856. 4. 84–89.
Wanderungen durch Newyork: Ein Blick auf die Schulen.
Newyork, March, 1856. 17. 407–8.
Strenger Winter—Der amerikanische Typus.
Newyork, March 1856 (Fortsetzung). 18. 431–32.
Die Amerikanerinnen—Die Irländer—Die Farbigen—Die Chinesen.
Korrespondenz-Nachrichten. Newyork, March 1856 (Schluss). 19. 453–56.
Die Chinesen—Die Indianer—Jochpleseleila—Zigeuner.
Newyork 1856. 26. 613–17.
Spaziergänge in Newyork.
Newyork 1856. 46. 1094–98.
Sommerwanderungen um Newyork:
Ein Seebad—Howe's Höhle.
Newyork 1856. 49. 1167–69.
Sommerwanderungen um Newyork: Niagara—Greenwood.

Newyork, November 1856. 50. 1173–76.
Die Präsidentenwahl und die Sklavereifrage.
Newyork, December 1856. 1. 22–24.
Die Präsidentenwahl—Theater—Kunst- und Industrieausstellung.
Newyork, December, 1856 (Schluss). 2. 46–48.
Kunst- und Industrieausstellung—Eine woman's right convention.

1857
Correspondenz-Nachrichten, Newyork, February 1857. 15. 352–56.
Ein Criminalfall—Unsicherheit—Wintersaison—Eine amerikanische Rachel—Kunst—
    Wendell Phillips—Eine Gift Enterprise.
Newyork, May 1857. 25. 598–600.
Hoboken.
Newyork, June 1857. 29. 695–96.
Amerikanische Justiz—Sitzung der Antisklavereigesellschaften—Der Redner Doug-
    lass.
Newyork, June 1857 (Schluss). 718–20.
Der Redner Douglass—Kunst—Geisterseherei.
Newyork, July 1857. 32. 766–68.
Zwei Polizeien—W. Walker—Eine Baptistentaufe.
Correspondenz-Nachrichten: Newyork, October 1857. 48. 1168–70.
Die Geldkrisis—Rechtspflege—Bewegungen in der Antisklaverei—Die Industrieausstel-
    lung.
50. 1160–65.
Skizzen aus dem Norden Amerikas: Von Niagara nach Montreal—Montreal—
    Quebec.
Skizzen aus dem Norden Amerikas: Mount Washington—Der Saguenay. 51. 1214–18.
Newyork, December 1857. 4. 93–96.
Die Mayorswahl—Kunst—Ein flüchtiger Sklave—General Worths Leichenbegäng-
    niss.

1858
Correspondenz-Nachrichten: Newyork, February 1858. 13. 307–11.
Der Streit wegen Kansas—Vorlesung der Lola Montez—Öffentliche Vorträge—
    Verbrechen und Justiz—Eine spiritualistische Sitzung.
Newyork, March 1858. 16. 382–84.
Religious revivals—Convention for woman's rights—Weibliche Kleiderreform—Frauen
    in Aemtern.
Correspondenz-Nachrichten: Newyork, March 1858 (Schluss). 17. 404–6.
Ein türkischer Besuch—Plane [sic] "for the relief of Broadway."
Correspondenz-Nachrichten: Newyork, April 1858. 21. 498–501.
Kansas—Revivals—Speisung der Armen—Drei- bis Zwölf-Cents-Herbergen—
    Aus-wandererschiffe.
Newyork, May 1858. 23. 551–52.
Untergang der oceanischen Dampfschiffahrt—Musards Orchester.

Newyork, May 1858 (Schluss). 24. 570–72.
Musik—Die photographische Diebsgallerie—Barnums Museum.
Correspondenz-Nachrichten: Newyork, June 1858. 27. 642–44.
Kansas—Anniversaries.
Correspondenz-Nachrichten: Newyork, June 1858. 31. 738–41.
Eine Excommunication—Die Sklaverei und die Deutschen—Ein deutsches Fest.
Newyork, August 1858. 36. 846.
Sommerhitze.
Newyork, August 1858 (Schluss). 37. 886–88.
Gemäldeausstellung—Winterlandschaft vor Gignour—Genrebilder von Mrs. Spencer—
Versammlung von Malcontenten—Durchreise indianischer Häuptlinge—Wieder-
holtes Leichenbegängnis Präsident Monroe's—Misshandlung eines Nichtsclavenhalters
in Maryland.
Correspondenz-Nachrichten: Newyork, October 1858. 45. 1072–75.
Die Telegraphenfeier und ihre Folgen—Zerstörung der Quarantäne—Ein aufgebrachtes
Sklavenschiff.
Newyork, November 1858. 48. 1150–52.
Der Brand des Crystallpalastes—Revivals und Spiritualismus.
Correspondenz-Nachrichten: Newyork, November 1858. 52. 1240–42.
Die Staats- und Kongresswahlen—Die Sklavenfrage—Eine Amerikanerin über Deutsch-
land—Faustkämpfe—Pedestrians—Wahrsagerinnen.
Newyork, December 1858. 5. 115–18.
Verwaltungsgreuel—Neue Bestrebungen für Colonisation der Neger—Die Botschaft des
Präsidenten—Theater.

1859

Newyork, January 1859. 9. 214–16.
Clima—Beglückwünschte Demokraten—Orr—Douglass—Die Eisenbahn an das stille Meer.
Newyork, January 1859 (Schluss). 10. 240
In der Wildnis.
Newyork, February 1859. 14. 332–35.
Cuba—Öffentliche Vorträge—Mount Vernon Fund Association—Loskauf eines
Sklaven—Eine verschwundene Dame.
Newyork, March 1859. 17. 407–8.
Sickles und Key.
Newyork, April 1859. 22. 526–28.
Frühling—Französisches Theater—Ein fashionabler Prediger—Klopfgeister—Sickles und Key.
Correspondenz-Nachrichten: Newyork, May 1859. 25. 593–96.
Ausgang des Sickles'schen Processes—Gefängniss, Arbeitshaus, Irrenhaus auf Blackwell's
Island—Anniversaries.
Newyork, June 1859. 28. 671–72.
Der Sklavenhandel—Amerikahass.
Correspondenz-Nachrichten: New York, June 1959 (Schluss). 29. 693–95.
Der Amerikafresser—Ausstellung amerikanischer Maler—Ausstellung der deutschen
Künstler—Morphys Schachspiel.

Newyork, July 1859. 34. 816.
 Witterung—Das Broadway.
Newyork, July 1859 (Schluss). 35. 837–40.
 Broadway—Die Newyork Tribune—Sklavenwesen 35.837–40.
Newyork, November 1859. 51. 1223–24.
 Blondin und de Lave—Frederick Douglass—Rowdythum.
Newyork, November 1859 (Schluss). 52. 1245–46.
 Kunstausstellungen—Muskitos.

1860

Newyork, January 1860. 9. 216
 Der Süden gegen den Norden.
Newyork, January 1860 (Schluss). 10. 237–38.
 Der Süden gegen den Norden—Einsturz der Pemberton Mills—Der "Wanderer."
Newyork, February 1860. 11. 263–64.
 Literarischer Krieg des Nordens gegen den Süden—Die Octoroon.
Newyork, March 1860. 17. 407–8.
 Die Strassen der Stadt im Winter—Lecturers.
Newyork, March 1860 (Schluss). 18. 430–31.
 Lecturers—Malerei—The Cooper Institute—Prozess wegen Eheversprechens.
Correspondenz-Nachrichten: Newyork, April 1860. 22. 522–24.
 Der Mormonismus—Vorbereitungen zur Präsidentenwahl—Snuff diggers.
Correspondenz-Nachrichten: Newyork, May 1860. 26. 617–19.
 Die Candidaten zur Präsidentschaft—Anniversaries—Unterschleife von Beamten—
  Humboldts Briefe an Varnhagen.
Newyork, July 1860. 34. 811–13.
 Vorbereitung auf die Präsidentenwahl—Die japanische Gesandtschaft—Der Great Eastern.
Correspondenz-Nachrichten: Newyork, October, 1860. 48. 1147–50.
 Aussichten auf die Präsidentenwahl—Epidemische Angst im Süden—Convention of Infidels.
Correspondenz-Nachrichten: Newyork, November 1860. 52. 1242–45.
 Die Präsidentenwahl—Republikaner und Demokraten.

1861

Newyork, January 1861. 6. 141–44.
 Die Bewegung im Süden der Union—Kunstausstellung.
Correspondenz-Nachrichten: Newyork, January 1861. 9. 209–11.
 Die staatliche Krisis—Rarey der Pferdebändiger.
Newyork, March 1861. 17. 407–8.
 Die Krisis—Das Theater.
Newyork, March 1861 (Schluss). 18. 430.
 Theater—Der neue Zolltarif.
Correspondenz-Nachrichten: Newyork, May 1861. 23. 548–50.
 Ausbruch der Feindseligkeiten—Kriegerische Begeisterung.

Newyork, May 1861: 25. 598–600.
Eine Mormonenpredigt—Spekulation der Spiritualisten—Justiz—Kunst.
Newyork, May 1861. 27. 644–46.
Der Krieg.
Correspondenz-Nachrichten: Newyork, August, 1861. 37. 883–85.
Der Krieg—Douglas—Die Deutschen in Missouri—Ein schwarzer Held und Barnum.
Newyork, October 1861. 48. 1147–49.
Der Bürgerkrieg—Fremont und die Regierung—Die Spitzbubengallerie.
Correspondenz-Nachrichten: Newyork, November 1861. 52. 1245–47.
Die grosse Telegraphenlinie—Fremont—Scott—Auswanderung von Farbigen nach Hayti—Barnum.

1862

Newyork, January 1862. 7. 163–66.
Der Krieg—Das Sklavenwesen—Der Brand von Charleston—Ein wichtiges Aktenstück.
Newyork, February 1862. 13. 310–12.
Die Sklaverei und die Unionsregierung—Verhältniss des weiblichen Geschlechts zur Sklaverei—Reguläre und Freiwillige—Armeelieferanten.
Newyork, March 1862. 16. 382–84.
Umschwung der Dinge—Die südliche Ritterschaft—Hinrichtung eines Sklavenhändlers.
Newyork, May 1862. 24. 572–74.
Der Krieg—Die Sklavenfrage—Farbenvorurtheil—Kunstausstellung.
Correspondenz-Nachrichten: Newyork, End of May. 28. 665–68.
General Hunter und die Regierung—Die Schwarzen—Sommer—Hundeausstellung—Commodore Nutt—Die Homestead-Bill.
Correspondenz-Nachrichten: Newyork, October 1862. 47. 1126–28.
Die Emancipation der Sklaven.
Newyork, November 1862. 1. 22–24.
Unerwartete Wirkungen des Krieges—Die Wahlen für den Congress—McClellan.
Newyork, December 1862. 5. 116–18.
Neue Niederlage—Corruption—Religiöse Zustände.

1863

Newyork, January 1863. 9. 214–16.
Die Emancipationsproclamation—Zustände im Staate Mississippi.
Newyork, March 1863. 14. 332–34.
Humbug—Psychologie—Die Zwergenhochzeit—Verhalten der Neger im Süden.
Newyork, April 1863. 22. 523–26.
Die Kupferschlangen—McClellan.
Newyork, November 1863. 50. 1194–96.
Amerikanische Zustände—Pöbelherrschaft.
Newyork, November 1863. 52. 1241–44.
Die bewaffneten Farbigen—Theuerung—Luxus—Bewegungen unter den Arbeitern—Bloomerismus.

1864

Newyork, January 1864. 6. 140–43.
Der Sitzungstag der Antisklavereigesellschaft—Unglücksfälle—Seeräuber.
Newyork, January 1864. 11. 262–64.
Einfluss des Krieges auf die gesellschaftlichen Verhältnisse und auf die Sklavereifrage.
Newyork, February 1864. 15. 354–57.
Die Flucht der gefangenen Unionsoffiziere—Überraschende Wirkungen des Kriegs.
Newyork, March 1864. 17. 406–8.
Ein Negerregiment—Die Ausstellung der Sanitätscommission—Die radicalen Deutschen.
Correspondenz-Nachrichten: Newyork, April 1864. 22. 520–23.
Die grosse Ausstellung.
Newyork, May 1864. 26. 621–22.
Der Krieg—Die grosse Ausstellung.
Newyork, May 1864 (Schluss). 27. 648.
Frauenverein gegen Kleiderluxus—Kunstausstellung.
Newyork, September 1864. 43. 1031–32.
Die Präsidentenwahl.
Newyork, September 1864 (Schluss). 44. 1052–53.
Die Präsidentenwahl.
Correspondenz-Nachrichten: New-York, November 1864. 49. 1169–71.
McClellans Brief.
Newyork, November 1864. 52. 1243–46.
Die Präsidentenwahl.
Correspondenz-Nachrichten: Newyork, December 1864. 5. 117–119.
Stimmung nach der Präsidentenwahl—Thanksgiving day—Das Feuercomplot.

1865

Newyork, January 1865. 11. 262–64.
Weihnachten und Neujahr—Die Sklavereifrage—Everett—Ein neues deutsches Buch.
Newyork, March 1865. 15. 356–59.
Gesetzliche Abschaffung der Sklaverei.
Correspondenz-Nachrichten: Newyork, March 1865. 18. 425–28.
Die Übergabe von Charleston—Volksfest—Corruption.
Correspondenz-Nachrichten, Newyork, April 1865. 22. 520–23.
Siegesjubel und Trauer.
Newyork, May 1865. 27. 645–47.
Der Prozess—Trauerfeierlichkeiten—Reconstituierung—Jefferson Davis.
Correspondenz-Nachrichten, Newyork, August 1865. 39. 929–32.
Die Mörder Lincolns und Jefferson Davis—Die Emancipationsfrage—Barnum.
Correspondenz-Nachrichten: Newyork, September 1865. 45. 1072–75.
Politik des Präsidenten—Negerverfolgungen—Erbitterung der Südländer—Neue Enthüllungen über die Behandlung der Gefangenen in den Südstaaten.

Newyork, November 1865. 50. 1200.
  "Der Sieg des Südens".
Correspondenz-Nachrichten: Newyork, November (Schluss). 51. 1220–22.
  Die Halben und die Ganzen—Der Spiritualismus—Ein literarisches Institut der Far-
  bigen.

Articles in *Beiblatt zur Zeitschrift für Bildende Kunst*

1872

No. 7	Vinnie Ream	121–24
No. 7	Korrespondenzen	124–27
No. 14	Korrespondenzen	255
No. 21	Korrespondenzen	381–85

1874

| No. 36 | Die Ausstellung der New Yorker Akademie | 569–74 |
| No. 37 | New York | 596–97 |

1876

No. 18	Kunstunterricht in Amerika	282–83
No. 43	Die Ausstellung des Kunstvereins für die Rheinlande und Westfalen	687–91
No. 51	Aus Düsseldorf	820–21

1877

No. 2	Prof. Wislicenus	23–24
No. 8	Düsseldorf	122–23
No. 14	Düsseldorf	225–27
No. 22	Düsseldorf	354–57
No. 23	Düsseldorf	366–70
No. 31	Düsseldorf	499–501
No. 33	Düsseldorf	531–33
No. 38	Düsseldorf	609–10
No. 41	Düsseldorf	661–62
No. 42	Düsseldorf	676–77

1878

No. 3		45–46
No. 5		76
No. 6		92–94
No. 8		127–29
No. 17	Düsseldorf	275–77
No. 17	Konkurrenzen	322–24
No. 23	Das städtische Museum in New York	361–64
No. 25	Aus dem Salon Schulte in Düsseldorf	399–401

No. 27	Aus den permanenten Ausstellungen . . .	433–35
No. 27	Korrespondenz	428–31
No. 28	Düsseldorf	451–53
No. 40	Kunstausstellung in New York	638–41
No. 42	Düsseldorf	675–76
No. 48	Düsseldorf	775
No. 48	Düsseldorf	778

1879

No. 14	Die Corcoran Galerie in Washington	221–24
No. 23	Korrespondenz	365–68
No. 30	Prof. P. Jansen	485
No. 30	Kunstauktion in New York	486
No. 32	Amerikanische Kunstausstellungen	505–7
No. 39	Amerikanische Kunstausstellungen II	628–30
No. 40	Museum in New York	665–66

1880

No. 12	Korrespondenz	185–89
No. 23	Korrespondenz	368–71
No. 33	Korrespondenz	523–30

1881

No. 10	Cesare Sighinolfi	163–64
No. 18	Cyprische Statuen in New York	289–93
No. 25	Cesnolas Rechtfertigung	401–4
No. 25	Korrespondenz	406–10
No. 36	Korrespondenz	584–87
No. 37	Korrespondenz (Schluss)	599–602
No. 43	Die Farragut-Statue	725–26

Articles in *Süddeutsche Post*

6 November 1882	Die amerikanischen Wahlen
22 December 1882	Amerikanische Freidenker
24 December 1882	Amerikanische Freidenker
13 November 1883	Zyr Rassenhetze in Amerika
22 December 1883	Von Deutschland nach Italien

Numerous articles in *National Era* and *New National Era* between 1868 and 1874

(*b*) UNPUBLISHED MANUSCRIPTS

"Ein Besuch bei Gerrit Smith," undated, *Schillermuseum Marbach am Neckar.*

"Der Aufstand bei Harpers Ferry," October, November, December 1859, *Schillermuseum Marbach am Neckar.*

"Die Farbigen in New York," undated, *Schillermuseum Marbach am Neckar.*

(*c*). UNPUBLISHED TEXTS

"Letters to Ludmilla Assing, 1864–1880." Biblioteka Jagiellonska Krakowa. Varnhagen Collection.

"Letters to Frederick Douglass, 1870–1879." Washington DC: Library of Congress, Frederick Douglass Papers, Reels 2–3.

"Miss Assing's Will." New York, November 9, 1871. Washington DC: Library of Congress, Frederick Douglass Papers. Container No. 45. Reel 30.

"Codicil." Florence, April 7, 1883. Washington DC: Library of Congress, Frederick Douglass Papers. Container No. 45. Reel 30.

2. Frederick Douglass

Autobiographies. Narrative of the Life of Frederick Douglass, an American Slave; *My Bondage and My Freedom*; *Life and Times of Frederick Douglass*. New York: Library of America, 1994.

Blassingame, John W., and McKivigan, John eds. *The Frederick Douglass Papers.* 5 vols. New Haven: Yale UP, 1979.

Foner, Philip S., ed. *The Life and Writings of Frederick Douglass.* 5 vols. New York: International, 1950–55.

Foner, Philip S., ed. *Frederick Douglass on Women's Rights* Westport, Conn.: Greenwood, 1976.

Sclaverei und Freiheit: Autobiographie von Frederick Douglass—aus dem Englischen. Trans. Ottilie Assing. Hamburg: Hoffmann und Campe, 1860.

"What I Found at the Northampton Association." *History of Florence, Massachusetts: Including a Complete Account of the Northampton Association of Education and Industry.* Ed. Charles A. Sheffield. Florence, Mass.: Charles A. Sheffield, 1895. 131–32.

3. Ludmilla Assing

Gräfin Elisa von Ahlefeld, die Gattin Adolfs von Lützow, die Freundin Karl Immermanns: Eine Biographie. Berlin: Duncker, 1857.

Vita di Piero Cironi. Prato: Tipografia FF. Giachetti, 1865.

"Erinnerungen an Rudolf von Gottschall." *Die Gartenlaube* (1880): 298–300.

4. Rosa Maria Assing/David Assing

Assing, David A., ed. *Rosa Maria's poetischer Nachlass.* Altona: Johann Friedrich Hammersch, 1841.

V. NINETEENTH-CENTURY NEWSPAPERS AND PERIODICALS

Alpha
Atlantische Studien
Deutsche Blätter: Beigabe zur Gartenlaube
Douglass' Monthly
Frederick Douglass' Paper
Die Gartenlaube
Illustrierte Zeitung
Jahreszeiten
Leipziger Zeitung für bildende Kunst

The Liberator
Morgenblätter für gebildete Leser
Morgenblätter für gebildete Stände
National Anti-Slavery Standard
Die neue Zeit
New National Era
New Yorker Abendzeitung
New Yorker Correspondenzen
New Yorker Criminal Zeitung und Belletristisches Journal
New Yorker Staats Zeitung
The North Star
Philadelphia Press
Der Pionier
Privilegierte wöchentliche gemeinnützige Nachrichten von und für Hamburg
Rochester Abendblatt
Rochester Demokrat und Chronicle
Rochester Daily Union and Advertiser
Rochester Täglicher Beobachter
Rochester Volksblatt
Süddeutsche Post
Der Volkstribun
Westermann's Illustrierte Monatshefte

VI. SECONDARY SOURCES

Aaron, Daniel. "The 'Inky Curse.' Miscegenation in the White Literary Imagination." *Social Science Information* 22 (1983): 169–90.

Adler, Hans. *Soziale Romane im Vormärz: Literatursemiotische Studie*. Munich: Wilhelm Fink, 1980.

Akinsha, Konstantin, Grigorii Kozlov, and Sylvia Hochfield. *Beautiful Loot: The Soviet Plunder of Europe's Art Treasures*. New York: Random House, 1995.

Allen, Theodore. *The Invention of the White Race*. Vol. 1: *Racial Oppression and Social Control*. New York: Verso, 1994.

Alt, Arthur Tilo, ed. *Hebbel-Briefe: Neue und ergänzte Briefe von und an Friedrich Hebbel nebst Register und Regesten der bisher gedruckten Briefe*. Berlin: Erich Schmidt, 1989.

Altman, Janet Gurkin. *Epistolarity: Approaches to Form*. Columbus: Ohio State UP, 1982.

Alvarez, A. *The Savage God: A Study of Suicide*. New York: Random House, 1970.

Anderson, Patricia. *When Passion Reigned: Sex and the Victorians*. New York: Basic Books, 1995.

Andrews, William L. "Frederick Douglass, Preacher." *American Literature* 54 (1982): 455–75.

———. "Reunion in the Postbellum Slave Narrative: Frederick Douglass and Elizabeth Keckley." *Black American Literature Forum* 23 (Spring 1989): 5–16.

———, ed. *Critical Essays on Frederick Douglass*. Boston: G. K. Hall, 1991.

Aptheker, Herbert. "An Unpublished Frederick Douglass Letter." *Journal of Negro History* 44 (1959): 278–80.

Arendt, Hannah. *Rahel Varnhagen: The Life of a Jewess*. London: Institute by the East & West Library, 1957.

Arndt, Karl J. R., and May E. Olsen. *Deutsch-amerikanische Zeitungen und Zeitschriften, 1732–1955*. Heidelberg: Quelle und Mayer, 1961.

Ascher, Louise deSalvo, and Sara Ruddick, eds. *Between Women: Biographers, Novelists, Critics, Teachers and Artists Write About Their Work on Women*. Boston: Beacon, 1984.

Ayers, Edward L. *The Promise of the New South: Life After Reconstruction*. New York: Oxford UP, 1992.

Azevedo, Aluisio. *Mulatto*. Rutherford, N.J.: Fairleigh Dickinson UP, 1990.

Bade, Klaus J., ed. *Deutsche im Ausland — Fremde in Deutschland: Migration in Geschichte und Gegenwart*. Munich: Beck, 1992.

Baker, Houston, Jr. *Blues, Ideology, and Afro-American Literature*. Chicago: U Chicago P. 1984

Barba, Preston A. "Emigration to America as Reflected in German Fiction." *German-American Annals* 12 (1914): 193–227.

Barthes, Roland. *Mythologies*. 1957. Paris: Seuil, 1970.

Basler, Roy P. *Abraham Lincoln: His Speeches and Writings*. New York: World Publishing, 1969.

Bausch, Mary. "America in German Fiction, 1880–1914." Diss. U of Wisconsin, 1921.

Bauschinger, Sigrid, Horst Denkler, and Wilfried Malsch, eds. *Amerika in der deutschen Literatur: Neue Welt-Nordamerika-U.S.A.* Stuttgart: Reclam, 1965.

Baylin, Bernard. *From Protestant Peasants to Jewish Intellectuals: The Germans in the Peopling of America*. Oxford: Berg Publishers, 1988.

Bayor, Ronald, and Timothy J. Meagher. *The New York Irish: Essays Toward a History*. Baltimore: Johns Hopkins UP, 1995.

Beane, Carol Anne. "The Characterization of Blacks and Mulattoes in Selected Novels from Colombia, Venezuela, Ecuador, and Peru." Ph.D. diss., U of California, Berkeley, 1980.

Beatty, Bess. *A Revolution Gone Backwards: The Black Response to National Politics, 1776–1896*. Westport, Conn.: Greenwood, 1987.

Bebler, Emil *Gottfried Keller und Ludmilla Assing*. Zürich: Rascher, 1952.

Behmer, Britta. "Von deutscher Kulturkritik zum Abolitionismus: Literarische und journalistische Betrachtungen der Emigrantin Ottilie Assing." MA thesis, University of Munich, Germany, 1996. Unpublished manuscript.

Behn, Aphra. *Oroonoko, The Rover, and Other Works*. Ed. Janet Todd. London: Penguin, 1992.

Belz, Herman. "Law, Politics, and Race in the Struggle for Equal Pay During the Civil War." *Civil War History* 22 (September 1976): 197–222.

Benstock, Shari, ed. *The Private Self: Theory and Practice of Women's Autobiographical Writings*. Chapel Hill: U of North Carolina P, 1988.

Berg, Barbara. *The Remembered Gate: Origins of American Feminism: The Woman and the City, 1800–1860*. Oxford: Oxford UP, 1978.

Bergland, Betty. "Immigrant History and the Gendered Subject: A Review Essay." *Ethnic Forum* 8 (1988): 24–39.

Bernstein, Iver. *The New York City Draft Riots: Their Significance for American Society and Politics in the Age of the Civil War.* New York: Oxford UP, 1990.

Berzon, Judith. *Neither White Nor Black: The Mulatto Character in American Fiction.* New York: New York UP, 1978.

Betz, Otto, et al. *Abraham unser Vater: Juden und Christen im Gespräch über die Bibel.* Leiden: E. J. Brill, 1963.

Bianquis, Geneviève. *Amours en Allemagne à l'Epoche Romantique.* Paris: Hachette, 1961.

Bittinger, Lucy. "Emigration to America Reflected in German Fiction." *Lutheran Quarterly* 43 (1913): 375–88.

Blackwell, Jeannine, and Susanne Zantop, eds. *Bitter Healing: German Women Writers, 1700–1830.* Omaha: U of Nebraska P, 1990.

Blassingame, John W. *The Slave Community. Plantation Life in the Ante-Bellum South.* New York: Oxford UP, 1972.

———. *Frederick Douglass: The Clarion Voice.* Washington, DC: National Park Service Division of Publications, 1976.

Blight, David W. *Frederick Douglass' Civil War: Keeping Faith in Jubilee.* Baton Rouge: Louisiana State UP, 1989.

Bloch, J. M. *Miscegenation, Melaleukation, and Mr. Lincoln's Day.* New York: Schaum C., 1958.

Bloom, Harold, ed. *Modern Critical Views: Toni Morrison.* New York: Chelsea, 1990.

Blumin, Stuart. "Explaining the New Metropolis: Perceptions, Depictions and Analysis in Mid-Nineteenth-Century New York City." *Journal of Urban History* 11 (November 1984): 9–30.

———. *The Emergence of the Middle Class: Social Experience in the American City, 1760–1900.* Cambridge: Cambridge UP, 1989.

Bolin, Wilhelm. *Ludwig Feuerbach: Sein Wirken und seine Zeitgenossen.* Stuttgart: Cotta'sche Buchhandlung, 1891.

———, ed. *Ausgewählte Briefe von und an Ludwig Feuerbach.* Leipzig: Otto Wigand, 1904.

Bontemps, Arna W. *Free at Last: The Life of Frederick Douglass.* New York: Dodd; Mead, 1971.

Börnstein, Heinrich. *75 Jahre in der Alten und Neuen Welt: Memoiren eines Unbedeutenden.* 2 vols. Leipzig: Peter Lang, 1986.

Bornstein, Paul, ed. *Friedrich Hebbels sämtliche Werke nebst den Tagebüchern und einer Auswahl der Briefe.* 4 vols. Munich: Georg Müller, 1911–26.

Boyd, Willis D. "James Redpath and American Negro Colonisation in Haiti, 1860–1862." *Americas* (12 Oct. 1995): 169–82.

Brantley, Daniel. "Black Diplomacy and Frederick Douglass' Caribbean Experiences, 1871 and 1889–1891: The Untold History." *Phylon* 45 (September 1984): 197–209.

Braude, Ann. *Radical Spirits: Spiritualism and Women's Rights in Nineteenth-Century America.* Boston: Beacon, 1989.

Bremer, Fredrika. *The Homes of the New World: Impressions of America.* Trans. Mary Howitt. 2 vols. New York: Harper, 1853.

Bretting, Agnes. *Soziale Probleme deutscher Auswanderer in New York City 1800–1860.* Wiesbaden: Steiner, 1981.

———. "Die Konfrontation der deutschen Einwanderer mit der amerikanischen Wirklichkeit in New York City im 19. und 20. Jahrhundert." *Amerikastudien/American Studies* 27 (1982): 247–57.

———. "Frauen als Einwanderer in der Neuen Welt: Überlegungen anhand einiger Selbstzeugnisse deutscher Auswanderinnen." *Amerikastudien/American Studies* 33 (1988): 319–27.

———. *Auswanderung und Schiffahrtsinteressen: "Little Germanies" in New York.* Stuttgart: Steiner, 1992.

Breuer, Edward. *The Limits of Enlightenment: Jews, Germans and the Eighteenth-Century Study of Scripture.* Cambridge, Mass.: Harvard UP, 1996.

Brodie, Fawn. *Thomas Jefferson: An Intimate History.* New York: W. W. Norton, 1974.

Brown, Gillian. *Domestic Individualism: Imagining Self in Nineteenth-Century America.* Berkeley: U of California P, 1990.

Brown, Harry J., and Frederick D. Williams, eds. *The Diary of James A. Garfield.* 4 vols. East Lansing: Michigan State UP, 1967–81.

Brown, Sterling A., Arthur P. Davis, and Ulysses Lee, eds. *The Negro Caravan: Writings by American Negroes.* 1941. Repr. New York: Arno P, 1970.

Bruer, Albert. *Geschichte der Juden in Preussen: 1750–1820.* Frankfurt, N.Y.: Campus, 1991.

Bruncken, Ernest. "German Political Refugees in the United States During the Period from 1815–1860." *Special Print from Deutsch-amerikanische Geschichtsblätter,* 1904. San Francisco: R and E Research, 1970.

Brunk, Otfried. *Die Atheismus-Anschuldigung gegen Johann Gottlieb: Die Geisteshaltung Goethes und anderer Zeitgenossen in Briefen und anderen erhaltenen Dokumenten.* Radolfzell: Edition Löwengasse, 1985.

Bryant, William Cullen. *The American Landscape.* New York: E. Bliss, 1830.

Bundesverband der Sudentendeutschen Landsmannschaft, ed. *Sudeten-deutsche Amerikaner: Festschrift zur 200-Jahresfeier der Vereinigten Staaten von Amerika.* Munich, 1976.

Bürger, Christa. *Leben schreiben: Die Klassik, die Romantik und der Ort der Frauen.* Stuttgart: Metzler, 1990.

Burke, Donald K. *Frederick Douglass: Crusading Orator for Human Rights.* New York: Garland, 1996.

Burkhardt, Marianne, ed. *Gestaltet und gestaltend: Frauen in der deutschen Kultur.* Amsterdam: Amsterdamer Beiträge zur neueren Germanistik, 1980.

Bussmann, Hadumod, and Renate Hof, eds. *Genus: Zur Geschlechterdifferenz in den Kulturwissenschaften.* Stuttgart: Kröner, 1995.

Camper, Carol, ed. *Miscegenation Blues: Voices of Mixed Race Women.* Toronto: Sister Vision P, 1994.

Carby, Hazel. *Reconstructing Womanhood: The Emergence of the Afro-American Novelist.* Oxford: Oxford UP, 1987.

Carlebach, Julius. *Karl Marx and the Radical Critique of Judaism.* London: Routledge, 1978.

———, ed. *Zur Geschichte der jüdischen Frau in Deutschland.* Berlin: Metropol, 1993.

Castro, Carlos de. *Grundriss der Geschichte der Familie de Castro.* Paderborn: Selbstverlag, 1934.

Chambers, Theodore F. *The Early Germans of New Jersey: Their History, Churches, and Genealogies.* Baltimore: Genealogical, 1969.

Chesnutt, Charles W. *Frederick Douglass.* Boston: Small & Maynard, 1899.

Christiansen, Rupert. *Romantic Affinities: Portraits from an Age 1780–1830*. New York: G. P. Putnam's Sons, 1988.

Clebsch, William. "Christian Interpretations of the Civil War." *Church History* 30 (June 1961): 212–22.

Clinton, Catherine. *The Other Civil War: American Women in the Nineteenth Century*. New York: Hill and Wang, 1984.

Clyde, Debra. " 'A People Called Methodists.' The Van Coortlandts and Methodism in Early America, Historic Hudson Valley, Tarrytown, NY." *Westchester Historian* 66 (Summer 1990): 51–56.

Cocalis, Susan L. "Der Vormund will Vormund sein: Zur Problematik der weiblichen Unmündigkeit im 18. Jahrhundert." *Gestaltet und Gestaltend: Frauen in der deutschen Kultur*. Ed. Marianne Burkhardt. Amsterdam: Amsterdamer Beiträge zur neueren Germanistik, 1980. 33–55.

Cohen, Naomi W. *Encounter with Emancipation: The German Jews in the United States, 1830–1914*. Philadelphia: Jewish Publication Society of America, 1984.

Condoyannis, George Edward. "German-American Prose Fiction from 1850–1914." Diss. Columbia U, 1953.

Cooper, Mark Anthony, Sr., ed. *Dear Father: A Collection of Letters to Frederick Douglass from His Children 1859–1894*. Philadelphia: Fulmore, 1990.

Cronholm, Anna-Christie. *Die nordamerikanische Sklavenfrage im deutschen Schrifttum des 19. Jahrhunderts*. Berlin: Philosophische Fakultät, 1958.

Cruden, Robert. *The Negro in Reconstruction*. Englewood Cliffs, NJ: Prentice-Hall, 1969.

Curtis, L. Perry, Jr. *Apes and Angels: The Irishman in Victorian Caricature*. Washington, D.C.: Smithsonian Institution Press, 1996.

Danton, George H. "Amalia Weise Schoppe: Schenectady's Most Prolific Author." *Proceedings of the New York State Historical Society* 37 (1939): 425–35.

Davis, Allison. *Leadership, Love, and Aggression*. San Diego: Harcourt Brace Jovanovich, 1983.

Davis, Natalie Zemon. *Women on the Margins: Three Seventeenth-Century Lives*. Cambridge, Mass.: Harvard UP, 1997.

Dearborn, Mary V. *Pocahonta's Daughters. Gender and Ethnicity in American Culture*. New York: Oxford UP, 1986.

Degener, Hermann A. L., ed. *Wer ist's?: Unsere Zeitgenossen*. Leipzig: Selbstverlag, 1909.

DePietro, Thomas, "Vision and Revision in the Autobiographies of Frederick Douglass." *College Language Association Journal* 26 (June 1983): 384–96.

Devrient, Eduard. *Geschichte der deutschen Schauspielkunst*. Berlin: Eigenbrödler, 1929.

Dick, Jutta. "Freundinnen: Rahel de Castro, Ludmilla Assing, Ottilie Assing." *Menora: Jahrbuch für deutsch-jüdische Geschichte*. Eds. Julius H. Schoeps et al. Bodenheim: Philo, 1977. 181–98.

———, and Marina Sassenberg, eds. *Jüdische Frauen im 19. und 20. Jahrhundert: Lexikon zu Leben und Werk*. Reinbek: Rowohlt, 1993.

———, and Barbara Hahn, eds. *Von einer Welt in die andere: Jüdinnen im 19. und 20. Jahrhundert*. Vienna: Brandstätter, 1993.

———, and Julius H. Schoeps, eds. *Salomon Ludwig Steinheim und Johanna Steinheim: Briefe*. Hildesheim: Olms, 1996.

Die Deutschen in Amerika: Atlantische Studien. 5 vols. Göttingen: Georg Heinrich Wigans, 1853.

Diner, Hasia. *In the Almost Promised Land: American Jews and Blacks, 1915–1935.* Baltimore: Johns Hopkins UP, 1995.

Dinnerstein, Leonard. *Antisemitism in America.* New York: Oxford UP, 1994.

Dobert, Eitel Wolf. *Die Schriften der deutsch-amerikanischen Achtundvierziger.* Baltimore: U of Maryland P, 1954.

———. *Deutsche Demokraten in Amerika: Die Achtundvierziger und ihre Schriften.* Göttingen: Vandenhoeck & Ruprecht, 1958.

———. *Karl Gutzkow und seine Zeit.* Bern: Francke, 1968.

Doerries, Reinhard R. "Organization and Ethnicity: The German American Experience." *Amerikastudien/American Studies* 33 (1988): 309–17.

Donald, David Herbert. *Lincoln.* New York: Simon & Schuster, 1995.

Dorn, Adelaide E. "A History of the Anti-Slavery Movement in Rochester and Vicinity." MA thesis, University of Buffalo, 1932.

Douai, Adolf. *Personen, Land und Zustände in Nord-Amerika: Rathgeber für Auswanderer.* Berlin: Otto Janke, 1965

———. *Better Times!* Chicago: Executive Committee, Workingmen's Party of the United States, 1877.

Douglass, Helen. *In memoriam: Frederick Douglass.* Philadelphia: J. C. Yorston, 1897.

Drescher, Martin. "Deutsche Erzähler in Amerika: Eine Studie." *Jahrbuch der Deutschamerikaner* 4 (1918): 89–109.

Duberman, Martin, ed. *The Antislavery Vanguard.* Princeton, N.J.: Princeton UP, 1965.

DuBois, Eugene E. *The City of Frederick Douglass: Rochester's African-American People and Places.* Rochester, NY: Landmark Society of Western New York, 1994.

Du Bois, W. E. B. *Black Reconstruction.* New York: Russell & Russell, 1935.

duCille, Ann. *The Coupling Convention: Sex, Text, and Tradition in Black Women's Fiction.* New York: Oxford UP, 1993.

Dulon, Rudolf. *Aus Amerika: Über Schule, deutsche Schule, amerikanische Schule und deutsch-amerikanische Schule.* Leipzig: C. F. Winter, 1866.

Early, Gerald, ed. *Lure and Loathing: Essays on Race, Identity, and the Ambivalence of Assimilation.* New York: Penguin, 1993.

Ebersberger, Thea, ed. *Erinnerungsblätter aus dem Leben Luise Mühlbach's: Gesammelt und Herausgegeben von ihrer Tochter.* Leipzig: H. Schmidt & C. Günther, 1902.

Eiseman, Alberta. *Rebels and Reformers: Biographies of Four Jewish Americans: Uriah Phillips Levy, Ernestine L. Rose, Louis D. Brandeis, Lillian D. Wald.* Garden City, N.Y.: Zenith (Doubleday), 1976.

Ericson, Edward L. *The Free Mind through the Ages.* New York: Frederick Ungar, 1985.

Ermatinger, Emil. *Gottfried Kellers Leben.* Zürich: Artemis, 1950.

Fabre, Michel, ed. *Regards sur la littérature noire américaine.* Paris: Publications du Conseil Scientifique de la Sorbonne Nouvelle-Paris III, 1980.

Favret, Mary A. *Romantic Correspondence: Women, Politics and the Fiction of Letters.* Cambridge: Cambridge UP, 1993.

Feilchenfeldt, Konrad. *Varnhagen als Historiker.* Amsterdam: Erasmus, 1970.

————, ed. *Varnhagen von Ense, Karl August: Werke in Fünf Bänden*. Frankfurt: Deutscher Klassiker Verlag, 1987–97.

Felden, Tamara. "Reiseliteratur von Vormärzlerinnen: Zur literarischen Repräsentation der Geschlechterrollenerfahrung." Diss. U of Maryland, 1990.

————. "Ottilie Assing's View of America in the Context of Travel Literature by 19th Century German Women." *German Quarterly* (1992): 340–48.

Felden, Tamara. *Frauen Reisen: Zur literarischen Repräsentation weiblicher Geschlechterrollenerfahrung im 19. Jahrhundert*. New York: Peter Lang, 1993.

Feyl, Renate, ed. *Sein ist das Weib, Denken der Mann: Ansichten und Äusserungen für und wider die gelehrten Frauen*. Darmstadt: Luchterhand, 1984.

Finkelmann, Paul, ed. *His Soul Goes Marching on: Responses to John Brown and the Harpers Ferry Raid*. Charlottesville: U of Virginia P, 1995.

Fischer, Hermann, ed. *Ludwig Uhland: Gesammelte Werke*. Darmstadt: Wissenschaftliche Buchgesellschaft, 1977.

Fishkin, Shelley Fisher. "Interrogating 'Whiteness,' Complicating, 'Blackness': Remapping American Culture." *American Quarterly* 47 (September 1995): 428–66.

Foner, Philip Sheldon. *Frederick Douglass: A Biography*. New York: Citadel P, 1964.

————, ed. *Alexander von Humboldt on Slavery in the United States*. Berlin: Humboldt University, 1981.

————, ed. *Alexander von Humboldt über die Sklaverei in den USA: Eine Dokumentation mit einer Einführung und Anmerkungen*. Berlin: Humboldt-Universität zu Berlin, 1981.

Foster, Edward Halsey, and Geoffrey W. Clark, eds. *Hoboken: A Collection of Essays*. New York: Irvington, 1976.

Fout, John C., ed. *German Women in the Nineteenth Century: A Social History*. New York: Holmes and Meier, 1984.

————, and Maura Shaw Tantillo, eds. *American Sexual Politics: Sex, Gender, and Race Since the Civil War*. Chicago: U of Chicago P, 1993.

Frankel, Zacharias, ed. *Monatsschrift für Geschichte und Wissenschaft des Judenthums*. Hildesheim: Georg Olms, 1969.

Frankenberg, Ruth. *The Social Construction of Whiteness: White Women, Race Matters*. London: Routledge, 1993.

Franklin, John Hope. *Reconstruction after the Civil War*. Chicago: U of Chicago P, 1961.

Franz, Eckhardt G. *Das Amerikabild der deutschen Revolution von 1848/49: Zum Problem der Übertragung gewachsener Verfassungsformen*. Heidelberg: Winter, 1958.

Fredrickson, George M. *The Inner Civil War: Northern Intellectuals and the Crisis of the Union*. New York: Harper & Row, 1965.

————. *The Black Image in the White Mind: The Debate on Afro-American Character and Destiny, 1817–1914*. New York: Harper & Row, 1971.

————. *A Nation Divided: Problems and Issues of the Civil War and Reconstruction*. Minneapolis: Burgess, 1975.

————. *The Arrogance of Race: Historical Perspectives on Slavery, Racism, and Social Inequality*. Middletown, Conn.: Wesleyan UP, 1988.

Freeman, Rhoda Golden. "The Free Negro in New York City in the Era Before the Civil War." Diss. Columbia University, 1966.

Freimark, Peter, Ina Lorenz, and Gunter Marwedel. *Judentore, Kuggel, Steuerkonten: Untersuchungen zur Geschichte der deutschen Juden, vornehmlich im Hamburger Raum*. Hamburg: Hans Christians, 1983.

————, ed. *Juden in Preussen, Juden in Hamburg*. Hamburg: Hans Christians, 1983.

Freimark, Peter, and Franklin Kopitzsch, eds. *Spuren der Vergangenheit sichtbar machen: Beiträge der Juden in Hamburg*. Hamburg: Landeszentrale für Politische Bildung, 1991.

Friedman, Lawrence J. "The Gerrit Smith Circle: Abolitionism in the Burned-Over District." *Civil War History* 26 (March 1980): 18–38.

————. *Gregarious Saints: Self and Community in American Abolitionism, 1830–1870*. New York: Cambridge UP, 1982.

Friedrichs, Elisabeth, ed. *Die deutschsprachigen Schriftstellerinnen des 18. und 19. Jahrhunderts*. Stuttgart: Metzler, 1981.

Friesen, Gerhard. "H. C. E. von Gagern and German Emigration to America. Some Preliminaries." *Amerikastudien/American Studies* 26 (1981): 4–10.

Funderburg, Lise. *Black, White, Other: Biracial Americans Talk About Race and Identity*. New York: William Morrow, 1994.

Gabaccia, Donna. *From the Other Side: Women, Gender, and Immigrant Life in the United States, 1820–1990*. Bloomington: Indiana UP, 1994.

Gagern, Carlos von. *Todte und Lebende*. 2 vols. Berlin: Abenheimischer Verlag, 1884.

Gallois, Dr. J. G. *Geschichte der Stadt Hamburg*. Hamburg: Oncken, 1867.

Gardner, Howard. *Frames of Mind: The Theory of Multiple Intelligences*. New York: Basic Books, 1985.

Garvey, John, and Noel Ignatiev, eds. *Race Traitor*. New York: Routledge, 1996.

Gates, Henry Louis, Jr., ed. *Figures in Black: Words, Signs, and the "Racial" Self*. New York: Oxford UP, 1987.

————. "A Dangerous Literacy: The Legacy of Frederick Douglass." *The New York Times Book Review* (28 May 1995): 3, 5.

Gay, Peter. *Education of the Senses*. New York: Oxford UP, 1984.

————. *The Tender Passion*. New York: Oxford UP, 1986.

————. *The Naked Heart: The Bourgeois Experience, Victoria to Freud*. New York: W. W. Norton, 1995.

Gebauer, Curt. "Studien zur Geschichte der bürgerlichen Sittenreform des 18. Jahrhunderts." *Archiv für Kulturgeschichte* 15 (1923): 97–116.

Geiger, Ludwig, ed. *Musenalmanach auf das Jahr 1806, Herausgegeben von L. A. Chamisso, K. A. Varnhagen*. Berlin: Gebrüder Paetel, 1889.

Geiger, Ruth-Esther, and Sigrid Weigel. *Sind das noch Damen?: Vom gelehrten Frauenzimmer-Journal zum feministischen Journalismus*. Munich: Frauenbuchverlag, 1981.

Gelberg, Birgit. *Auswanderung nach Übersee: Soziale Probleme der Auswandererbeförderung in Hamburg und Bremen von der Mitte des 19. Jahrhunderts bis zum 1. Weltkrieg*. Hamburg: Hans Christians, 1973.

Germans in Boston. Boston: Goethe Society of New England, 1981.

Giddings, Paula. *When and Where I Enter: The Impact of Black Women on Race and Sex in America*. New York: Bantam, 1984.

Gilman, Sander L. *The Jew's Body*. New York: Routledge, 1991.

————. *Rasse, Sexualität und Seuche: Stereotype aus der Innenwelt der westlichen Kultur.* Reinbek bei Hamburg: Rowohlt, 1992.

————, and Steven T. Katz, eds. *Anti-Semitism in Times of Crisis.* New York: New York UP, 1991.

Gilroy, Amanda, and W. M. Verhoeven, eds. "Correspondences: A Special Issue on Letters." *Prose Studies. History, Theory, Criticism* 19 (August 1997).

Glasenapp, Gabriele von, and Michael Nagel. *Das jüdische Jugendbuch.* Stuttgart: Metzler, 1996.

Goldammer, Peter, ed. *Kellers Briefe in einem Band.* Berlin: Aufbau-Verlag, 1982.

Goldberger, Avriel H., ed. *Woman as Mediatrix: Essays on Nineteenth-Century European Women Writers.* New York: Greenwood, 1987.

Golden, Marita, and Susan Richards Shreve, eds. *Skin Deep: Black Women and White Women Write About Race.* New York: Anchor Books, 1995.

Goldstein, Leslie Friedman. "Violence as an Instrument for Social Change: The Views of Frederick Douglass." *Journal of Negro History* 61 (1976): 61–72.

Gordon-Reed, Annette. *Thomas Jefferson and Sally Hemings: An American Controversy.* Charlottesville: UP of Virginia. 1997.

Gottschall, Rudolf von. "Erinnerungen an Ludmilla Assing." *Die Gartenlaube. Illustriertes Familienblatt* 18 (1880): 298–99.

Grab, Walter. *Der deutsche Weg der Judenemanzipation: 1789–1938.* Munich: Piper, 1991.

————, and Julius H. Schoeps, eds. *Juden im Vormärz und in der Revolution von 1848.* Stuttgart: Burg, 1983.

Green, Constance McLaughlin. *The Secret City: A History of Race Relations in the Nation's Capital.* Princeton, N.J.: Princeton UP, 1967.

Gregory, James M. *Frederick Douglass: The Orator.* Springfield, Mass.: Willey & Co., 1893.

Griffiths, Julia, ed. *Autographs for Freedom.* Boston: Jewett, 1853.

Grün, Karl. *Ludwig Feuerbach in seinem Briefwechsel und Nachlass sowie in seiner Philosophischen Charakterentwicklung.* 2 vols. Leipzig: C. F. Winter, 1874.

Gutman, Herbert G. *The Black Family in Slavery and Freedom.* New York: Random, 1977.

Gutzkow, Karl. "Rosa Maria." *Gesammelte Werke von Karl Gutzkow.* Ed. Karl Gutzkow. Frankfurt: Literarische Anstalt, 1845. Vol. 6: 291–302.

————. "J. D. Assing." *Gesammelte Werke von Karl Gutzkow.* Ed. Karl Gutzkow. Frankfurt: Literarische Anstalt, 1845. Vol. 6: 303–16.

————. *Rückblicke auf mein Leben.* Berlin: A. Hofmann, 1875.

Hagstrum, Jean H. *Sex and Sensibility: Ideal and Erotic Love from Milton to Mozart.* Chicago: U of Illinois P, 1980.

Hahn, Barbara. "Suche alle meine Briefe: Die wiederaufgefundene Sammlung Varnhagen." *Frankfurter Allgemeine Zeitung* (1 April 1986).

————, and Ursula Isselstein. *Rahel Levin Varnhagen: Die Wiederentdeckung einer Schriftstellerin.* Göttingen: Vandenhoeck & Ruprecht, 1987.

Hahn, Barbara, ed. *Antworten Sie mir!: Rahel Levin Varnhagens Briefwechsel.* Frankfurt: Stroemfeld, Roter Stern, 1990.

Hahn, Barbara. *Unter falschem Namen: Von der schwierigen Autorenschaft der Frauen.* Frankfurt: Suhrkamp, 1991.

Hallowell, Anna Davis. *James and Lucretia Mott: Life and Letters*. Boston: Houghton, 1884.

Halttunen, Karen. *Confidence Men and Painted Women: A Study of Middle Class Culture in America, 1830–1870*. New Haven: Yale UP, 1983.

Hamilton, Ronin, and Nicolas Soames, eds. *Intimate Letters*. London: Marginalia P, 1994.

Handlin, Oscar, ed. *This Was America*. New York: Harper, 1949.

Hans Kudlich und die Bauernbefreiung in Niederösterreich. Ed. Amt der Niederösterreichischen Landesregierung. Bad Vöslau: Grasl, 1983.

Hansen, Klaus P. *Die retrospektive Mentalität: Europäische Kulturkritik und amerikanische Kultur*. Tübingen: Gunter Narr, 1984.

Hansen, Marcus Lee. "The Revolutions of 1848 and German Emigration." *Journal of Economic and Business History* 2 (1964): 630–58.

Harding, Vincent. *There Is a River: The Black Struggle for Freedom in America*. New York: Harcourt Brace Jovanovich, 1981.

Harris, Horton. *David Friedrich Strauss and His Theology*. London: Cambridge UP, 1973.

Harris, Trudier. *From Mammies to Militants: Domestics in Black American Literature*. Philadelphia: Temple UP, 1978.

Harris, William Torrey. "German Reform in American Education: An Essay Read Before the German American Teachers' Association, August 3, 1872." St. Louis: E. F. Hobart, 1872.

Hartmann, Julius, ed. *Uhlands Briefwechsel: 1795–1815*. Vol. 1. Stuttgart: Cotta'sche Buchhandlung, 1911.

Hebbel, Friedrich. *Werke*. Munich: Carl Hanser, 1966.

Heid, Ludger, and Joachim H. Knoll, eds. *Deutsch-jüdische Geschichte im 19. und 20. Jahrhundert*. Stuttgart: Burg, 1992.

Heinzen, Karl. *What Is Humanity?: A Lecture*. Indianapolis: Society for the Diffusion of Radical Principles, 1877.

———. *Communism and Socialism*. Indianapolis: H. Lieber, 1881.

Helbich, Wolfgang Johannes. *Alle Menschen sind dort gleich: Die deutsche Amerika-Auswanderung im 19. und 20. Jahrhundert*. Düsseldorf: Schwann, 1988.

Helbling, Carl, ed. *Kellers Gesammelte Briefe*. Bern: Benteli, 1951.

Henkel, Heinrich. *Geschichte der Familie Lich aus der Rabenau*. Pohlheim: Henkel, 1989.

Hertz, Deborah Sadie. "The Varnhagen Collection Is in Krakow." *American Archivist* 44 (1981): 223–28.

———. *Jewish High Society in Old Regime Berlin*. New Haven: Yale UP, 1988.

Herzig, Arno, ed. *Die Juden in Hamburg, 1590–1990*. Hamburg: Dölling und Galitz, 1991.

Higginbotham, A. Leon, and Barbara Kopytoff. "Racial Purity and Interracial Sex in the Law of Colonial and Antebellum Virginia." *Georgetown Law Journal* 77 (August 1989): 1967–2029.

Hildebrand, Janice. *Sheboygan County: 150 Years of Progress: An Illustrated History*. Northridge, Calif.: Windsor, 1988.

Hill, Mike, ed. "The White Issue." *Minnesota Review* 47 (1996).

Hilmes, Carola. *Die Femme fatale: Der Weiblichkeitstypus in der nachromantischen Literatur*. Stuttgart: Metzler, 1990.

Hinners, Wolfgang. *Exil und Rückkehr: Friedrich Kapp in Amerika und Deutschland, 1824–1884.* Stuttgart: Heinz, 1987.

Hinrichs, Beate. *Deutschamerikanische Presse zwischen Tradition und Anpassung: Die Illinois Staatzeitung und Chicagoer Arbeiterzeitung 1879–1890.* Frankfurt: Peter Lang, 1989.

Hipp, Hermann. *Freie und Hansestadt Hamburg: Geschichte, Kultur und Stadtbaukunst an Elbe und Alster.* Cologne: DuMont, 1989.

Hirschler, Eric E., ed. *Jews from Germany in the United States.* New York: Farrar, Straus and Cudahy, 1955.

Höfle, Frieda. "*Cottas Morgenblatt für gebildete Stände* und seine Stellung zur Literatur und zur literarischen Kritik." Munich: Univ. diss., 1933.

Holland, Frederic M. *Frederick Douglass: The Colored Orator.* 1891. Westport, Conn.: Negro UP, 1970.

Hömberg, Walter. *Zeitgeist und Ideenschmuggel.* Stuttgart: Metzler, 1975.

Homberger, Eric, and John Charmley, eds. *The Troubled Face of Biography.* Houndsville: Macmillan, 1988.

Homolka, Walter, and Albert H. Friedlander, eds. *The Gate to Perfection: The Idea of Peace in Jewish Thought.* Oxford: Berghahn, 1994.

Honan, Park. "The Theory of Biography." *Novel* 13 (Fall 1979): 109–20.

Honegger, Claudia, and Bettina Heintz, eds. *Listen der Ohnmacht: Zur Sozialgeschichte weiblicher Widerstandsformen.* Frankfurt: Campus, 1981.

Horton, James O. *Free People of Color: Inside the African American Community.* Washington, D.C.: Smithsonian Institution, 1993.

Houben, H. H., ed. *Gutzkow-Funde: Beiträge zur Literatur- und Kulturgeschichte des neunzehnten Jahrhunderts.* Berlin: Arthur L. Wolff, 1901.

Huggins, Nathan I. *Slave and Citizen: The Life of Frederick Douglass.* Boston: Little, Brown, 1980.

Humboldt, Alexander von. *Versuch über den politischen Zustand des Königreichs Neu-Spanien.* Tübingen: Cotta, 1809.

Ignatiev, Noel. *How the Irish Became White.* New York: Routledge, 1995.

Isselstein, Ursula. *Der Text aus meinem beleidigten Herzen: Studien zu Rahel Levin Varnhagen.* Torino: Tirrenia Stampatori, 1993.

Jackson, Ronald Vern, et al., eds. *Hoboken & Jersey City, New Jersey, 1870 Federal Census Index.* North Salt Lake: Accelerated Index Systems International, 1988.

Jaher, Frederic Cople. *A Scapegoat in the Wilderness: The Origins and Rise of Anti-Semitism in America.* Cambridge, Mass.: Harvard UP, 1994.

Janssen, Albrecht. *Die Frauen rings um Friedrich Hebbel: Neue Materialien zu ihrer Erkenntnis mit einem Anhang aus Hebbels Freundeskreis.* Berlin: Behr, 1919.

Jantz, Harold. "America and the Younger Goethe." *Modern Language Notes* 97 (1982): 515–45.

Joeres, Ruth-Ellen Boetcher. "1848 from a Distance: German Women Writers on the Revolution." *Modern Language Notes* 97 (1982): 590–614.

———, and Mary Jo Maynes, eds. *German Women in the Eighteenth and Nineteenth Centuries: A Social and Literary History.* Bloomington: Indiana UP, 1986.

Johnson, Michael P. "Twisted Truth: Sojourner Truth: A Life, a Symbol, by Nell Irvin Painter." *The New Republic*, 4 November 1996, 37–41.

Jolowicz, Heymann. *Geschichte der Juden in Königsberg*. Vol. 1 *Ein Beitrag zur Sittengeschichte des preussischen Staates*. Posen: 1867.

Jones, Jacqueline. *Labor of Love, Labor of Sorrow: Black Women, Work, and the Family from Slavery to the Present*. New York: Basic Books, 1985.

Jordan, Glenn, and Chris Weedon. *Cultural Politics: Class, Gender, Race and the Postmodern World*. Oxford: Blackwell, 1995.

Kaplan, Amy, and Donald E. Pease, eds. *Culture of United States Imperialism*. Durham, N.C.: Duke UP, 1993.

Kaplan, Marion A. *The Making of the Jewish Middle Class: Women, Family, and Identity in Imperial Germany*. New York: Oxford UP, 1991.

Kaplan, Sidney. "The Miscegenation Issue in the Election of 1864." *Journal of Negro History* 34 (July 1949): 274–343.

Kapp, Friedrich. *Geschichte der Sklaverei in den Vereinigten Staaten von Amerika*. Hamburg: Otto Meissner, 1861.

———. *Briefe: 1843–1884*. Frankfurt: Insel, 1969.

———. *Geschichte der Deutschen im Staate New York bis zum Anfange des neunzehnten Jahrhunderts*. New York. E. Steiger, 1869.

———. *Immigration and the Commissioners of Emigration in the State of New York*. New York, 1870.

———. *Aus und über Amerika: Thatsachen und Erlebnisse*. 2 vols. Berlin: Julius Springer, 1876.

———, and Philip Bissinger. *Report of Messrs. Kapp & Bissinger to the Board of Commissioners of Emigration on the Condition of the Emigrant-Ship Leibnitz, of Sloman's Hamburg Line*. New York: Stone & Barron, 1868.

Katz, Michael, ed. *The "Underclass" Debate: Views from History*. Princeton, N.J.: Princeton UP, 1993.

Kaufman, Linda S. *Discourse of Desire: Gender, Genre, and Epistolary Fiction*. Ithaca, N.Y.: Cornell UP, 1986.

Kern, Stephen. *The Culture of Love: Victorians to Moderns*. Cambridge, Mass.: Harvard UP, 1992.

Kerner, Justinus, et al., eds. *Deutscher Dichterwald*. Tübingen: I. F. Heerbrandt'sche Buchhandlung, 1813.

———. *Die Reiseschatten*. Weimar: G. Kiepenheuer, 1917.

Kerner, Theobald, ed. *Justinus Kerners Briefwechsel mit seinen Freunden*. 2 vols. Stuttgart: Deutsche Verlagsanstalt, 1897.

Kerner, Theobald. *Das Kernerhaus und seine Gäste*. Stuttgart: Deutsche Verlagsanstalt, 1897.

Kessler, Gerhard. "Judentaufe und judenchristliche Familien in Ostpreussen," *Familiengeschichtliche Blätter* 35. Ed. Zentralstelle für Deutsche Personen- und Familiengeschichte (1938): 8–11, 201–32, 262–72, 298–306.

Kisch, Guido. *Judentaufe: Eine historisch-biographisch-psychologisch-soziologische Studie besonders für Berlin und Königsberg*. Berlin: Einzelveröffentlichung der Historischen Kommission zu Berlin 14, 1973.

Kletke, Hermann, ed. *Deutschlands Dichterinnen*. Berlin: Hollstein, 1854.

Kobrin, David. *The Black Minority in Early New York*. Albany: New York State American Bicentennial Commission, 1975.

Kolodny, Annette. "A Map for Rereading, or, Gender and the Interpretation of Literary Texts." *New Literary History* 11 (1980): 451–67.

Kopitzsch, Franklin. *Grundzüge einer Sozialgeschichte der Aufklärung in Hamburg und Altona*. Hamburg: Hans Christians, 1982.

Krohn, Helga. *Die Juden in Hamburg 1800–1850: Ihre soziale, kulturelle und politische Entwicklung während der Emanzipationszeit*. Frankfurt: Europäische Verlagsanstalt, 1967.

Krommer, H., and P. Raimann, eds. *"Verlass das alldeutsche Narrenschiff!": Hans Kudlichs politisches Testament*. London: Einheit, 1944.

Kudlich, Hans. *Rückblicke und Erinnerungen*. Vienna: A. Hartleben, 1873.

———. *Die Deutsche Revolution des Jahres 1848: Vortrag Gehalten im Deutschen gesellig-wissentschaftlichen Verein von New York am 24. März 1898, von Dr. Hans Kudlich*. New York: Verlag des Deutschen gesellig-wissenschaftlichen Vereins, 1898.

Kühn, Joachim, ed. *Alexander von Sternberg: Erinnerungsblätter aus der Biedermeierzeit*. Potsdam: Gustav Kiepenheuer, 1919.

Kunsthalle zu Hamburg, ed. *Katalog der neueren Meister*. Hamburg: Lütcke & Wulff, 1910.

Lang, Barbara. *The Process of Immigration in German-American Literature from 1850 to 1900: A Change in Ethnic Self-Definition*. Munich: Wilhelm Fink, 1988.

Lange, Hermann. "Die christlich-jüdische Ehe: Ein deutscher Streit im 19. Jahrhundert." *Menora: Jahrbuch für deutsch-jüdische Geschichte*. (1991): 47–80.

Lapham, James S. "The German-Americans of New York City, 1860–1890." Diss. St. John's U, 1977.

Larkin, Oliver W. *Art and Life in America*. New York: Holt, Rinehart and Winston, 1949.

Lea, Charlene A. *Emancipation, Assimilation and Stereotype: The Image of the Jew in German and Austrian Drama, 1800–1850*. Bonn: Herbert Grundmann, 1978.

Leberman, J. E. *One Hundred Years of Sheboygan, 1846–1946*. Sheboygan, Wisc.: 1946.

Lerner, Michael, and Cornel West, eds. *Jews and Blacks: A Dialogue on Race, Religion, and Culture in America*. New York: Plume, 1996.

Leuchs, Frederick A. H. *Early German Theater in New York: 1840–1872*. New York: Columbia UP, 1928.

Leverenz, David. *Manhood and the American Renaissance*. Ithaca, N.Y.: Cornell UP, 1989.

Levine, Bruce C. *The Spirit of 1848: German Immigrants, Labor Conflict, and the Coming of the Civil War*. Urbana: U of Illinois P, 1992.

Levine, Robert S. *Martin Delany, Frederick Douglass, and the Politics of Representative Identity*. Chapel Hill: U of North Carolina P, 1997.

Lewald, Fanny. *Gefühltes und Gedachtes: 1838–1888*. Ed. Ludwig Geiger. Dresden: Heinrich Minden, 1900.

———. *Römisches Tagebuch: 1845/46*. Ed. Heinrich Spiero. Leipzig: Klinkhardt & Biermann, 1927.

———. *Jenny*. 1842. Berlin: Morgen, 1967.

———. *Erinnerungen aus dem Jahre 1848*. Ed. Dietrich Schaefer. Frankfurt: Insel, 1969.

———. *Meine Lebensgeschichte*. Ed. Ulrike Helmer. 3 vols. Frankfurt: Ulrike Helmer, 1988–89.

————. *The Education of Fanny Lewald: An Autobiography.* Ed. and trans. Hanna Ballin Lewis. Albany: State U of New York P, 1992.

Lewis, Hanna B. "Fanny Lewald and George Sand." *George Sand Studies* 8:1&2 (1986–87): 38–45.

Litwack, Leon. *North of Slavery: The Negro in the Free States.* Chicago: U of Chicago P, 1961.

Logan, Rayford. *The Negro in American Life and Thought: The Nadir, 1877–1901.* New York: Dial P, 1954.

Löher, Franz von. "Talvj." *Deutsches Museum* 3 (1853): 460–63.

————. "Talvj: Ein deutsches Frauenleben." *Beilage zur Augsburgischen Allgemeinen Zeitung,* 9 and 10 June 1870.

Lohrer, Liselotte. *Cotta: Geschichte eines Verlags, 1659–1959.* Ludwigsburg: Süddeutsche Verlagsanstalt und Druckerei, 1959.

Lougée, Carolyn C. *"Le Paradis des Femmes": Women, Salons, and Social Stratification in Seventeenth-Century France.* Princeton, N.J.: Princeton UP, 1976.

Lowenstein, Steven M. *The Berlin Jewish Community. Enlightenment, Family, and Crisis, 1770–1830.* New York: Oxford UP, 1994.

Ludges, Juachim H., and Joachim H. Knoll, eds. *Deutsch-jüdische Geschichte im neunzehnten und zwanzigsten Jahrhundert.* Stuttgart: Burg, 1992.

Mabee, Carleton. *Sojourner Truth: Slave, Prophet, Legend.* New York: New York UP, 1993.

Machann, Clinton. *The Genre of Autobiography in Victorian Literature.* Ann Arbor: U of Michigan P, 1994.

Mackowsky, Hans. "Rahels Haus Mauerstrasse 36." *Kunst und Künstler: Monatsschrift für Bildende Kunst und Kunstgewerbe* 10 (October 1911).

Magonet, Jonathan, ed. *Jewish Explorations of Sexuality.* Oxford: Berghahn, 1995.

Mania, Marino. *Deutsches Herz und amerikanischer Verstand: Die nationale und kulturelle Identität der Achtundvierziger in den U.S.A.* Frankfurt: Peter Lang, 1993.

Martin, Waldo E., Jr. *The Mind of Frederick Douglass.* Chapel Hill: U of North Carolina P, 1984.

Marwedel, Günter, ed. *Die Privilegien der Juden in Altona.* Hamburg: Hans Christians, 1976.

Matlack, James. "The Autobiographies of Frederick Douglass." *Phylon* 40 (1979): 15–28.

Matthews, Harry Bradshaw. *Tracing the Family of Frederick Douglass, 1817–1928: A Genealogy Case Study of a Historical Role Model.* Baldwin, NY: Matthews Heritage Service, 1993.

Mayer, Karl. *Ludwig Uhland: Seine Freunde und Zeitgenossen.* Stuttgart: Adolph Krabbe, 1867.

McCarthy, Florence Lindner. *The Lindner and McCarthy Families of Hoboken, Newark, and Elizabethport, New Jersey.* Baltimore: Gateway, 1988.

McCormick, E. Allen, ed. *Germans in America: Aspects of German-American Relations in the Nineteenth Century.* New York: Brooklyn College Press, 1983.

McDowell, Deborah, and Arnold Rampersad, eds. *Slavery and the Literary Imagination.* Baltimore: Johns Hopkins UP, 1989.

McDowell, Deborah. *"The Changing Same": Black Women's Literature, Criticism, and Theory.* Bloomington: Indiana UP, 1995.

McFeely, William S. *Frederick Douglass.* New York: Norton, 1990.

McGinty, Ulrike. *150 Jahre Deutscher Verein: 1842–1992.* New York: Deutscher Verein, 1992.

McGuire, Horace. "Two Episodes of Anti-Slavery Days." *Publications of the Rochester Historical Society* 4 (1925): 219.

McKelvey, Blake, ed. *Rochester in the Civil War.* Rochester, N.Y.: The Historical Society, 1944.

McKelvey, Blake. *Rochester: The Water-Power City, 1812–1854; The Flower City, 1855–1890.* Cambridge, Mass.: Harvard UP, 1945.

———. *Susan B. Anthony.* Rochester, N.Y.: Rochester Public Library, 1945.

———. "The Germans of Rochester, Their Traditions and Contributions." *Rochester History* 20 (January 1958): 1–28.

———. "Lights and Shadows in Local Negro History." *Rochester History* 21 (October 1959): 1–27.

McPherson, James M. *The Negro's Civil War: How American Negroes Felt and Acted During the War for the Union.* New York: Pantheon, 1965.

Meese, Elizabeth, and Alice Parker, eds. *The Difference Within: Feminism and Critical Theory.* Amsterdam, Philadelphia: Benjamins, 1989.

Mehegan, David. "Scenes from the Lives: The Seduction of Biography." *The Boston Sunday Globe,* 7 September 1997: N34.

Merrill, Walter M., and Louis Ruchames, eds. *The Letters of William Lloyd Garrison.* 6 vols. Cambridge, Mass.: Harvard UP, 1971–81.

Metzner, Henry Christian Anton. *History of the American Turners.* Rochester, N.Y.: National Council of the American Turners, 1974.

Meyer, Hildegard. *Nordamerika im Urteil des deutschen Schrifttums bis zur Mitte des 19. Jahrhunderts: Eine Untersuchung über Kürnbergers* Amerika-Müden. Hamburg: Friederichsen, de Gruyter, 1929.

Meyer, Michael A. *German Political Pressure and Jewish Religious Response in the Nineteenth Century.* New York: Leo Baeck Institute, 1981.

———. *Jewish Identity in the Modern World.* Seattle: U of Washington P, 1990.

———. *The German Jews: Some Perspectives on Their History.* Syracuse: Syracuse UP, 1991.

Meyerowitz, Raphael. *Transferring to America: Jewish Interpretations of American Dreams.* Albany: State U of New York P, Cornell UP, 1995.

Mikoletzky, Juliane. *Die deutsche Amerika-Auswanderung des 19. Jahrhunderts in der zeitgenössischen fiktionalen Literatur.* Tübingen: M. Niemeyer, 1988.

Miller, Douglas T. *Frederick Douglass and the Fight for Freedom.* New York: Facts on File, 1996.

Miller, Edmund E. "Das New Yorker Belletristische Journal." *American-German Review* 8 (1941): 24–27.

Möhrmann, Renate. *Die andere Frau: Emanzipationsansätze deutscher Schriftstellerinnen im Vorfeld der Achtundvierziger-Revolution.* Stuttgart: Metzler, 1977.

Moltmann, Günter, ed. *Deutsche Amerikaauswanderung im 19. Jahrhundert: Sozialgeschichtliche Beiträge.* Stuttgart: Metzler, 1976.

Moorhead, James H. *American Apocalypse: Yankee Protestants and the Civil War, 1860–1869.* New Haven, Conn.: Yale UP, 1978.

———, "Between Progress and Apocalypse: A Reassessment of Millennialism in American Religious Thought, 1800–1880." *Journal of American History* 71 (December 1984): 524–42.

Moses, Wilson J. *The Golden Age of Black Nationalism: 1850–1925.* Hamden, Conn.: Archon Books, 1978.

———. *Black Messiahs and Uncle Toms: Social and Literary Manipulations of a Religious Myth.* University Park: Pennsylvania State UP, 1982.

Mosse, George. *German Jews: Beyond Judaism.* Bloomington: Indiana UP, 1985.

Mühlbach, Luise. *Aphra Behn.* 3 vols. Berlin: M. Simion, 1849.

———. *The Works of Luise Mühlbach in Eighteen Volumes.* London: The Chesterfield Society, 1866–93.

Nadel, Ira Bruce. *Biography: Fiction, Fact and Form.* New York: St. Martin's P, 1984.

Nadel, Stanley. "Jewish Race and German Soul in Nineteenth-Century America." *American Jewish History* 77 (1987): 6–26.

———. "From the Barricades of Paris to the Sidewalks of New York: German Artisans and the European Roots of American Labor Radicalism." *Labor History* 30 (1989): 47–75.

———. *Little Germany: Ethnicity, Religion, and Class in New York City, 1845–80.* Urbana: U of Illinois P, 1990.

Nagler, Jörg. *Fremont contra Lincoln: Die deutsch-amerikanische Opposition in der Republikanischen Partei während des amerikanischen Bürgerkrieges.* Frankfurt: Peter Lang, 1984.

Nalter, Bernard C. *Strength for the Fight. A History of Black Americans in the Military.* New York: Free Press, 1986.

Nelson, Dana D. *The Word in Black and White: Reading "Race" in American Literature, 1638–1867.* New York: Oxford UP, 1992.

Noble, John Friend. "Christian and Henry Bergh: A Biographical Sketch of Christian Bergh, one of the Leading Shipbuilders in New York in the Early Nineteenth Century, and of his Son, Henry Bergh, the Leader of the First Organized Humane Movement in the United States, and the Founder of the American Society for the Prevention of Cruelty to Animals." *Prize Essay for the New-York Historical Society,* (May 1933). MS Collection.

Nott, Josiah C. "The Mulatto a Hybrid—probable extermination of the two races if the Whites and Blacks are allowed to intermarry." *American Journal of Medical Sciences* 66 (July 1843).

———, and George R. Gliddon. *Types of Mankind, or, Ethnological Researches.* Philadelphia: Lippincott; London: Trübner, 1854.

Oates, Stephen D. *To Purge This Land with Blood: A Biography of John Brown.* Amherst: U of Massachusetts P, 1984.

Oelsner, Elise. *Die Leistungen der deutschen Frau in den letzten vierhundert Jahren: Auf wissenschaftlichem Gebiete.* Guhrau: Lemke, 1894.

Ong, Walter J. *Orality and Literacy: The Technologizing of the Word.* London: Methuen, 1982.

Osthaus, Carl R. *Freedmen, Philanthropy, and Fraud: A History of the Freedman's Savings Bank.* Urbana: U of Illinois P, 1976.

Painter, Nell Irvin. *Exodusters: Black Migration to Kansas After Reconstruction.* 1977. Repr. New York: W. W. Norton, 1992.

———. "Representing Truth: Sojourner Truth's Knowing and Becoming Known." *Journal of American History* 81 (1994): 461–92.

———. *Sojourner Truth: A Life, a Symbol.* New York: W. W. Norton, 1996.

Parker, Jane Marsh. "Reminiscences of Frederick Douglass." *Outlook* 2 (April 6 1895): 552.

Pease, William Henry, and Jane H. Pease, eds. *Black Utopia: Negro Communal Experiments in America*. Madison: State Historical Society of Wisconsin, 1963.

Pelz, Annegret. *Reisen durch die eigene Fremde: Reiseliteratur von Frauen als autogeographische Schriften*. Köln: Böhlau, 1993.

Pelz, Eduard. *New York und seine Umgebung*. New York: Hoffmann, 1867.

Pennington, James W. C. *The Fugitive Blacksmith; or, Events in the History of James W. C. Pennington Pastor of a Presbyterian Church*. London: Gilpin, 1849.

Peters, Günter. *Der zerrissene Engel: Genieästhetik und literarische Selbstdarstellung im achtzehnten Jahrhundert*. Stuttgart: Metzler, 1982.

Pfaefflin, Herman. *Hundertjährige Geschichte des Deutschtums von Rochester*. Rochester: Deutsch-Amerikanischer Bund von Rochester, 1915.

Pickett, Terry H. *The Unseasonable Democrat K. A. Varnhagen von Ense: 1785–1858*. Bonn: Herbert Grundmann, 1985.

———. "Perspectives on a National Crisis: A German Correspondent Reports on America, 1853–1865." *Tamkang Journal of American Studies* 4 (Spring 1988): 5–15.

———. "The Friendship of Frederick Douglass with the German Ottilie Assing." *Georgia Historical Quarterly* 73 (Spring 1989): 88–105.

Pittenger, Mark. "A World of Difference: Constructing the 'Underclass' in Progressive America." *American Quarterly* 49 (March 1997): 26–65.

Pochmann, Henry A. *Bibliography of German Culture in America to 1940*. Millwood: Kraus International, 1982.

Pollnick, Carsten. "Lola Montez: Geschichte und Legende." *Mitteilungen aus dem Stadt- und Stiftsarchiv Aschaffenburg* 3 (1990–92): 138–45.

Pörnbacher, Karl, ed. *Das Leben des Justinus Kerner: Erzählt von ihm und seiner Tochter Marie*. Munich: Kösel, 1967.

Prinz, Friedrich. *Hans Kudlich, 1823–1917: Versuch einer historisch-politischen Biographie*. Munich: R. Lerche, 1962.

Procter, Mary, and William Matuszeski. *Gritty Cities: A Second Look at Allentown, Bethlehem, Bridgeport, Hoboken, Lancaster, Norwich, Paterson, Reading, Trenton, Troy, Waterbury, Wilmington*. Philadelphia: Temple UP, 1978.

Pula, James S., ed. *Ethnic Rochester*. Lanham, Md.: UP of America, 1985.

Pye, Michael. *Maximum City: The Biography of New York*. London: Picador, 1991.

Quarles, Benjamin. "Frederick Douglass and the Women's Rights Movement." *Journal of Negro History* 25 (January 1940): 35–44.

———. *Frederick Douglass*. Washington, DC: Associated Publishers, 1948.

———. *The Negro in the Civil War*. Boston: Little, Brown, 1953.

———. *Lincoln and the Negro*. New York: Oxford UP, 1962.

———, ed. *Blacks on John Brown*. Urbana: U of Illinois P, 1972.

———. "Frederick Douglass: Black Imperishable." *Quarterly Journal of the Library of Congress* 29 (July 1972): 159–69.

———. *Allies for Freedom: Blacks and John Brown*. New York: Oxford UP, 1974.

Racowitza, Prinzessin Helene von. *Von Andern und Mir: Erinnerungen anderer Art*. Berlin: Paetel, 1911.

Randall, G. A., & Co. *Illustrated Historical Atlas of Sheboygan County, Wisconsin.* Oshkosh, Wisc.: G. A. Randall, 1875.

Rattermann, Heinrich Armin. "Deutsch-amerikanische Schriftsteller- und Künstler-Pseudonyme." *Deutsch-amerikanisches Magazin* 1 (1886–87): 143–56.

Rauh, Reinhold, and Bruce Seymour. *Ludwig I. und Lola Montez: Der Briefwechsel.* Munich: Prestel, 1995.

Reich-Ranicki, Marcel. *Über Ruhestörer: Juden in der deutschen Literatur.* Stuttgart: Metzler, 1989.

Reiter, Herbert. *Politisches Asyl im 19. Jahrhundert: Die deutschen politischen Flüchtlinge des Vormärz und der Revolution von 1848/49 in Europa und den USA.* Berlin: Duncker & Humblot, 1992.

Remy, Nahida. *The Jewish Woman.* Trans. Louise Mannheimer. New York: 1895.

Renehan, Edward J., Jr., *The Secret Six: The True Tale of the Men Who Conspired with John Brown.* Columbia: U of South Carolina P, 1997.

Rippley, LaVern. *The German-Americans.* Boston: Twayne, 1976.

Robinson, Therese. *The Exiles.* New York: G. P. Putnam, 1853.

Robinson, Therese (Talvj). "Slavery in Russia." *North American Review* (April 1856): 292–318.

———. "Ein Ausflug nach dem Gebirge Virginiens im Sommer 1856." *Westermann's Illustrierte Deutsche Monatshefte* 4 (1856): 373–81.

———. "Ein Bild aus seiner Zeit." *Westermann's Illustierte Deutsche Monatshefte* 69–72 (1870): 295–307, 394–408, 511–23, 586–604.

Rochester Directory. Rochester, N.Y.: Sampson & Murdock, 1868–1939.

Rogers, William B. *"We are all together now": Frederick Douglass, William Lloyd Garrison, and the Prophetic Tradition.* New York: Garland, 1995.

Rose, Ernestine L. *A Defense of Atheism: Being a Lecture Delivered in Mercantile Hall, Boston, April 10, 1861.* Boston: Mendum, 1889.

Rotundo, E. Anthony. *American Manhood: Transformations in Masculinity from the Revolution to the Modern Era.* New York: Basic Books, 1993.

Roy, Ratna. "The Marginal Man: A Study of the Mulatto Character in American Fiction." Ph.D. diss., University of Oregon, 1973.

Runge, Mita, and Lieselotte Steinbrigge, eds. *Die Frau im Dialog: Studien zur Theorie und Geschichte des Briefes.* Stuttgart: Metzler, 1991.

Russell, Mary. *The Blessings of a Good Thick Skirt: Women Travellers and Their World.* London: Collins, 1988.

Salzman, Jack, Adina Back, and Gretchen Sullivan Sorin, eds. *Bridges and Boundaries: African Americans and American Jews.* New York: George Braziller, 1992.

Salzman, Jack, and Cornel West, eds. *Struggles in the Promised Land: Towards a History of Black-Jewish Relations in the United States.* New York: Oxford UP, 1997.

Sarna, Jonathan D, and Ellen Smith, eds. *The Jews of Boston.* Boston: Northeastern UP, 1995.

Sass, Hans-Martin. ed. *Ausgewählte Briefe von und an Ludwig Feuerbach.* Vols. 12–13. Stuttgart: Friedrich Frommann, 1964.

Schindel, Carl Wilhelm Otto August von. *Die deutschen Schriftstellerinnen des neunzehnten Jahrhunderts.* Hildesheim: Georg Olms, 1978.

Schinnerer, Paul Otto. *Karl Heinzen: Reformer, Poet and Literary Critic*. Chicago: U of Chicago P, 1915.

Schleucher, Kurt. *Das Leben der Amalie Schoppe und Johanna Schopenhauer*. Darmstadt: Turris, 1978.

Schmidt-Linsenhoff, Viktoria, ed. *Sklavin oder Bürgerin: Französische Revolution und Neue Weiblichkeit 1760–1830*. Frankfurt: Historisches Museum Frankfurt, 1989.

Schneider, Gabriele. *Fanny Lewald*. Reinbek bei Hamburg: Rowohlt, 1996.

Schöberl, Ingrid. *Amerikanische Einwandererwerbung in Deutschland: 1845–1914*. Stuttgart: Steiner, 1990.

Schoeps, Hans-Joachim, Heinz Mosche Graupe, and Gerd-Hesse Goeman, eds. *Salomon Ludwig Steinheim: Leben und Werk*. *Salomon Ludwig Steinheim zum Gedenken*. Hildesheim: Olms, 1987.

Schultz, Hans-Jürgen, ed. *Frauen: Porträts aus zwei Jahrhunderten*. Stuttgart: Kreuz, 1981.

Schüppen, Franz B., ed. *Neue Sealsfield-Studien: Amerika und Europa in der Biedermeierzeit*. Stuttgart: Metzler, 1995.

Schuricht, Hermann. *Geschichte der deutschen Schulbestrebungen in Amerika*. Leipzig: 1884.

Scott, Daryl Michael. *Contempt and Pity: Social Policy and the Image of the Damaged Black Psyche, 1880–1996*. Chapel Hill: U of North Carolina P, 1997.

Scott, Joan W. "The Evidence of Experience." *Critical Inquiry* 17 (Summer 1991): 773–97.

Seibert, Peter. *Der Literarische Salon: Literatur und Geselligkeit zwischen Aufklärung und Vormärz*. Stuttgart: Metzler, 1993.

Seidman, Steven. *Romantic Longings: Love in America, 1830–1980*. New York: Routledge, 1991.

Seifert, Walter. *Der Bauernbefreier Hans Kudlich*. Grettstadt: Burgberg, 1954.

Seller, Maxine Schwartz. *Immigrant Women*. Philadelphia: Temple UP, 1981.

Senger und Etterlin, Stefan von. *Neu-Deutschland in Nordamerika: Massenauswanderung, nationale Gruppenansiedlungen und liberale Kolonialbewegung, 1815–1860*. Baden-Baden: Nomos, 1991.

Sewell, Richard E. *A House Divided: Sectionalism and Civil War, 1848–1865*. Baltimore: Johns Hopkins UP, 1988.

Seymour, Bruce. *Lola Montez: A Life*. New Haven: Yale UP, 1996.

Shaplen, Robert. *Free Love and Heavenly Sinners: The Story of the Great Henry Ward Beecher Scandal*. New York: Alfred A. Knopf, 1954.

Sharpe, William, and Leonard Wallock, eds. *Visions of the Modern City*. New York: Columbia UP, 1983.

Shavit, Zohar, and Hans-Heino Ewers, eds. *Deutsch-jüdische Kinder- und Jugendliteratur von der Haskala bis 1945*. Stuttgart: Metzler, 1996.

Sheffield, Charles A., ed. *History of Florence, Massachusetts: Including a Complete Account of the Northampton Association of Education and Industry*. Florence, Mass.: Charles A. Sheffield, 1895.

Shelley, Percy Bysshe. *The Necessity of Atheism, and Other Essays*. Buffalo: Prometheus Books, 1993.

Shepherd, Naomi. *A Price Below Rubies: Jewish Women as Rebels and Radicals*. Cambridge, Mass.: Harvard UP, 1993.

Shore, Elliott, Ken Fones-Wolf, and James P. Danky, eds. *The German-American Radical Press: The Shaping of a Left Political Culture, 1850–1940.* Urbana: U of Illinois P, 1992.

Simmel, Monika. *Erziehung zum Weibe: Mädchenbildung im 19. Jahrhundert.* Frankfurt: Campus, 1980.

Smith, Henry B., and Roswell D. Hitchcock. *The Life, Writings and Character of Edward Robinson.* New York: Anson D. F. Randolph, 1863.

Smith, Lacey Baldwin. *Fools, Martyrs, Traitors: The Story of Martyrdom in the Western World.* New York: Alfred A. Knopf, 1997.

Smith, Theodore Clarke. *James Abraham Garfield: The Life and Letters.* 2 vols. New Haven: Yale UP, 1925.

Sollors, Werner. "Of Mules and Mares in a Land of Difference; or, Quadrupeds All?" *American Quarterly* 42 (June 1990): 167–90.

———. *Theories of Ethnicity. A Classical Reader.* Basingstoke, Eng.: Macmillan, 1996.

———. *Neither Black Nor White Yet Both: Thematic Explorations of Interracial Literature.* New York: Oxford UP, 1997.

Sontag, Susan. *On Photography.* New York: Farrar, Straus & Giroux, 1977.

Sorin, Gerald. *Tradition Transformed: The Jewish Experience in America.* Baltimore: Johns Hopkins UP, 1997.

Sorkin, David. *The Transformation of German Jewry: 1780–1840.* New York: Oxford UP, 1987.

Spiero, Heinrich. *Geschichte der deutschen Frauendichtung seit 1800.* Leipzig: B. G. Teubner, 1913.

Sprague, Rosetta Douglass. *Anna Murray Douglass: My Mother as I Recall Her. Delivered Before the Anna Murray Douglass Union W.C.T.U., Washington, D.C. May 10, 1900.* Repr. Washington, D.C., 1923. FDP. LC.

Stanton, Elizabeth Cady, Susan B. Anthony, and Matilda Joslyn Gage, eds. *History of Woman Suffrage.* Vol. 2. 1882. Repr. Salem, N.H.: Ayer Company, 1985.

Steig, Reinhold. "Briefwechsel zwischen Jacob Grimm und Therese von Jakob." *Preussische Jahrbücher* 77 (1894): 345–66.

Steiger, Ernst. *Dreiundfünfzig Jahre Buchhändler in Deutschland und Amerika: Erinnerungen und Plaudereien.* New York: E. Steiger, 1901.

Steinhauer, Marieluise. *Fanny Lewald, die deutsche George Sand.* Berlin: Karl und Richard Hoffmann, 1937.

Stern, Carola. *Der Text meines Herzens: Das Leben der Rahel Varnhagen.* Reinbek bei Hamburg: Rowohlt, 1996.

Steward, Austin. *Twenty-two Years a Slave, and Forty Years a Freeman; Embracing a Correspondence of Several Years, While President of Wilberforce Colony.* London: W. Alling, 1857.

Still, William. *The Underground Railroad.* Philadelphia: Porter & Coates, 1872.

Stocking, George W., ed. *Race, Culture, and Evolution: Essays in the History of Anthropology.* New York: Free Press, 1968.

Stonequist, Everett V. *The Marginal Man: A Study in Personality and Culture Conflict.* 1937. Repr. New York: Russell & Russell, 1961.

Stout, Janis T. *The Journey Narrative in American Literature: Patterns and Departures.* Westport, Conn.: Greenwood, 1983.

Studemund-Halévy, Michael, and Peter Koj, eds. *Die Sefarden in Hamburg: Zur Geschichte einer Minderheit.* Vol. 1. Hamburg: Helmut Buske, 1994.

Suhl, Yuri. *Eloquent Crusader: Ernestine Rose.* New York: Messner, 1970.

Sundquist, Eric J. *To Wake the Nations: Race in the Making of American Literature.* Cambridge, Mass.: Harvard UP, 1993.

————, ed. *Frederick Douglass: New Literary and Historical Essays.* Cambridge: Cambridge UP, 1990.

Swift, David. *Black Prophets of Justice: Activist Clergy Before the Civil War.* Baton Rouge: Louisiana State UP, 1989.

Takaki, Ronald T. *Violence in the Black Imagination: Essays and Documents.* New York: Putnam, 1972.

Tanser, Harry A. *The Settlement of Negroes in Kent County, Ontario.* Chatham, Ont.: Shepherd, 1939.

Tatlock, Lynne. "The Young Germans in Praise of Famous Women: Ambivalent Advocates." *German Life and Letters* 39 (1986): 192–209.

Taylor, Clarence. *The Black Churches in Brooklyn.* New York: Columbia UP, 1994.

Tenzer, Lawrence E. *A Completely New Look at Interracial Sexuality: Public Opinion and Select Commentaries.* Manahawkin, N.Y.: Scholar, 1990.

Tewarson, Heidi Thomann. *Rahel Varnhagen.* Reinbek: Rowohlt, 1988.

Thies, Erich, ed. *Ludwig Feuerbach.* Darmstadt: Wissenschaftliche Buchgesellschaft, 1976.

Thomas, Herman Edward. *James W. C. Pennington: African American Churchman and Abolitionist.* New York: Garland, 1995.

Thompson, James H., ed. *The Real Diary of a Rochester Boy, 1864.* Rochester, N.Y.: Rochester Herald, 1917.

Thompson, John W. *An Authentic History of the Douglass Monument; Biographical Facts and Incidents in the Life of Frederick Douglass.* Rochester, N.Y.: Rochester Herald, 1903.

Tilton, Theodore. *Sonnets to the Memory of Frederick Douglass.* Paris: Brentano, 1898.

Todorov, Tzvetan. *On Human Diversity: Nationalism, Racism, and Exoticism in French Thought.* Cambridge, Mass.: Harvard UP, 1993.

Tolzmann, Don Heinrich, ed. *German-American Literature.* Methuen, N.J.: Scarecrow P, 1977.

Toth, Carolyn. *German-English Bilingual Schools in America: The Cincinnati Tradition in Historical Context.* New York: Peter Lang, 1990.

Towers, Frank. "African-American Baltimore in the Era of Frederick Douglass." *American Transcendental Quarterly* 9 (September 1995): 165–80.

Traux, Rhoda. *The Doctors Jacobi.* Boston: Little, Brown, 1952.

Trefousse, Hans L. *Lincoln's Decision for Emancipation.* Philadelphia: Lippincott, 1975.

Trollope, Frances. *Domestic Manners of the Americans.* 1832. Ed. Donald Smalley. New York: Vintage, 1960.

Trommler, Frank, and Joseph McVeigh, eds. *America and the Germans: An Assessment of a Three-Hundred-Year War.* 2 vols. Philadelphia: U of Pennsylvania P, 1985.

Troxler, Ignaz Paul Vital. *Der Briefwechsel zwischen Ignaz Paul Vital Troxler und Karl August Varnhagen von Ense, 1815–1858.* Aarau: H. R. Sauerländer, 1953.

Tuan, Yi-Fun. *Space and Place: The Perspective of Experience*. Minneapolis: U of Minnesota P, 1977.

Turner, James. *Without God, Without Creed*. Baltimore: Johns Hopkins UP, 1986.

Tuttleton, James W. "The Many Lives of Frederick Douglass." *The New Criterion* 12 (February 1994): 16–26.

Tuveson, Ernest Lee. *Redeemer Nation: The Idea of America's Millennial Role*. Chicago: U of Illinois P, 1968.

Uhde, Hermann. *Das Stadttheater in Hamburg 1827 1877: Ein Beitrag zur deutschen Culturgeschichte*. Stuttgart: Cotta'sche Buchhandlung, 1879.

Uhland, Emilie V., ed. *Ludwig Uhlands Leben: Aus dessen Nachlass und eigener Erinnerung zusammengestellt von seiner Witwe*. Stuttgart: Cotta'sche Buchhandlung, 1874.

Vagts, Alfred. *Deutsch-amerikanische Rückwanderung*. Heidelberg: C. F. Winter, 1960.

Van Deburg, William L. "Frederick Douglass: Maryland Slave to Religious Liberal." *Maryland Historical Magazine* 69 (Spring 1974): 27–43.

van Rheinberg, Brigitta. *Fanny Lewald. Geschichte einer Emanzipation*. Tübingen: Selbstverlag, 1987.

Varnhagen von Ense, Karl August. *Tagebücher: Aus dem Nachlass Varnhagens von Ense*. 15 vols. Ed. K. Feilchenfeldt. Bern. II. Lang, 1972

Venske, Regula. " 'Ich hätte ein Mann sein müssen oder eines grossen Mannes Weib!': Widersprüche im Emanzipationsverständnis der Fanny Lewald." Ed. Ilse Brehmer et al. *Frauen in der Geschichte IV*. Düsseldorf: Schwann, 1983. 368–97.

Voigt, Irma Elizabeth. "The Life and Works of Mrs. Therese Robinson Talvj." Diss. U of Illinois. *Deutsch-amerikanische Geschichtsblaetter: Jahrbuch der Deutsch-amerikanischen Historischen Gesellschaft von Illinois* 13 (1913): 7–148.

Volger, Bruno, ed. *Sachsens Gelehrte, Künstler und Schriftsteller in Wort und Bild*. Leipzig: Selbstverlag, 1908.

Vordtriede, Werner, ed. *Therese von Bacheracht und Karl Gutzkow: Unveröffentlichte Briefe. 1842–1849*. Munich: Kösel, 1971.

Voss, Abraham. *Deutschlands Dichterinnen*. Düsseldorf: Buddens, 1847.

Wagner, Ludwig. *Talvj, 1797–1870: Biographische Skizze zur Erinnerung an ihren 100. Geburtstag*. Pressburg. 1897.

Wagner, Maria. *Mathilda Franziska Anneke in Selbstzeugnissen und Dokumenten*. Frankfurt: Fischer, 1980.

———, ed. *Was die Deutschen aus Amerika berichten, 1828–1865*. Stuttgart: H. D. Heinz, 1985.

Walker, George. "The Afro-American in New York City, 1827–1860." Diss. Columbia University, 1975.

Walker, Mack. *Germany and the Emigration. 1816–1885*. Cambridge, Mass.: Harvard UP, 1964.

Walker, Peter. *Moral Choices: Memory, Desire, and Imagination in Nineteenth-Century American Abolitionism*. Baton Rouge: Louisiana State UP, 1978.

Ware, Susan, ed. *New Viewpoints in Women's History: Working Papers from the Schlesinger Library 50th Anniversary Conference, March 4–5, 1994*. Cambridge, Mass.: Radcliffe College, 1994.

Ware, Vron. *Beyond the Pale: White Women, Racism and History*. London: Verso, 1992.

Washington, Booker T. *Frederick Douglass*. Philadelphia: George W. Jacobs, 1906.

Washington, Joseph R. *The First Fugitive Foreign and Domestic Doctor of Divinity: Rational Race Rules of Religion and Realism Revered and Reversed or Revised by the Reverend Doctor James William Charles Pennington*. New York: E. Mellen Press, 1990.

Washington, Mary Helen. "These Self-Invented Women: A Theoretical Framework for a Literary History of Black Women." *Radical Teacher* 17 (1980): 3–6.

Waters, Mary C. *Ethnic Options: Choosing Identities in America*. Berkeley: U of California P, 1990.

Weber, Ernst. *Lyrik der Befreiungskriege: 1812–1815*. Stuttgart: Metzler, 1991.

Weber, Marta. *Fanny Lewald*. Rudolfstadt: Eugen Renthsch, 1921.

Weber, Paul C. *America in Imaginative German Literature in the First Half of the Nineteenth Century*. New York: Columbia UP, 1966.

Weedon, Chris. *Poststructuralist Theory and Feminist Practice*. Oxford: Blackwell, 1987.

Wegner, Judith R. *Chattel or Person?: The Status of Women in Mishnah*. New York and Oxford: Oxford UP, 1988.

Wehl, Feodor. *Hamburgs Literaturleben im achtzehnten Jahrhundert*. Leipzig: F. A. Brockhaus, 1856.

———. *Das Junge Deutschland: Ein kleiner Beitrag zur Literaturgeschichte unserer Zeit. Mit einem Anhange seither noch unveröffentlichter Briefe von Th. Mundt, H. Laube und K. Gutzkow*. Hamburg: F. F. Richter, 1886.

———. *Zeit und Menschen: Tagebuchaufzeichnungen aus den Jahren von 1863–1884*. 2 vols. Altona: A. C. Reher, 1889.

Welter, Barbara. *Dimity Convictions: The American Woman in the Nineteenth Century*. Columbus: Ohio State UP, 1975.

Werner, Richard Maria, ed. *Friedrich Hebbels Briefe*. Berlin: Behr, 1900.

———, ed. *Friedrich Hebbels Sämtliche Werke: Historische-kritische Ausgabe*. Bern: Herbert Lang, 1904–7.

West, Shearer, ed. *The Victorians and Race*. London: Scolar P, 1996.

Westhoff-Krummacher, Hildegard. *Als die Frauen noch sanft und engelsgleich waren: Die Sicht der Frau in der Zeit der Aufklärung und des Biedermeier*. Münster: Westfälisches Landesmuseum für Kunst und Kulturgeschichte, 1996.

Whaley, Joachim. *Religious Toleration and Social Change in Hamburg, 1529–1819*. Cambridge: Cambridge UP, 1985.

White, Hayden V. *Topics of Discourse: Essays in Cultural Criticism*. Baltimore: Johns Hopkins UP, 1992.

Wiedenmann, Ursula. *Karl August Varnhagen von Ense: Ein Unbequemer in der Biedermeierzeit*. Stuttgart: Metzler, 1994.

Wiegand, Johannes. *Die Frau in der modernen Literatur: Plaudereien*. Bremen: Carl Schünemann, 1903.

Wilk, Gerard. *Americans from Germany*. New York: German Information Center, 1976.

Williams, T. Harry. *Lincoln and His Generals*. New York: Vintage, 1952.

Wilson, Hill Peebles. *John Brown, Soldier of Fortune: A Critique*. Lawrence, Kans.: Wilson, 1913.

Winks, Robin W. *The Blacks in Canada: A History*. Montreal: McGill-Queen's UP; Yale UP, 1971.

Wintersteiner, Marianne. *Lola Montez*. Munich: Nymphenburger, 1990.

Wistrich, Robert. *Revolutionary Jews from Marx to Trotsky*. London: Harrap, 1976.

Wittke, Carl. *Against the Current: The Life of Karl Heinzen*. Chicago: U of Chicago P, 1945.

———. *Refugees of Revolution*. Philadelphia: U of Pennsylvania P, 1952.

———. *The German Language Press in America*. Lexington: U of Kentucky P, 1957.

Wolf, Gerhard, ed. *Fanny Lewald: Freiheit des Herzens. Lebensgeschichte, Briefe, Erinnerungen*. Berlin: Morgen, 1987.

Wolff, Oskar Ludwig Bernhard, *Poetischer Hausschatz des deutschen Volkes: Ein Buch für Schule und Haus*. Leipzig: Weigand, 1853.

Wood, Forrest G. *Black Scare: The Racist Response to Emancipation and Reconstruction*. Berkeley: U of California P, 1970.

Woodson, Leroy H. *American Negro Slavery in the Works of Friedrich Strubberg, Friedrich Gerstäcker and Otto Ruppius*. Washington, D.C.: Catholic U of America P, 1949.

Woodward, C. Vann. *The Strange Career of Jim Crow*. 2d rev. ed. New York: Oxford UP, 1966.

Wust, Klaus German. *Guardians on the Hudson: The German Society of the City of New York, 1784–1984*. New York: German Society, 1984.

Yellin, Jean Fagan. *Women and Sisters: The Antislavery Feminists in American Culture*. New Haven: Yale UP, 1989.

———, and John C. Van Horner, eds. *An Untrodden Path: Women's Political Culture in Antebellum America*. Ithaca: Cornell UP, 1994.

Zack, Naomi. *Race and Mixed Race*. Philadelphia: Temple UP, 1993.

Zakrzewska, Maria E. *A Woman's Quest: The Life of Maria E. Zakrzewska*. Ed. Agnes C. Vietor. New York: Appleton, 1924.

Zeise, Heinrich. *Aus dem Leben und den Erinnerungen eines norddeutschen Poeten*. Altona: Reher, 1888.

Zimmermann, Erich, "Erinnerungen des Hamburger Bibliothekars Meyer Isler (1807–1888)." *Zeitschrift des Vereins für Hamburgische Geschichte* 47 (1961): 45–86.

Zimmermann, Mosche. *Hamburgischer Patriotismus und deutscher Nationalismus: Die Emanzipation der Juden in Hamburg, 1830–1865*. Hamburg: Hans Christians, 1979.

Zlocisti, Theodor. *Mitwirkung der Juden an der freiwilligen Krankenpflege in den Befreiungskriegen*. Berlin: 1898.

Zucker, Adolf Eduard, ed. *The Forty-Eighters: Political Refugees of the German Revolution of 1848*. New York: Columbia UP, 1950.

Illustration Credits

Page   21: *Karl August Varnhagen von Ense.* Contemporary copper engraving. By permission
and courtesy of the Bildarchiv Preussischer Kulturbesitz Berlin. 182/1512, 1997.
Rahel Varnhagen von Ense. Dotted engraving by C. E. Weber, 1817. By permission
and courtesy of the Bildarchiv Preussischer Kulturbesitz Berlin. 921/28, 1997.
Salomon Ludwig Steinheim. By permission and courtesy of Gidal-Bildarchiv,
Salomon Ludwig Steinheim-Institut für deutsch-jüdische Geschichte, Duisburg,
Germany. A copy of this portrait is also in Ottilie Assing's personal photo album,
now at the Museum and Archeological Research and Supplies at Glen Dale, MD.
Amalie Schoppe. Drawing by Jürgen Sickert, 1828. Kurt Schleucher, *Das Leben
der Amalie Schoppe und Johanna Schopenhauer.* Darmstadt: Turris-Verlag, 1978,
p. 64.

Page   62: *Karl Gutzkow.* From Ottilie Assing's photo album. By permission and courtesy
of the National Park Service, Frederick Douglass Historic Site. *Fanny Lewald.*
Steel engraving by Auguste Küssener after a drawing by E. Ratti, around 1850.
By permission and courtesy of the Bildarchiv Preussischer Kulturbesitz Berlin.
944/1512, 1997. *Clara Mundt, alias Luise Mühlbach.* From the author's collection.

Page 115: *Ottilie Assing; Emilie Nickert.* From Ottilie Assing photo album. By permission
and courtesy of the National Park Service, Frederick Douglass Historic Site. *The
Kudlich family in Hoboken, New Jersey.* By permission and courtesy of Dr. Jörg
Kudlich, Mossbichlerweg 1, D 82237 Wörthsee, Germany.

Page 151: *Frederick Douglass. Title page of* My Bondage and My Freedom, *first edition of 1855.*
Engraved by J. C. Buttre from a daguerreotype. From the author's collection. *Title page of the first German edition of* Sclaverei und Freiheit. *1860.* Rochester. By
permission and courtesy of Department of Rare Books and Special Collections,
Rush Rhees Library, University of Rochester.

Page 189: *Anna Murray Douglass; Rosetta Douglass.* From Ottilie Assing photo album. By
permission and courtesy of the National Park Service, Frederick Douglass Historic Site.

Page 225: *John Brown; Ludwig Feuerbach.* From Ottilie Assing photo album. By permission
and courtesy of the National Park Service, Frederick Douglass Historic Site.
*Autographs of Frederick Douglass and Ottilie Assing from the autograph album of Lucy
Coleman.* By permission and courtesy of Between the Covers—Rare Books, Inc.,
Merchantville, NJ.

Page 249: *Charles Douglass; Lewis Douglass.* By permission and courtesy of the Photographer Collection, Moorland-Springarn Research Center, Howard University. *Frederick Douglass, Jr.* From Ottilie Assing photo album. By permission and courtesy of the National Park Service, Frederick Douglass Historic Site.

Page 281: *Sylvester Rosa Koehler; Amalie Koehler; Hedwig and Walter Koehler; Karl Heinzen; Ottilie Assing.* From Ottilie Assing photo album. By permission and courtesy of the National Park Service, Frederick Douglass Historic Site.

Page 321: *Frederick Douglass in travel outfit.* By permission and courtesy of the National Park Service, Frederick Douglass Historic Site. *Ludmilla Assing; Gino Grimelli.* From Ottilie Assing photo album. By permission and courtesy of the National Park Service, Frederick Douglass Historic Site.

Page 353: *The Douglass house on Washington's A Street.* By permission and courtesy of the National Park Service, Frederick Douglass Historic Site. *Robert Ingersoll; Cedar Hill.* From Ottilie Assing photo album. By permission and courtesy of the National Park Service, Frederick Douglass Historic Site.

Page 356: *Frederick Douglass in his library at Cedar Hill; Helen Pitts; Frederick Douglass; Ottilie Assing.* From Ottilie Assing photo album. By permission and courtesy of the National Park Service, Frederick Douglass Historic Site.

Index

Abelard and Héloïse, letters of, 317
abolitionists, xvi, 116–17, 124, 206, 210, 225, 253, 262, 285, 298, 304; Anna Murray Douglass and, 135, 178–79, 182; black, 208; and cult of domesticity, 187; and Douglass' oratory, 174, 176; feminists and, 159; Lincoln criticized by, 240; persecution of, 158; and use of violence, *see* Harpers Ferry, Brown's raid on; white, racism of, 160, 208, 238, 257
African Methodist Episcopal (AME) Zion Church: in New Bedford, 177, 228; in Rochester, 237, 253
Agassiz, Louis, 257
Ahlefeld, Countess Elise von, 53, 68, 70, 149, 311
Allgemeine Zeitung des Judenthums, 32
Alpha (journal of Moral Education Society), 350, 358, 418n74
American Abolitionist Society, 144, 159, 166, 203
American Anti-Slavery Society, 86, 267, 292
American Equal Rights Association, 289–91
American Revolution, 83, 247
American Society for the Prevention of Cruelty to Animals (ASPCA), 310, 379
Andersen, Hans Christian, 85, 141
Anderson, Jeremiah G., 212
Anthony, Aaron, xxiii, 6, 253, 386n4, n7
Anthony, Lucretia, 6, 253
Anthony, Susan B., 183, 209, 210, 289–91
anti-Semitism, xxii, 13, 14, 24–27, 35–36, 48, 75, 81, 83, 108

Aphra Behn (Mundt), xxii, 43, 62, 84–85, 87, 127, 128, 139, 144, 185, 187, 199–203 (quoted), 393n114
Aristotle, 118
Arnim, Achim von, 28
Arnim, Bettina Brentano von, 53
Assing, (Assur) David (OA's father), 7, 11–27, 31, 48, 73, 95, 196, 420n113; and anti-Semitism, 24–26; birth of, 12; birth of children of, 18; conversion of, 17, 24, 35; death of, 41, 44, 59, 192, 371, 372; early life of, 12–14; family background of, 11–12; as father, 19–20, 22, 27; marriage of, 16–19, 22–23; physical appearance of, 15–16; political views of, 33, 35; and wife's death, 4–6, 38–40, 51, 77–78, 204
Assing, Ludmilla (OA's sister), xvii–xix, xxv–xxvii, 4–6, 43, 46, 65, 70, 97, 100, 101, 115, 145, 223, 280, 328, 330, 332, 365, 377, 380, 382, 390n20, 392n89, 393n112, 394n11, n20; in Berlin, 47–51, 53–59; and biography of Cironi, 311, 414n32, n33; birth of, 7, 18; childhood and adolescence of, 7, 11, 19, 20, 22–24, 26–29, 32–34; conflicts and reconciliations of OA and, 59–61, 78–79; death of, 354–55, 357, 358; disinheriting of OA by, 355, 361–62, 370; during Hamburg fire, 44–45; letters from OA in America to, 97, 153, 184, 190, 255, 268, 272, 275, 277, 279, 281–83, 285, 287, 293, 294, 296, 298, 303–4, 308, 310, 317–20, 322, 335, 337, 353, 399n41, n45, 404n25, 406n69; and

Assing, Ludmilla (*cont.*)
liaison with Cironi, 78, 312, 414*n*33; marriage of, 311–16, 320, 321; OA's bequest to, 379, 380; and OA's departure for America, 81, 82; and OA's liaison with Baison, 67, 68, 72, 73, 76, 77, 392*n*79; and OA's translation of Douglass' autobiography, 149, 163, 203; and parents' deaths, 4–6, 38–41; reunion of OA and, 323–26, 331; and Varnhagen's death, 203–4

Assing, Ottilie: and American women's movement, 209–10, 290–91; anti-Semitism experienced by, 25, 35, 83; articles on FD by, 136–42, 154, 162–64, 206–7; atheism of, 33–34, 101, 113, 126, 191, 293; attitude toward FD's wife of, 184–88; Berlin circle of, 54–55; birth of, 7, 18; books on slavery read by, 84–85; in Boston, 288, 322, 337–38; and Brown's raid on Harpers Ferry, 212–23; and burning of FD's Rochester home, 303–4, 306–7; in Canada, 145–47, 150, 152–54; childhood and adolescence of, 7, 18–20, 22–37; during Civil War, 231–33, 236–47, 250–56; conflicts between LA and, 5, 56, 58–61, 78–79, 205, 323–26; during convention weeks, 144–45, 159–61, 209; correspondence of FD and, 142–43, 196, 317, 346–47, 359; criticism of FD's politics by, 346–49; destruction of papers of, xvii, xviii, xxiii; disinherited by LA, 355, 357–62, 370; early writing career, 63–64, 79–81; education of, 23–24, 27–28; emigration to America of, 43–44, 80–83, 86–87, 93–97; estrangement of LA and, 349–51; European tours of, 288, 320, 322–30, 331–32, 335, 361–66, 370–71; family background of, 7–17; and father's death, 41, 44; and FD's appointment as Marshal of District of Columbia, 332–35; and FD's children, 149, 150, 193–96, 277, 297, 336–37, 342–45;

and FD's exile, 218–19, 223–24, 226–27; and FD's second marriage, 368–70; first meeting of FD and, xvii, 128–29, 131–36; and Franco-Prussian War, 309–10; German accounts of relationship of FD and, xv–xvi; during Hamburg fire, 44–45; in Hoboken, 112–16, 143, 203, 260–62, 264, 275–76, 278–80, 282, 298, 302–3, 309, 340–42; ignored in Douglass biographies, xxiv–xxv; interpretation of relationship with FD constructed by, xix–xxi, 166–67, 190–93, 197–98, 258, 312, 366–67; and issues of race, xxviii–xxix, 117–22, 205–6, 256–58; journalistic collaboration of FD and, 294–97, 318; and LA's death, 354–55; and LA's marriage, 312–16; last meeting of FD and, 360–61; lectures by, 285–87; letters to LA from, xviii–xix, 97, 153, 184, 190, 255, 268, 272, 275, 277, 279, 281–83, 285, 287, 293, 294, 296, 298, 303–4, 308, 310, 317–20, 322, 335, 337, 353, 399*n*41, *n*45, 404*n*25, 406*n*69; letter to Feuerbach from, 225, 259–60, 293; and liaison with Baison, 64–68, 71–78; Methodist camp meeting attended by, 89–93; Midwestern trip of, 104–11; Montez and, 154–57; and mother's death, 2–6, 37–38, 44; moves to Berlin, 45–49; in New York, 97–104, 111–12, 116, 119; Pennington and, 122–27; and planned Haitian trip with FD, 235–36; Racowitza and, 351–52, 354; and Reconstruction, 262–63, 265–70, 272, 274–75, 293, 345; suicide attempt of, 56–57; suicide of, 371–75, 377–79; summers spent in Rochester by, 147–50, 161–63, 169–71, 203, 206–12, 227–30, 253, 273, 274; translation of FD's autobiography by, 142, 147–49, 151, 163, 203, 206, 211–12, 222, 223; as tutor, 61, 63; and Varnhagen Collection, xxv–xxvii; Varnhagen denounced by, 21, 52, 57–58; in

Varnhagen household, 50–56; and Varnhagen's death, 203–5; views on extramarital relationships of, 68–71, 157–59, 174–75; in Washington, 282–85, 307–9, 311, 317–19, 336, 338–40, 353, 356–58; will of, 379–81

Assing, Rosa Maria (née Varnhagen) (OA's mother), 7–11, 14–33, 35, 41, 51, 61, 71, 77–78, 94, 95, 99, 170, 282, 355, 420n113; birth of, 8; birth of children of, 18; death of, 3–6, 37–40, 44, 46, 59, 204, 371; education of daughters by, 23–24, 27–29, 75, 192; family background of, 7–8; feminism of, 68–70, 103; marriage of, 16–19, 22–23; as mother, 19–20, 22; physical appearance of, 4, 5, 20; poetry and stories by, 10–11, 18, 29–30, 37–38, 67, 372, 377; salon of, 32–33, 135; Schoppe and, 21, 203, 386n18

Assur, David, see Assing, (Assur) David
Augsburger Allgemeine Zeitung, 79
Auld, Hugh, 7, 86, 175, 178
Auld, Lucretia Aaron, 173, 216
Auld, Sophia, 173, 289
Auld, Thomas, 335, 386n7
Autographs for Freedom (Griffiths, ed.), 208

Bacheracht, Therese von, 63, 70
Bailey, Betsy, 6, 171, 173
Bailey, Harriet, xxiii, 6, 171, 173
Bailey, Hester, 6
Bailey, Isaac, 6
Baison, Caroline Sutorius, 43, 64, 67, 71–72, 74, 76–77, 82, 87, 97, 126, 137, 145
Baison, Jean Baptiste, 64–67, 71–78, 81, 82, 84, 91, 95, 122, 126, 144, 204, 392n79, 394n11
Baison, Josephine, 145
Baker, Houston, Jr., 138, 175
Bakunin, Mikhail, 51, 192
Bassett, Ebenezer D., 291

Battaglia family, 355, 362
Beecher, Henry Ward, 165, 186n, 228, 319
Behn, Aphra, 85, 103, 127–28, 139, 140, 222, 370, 393n114; see also Aphra Behn (Mundt)
Bergh, Henry, 310, 375, 379–81
Bericht über eine Reise nach den westlichen Staaten Nordamerikas (Duden), 104
Biedermeier culture, 54, 63
Birkenstock, Maria, 61, 67, 365
Birkenstock, Wilhelm Christian, 45, 61, 67
Bismarck, Otto von, 310, 329
Black Codes, 266, 269
Blake, William, 83
Blassingame, John W., xxv
Blight, David W., xxv, xxix, 210, 234
Bonaparte, Jérôme, 51
Bontemps, Arna W., xxv
Booth, Edwin, 291
Brandt, Marion, 414n33
Bremer, Fredrika, 93, 180, 184
Brentano, Clemens, 28
Brontë, Charlotte, 185
Brontë sisters, 71
Brooks, Preston S., 239
Brown, John, xxiv, 137, 206, 212–25, 229, 234, 285–87, 308, 340, 404n25, n27
Brown, John, Jr., 212, 213
Brown, William Wells, 126, 224
Bryant, William Cullen, 113
Buchanan, James, 162, 216, 219, 285, 286
Bug-Jargal (Hugo), 199
Burney, Charles, 15
Byron, George Gordon, Lord, 186n

Carlyle, Thomas, 278
Cartesianism, 69
Catholicism, see Roman Catholic Church
Chamisso, Adelbert von, 9, 28
Chase, Salmon P., 262
Chesnutt, Charles W., xxiv, xxv
Child, Lydia Maria, 186, 221

"Chimney Sweeper, The" (R. M. Assing), 30

Christianity, 13; conversion of Jews to, xxii, xxvi, 17, 36, 54; Douglass and, 227–29, 293; see also specific denominations

Cironi, Piero, 78, 311, 312, 414n33

Civil Rights Act (1875), 332

Civil War, 232–33, 236–58, 261, 266, 287, 304, 305, 348

Clementine (Lewald), 70

Clotel, or, The President's Daughter (Brown), 224

Coates, Benjamin, 407n7

Code noir, 85

Coleman, Lucy, 225

colonization, by ex-slaves, 150, 152, 270

Columbus, Christopher, 82

Commager, Henry Steele, 83

Congress, U.S., 239, 245, 268, 279, 307, 316, 357

Constitution, U.S., 86, 226; Thirteenth Amendment, 268; Fourteenth Amendment, 210; Fifteenth Amendment, 210, 275, 276, 287, 290–93

Convention of Colored Men (1866), 269

Cooper, James Fenimore, xviii, 104, 106

Cotta, Carl, 79, 87, 123, 125, 137, 148, 163, 219, 263, 392n95

Coupling Convention (duCille), xxix

Crofts, H. O., 183, 223

Crofts, Julia Griffiths, xxiii, 149, 150, 171, 179–85, 188, 194, 195, 208–9, 262, 289; and FD's second marriage, 369, 382, 420n11; Garrisonian campaign against FD and, xxiv, 86, 117, 148, 182–83, 210, 306; managerial talents of, 192; marriage of, 183–84, 223; return to England of, xvi–xvii, 183, 402n45

Croly, David Goodman, 256

Culver, Erastus Dean, 158

Dallas, George, 224

Davis, Jefferson, 248

Davis, Natalie Zemon, xxix

Day, William H., 182

de Castro, Anna, 338

de Castro, Joseph, 98, 394n11

de Castro, Rahel, 32, 43, 68, 78, 99, 145, 226, 338, 392n79, 393n112; correspondence of OA and, 98, 121, 142, 223, 224, 235, 394n11; OA's and LA's vacations with, 47, 60; OA's 1877 visit to, 329; and OA's liaison with Baison, 72, 74, 76;

de Castro family, 26, 32, 35, 45

Dean, Phebe, 409n7

Declaration of Independence, 83, 268

Delany, Martin R., 214, 407n7

Democracy in America (Tocqueville), 83

Democratic Party, 224, 239, 242, 256, 279, 290, 304, 333, 335, 358

Dennett, Lydia, 150

Deutsche Literaturarchiv (Marbach, Germany), 137

Dick, Jutta, xxvii

Dickens, Charles, xviii, 284

Dickinson, Anna, 271–72, 276

Dickinson, Emily, 71

Diede, Charlotte, 69

domesticity, cult of, 187–88

Domestic Manners of the Americans (Trollope), 87

Douai, Alfred, 148, 245

Douglas, Stephen A., 116

Douglass, Amalia Loguen (Lewis' wife), 411n66

Douglass, Anna Murray (FD's wife), xxviii, 150, 171, 189, 192–94, 217, 230, 237, 254, 255, 276, 284, 289, 344, 345, 350, 367; burning of Rochester home of, 303, 306; death of, xvii, 363, 366, 368, 369, 380; death of youngest daughter of, 226; and FD's exile, 219; marriage of FD and, 171, 175–88; OA's disparagement of, 189, 215–16, 282, 306–7, 315, 319, 337, 343, 406n69; OA's first meeting with, 135, 136; Rosetta's relationship with, 194–96, 273–74; in Washington, 319, 337, 339, 342, 358, 410*n41*

Douglass, Annie (FD's daughter), 149, 181, 194, 223, 224, 226, 227, 254

Douglass, Charles (FD's son), 149, 175, 249, 272–73, 276–78, 282, 283, 291, 295–97, 318–19, 336, 343–44, 358, 368, 369

Douglass, Frederick, xv–xxix, 28, 37, 67, 72, 75, 86, 126–29, 145–46, 156, 167, 170–71, 259, 264, 312, 354, 355, 377–78, 381–82, 399*n45*, 406*n81*, *n82*; articles about, 136–42, 154, 162–64, 206–7; birth of, 6, 386*n4*; Brown and, 212–18, 220–24, 234, 405*n45*; burning of Rochester home of, 303–7; children's relationship with, 193–96, 224, 226, 342–45; cigar smoking by, 204, 340–41, 363; on civil rights, 267, 287, 298; during Civil War, 232–33, 236–38, 240, 241, 244–48, 250–55, 257–58, 407*n7*; and controversy with Garrisonians, 117, 144, 148, 161, 182–83, 210; correspondence of OA and, 142–43; cultural interests of OA and, 149–50; early life of, 6–7, 282; Elgin Association visited by, 150, 152–54; escape from slavery of, 7, 46, 173, 175, 217; estrangement of OA and, 349–51; in exile, 218–19, 223–24, 226–27; first meeting of OA and, 131, 133–36; and first wife's death, 363, 364, 366–68; in Hoboken, 115, 261, 262, 278–79, 281, 282, 291, 298, 302; homecoming to Talbot County of, 335–36; last meeting of OA and, 360–61; lecture tours of, 145, 150, 312, 320, 321, 326–27; marriage to Anna Murray, 171, 175–88; marriage to Helen Pitts, 368–70, 380, 420*n111*; nature of relationship of OA and, 188–93, 196–97, 314, 315; at New York City conventions, 130–31, 159–60; OA's bequest to, 379, 380–81; and OA's European trip, 320, 322, 324–29; and

OA's suicide, 57, 371–75, 380; OA's translation of autobiography of, 142, 148–49, 151, 163–66, 206, 211–12, 340; oratory of, 130–31, 164–66, 174; and planned Haitian trip, 233–36; post-Reconstruction political views of, 345–49, 417*n44*; during Reconstruction, 262–63, 265–80, 282–97, 409*n5*, *n7*, 410*n41*; relationships to women of, 171–74; religious views of, 227–30; on Santo Domingo commission, 297–99, 413*n124*; and Underground Railroad, 205, 212, 218; in Washington, 307–10, 316–19, 327–28, 332–39, 341, 342, 345, 353, 356–59, 418*n74*; white abolitionist friends of, 208–11

Douglass, Frederick, Jr. (FD's son), 149, 175, 249, 272, 273, 276, 295–97, 318, 319, 368, 410*n41*

Douglass, Lewis Henry (FD's son), 149, 175, 217, 247, 249, 269, 272–73, 276–77, 279, 294–97, 318–19, 332, 368, 411*n66*, 413*n123*

Douglass, Libbie Murphy (Charles' wife), 272–74, 276, 282, 283, 318, 336, 344

Douglass, Rosetta (FD's daughter), *see* Sprague, Rosetta Douglass

Douglass' Monthly, 233, 237, 244, 250, 251, 295, 303

Downing, George T., 269, 291, 294, 347

Downs, Perry, 277–78, 344, 358

Drayton, Michael, 83

Du Bois, W. E. B., 252

duCille, Ann, xxix, 188

Duden, Gottfried, 104

Dumas, Alexandre (*père*), 155

East Baltimore Mental Improvement Society, 175

Easton Gazette, 346

Echtermeyer, Theodor, 34

Elective Affinities (Goethe), 29

Elgin Association (Buxton, Ontario), 150, 152–54

Eliot, George (Mary Anne Evans), 71, 227, 260

Elter, John, 304

Emancipation Proclamation, 240–42, 258, 266

Engels, Friedrich, 52

Enlightenment, 24, 31, 32, 37, 68, 69, 235; Jewish, 12–14, 26, 35

Essence of Christianity, The (Feuerbach), 113, 225, 227, 228, 260

Estlin, J. B., 182

Evans, Mary Anne, *see* Eliot, George

"Exodusters," 348

"Farewell and Covenant" (R. M. Assing), 16

Favret, Mary A., xix

Fehr, Julius, 340

Fehr, Linn, 341–42

Felden, Tamara, xxvii

Feuerbach, Ludwig, 113, 114, 225, 227–29, 281, 288, 328, 356, 406n82; letter to, 225, 259–60, 293

Fichte, Johann Gottlieb, 69

Finck von Fickenstein, Karl Graf, 68

Flaubert, Gustave, 63

Foner, Eric, xxv, 174

Forbes, Hugh, 220

Foster, Abby Kelley, 116, 258, 292

Foster, Stephen, 258

Franchot, Jenny, xxix, 177

Franco-Prussian War, 294, 305, 309, 324

Frankenberg, Ruth, 398n15

Frauenstein, Gustav, 126, 275, 276, 280, 282, 291, 308, 310, 314, 320, 342, 381–82

Frederick Douglass's Paper, 127, 295, 303, 407n7

Frederick William, King of Prussia, 47, 51, 74, 309

Freedman's Savings and Trust Company

(Freedman's National Bank), 288, 316–17

Freedmen's Bureau, 266, 270, 276, 296

Frémont, Gen. John C., 241, 250

French Revolution, 8, 9, 149, 386n15

Friedländer family, 26, 32, 35

Fugitive Blacksmith, The (Pennington), 122, 125, 127

Fuller, Margaret, 71

Gagern, Carlos von, xv–xvi, 261, 374–75

Garbardi, Countess, 362

Garfield, James A., 357–59, 418n74

Garfield, Lucretia, 358

Garibaldi, Giuseppe, 220

Garies and Their Friends, The (Webb), 224

Garnet, Henry Highland, 144, 182, 214, 269, 292, 347

Garrison, William Lloyd, xxiv, 86, 116, 122n, 179, 182–83, 267, 288, 347, 403n4

Garrisonians, 7, 86, 144, 148, 161, 176, 182, 210, 253, 306

Gartenlaube, Die, 97, 103, 148, 153, 263

Gaskell, Elizabeth, 71

Gates, Henry Louis, Jr., xviii, xxix, 144

Gay, Peter, xix, xxiv, 22, 71

German-Americans, xix, 95–96, 245, 261, 275, 286; Bismarck supported by, 310, 329; in Rochester, 210, 304–6; *see also* Revolution of 1848, exiles from

German Confederation, 52, 74

German War of Independence (1813–15), 16

Gibbons, Abigail Hopper, 221

Giddings, Joshua R., 216

Gilbert, Eliza Dolores, *see* Montez, Lola

Gilroy, Amanda, 385n13

Gliddon, George R., 257

Goethe, Johann Wolfgang von, xx, 23, 29, 33, 57, 58, 65, 69, 75, 79, 83, 106, 132, 190, 197, 372

Golden, Marita, xxix

Government Printing Office, 296
Grant, Ulysses S., xxiv, 285, 287–89, 291–
    93, 297, 299, 305, 310, 317, 340, 379
Greeks, ancient, 82
Greeley, Horace, 220, 263, 305
Green, Beriah, 144
Green, Shield, 213, 215, 404n27
Greene, Martha, 206, 368, 371
Greener, Richard T., 347
Greenwood, Grace, 366
Gregory, James M., xxiv
Griffing, Josephine Sophie White, 289
Griffiths, Julia, see Crofts, Julia Griffiths
Grimelli, Gino, 312, 313, 321, 325, 331,
    362
Grimké, Francis, 368
Güderode, Karoline von, 373
Gutzkow, Amalie, 70
Gutzkow, Bertha, 361–62
Gutzkow, Karl, 18, 31, 33–36, 39, 40, 47,
    53, 62, 73, 121, 126, 362; anti-
    Semitism of, 36, 81; Baison and, 65; ex
    tramarital affair of, 70; last meeting of
    OA and, 323–24; OA's correspondence
    with, 50, 61, 63, 67, 77, 104, 109, 114,
    235, 372; obituaries of David and Rosa
    Maria by, 20, 23, 25, 29; suicide at-
    tempt of, 320, 323; in Young Germany
    movement, 32, 34, 52, 55, 81

Haitian Revolution, 84, 235, 393n112
Hallgarten & Company, 264, 310
Hambach Festival, 28, 52
Hamburger Correspondent, 63
Hamburger Telegraph, 63, 87
Hampton Institute, 350
Hampton Singers, 413n112
Handels Zeitung, 374
Hard Times (Dickens), 284
Hardenberg, Count Karl von, 31
Harding, Vincent, 253
Harpers Ferry, Brown's raid on, 212, 215–
    23, 227, 234, 253, 285, 286, 404n27

Hawthorne, Nathaniel, xviii
Hayes, Rutherford B., 288, 327, 332–34,
    345, 348, 358
Hebbel, Friedrich, 32, 58, 70
Hegelianism, 33
Heidelberg, University of, 84, 113, 122
Heine, Heinrich, 28, 32, 33, 52, 63, 81, 83
Heine, Salomon, 31, 35, 45
Heinzen, Karl, 114, 148, 281, 288
Herbert, Philemon T., 239
Herbert, William, 83
Hern, James, 217
"Heroic Slave, The" (Douglass), 178, 245
Hertz, Dr., xxiin
Hertz, Fanny, 9, 31, 35
Hertz, Henriette, 31, 351
Higginson, Thomas Wentworth, 214
Hildebrand, Janice, 107
Hildreth, Richard, 224
Hilton, Judge, 334
Hirschfeld, Bertha, 380
Hoboken Academy, 113
Hoffmann und Campe, 151, 223
Holland, Frederick May, xxiv
House of Representatives, U.S., 269, 279
Howard, O. O., 270, 276
Howard, William, 304
Howe, Julia Ward, 214, 221, 292
Howe, Samuel Gridley, 214, 216
Huggins, Nathan I., xxv, 174, 270
Hugo, Victor, 22, 199
Humboldt, Alexander von, 84, 93, 204, 377
Humboldt, Wilhelm von, 69, 377
Hunt, Harriet K., 211
Huntington family, 338, 357
"hybrid vigor," theory of, 22, 24, 139
Hyers, Anna Madah, 413n112
Hyers, Emma Louisa, 413n112
Hymer, Mrs., 360, 381

Immerman, Karl, 70
Industrial Revolution, 112
Ingersoll, Robert, 353, 358

Jacobs, Harriet, 208
Jagiellonian Library (Krakow), xix, xxvi–xxvii
Jahreszeiten, 63, 94, 97, 102, 103
James, Thomas, 228
Jane Eyre (Brontë), 185
Jenny (Lewald), 55
Jesuits, 156
Jesus, historical, 33–34
Jews, 15, 22, 30, 33, 73, 348, 351; conversion to Christianity of, xxii, xxvi, 17, 36, 54; discrimination against, *see* anti-Semitism; emancipation of, 35–36, 74; in German intelligentsia, 8–9, 12–14, 31, 35, 68, 108; orthodox, 11–12
Johnson, Andrew, 266, 268–71, 276, 279, 282, 283

Kagi, John Henry, 215
Kansas-Nebraska Act, 116, 206
Kant, Immanuel, 11
Kapp, Friedrich, 100, 113, 114, 148, 220, 245, 310
Keller, Gottfried, 53, 204, 311, 313, 315, 321, 325, 354, 357, 399n44
Kerner, Justinus, 9–11, 14–17, 28, 48, 386n18
Key, Philipp Barton, 239
Kientzel, Rinaldo, 355, 374, 375
King, William, 152–54
Kleist, Heinrich von, 23, 84, 235
Koehler, Amalie, 126, 275–76, 279–81, 288, 307, 320, 322, 337, 343, 352, 357–64, 369, 370, 380, 381
Koehler, Hedwig, 281
Koehler, Sylvester Rosa, 126, 263, 281, 288, 307, 310, 320, 322, 326, 337, 342, 360, 406n81; *Art Review* published by, 341; bequest to, 380, 381, 420n7; moves to Boston, 279–80; OA boards with, 275–76; OA's correspondence with, 324n, 340, 343, 347, 352, 353, 357–59, 361–63, 370; and OA's suicide, 374

Koehler, Walter, 281
Kompass, 97, 148
Ku Klux Klan, xxv, 289–90, 303, 333
Kudlich, Hans, 113, 115, 126, 143, 148, 245, 282, 309, 310, 323
Kudlich, Hermann C., xvii, 115, 280, 374, 381, 388n54, 420n7
Kudlich, Luise, 113, 115, 126, 143, 280, 282, 323, 370

Lamarckianism, 109
Lange, Johannes D., 262, 275, 276, 279, 280, 282, 290, 310, 342, 369n, 374, 406n81
Langston, Charles S., 182
Langston, John M., 347
la Roche, Sophie de, 311
Lassalle, Ferdinand, 192, 351
Laube, Heinrich, 55, 75, 372
Lawson, Charles, 177, 228
Leatherstocking Tales, The (Cooper), 104
Lensing, Elise, 70
Lessing, Gotthold Ephraim, 12
Leutze, Emanuel Gottlieb, 119
Leverenz, David, xxix, 178
Levy, Ascher, 11
Levy, Caja, 11
Lewald, Fanny, 11, 12, 26, 48–49, 51–55, 62, 70–71, 186n, 290, 373, 399n44
Lewes, George Henry, 71, 186n
Liberal Republican Party, 295, 305, 310, 334
Liberator, The, 179, 182, 183
Liberty Party, 86
Library of Congress, 317, 319
Liebknecht, Wilhelm, 309
Life and Times of Frederick Douglass, The (Douglass), xvii, xxiii, xxv
Life of Jesus, The (Strauss), 33
Lincoln, Abraham, 230, 233, 234, 237, 240, 248, 250, 251, 254, 262, 268, 269, 340
Liszt, Franz, 71, 154

Loewenthal, Dr. E. J., 143, 275, 280, 282, 291, 309, 363, 364, 381*n*

Loguen, Jermain Wesley, 214

Lorimer, Douglas, xxviii–xxix

Löscher, Madame, 112

Louis Ferdinand, Prince of Prussia, 69

Louisiana Purchase, 116

Lucinde (Schlegel), 69

Ludwig I, King of Bavaria, 155, 157*n*

Lumpensammler, Der, 64

Lutheranism, 7, 8, 30, 35

McClellan, Gen. George B., 241

McDowell, Deborah, xix, 187

McFeely, William, xxvii, xxix, 124, 172, 224, 386*n*7, 411*n*66

McKibbon, Joseph Chambers, 239

McKim, J. Miller, 266

McPherson, James M., 252

Malchow, H. L., 25, 138

Marks, Mrs., 143, 217, 218, 260, 275

Markus, Zippora Assur, 12, 26

Martin, J. Sella, 294

Martin, Waldo E., Jr., xxv, xxix, 228

Martineau, Harriet, 93

Marvell, Andrew, 83

Marx, Karl, 81, 192, 266

Massachusetts 54th Regiment, 247–48, 250

Massachusetts Society, 178

Maurice (theatrical entrepreneur), 64

May, Samuel, Jr., 182

Mayer, Karl, 9, 11

Mazzini, Giuseppe, 192, 311, 312

"Meeting of Two Friends After a Long Separation, The" (Douglass), 360–61

Mendelssohn, Jette, 51

Mendelssohn, Moses, 12

Mendelssohn-Veith, Dorothy, 69, 71

Merlau, Henry, 304

Methodism, 91, 120, 228; *see also* African Methodist Episcopal (AME) Zion Church

Mexican Revolution, 261

Miller, Elizabeth, 211

Milton, John, 237

Missouri Compromise, 116

Mitchell, Eliza, 277, 335

Montez, Lola (Eliza Dolores Gilbert), 154–57, 162, 186*n*, 351

Moral Education Society, 350

moral suasion, Garrisonians' reliance on, 86

More, Thomas, 83

Morgenblatt für gebildete Leser, xix, xxii*n*, xxvii, 79–81, 87, 97, 103, 107, 111, 147, 211, 226, 250, 266, 268, 283, 295, 349, 384*n*5; American women's movement described by OA in, 209; Canadian articles by OA in, 145–46; ceases publication, 263–64, 274; Civil War articles by OA in, 237, 242, 256; Culver article by OA in, 158; Douglass portraits by OA in, xvii, 136–42, 163–65, 206–7, 399*n*45; Harpers Ferry raid reported by OA in, 219, 225, 286; Montez article by OA in, 155–57; New York articles by OA in, 102, 105; and OA's planned Haitian trip, 235; Pennington article by OA in, 123, 126; slavery articles by OA in, 83, 137, 205, 206, 285; social problems described by OA in, 112, 118–19; Varnhagen denounced by OA in, 57–58

Mormons, 351

Morrison, Toni, 349

Motley, John, 284

Mott, Lucretia, 159, 292

Mount Holyoke Seminary, 350

Mühlbach, Luise, *see* Mundt, Clara

Mulatten (Andersen), 85, 141

Mundt, Clara (pseudo Luise Mühlbach), xxii, 60, 84–85, 87, 127, 128, 139, 144, 185, 187, 199, 377, 393*n*114; marriage of, 48; OA's friendship with, 55, 56, 61, 62, 290; Varnhagen and, 52

Mundt, Theodor, 48, 52, 56, 311, 390*n*13

Municipal Theater (Hamburg), 63–64, 67

Murray, Anna, *see* Douglass, Anna Murray

My Bondage and My Freedom (Douglass), xvii, xxiii, 67, 126, 127, 137, 174, 187, 245; German translation of, 142, 147–49, 151, 163, 203, 206, 211–12, 222, 223

My Relationship with Ferdinand Lassalle (Racowitza), 352

Napoleon III, Emperor of the French, 224, 294, 305

Napoleonic Wars, 16, 31, 247

Narrative of the Life of Frederick Douglass (Douglass), xxiii, 86, 127, 138, 148, 173–74, 178, 245

National Anti-Slavery Standard, 182, 270

National Negro Convention, 122

National Republican, 333

National Woman's Rights Convention, 159

Nazis, and Varnhagen papers, xxvi

Neither Black nor White (Sollors), xxix

Nell, William Cooper, 208, 402*n*45

New National Era, 288, 293–96, 305, 308–10, 318, 344, 379, 381*n*, 413*n*124

New York Herald, 220

New York Times, The, 304, 333, 369

New York Tribune, 220

New York World, 256

Nickert, Emilie (née Reihl), 61, 99–100, 111, 115, 128, 136, 282, 283, 341, 354, 362, 379, 380, 394*n*11, 411*n*66

Nickert, Mary, *see* Walpuski, Mary Nickert

Nickert, Peter, 100, 111, 128

North Star, The, xvi, 86, 117, 181, 182, 210, 295, 303

Nott, Eliphalet, 99

Nott, Josiah Clark, 257

Nott, Urania Sheldon, 99, 101

Ochs, Cäcilia, 304

Ochs, Nicholas, 304

Oroonoko, or, The Royal Slave (Behn), 85, 393*n*114

Othello (Shakespeare), 291

Owen, Robert, 103

Painter, Nell I., 122, 178, 180, 208, 402*n*33

Pappenheim, Jenny von, 51

Paradise Lost (Milton), 237

Parker, Theodore, 214, 229

Paulsen, Madame, 80

Pelz, E., 102

Pennington, Almira Way, 124

Pennington, James W. C., 84, 121–27, 135, 160–61, 235, 246

Pestalozzi, Johann Heinrich, 23

Phillips, Wendell, 116–17, 134, 159, 229, 257, 267, 276, 292, 347

Pickett, Terry H., xxvi–xxvii, 51

Pitts, Helen, xvii, xxiii, xxiv, 171, 350–51, 356, 361, 366–69, 380–82, 418*n*59, *n*74, 420*n*111

Pitts, Hiram, 350

Plessy v. Ferguson (1896), xxv

polyphony, xxviii

Porter, Samuel D., 208–9, 253, 327, 417*n*44

Porter, Susan, 208, 253

Post, Amy, 183, 208, 218, 219, 253, 344, 402*n*45, 405*n*45, 409*n*7

Post, Isaac, 208, 218, 219, 253

Prang Company, 341

Preston, Dickinson J., xxix, 386*n*4

Printers' Union, 296

Private Heart, The (Gay), xxiv

Privilegierte wöchentlich gemeinnützige Nachrichten von und für Hamburg, 63, 73, 148, 162

Protestantismus und die Romantik, Der (Ruge and Echtermeyer), 34

Pückler-Muskau, Prince Hermann von, 204, 311

Purvis, Robert, 116, 292

Putnam, Caroline Remond, 288, 292, 325

Quadroons, The (Child), 186
Quarles, Benjamin, xxv, 127, 173, 194, 252

racism, 84, 101, 148, 152, 206, 230; of Johnson, 270; Northern, 124, 126, 159–60, 183, 241, 243
Racowitz, Janko von, 351
Racowitza, Helene von, xvi, xxi–xxii, 351–52, 354, 356, 418n59
radical Republicans, xxiv, 271, 272, 289, 351
Reconstruction, xxv, 262–99, 332, 345
Red, White, and Blue Mining Company, 272
Redpath, James, 235
Reihl, Anna Maria, 380
Remde (artist), 98
Remond, Charles Lenox, 144, 288
Remond, Sarah, 288
Republican Party, 220, 240, 256, 291, 335, 346, 349; Douglass and, 274, 287, 327, 328, 333, 334, 357, 358; and Franco-Prussian War, 305; and impeachment of Johnson, 283; and Reconstruction, 276, 285; split between Liberal Republicans and, 295, 310, 334; *see also* radical Republicans
Restoration Germany, 31, 32, 51, 54, 268
Revolution of 1848, 32, 74–75, 81, 84, 85, 155, 268; exiles from, 100, 108, 112, 114, 115, 148, 241, 281, 285, 288, 305, 309
Reybaud, Mme Charles, 85
Riehl, W. H., 54
Riesser, Gabriel, 32, 35, 36, 52, 75, 81
Riotte, C. N., 282, 291, 310, 329, 411n69
Rise of the Dutch Republic, The (Motley), 284
Robinson, Edward, 100
Robinson, Therese (Talvj), 100–1, 112, 135, 290
Rochester Daily Union and Advertiser, 303–6
Rochester Democrat and Observer, 222

Rochester Ladies Anti-Slavery Society, 208
Rodenberg, Julius, 50
Roman Catholic Church, 7–8, 30, 155–58, 324
"Romance" (R. M. Assing), 10
Romantic Correspondence (Favret), xix
Romanticism, 9–11, 14, 16–19, 23, 24, 28, 32, 39–40, 57, 68, 69, 90, 104, 186, 235
Rose, Ernestine, 103, 209
Rosenthal family, 93, 105, 107–8, 110–11, 145, 399n38
Royal Danish Theater, 85
Ruge, Arnold, 33, 34

Saaling, Marianne, 51
Sanborn, Franklin, 214, 216
Sand, George, 23, 27, 28, 33, 50, 54, 59, 71, 103
Santo Domingo commission, 297–99, 305, 307
Schewitsch, Baron Serge von, 351
Schiller, Friedrich von, 69, 79
Schirges, Georg, 58–59, 63
Schlegel, Friedrich, 69, 71
Schleiermacher, Friedrich E. D., 69
Schoppe, Alphons, 76, 80, 161, 203, 253, 394n20
Schoppe, Amalie, 18, 63, 65, 70, 79, 96, 97, 99, 108, 394n20; in Assing salon, 32, 35; death of, 162, 253; emigration of, 80; on OA's liaison with Baison, 71–72, 76; Rosa Maria's friendship with, 21, 203, 386n18; in Schenectady, 101, 128, 132, 161
Schurz, Carl, 305, 309, 310, 334, 378
Schwab, Gustav, 9, 11, 17, 28
Schweizer, Mrs., 97
Sclaverei und Freiheit (Douglass, tr. by OA), 151
Scott, Dred, 144, 206, 224
Scott, Sir Walter, 100
Sealsfield, Charles, 79, 104

Sears, Amanda Auld, 216–17, 289
Sears, John, 216
Secret Six, 214
Senate, U.S., 224, 299, 327; Finance Committee, 317; Foreign Relations Committee, 297
Seward, William Henry, 262
Seymour, Horatio, 232, 242
Shakers, 120
Shakespeare, William, 23, 64, 65, 83, 127, 190, 344
Sherman, John, 317, 358
Sherman, Gen. William Tecumseh, 273
Shiloh Presbyterian Church (New York), 122, 124, 126, 144, 159, 160
Sickle, Daniel S., 239
Sigel, Franz, 241, 309
Skin Deep (Golden), xxix
Slade, William, 270
Slave, The; or, Memoirs of a Fugitive (Hildreth), 224
slavery, 83–84, 93, 137, 148, 161, 175, 205, 267, 294; abolition of, 187, 242, 243, 254–56, 258, 268, 269 (*see also* abolitionists); British opposition to, 86; Douglass' escape from, 7, 46, 173, 175, 217, 261; Johnson and, 270; Lincoln and, 234, 241, 242; Northern attitudes toward, 116–17; OA's articles on, 83, 137, 205, 206, 285; Pennington's preaching against, 122–25; religion and, 177, 228, 292; violent resistance to, 214 (*see also* Harpers Ferry, Brown's raid on)
Smalls, Robert, 245–46, 265
Smith, Ann, 210–11, 213, 216
Smith, Gerrit, 86, 117, 134, 180, 182, 210–11, 213, 214, 216, 278, 296, 307, 317, 318
social Darwinism, 346
Social Democrats (Munich), 365
Sollors, Werner, xxix
Solmar, Henriette, 51, 52, 81–82
"Song of Spring" (R. M. Assing), 10
Sontag, Susan, 181

Sorge, Friedrich, 309
Sorrows of Young Werther, The (Goethe), 29, 197, 372
Southern Redeemers, 332, 348
Spelman, J. J., 277
Spinoza, Baruch, 122
Sprague, Annie, 273–74, 303, 307, 336, 363
Sprague, Harriet, 276, 303, 307, 336
Sprague, Louisa, 311, 336–37, 344, 358, 363, 368–69, 410$n41$
Sprague, Nathan, 190, 272–74, 276, 303, 307, 317, 319, 336, 342, 343
Sprague, Rosetta Douglass, 149, 150, 179–81, 183, 212, 232, 276, 307, 319, 336, 358; birth of, 175; and burning of Rochester home, 303; education of, 172; FD's correspondence with, 191, 223, 310–11, 320, 410$n41$; and FD's remarriage, 368, 369; marriage of, 254, 343; and mother's death, 363; OA's friendship with, 170–71, 189; pregnancies of, 272; relationship with mother, 194–96, 273–74; and sister's death, 224, 226
Stahr, Adolf, 71, 186n, 399$n44$
Stanton, Edwin, 248, 251
Stanton, Elizabeth Cady, 191, 289, 290
Stearns, George Luther, 214
Stearns, Mary, 214
Steinbach, Erwin von, 27
Steinbach, Sabina von, 13, 27, 103
Steinheim, Johanna, 20, 26, 32, 35, 39, 61, 118, 313, 365, 372; correspondence of Ludmilla and, 49, 53, 78, 312, 320, 325, 330; during Hamburg fire, 45; in Italy, 76; and OA's liaison with Baison, 71, 81, 392$n89$; OA's visits in Zurich with, 323, 324n, 329
Steinheim, Salomon Ludwig, 20, 26, 32, 34, 35, 39, 52, 61, 118, 372; conversion of Jews opposed by, 13, 21; and David's death, 41, 59; during Hamburg fire, 45; in Italy, 76; Ludmilla's correspondence with, 53, 58; paternalism of, 46; poetry by, 3; and Rosa Maria's death, 4

Stephens, Alexander H., 241
Sternberg, Alexander von, 47n, 52
Steward, Austin, 144, 250
Stietzing, Dr., 41
Stout, Janis, 82
Stowe, Harriet Beecher, 84, 127, 135, 148, 257–58, 393n112, 399n41
Strauss, David Friedrich, 33–34, 229, 356, 406n82
Strothers, Henry, 272–73
Süddeutsche Post, 331, 363, 365
suffrage, black, 289–92
Sumner, Charles, 229, 239, 297–98, 340
Supreme Court, U.S., xxv, 144, 332
Swift, Jonathan, 83

Täglicher Beobachter, 303
Tappan, Lewis, 126
Tempest, The (Shakespeare), 83
Tenure of Office Act, 279
Thalia Theater (Hamburg), 64
Thayer, Phebe, 172, 194
"Theater War" (Hamburg), 63–64, 74, 75
Thomas, Gen. Lorenzo, 250
Tieck, (Johann) Ludwig, 28
Tillman, William, 243–44, 246, 265
Tilton, Elizabeth, 319n
Tilton, Theodore, 186n, 271, 278, 289, 319
Tocqueville, Alexis de, 83, 93
Toussaint L'Ouverture, 84, 127, 229, 235, 236
Transcendental Unitarianism, 229
Trollope, Frances, 87, 93, 113, 133, 283
Truth, Sojourner, 177, 178, 181, 208, 347, 402n33
Tubman, Harriet, xvi, 214, 221
Turner, Franklin, 217
Types of Mankind (Clark and Gliddon), 257

Uhland, Ludwig, 9–11, 14, 28, 33, 386n18

Uncle Tom's Cabin (Stowe), 84, 148, 163–64, 393n112
Underground Railroad, 152, 205, 212, 218, 253
Underwood, John Curtis, 262
Union College (Schenectady), 99
Unitarianism, 229
Uriel Acosta (Gutzkow), 62, 73, 121
Urquijo, Raphael d', 68
Utopia (More), 83

Varnhagen, Anna Maria, 7–8
Varnhagen, Johann Andreas Jakob, 7–8
Varnhagen von Ense, Karl August, xxvi, 14, 19, 28, 35, 38, 41, 43, 45–58, 61, 69n, 76, 99–101, 109, 124, 135, 311, 331, 377, 380, 390n20; death of, 203; denounced by OA, 21, 52, 57–58; family background of, 8; Humboldt and, 84; marriage of, 17, 68; OA's break with, 56–58; and OA's emigration, 81–82; and OA's translation of Douglass' autobiography, 163; and wife's death, 40, 50–51, 78, 204
Varnhagen von Ense, Rahel Levin, xxv–xxvi, 28, 47, 53, 54, 76, 103, 149, 282; affairs of, 68; conversion to Christianity of, xxvi, 13, 17, 24; death of, 40, 47, 50–51, 78, 204; feminism of, 27, 69; marriage of, 17, 68; salon of, 21, 31, 52, 70, 311, 351, 377
Varnhagen von Ense Collection, xix, xxvi–xxvii, 78, 355
Verhoeven, W. M., 385n13
Victoria, Queen of England, 162
Viereck family, 363–65
Villard, Fanny Garrison, 288
Villard, Henry, 288

Waggoner, Henry O., 311
Wagner, Maria, xxvii
Wakeman, George, 256

Walker, George, 374

Walker, Peter, xviii, xxiii, xxv, 174

Walpuski, Mary Nickert, 128, 341, 354

Ward, Edgar E., 359

Washington, Booker T., xxiv

Washington, George, 283–84

Washington, Mary Helen, xxix, 176

Washington *Evening Star*, 333

Washington Exhibition (1853), 119

Waters, Mary, 397*n*97

Webb, Frank, 224

Wehl, Feodor, 15, 26, 28, 31–33, 50, 54, 63, 65, 67, 68, 73, 97, 311, 313, 355

Weise, Amalie, 9

Welsh, William L., 380

Werpup, Mrs., 291, 340, 342, 360

West, Cornel, 349

Westermann's Monatshefte, 97, 148, 153, 263

Western New York Anti-Slavery Society, 208

"What Am I to You" (Douglass), 367–68

Wheatley, Phillis, 191

Wiesel, Pauline, 69

Wilberforce, William, 179

Wilberforce Colony (Ontario), 150, 152

Williams, James, 292–93

Winslow, Caroline B., 350

Wise, Henry, 216, 218, 221

Wittgenstein, Ludwig, 24

Wolff family, 61, 67–68

women's suffrage, 289–90

World War I, 247

World War II, xxvi, 97

Wright, Theodore S., 182

Württemberg, Herzog Paul Wilhelm von, 79

Yarborough, Richard, xxix, 144

Young Germany movement, 32–34, 51–53, 55, 59, 81, 83, 95, 108, 112, 113, 117, 235

"Young Lady and the Fisherman, The" (R. M. Assing), 29

Zakrzewska, Dr. Maria, 288

Zecher, Wilhelm, 211

Zeise, Heinrich, xvi, 32, 35, 39, 52, 115

Zeit und Menschen (Wehl), 31

Zeitschrift für bildende Kunst, 263, 295